British Idealism

British Idealism

A History

W. J. Mander

OXFORD
UNIVERSITY PRESS

OXFORD
UNIVERSITY PRESS

Great Clarendon Street, Oxford OX2 6DP

Oxford University Press is a department of the University of Oxford.
It furthers the University's objective of excellence in research, scholarship,
and education by publishing worldwide in

Oxford New York

Auckland Cape Town Dar es Salaam Hong Kong Karachi
Kuala Lumpur Madrid Melbourne Mexico City Nairobi
New Delhi Shanghai Taipei Toronto

With offices in

Argentina Austria Brazil Chile Czech Republic France Greece
Guatemala Hungary Italy Japan Poland Portugal Singapore
South Korea Switzerland Thailand Turkey Ukraine Vietnam

Oxford is a registered trade mark of Oxford University Press
in the UK and in certain other countries

Published in the United States
by Oxford University Press Inc., New York

British Library Cataloguing in Publication Data

Data available

Library of Congress Cataloging in Publication Data

Data available

Typeset by SPI Publisher Services, Pondicherry, India
Printed in Great Britain
on acid-free paper by
MPG Books Group, Bodmin and King's Lynn

ISBN 978–0–19–955929–9

1 3 5 7 9 10 8 6 4 2

To Avril

Contents

Detailed Contents

Preface

When I started researching twenty years ago it would not have been possible to write this history of British Idealism for, even if it remains a topic of minority attention, during that time there has been something of a reawakening of interest in this field, with a small band of scholars working carefully to recover a wealth of philosophical material which the modern discipline has forgotten. Only by adding the fruit of that work to my own researches has it become possible to produce a fully synoptic history such as this. A more friendly and encouraging set of co-workers could not have been hoped for, and to the writings, conference presentations, and conversations of them all I owe many debts—more, no doubt, than I can now precisely recall and enumerate, but I would particularly like to thank for their help: James Allard, Leslie Armour, Pierfrancesco Basile, Jan Olof Bengtsson, David Boucher, James Connelly, Maria Dimova Cookson, Philip Ferreira, Peter Nicholson, Stamatoula Panagokou, Avital Simhony, the late Timothy Sprigge, Guy Stock, Will Sweet, Elizabeth Trott, Colin Tyler, Andrew Vincent, and Ben Wempe. Several colleagues were kind enough to read parts of the manuscript and to them I owe special thanks for a great many helpful suggestions, as I do to the two anonymous readers for Oxford University Press.

This work draws on many of my own previous publications, but always as a starting point for thorough revision and in no case have earlier writings been simply reproduced. In each case I would like to thank the editors and publishers for their kind permission to make use of this material here.

I would like to thank Peter Momtchiloff at Oxford University Press for his help with the book, the Principal and Fellows of Harris Manchester College for their continued support over many years, as well as the British Academy for the award of a Senior Research Fellowship in 2008–9 which allowed me to bring my many researches together into a final manuscript. Most of all I would like to thank Avril, Sam, and Breesha, whose love and encouragement contribute much more than they know.

Article Acknowledgements

An Introduction to Bradley's Metaphysics, Clarendon Press, 1993.

Introduction to *T.H. Green: Ethics, Metaphysics and Political Philosophy*, OUP, 2006.

Introduction to *Dictionary of Nineteenth-Century British Philosophers*, Thoemmes Press, 2002.

Introduction to *Anglo-American Idealism, 1865–1927*, Greenwood Press, 2000.

Introduction to *The Collected Works of F.H. Bradley*, Thoemmes Press, 1999.

Introduction to *Perspectives in the Logic and Metaphysics of F.H. Bradley*, Thoemmes Press, 1996.

'Bradley's Logic', in D. Gabbey and J.H. Woods (eds), *Handbook of the History of Logic, Volume Four: British Logic in the Nineteenth Century*, Elsevier, 2007.

'In Defence of the Eternal Consciousness', in *T.H. Green: Ethics, Metaphysics and Political Philosophy*, OUP, 2006.

'Life and Finite Individuality; the Bosanquet/Pringle-Pattison Debate', *British Journal for the History of Philosophy*, 2005.

'Bradley & Green on Relations', in W. Sweet (ed.), *Idealism, Metaphysics and Community*, Aldershott: Ashgate, 2001.

'Bosanquet and the Concrete Universal', *The Modern Schoolman*, 2000.

'Caird's Developmental Absolutism', in *Anglo-American Idealism, 1865–1927*, Greenwood Press, 2000.

'John Caird—Theologian and Philosopher', *New Blackfriars*, 1999.

'Edward Caird's Neo-Kantian Idealism', *The Modern Schoolman*, 1998.

'McTaggart on Time and Error', *The Modern Schoolman*, 1998.

'McTaggart's Argument for Idealism', *Journal of Speculative Philosophy*, 1997.

'On McTaggart on Love', *History of Philosophy Quarterly*, 1996.

'The Role of the Self in Bradley's Argument for Idealism', in *Perspectives in the Logic and Metaphysics of F.H. Bradley*, Thoemmes Press, 1996.

'What's So Good about the Absolute?' *British Journal for the History of Philosophy*, 1996.

'Levels of Experience in F.H. Bradley', *The Southern Journal of Philosophy*, 1995.

'Bradley's Philosophy of Religion', *Religious Studies*, 1995.

'F.H. Bradley and the Philosophy of Science', *International Studies in the Philosophy of Science*, 1991–2.

'British Idealist Ethics' in R. Crisp (ed.), *Handbook of the History of Ethics*.

Entry on Bradley's Absolute Idealism, in Robin Le Poidevan, Peter Simons, Andrew McGonigal, Ross Cameron (eds), *Routledge Companion to Metaphysics*, 2009.

Entry on British Idealism, in A.C. Grayling, A. Pyle, and N. Goulder (eds), *Continuum Encylopeadia of British Philosophy*, Thoemmes Continuum, 2006.

Entry on British Idealism, in J. Protevi (ed.), *The Edinburgh Dictionary of Continental Philosophy*, Edinburgh University Press, 2005.

Entries on A.C. Ewing, Millicent MacKenzie, C.R. Morris, and May Sinclair, in *Dictionary of Twentieth-Century British Philosophers*, Thoemmes Press, 2005.

Entries on J. Caird, A.S. Pringle-Pattison, H.H. Joachim, W.R. Sorley, J.H. Muirhead, R.B. Haldane, J.S. Mackenzie, J. Seth, A.E. Taylor, A. Gifford, C.B. Upton, W. Graham, A.C. Bradley, J. Maccunn, J.S. Haldane, and G. Jamieson, in *Dictionary of Nineteenth-Century British Philosophers*, Thoemmes Press, 2002.

'John McTaggart Ellis McTaggart', in Philip B. Dematteis, Peter S. Fosl, and Leemon McHenry (eds), *Dictionary of Literary Biography: volume 259: British Philosophers, 1800–2000*, Gale Research Co., 2002.

'British Idealism', in S. Glendinning (ed.), *The Edinburgh Encyclopaedia of Continental Philosophy*, Edinburgh University Press, 1999.

'F.H. Bradley,' in R.L. Arrington (ed.), *A Companion to the Philosophers, Blackwells*, 1999.

Picture Acknowledgements

Edward Caird, John Caird, Henry Jones, A.C. Bradley, and H. Hetherington—Glasgow University

F.H. Bradley—Merton College

R.B. Haldane, A.E. Taylor, W.R. Sorley, J.M.E. McTaggart, H.H. Joachim—The National Portrait Gallery

Radhakrishnan—Harris Manchester College

1

Introduction

1.1 The importance of British Idealism

This book sets out the history of British Idealism, a philosophical movement which flourished during the last third of the nineteenth century and the first third of the twentieth. But before beginning what is, admittedly, a rather long book the reader may well ask what profit to expect from such an undertaking?

The power and value of the history of philosophy lies in its ability to surprise and challenge us with unfamiliar thoughts or arguments, but it can only do this if we allow ourselves to stray from our usual routes or haunts; to move outside the compass of time-honoured philosophies (or interpretations of philosophies) with which we have grown up into the alien concept-world outside. To the average British philosopher today, a short step back of little more than a hundred years amounts to just such a shift; for it takes us to a period in our philosophical history that is almost wholly unknown. The chronicle of British philosophy as taught in our universities stops at Mill to start again with Russell and Moore, as though nothing at all happened in the intervening period. But when we seek to fill this gap what a surprise meets us! Not only do we encounter a whole world of forgotten and unexplored philosophy, but we find it to be of a character markedly different in kind to anything of more recent currency. For at the close of the nineteenth century the philosophical landscape in Britain was predominantly idealist—the problems, concepts, methods, and history of the discipline all taken from a point of view opposed at almost every juncture to that which prevails today. To recover this lost period in our philosophical history is the primary purpose of this work. To this end I have tried as far as possible to let the philosophers in question speak again for themselves and, rather than rushing into the mêlée of criticism and engaging with as many as possible of their various detractors or defenders, concentrated the bulk of my attention on their primary texts.

Not everything which is lost is worth finding again, and it may be objected that there are good reasons why British Idealism has been neglected; for among the few today who know of their existence the predominant belief is that its philosophers had nothing to say of any interest or value. But this attitude, if we search out its origins, reveals itself to be one of the founding myths of the school of philosophy commonly called Analytic, within whose broad tradition nearly all contemporary Anglo-American philosophers still work. That early twentieth-century movement came to prominence precisely by attacking Idealism, whose views it sought to portray as old-fashioned and worthless (caring little whether the representation was accurate or not) and the resulting prejudice has persisted. It so stretches credulity to suppose that for some forty years in Britain there existed no philosophical talent at all that the negative assessment almost wholly condemns itself. But it is still common, and so another of the fundamental motivations for this work is to demonstrate its falsity. Once we *understand* British Idealist philosophy it will be seen that we may find much of intrinsic merit in it. Neither hopelessly confused nor obviously wrong, it is a philosophy well worth studying in its own right.

Such besmirching of predecessors is hardly new. Intellectual movements have always emerged by rudely pushing out the current incumbents. Indeed, the Idealists themselves came to the fore by attacking their empiricist and utilitarian forebears. To note this is to light up another perspective from which their story may further teach us, namely, as an instance of something more general in intellectual history. Ideas flourish and die—those which press themselves upon us so forcibly today will lose their shine as inevitably as those of the past—and we can learn something more about this ongoing life-cycle of thought by looking at specific historical case studies. By studying their genesis, development, procreation, and decay we can begin to appreciate the forces that form an intellectual landscape and so better understand the shapes and dynamics of our own thought-world.

But the story of British Idealism is of more than just generic historical interest; it is an episode recent enough for us to be able to see its effects today. We cannot understand the philosophical tradition in which we now work without understanding its origins, and a crucial thing to appreciate about those origins was that Analytic philosophy did not just magically replace the earlier Idealism, but rather developed alongside and in conscious opposition to it, and in this process Idealism shaped its successor; as truly as any parent shapes the child who rebels against it. There have been valuable recent studies of the early anti-idealist efforts of Bertrand Russell and G.E. Moore,[1] but it should also be recognized that the emancipation process did not stop with them, and one lesson of this book will be that long after what analytic philosophers might like to regard as its 'refutation' Idealism continued both to be taught and to be developed, remaining as a doctrine against which those who styled themselves as pragmatists, realists, or positivists developed their own views. Its shadow of influence was longer lasting than has been appreciated and, to pick just a few examples, can be seen not only in those domains where contemporary philosophy rejects Idealism, such as its naturalist

---

[1] P. Hylton, *Russell, Idealism and the Emergence of Analytic Philosophy*; N. Griffin, *Russell's Idealist Apprenticeship*; S. Candlish, *The Russell/Bradley Dispute and its Significance for Twentieth Century Philosophy*.

assumptions, its ongoing distrust of constructive metaphysics or its widespread devalu-ation of the history of philosophy, but also in those Idealist insights which it in fact adopted, such as the self-understanding of philosophy as a distinct discipline separate from any of the special sciences or the rejections of associationist empiricism and classical hedonistic utilitarianism.[2]

While other disciplines banish their earlier ideas into history, the notions of philos-ophy do not cease to be philosophical for being past, and in the end no more justification is needed for considering any philosophical ideas than their intrinsic interest and relevance to contemporary questions. That Idealism holds its own on this score will become apparent. To a large extent the questions of philosophy are perennial—only the idiom changes—and, once we learn to speak its language, Ideal-ism is seen to have much to say on many vital questions; its contributions all the more valuable for coming from a slightly different perspective than we are used to.

1.2 Common themes in British Idealism

To speak of 'British Idealism' is to imply something like a school or movement and it is one of the theses of this book that that was in fact the case; that among the individual philosophers in question we find deep and wide-ranging unity of thought; more indeed than we characteristically discover between the adherents of other schools, such as 'the British empiricists', 'pragmatists', or 'analytic philosophers'. In many respects theirs was a collaborative endeavour. For the most part personally acquainted, they knew and cited each other's work, to which they often deferred, in effect dividing up the domain of philosophy between them, and they had a definite sense of themselves as a common school. This unity becomes especially clear if we take time to look also at the lesser figures of the movement rather than just the major ones, for some of latter (such as Bradley and McTaggart) were somewhat atypical of the broader school. Of course, it must be the work of this book to bring out and justify this assertion of doctrinal unity, but by way of orientation, it may be helpful to begin by mentioning some common themes in British Idealism.

The Idealists had a distinctive conception of the world of knowledge, and of the place of philosophy within it. They insisted on its essential underlying *unity*, arguing that all ideas were systematically linked together into one whole with no fundamental divisions between the different departments of learning, the concepts and principles of one leading into those of another. As Haldane put it, 'Between the pure mathematician and the poet and the preacher there are no gulfs fixed.'[3] Similarly Jones argues that, 'Physics, chemistry, biology, and the other sciences . . . necessarily presuppose the unity

---

[2] Modern philosophy saw no reason to reverse Idealism's attack on John Stuart Mill and, compared with its once high-water mark, his system still stands at a low ebb.

[3] *The Philosophy of Humanism*, 93.

of knowledge, and attempt in their own way and in their own sphere to discover it.'[4] In addition to being thought of as a connected whole, knowledge was often conceived of in hierarchical terms, with various different orders of truth emerging in sequence at different levels.[5] Notwithstanding the fact that modern knowledge is perhaps more fragmented than ever, the inter-disciplinary nature of learning is once again a fashionable article of faith and therefore an earlier incarnation of this ideal must all the more command our attention.

Philosophy, for the Idealists, occupied a vital place in this scheme. It was knowledge-giving, not some species of linguistic analysis or conceptual therapy, although it lacked any distinctive subject matter of its own. Its area of interest was simply reality; but reality considered *as a whole*—'the connected vision of the totality of things.'[6] Making this same point, Mackenzie argued that 'the more speculative aspects of philosophy aim at a comprehensive survey of the universe, which brings them into close relation to the larger utterances of poetry and the deeper kinds of religion',[7] demonstrating at the same time that this universal concern was not thought unique to philosophy.

Putting together these two points about the subject-matter of philosophy and the unity of knowledge, we are led to a conception of philosophy itself as a unified whole. Unlike subsequent and indeed contemporary philosophers who have been more inclined to take a piecemeal approach—where your standpoint on one topic does not generally determine your standpoint on another—the Idealists saw philosophy as an integrated system, their idealistic creed permeating through to every part, so that logic, ethics, metaphysics, even aesthetics, were all conceived as expressions of a single underlying view. Here we find a further justification for the precise nature of this current investigation, for the following work differs from anything previously attempted in respect of its *scope*. While various studies have been made to date of isolated aspects of the Idealists' output (such as their ethics, politics, or religion) this book considers their philosophy *as a whole*, permitting the full range and unity of their philosophical vision to emerge.

Early modern philosophy emphasizes epistemology, twentieth-century philosophy is anchored in the philosophy of language, and in similar fashion the department of philosophy that most characterizes British Idealism is metaphysics. While one of the things to be shown is that there was more disagreement about *precise* metaphysical doctrine than simplistic pictures might suggest, the common point that stands out in all of their thinking is the utter centrality of metaphysics *itself*. To the Idealists, philosophical questions, from religion to logic to ethics, are first and foremost metaphysical

---

[4] *Browning as a Philosophical and Religious Teacher*, 36.

[5] 'knowledge discloses itself as of degrees and at levels which are determined by the character of the concepts it employs. But these degrees and levels imply each other. They are not distinct entities apart' (Haldane, *Reign of Relativity*, 128).

[6] Bosanquet, 'Science and Philosophy', 25–6.

[7] *Outlines of Social Philosophy*, 237.

questions. This follows from their fundamentally idealist perspective which, assimilating idea and reality, identifies logic and metaphysics, and cuts out the need for epistemology or philosophy of language. But the point is linked also to that just made above about the structure and unity of all knowledge, for the thought behind it is that the more one presses an area—the more one approaches its core or foundations—the more one finds oneself involved in metaphysics. Simply to illustrate now what we shall observe in greater detail in due course, the new conceptions which they put forward of self, society, right and duty grew directly out of a new metaphysics of human nature, in which individuality was something born out of membership of a wider social whole. Nor could this understanding be omitted if the resultant ethics was rightly to be understood. In defence of what he feared would be dismissed as unintelligible mysticism, D.G. Ritchie was quite explicit on this point. 'The metaphysics seem to me, indeed, necessary for a *complete* account of the basis of ethics and politics', he argued.[8]

The movement is known as British *Idealism*, and here too we find a vital point of unity; a common affiliation—not to Berkeley but to Plato, Kant, and Hegel—which bound a generation together. In 1860 there were scarcely any idealists, by 1900 the majority of philosophers so designated themselves, but thirty years later they were rare again. Yet it will not do just to leave matters at that; for although they were all idealists, the philosophers to be studied were not all idealists in the same way. Indeed as the movement progressed there came to be developed a great variety of such positions, ranged against a set of outlooks they variously called empiricism, materialism, or dualism,[9] many incompatible with each other and some scarcely distinguishable from those of their opponents. One of the chief tasks of this study will be to bring out in detail the wide range of different ways in which 'idealism' was taken up, but it will be argued too that these various positions display a family resemblance which makes it quite appropriate to take them all together in one tradition.

Still trying to fix their 'idealism', it might be suggested that we could say at least that they were all *philosophical* idealists, rather than simply 'idealists' in the ordinary sense of that term, that is, those who believe in or aspire to the highest standards, principles, and purposes. But this will not do; for very typically the British Idealists have also the optimism, the faith in progress (both human and cosmic), the high ethical standards, and the religious aspirations that mark off 'idealists' as that word is commonly understood. Nor is this fact unconnected with their more philosophical orientation, the latter providing the metaphysical ground of the former. On the other side, however, it must be added that they were not idealists in any utopian, visionary or mystical sense. To them, the realm of ideals is just the realm of the here and now, transformed. They are

---

[8] *Natural Rights*, 97.
[9] 'The real enemy of idealism, as Caird always recognised, is not materialism but dualism' (J.S. Mackenzie, 'Edward Caird as a Philosophical Teacher', 515).

not drawn beyond this world to some other, but rather make a division within this world, between the higher and the lower.[10]

Another unifying theme is the philosophy of religion; few, if any, of the Idealists lacked a pervasive religious dimension to their thought. And even in those for whom the religious motivation seemed reduced or lacking, it can be argued that their conceptualization of ethical and political duty turns moral and social life into a surrogate for religion. In this respect the difference is very great from contemporary philosophy where we meet with faith only in that small reserve designated 'philosophy of religion'. This ghettoization is the result of a narrowing in outlook on the part of both philosophy and religion, the one unwilling to contemplate reality *as a whole*, the other granting to philosophy only a precisely delineated set of concepts and arguments. The Idealists, by contrast, made no such restrictions, finding that nearly every topic if pushed far enough would touch upon ultimate questions that might properly be designated religious.

The other great area of common interest that characterizes all British Idealist thought is its focus on social and political questions. By the last third of the nineteenth century rapid industrialization and urbanization, pursued under a night-watchman or minimal state committed to the classical liberal value of *laissez faire*, had allowed to develop social and economic conditions so deplorable that nearly everyone felt simple continuation as before was no longer an option. Concern over 'the Social Problem' was widespread. In this sentiment the Idealists were in company with many other reforming minds, but what was new and distinctive to them was the social theory in which they embedded their response. They put forward an innovative and powerful conception of the individual and society which contributed substantially to a fundamental shift in political thinking in Britain. Allowing that there were significant differences between them—differences that it will be the work of this study to explore—we can nonetheless pick out four key points which might be said to characterize 'Idealist social thought'. First, as noted above, they advanced a societal conception of the individual. They argued that people could not be understood as distinct individuals, but made sense only in the context of a community which gave to them their thoughts, character and role in life. Rather than society being some aggregate of individuals, the individuals themselves were abstractions from the wider society. Secondly, this holist conception of society in turn allowed them to conceive a new and increased role for the political state. Where before it was simply the guardian of liberty, a position which required standing back as far as possible, they advanced the notion that the state could and should intervene far more to help people make the best of themselves. Thirdly, (and here their views chime far less with those current today) the Idealists advanced a social conception of rights, holding them neither absolute nor natural, but instituted through mutual recognition by a society for its own purposes. Fourthly, they saw an

---

[10] See, for example, Bosanquet, 'On the True Conception of Another World'.

intimate connection between theory and praxis. In many ways their political faith was like religious faith, and just as religion calls for more than simply belief, so the new political philosophy was practically orientated. This was no 'ivory tower' movement, and nearly all of the Idealists were involved in the practical application of their ideas.

So far I have characterized the unity of British Idealism in thematic terms, but it should be acknowledged also that this integrity held at a personal and an institutional level as well, in that there obtained a set of extraordinarily close interconnections between its members. The vast majority of them knew each other well, either as student and teacher, or from working together in academic ventures or on behalf of various societies, committees, and commissions. Some measure of this unity may be seen from the following overview.

Essays in Philosophical Criticism,[11] published in 1883, was a kind of manifesto for the Idealist movement. It was dedicated to T.H. Green, for he was regarded by most of the Idealists as a kind of founder. Green was at Balliol College, Oxford, from 1855 to 1882, first as a student then as a tutor. Bosanquet (1860–70), Nettleship (1864–92), and Wallace (1865–7) were all students of Green's at Balliol; Nettleship remaining as a Fellow, while Bosanquet went on to University College and Wallace to Merton College. At the same time F.H. Bradley, though a student at University College (1865–9), certainly attended his lectures, before taking up a fellowship at Merton as a colleague of Wallace.

Besides Oxford the second great centre of Idealism was Glasgow, where John and Edward Caird were both students, and where from 1862 and 1866 respectively both taught, one in the Chair of Theology the other in the Chair of Moral Philosophy. Nor were these two centres unconnected. In 1860 Edward Caird came as a student to Balliol, forming a close attachment to Green, and returning again in 1893 to take over from Jowett as Master of the college. Like those of Green, Edward Caird's pupils did much to spread Idealism. John Watson studied under him (1866–72) as did Henry Jones (1875–82)—who, indeed, went on to become first his teaching assistant and then his successor—and J.S. Mackenzie (1877–86). Some of his pupils even went on to strengthen the Glasgow–Oxford connection he had begun: John Maccunn first studied in Glasgow, where he was taught by Caird and then at Balliol (1872–6) where he was taught by Green. Another of Caird's pupils to take the same path was J.H. Muirhead, who also went on to study under Green at Balliol (1875–9).

Edinburgh too was a centre of Idealistic thinking. D.G. Ritchie, W.R. Sorley, and R.B. Haldane were all students there; Ritchie moving on to Green's Balliol (1874–8) and then Jesus College, Sorley going on to Trinity College, Cambridge, and Haldane moving to Göttingen where he studied under Lotze. Another Edinburgh graduate

---

[11] This volume was edited by Andrew Seth Pringle-Pattison and R.B. Haldane, both of whom contributed articles, as did B. Bosanquet, D.G. Ritchie, H. Jones, and J.S. Haldane. Individual articles are cited throughout by title and listed in the Bibliography under the author's name.

who went on to study under Lotze was Andrew Seth Pringle-Pattison. After posts in Cardiff and St Andrews, in 1891 he returned to Edinburgh to take up the Chair of Logic and Metaphysics which he occupied until 1919, during most of which time his younger brother, James, also an Edinburgh graduate, held the Chair of Moral Philosophy.

Oxford continued to be a centre for the movement. J.R. Illingworth was educated at Corpus Christi College, Oxford, after which he became Fellow of Jesus College in 1872. A.C. Bradley, the younger brother of F.H. Bradley, went up to Balliol in 1869 where he was first a student and then, alongside Green until 1882, a fellow. Arnold Toynbee too was taught by Green at Balliol in the 1870s and afterwards went on to lecture there, before his early death in 1883. H.H. Joachim was at a student at Balliol in the second half of 1880s, taught by Nettleship. In 1897 he became a fellow of Merton and colleague of Bradley. Another Merton figure from this period was the New College educated A.E. Taylor, who held from 1891–8 a prize fellowship at the College. He too became an intimate of Bradley.

Cambridge played a lesser role, but it should not be forgotten. After studying under Caird, J.S. Mackenzie (like Sorley) went for some years to Trinity College, Cambridge; a significant episode for it was here that he formed a close friendship with McTaggart, also a Trinity man—first one of its students and then one of its fellows. And it was McTaggart who went on to create one of the most original of the Idealist systems.

There is, then, plenty to justify taking the British Idealists together as a single group, but from the start, least a mistaken impression arise, a warning must be issued. For all their agreement, the Idealists were not homogeneous. There was no single party doctrine or manifesto to which they all signed up. Shorter accounts of the movement, by concentrating on only a few figures, have tended to obscure this, and one of the main justifications of this longer work is precisely to bring out the interesting variety and range of opinion that existed within their basic commonality. This is most clear to see in the debate that we observe taking place *between* them. Philosophy is not the enterprise of single isolated thinkers, but an ongoing and developing discussion across a discipline, and for that reason this study has emphasized the internal dialogue to be found within the movement. A favourite British Idealist watchword was 'identity in difference' and, whatever value it may have as a *philosophical* term,[12] it is in fact an excellent expression to describe their own tradition; for close examination brings out the commonality of assumption, history, orientation, and sympathy that they share which, at the same time, not only contains, but itself permits, the vital diversity, modification, disagreement, and exchange that made the movement such a vital one.

---

[12] See pp.41, 44, Chapters 8.2, 8.3.4, and 8.4.1 (p.312) below.

1.3 Terms of reference

To study anything one must draw limits but, even if limits are necessary, those selected must still be chosen; which calls for justification. Since this is an historical study, we may begin with its temporal limits. The dating of intellectual currents must always involve a certain element of arbitrary fiat, but we will not go far wrong if we think of the movement as beginning in 1865, the year in which James Hutchison Stirling published his *The Secret of Hegel*, or in 1866, the year of T.H. Green's appointment as college tutor at Balliol and Edward Caird's election as Professor of Moral Philosophy in Glasgow. By this date the philosophies of Kant and Hegel had been well assimilated[13] and, arising out of them, a new sustained and independent kind of philosophical voice began to make itself heard on the intellectual scene. It might be tempting to place the starting date of the movement a little later, for the flood of idealist publications did not begin until the mid-1870s, but to do so would be to miss the extent to which the school was one of teachers and pupils, not just authors and readers. Green, Caird, Nettleship, and Wallace all inspired a large body of former students who publicized and popularized their teachers' views, independently and in advance of any published works.

To fix an end date for the movement is much harder. For while it burst forth onto the scene with an explosion, its departure was a very drawn-out affair. It could be argued that there was no significant new idealist philosophy after the turn of the century,[14] but it remained a real force in Britain for years after that, and it is equally possible to trace idealism in direct descent from the tradition of Green still being taught into the 1960s. Neglected in most treatments,[15] this long 'after-life' of Idealism will be considered in the second half of the book and especially in the concluding chapter.

A further limitation of this study, not historical this time but geographic, lies in the restriction of its attention to *British* Idealism. For the rise of idealism during this period was not a solely British phenomenon. With respect to English-language philosophy, from the beginning, parallel movements may be found in several countries—involving such figures as, in America, George Holmes Howison, Borden Parker Bowne, Josiah Royce, and James Edwin Creighton; in Canada, George Paxton Young and John Watson; in Australia, Francis Anderson and W.R. Boyce Gibson; and in South Africa, R.F.A. Hoernlé and Arthur Ritchie Lord. Nor were these movements unconnected, either with each other or with work in Britain. Idealists from different countries all read and reacted to each other's works, and there was even a certain exchange of philosophers themselves. Many British trained idealists went to work in other English-speaking countries—some temporarily, some for good—while visits such as those of

---

[13] See Chapter 2.2 to 2.4 below.

[14] This most obvious counter-example to such a claim is the system of McTaggart. But although this did not appear in its final form until 1921–7, its essentials were put forward as early as 1893 in his paper 'Further determination of the Absolute'.

[15] It has been noted briefly by Anthony Quinton, 'Absolute Idealism', 125–6.

Josiah Royce and John Watson to deliver Gifford lectures in 1899–1900 and 1910–12 respectively[16] influenced the development of British Idealism in return. And moving away from English-language philosophy, somewhat later on, there was also a new growth in idealism centred around the Italians Benedetto Croce and Giovanni Gentile which also influenced British Idealism. A history of world idealism would be impossibly large, and yet (as the brief review above sufficiently demonstrates) to exclude all reference to philosophy done outside the British Isles would fundamentally distort our understanding of what happened here. For this reason the restriction to *British* philosophy has not been adhered to with absolute rigour.

A further limitation must also be mentioned. Although aiming to be a comprehensive history of British Idealism, this work does not include discussion of all British idealists at work during the period in question. To explain this paradox, it must be pointed out that one consequence of the contemporary neglect of idealism is a failure to comprehend its breath. For just as not everyone called Smith is related, not all 'idealists' belong to the same clan. The central concern of this book is with the Kantio-Hegelian tradition in idealism which flows out of the philosophy of Green and Edward Caird. It accounts for most, but not quite all, British idealists of the period. Indeed, since it was a tradition that (increasingly) mixed and came into contact with idealisms of a different stamp and lineage, probably no one has been left wholly unmentioned, but some figures have been given only very small walk-on parts.[17]

To sketch a plan of the material ahead, after a chapter outlining the influences on and earliest origins of British Idealism, Chapters 3 to 9 examine Idealist contributions to each of the main areas of philosophy prior to the end of the nineteenth century. Chapters 10 to 14 continue the story, taking up developments in the years after the turn of the century, while the concluding chapter traces the long process by which Idealism decayed and finally disappeared. Although the turn of the century might well be regarded as the high-water mark of Idealism, no special significance attaches to this date, the method of arrangement having been chosen principally in order to keep broadly contemporaneous material together. Where it has best served the story to depart from this scheme of division, I have done so.

1.4 The history of philosophy

Last of all, a word is in order about the kind of study to be embarked upon. What is offered is a work in the history of philosophy and, although the history of philosophy has experienced something of a recovery after its long period of neglect in the Anglo-American tradition, it is still a subject in need of explanation and defence.

---

[16] Subsequently published as *The World and the Individual* and as *The Interpretation of Religious Experience*.
[17] To anticipate a little, figures such as Belfort, Bax, Ward, Wildon Carr, Collingwood, and Whitehead, could all claim (in their various different ways) to be 'idealists' but have little connection with the central current of the story.

We may begin by trying to differentiate it. Although it will be of interest to social, cultural, or political historians—by any measure British Idealism was a movement of great consequence, whose thinking had a deep impact on the culture of its day, and it is impossible to fully understand turn of the century Britain without understanding this its favoured style of philosophical thinking—what is to be offered is not that sort of history. For its concern is with ideas themselves, not their role in history. And likewise, although there will be much here of interest to historians of ideas, our concern is not simply to trace lines of intellectual descent, as we might, say, fashions or trends in art. The focus is rather on the philosophic value of the ideas, the attempt to explain their meaning and to assess their correctness.

In the twentieth century the analytic tradition more or less abandoned the history of philosophy. Past philosophies, where treated at all, were seen as continuous with present ones; their questions, methods, and meanings the same as those of their expositor, as though they had stepped off the pages of a contemporary journal. It is now widely recognized that this approach led to massive distortion and caricature and it has been largely abandoned in favour of a more contextual one. To understand a philosopher one needs to attempt the difficult task of seeing through their eyes. But there is danger too in excessive contextualization. For it is no aid to understanding to find ourselves swamped under a massive sea of ideas, all connected to each other, but none connected to anything we might think today. Too much context leads to an uncritical descriptivism.

The history of philosophy, properly conceived, attempts to avoid both of these opposed errors. For it is neither just history nor just philosophy, but a subject *sui generis* standing between the two, and as such, a challenge to traditional lines of academic demarcation of precisely the same sort as idealism itself. The history of philosophy is that discipline which allows the present to talk with the past. It is sensitive to historically different points of view (it attempts to understand what a philosophy meant *in its time*) but at the same time it will not lose sight of the essential point that philosophy is nothing if not *an engagement with real living ideas*. To object that it is neither properly philosophical nor properly historical is like complaining of a bridge that it is on neither one bank nor the other. It is sometimes urged that the task it attempts is impossible, that we can see through present eyes or past eyes but never both. However, this is a mistake, for ages, languages, and communities are never so sharply separated that they do not partially overlap, making communication a possibility. The establishment of such dialogue is, of course, a project fraught with difficulty, but the very feature that makes it difficult is the feature that makes it worthwhile.

For example, the history of philosophy is often presented as the story of how-we-got-to-be-where-we-are, and so we look back in time to find and posthumously praise all of those whose vision of the world was closest to our own, to trace the early anticipations of the things we now want to say. In this way the philosophers of the past turn out to be reassuringly familiar figures, and overall their message endorses and reinforces our modern sense of what we are dong and how we do it. Such an approach to the history of philosophy is not just suspiciously cosy, but culpably selective, for when we actually turn to pick up old texts themselves very often what we are confronted with is not similarity but bewildering difference. Yet though different, the past is never so different as to be unintelligible, irrelevant, or uninteresting to us, and if we attempt the difficult task of breaking out of our bonds, and coming to understand new conceptions of the scope, methods, problems, and purpose of philosophy, instead of simple confirmation of what we believe, the effort holds out promise of a much more valuable stimulus to new thought.

We show scant respect to past philosophers unless we make proper effort to understand their ideas but, having done so, it shows just as little respect for their thought if we fail to engage critically with it and assess its worth. However lovingly preserved or re-created, ideas do not like to be placed in museums; ideas live to be challenged and questioned. But that, of course, is something we can only do from our own perspective. Seeking first to understand as a prelude to criticism, past ideas must be approached with the same goal as any others—it is irrelevant whether their proponents are now living or dead. For this reason, I have seen no need in the foregoing study to keep quiet about what seems to me right or what wrong, what looks promising or what less so.

2

Beginnings and Influences

The out-pouring of new ideas that marked the beginning of the British Idealist movement was dated to the mid-1860s. But, of course, no revolution can spring into life *ex nihilo*, and this flowering could never have happened without the considerable preparation of the ground that had taken place beforehand. It is these antecedents that form the subject of this chapter.

In tracing the story backwards to its various roots and forerunners the aim is not to deny that the rise of British Idealism constituted a truly transformational episode, the breaking in of something markedly unlike what went before, rather the point is to insist that the change—however radical it was—was not some freak or random surd, but something which may be *explained*. For even without committing ourselves Whiggishly to a view of the nineteenth century as somehow destined to culminate in idealism, it is undeniable that a variety of factors came together which the Idealists then exploited in making their new move.

Location of its historical origins uncovers vital clues to understanding the character of the movement. But no one is just the child of their ancestors and, as the biographer who spends too long considering the parents, grandparents, and even great-grandparents of his chosen subject risks losing his reader's patience and interest before he ever begins his main task, wary of courting a similar fate, although it is always possible to specify more detail or go further back, this discussion of the origins of British Idealism will be kept to a minimum. In brief and to anticipate, it will be seen that the idealistic movement occurred when the native philosophical tradition proved itself largely moribund and unable to respond to the challenges of the day, and people began to look further afield for new ideas; to literature, and to the philosophies of Germany and of the Ancient Greeks. Initial steps were tentative but important insofar as they paved the way for the rush that was to follow.

2.1 British philosophy in the mid-nineteenth century

British Philosophy in the late 1850s and early 1860s was dominated by two main schools of thought, both with a strong geographical affiliation. In Scotland, there reigned supreme what was even then known as the Common Sense school (or the school of Intuition). Taking its origin in Reid's response to Hume, the school offered a mode of thought which, while remaining empiricist, aimed to uphold pre-reflective understandings of ethics and metaphysics in the face of philosophical doubt. Developed through the efforts of such people as Dugald Stewart and Thomas Brown, by the mid-nineteenth century its mantle had passed to Sir William Hamilton, whose 'philosophy of the unconditioned', while an anti-sceptical assertion of the primacy of belief, was also influenced by Kant insofar as it maintained that all knowledge was relative and that there could be no positive understanding of the ultimate nature of things. Following Hamilton's death in 1856, the Oxford theologian Henry Longueville Mansel, who was responsible (with John Veitch) for posthumously publishing Hamilton's lectures, himself took up the common sense cause continuing the Kantian bent; though his concern was principally to apply it to matters of religion, where he argued the case for 'theological agnosticism'.[1] Since to think is to 'condition', the endeavour to comprehend God or the infinite, the 'unconditioned', was for Mansel precisely the attempt to think the unthinkable.

South of the border the situation was different. No less empiricist, philosophy there was of a more psychologistic character, tracing its origins back to Bacon, Hobbes, and Locke. Much developed since those times, in the nineteenth century it found its champion in the figure of John Stuart Mill, whose *System of Logic* (1843) set out his massively influential inductive philosophy which extended even to mathematics, social science, and ethics, and whose *Utilitarianism* (1863), developing the earlier hedonism of such thinkers as Jeremy Bentham and his own father, James Mill, rapidly established itself as the definitive statement of consequentialist moral thinking. Although others such as Alexander Bain continued the psychologistic tradition, it saw little by way of advance after Mill.[2]

In general terms, it is not unfair to say that most British philosophy in the mid-nineteenth century was at low ebb. Reid's system of common sense first emerged in confutation of Hume's psychologistic scepticism and the fight between the two schools continued into the nineteenth century, becoming increasingly sterile. Indeed, that in 1865 one of the chief philosophical publications of the year was Mill's *An Examination of Sir William Hamilton's Philosophy*, defending his own phenomenalism against Hamilton's theory of perception, illustrates how the battle lines in philosophy had barely changed

---

[1] To use Reardon's phrase (*Oxford Dictionary of National Biography*). An Anglican clergyman, Mansel, somewhat in the manner of Kant, sought to limit the pretentions of reason in order to make proper room for revelation and faith.

[2] Utilitarianism, it turned out, was not quite a spent force and, contemporaneously with the development of Idealism, received further development at the hands of Henry Sidgwick. (See below pp.186, 202, 214.)

over the previous fifteen or twenty years, when the positions of these authors were first put forward. Philosophy seemed caught in a narrow range of polarized options; the physical world was either an external reality given in immediate perception or a mere phenomenal construction, its ultimate metaphysical basis was either a matter of un-avoidable agnosticism or of simple empirical faith, while moral duty lay in either unchanging conservative intuition or radically progressive but hedonistic and mechanical utility. Meanwhile, of course, history moved on and the scientific, social, political, religious, and aesthetic worlds of the second half of the nineteenth century were vastly different from those of the early years of the century in which these philosophical systems had first been developed.

Not everything in philosophy was static, however, and to complete the picture note must be taken of a new and strident species of naturalism that was beginning to make itself felt as, year on year, the advances of science seemed to confirm a materialist view of the world. Specifically, growing numbers of thinkers began, in one form or another, to speak out for the idea of evolution. Darwin published *The Origin of Species* in 1859, but even before then Herbert Spencer was developing an all-embracing conception of evolution which took into its compass the progressive development of the physical world, biological organisms, and the human mind, as well as human culture and society. And following him others, such as Thomas Henry Huxley, George Henry Lewes, and Leslie Stephen, took up the cause of scientific naturalism and evolution. But if this growth of evolutionary naturalism represented a new departure in philosophy, it was one that aroused as much discomfort and resistance as it did support. Moreover, from the point of view of its critics, the powerlessness of existing systems to supply clear or decisive refutation of the perceived threat turned the otherwise depressed state of philosophical speculation of that period into one of crisis.

2.2 Kant

The jibe that 'bad German philosophers, when they die, go to Oxford'[3] was, no doubt, unfair to both German philosophers and Oxford, but it is nonetheless true that a vital factor behind the emergence of British Idealism was a leavening of the native tradition with the ideas of German philosophy. The process by which this happened was a long one involving many people, the full details of which need not detain us,[4] but some highlights should be noted.

While perhaps the earliest English writings on Kant appeared in the 1790s,[5] it is necessary to move forward quite some years before one may find any significant use of

---

[3] Quoted in Webb, *A Study of Religious Thought in England*, 97.
[4] For more extensive discussion see J.H. Muirhead, *The Platonic Tradition*, 147–73; René Wellek, *Immanuel Kant in England*; R. Metz, *A Hundred Years of British Philosophy*, 29–268; James Bradley, 'Hegel in Britain'; Peter Robbins, *The British Hegelians*, chs 2–5; A.P.F. Sell, *Philosophical Idealism and Christian Belief*, ch. 1; Sandra den Otter, *British Idealism and Social Explanation*, 19–33.
[5] Metz, *A Hundred Years of British Philosophy*, 240 note.

his ideas and, with a view to the subsequent idealist legacy, the first person we should note is Samuel Taylor Coleridge.[6] In his *Biographia Literaria* (1817) Coleridge did much to introduce the ideas of Kant, as well as those of Fichte and Schelling, to a new audience. Subsequent accusations of misrepresentation and plagiarism[7] have dented Coleridge's reputation in this matter, but his importance at the time cannot be doubted. To Coleridge, who moved over from a youthful support for John Locke and David Hartley to embracing something like Schelling's *Naturphilosophie*, the discovery of Kant was a decisive moment. Kant's writings, Coleridge says, 'took possession of me as with a giant's hand.'[8] Crucial to Coleridge was the conception of mind as something which, instead of just passively copying experience, had the power to shape it—and even to penetrate through appearances to the spiritual realm behind. For while his presentation of the claim that understanding cannot establish the fundamental truths of noumenal reality is Kantian enough, drawing much out of the distinction between understanding and reason, Coleridge's development of that point as the thesis that we are nonetheless entitled to claim not simply practical knowledge but 'faith' or 'immediate awareness', of God, freedom, immortality, and even of things in themselves, moves out considerably on its own.

Another figure of great significance to idealism in the introduction of Kantian ideas was Thomas Carlyle, whose 1827 essay on the 'State of German Literature' did much to introduce Kant (as well as Fichte) to the wider reading public. Although he had perhaps even less direct knowledge of Kant than did Coleridge, Carlyle was equally convinced of his importance. Endorsing Schlegel's claim, he advertised to his readers that the critical philosophy, 'in respect of its probable influence on the moral culture of Europe . . . stands on a line with the Reformation.'[9] Like Coleridge, he takes the crucial message of Kant to be that there exist in man two faculties, understanding and reason. Understanding cannot demonstrate the existence of God, virtue, freedom, or immortality and, if it attempts to do so, only ends up in contradiction or proof of the opposite. But 'to discern these truths is the province of Reason, which therefore is to be cultivated as the highest faculty in man. Not by logic and argument does it work; yet surely and clearly may it be taught to work: and its domain lies in that higher region whither logic and argument cannot reach; in that holier region, where Poetry, and Virtue and Divinity abide.'[10] Not claiming himself fully to understand or to pass judgement on it, Carlyle nonetheless insisted that Kant's philosophy was neither impossibly obscure nor mystical, and his call for its further study was effective.

---

[6] For more detail see J.H. Muirhead, *Coleridge as Philosopher*.

[7] Whole pages were copied unacknowledged from Schelling and Maasz, a point proved by J.F. Ferrier in 1840 in *Blackwood's Magazine*.

[8] *Biographia Literaria*, ch. IX, 76.

[9] 'State of German Literature', 66.

[10] 'State of German Literature', 70.

Indeed, it is fair to say that by 1860 the ideas of Kant were well assimilated. It was possible to read his main work in English translation[11] and to find broadly reliable and reasonably engaged discussions of his views. Hamilton, Whewell, Martineau, and Mansel, for example, all knew Kant's philosophy and modulated their views in the light of that knowledge. But what had not yet occurred at this time, however, was detailed analytical engagement on the part of British philosophers with the critical system of thought.

2.3 Hegel

The philosophy of Hegel was of immense influence on British Idealism but when we turn to the story of its introduction we find that, although it is possible to trace very early references,[12] Hegel's philosophy in general made much slower inroads into British thought than did Kant's, and the 1830s, 1840s, and 1850s saw only a trickle of information. The difference calls for some consideration. Muirhead in his history paints a picture of sheer ignorance of foreign trends fed by the insularity of, especially, Scottish Common Sense philosophy, but James Bradley challenges this interpretation suggesting there was far more awareness of Hegel than that would suggest, a point with which den Otter concurs, arguing that the state of philosophy at this time was less one of ignorance about Hegelianism as one of positive hostility to it.[13] Typical of such a view was Sidgwick, who of his 1870 trip to Germany, wrote later to a friend 'before I left Halle I had made up my mind about Hegel for the present. No, I shall read no more of it: not of Hegel in the German language. But if Hegelianism shows itself in England I feel equal to dealing with it. The *method* seems to me a mistake, and therefore the system a ruin.'[14]

In consequence of such attitudes, by the early 1860s accurate translation, unbiased commentary, and detailed discussion of Hegel's philosophy were all still in limited supply in Britain, however, this situation changed in 1865 with the publication of

---

[11] A list of the main early translations of Kant: *Essays and Treatises on Moral, Political and Various Philosophical Subjects* (J. Richardson, 1798–9), *Metaphysic of Morals* (J. Richardson, 1799), *Prolegomena to any Future Metaphysics* (J. Richardson, 1819), *Lectures on Logic* (J. Richardson, 1819), *The Metaphysic of Ethics* (J.W. Semple, 1836, extracts), *The Critick of Pure Reason* (Francis Haywood, 1838), *Religion within the Boundary of Pure Reason* (J.W. Semple, 1838), *The Critique of Pure Reason* (J.M.D. Meiklejohn 1855), *Kant's Critical Philosophy for English Readers* (J.P. Mahaffy, 1872, extracts; rev edn with J.H. Bernard, 1889), *Kant's Theory of Ethics or Practical Phiulosophy* (T.K. Abbott, 1873), *The Critique of Pure Reason* (J. Max Müller, 1881), *Text-book to Kant* (James Hutchison Stirling, 1881, extracts), *The Philosophy of Kant* (John Watson, 1882, extracts), *Kant's Prolegomena and Metaphysical Foundations of Natural Science* (Ernest Belfort Bax, 1883; revised 1891), *Kant's Introduction to Logic* (T.K. Abbott, 1885), *The Philosophy of Law* (W. Hastie, 1887).

[12] The earliest (if passing) reference to Hegel has been credited to William Hamilton in his 1829 essay on 'The Philosophy of the Unconditioned' (James Bradley, 'Hegel in Britain' 4–5).

[13] Muirhead, *The Platonic Tradition*, 148–54, 160; James Bradley, 'Hegel in Britain' 1–2, 6–7; den Otter, *British Idealism and Social Explanation*, 12–13. For further discussion of Hegel's early reception in Britain see Willis, 'The introduction and Critical Reception of Hegelian Thought in Britain 1830–1900'.

[14] Letter of 8th September 1870 quoted in A.S. Sidgwick and E.M. Sidgwick, *Henry Sidgwick: A Memoir*, 238.

J.H. Stirling's book, *The Secret of Hegel*.[15] James Hutchison Stirling had attended the University of Glasgow, where he fell under the spell of both philosophy and Carlyle. He proceeded, however, to medical school and thence to medical practice; but, on receiving an inheritance at the death of his father, he became able to devote himself to philosophy, and in 1852 he relocated initially to France and then to Germany. He returned five years later, but it was not until 1865 that the fruit of his studies abroad saw light of day and he published *The Secret of Hegel*. The book was a considerable success, and he hoped that it might lead to an academic career, but despite numerous lectures, further publications and (eventually) honours, that hope was never realized.

The Secret of Hegel: being the Hegelian system in origin, principle, form, and matter, to give the book its full title, is a curious amalgam of differing elements; a personal account of the author's struggle to make sense of his subject, notes towards a true understanding, direct translation, paraphrase, textual commentary, and consideration of rival interpretations. Moreover, its writing style, full of exclamation and mock-quotation, is so much influenced by Carlyle as to be in places almost unreadable; and it was joked at the time that if Stirling 'knew the secret of Hegel he had managed to keep it to himself.'[16]

What is most notable about Stirling's book is its initiation of many of the elements that were to become characteristic markers of the British Idealist reading of Hegel. First, he champions Hegel as one offering an answer to the 'crisis of faith'. He recalls how he was led to study him by the report that Hegel 'had not only completed philosophy, but, above all, reconciled to philosophy Christianity itself. *That struck!*'[17] 'Kant and Hegel' he goes on to tell us 'have no object but to restore Faith—Faith in God—Faith in the immortality of the Soul and the Freedom of the Will—nay, Faith in Christianity as the Revealed Religion.'[18] The way in which Hegel achieved this, he felt, was through a doctrine of divine immanence. 'Here lies the germ of the thought of Hegel that initiated his whole system. The universe is but a materialisation, but an externalisation, but a heterisation of . . . the thoughts of God. . . . God has *made* the world on these thoughts. In them, then, we know the thoughts of God, and, so far, God himself.'[19] A rounding up, not down, such immanence involved, for Stirling, strong opposition to Darwinism, a cause in which he enlists Hegel's direct help.[20] A second key point is his insistence that the only proper way to understand and see the significance of Hegel is through Kant; 'the secret of Kant is the secret of Hegel.'[21] As Kant completes what Hume set in train, so Hegel finishes Kant,[22] and in doing so closes the modern world as Aristotle did the ancient.[23] The point, on this way of thinking, is that Kant cut off half-way the natural line of thought. Because he retained the thing-in-itself, Kant's categories remained only abstract, but by beginning with the

---

[15] For more detail see G.D. Stormer, 'Hegel and the Secret of James Hutchison Stirling' and J. Allard, *Logical Foundations of Bradley's Metaphysics*, 6–11.
[16] Muirhead, *Platonic Tradition*, 171.   [17] *Secret*, xviii.   [18] *Secret*, xxii.
[19] *Secret*, 85.   [20] *Secret*, 745–6.
[21] *Secret*, 98.   [22] *Secret*, 185.   [23] *Secret*, 78, 97.

most abstract (being) and showing how it develops itself into the most concrete of all (the Absolute) Hegel showed that thought instantiates itself and is therefore really concrete.[24] In consequence, 'The secret of Hegel may be indicated at shortest thus: As Aristotle—with considerable assistance from Plato—made *explicit* the *abstract* Universal that was *implicit* in Socrates, so Hegel—with less considerable assistance from Fichte and Schelling—made *explicit* the *concrete* Universal that was *implicit* in Kant.'[25] As we shall see, this emphasis on the concrete universal was a third point subsequently picked up by the British Idealists. It also explains a fourth and final point of influence, namely his choice of Hegel's *Science of Logic* as his most important work. Nearly all of the Idealists followed Stirling in this choice of text.

For all its faults, Stirling's book was well received; Green, Jowett, Carlyle, Emerson, Edward Caird, and R.B. Haldane were all admirers.[26] But its significance lay less in itself—despite his great efforts and profound conviction of the truth of the Hegelian system, there were doubts about how well Stirling had really understood his subject[27]—than in the new impetus it gave to future study.[28] For undoubtedly it is the first work in English seriously to engage with Hegel and to present before its readers the details of his words and arguments. In many ways it heralds the start of the Idealist movement.

2.4 A German import?

Slowly at first but then with growing momentum British minds woke up to the ideas of German idealism, recognizing in them a potential way through the impasse between intuitionism and scepticism, a line of reasoning whereby human knowledge might reach the metaphysical, spiritual, and moral foundations it had been seeking. Long after they had run their course in their native land they began to take on new life in a foreign country. There can be no doubt that this embracing of Kant and (especially) Hegel was a crucial factor in the emergence of British Idealism. As the school burst forth they were expounded at length and in detail, and their views presented as a crucial step forward in

---

[24] *Secret*, 191.   [25] *Secret*, xxii.

[26] Amelia Hutchison Stirling, *James Hutchison Stirling*, 66–70; Muirhead, *Platonic Tradition*, 170–1; for Green's high opinion see *Collected Works* V:454n. R.B. Haldane wrote the Preface to Amelia Hutchison Stirling's account of her father.

[27] Bosanquet wrote, 'I should not like to say it in public, but I am convinced that Stirling never understood Hegel' (*Bernard Bosanquet and his friends*, 52–3).

[28] It is possible to see this explosion of activity from the rate of translations, many made by the Idealists themselves. H. Sloman and J. Wallon's summary of *The Subjective Logic of Hegel* (1855); T.C. Sandars' summary of Hegel's *Philosophy of Right* (1855); *Hegel's lectures on the Philosophy of History* (J. Sibree, 1857); *The Secret of Hegel* (J.H. Stirling, 1865, extracts); *Hegel's Logic* (William Wallace, 1874); *The Introduction to Hegel's . . . Philosophy of Fine Art* (Bernard Bosanquet, 1886); *Hegel's Lectures on the History of Philosophy* (E.S. Haldane and F.H. Simson, 1892–6); *Hegel's Philosophy of Mind* (William Wallace, 1894); *Hegel's Lectures on the Philosophy of Religion* (E.B. Spiers and J. Burdon Sanderson, 1895); *Hegel's Philosophy of Right* (S.W. Dyde, 1896); *Hegel's Phenomenology of Spirit* (J.B. Baillie, 1910); *Hegel's Science of Logic* (W.H. Johnson and L.G. Struthers, 1929).

philosophy. But many commentators have gone further than this insofar as the Idealists themselves have often been described as 'Hegelians' or 'neo-Hegelians'—implying a relationship less of influence than discipleship.[29] Not a designation they were necessarily happy with themselves (Collingwood has argued that it was primarily their enemies who called them this)[30] the charge must nonetheless be investigated. And although adjudication on this complex question can only emerge gradually, three points seem worth making at this early stage.

First of all, it should be remembered that philosophical schools lack precise membership criteria and that, similarity and difference being matters of degree, it is always possible for one person to see close adherence where another sees creative influence. The question, 'Was he a Kantian or Hegelian?' merits an unqualified affirmative only in the cases of Kant and Hegel themselves. Moreover, the distribution of membership badges is no business of the history of philosophy, merely the tracing such lines of connection as aid our understanding.

A second equally obvious point is that, for all their agreements, the many differences between the various philosophers of the Idealist School call for separate answers in each case to the question of how Kantian or Hegelian their system is. A charge which might perhaps be made to stick against one would be harder to prosecute against a second and frankly untenable against a third.

Thus, for example, Haldane's Gifford Lectures begin with the blunt admission: 'all that is in these lectures I have either taken or adapted from Hegel, and . . . in Hegel there is twice as much again of equal importance.'[31] While McTaggart says at the end of his *Commentary on Hegel's Logic*, 'I would wish, therefore, in concluding the exposition of Hegel's philosophy which has been the chief object of my life for twenty one years, to express my conviction that Hegel has penetrated further into the true nature of reality than any philosopher before or after him.'[32] Bradley, by contrast, takes pains to place considerable distance between himself and Hegel. In the Preface to his *Principles of Logic* he rejects any affiliation, 'partly because I can not say that I have mastered his system, and partly because I could not accept what seems his main principle, or at least part of that principle.'[33] Standing between these two extremes, Green had a much more complex relation to Hegel,[34] the two sides of which were recalled by Sidgwick:

---

[29] See e.g. T.M. Lindsay, 'Recent Hegelian Contributions to English Philosophy', 476. Bertrand Russell often called them this (e.g. *History of Western Philosophy*, 701, 762, *My Philosophical Development*, 32) but the term has stuck, e.g. P. Robbins, *The British Hegelians*.

[30] 'As for the "Hegelian School" which exists in our reviews, I know no one who has met with it anywhere else' (Bradley, *Principles of Logic*, x); Collingwood, *Autobiography*, 15.

[31] *Pathway to Reality*, 309.

[32] *Commentary*, 311.

[33] *Principles of Logic*, x.

[34] For a detailed account of Green's view of Hegel see Wempe, *Beyond Equality*, ch. 1.

I remember writing to him after a visit to Berlin in 1870, and expressing a desire to 'get away from Hegel': he replied that it seemed to him one might as well try to 'get away from thought itself.' I remember, on the other hand, that in the last philosophical talk I had with him, he said, 'I looked into Hegel the other day, and found it a strange *Wirrwarr*': the sentence startled me; and the unexpected German word for 'chaos' or 'muddle' fixed it firmly in my mind.[35]

Green was keen to direct attention towards the study of Hegel, yet he admitted the whole Hegelian scheme, though in a sense valid, needed to be reworked. 'It must all be done over again,' he said.[36] The same complex relation may be seen in his 1880 review of John Caird's *Introduction to Philosophy of Religion*, where he complains that Hegel fails properly to persuade us, despite having produced 'the last word of philosophy.'[37] It may be true that the ultimate reality of things lies in thought, he continues, but we must remain armchair Hegelians—Hegelians, so to speak, on the Sundays of 'speculation' rather than the weekdays of 'ordinary thought'—so long as we understand the second of these terms by reference to our own inner experience rather than the inherent structure of the objective world.[38] Peter Nicholson concludes of Green that he was 'an original and independent thinker who works everything out for himself,' but he adds that 'he would not have thought the way he did but for his encounters with Hegel.'[39]

In no case can a charge of pure discipleship be upheld. Their readings are (by modern lights) quite odd and, very often, the Idealists make a point of disagreeing with their sources, for undoubtedly they thought of themselves as *going beyond* both Kant and (to a lesser degree) Hegel. In his Preface to the 1883 T.H. Green memorial volume, *Essays in Philosophical Criticism*, Edward Caird argues that however valuable Hegel may be found, it is as impossible as it is undesirable simply to transplant past philosophies to a new time and place,[40] a suggestion Wallace too in his *Prolegomena to Hegel* dismisses as 'absurd' and 'impossible.'[41] In this last point we find one explanation of why, after so long, the ideas of German idealism were suddenly taken up with such enthusiasm. The key to the explosion of constructive work, as well as of detailed textual study, was the realization that Kant and Hegel could be treated as *resources*, to be selectively mined and adapted, and not just systems requiring to be taken up, or resisted, *as complete wholes*. Their thoughts could be here accepted, there dismissed, here taken in spirit, but there ignored in detail, held to possess insight, but to be in need also of new working out or supplementation by rivals. Paradoxically, denying discipleship, it was precisely because

---

[35] H. Sidgwick, 'The Philosophy of T.H. Green', 19.

[36] From Edward Caird's Preface to Seth Pringle-Pattison and Haldane (eds), *Essays In Philosophical Criticism*, 5.

[37] 'Review of John Caird's *Introduction to the Philosophy of Religion*', 141.

[38] 'Review of John Caird's *Introduction to the Philosophy of Religion*', 142–6.

[39] 'T.H. Green's Doubts about Hegel's Political Philosophy', 62.

[40] *Essays in Philosophical Criticism*, Preface, 2.

[41] Wallace, *Prolegomena to . . . Hegel*, 12.

they were freed from the obligation of taking *everything*, that the Idealists were able to take *so much* from German idealism.

A third point to note is that whatever we decide about the measure of influence of Kant and Hegel on British Idealist thought, that should not blind us to the various other influences which were at work upon them; some of which I now turn to, others of which will be considered in the next chapter.

2.5 Herman Lotze

Philosophical influences from the continent were not limited to those of classical German idealism. By the mid-nineteenth century that school had collapsed, but reformed academic structures created a period of growth in philosophy, and many contemporary German philosophers were read in Britain. These included such figures as Herbart, Fechner, Fischer, Sigwart, and Wundt, but without doubt the most important of them was, the now largely forgotten, Lotze.

Rudolph Hermann Lotze held the chair of philosophy at Göttingen, between 1844 and 1880, from whence he propounded a complex philosophy which, although emphasizing organic unity and maintaining that the underlying nature of reality was spiritual, nonetheless broke clearly with Hegelian Absolute Idealism, drawing sharply the distinction between thought and reality. Yet if he was opposed to Hegelian panlogicism, he was equally critical of any psychologistic alternative, and argued strongly against any reductive materialism that would remove 'soul' or 'purpose' from the world. Rejecting the constraints of 'system' which he saw as straight-jacketing both Hegelians and Materialists, his philosophy was eclectic and of doubtful overall coherence, but it was immensely successful. He became especially influential in the English-speaking world in the 1870s and 1880s.[42] Many visited Göttingen to study under him, including the British Idealists, Haldane, Seth Pringle-Pattison, and James Ward, the American Idealists Josiah Royce, Borden Parker Bowne, and Jacob Gould Shurman, as well as others, such as John Cook Wilson.[43] And a host of further figures were influenced by his thought, including Green, Bradley, Wallace, Bosanquet, Sorley, and Rashdall. We get a snapshot of his importance at this time if we note the vast amount of work done translating his writings, much of it undertaken by the Idealists.[44]

---

[42] For details see Devaux, *Lotze et son Influence sur la Philosophie Anglo-saxonne*, and Kuntz, 'Introduction' to George Santayana's *Lotze's System of Philosophy*, 48–68.

[43] R.B. Haldane, *Autobiography*, 12–17; G.F. Barbour, 'Memoir of Andrew Seth Pringle-Patton', 28–30; P.K. Kuntz, 'Introduction', 48–64. Trips to Germany for study purposes were common at the time and taken by many of the Idealists, including Green, Mackenzie, and Sorley.

[44] *System of Philosophy: Logic* [1874] (R.L. Nettleship, F.H. Peters, F.C. Conybeare, B. Bosanquet, 1884); *System of Philosophy: Metaphysic* [1879] (T.H. Green, B. Bosanquet, C.A. Whittuck, A.C. Bradley, 1884); *Microcosmus* [1856–64] (E. Hamilton and E.E. Constance Jones, 1885). G.T. Ladd translated a series of his lecture notes: *Outlines of Metaphysic* (1884); *Outlines of Philosophy of Religion* (1885); *Outlines of Practical*

Many of the Idealists felt they could regard him as an ally. For instance in 1885 William Wallace wrote, 'on the whole he executes a retreat from the advanced idealist philosophy of the absolute and *to* a more generally human ground. But the retreat is not equivalent to a surrender. All that was precious in idealism may still be kept, but kept partly as a faith and a conviction, partly as a series of inferences gradually reached by confronting these ideals with the data of everyday experience.'[45] Both Green and Bradley drew heavily on Lotze's view of relations while, since he set himself equally against naturalism and Absolute Idealism, in affirmation of the fundamental truths of moral and spiritual experience, he was able to appeal also to Personal Idealists like Seth Pringle-Pattison.[46]

More divisive, however, was his apostasy from Hegelian rationalism. Seth Pringle-Pattison had sympathy for Lotze's instinct that room must be made in knowledge for particular feelings or intuitions in addition to universal ideas, since thoughts are true of the things we experience but they are not those things themselves, and, even if he felt that Lotze had not managed perfectly to state the relation between thought and reality, he agreed with the insistence that a necessary relation between them is not the same as an identity.[47] Nor was Seth Pringle-Pattison his only champion in this regard. The rejection of Hegel's key identification of thought and reality was precisely where Bradley found a point of connection, and of all recent writers, Bradley admits, it is Lotze to whom he owes the most.[48] Henry Jones, by contrast, was far less supportive of the break. His 1895 book, *The Philosophy of Lotze*,[49] has been described as 'a vigorous attempt, from a neo-Hegelian point of view, to stem the tide of Lotze's influence'[50] for, instead of expository endorsement, it attempts to drag Lotze forth 'as an unwilling witness'[51] in support of idealism, by exposure of the weaknesses and contradictions of his opposition to Hegel; his view of thought as representative rather than constitutive of reality. A key complaint for Jones is the consequent emphasis Lotze places on feeling as our only genuine access to reality, leaving thought to work with a material quite foreign and alien to it, something which can only lead to scepticism.[52] Jones agrees with Lotze that we must avoid 'panlogicism', the replacement of living concrete reality by the dead abstractions of thought, but the idealism of Kant and especially of Hegel he understands as the rejection of just such an error, treating as it does the pure universal of

---

Philosophy (1885); *Outlines of Psychology* (1886); *Outlines of Aesthetics* (1886); *Outlines of Logic* (1886); *Outlines of Philosophy of Religion* (F.C. Conybeare, 1892).

[45] 'Lotze', 509–10.
[46] See Chapters 4 and 10.
[47] Review of Henry Jones' *The Philosophy of Lotze*, 528 and *passim*.
[48] *Principles of Logic*, ix.
[49] An expansion of some previous articles, this was the first of two volumes planned—one on thought, one on reality—although only the first was ever written (*Old Memories*, 219).
[50] Passmore, *One Hundred Years of Philosophy*, 536.
[51] *The Philosophy of Lotze*, Preface, xiv.
[52] *The Philosophy of Lotze*, 331, 333.

thought and the pure particular of sense alike as nothing but logical abstractions.[53] Given the strength of his opposition to Lotze's system, one might wonder why Jones should write an entire book discussing a philosophy he thought so misguided, but that he should do so shows even among the most loyal supporters of Hegel a recognition that the supposed identity of the real and the rational was not unproblematic.[54]

2.6 Literary influences on Idealism

Philosophy is today a highly professionalized discipline; its exponents read and react to each other, but hardly ever to outside voices. The British Idealists were certainly aware of contemporary and preceding philosophy, but it is absolutely crucial to realize that for them the influence of non-philosophical writers was equally important.[55]

This is to be explained partly by the fact that, in their view, the matters with which philosophy dealt were ones which could legitimately be approached from more than one angle, and in this regard the influence of religious writings (notably, the Gospels, St Paul, and Luther) and of poetry (notably, Dante, Wordsworth, Coleridge, Browning, and Tennyson) were both important, and will be discussed in detail in subsequent chapters.

But there was another side to this interest which they might, perhaps, have put by saying that the true spirit of philosophy will always find expression, and if it is blocked in one direction it must flow out in another. Thus Bosanquet in an 1889 Aristotelian Society paper,[56] emphasized the currently moribund state of 'technical' British Philosophy, and the vital role played by more 'literary', 'prophetic', or 'sage' writers, nurturing and feeding speculative thought. With metaphysics dominated by common sense, psychologism, and materialism, and ethics ruled by traditional intuition or calculations of utility, the ingredient lacking from nineteenth-century British philosophy was a sense of 'spirit', any penetration above, beyond, or beneath the appearances of things to a world of greater significance or value. And these writers provided that. The figures of note here are various. On the Continent, we should record Rousseau, Lessing, Herder, Schiller and, perhaps most important of all, Goethe;[57] while native writers of importance include Coleridge, Walter Scott, John Ruskin, George Eliot, Matthew Arnold, William Morris, and Walter Pater.

---

[53] *The Philosophy of Lotze*, 69.

[54] Allard, *Logical Foundations of Bradley's Metaphysics*, 22.

[55] See Lindsay, 'Idealism of Jones and Caird', 176.

[56] 'The Part Played by Aesthetic in the Development of Modern Philosophy'.

[57] Goethe was in Jones' eyes ones of those poet-philosophers who 'teach the world as it never was taught before, in any age, how sacred it all is and how interfused with the light divine' (*Idealism as Practical Creed*, 101) while for Haldane he was 'the greatest critic of life that has spoken in modern times' (*Pathway*, 323). Between 1898 and 1912 Haldane (together with Peter Hume Brown, the Scottish historian, who shared his passion) made annual trips to Weimar where Goethe had lived; he was for a while president of the English Goethe Society, and Volume II of his *Pathway to Reality* includes a portrait of Goethe as its frontispiece. Sorley cites as

While clearly neither possible nor appropriate to offer detailed examination of all these figures, it is worth considering one especially dear to the Idealists, and that is Thomas Carlyle. Carlyle was influential on Victorian society generally, of course, but his particular significance to the British Idealists can hardly be overstressed. He was the writer of their youth. Naming him the greatest literary influence of his own student days, Edward Caird recalled that 'at that time, Carlyle was the author who exercised the most powerful charm upon young men who were beginning to think. It is hardly possible for those who now for the first time take up Carlyle's works to realise how potent that charm was.'[58] And both R.B. Haldane[59] and Andrew Seth Pringle-Pattison[60] recollect that what was true for Scottish undergraduates in the 1860s held equally in the 1870s. Not that the lessons Carlyle had to teach were limited to Scotland. The youthful Green was much influenced,[61] Nettleship admiringly suggested in a letter to Henry Scott Holland that his work ought to be available in pocket form so that 'one might drink of him whenever one felt faint,'[62] to Henry Jones he was 'probably one of the greatest spiritual forces in this country in the nineteenth century,'[63] while Bosanquet described Carlyle and his wife as 'about as noble a pair of human beings as ever lived', adding that 'his work, which was made possible by her, has had an influence on English life that cannot be calculated.'[64] What was it that all these people found so important and inspiring in the sage of Chelsea's writing? Of the myriad insights to be taken away from Carlyle, the following perhaps stand out.

Though not a particularly Christian thinker, Carlyle is a deeply *religious* one. 'A man's religion is the chief fact with regard to him',[65] he urged, the need to find one's proper home in the universe an imperative second to none. In June 1821, in Leith Walk Edinburgh, Carlyle experienced a striking spiritual awakening which is (partially) related in his extraordinary novel, *Sartor Resartus*. He there describes a state of existential hopelessness into which the book's narrator and hero, Teufelsdröckh, falls having lost his religious faith, a state in which, 'To me the Universe was all void of Life, of Purpose, of Volition, even of Hostility: it was one huge, dead, immeasurable Steam-engine, rolling on, in its dead indifference, to grind me limb from limb.'[66] Against this despair rises up the sudden realization that he himself is quite *other* than this world and

---

meriting special approval Goethe's recognition of the way in which analysis can kill the life of something (*Moral Values*, 248).

[58] 'The Genius of Carlyle', 231.

[59] 'The Conduct of Life', 6–8.

[60] Preface to *Selected Essays of Thomas Carlyle*, viii.

[61] A.V. Dicey wrote to Green's widow of the 'great admiration which when I first knew your husband, he felt for Carlyle' (A.V. Dicey to Mrs Green, 17th September 1882, T.H. Green papers; quoted in Gordon and White, *Philosophers at Educational Reformers*, 59).

[62] Holland, *Henry Scott Holland: Memoir and Letters*, 28.

[63] *A Faith that Enquires*, 7.

[64] Letter of 24 December 1887 quoted in Helen Bosanquet, *Bernard Bosanquet, A Short Account of his Life*, 41.

[65] *On Heroes, Hero-Worship and the Heroic in History*, 2. cf. Bosanquet, *What Religion is*, vii.

[66] *Sartor*, 196.

can stand defiantly against it, a fundamental recognition that spiritual life itself can never be reduced away. To such a unresponsive cosmos he protests, '*I* am not thine, but Free, and forever hate thee!' ('The Everlasting No').[67]

Teufelsdröckh is a philosopher and born out of this spiritual rebirth puts forward what he calls a 'clothes philosophy' whose message is that Nature, Life, and the Universe are but a 'living garment' or 'symbol' of God or Spirit,[68] for 'All visible things are emblems; what thou seest is not there on its own account; strictly taken, is not there at all: Matter exists only spiritually, and to represent some Idea, and body it forth. Hence Clothes, as despicable as we think them, are so unspeakably significant.'[69] This position, which he characterized as a 'high Platonic Mysticism',[70] was also (of course) idealism. Its greatest attraction, perhaps, lay in the fact that it offered not just an altered vision of the world but of human nature itself, for what holds of objects holds even more of the soul. To Carlyle, it is because we are more than we know that we cannot be satisfied with any lower view of our nature. 'Man's Unhappiness, as I construe, comes of his Greatness; it is because there is an Infinite in him, which with all his cunning he cannot quite bury under the Finite.'[71] Carlyle's consequent attacks on the demeaning hedonism and utilitarianism that were dominant in his day were another aspect of his thought that resonated with the Idealists. In its emphasis on pleasure, utilitarianism is satirized as 'pig philosophy' in which paradise consists in the unlimited attainability of Pig's-wash.[72] But his opposition was not such as could be dissolved by something as easy as Mill's distinction between higher and lower satisfactions, for what he really objected to was the very notion that we should make happiness at all the goal in life. As Teufelsdröckh reflects further, he sees that the human problem lies precisely in the search for individual contentment. We must seek not happiness, but blessedness. We must love not pleasure, but God ('The Everlasting Yea').[73]

Though in many ways an anti-philosopher, with contempt for logical proof in general, Carlyle drew on philosophical sources (as we have seen) and his ideas had much philosophical potential. To many of the British Idealists, it seemed that they were simply reformulating (in more detailed and philosophical a fashion) the idealism they had first read as students in Carlyle. It should not be supposed, however, that the Idealists approved of, or followed, everything that their exalted spiritual guide advanced. Carlyle championed the natural equality of all and supported social change, but his was a radicalism quite unlike that of those to whom the term is more usually applied. The stern calling he prescribed for individuals he repeated for society, leading

---

[67] *Sartor*, 198. Jones (*Browning as Philosophical and Religious Teacher*, 55–6) and Haldane ('Conduct of Life', 6–8) both testify to the importance of this passage.

[68] *Sartor*, 220, 236, 254.

[69] *Sartor*, 89.

[70] *Sartor*, 81.

[71] *Sartor*, 221. This idea is echoed in Bosanquet especially.

[72] *Latter-Day Pamphlets*, VIII, 379–80,

[73] *Sartor*, 223–4. *Past and Present*, bk. 3, ch. 4.

him to express an elitist love of heroes and a loathing for democracy. This strong individualism offended the Idealists' social holism, and Caird, Macunn, and Mackenzie all took him to task in their various ways for his failure to value the unity and solidarity of civic life.[74]

2.7 Forerunners of Idealism

2.7.1 James Frederick Ferrier

Although the idealist movement proper did not begin until the 1860s, there were a few philosophers before then who may be thought of as forerunners, figures who began to sense the possibility of new lines of thought and who freed up the ground for others to go further. The first such person to consider is James Frederick Ferrier, a Scot, who was educated in the Universities of Edinburgh, Oxford, and Heidelberg, before finally he became Professor of Moral Philosophy at St Andrews.[75]

His principal work, *Institutes of Metaphysics* (1854), marks something new in both message and method. It is divided into three sections. Section I, *The Epistemology or Theory of Knowing*, uses Berkeleian ideas to argue for the relativity of subject and object, section II, *The Agnoiology or Theory of Ignorance*, uses this idealist result to urge that knowledge of either subject or object as it is in itself out of all relation to the other is an utter impossibility, even for a supreme intelligence, and so not really ignorance at all, thereby opposing Hamilton's doctrine of the unconditioned (although the case it makes is equally applicable to Kant also),[76] while section III, *The Ontology or Theory of Being*, puts forward a positive metaphysic of monistic idealism. The approach throughout is rationalistic (it even adopts a geometrical model of presentation) and opposed to both the common sense and the psychological styles of its day.

To assess the historical significance of this work is not easy. Ferrier's thought is sometimes proposed as a vital step in the story of how Hegel came to Britain. He wrote two detailed articles on Hegel and Schelling for the *Imperial Dictionary of Universal Biography* (1857–63)[77] and his *Institutes* ranks Hegel (above Kant) with Plato, Leibniz, and Spinoza.[78] Moreover, the position he ultimately advances is unquestionably an Absolute Idealist one. At the same time, however, he is openly doubtful just how much can be usefully got out of Hegel's writing,[79] and responding to criticisms of the book, he absolutely denied that there had been any influence.

---

[74] 'Genius of Carlyle', 264; *Six Radical Thinkers*, 152; 'Dangers of democracy', 164–8.

[75] For further details on Ferrier see Keefe, 'The Return to Berkeley', 'James Ferrier and the Theory Of Ignorance'.

[76] It is worth noting that we find similar arguments against the 'unconditioned' in both J. Caird *Introduction* (ch. I) and E. Caird *Evolution of Religion* (ch. IV).

[77] James Bradley, 'Hegel in Britain', 8.

[78] *Institutes*, 42.

[79] 'who has ever yet uttered one intelligible word about Hegel? Not any of his countrymen, not any foreigner, seldom even himself' (*Institutes*, 91). He has a similarly low opinion of Kant. 'Kant had glimpses of

Some of my critics assert that my philosophy is nothing but an echo of Hegel's.... The exact truth of the matter is this: I have read most of Hegel's works again and again, but I cannot say that I am acquainted with his philosophy. I am able to understand only a few short passages here and there in his writings.... If others understand him better, and to a larger extent, they have the advantage of me, and I confess that I envy them the privilege. But, for myself, I must declare that I have not found one word or one thought in Hegel which was available for my system, even if I had been disposed to use it.[80]

Nor is the question of his relation to the British Idealists any clearer. James Seth, Sorley, and Muirhead all include him in their histories, Muirhead describing him as a 'pioneer' of the Idealist movement,[81] and certainly his system is a striking anticipation of theirs. But was there any more direct influence? Arguably so. His university career interrupted by ill health, Edward Caird was for a short while (1856–7) at St Andrews. It is not known for certain whether he attended Ferrier's classes, but undoutedly in subsequent years he advised his students to read Ferrier.[82] Less conjecturally we know it was Ferrier who first awoke an interest in philosophy on the part of William Wallace when he was a student at St Andrews.[83] Nor was Ferrier's influence confined to St Andrews. R.B. Haldane wrote in the introduction to his sister's life of Ferrier that when he was a student at Edinburgh in 1875, Ferrier's writings were much read; indeed, that although he had died more than ten years earlier, the memory of his personality was still a living influence. To the students of that time 'Ferrier had pointed out a path which seemed to lead us in the direction of Germany if we would escape from Mill, and Stirling was urging us in the same sense.'[84]

2.7.2 John Grote

The second pioneering figure to consider is John Grote, younger brother of the more famous utilitarian, George Grote. Educated in Cambridge, where he finally became Knightbridge Professor of Moral Philosophy, the first volume of his *Exploratio Philosophica* was published in 1865—the same year as Stirling's *Secret*. His *Examination of the*

---

the truth; but his remarks are confused in the extreme in regard to what he calls the unity (analytic and synthetic) of consciousness' (*Institutes*, 90).

[80]   In an 1856 pamphlet entitled 'Scottish Philosophy, the old and the new'. This was partially reproduced in Volume I of his posthumous *Lectures on Greek Philosophy and other Philosophical Remains* as 'Appendix to the *Institutes of Metaphysics*'. The quotation is from p.486 of this volume.

[81]   Seth, *English Philosophers*, 332–9; Sorley, *History of English Philosophy*, 284–6; Muirhead, *The Platonic Tradition*, 162.

[82]   Jones, E. *Life and Philosophy of Edward Caird*, 19, 78.

[83]   Caird's 'Biographical Introduction' to Wallace's posthumous *Lectures and Essays*, viii. Wallace graduated in 1864, the year Ferrier died.

[84]   Elizabeth S. Haldane, *James Frederick Ferrier,* 7. The younger sister of R.B. Haldane and J.S. Haldane, Elizabeth Haldane—who never married but lived with her philosopher-statesman brother at Cloan and London—was notable also as a philosopher. She collaborated on translations of *Hegel's Lectures on the History of philosophy* (1892–6) and *The Philosophical Works of Descartes* (1911–12) as well as writing three philosophical monographs, *The Wisdom and Religion of a German Philosopher* (1897), *James Frederick Ferrier* (1899), and *Descartes, his Life and Times* (1905).

Utilitarian Philosophy (1870) and the second volume of the *Exploratio Philosophica* (1900) were published posthumously.[85]

Through written in the knowledge of and with affinities to, both Hegel and Ferrier, Grote's metaphysics traces its own path to idealism. The current field he finds to be occupied by three sorts of philosophy. *The Philosophy of the Human Mind or Psychology*, by which he means the empirical tradition from Locke to Mill that seeks to explain consciousness by treating us, its possessors, as one object among a universe of similar objects,[86] and *ultra-phenomenalism*, *mis-phenomenalism* or (more helpfully) *positivism*, by which he means the scientific or naturalistic attempt to treat mind as a just species of animal intelligence, and which he regards as 'not properly philosophy',[87] are both rejected as of only limited value relative to 'the true and real philosophy',[88] which he calls both *idealism* and *personalism*,[89] and which takes as its given or basic starting point our consciousness of reality. Such a philosophy is not without danger and he warns of both *notionalism*, which illegitimately reifies what are philosophical notions,[90] and subjectivism or scepticism to which Kant and Berkeley in their different ways alike fell prey.[91] Grote's idealism itself is given more flesh in the second volume of the *Exploratio* where he argues that 'Knowledge is really a phase or mode of consciousness and, the object as well as the subject being a part of itself, it is really *mind* that is its object as well as its subject; and existence, the more immediate object, is such, in virtue of its being looked upon as the result of mind or intelligence. Knowledge is the sympathy of intelligence with intelligence, through the medium of qualified or particular existence.'[92]

Of even greater interest with regard to subsequent thought is Grote's moral philosophy, and that more so in its negative than in its positive aspect, for he was as determined a critic of egoistic hedonism and utilitarianism as the Idealists who followed him. He gives a thorough exploration of the many problems and fallacies of Mill's system, but his fundamental point is that while pleasure or happiness is a legitimate goal, it is but one small part of ethics (he calls it 'eudaimonics') next to a far greater part ('aretics'), dealing with non-consequential value. The utilitarian viewpoint must, therefore, be widened to include, on one side, motive, and on the other, such ideals as virtue, duty, and the perfection of character. Grote gives particular emphasis to justice, distribution, and self-sacrifice, all areas in which utilitarianism is notoriously weak. While Grote's work undoubtedly contains many such idealist themes, his precise influence on British Idealism, however, is harder to discern. It has been argued that he helped shape the movement in so far as it developed in Cambridge,[93] and that is not

---

[85] For a detailed discussion of Grote see John Gibbins, *John Grote*.   [86] *Exploratio*, I:ix.
[87] *Exploratio*, I:xiii.   [88] *Exploratio*, I:xi.   [89] *Exploratio*, I:146.
[90] *Exploratio*, I:73.   [91] *Exploratio*, I:114.
[92] *Exploratio*, II:296.   [93] John Gibbins, *John Grote*, ch. 10.

unlikely, but it must be allowed that the chief Cambridge Idealists were mainly influenced from outside.[94]

2.7.3 Benjamin Jowett

Benjamin Jowett, although not a *forerunner* of Idealism in the sense of someone who, like Ferrier or Grote, clearly advocated such a position, was nonetheless absolutely crucial in its emergence. For many years a tutor at Balliol, before becoming its Master, and a long-serving Professor of Greek in the University at large, Jowett re-energized classical studies at Oxford (and, indeed, nationally.) This he did in large part through his *Dialogues of Plato translated into English with Analyses and Introductions* which first appeared in 1871. His original intention had been to produce a commentary on the *Republic*, but for an adequate account of that he found it necessary to bring in Plato's other dialogues, and the scheme was expanded. As the title suggests, what Jowett presented was more than just translation, but combined analysis and interpretation which, together with the manifest literary qualities of his translations (many of which are still read today), made him the unsurpassed Plato expert of the age. He also published a translation of Aristotle's *Politics*—in which he challenged the traditional picture of Aristotle as simply an empiricist[95]—but his principal influence at Oxford, was to direct attention to Plato and to raise him up on the same level as Oxford's more traditionally favoured ancient philosopher, for example, by getting the *Republic* designated in 1853 a 'set text' for Greats, alongside those of Aristotle. Jowett also injected more modern philosophy into the course, helping further to free it from a *purely* historical or literary focus.[96]

The second important fact about Jowett was his early appraisal of the significance of German philosophy. Before he turned in his later years to Plato, Jowett's first interests had been in theology, and these had taken him, as early as 1844 and 1845, to Germany where he learnt about Hegel. On returning, he set to a more thorough study of Hegel,

[94] Sorley's (Cambridge 1879–88, 1900–33) formative education was in Edinburgh and MacKenzie's (Cambridge 1886–96) in Glasgow. Mackenzie introduced his Glasgow Hegelianism to Cambridge and, in particular to McTaggart (Cambridge 1885–1925) (*John Stuart Mackenzie*, 50), although McTaggart was also was much inspired by Oxford's Bradley. G.E. Moore recalls McTaggart saying of an occasion when he met Bradley at Oxford that, when Bradley entered, he felt 'as if a Platonic Idea had walked in the room' ('Autobiography', 22).

[95] 'Aristotle is thought to have been the first who based knowledge on experience, but ever and anon the ideal or poetical image which was always latent in Greek philosophy, though clothed in an unpoetical dress, and reduced to a skeleton, returns upon him. It would have been a surprise to himself, and still more to his school, if he could have recognised how nearly he approached in reality to some of those conceptions on which he was making war' (*The Politics of Aristotle*, 'Introduction', xix).

[96] 'The teaching of philosophy in Oxford at this time centred round certain works of Aristotle, to which portions of Plato had recently been added. . . . The study of Plato and Aristotle had lately entered on a new phase. With an increased knowledge of German philosophy, and especially of German history of philosophy, working through men like Jowett and Pattison, it had become (to use a current antithesis) less "literary" and more "philosophical." In other words, their works had begun to be treated less as instructive analyses or brilliant criticisms of the commonplaces of culture, and more as partial expressions of systematic views of human life and the world' (Nettleship, 'Memoir', lxx).

beginning a translation of the *Logic*, and becoming embroiled in some controversial biblical scholarship. The precise influence of Hegel on his own thinking is contested. Although never a follower and, indeed, as he grew older, more and more critical, of Hegel's thought,[97] he had no doubt of its importance. Nor did he keep this to himself. His great significance to the story lies in the fact that as a fellow and then Master of Balliol College until his death in 1893 he passed his interest in Hegel on to Green, Caird, Bosanquet, Ritchie, Wallace, and Arnold Toynbee, all of whom were Balliol students. Jowett, we may say, was the route by which Hegel came finally into Oxford.

Jowett's two interests were not unconnected, of course, for he saw a fundamental affinity between Platonic and Hegelian idealism. He knew not only Hegel, but Hegel's account of ancient philosophy, and in his commentaries he made use of these ideas to explain Plato. Moreover, his 'Hegelian' belief in the development or evolution of ideas led him to see a continuity between their positions. It allowed him to see modern thought as a fuller understanding of the things Plato had been trying to say, which is as much as to say it allowed him to see in Plato anticipations of more modern thinking.[98] At times, it must be allowed, Jowett's Plato is made to speak in an anachronistically Hegelian idiom—'The Platonic unity of differences or opposites', for example, is explained as a forerunner of 'the Hegelian concrete or unity of abstractions'.[99] But for the most part Jowett is more catholic. His general aim, he admits 'has been to represent Plato as the father of Idealism',[100] that doctrine 'which places the divine above the human, the spiritual above the material, the one above the many, the mind before the body'.[101] And in this broad spirit he tries also to present Plato as criticizing sensational empiricism,[102] and as preaching an ideal ethic of self-sacrifice to the higher common good.[103]

Jowett shaped classics at Oxford for a generation. Looking back, from the idealist-unfriendly perspective of 1959, C.S. Lewis, the celebrated Christian writer who first went up to Oxford in 1917, wrote

The tradition of Jowett still dominated the study of ancient philosophy when I was reading Greats. One was brought up to believe that the real meaning of Plato had been misunderstood by Aristotle and wildly travestied by the neo-Platonists, only to be recovered by the moderns. When recovered, it turned out (most fortunately) that Plato had really all along been an English Hegelian, rather like T.H. Green.[104]

---

[97] Jowett felt, in particular, that Green had gone too far in his Hegelianism. His Notebooks complain that Green had become a servant of the Hegelian system rather than its master (Robbins, *The British Hegelians*, 44) while in a letter to Florence Nightingale he says Green has become so swamped by Hegelian metaphysics as to have become unintelligible to his students (den Otter, *British Idealism and Social Explanation*, 10).

[98] He did not, of course, equate them, not least because as his thought developed he became increasingly critical of Hegelianism, but finding in Plato 'the germs of many thoughts which have been further developed by Spinoza and Hegel' he confessed to 'difficulty in separating the germ from the flower, or in drawing the line which divides ancient from modern philosophy' (*Dialogues of Plato*, IV:316).

[99] *Dialogues of Plato*, IV: 314, 316.   [100] *Dialogues of Plato*, I: xi.

[101] *Dialogues of Plato*, II: 19.   [102] *Dialogues of Plato*, IV: Intro to *Theaetetus* passim.

[103] *Dialogues of Plato*, II: 295–6.   [104] 'Fern Seeds and Elephants', 247.

2.7.4 James Martineau

A number of the Idealists were drawn towards Unitarianism, and at least two even contemplated careers in the Unitarian ministry,[105] it is therefore worth briefly considering this intellectual tradition with which they felt so closely at home. The intellectual champion of Unitarianism at this time was James Martineau. The strong ethical tenor of his mind led him to reject what he saw as the barren materialism of Locke, Hartley, and Priestley on which he had been brought up, replacing deism with theism and materialistic necessitarianism with a quasi-Berkeleian idealism that emphasized the role of free will.

Green and Martineau were on warm terms with each other, a friendship fed by the close affinity in both their views and their characters.[106] As a Unitarian, Martineau regarded the figure of Jesus unique in degree rather than in kind, that is, he saw him as a man vastly more inspired than any other by the spirit of God, thereby revealing the potentiality for fellowship with God that lies in us all.[107] As we shall see later on, this same line was taken up by Green (and many of the other Idealists) and, more than just coincidence on a technical point in Christology, it represents a deep point of sympathy in their respective understandings of human nature. For both, the 'indwelling of God' is a literal truth about the proper nature and potential of human character; the development of the human moral consciousness is to be understood as nothing less than the progressive self-realization and revelation of God. As Martineau's pupil and later colleague, C.B. Upton put it, 'Where Martineau and Green were entirely at one was in the conviction that the eternal Thinker, of whose thought the universe is the expression, progressively reveals Himself and His character in the human soul.'[108] And as Martineau himself put it in an early sermon, anticipating several of the later idealists,

---

[105]   A career in the dissenting ministry was one option Green considered, once admitting (in 1861) that 'a modified unitarianism suits me very well' (Nettleship, 'Memoir', xxxv). From 1885 to 1888 J.H. Muirhead studied philosophy and theology at Manchester New College (then in London) where James Martineau was Principal, with a view perhaps to becoming a Unitarian minister (Muirhead, *Reflections by a Journeyman*, ch. V). A contemporaneous novel that brings together Unitarianism and the Victorian crisis of faith is William Hale White's *The Autobiography of Mark Rutherford*.

[106]   Upton recalls that 'with T.H. Green he cherished a warm and much valued friendship. He delighted to recall his visits to Balliol and the conversations he there enjoyed' (*Dr Martineau's Philosophy*, xviii). Muirhead confirms that Martineau 'was himself strongly attracted both by the teaching and the personality of T.H. Green' (*Reflections by a Journeyman*, 67).

[107]   'The Incarnation is true, not of Christ exclusively, but of Man universally and God everlastingly. He bends into the human to dwell there; and humanity is the susceptible organ of the divine' (Letter 5 June 1895, cited in J.E. Carpenter, *James Martineau Theologian and Teacher*, 404). 'The Divineness which I meant to claim for Jesus is no other than that which I recognise in every human soul, which realises its possible communion with the Heavenly Father. And the pre-eminence which I ascribe to him is simply one of degree, so superlative, however, as to stand out in strong relief from the plane of ordinary history' (letter 13 August 1894 to Rev. Valentine Davis. MS in the library of Harris Manchester College, Oxford). We find the same view in his pupil, C.B. Upton: 'the Incarnation here contended for, though, in my view, most completely manifested in the personality and teachings of Jesus of Nazareth, is by no means peculiar to him, but is, in its essence, the intrinsic property and highest privilege of all rational souls' (*Lectures on the Bases of Religious Belief*, viii).

[108]   *Dr Martineau's Philosophy*, xviii.

'no merely finite being can possibly believe the infinite'.[109] At first sight their views may seem rather different. For Martineau conscience is necessarily dualistic, a state in which Self stands face to face with the higher moral authority of God, whereas for Green 'it is the very essence of moral duty to be imposed by a man upon himself.' But the difference disappears when we remember that for Green the self-legislating moral consciousness in time is precisely the communication of an eternal consciousness.[110] There was affinity too in the profoundly ethical cast of both their minds. Equally opposed to the hedonism and utilitarianism of the day, they both took from Kant the overwhelming importance of *motives* in moral action.[111]

But any assessment of his significance for Green must note too Martineau's deep dissent from what he regarded as the Hegelian element in the system. (Although at heart he always felt Green was really more of a Kantian.[112]) With what amounted almost to a horror of pantheism, he could not accept any wholesale absorption of the finite into the infinite spirit, while the primacy he accorded to the freedom of contingency, prevented him from resting even in the non-natural freedom of self-determination that Green worked so hard to secure. It was, admitted Martineau, no easy task to draw a line that separates God's being from our own, but if in a region higher than volition there is some sense in which we are one with God, the decisions of our will at least are unimpeachably our own.[113] In both of these worries Martineau was followed by his colleague C.B. Upton, who was an important early critic of British Idealism in its Absolutist form.[114]

Not surprisingly this antipathy meant that Martineau never fully appreciated or anticipated the importance Idealism was to have. He doubted Green's thought would have any 'permanent influence' and, thinking the condition in which he left it quite unstable, looked forward to the next advance of the Greenian school.[115] This he thought he saw in the idealism of Andrew Seth Pringle-Pattison and his brother James Seth.[116] And certainly Martineau's position, often described as 'ethical theism', with its

---

[109] 'The Spirit of Life in Jesus Christ', 2.

[110] *Types of Ethical Theory*, II:5; *Prolegomena to Ethics*, §324; *Types of Ethical Theory*, II:99.

[111] *Types of Ethical Theory*, II:23; Drummond and Upton, *The Life and Letters of James Martineau*, II:390.

[112] Drummond and Upton, *The Life and Letters of James Martineau*, II:360. In a letter dated 6 December 1892 to a former pupil, Alexander Craufurd, Martineau even suggests that in the end Green experienced something of a change of heart, writing 'I know Hegel's "Philosophy of Religion"; but neither in it, nor in his English interpreters, have I found any future life that does not disappoint its name. The genuine hope dawned upon Thomas Hill Green on his death-bed, I am assured; not, however, as a corollary from his Hegelianism, but rather as an emergence from it' (Craufurd, *Recollections of James Martineau*, 221–2).

[113] 'Lo! God is here', 83.

[114] Upton, Review of *Prolegomena to Ethics*, 831; *Lectures on the Bases of Religious Belief*, ch.VIII.

[115] Drummond and Upton, *The Life and Letters of James Martineau*, II:226; J.E. Carpenter, *James Martineau*, 571.

[116] Upton, *Dr Martineau's Philosophy*, 155–6. On 29 November 1893 Martineau, then in his eighty-ninth year, wrote to Seth Pringle-Pattison: 'I have read your essay on Man's Place in Nature with the keenest interest, and with all but unqualified assent to its reasoning and its critical estimates through out. I would fain express to you, if I could, the happy confidence with which, at the end of life, I anticipate from you the much-needed reaction from the dominant Hegelian form of Idealism. My hopes in this respect used to rest, as

strong emphasis on the individual or personal character of moral life, was really more influential on the Personal Idealists. His conception that in conscience or moral obligation we are confronted with a consciousness both *other* and *higher*,[117] is clearly echoed in Illingworth, and openly acknowledged as a source—if with a greater degree of reserve—by both Seth Pringle-Pattison and Webb.[118]

2.8 The success of Idealism

When, from all these beginnings the British Idealist philosophy began to spring forth, it was by any measure, immensely successful; a fact which, before we chart the details of its course, we should stop to note. The few pioneering works of the 1860s were followed by a flood of writings in the 1870s and 1880s, as a whole generation of idealist philosophers emerged. They were especially successful at Glasgow and Oxford; although Edinburgh, St Andrews, and Cambridge all contributed as well (as, in due time, did the new provincial universities.)[119] Nor was this some mere fashion, as rapid in its passing as in its arrival; Idealism continued to dominate the philosophical scene for at least thirty years, and to be a formidable force for many more. It must not be forgotten that philosophical theories are adopted because they are perceived to be true and the arguments in their support to be sound, but it should be remembered as well that such a sense is unlikely to occur unless the theory is perceived also to answer certain questions, meet certain needs or solve certain problems that press at that time.[120] It is, therefore, worth enquiry into the contributory factors that made idealism intellectually so successful.[121]

The late nineteenth century saw a series of threats to the spiritual or religious view of humanity and its place in the universe—from the advance of science to the advent of evolutionary theory to the results of Biblical Criticism—which so overwhelmed previous certainties as to constitute nothing short of an intellectual crisis. Not just the

---

I often told him, on Thomas Hill Green, whose noble moral nature was always pressing him in that direction. And now it is my fancy that his mission has devolved on you. It is a great trust; and may be executed with full acknowledgment of the lofty influence, intellectual and ethical, exercised by his genius and Edward Caird's during their period of ascendancy. But they have not said the last word in philosophy, and would be the first to repudiate the pretension' (Barbour, 'Memoir of Pringle-Pattison', 80).

[117] 'it takes two to establish an obligation' (*Types of Ethical Theory* II:100). 'In the act of Perception,' says Martineau, 'we are immediately introduced to an *other than ourselves that gives us what we feel*; in the act of Conscience we are immediately introduced to a *Higher than ourselves that gives us what we feel*' (*Study of Religion*, II:27).

[118] Seth Pringle-Pattison, 'Martineau's Philosophy', 95–6; Webb, *Divine Personality and Human Life*, 123. (Note: Andrew Seth Pringle-Pattison's works can all be found together in the Bibliography under Pringle-Pattison.

[119] It was a success repeated also in America. Rogers wrote in 1922 that, 'This English adaptation of German Idealism attracted during the last quarter of the century a large proportion of the best speculative intellect of England and America, attaining in the universities a dominance that for a time was almost complete' (*English and American Philosophy Since 1800*, 208).

[120] To admit the necessity of such a condition is not, of course, to admit its sufficiency.

[121] For further detailed discussion of these factors see Quinton, 'Absolute Idealism', 126–39.

articles of faith, but the sense of self and of moral value, appeared under threat from a growing naturalism and materialism. Crucially, the old division between the school of Mill and Hamilton seemed unable to respond to this challenge, quite lacking the resources to deal with it. The 'unknown' was too thin and abstract a notion to ground real hope, but honesty ruled out any faith that called on one simply to close one's eyes to intellectual progress. It was in this frame of mind that many began to look to idealism, whether classical or German, for help. On an idealist understanding the infinite was no longer beyond the reach of human cognition but rather to be encountered, in a world transfigured, all around us. Whether they found explicit defence of Christianity, or simply a friendlier universe, all heard Carlyle's call for a higher self in a higher world. This will be discussed further in Chapter 5.

Other factors that aided the idealist cause were more temporal. By any measure late nineteenth-century social conditions were appalling, a deep indictment on the political philosophy of the preceding century that had allowed them to develop. Idealism offered a moral and political theory which addressed these concerns and that was a large factor in its success. In this regard, the success of idealist philosophy needs to be considered alongside and even to a degree as overlapping with the broader parallel movement known as 'the new liberalism' which, without going so far as socialism, argued for increased state intervention in social, economic, and cultural life. The Idealists (especially Green, Ritchie, and Haldane) are sometimes included in their number, and certainly there are similarities, but both the New Liberals and the Idealists were very diverse groups, the former including figures such as L.T. Hobhouse who were suspicious of, and unfriendly towards, idealism, while the latter included such figures as Jones, Bosanquet, and Muirhead who were suspicious of the collectivism of the New Liberals.[122] The success of idealist philosophy in the social field sprang also in part from its close connection with praxis. To the Idealists it was not enough to understand what needed to be done, one had to go out and do it. They took their ideas right into their own lives, and this stimulated the creation of ethical societies, university settlements, and such like, which were important to its spread insofar as they gave to the movement a real life and impetus of its own, which it would have lacked had it simply remained in the universities. For beyond mere beliefs, or individual efforts, such institutions—many of which are still with us—have themselves a power to carry ideas forward. These matters will be discussed further in Chapter 7.

Another factor that Idealists both benefited from and contributed to concerned the life of the universities. Mark Pattison in his 1876 *Mind* account of 'Philosophy at Oxford' complains of the 'stagnation of philosophical thought' at the university,[123] while some time later William Wallace makes a similar complaint that in England generally 'the fountain head of the philosophical stream has not been in the Universities.' And he contrasts the case with Germany where the universities were the centre

---

[122] Collini, *Liberalism and Sociology*, 45; Vincent and Plant *Philosophy Politics and Citizenship*, ch. 5.
[123] 'Philosophy at Oxford', 86.

of philosophy. Institutional organization, he argued, provides at the very least a continuous tradition with more or less uniform vocabulary and usage which allows for a kind of progress that individual disorganized or even eccentric private efforts can never produce.[124] Like German philosophy, German educational systems were widely admired and played a significant role in fuelling a major programme of educational and academic reform in Britain; these processes included the establishment of new chairs and lectures, and led in the next century to the creation of the new universities. Idealism both contributed to and benefitted from these developments. One part of this change was the emergence of philosophy itself as an autonomous academic subject, distinguished from either theology or classics and marked, for example, by the setting up of specialized journals.[125] Green himself has been heralded as 'the man who for the first time established philosophy as an independent discipline at Oxford.'[126] In this sense philosophy was a new subject, calling for a new methodology and new body of professional exponents, and Welchman has argued that the rise of Absolute Idealism may be explained in part by the fact that it was the only school willing or able to take up this challenge and to defend the legitimacy of philosophy itself.[127]

One last point must be mentioned. Lakatos argued that no existing scientific research programme is ever abandoned unless a stronger one presents itself as available replacement, nor any new one adopted unless the current programme is perceived as relatively weaker.[128] The same is true of philosophical theories and in this regard it must be noted that had there been more vigour in native philosophy at this time the Idealist story might well have been different, but (as we saw at the beginning of this chapter) British Philosophy in the early 1860s was in a moribund state; and so one final (albeit negative) factor in the success of Idealism must be the fact that (in Quinton's words) 'it arose in something very like a philosophical vacuum'.[129]

This brief discussion of the success of Idealism should not conclude without one further, negative, point. It must not be forgotten that Idealism, even at its most successful, was not *all-conquering*. Collingwood says that the movement never dominated philosophical thought and teaching at Oxford and, taking the year 1900, he points out that Bosanquet had long left for London, T.H. Green, Toynbee, Nettleship, and Wallace had all died young, Caird was lost to administration and Bradley a recluse.[130] Oxford Examination papers from the 1870s onwards show the increasing

---

[124]   *Schopenhauer*, 11–12.

[125]   *Mind* (1897), *Proceedings of Aristotelian Society* (1887), *Philosophical Review* (1892), *International Journal of Ethics* (1876), *Hibbert Journal* (1902).

[126]   Richter, *Politics of Conscience*, 9. Bain and Sidgwick were comparable figures in Scotland and Cambridge respectively (Schneewind, *Sidgwick's Ethics and Victorian Moral Philosophy*, 6).

[127]   *Dewey's Ethical Thought*, 18–19. She suggests too that it fell into decay at the turn of the century once the status of philosophy as a discipline became once again secure.

[128]   Lakatos, 'Methodology of Scientific Research Programmes'.

[129]   'Absolute Idealism', 126, 135–9.

[130]   Collingwood, *Autobiography*, 16. Boucher has argued that Collingwood is probably deliberately downplaying the impact of idealism here (*The Social and Political Thought of R.G. Collingwood*, 9–10).

influence of idealism, with questions on Kant, Hegel, and Bradley making an appearance, but it did not wholly take over and, as Walsh notes, at the very height of its influence it was still possible to do well in Greats without being an idealist.[131] Even if we move from teaching to publication, and from Oxford to Britain at large, allowing a case to be made for greater dominance, it is nonetheless true that there remained at all times a group of thinkers opposed to Idealism: the evolutionists such as Spencer, Huxley, and Leslie Stephen continued to speak out, Utilitarianism found a fresh champion in Henry Sidgwick, realism was defended by Shadworth Hodgson and given powerful new voice by Cook Wilson, while F.C.S. Schiller developed the novel line of thought that was in America called 'pragmatism', though he himself preferred the term 'Humanism'.

---

[131] Mure 'Oxford and Philosophy', 298–9; Walsh, 'The Zenith of Greats', 314.

3

The History of Philosophy

The British Idealists, as we shall see in subsequent chapters, looked always for historical explanation.[1] Everything develops, they thought, and only when we see where something has come from can we understand its true nature and predict its next step. This approach they applied no less to their own subject, philosophy. Whatever ideas might be put forward, their proper assessment could only be as but the latest contribution to an ongoing dialogue and so, if philosophy is to be pursued usefully, it must be done in self-conscious understanding of its own history. Thus one very notable feature of the British Idealist movement, especially of its beginning period, absent before that time[2] and largely absent since, was its emphasis on the history of philosophy. So important was this exercise in historical self-understanding that I shall devote an entire chapter to its consideration.[3] A history of the history of philosophy may feel to some readers an uncongenial place to start, but no one should be tempted to skip this chapter and press on to see what the Idealists had to say about more current issues, for this is where the Idealists *themselves* started from, and to have arrived at an appreciation of how they viewed their predecessors is to have done the bulk of the work of understanding where they stood on those other more topical questions.

The investigation will also serve as a useful reminder of how our common history of philosophy has been read in very different ways by different generations of philosophers; for their histories are quite unlike any that might be produced today. They differ not simply in their cast lists—which figures they include or emphasize—but in their very style and approach. The precise character of the historical studies the Idealists

---

[1] A notable exception to this claim is F.H. Bradley who, after his *Ethical Studies* (1876), rarely takes a historical perspective. However, he would not dissent from the general idea that Reality, while not itself something which develops, is nonetheless something which progressively realizes itself in time (*Essays on Truth and Reality*, 344).

[2] Of course, their predecessors had paid some measure of attention to the past, but in their quest for philosophical understanding the Idealists introduced a hitherto unprecedented level of detailed historical engagement.

[3] My focus here is mainly on metaphysics and epistemology, their discussions of the history of ethics and aesthetics will be considered in Chapters 6 and 9.

produced was much influenced by the broadly Hegelian conception of the history of philosophy to which they subscribed. Like him they regarded it, not simply as a compendium of ideas, but as a *story* or developing sequence in which no philosophy is ever strictly or simply 'refuted' but rather 'absorbed' into a higher viewpoint which takes up its insights while correcting its errors.[4] In consequence their studies focus as much on where ideas 'come from' or 'lead to' as on their actual role in the theories examined; although it should be noted that the notion of 'influence', as central to this approach as it is problematic in many modern eyes, is treated lightly because it is a story conceived, not in historical terms of who read what, but in terms of the logic of ideas themselves, the lines and currents of which their authors may well be unaware.

The greater the role of influence the less room is left for agency or originality; and the British Idealists tended to view the history of philosophy largely as the story of a single set of problems and ideas, variously manifested over time. They saw the constant change and upheaval that characterize the philosophical record, not as the continual replacement of outworn ideas by fresh rivals, but rather as a sequence of differing expressions of a single underlying core. Thus argues Haldane, 'between the teaching of the great schools of Grecian thinkers, those schools which were led by such men as Plato, Aristotle, and Plotinus, and the teaching of the great idealists of the modern world, there is no insuperable gulf. If we strip the forms of such teaching of the mere setting that has been due to the times, the agreement is more marked than is the difference.'[5] Originality, suggests John Caird, must not be misconstrued; 'the originality of a philosophical writer is not to be determined simply by the measure in which his ideas are traceable to earlier sources, or by the suggestions he has caught up from other minds. To lend real value to any contribution to philosophy it *must* reproduce the past, the sole question is whether the reproduction is a dead or living reproduction.'[6] No doubt this tendency could be carried to excess,[7] but the Idealists themselves were not unaware of that danger,[8] and never meant to claim that ideas are passed down unchanged—that the whole of Hegel is already in Kant, Hume in Locke, or modern in ancient thought—only to insist on development rather than creation.

It was an axiom of this understanding of history that philosophical development occurred always in the direction of increasing adequacy or completeness, making it a matter of vital importance to identify that underlying drift; to correctly locate any theory's strengths, weaknesses and 'natural next step'. The Idealists' interest in past philosophers was less in uncovering the details of what they had believed or intended

---

[4] Hegel, *Lectures on the History of Philosophy*, 1:37.

[5] *Reign of Relativity*, 8.

[6] *Spinoza*, 37.

[7] 'Indeed, it was to some extent a defect in [Edward] Caird's teaching of the history of philosophy that he sometimes gave one the impression that all the philosophers who were worth considering had said the same thing, though they had not always realized it themselves, and that he tended to minimize or neglect their differences' (Lindsay, 'Idealism of Jones and Caird', 177).

[8] See, for example, Green, 'Popular Philosophy In Its Relation To Life', 93; and E. Caird, *Evolution of Greek Theology*, II:30.

than in ascertaining what they had got right and what might be learnt from their mistakes. To the objection that one ought not to pass judgment on people before it has been determined just what they were trying to say, their response was that as often as not thinkers are caught up in intellectual currents larger than themselves, and are not the best guides to the true import of their ideas. For example, although few would care to cast themselves in such a role, a philosopher's greatest contribution to posterity may lie in his mistakes. As interested in what they 'should have' said as in what they did, the Idealists were happy to 'correct' past philosophers where it was thought they had gone wrong, or to point out the 'true' significance of their contribution where it differed from their own assessment. Modern history of philosophy tends to be based on an assumption of charity; where ideas look wrong or inconsistent the first thought is that *we* have misinterpreted them. Regarding error less of black mark against any philosophy, the Idealists were quicker to judge. For instance, in response to the objection that we ought at least to attribute consistency to past thinkers, Ritchie responds that really that is 'a poor virtue' to accord their thoughts, insultingly suggestive of a 'ready-made' system with no potential for development or growth.[9]

3.1 Hegel

Although the actual development of concepts proceeds from oldest to most recent, since we lie at the near-end of this sequence, our examination of this history must proceed in the opposite direction, reading each philosophy through the lens of those which it brought about after it. The focus is on what each added to its predecessors, but the story is always interpreted in retrospect and, told in historical order, can seem contrived or false. To those actually riding the dialectical train, its crazy switchback seems anything but goal-directed. Therefore this chapter will begin with Hegel, and work backwards. The 'British Idealist Hegel' that emerges from their various studies has a clear character distinguishing him from, for example, contemporary readings. But if in general they saw his philosophy as religious, metaphysically laden, and driven most strongly by logic, we should not make the mistake of thinking that his Idealist commentators all interpreted him in exactly the same way, for, as the following series of sketches show, there was considerable variety in the pictures they painted.

Idealist work on Hegel began early. From about 1866 or 1867, in Oxford and in Glasgow respectively, both Green and Caird were offering lectures which made heavy use of Hegel's philosophy. The lectures, however, were never published, and neither was really working to *expound* Hegel.[10] That role fell some few years later to William Wallace, Green's Oxford colleague and fellow Balliol graduate.

---

[9] Ritchie, 'On Plato's *Phaedo*', 13–14.
[10] Our knowledge of Green's lectures (which deal with much else besides Hegel) is from Bradley's undergraduate notebooks, the notes from which have been reproduced in the collected works of both Bradley (ed. C.A. Keene, I:57–136) and Green (ed. R.L. Nettleship and P.P. Nicholson, V:105–82). Caird's lectures are reproduced in Tyler, *Unpublished Manuscripts in British Idealism*, II:40–152.

3.1.1 William Wallace

William Wallace is chiefly remembered as the finest of Hegel's early translators into English. In 1874 he put Hegel scholarship on a new footing by publishing an edition of the first part[11] of the *Encyclopaedia of the Philosophical Sciences*—entitled by Wallace *The Logic of Hegel*—together with a substantial *Prolegomena* to Hegel's philosophy as a whole. Compared with Stirling's effort of nearly a decade before, the accuracy and literary merit of the translation was much higher, and the commentary less idiosyncratic and extravagant—although the latter remained general, seeking merely 'to remove certain obstacles, and to render Hegel less tantalizingly hard to those who approach him for the first time.'[12] Exploratory and unsystematic, it actively resists the suggestion of its celebrated predecessor that there is some 'key' or 'secret' to understanding Hegel; all that is called for is the patient unravelling of the many knots and intricacies of his thought.[13] Nonetheless the work was a great success, and a revised translation appeared in 1892, with an expanded *Prolegomena*, now longer than the translation itself, appearing as a separate volume in 1894.[14] In the same year Wallace also produced a translation of the third part of the *Encyclopaedia*—*Hegel's Philosophy of Mind*, itself prefixed by five lengthy 'Introductory Essays' which aim to explain what 'philosophy of Mind' covers in Hegel's system and to distinguish it from the psychology of such contemporary figures as Spencer and Herbart.

Wallace's choice to start with the Logic was hardly accidental, since (as had Stirling before him) he finds this to be the very centre of Hegel's system. A modern day rival to that of Aristotle,[15] its task—'the fundamental problem of philosophy'—is to demonstrate the identity (in difference) of subject and object,[16] to discover the underlying 'primeval unity' which manifests itself in the duality of mind and nature;[17] for it was in this insight that Hegel 'solved the problem of Metaphysics', argues Wallace, 'by turning it into Logic',[18] that is, by demonstrating that the key to reality is to be found in reason.

But he is keen to guard against any misunderstanding of so rationalist a claim. If not absurd, it is at least misleading, to speak of Hegel's system as 'panlogism'[19]—the replacement of solid experience by a world of abstract thought—since this new species of idealism seeks not to escape from reality, but to uncover it. 'It is true the ideal is, in a way, always another world: but not a *mere* other world; it is another, and yet not another, but the same, seen, if you like to say, transfigured, idealised.'[20] Simultaneous with its insistence on the ideality of material nature, this view calls no less for the real and physically manifested character of thought,[21] and thus what German idealism ushers in is a *true* Age of Reason, suggests Wallace, where reason is not simply

---

[11] The so-called 'lesser logic'.   [12] *Prolegomena*, xiii.   [13] *Prolegomena*, 19, 40.
[14] This last was dedicated to Jowett, who died in 1893.
[15] 'What Aristotle did for the theory of demonstrative reasoning, Hegel attempted to do for the whole of human knowledge' ('Hegel', 619).
[16] *Prolegomena*, 148.   [17] *Prolegomena*, 209.   [18] *Prolegomena*, 297.
[19] *Prolegomena*, 61.   [20] *Prolegomena*, 145.   [21] *Prolegomena*, 146.

disembodied intellect or uninstantiated intelligence, 'but intelligence, charged with emotion, full of reverence, reverent above all to the majesty of that divinity which, much disguised, and weather-beaten, like Glaucus of the sea, resides in common and natural humanity.'[22] It is in this context that we must understand the otherwise paradoxical way in which Hegel employs the notions *abstract* and *concrete*. Almost exactly reversing the common understanding which regards intellect as something that abstracts away from the concrete reality given in sense experience, for Hegel, mere sense yields a world which wants all system or unity, a world which is made up of bits imperfectly adjusted to each other. It is only the beginning of knowledge, it looks beyond itself for rational explanation, it is incomplete and in need of thoughts or concepts to raise it to an intelligible totality; and any such partial apprehension is what Hegel terms 'abstract'.[23]

Two further aspects of Wallace's Hegel should be noted, both influential on and typical of British Idealism generally. The first is his emphasis on theology. Reporting Hegel's claim that philosophy seeks to apprehend in reasoned knowledge the same truth which the religious mind grasps in faith, he presents Hegel's philosophy as nothing less than the explication of God, and wholly assimilable to Christianity.[24] 'Hegel, on his own showing, came to prove that the real scope of philosophy was God;—that the Absolute is the 'original synthetic unity' from which the external world and the Ego have issued by differentiation, and in which they return to unity.'[25] Just how easy all Christians would find such a claim may be doubted for, as Wallace readily admits, this is 'God in the actuality and plenitude of the world, and not as a transcendent Being.'[26]

A second feature of his interpretation, just as crucial to his acceptance at the time, was the measure of harmony he finds between the Hegelian and Darwinian pictures of evolution.[27] Wallace even locates a similarity in the method by which they were discovered; just as Darwin was able to unlock the more general workings of evolution by natural selection through looking at cases of artificial selection, so for Hegel the history of philosophy gives a clue to the wider evolution of thought that underlies all of human history.[28] But Wallace was alive also to their differences, noting that where Darwinism draws an unwelcome distinction between a living thing and its circumstances, between the organic and the inorganic, philosophy's broader vision finds a wider sense of living unity among all things, and that where philosophy's true interest is in the purely conceptual development of ideas, only incidentally manifested in

---

[22] *Prolegomena*, 143–4. As he elsewhere puts it, in its modern conception, 'Philosophy is not the work of abstract or 'unassisted Reason'. . . . the pure reason of philosophy is a reason which has been purified of dross, corruption, and sluggishness by the discipline of the sciences, by the heroism and conscientiousness of religion, by the fair and noble intuitions of art. Otherwise it is little worth' (Review of Balfour's *Foundations of Belief*, 544).

[23] *Prolegomena*, 233.   [24] *Prolegomena*, 22–3.   [25] *Prolegomena*, 208–9.

[26] *Prolegomena*, 22.

[27] *Prolegomena*, 61–3, 117. In this he may be contrasted with Stirling.

[28] *Prolegomena*, 288–9.

temporal sequence, the Darwinian's interest remains rooted in the actual historical development of things.[29]

3.1.2 Edward Caird

In 1883, just short of a decade after Wallace's *Logic*, appeared another milestone in the idealist interpretation of Hegel, a brief monograph for the Blackwood's Philosophical Classics series by Edward Caird, simply entitled *Hegel*.

That, in comparison to his voluminous writings on Kant, Caird produced far less on Hegel is not a reflection on his view of their relative importance.[30] It represents rather his understanding of Hegel's idealism as the culminating step in a logical sequence. Our interest is in the result, but properly to understand that result, we must look to the origin, for the product is meaningless except in the light of the process by which it is reached.[31] In consequence, even the book on Hegel spends a great deal of time discussing his historical antecedents and early development—taking up nearly two-thirds of what is only a short book—before it reaches the system proper. In this approach he was followed by Wallace; one of the largest additions to the revised *Prolegomena* of 1894 is the group of eight chapters on the historical development of philosophy up to Hegel's *Logic*.

Caird regarded Kant as a great pioneer, but one who had, for all his insight, left the task half done. He failed to carry his argument through to its proper conclusion, and in consequence his position is marred by an irreconcilable dualism between the subject and object, a dichotomy which manifests itself in a whole series of sub-dualisms: sense and understanding, experience and reason, phenomena and noumena, nature and spirit, necessity and freedom, knowledge and faith.[32] While they mark real differences, these contrasts cannot be accorded final legitimacy, for like all distinctions they are only possible within the context of a greater unity. Only inside such a framework can they oppose one another. But while it is easy enough to say that opposition presupposes unity, finding the precise mechanism by which to draw out this fact was much harder, as the history of post-Kantian thought shows. Fichte sought to impose unity by so accentuating one side that, in effect, it swallowed up the other; for, in over-emphasizing the creative work of the subject, he paid insufficient attention to the autonomous reality (albeit of a lower kind) of the object, turning nature into a mere shadow of mind.[33] Schelling on the other hand, reacting against Fichte's downgrading of the object, insisted that the Absolute manifest itself in subject and object alike. But in so doing he over-emphasized their unity, reducing the very difference between them.[34] What was needed was a unifying mechanism which could do equal justice to their

---

[29] *Prolegomena*, 119–20.
[30] He describes Hegel as 'the last great philosopher who deserves to be placed on the same level with Plato and Aristotle in ancient, and with Spinoza and Kant in modern times, and who, like them, has given an 'epoch-making' contribution to the development of the philosophic . . . interpretation of the world' (*Hegel*, 223).
[31] *Critical Philosophy of Immanuel Kant*, I:52.   [32] *Hegel*, 122.   [33] *Hegel*, 127.
[34] *Hegel*, 128.

identity and their difference—an 'organic unity' or 'self-differentiating principle' which both reconciles and realizes itself in diversity. This Hegel found when he proposed that 'self-consciousness itself was the ideal unity, by which, or in reference to which, the world must be explained',[35] for the self-conscious individual in being 'conscious of himself in *opposition* to that which is not himself . . . is at the same time conscious of self and not-self in *relation* to each other; and that implies that he is conscious of the unity that includes both.'[36] To Caird, 'the opposition between mind and matter is not an opposition between consciousness and something else than consciousness, but an opposition between two factors of consciousness. The unity of experience embraces both the inner and the outer.'[37]

Kant held the key but was too afraid to use it, thinks Caird. He recognized the constructive role of thought, or self-consciousness, in our experience of things, but instead of embracing this as the very criterion of reality and thereby concluding that rational thought, that is, science and philosophy, have the power to bring us to the truth, he takes the opposite line and, precisely because they are mixed up with thought, takes these pursuits as fit only to uncover appearances of an otherwise unknowable reality. He was right, of course, that the things they reveal to us cannot claim to be ultimate reality, but instead of explaining this as a matter of their being early stages on the way to truth, he forever condemns them as appearances of an unknown and unknowable noumena beyond.

There are several aspects of this Hegelian result that Caird chooses to stress. One is *rationality*. To Caird, Hegel reasserted against Kantian scepticism the power of the understanding to penetrate reality. Kant recognized the unity of thought and being, but limited it to certain general features—the categories. Hegel saw no need to hold back and extended the identity across the board. Reality lies, not in the mere individual taken by itself, but rather in the system of relations that locate it in the world, not in what is particular but in what is universal; 'or, to express all in a word, "the real is the rational or intelligible"; i.e., it is that which is capable of being thoroughly understood by the intelligence, just because it has in it the essential nature of the intelligence or self-consciousness.'[38]

The power of the Hegelian insight was to reconcile difference and to overcome opposition, and therefore its most fundamental drift was in the direction of *monism*. Diversity is not denied but in the last analysis always falls within a greater unity. This for Caird was axiomatic, and from now on, he argued, 'the only reasonable controversy between philosophers must be, on the one hand, as to the nature of the all-embracing unity on which every intelligible experience must rest, and on the other hand, as to the nature of the differences which it equally involves. . . . The problem of knowledge is to find out how the real unity of the world manifests itself through all its equally real

---

[35] *Hegel*, 129.   [36] *Hegel*, 154.
[37] *Critical Account of the Philosophy of Kant*, 387.   [38] *Hegel*, 176.

differences.'[39] Caird goes to great pains to stress that such an Absolute does not 'swamp' its contents. It is not like the universe of Spinoza in which all differences are absorbed.[40] It is only through the diversity of its members that the one whole exists.

Discovery that the world is a rational unity leads in the last analysis to *idealism*. Rather than dead matter in external relation to thought, reality is an expression of self-consciousness, the known is fundamentally continuous with the knowing of it. But it would be a mistake to think here in terms of any crude dichotomy between matter and mind. Instead we need to imagine a continuum of progressively more adequate ways of understanding reality; the more we see in things the working of thought the truer our account becomes. In this way space is left for the intermediary notion of organic unity, for Hegelianism on Caird's reading teaches us to regard the world as an organism, as living rather than mechanical, which is one step on the way to recognizing it as fully spiritual.[41] Like Wallace, Caird is keen to downplay all suggestions of other-worldliness in Hegel's idealism. The ideal is not one kind of thing opposed to another, nor the idealist someone who denies one kind of reality to replace it with another. As he puts it, 'the world of intelligence and freedom cannot be different from the world of nature and necessity; it can only be the same world, seen in a new light, or subjected to a further interpretation.'[42]

For Caird, as for Wallace, Hegel was the great champion of religion. Religion he understands as the search beyond our divided and fragmentary existence for a higher unity,[43] and what Hegel called the Absolute idea, 'the absolute principle to which, as their unity, we must refer all things and beings', is to Caird nothing less than God.[44] But more specifically, he believes that Hegel's philosophy is Christian, indeed, the discovery and expression of 'the essential meaning of Christianity.'[45] Hegel's doctrine of coming to self-consciousness through self-diremption into the other, of affirmation through negation, of reconciliation through opposition is, argues Caird, the very same as the essential Christian message 'Die to live'. The moral principle that we must lose our lives to save them, that we must die to the passionate flesh to live the life of the rational spirit, that we must leave behind the life of the selfish individual to take up the moral life of the whole has a metaphysical counterpart; the law that holds for man holds for God in that only by giving up his isolation and manifesting himself in reality may he too find himself.[46] This is an idea which recurs in Caird again and again.[47]

Unlike his treatment of Kant, Caird's account of the philosophy of Hegel is expounded in almost entirely positive terms, and so it may reasonably be asked

---

[39] 'Idealism and the Theory of Knowledge', 102.
[40] See section 3.4.1 below.
[41] *Hegel*, 190–2. On 'organic unity' see Chapter 7.3 below.
[42] *Hegel*, 125.
[43] *Critical Philosophy of Immanuel Kant*, II:68; *Evolution of Theology in the Greek Philosophers*, I:32.
[44] *Hegel*, 218.
[45] *Hegel*, 218. See also 'Metaphysic', 534–6.
[46] *Hegel*, 43–4, 211–18.
[47] See below especially § 6.3.5.

whether he was an Hegelian? But, if he was, his Hegelianism resided more in the spirit of his thinking than in any detailed following. He is, for example, sharply critical of Hegel's philosophy of nature. He accepts the general principle of a continuity between spirit and nature, but he thinks that Hegel succumbs too swiftly to the temptation to move ahead and prescribe a path for advancing knowledge. Natural science will give way first to an organic and then a spiritual conception, but it must do so from its own resources and in its own time.[48]

3.1.3 Further idealist scholarship on Hegel

Following the lead set by Green, Wallace, and Caird, many other idealists turned their attention to Hegel. Graduating from Edinburgh with first class honours in 1878, the recommendation of James Martineau helped Andrew Seth Pringle-Pattison to win a Hibbert travelling scholarship, which allowed him to spend two years studying in Berlin, Jena, and Göttingen. The fruits of that research, an article on Hegel which appeared in *Mind* in 1881 and his first book, *The Development from Kant to Hegel*, which appeared in 1882, both attempted to show that idealistic philosophy had developed under its own necessary internal logic from Kant, through Fichte and Schelling, to its culmination in Hegel. 'Indeed,' he claims, a little optimistically, that 'anyone so minded might put together a statement out of Fichte, still more out of Schelling, which would seem to anticipate all the results of Hegel.'[49]

Another important commentator on Hegel from this time was D.G. Ritchie who, after gaining a first degree from Edinburgh four years before Seth Pringle-Pattison, had proceeded to Balliol College where he had been tutored by Green. His applications of Hegelian ideas to political theory and to Darwinian evolution will be considered in Chapter 7, but note should be taken here of his first published essay, 'The Rationality of History', which appeared in the volume, *Essays in Philosophical Criticism*, published in 1883 under the editorship of Andrew Seth Pringle-Pattison and R.B. Haldane. Praising Hegel's opening up of this field, he argues the need for and possibility of 'philosophy of history', that discipline which seeks to interpret the facts of the past by looking for the underlying principle or idea behind them,[50] their spirit or meaning, something best seen in the direction towards which they are tending. Such history, he notes, implies a teleological view;[51] it assumes that events are part of a plan and 'that history is the work of reason.'[52]

The Hegel of whom Bertrand Russell often speaks so disparagingly was a sort of rationalistic metaphysician of the Absolute,[53] quite unlike the Hegel that finds favour

---

[48] *Hegel*, 201.
[49] *Development*, 86. His view of Hegel at this stage was entirely in line with that of Green, Wallace, and Caird. As will be seen in Chapter 10 he later became highly critical of Hegel.
[50] 'The Rationality of History', 126, 127.
[51] 'The Rationality of History', 129.
[52] 'The Rationality of History', 132.
[53] See e.g. his *History of Western Philosophy*, ch. 22.

with modern scholars, and if an origin is sought for such a wrong-headed conception people are often tempted to look to the British Idealists from whom, after all, Russell learned his Hegel. J.N. Findlay, for example, took just such a dim view of the British Idealist Hegel, complaining that their picture of him as a transcendent metaphysician asserting the existence of an Absolute Spirit beyond all human experience is one that should be dismissed as a complete fiction.[54] But in fact the fiction here is Findlay's, for while it is true that their reading of Hegel often emphasized metaphysics, the British Idealists were far from regarding his work as one of transcendent construction. In an empirically minded nation like Britain, perhaps the greatest obstacle to the acceptance of Hegelianism, or any other philosophy that might claim kinship with it (such as Platonism, Kantianism, or Christianity) is the sense of 'other-worldliness' that clings to its assertions. Does it not locate true being in some realm of insubstantiality, with everything that appears in space and time condemned as somehow unreal? Well aware of this native prejudice, the Idealists worked hard to counter it. We have already noted Wallace's and Caird's claims in this regard, but the charge is perhaps rebutted most strongly in an essay, 'On the True Conception of Another World' first published by Bernard Bosanquet as the Preface to his 1886 translation of the Introduction to *Hegel's Aesthetik*.

For Hegel (argues Bosanquet) the 'other world', the world of 'things not seen', is not some ghostly or super-sensible double of the existing world.[55] His aim was only ever to draw a distinction *within* the world we know, not *between* it and some further realm.[56] He seeks only to draw out the difference between the higher—the rational and spiritual—and the lower—the material and the everyday.[57] The difference is one of the *same* world, transformed.[58] To take some examples, the Hegelian idea of the infinite is that which may be taken as self-complete without reference beyond itself and, as such, it is something 'present, concrete, and real',[59] (unlike the 'common' or 'false' infinity of enumeration without end which is indeed suspiciously remote and mysterious). Similarly, rather than in some (noumenal) realm of metaphysical abstraction, human freedom is to be found in the same world in which our humanity is realized, that is the world of family, property, law, and society—'it is only in civilization that man becomes human, spiritual, and free'.[60] Even the nature of Absolute Spirit itself, God, is something to be understood not as transcendent but in terms of immanence, in the natural world also, but primarily in human intelligence—'God in us'.[61]

A last figure to note in this section, James Black Baillie, continued the Idealist tradition of Hegel scholarship into the twentieth century, publishing a general intro-

[54] *Hegel: a Re-Examination*, 20–6.
[55] 'On the True Conception of Another World', xvii.
[56] 'On the True Conception of Another World', xviii.
[57] 'On the True Conception of Another World', xix.
[58] 'On the True Conception of Another World', xxi.
[59] 'On the True Conception of Another World', xxviii.
[60] 'On the True Conception of Another World', xxx.
[61] 'On the True Conception of Another World', xxxi.

duction to Hegel's system, a work of constructive metaphysics in the same vein, as well as a translation of the *Phenomenology of Mind*.[62] Perhaps most conservative of all the British Idealist commentators, where thinkers such as Green, Caird, and McTaggart re-worked the ideas they found, Baillie tended always to go back to the historical Hegel himself; whose very idiom also he swallowed, much detracting from the overall clarity and coherence of his writing. After the First World War he rejected Hegelianism; though not perhaps its spirit, since like many of the Idealists he went into university administration, rising to become vice-chancellor of the University of Leeds in 1924, for which he was knighted in 1931.

3.1.4 McTaggart

Of all the British Idealist commentators the most dedicated Hegel scholar was the Cambridge philosopher McTagggart.[63] Though in later life (as we shall see) he developed his own distinctive variety of idealism, the first half of his career was dominated by the study of Hegel, the main output of which was three books—*Studies in the Hegelian Dialectic* (1896), *Studies in Hegelian Cosmology* (1901), and *A Commentary on Hegel's Logic* (1910)—each marked by its great familiarity with the details of that system. McTaggart's Hegel stands out from that of, say, Wallace or Caird, for the extreme precision and clarity of his views.[64] In a memorable passage, Broad joked that 'If Hegel be the inspired, and too often incoherent, prophet of the Absolute; and if Bradley be its chivalrous knight, ready to challenge all who dare to question its pre-eminence; McTaggart is its devoted and extremely acute family solicitor.'[65]

It has already been observed how the Idealists looked to Kant in reading Hegel, and McTaggart takes this approach even further, urging that Hegel's methodology is essentially Kantian in the sense that it starts from some category which we cannot help but assume in thinking and proceeds by uncovering its necessary presuppositions, which it then appropriates as a categorical result.[66] What is new is that the method is

---

[62] *The Origin and Significance of Hegel's Logic* (1901); *An Outline of the Idealistic Construction of Experience* (1906); *The Phenomenology of Mind* (1910).

[63] Coming up to Trinity College Cambridge in 1885, McTaggart was awarded a Fellowship there in 1891, which he held until his death in 1925.

[64] This fact in itself might seem to distance them from their source, and it is true that subsequent scholarship has not thought highly of McTaggart's Hegel. It is often 'hard to believe that Hegel had ever imagined, or would have accepted, the doctrines which McTaggart ascribed to him,' wrote Broad, 'if McTaggart's account of Hegelianism be taken as a whole and compared with Hegel's writings as a whole, the impression produced is one of profound unlikeness' ('McTaggart', xxi). Geach claimed that 'his acquaintance with Hegel's writings was like the chapter-and-verse knowledge of the Bible that out-of-the-way Protestant Sectarians often have; the unanimous judgement of Hegel experts appears to be that McTaggart's interpretations were as perverse as these sectarians' interpretations of the Bible' (*Truth, Love and Immortality*, 17).

[65] Broad, 'McTaggart', xxviii.

[66] In the first edition McTaggart even describes this method as 'trancendental'. By the second edition, however, this epithet is withdrawn, on the grounds that Kant's starting points are ones simply *known* to be true of experience while Hegel commences from something—the category of being itself—which it would be self-refuting to deny (*Hegelian Dialectic*, 21).

then reapplied to the higher category, whose own necessary presuppositions lead to an even higher category, and so on, until we reach the highest category of all, the Absolute. In this way he holds that, 'The Hegelian logic, from an epistemological point of view, does not differ greatly I believe from that of Kant.'[67] For McTaggart, Hegel's logic is simply a more rigorous version of Kant's. Equally familiar from the earlier Hegel studies we have already considered is McTaggart's desire to resist the charge of excessive abstraction, the objection that the dialectic is but an empty dance of pure thought. He therefore insists that Hegel's logic cannot be understood without reference to experience, arguing that 'the process, although independent of the matter of intuition, can only be perceived when the pure notion is taken in conjunction with matter of intuition—that is to say when it is taken in experience—because it is impossible to grasp thought in abstract purity, or except as applied to an immediate *datum*.'[68] This point too McTaggart refers back to Kant, recalling his famous dictum that 'pure' thoughts are as *empty* as 'pure' intuitions are *blind*.[69]

But, if on these points McTaggart was in broad agreement with his fellow Idealist interpreters, on others he was at sharp variance. While all could agree that the heart of Hegel's philosophy was to be found in his logic, his outline of the dialectical development of the categories which structure experience, that process itself was not without paradox. For Hegel the engine which drives the dialectical process was the tendency to contradiction which besets thought and keeps pushing it on to higher and higher stages in search of relief, but if at the same time he was claiming an identity between thought and reality, this seemed to amount to a paradoxical claim that reality *itself* was contradictory. While commentators such as Caird sought to explain in what sense that might be so, McTaggart boldly rejected any suggestion that Hegel was violating the law of non-contradiction.[70] He downplays the role of negation and contradiction in thought's actual evolution—'The really fundamental aspect of the dialectic is not the tendency of the finite category to negate itself but to complete itself'[71]—but his chief response is to insist that dialectical transition takes place nowhere but in our minds. An object may seem flawed, but its 'imperfection and contradiction are really, according to Hegel, due only to our manner of apprehending the object,'[72] forcing us on to a superior conception. Connected to this point is the question of the relation between spirit and nature. McTaggart notes that Hegel has often been accused of attempting to deduce existence from essence, and in considering this charge he distinguishes between two ways in which dialectic might claim ontological significance.

It may mean only that the system rejects the Kantian thing-in-itself, and denies the existence of any reality except that which enters into experience, so that the results of a criticism of knowledge are valid of reality also. But it may mean that it endeavours to dispense with or transcend all *data* except the nature of thought itself, and to deduce from that the whole existing

---

[67] *Hegelian Dialectic*, 25.   [68] *Hegelian Dialectic*, 17–18.   [69] *Hegelian Dialectic*, 17.
[70] *Hegelian Dialectic*, 8.   [71] *Hegelian Dialectic*, 10.   [72] *Hegelian Dialectic*, 7.

universe. The difference between these two positions is considerable. The first maintains that nothing is real except the reasonable, the second that reality is nothing but rationality.[73]

McTaggart claims that Hegel endeavours only the first, and must be acquitted of any attempt at the second, which is something quite impossible. There can be no deduction—no emanation—of existence itself from thought. In drawing so sharp a distinction between thinking and being, McTaggart certainly set himself at odds with other commentators, such as Caird,[74] but his was not a lone voice. That reality itself was not contradictory was stressed too by Bradley, and that there was no bridge from Hegelian dialectic to existence itself was a key element of Seth Pringle-Pattison's apostasy.[75]

A further wedge between McTaggart and the rest of the British Idealists is found in his efforts to sever the link between Hegelian philosophy and theology. He argues against Hegel's contention that the dialectic entails Christianity; its claims about the Trinity, the incarnation, morality, and sin are, he insists, quite different from anything ordinary people would recognize as 'Christian'.[76] He argues also against viewing the Absolute as a unitary spirit, something it might be appropriate to call 'God', preferring to regard it as a *community* of such selves.[77] Finally, he rejects any pretension of Hegel's to offer a form of perfect existence that might stand stead for the perfection of deity. Regarding the Absolute as something timelessly real rather than something future towards which reality is developing, Hegel is unable to account for the undeniable appearance of imperfection or contingency. We may call it a delusion, but then we must account for why we who are deluded, though we belong to the perfect Absolute, are not ourselves perfectly rational. Alternatively, we may think it a consequence of viewing piecemeal *in time* what really exists as a whole *sub specie aeternitas*, but then we must give reasons why the undistorted Absolute manifests itself through the distorting facade of time whose appearance it is. Either we deny outright the existence of evil and contradict the blatant facts of experience, or we hold it to be some kind of appearance, whose ultimate cause we must by one route or another refer back to the Absolute, contradicting its perfection.[78]

Reviewing these various commentaries on Hegel by the British Idealists we are struck by both similarities and differences. There was widespread agreement that the heart of Hegel's thought lay in his logic and his philosophy of religion, while that his subject matter was ultimate reality and not simply human conception was also unques-

---

[73]   *Hegelian Dialectic*, 26.
[74]   For Caird's understanding of the dialectic see Chapter 8.2 below. For his criticism of McTaggart's interpretation of Hegel see his reference written in connection with McTaggart's application for a Cambridge D.Litt. (in Tyler, *Unpublished Manuscripts in British Idealism*, II:204–8); also Mackenzie 'Edward Caird as Philosophical Teacher', 517–18; H. Jones and J.H. Muirhead, *Life and Philosophy of Edward Caird*, 237–38, 298 note, 353.
[75]   For Bradley see below Chapters 4 and 8. For Seth Pringle-Pattison see below Chapter 10.
[76]   *Hegelian Cosmology*, ch.VII.
[77]   *Hegelian Cosmology*, ch.IX. For further discussion of this view see Chapters 10.1.3 and 11.4 below.
[78]   *Hegelian Dialectic*, 169–80. This problem (which, he notes, theism is no more able to solve than Hegelianism) was one he picked up years later in his own constructive work. See pp.467.

tioned. (The *Phenomenology of Spirit* was accorded nothing like the attention it now receives.) The Hegel whom the British Idealists discovered was in large measure a reaction against prevailing philosophical habits of thought; a figure who—contra intuitionism—argued for an underlying rationality behind the universe and its development and who—contra psychologism—found the universal or the ideal present within experience from the very start. But interpretation was not a monolithic block. It was loose enough to permit different approaches, emphases, and applications, and it was far from a uniform acceptance of the doctrines it found. While the majority embraced what they took to be Hegel's central claim of the identity of logic and metaphysics, other such as McTaggart, Bradley, and Seth Pringle-Pattison insisted that the study of thoughts must never be conflated with the study of things. Again, while most accepted that Hegelianism might bolster religion, McTaggart and Bradley were very clear that it could not support any thing like theism.

3.2 Kant

As will be noted in the final chapter, Idealist scholarship on Hegel continued well into the twentieth century (with the work of G.R.G. Mure, for example) but for now it may be left and the focus switched to his predecessor, Kant. With each step back the number of lenses through which past philosophies are read increases, but with regard to our story the first of these shifts is perhaps the most important, for the Idealists' most constant tool in looking to past philosophy was Hegel's own *Lectures on the History of Philosophy*. So important was this work that, without taking back what has been said about his logic or philosophy of religion, it should be added it was in large part through his history of philosophy that Hegelian ideas first entered into British philosophy. Nowhere is this clearer than with the philosophy of Kant—accorded a vast interpretative effort by the Idealists—which was understood, essentially, as a kind of forerunner or harbinger to Hegel. Kant was painted as a kind of flawed genius; as one who had penetrated through the conceptual barriers that had held philosophy back for centuries opening up for it a entirely new age, but who had, at the same time, only a partial grasp of what he had done or insufficient courage to press though his insight to its full outcome. But no more than was the case with Hegel commentary, did all the Idealists agree exactly on how to read Kant, as the following accounts show.

3.2.1 T.H. Green

In the years 1874–6 Green was lecturing to his own students at length on Kant; material posthumously published in his *Works*. In view of the previous chapter's claim that Kant's philosophy was already familiar in Britain by that time, it might be wondered why he felt the need to do so. But the fact is, that, although known, Kant was still not known *in detail* or with great *accuracy*. Green complains that earlier writers gave to previous generations highly misleading interpretations of Kant, as a champion of 'reason' (Coleridge) or the great advocate of the contrast between phenomena and noumena (William Hamilton).[79] With Green and the Idealists that followed, Kant scholarship really entered a new level.

Given his view that those in search of any living or progressive philosophy must look to Kant, the first thing to strike us is how *critical* Green is. The empiricist conception of knowledge as a passive encounter with external reality is seen off, to Kant's credit, but he continues to believe in a fatal distinction—which comes to him through Locke and Hume—between 'objects affecting the senses' and 'the mind', with a corresponding distinction of judgements into the empirical, particular, and contingent and the a priori, universal, and necessary, when the proper lesson of the Kantian insight into the essential role of thinking in experience, suggests Green, is that 'it is as impossible to divide knowledge into elements, one contributed by feeling, the other by thought, as to analyse the life of an animal into so much resulting from the action of the lungs, so much from the action of the heart; and accordingly equally impossible to divide judgments into empirical and a priori.'[80]

In Green's eyes Kant has failed fully to follow through his new insights, that is, fully to leave behind the old positions from which he started. In consequence we find in his system two inconsistent notions of 'object' continually struggling with each other: there is the notion that an object is something given independently of thought, and there is the newer idea that something first becomes an object only through a certain action of the mind upon some 'matter' given in sensation. It is, of course, the second that Green endorses, but he complains that Kant fails to see how it simply cuts away the ground from under the first; for if objects are essentially made by thought, there is no longer any sense in talking about 'things in themselves' or in drawing any hard and fast contrast between 'intuition' and 'conception.'[81] The distinction is baseless because 'real', 'individual', and 'object' are all conceptual terms and hence the class of intuitions picks out nothing fundamentally different from the class of concepts.[82]

At bottom, thinks Green, Kant does not really understand what an 'idea' is, for (like many) he thinks that to call something 'ideal' is the opposite of calling it 'real'. But that is a mistake. We think of 'idea' and 'reality' as diametrically opposed notions, argues Green, because ideas constantly change while reality, we suppose, is fixed and permanent. But this mutability can be accounted for just as well by the suggestion that ideas are communicated to us only gradually, and that our initial grasp of them is only partial. There is always more in our ideas than first we know. Indeed, urges Green, 'the progressive character of our knowledge is *better* explained as a revelation of the actually existing ideas through which possibilities of them in us are gradually actualised, than as the result of an operation of things which are not ideas, on us.'[83] For Green, although

[79] Review of Edward Caird's *The Philosophy of Kant*, 127.

[80] *Lectures on Kant*, 6.

[81] *Lectures on Kant*, 8–9.

[82] *Lectures on Kant*, 12. The terms here are all relational ones (an 'object' is what stands in relation to consciousness, an 'individual' what stands in a relation of distinctness to other objects, and the 'real' what relates present with previous perceptions) but for Green anything relational is thereby conceptual.

[83] *Lectures on Kant*, 10. Italics added.

the 'work of the mind', ideas in themselves reside neither in individual subjects nor in time—that would be to mistake them for the subjects of psychological science—for, while not so separate from intuition as Kant would have us believe, they are always universal and as such actively grasped in understanding rather than just passively given in perception.

Another way to put the realist's worry would be this. If reality is only possible in relation to a thinking subject, how can that claim be squared with the fact we think we all know that the world existed long before there was ever any consciousness of it? To this Green responds, in the first place, that events revealed to us by science as having taken place before there was any sentience should not be thought of as though they did not belong to our phenomenal world. Limit 'our experience' to simply our current feelings and it is no 'world' at all; extend it to include the factors that *determine* those feelings and there is no reason why it cannot stretch back before the emergence of sentience.[84] This answer is relatively Kantian, but his further response goes well beyond Kant. When we feel inclined to complain that a world constituted by the presence to consciousness of various representations does not seem objective enough we tend to have in mind the succession of experiences enjoyed by the inner self or empirical ego. But this, urges Green, is to take too narrow and abstracted a view. Objective reality must certainly amount to more than just ourselves and our states of consciousness *as we commonly experience them*; but it does not follow that it is other than these things *in their full reality*.

I do not 'make nature' in the sense that nature = a succession of states of consciousness, beginning with my birth and ending with my death. If so, the 'objectivity' of nature would doubtless disappear; there would be as many 'natures' as men. But only by a false abstraction do we talk of such a succession of states. Their reality lies in eternal relations; relations which are there before what I call my 'birth,' and after my 'death.'[85]

This notion of 'eternal relations' whose full reality presupposes the presence of a wider 'eternal consciousness' we shall meet with again in the next chapter.

3.2.2 Edward Caird

At the same time as Green in Oxford was lecturing on these matters, Caird in Glasgow was working on a book about Kant, *A Critical Account of the Philosophy of Kant*, which he published in 1877. The book was well received; not least by Green who in his review pronounced that, 'we find no holes to pick in it; and a statement that it contributes more to an understanding of the central questions of philosophy than any other treatise which this generation of Englishmen has produced would perhaps be ascribed to the partiality of a reviewer with whose views it happens exactly to correspond.'[86] But Caird did not stop there. Twelve years later in 1889 he published a

---

[84] *Lectures on Kant*, 74.   [85] *Lectures on Kant*, 32.
[86] Review of Edward Caird's *The Philosophy of Kant*, 136.

second, even larger volume, *The Critical Philosophy of Immanuel Kant,* in all subjecting Kant to a level of critical scholarly attention unequalled before or since in the English-language.[87]

Though immensely detailed, the books are not simply exposition. They aim not just to tell us what Kant said, but to demonstrate its value and significance, and to explain where he was correct and where he went wrong.[88] In this regard their approach is quite unlike that of modern history of philosophy, not least in the fact that it is often hard to separate out the Kant from the Caird. That he devoted so much time to Kant was a mark of the great advance he thought the Critical Philosophy had achieved, for Caird held it to have made a decisive break in thought; so much so, he claims, that 'there is not a single problem of philosophy that does not meet us with a new face; and it is perhaps not unfair to say that the speculations of all those who have not learned the lesson of Kant are beside the point.'[89] Yet, like Green, for all his importance, he believed that Kant had been fundamentally misunderstood by most of his commentators, and a major purpose of both books was to set that right.

To Caird, Kant's great claim to fame is that it was he who first brought to 'the consciousness of the modern world' the idea of 'the relativity of thought and being'.[90] He taught us that the world we know acquires its being and its character from our knowing of it. In Caird's own words, 'it is only from the point of view of man, i.e., of a being who has such a sensibility as ours, that we can talk of space and of extended things, or of time and events happening in it',[91] for 'divest the world of all its relations to a subject, and it sinks into a "thing in itself", a *caput mortuum* of abstraction, of which nothing can be said.'[92]

Caird was concerned, however, that Kant's message had been all too often misunderstood. One misreading he was especially keen to counteract was that which takes Kant's thesis of the world's relativity to thought as a claim that the 'external' world is really just the same as the 'inner' world and that all the objects of our awareness are strictly speaking mental in nature. Caird is quite adamant that that is not the way to understand Kant's idealism. It is, he thinks, more or less to assimilate it to the idealism of

---

[87]   The first book (*Critical Account of the Philosophy of Kant*) aimed to show how the Kantian philosophy developed out of what came before. Accordingly the first 180 pages are historical, discussing the schools of Descartes, Locke, Leibniz, and Wolff, as well as an account of Kant's pre-critical writings. The intention was then to give a general account of his philosophy without going too far into the detail of its presentation. The historical precursors are not omitted in the second book (*Critical Philosophy of Immanuel Kant*), but the emphasis is much more on Kant's text itself and the discussion expanded greatly. There is also added an account of Kant's ethical and aesthetic philosophy.

[88]   Although, as Henry Jones noted, unmotivated to seek independence or originality for their own sake, Caird was always far more interested in finding out what *truths* previous writers had discovered rather than what *errors* they had made ('Is the Order of Nature Opposed to the Moral Life?', 4).

[89]   *Critical Account of the Philosophy of Kant*, 120–1.

[90]   'Metaphysic', 404; cf. *Hegel*, 121.

[91]   *Critical Philosophy of Immanuel Kant*, I:300.

[92]   *Evolution of Religion*, I:127–8.

Berkeley, a view for which he has no sympathy at all. True idealism, he urges, 'has no special kindred with the philosophy of Berkeley'.[93]

Just how far such a mentalistic reading stands from the correct way to interpret the Critical Philosophy may be seen from Caird's discussion of the question of other minds.[94] Pre-reflectively we might suppose our belief in other minds to be an inference based on analogy with our own case. But to think so is to commit two errors. In the first place it is a mistake to think of a person's body as given in perception and his soul as reached by inference. In both cases the mind makes an interpretation of given feeling, relating together a collection of elements either as a body or a mind. But, secondly, in neither case should we think of this as a transition in thought from some inner experience to an outer object, as though we know first our own self and then work outwards from there; for it is only in differentiating the known object (be it a body or a soul) that we differentiate the knowing subject (ourselves.) The starting point of knowledge is an undifferentiated feeling in which neither subject nor object has as yet appeared and, rather than the inner being the foundation from which we might hope to move on to the outer, knowledge of the not-self is a precondition of self-knowledge. If we remove the former, we lose the latter also. As Caird puts it, 'if we reduce the inner life to mere sensations, it ceases to be a consciousness of an inner any more than of an outer world; and, therefore, such a reduction cannot be said to *prove* that there is no outer world, but only an inner world . . . we have not in this sense a consciousness of our inner life *except* as mediated by a consciousness of the outer world.'[95] In short, mentalism fails precisely to learn the lesson of the Transcendental Deduction.

Another very common reading of Kant's philosophy is to take him as saying that objects of experience are, in effect, a joint-product, coming partly from within and partly from without. The conceptual matter of experience is supplied by us while its object matter is supplied by the world. But Caird thought this too a misreading; for to speak in this way of two distinct sources implies at least a possibility of their independent existence, while the whole point of the *Critique* was to show, against both the empiricists and the rationalists, that in themselves neither sense experience nor thought could ever provide us with any knowledge at all; indeed, that their separate existence was not even possible. They are not two independently real components somehow brought together to make up a third composite kind of experience, rather they are both abstractions—one-sided aspects or factors—of the only kind of experience there can be,[96] no more capable of real existence in their own right than shape without size or pitch without volume. In truth, form and matter, sense and understanding, perception and conception, a priori and a posteriori, necessary and contingent, our contribution and the world's—none of these can be separated in anything other than a relative

[93] 'Idealism and the Theory of Knowledge', 105.
[94] *Critical Philosophy of Immanuel Kant*, II:368–71.
[95] *Critical Philosophy of Immanuel Kant*, I:643.
[96] *Critical Account of the Philosophy of Kant*, 371, 393.

manner. We should note the elision of categories here, for Caird expresses the same point in many different ways. He is prepared to admit that critics cannot take *all* the blame for misinterpreting Kant here since, for much of the time Kant does seem to treat these elements—the 'form' of experience and its 'content'—as separable, in principle at least. He recognized their union, but continues to regard it as a bringing together, or external combination, of alien items. Caird allows that, 'the essential truth which Kant had to express . . . is marred in his statement of it by the persistent influence of the abstract division between contingent matter given from without and necessary principles supplied from within, a division essentially inconsistent with the attempt to show that the contingent matter is necessarily subsumed under these principles, and indeed exists for us only as it is so subsumed.'[97]

This novel understanding of the relationship between the a priori and the a posteriori is one of the most distinctive features of Caird's account of Kant. He took Kant to show that the a priori and the a posteriori 'are inseparable or organically united.'[98] There is a complete penetration of conception into perception, such that 'no element in experience can be purely *given*, purely a posteriori,'[99] and in consequence there can be no final separation between them. 'On this view,' he says, 'the a priori and a posteriori factors of experience do not really exist as two separate portions of knowledge. If they are severed each loses all its meaning . . . the a priori is the condition under which alone the a posteriori exists for us.'[100] More than just a framework to structure and bind together the matter of experience, thought, for Kant, was something operative from the start, something whose work is to bring forth the very subject–object framework, that unity-in-difference which grounds the distinction between inner and outer, a priori and a posteriori. Underlying all our experience there lies a deeper 'ideal principle' realizing itself in both subject and object. Caird is not saying that the distinction is vacuous, only that it lacks final legitimacy. Rather than the last word on matters, he suggests that it needs to be understood in terms of the stage of knowledge that one is discussing. At first knowledge is a posteriori, for how else but by experience can we learn about the world outside us? But this is only our starting point and gradually, in the end, all knowledge will be seen to be a priori, as experience which first seems to be an encounter between mind and what is alien to it gradually reveals its true character, that of mind expressing itself. Rather than its opposite, perception is just an undeveloped form of thought, whose appearance to the contrary is gradually unmasked as knowledge of the 'other' progressively shows its true colours as a kind of 'self-knowledge'.[101] 'The a posteriori is but the a priori in the making.'[102]

If experience cannot be conceived as a compound of the purely intelligible and the utterly unintelligible, it seems necessary that the distinction between a priori and a posteriori should disappear from a higher point of view; or should be used to indicate a difference not of the kinds,

---

[97] 'Metaphysic', 82.   [98] 'Metaphysic', 91.
[99] *Critical Account of the Philosophy of Kant*, 469.   [100] 'Metaphysic', 82.
[101] *Hegel*, 188.   [102] *Hegel*, 195.

but of the stages, of knowledge. On this supposition everything will at first be a posteriori, in the sense that, in the beginning of knowledge, the world appears to be a combination of things and events which have no relation to each other or to the mind. And everything at last must become a priori, in the sense that perfect knowledge would see all things in relation to each other and to the mind.[103]

Not all of the weaknesses of the Kantian system may be put down to misinterpretation, either by his critics or by Kant himself, admits Caird, for it must be allow that Kant made certain clear *mistakes* of his own. Most significantly, he downgraded the objects of experience as mere 'phenomena', postulating real, but unknowable, 'noumena' behind them. Caird argues that this is an absurd position. One cannot state that there exists a world beyond all knowing, for either one knows about it in which case it is not beyond knowing, or it is simply nothing to us and must drop out of the equation altogether. To condemn the world we experience as unreal 'phenomena' is to have, at least implicitly, a criterion of reality. Or to put things another way, there can be no epistemology that is not also metaphysics; we cannot split off 'knowledge' as a separate sphere and study that alone.[104]

Simply to say that Caird criticizes Kant as adhering to an untenable distinction between phenomena and noumena is, perhaps, to present that matter more brutally than it warrants. Caird was much concerned to balance Kant's earlier critical work with his later efforts which he saw as altogether more positive. With great charity he repeatedly stresses that Kant's first word on such matters cannot be taken as his last; 'it is a frequent . . . characteristic of Kant's method of exposition, that he first treats as entirely separate things what he afterwards shows to be merely elements or factors of a unity.'[105] He suggests Kant was not unaware that to deny the reality of phenomena was to implicitly appeal to a criterion of reality, even that he grasped in part what that criterion ought to be, but that he was unable clearly to express it. That honour goes to Hegel, for the criterion is precisely self-consciousness, but so generous is Caird to Kant that at times Hegel's role in story seems but a minor one. While most commentator's present Hegel as offering fundamental correctives to the Kantian system, Caird's Kant seems so prescient of the future direction of philosophical thought that poor Hegel is portrayed as offering little more than confirmation or clear expression of the modifications and developments that Kant himself was in the process of making.[106]

Though having demonstrated beyond doubt the general contribution of conceptual understanding to experience, Caird's Kant is judged less successful in his working out of the details. His categories are all seen to be problematic and of only limited value as, in Caird's hands, Kant's theory of fixed structures for, and limits to, human understanding becomes a thesis of the human mind's inherent tendency to self-transcendence.

---

[103] *Critical Account of the Philosophy of Kant*, 471.
[104] *Critical Account of the Philosophy of Kant*, 642; *Critical Philosophy of Immanuel Kant*, II:96, 153–3.
[105] *Critical Account of the Philosophy of Kant*, 219.
[106] Thus Kant is represented (in the Dialectic) as realizing that he needs some kind of identity-in-difference, but being held back from it by adherence to the logic of abstract identity (*Hegel*, 147).

Through a continual process of categorical development, it moves towards more and more satisfactory modes of knowing the world. The conceptual tools employed fail wholly to resolve its puzzles, leaving residual contradictions or externalities, which in turn call for new higher categories.[107] Crucially this process must, in the end, take understanding beyond the phenomenal into the heart of the noumenal. Kant's deduction of the categories, in setting out the chief elements of thought involved in the determination of objects, did vital work in spelling out what is meant by the unity or relativity of the subject and its object. But fatally on his scheme, the thinking self, the very source of the categories, cannot itself be brought under them, for it is not part of the phenomenal world. While he gives us a catalogue of the different elements out of which it makes up phenomenal reality, he does not show how, in the diversity of its operations, intelligence itself can still be one and conscious of itself as one. Yet this question cannot just be left open, for 'to know the world is not an accidental or external purpose of the intelligence . . . the various categories or forms of thought by which it makes the world intelligible, are not external instruments it uses, but modes of its own activity, or stages in its own development.'[108] In conceptual discovery we discover ourselves and in discovering ourselves we discover reality. Categories must therefore have more than just phenomenal validity.

3.2.3 Further idealist scholarship on Kant

The pioneering work of Green and Caird inspired a host of subsequent philosophers to follow them in the detailed study of Kant. Though he later turned away from idealism to become one of its fiercest critics, Robert Adamson's first publication, *On the Philosophy of Kant*, his Shaw Fellowship lectures of 1879, takes a similarly idealist reading.[109] Like Caird, he thinks Kant a poor spokesperson for his own theory. Though in himself quite clear that their union is organic—that none of their roles can be discharged without the other—his presentation never quite frees itself from the suggestion that we can somehow separate the contributions of sense, imagination, and understanding, with the result that their combination seems artificial and mechanical.[110] As well as taking issue with the tendency to read Kant from an individualist or psychological point of view, Adamson opposes those who see him as some sort of agnostic, limiting knowledge to experience. Although his distinction between phenomena and noumena is deeply flawed, as we advance into the *Dialectic*, we increasingly see that beneath it lies a more justifiable and less scepticism-generating distinction between understanding and reason.[111]

---

[107] *Critical Account of the Philosophy of Kant*, 351.
[108] *Hegel*, 142.
[109] Essentially the same line may be found in his 1881 article on 'Kant' for the *Encyclopedia Britannica*, although his later posthumously published *Development of Modern Philosophy* (1903) takes an altogether different approach.
[110] *On the Philosophy of Kant*, 48–9.
[111] *On the Philosophy of Kant*, 72–82.

Another Kant scholar of great influence was one of Caird's own students, John Watson. On graduation from Glasgow, he took up a post in Canada, at Queen's University Kingston, where he remained for the rest of his life.[112] In a sequence of secondary writings, translations, and more independent forays from 1880 onwards, he proceeded to disseminate a Cairdian view of Kant, although perhaps the most interesting from an historical point of view is one of the earliest of these, *Kant and his English Critics*, in which he attempts to demonstrate the superiority of the idealist reading over that of any of its contemporary rivals, for example, taking issue with A.J. Balfour's recent criticisms of Green and Caird's 'transcendentalism'.[113] Against the complaint that the first question of knowledge should be 'whether' not 'how' it is possible, Watson responds that the kind of knowledge which transcendental argument assumes is simply that proper to the special sciences, not that of any underlying (and controversial) metaphysic which might give it deeper truth; which is surely right, since whatever our view of the general character of the objects of knowledge the facts of science and mathematics remain what they are. Balfour is charged too with failing to understand the true nature of transcendental argumentation which is not some analysis of the deep implications of ordinary belief or experience, but a laying bare of those conditions without which there could be no experience at all.[114]

A similar view of Kant appears in the writings of Andrew Seth Pringle-Pattison. Though later to distance himself from Hegelian idealism, his early work—his 1882, *The Development from Kant to Hegel* and his 1883 contribution to the Green memorial volume 'Philosophy as Criticism of Categories'—presented an orthodox picture of Kant's philosophy as something pointing inevitably to Hegel. Resisting any psychological reading, he finds Kant's great contribution to lie in his discovery of 'the true nature of knowledge'; the recognition (notwithstanding the lingering remnant of dualism which clings to the phenomena/noumena distinction) that 'thinker and thing are both "as good as nothing at all for us," except as united in knowledge.'[115] Given this new conception of what it is to be real, in which the categories become 'the knot which binds man and the world together', several initially important Kantain themes fade into the background. The difference between necessary and contingent is judged not one of kind but one of degree, while form and matter are held to be 'shifting distinctions, relative to the point of view from which they are contemplated; and the same is true of the world and the mind, of which opposition, indeed, the other is only another form. From the standpoint of a theory of knowledge it will be found that the mind and the world are in a sense convertible terms.'[116] In short, the

---

[112] In 1894 he made at least two attempts to return, but was defeated first by Henry Jones for Caird's recently vacated Glasgow Chair, and then by D.G. Ritchie for the St Andrews Chair which Jones in consequence gave up. Ritchie had also stood unsuccessfully for the Glasgow chair.

[113] This being the term Balfour uses to designate their reading of Kant. See his 'Transcendentalism'.

[114] *Kant and his English Critics*, 1–33.

[115] *Development*, 8.

[116] 'Philosophy as Criticism of Categories', 13.

whole separation between *Aesthetic* and *Analytic*, sense and understanding, a posteriori and a priori begins to fade away. At the same time other points, at first only in the background, press to the front. For example, Kant's paradoxical use of self-consciousness, as that which is the condition of all unity yet itself unconditioned, leads us in the end beyond his own point of view to investigate further the true nature of the universal self.[117]

William Wallace in his 1882 volume for the Blackwood's series, *Kant*, like many of the others, stressed the origin and development of Kant's views giving extensive attention to his life story. And if the fact that Kant's ideas developed in response to the challenge of Hume constitutes one reason why interest in his thought should be so strong among Scottish Philosophers, in pointing out that Kant believed himself to be of Scottish origin Wallace suggests another.[118] But on the other hand, Wallace's commitment to Hegel precludes him from finding much significance in Kant beyond the further thoughts of others that he stimulated. 'At every step he carries us beyond his own lines, and hints at a systematic unity which might carry us over the breaks in his thought. These hints were followed out with various success by the succeeding systems of Fichte, Schelling, and Hegel. They were his children, though he disowned them, and though they . . . spoke hardly of their father.'[119]

It should not be thought that all consideration of Kant at this time was in the tradition of Green and Caird. In the 1870s and 1880s James Hutchison Stirling moved his attention from Hegel to Kant, producing a series of articles and a book which presented a rather different Kant.[120] Taking a thoroughly psychological reading, he sees Kant as buying the possibility of a priori foundations to science at the price of denying all knowledge of an independent external universe, leaving him quite unable to answer Hume. In view of this upshot, 'Kant's idealism, like all subjective idealism of what name soever, must perish' he concluded.[121] He allowed that the line of philosophy which culminated in Hegel began in Kant—'It is the Categories of Kant *made* Hegel'[122] he admits—but he thinks too that Hegel completely replaces and subverts that starting point, and he had no sympathy with any sort of 'back to Kant' sentiment. That one of the most 'Hegelian' of the British Idealists should have repudiated the affinity and transition between the two German idealists that nearly all of the rest of them affirmed reminds us of the diversity to be found within the movement.

Reviewing the various Idealist commentaries on Kant we are struck by their simultaneous extremes of endorsement and criticism. That Kant was first to recognize

---

[117] *Development*, 13.

[118] *Kant*, 8–9. Wallace, of course, was another Scot, although by this time at Oxford.

[119] *Kant*, 219.

[120] 'Philosophy of Causality: Hume and Kant' (*Princeton Review*, 1879); 'Schopenhauer in Relation to Kant' (*Journal of Speculative Philosophy*, 1879); 'Caird on Kant' (*Journal of Speculative Philosophy*, 1880); 'Criticism of Kant's Main Principles' (*Journal of Speculative Philosophy*, 1880); *Text-book to Kant* (1881); and 'Kant has not answered Hume' (*Mind*, 1885), *The Categories* (1903).

[121] 'Criticism of Kant's Main Principles', 374.

[122] *The Categories*, 151.

the input of the subject to the object and the vital importance of the transcendental unity of apperception all are agreed, but he is so accused of misunderstanding his own discovery that at times this acknowledgement can seem hollow. That there is no final distinction between subject and object, that the a priori / a posteriori distinction is a relative one, and that the unity of apperception offers a window into the nature of ultimate reality are all commonly regarded as the true import of Kantianism, though none would be recognized as Kantian today. But if Kant himself is found to fall short of the full promise of his insight, by quite how far is a point which varies. At one extreme Stirling finds a terrible mess that Hegel must correct, Green by contrast sees someone who is not fully aware of the significance of what he has done, while Caird attributes such prescience to Kant that Hegel merely underlines his achievements. These differences serve to warn us of something that will become more and more apparent as this study progresses, namely just how diverse the Idealists were in their understandings of 'idealism'.

3.3 The British Empiricist tradition

3.3.1 T.H. Green

3.3.1.1 The classical empiricist tradition: Locke, Berkeley, Hume
If the significance of Kant was to be found in the way his failures led to Hegel, the significance of British empiricism lay in the way its failures led to Kant. Kant himself described its sceptical shipwreck with David Hume at the helm as the event that woke him from his dogmatic slumbers.[123] But empiricism's defeat, felt Green, had never yet been recognized in its own land, and he therefore set himself the task of demonstrating to his countrymen the bankruptcy of their native philosophical tradition. His first effort in this direction—one of his earliest pieces—was an 1868 essay, 'Popular Philosophy in its Relation to Life,' in which he urges the inability of any purely passive account, in terms of feeling, to explain human knowledge, either metaphysical or moral. Where knowledge is *given*, man may think any input of his own a species of distortion that ought properly to be removed, but 'it is in vain that he seeks to place himself in the attitude of pure receptivity,' for it is only by first 'infecting' the world that he comes to know it at all.[124]

Green's main engagement with the British empirical tradition, however, is to be found a few years later in the 1874 *Introduction* he wrote to the four-volume edition of Hume's *Philosophical Works* that he edited together with T.H. Grose. Running to a massive 370 pages and entirely negative, not simply of Hume but of the whole tradition to which he belongs, this was Idealism's great assault on empiricism.

In saying that Green attacks empiricism, we need to distinguish the thesis that all knowledge comes from *experience* from the thesis that all knowledge comes from

---

[123] Kant, *Prolegomena*, Preface.   [124] 'Popular Philosophy', 95.

sensation. If empiricism asserts the former, then Green has no quarrel with it. The traditional empiricist dismissal of innate ideas is one of the few parts of the doctrine that escapes his censure. However, a serious philosophy cannot simply rest in experience, but must further seek to analyse it, to ask how it is composed and what makes it possible; and, if to this inquiry empiricism claims that all knowledge derives from *sense experience* or *sensation*, then Green certainly does take issue with it. We never go beyond *experience*, but, he thinks, in all experience we go beyond *sense*.[125] Empiricism as the doctrine that mind is wholly passive and derives all its materials from the action of the world upon it, he emphatically rejects.[126] It is quite unsustainable to regard experience simply as a matter of what is 'out there' or 'given' as opposed to what is 'made' 'by us'. All experience necessarily involves thought.

Just what, as Green saw it, was wrong with sensationalism? Simply this, that faithfully executed, it leaves the knowing subject mired in psychology and reduced to silence. As an attempt to construct the world from sensation alone, empiricism is doomed, when done strictly, to reduce itself to scepticism. Its classical exponents, of course, thought themselves to have done better than this, but if we look more closely into their supposed achievements, argues Green, we find again and again that they have begged the question, presupposing the very things they had hoped to derive.

This failure Green attempts to show in his *Introduction* by means of a critical account of the philosophical development from Locke, through Berkeley, to Hume; an account that would allow the reader to see how the whole empiricist project had by its own internal logic progressed to a point of complete and utter breakdown. The bulk of the essay in fact deals with Locke, for it is here thinks Green that the roots of sensationalism are laid. It is noteworthy too that Berkeley receives scarcely any attention. As an empiricist he adds but little to the story, thinks Green, while as an idealist he is of even less significance; his idealism being of the 'subjective' or 'psychological' variety. But it was in Hume, he thought, that empiricism had 'found its last word.'[127] That word was emphatically negative, for as Green saw it, Hume's great contribution—his 'splendid failure'[128]—was, by taking empiricism as strictly as possible and thereby running it into a sceptical brick wall, to have perfectly illustrated the fatal tendency of the school. That it *is* a fatal path, Green has no doubt, for scepticism is something he finds simply absurd. Like Kant, without argument, he just *assumes* that we possess knowledge of reality. Our task, as philosophers, is to analyse this knowledge and see how it is possible.[129] Unable to accept scepticism and brought to admit that

[125]   *Introduction*, §314.
[126]   *Prolegomena*, §34.
[127]   'Review of Caird's *Philosophy of Kant*', 133.
[128]   *Introduction*, §153. There is no small irony in the level of attention which Green paid to Hume. Remembered more for his historical than his philosophical work, prior to that point Hume was not regarded as a major thinker, but Green's spotlight on his 'failure' raised his profile and set the stage for the generation of philosophers that came after the Idealists to raise him up as their great champion.
[129]   Green's question is not '*Is* knowledge possible?' but '*How* is knowledge possible?' For the true task for philosophy 'is simply the consideration of what is implied in the fact of our knowing or coming to know a

experience is not wholly given, Green's own thought proceeds down a Kantian track which holds that the work of the mind itself is necessary to bring about the apprehension of reality.

To chart in more detail the path of destruction chronicled by Green in his *Introduction* it is useful to follow the key distinction, made by each of the classical empiricists, between simple ideas and the complex ones we make out of them. Beginning with the former, the alleged basic elements of our experience, Green's fundamental objection is that Locke's use of the term 'simple idea' continually confuses or equivocates between two quite different notions. He alternates between thinking of it as a physical sensation (something like a tickle, itch, or pain) and thinking of it as a perception of some real quality in things. He confuses the physical stimulation of an organism by a quality with the conscious perception of that quality. While the former may be necessary for, even the occasioning cause of, the latter, they are nonetheless quite different.[130] Hume for his part, attempting not to go beyond what is given in immediate consciousness, is less guilty than Locke of this conflation, but even he (argues Green) fails sufficiently to distinguish between feelings and things felt. The cause of an impression, the impression produced on the senses, and the resultant idea preserved by the mind are all on occasion elided, as Hume quietly benefits from the natural assumptions an uncritical reader tends to make.[131] A crucial aspect of this distinction between feeling or sensation, and perception, of which Green wishes to remind us, is *consciousness*. It is one thing to be affected physically but quite another to be conscious that one is so, and it is only when feelings enter into consciousness that they exist for us as objects. It is only then that we move beyond the mere fact that there has been some modification of our sense to the possession of an idea *of* something.

Green argues that empiricism is only plausible because of this unacknowledged equivocation between sensation and perception, and he spends much time demonstrating the variety of ways in which it gets covered up. He criticizes Locke's careless and seemingly interchangeable use of the terms 'idea' and 'quality',[132] and attacks particularly the metaphor of 'impression'. Locke in using this term conflates a supposed impression on the 'outward parts' (the body, brain, nerves, etc.) and a supposed impression on the 'tablet of the mind', and in this way (as Green puts it) 'a metaphor interpreted as a fact becomes the basis of his philosophical system.'[133] Once this equivocation is unmasked, the dilemma which it poses to the empiricist becomes only too apparent. The question, claims Green, 'whether the simple idea as the original of knowledge, is on the one hand a mere feeling, or on the other a thing or quality of a thing' comes to the fore as the key issue confronting

---

world, or, conversely, in the fact of their being a world for us to know'. 'The fact that there is a real external world of which through feeling we have direct experience...is one which no philosophy disputes' ('Mr Herbert Spencer and Mr G.H. Lewes', 374, 376); 'Philosophy does not precede but follows, that actual knowledge of things, which it is its office to analyse and reduce to its primitive elements' ('Philosophy of Aristotle', 48).

[130] *Prolegomena*, §59.   [131] *Introduction*, §201.   [132] *Introduction*, §18.
[133] *Introduction*, §14.

empirical psychology, for, he continues, 'adopting the one alternative, we have to face the difficulty of the genesis of knowledge, as an apprehension of the real, out of mere feeling; adopting the other we virtually endow the nascent intelligence with the conception of substance.'[134]

The point is not difficult to grasp. Suppose we take the simple idea to be nothing but feeling or sensation. Immediately it is hard to see how we could ever come to know anything. A single sensation is an isolated event, a mere point of experience. Without context or continuity it is ultimately without even character, and as such it can tell us nothing. If sensations are, as Hume argued, 'fleeting' and 'momentary' they must for that reason, insists Green, be 'unnameable' ('because, while we name it, it has become another') and 'the very negation of knowability'.[135] It cannot be, as the empiricist urges, that reality is given to us only in what is currently presented, for things have to be continuants, however short-lived, in order to possess any definite character at all. And it is not just our *descriptive* net that would be eluded by such sensations, for Green endorses the argument of Hegel's *Phenomenology* that we could not even *point* to such elements.[136] Demonstrative words like 'this', 'here', and 'now' are all implicitly relational, locating their referents in a net of other similarly identified items, a work of classification which implicitly involves generality.[137] The simple idea, considered merely as a physical sensation, could not even be picked out and is hence no basis for knowing anything.

But we do no better if we suppose, on the other hand, that simple ideas are basic perceptions of qualities. The reason for proposing them, as our supposed purely passive point of contact with reality, was to use them as the basic building blocks out of which to fashion our understanding of the world. But, argues Green, if we take them as perceptions rather than just sensations, they turn out to be far from simple and to contain within themselves great theoretical complexity. In thinking of the mind in its alleged primitive state we find that we have implicitly assumed its possession of a whole host of ideas which, according to the official doctrine, can be reached only after a gradual process of comparison, abstraction, and generalization. The mind's awareness of a real quality turns out to be no small affair. 'The simple idea has . . . lost its simplicity. It is not the momentary isolated consciousness, but the representation of a thing determined by relations to other things in an order of nature, and causing an infinite series of resembling sensations to which a common name is applied.'[138] In this way, saying far more than first they seemed to, when the empiricist speaks of simple ideas not

---

[134]   *Introduction*, §18.

[135]   *Introduction*, §22. The reason he gives here is the Heraclitean argument that Plato uses in the *Theaetetus* (180a–183c) to defeat the thesis that knowledge lies in perception; that in our very naming it, it would have become something different. Green himself recognizes that origin, reminding that it was Plato who 'long ago taught' that 'a consistent sensationalism must be speechless' (*Introduction*, §45).

[136]   *Phenomenology of Spirit*, §A.I. sense-certainty.

[137]   *Introduction*, §45, See also 'Philosophy of Aristotle', 52.

[138]   *Introduction*, §64.

as feelings but as representations, he in effect treats them as though they were complex and conscious *judgements* about the world. To put the point in a slightly different way, since the detail which the allegedly simple idea is found to contain turns out to be essentially relational (detailing how it stands to its cause, the self that entertains it, and to other sensations at various different times and places), and relations are (by the empiricists' own admission) quintessentially the work of the mind,[139] we must conclude that the simple idea turns out to be not really *given* at all, but in very large part our own *creation*. The idea of the purely given, as one more recent philosopher has put it, is a 'myth'.[140]

Simple ideas, then, are either silent or not so simple after all. But turning from simple ideas to the complex ones (such as substance, causation, identity, space, time, and the self) which empiricism supposes that we construct out of them, Green shows how our problem with the building material is transferred up to the structure created out of it. More specifically, the ambiguity in what is intended by 'simple idea' means that in each case where we attempt to derive a complex idea, one or other of two results ensue, both equally fatal. On the one hand, taking simple ideas more strictly as sensations, we find it simply impossible to arrive at the concepts we want. For, constructed as they are out of relations (especially spatio-temporal and causal ones), these concepts go far beyond what is given in immediate sensation, or even in everyday common-sense present-tense experience. On the other hand, taking simple ideas as perceptions of real qualities, the constructions we attempt are more or less successful but only, we then find, because we have begged the question. Since the supposedly simple ideas we employ are really quite complex, we find we have been smuggling in the very notions we had hoped to construct.[141]

The complex notion of substance serves well as an illustration. Locke continually equivocates in his attempt to arrive at the idea of substance, but his irrepressible common sense prevents him from seeing the problems which beset him when a stricter application of his principles would have made him keep silent. Berkeley and Hume show greater sensitivity to these problems and become more sceptical about substance as a result.[142] Green describes Berkeley as 'Locke purged'[143] and says that for him 'matter . . . with all its qualities, is a fiction except so far as these can be reduced to simple feelings', while Hume's account of substance too 'is simply Locke's, as Locke's would become upon elimination of the notion that there is a real "something" in which the collection of ideas subsist, and from which they result.'[144] Indeed, Hume (for Green) is even more of a subjective idealist than Berkeley, in whom the work of

---

[139] See Chapter 4.1.2.
[140] Sellars, 'Empiricism and the Philosophy of Mind', 195.
[141] This result, for Green, is no condemnation of experience but simply a recognition of the fundamental truth of idealism, that experience is unavoidably shaped by mind. However, for the sensationalist, who holds fast to the distinction between thought and reality, it is a damning failure.
[142] *Introduction*, §132.   [143] *Introduction*, §155.   [144] *Introduction*, §214.

scepticism is only 'half done'.[145] He at least made a move in the direction of consistency and completed Berkeley's sceptical shift by also abandoning altogether the notion of the thinking self.[146]

Nettleship in his *Memoir* complained that Green had written an introduction to Hume 'more difficult to master than the work itself.'[147] And there is no disputing that Green's *Introduction* is very inhospitable; it makes for long, complex, and turgid reading. It meanders without clear direction, is over-reliant on metaphor and continually mixes minor—often merely verbal—points with more significant insights. But for all that, it must be allowed, in conclusion, that the attack was immensely influential. Green finished his *Introduction* with an injunction to students to put away what he dismissed as the anachronistic systems of empiricism and turn instead to Kant and Hegel,[148] and that is what they did. When he first wrote, empiricism was pretty much the assumption of the day, but as a result of his extensive criticisms a whole generation of philosophers felt that it had been shown to be untenable and that they were thereby set free to work out alternatives. The later idealists felt able to assume that any more cautious sense-based approach was false, leaving the field free for idealist construction. And this state of affairs must largely be put down to the work of T.H. Green.[149]

3.3.1.2 The contemporary empiricist tradition: Spencer and Lewes Green wrote his *Introduction* because, in his view, contemporary British philosophy had simply failed to notice its own refutation and, blind to the lessons of the past, doggedly continued to mine a long-exhausted seam. Not surprising this charge was resisted and so, in a series of four articles published shortly afterwards, Green took it on himself to demonstrate explicitly how the philosophies of his contemporaries, Spencer and Lewes, had managed to do nothing more than repeat the errors and confusions of their more illustrious predecessors.[150]

For instance, examining Part Seven of his *Principles of Psychology* (1855) in which Spencer sets out the distinction between subject and object, Green claims that he has simply repeated Locke's equivocations. He tries to defend a view of knowledge as the result of the action upon a subject of some object existing outside or distinct from it, but at times this object is reduced to a series of fleeting states (resulting in an idealism akin to Berkeley or Hume's), while at times it is made to sit 'beyond consciousness', as that 'which causes our knowledge, an "unknowable" reality'.[151] As a result, 'consciousness' with Spencer has two different meanings, and his system turns on an

---

[145] 'Spencer and Lewes', 380.   [146] *Introduction*, §339.   [147] 'Memoir', lxxiv.

[148] *Introduction to Hume's Treatise*, Part II §64, 371.

[149] Peter Hylton, *Russell, Idealism and the Emergence of Analytic Philosophy*, 22.

[150] 'Mr Herbert Spencer and Mr G.H. Lewes' (The first three articles appeared in 1877–8, the fourth was withdrawn because of Lewes' death in 1878. They were all reprinted Green's *Works*, together with a reply to Shadworth Hodgson (which first appeared in 1881) defending himself against charges of having misinterpreted Spencer in the first article).

[151] 'Spencer and Lewes', 393.

equivocation between them. 'It means one thing when it is found to tell of an objective world; another thing when this world is shown to be independent of it. So long as consciousness is understood to be a mere succession of states, it is easy to show that the objective world is independent of it, but the consciousness which can alone tell of such a world is not such a succession.'[152]

Lewes's attempt to account for consciousness as having arisen by wholly natural process makes a similar mistake, for it is not possible that our experience of matter and force itself can be understood as resulting from the action of matter and force, our knowledge of nature cannot itself be a product of nature. The problem is that our experience is of things in relation, but all nature furnishes—in the world or within us— is a series of fleeting events, which cannot by itself account for knowledge of relations.[153] There is a world of difference between a sequence of feelings and consciousness of such a succession. The latter cannot be just one more member of the former, for, were it a term in the series, it could not be present to all the members of that series, as it must be in order to be a consciousness of the series.[154] For Lewes the emergence of mind is a matter of 'evolution' but that, complains Green, 'is to use the charm of a potent word to hide a confusion of thought,' for evolution implies identity as well as differentiation, some common point which is continued in modified form, but in the alleged move from repeated sensation to the development of consciousness there is no continuance at all; rather a magic transformation.[155]

In certain minds, of course, failure to learn the Kantian lesson might be held up as a badge of honour, a thoroughly sensible decision to avoid metaphysics and work at scientific psychology instead. But Green is unimpressed. 'If psychology could avoid being a theory of knowledge, or if a theory of knowledge were possible without a theory of the thing known, the reply might be effective,' he counters, 'but since this cannot be, it merely means that it is unaware of the assumptions which it uncritically makes in order to its own justification.'[156] Metaphysics is unavoidable; the only choice is whether it is done consciously and critically or unconsciously and blindly.

3.3.2 Edward Caird

Green's criticisms of empiricism were influential and, picked up by subsequent idealists, rapidly became something like an orthodox starting point in the history of philosophy. For example, essentially the same case is stated by Edward Caird, more succinctly, and with explicit reference to Green for those wishing to pursue the details,[157] in Chapter Four of his *Critical Account of the Philosophy of Kant* (1877).

In Caird's summary, Locke's philosophy is at best an awkward compromise, at worst an inconsistent oscillation, between two worldviews that cannot really be combined or reconciled. *Part of the time* his base idea is of a world in space of which the mind, in

---

[152] 'Spencer and Lewes', 298–9.   [153] 'Spencer and Lewes', 442–3.
[154] 'Spencer and Lewes', 450.   [155] 'Spencer and Lewes', 467.
[156] 'Spencer and Lewes', 375.   [157] *Critical Account of the Philosophy of Kant*, 58.

communion with a material body, is one component, *but at other times* his starting conception is one of the individual mind itself, something self-complete without essential relation to the world, which it then attempts to know through its own sensations. The second view is defeated by the fact all that sense yields is momentary sensations which, quite unrelated to one another, it is 'the work of the mind' to put together, with the result that no relation or complex idea may be taken to correspond beyond itself or have any more than subjective validity. According to the first model we simply assume such knowledge, but only to then face defeat by the deeper problem of how objects can ever interact with and be known by subjects.[158]

Berkeley may be understood as attempting to remove the inconsistency that marred Locke's vision; but thus trying to rid the world of matter and leave only spirit, says Caird, he failed to see that the weapon he used was a double-edged sword. He failed to see 'that in rejecting Locke's materialistic ontology, he was rejecting all ontology whatever and reducing reality to a series of feelings'—which is not *idealism* but *sensationalism*.[159] If we take away from our sensations all the constructive interpretation by which they are turned into perceptions of an objective world, what is left but a succession of isolated, fleeting, and (ultimately) meaningless points of feeling? The permanent order from which we might have hoped to demonstrate their divine origin, the enduring self that experiences them, even the stability required to speak of them— is quite lost to us.

Hume was the first clearly to see that Locke and Berkeley, although professing to work from the point of view of the individual mind, had nevertheless adopted the universal point of view of a spectator able to observe both mind and its object, and he determined to avoid this error and stick within the limits of his introspective sensation-alism. The sceptical lesson of this restriction was not lost on him, for he well saw that from such a point of view the problem is no longer whether or how we can know external reality, but rather why experience takes the shape it does. But when he tries to answer this question he fails. He attempts to show how the purely sensitive conscious-ness, itself nothing but a bundle of perceptions, constructs categories such as causation and identity simply by attending to the 'natural relations' (resemblance, contiguity, sequence) between its own ideas. But the account he offers presupposes the very categories in question; for there can be no permanent self able to compare sensations except in contrast to an equally permanent world of objects, and no such world except as determined by universal laws governing the coexistence or succession of distinct states.[160] Locke and Berkeley in their positive assertions went beyond the warrant of

---

[158]   *Critical Account of the Philosophy of Kant*, 60.

[159]   *Critical Account of the Philosophy of Kant*, 61, 62. Caird's description of his position as 'the so-called idealism of Berkeley' makes his view plain ('Mr Balfour on Transcendentalism', 112). His pupil Mackenzie echoed the assessment calling it a 'false Idealism' ('Edward Caird as Philosophical Teacher', 519).

[160]   *Critical Account of the Philosophy of Kant*, 71.

sensation but, in trying to explain how these illusions arise, and for all his caution, Hume unwittingly transgresses the same limits.

The idealist history of British empiricism is a history of scepticism, a history of how philosophy was led inexorably and hopelessly up a sceptical blind alley. It was a reading which did not really out-live idealism itself; Norman Kemp Smith in the 1940s popularizing the more naturalistic reading fashionable today. But, before leaving it, note should be taken that the sceptical problem which the Idealists identify is *not* the familiar 'veil of perception problem' commonly raised in contemporary discussions. Green (for example) had no interest in the known fact as it supposedly stands in abstraction from our knowledge of it. 'The existence of a world beyond consciousness' he holds is an 'essentially unmeaning phrase'.[161] For the Idealists, in rejecting scepticism, what is being assumed is not that we have some bridge to a world 'out there', but simply that experience is rational, that is, of a connected related whole. All that is rejected is a world of wholly disconnected sensations.

3.4 Spinoza

Looking back further into early modern thought, an additional figure that the Idealists all concurred in elevating among the pantheon of 'philosophical greats' was Spinoza.[162] They were very aware of the key role he had played in the eighteenth- and early nineteenth-century development of thinking in continental Europe, but his importance was not just historical, for they agreed with the words of Hegel that it was an essential precondition of philosophizing oneself that one must first bathe thoroughly in the sea of Spinoza.[163]

Nor is it hard to see what they found attractive in Spinoza. He was to them an idealist, one who asserted the presence of mind in all things; a rationalist, with a correspondingly high estimate of the role of philosophy; a monist, deeply imbued with a sense of the immanence of God; and his system though timeless was also (in its own fashion) strongly progressive. He makes central to his philosophy the human drive to moral and intellectual advance, which he understands at the same time as a progressive manifestation of God and, in this sense, for Green, he was a greater witness to the true doctrine of Christian resurrection than all the dogmatic theologians who would exclude him personally from it.[164] In the development of the history of philosophy he moved beyond Cartesian psychologism to set philosophy on a sounder *metaphysical* basis,[165] and as Henry Jones argues he was the only modern philosopher

---

[161] 'Spencer and Lewes', 396.

[162] Caird ranks him with Kant and Hegel as the three modern philosophers who stand on a par with Plato and Aristotle (*Hegel*, 223). In the last few years of his life Nettleship read little except Plato and Spinoza, and the books he took with him on his last trip to Switzerland were *The Ethics* and a selection of poems by Browning (*Philosophical Lectures and Remains*, I:xxx).

[163] *Lectures on the History of Philosophy*, III:257.

[164] 'Witness of God', 238.

[165] *Critical Philosophy of Immanuel Kant*, I:80.

before Hegel not to start out from the subjective point of view—even Kant was unable to claim that.[166] Lastly, extending Descartes' insight into the concept, and anticipating Hegel's notion of true infinity, he puts forward a conception of the infinite as wholly positive, a concept of finitude or determination as a species of negation.[167]

However, the Idealist view of Spinoza was not entirely positive. They all saw in his one substance doctrine a tendency for abstract empty monism and a lack of appreciation of concrete particularity.[168] In addition, philosophers persuaded by Green's argument that the subject which knows nature cannot itself be explained naturalistically, could not be quite comfortable with Spinoza's reductionism (exemplified, for instance, in his notorious claim that we should study man just as we would lines, planes, and figures.) And if there was a *nisus* or direction to his system, it was compatible with quite open and explicit denials of any sort of cosmic teleology or purpose.

3.4.1 Edward Caird

One of the first to consider Spinoza in any detail was Edward Caird who discussed him twice in the mid-1870s.[169] Caird sees a kindred spirit in Spinoza. His is a philosophy in which thought must rise—from sense and imagination to reason, from particular to universal, from finite to infinite, from temporal to eternal and, most importantly of all, from part to whole. For Caird, Spinoza is above all things the philosopher of *unity*. Most of what he says about Spinoza can be understood in that light. For example, he attributes to Spinoza a strongly *coherentist* conception of knowledge and truth. It is the work of the senses and the imagination to divide, whereas reason or intellect proceeds by connecting things together. Only knowledge of the whole is true, anything less not wholly so.[170] Such ideas are present in Spinoza, of course, but so too is a doctrine of adequate ideas, which Caird largely ignores, and his attribution to Spinoza of the thought that individual human minds make sense only as part of the great history of thought[171] sounds more like Hegel, or Caird himself, than *Spinoza*.

If the only true grasp is a complete grasp, then to fix one's eyes on any determinate detail is to distort. In this way Caird extracts what he takes to be the root of Spinoza's monism; the philosophical principle that ultimately all determination is false; *determinato negato est*.[172] What this means, thinks Caird, is that to reach reality we must abstract away from all

---

[166]   Jones, 'Idealism and Epistemology', 303.

[167]   Mackenzie, 'Infinite and Perfect', 358.

[168]   The claim that Spinoza's was an undifferentiated abstract unity is characteristic of the Idealists. In addition to those below, see Seth Pringle-Pattison, 'New Theory of the Absolute', 169, 174, 179–80; and James Seth, *Study of Ethical Principles*, 440.

[169]   The first longer account was in his 1876 article on 'Cartesianism' for the ninth edition of the *Encyclopaedia Britannica*, the second shorter account occurred as part of his 1877 volume *A Critical Account of the Philosophy of Kant with an historical introduction*. Both unsurprisingly consider Spinoza as one link in a wider story.

[170]   'Cartesianism', 344, 349.

[171]   'Cartesianism', 345–6.

[172]   The claim comes not from Spinoza's *Ethics* but one of his letters (*Correspondence of Spinoza*, letter 50, p.270). In itself of somewhat unclear significance, it was Hegel who elevated it to such centrality.

concrete differences.[173] But although this produces monism, it does so at a very high cost. Finding differentiation a species of error, 'Spinoza is driven, in spite of himself, to dissolve everything in the dead abstraction of substance, in a pure identity that has no difference in itself, and from which no difference can be by any possibility evolved.'[174] In the end the universe of Spinoza is one in which all distinctions and details are absorbed, transcended only because they are set aside. We are left with a blank and abstract nothing. Caird is prepared to admit that that was not Spinoza's intention, that what he was aiming at was some sort of inclusive concrete totality, which conception we may also glimpse at times through in his writing,[175] but ultimately he failed to reach that goal, for his underlying logic defeats him.[176] To take just one example, while he may try to explain human individuality, really the concept eludes him and for all his efforts he is left with nothing more than a mode of the infinite thought-attribute without any real independent existence.[177]

The great obstacle on the path to monism is, for Spinoza, the irreducible dualism of attributes (thought and extension) in which he finds himself obliged to follow Descartes. In the manner of Hegel, Caird takes a 'subjective reading' of this difference, that is, he treats it as a perceived rather than a real distinction.[178] The duality between thought and extension is merely relative to our understanding; these are but two languages in which reality is articulated to us. Although Spinoza does sometimes define substance positively, as 'consisting in an infinity of attributes' or as 'the unity of mind and matter', in truth, substance is not for him a principle of unity that explains or expresses itself in these differences, but rather just the common element behind them. The identity of thought and being is for him an arbitrary identity of two elements with no necessary relation to each other.[179] Nothing we know of reality itself necessitates its self-revelation in distinct modes or attributes at all.[180] It is in dealing with the relation between mind and matter, Caird feels, that Spinoza missed his great chance. He applauds the fact that extension is taken just as seriously as thought,[181] but regrets that in the end Spinoza can find them only externally related to one another, that is, as both just falling under the overarching category of substance. Had he been able to recognize their essential relativity to each other, he could instead have advanced to the category of subject.[182] Here of course, as elsewhere, Caird is following Hegel closely.[183]

[173] 'Cartesianism', 355, 357, 358, 366.
[174] *Critical Account of the Philosophy of Kant*, 48–9; see also *Hegel*, 179; *Evolution of Religion*, I:104–5; *Critical Philosophy of Immanuel Kant*, I:81.
[175] 'Cartesianism', 364.
[176] 'Cartesianism', 365; *Critical Account of the Philosophy of Kant*, 43–4.
[177] *Critical Account of the Philosophy of Kant*, 50.
[178] 'Cartesianism', 363.   [179] *Critical Account of the Philosophy of Kant*, 49.
[180] *Critical Account of the Philosophy of Kant*, 48.
[181] 'Cartesianism', 361–2.   [182] 'Cartesianism', 368–9.
[183] See *Phenomenolgy of Spirit*, Preface, paragraph 17.

3.4.2 John Caird

Many of these ideas are repeated in a short book on Spinoza by John Caird, Edward's elder brother, published in 1888 (at which time they were in almost daily contact in Glasgow).[184] Spinoza is accused of having reached his final system by a kind of 'short-cut.'[185] Holding determination a form of negation[186] he arrives at an infinite unity which is abstract and empty rather than concrete and organic.[187] But 'unity which carries with it no implication of diversity, becomes as meaningless a conception as that of a whole without parts, or a cause without effect'.[188] In face of the undeniable difference between thought and extension, monism is preserved by holding that this dualism of attributes resides not in substance itself but only in relation to intelligence,[189] which, Caird points out, is not only subjective but self-contradictory—finite intelligence cannot possibly create that by which it is itself created.[190] Not that the notion of cause is really available here for, as Caird notes also, if we pass beyond all finite categories, we pass beyond causality as well, with the consequence that there remains no meaningful sense in which Spinoza can claim as he wants to that God is the (immanent) cause of all things.[191]

But if in these respects John Caird is a somewhat harsher critic than his brother, in another respect he is perhaps more generous. For even more than his brother he sees that there is also, alongside this picture a second more positive Spinoza. This he locates especially in the final book of the *Ethics* in which Spinoza seems to restore in some measure the notions which he had appeared to destroy in the earlier books. The all-absorbing lifeless substance becomes the God who knows and loves both Himself and man with an infinite 'intellectual love', while the rejected doctrine of final cause is restored in the conception of the human mind as having in it an implicit drive towards the ideal, which, through reason and intuitive knowledge, it is capable of realizing.[192]

This is not to say that Caird sees Spinoza as having somehow solved or moved beyond his problems; the system is merely contradictory, simultaneously pulled in opposing directions. At times the infinite is so emphasized as to leave no place for the finite, objects Caird, while in other places the finite seems to be given such an independent reality as to leave no room for the infinite. But the more clearly we see these contradictions, the more we see the positive set alongside the negative, the more we can see him as anticipating later systems that *do* reconcile them.

---

[184]   The book would have been longer but, his brother recalls, he made a mistake about the length and had to cut out the 'life' (Memoir by E.Caird in *Fundamental Ideas of Christianity* I:cxxiii).

[185]   *Spinoza*, 133.   [186]   *Spinoza*, 4, 53, 123.

[187]   *Spinoza*, 139.   [188]   *Spinoza*, 145.

[189]   *Spinoza*, 146.   [190]   *Spinoza*, 151.

[191]   *Spinoza*, 167–8.

[192]   *Spinoza*, 120, 303. Wallace concurs with Caird that in conceiving his eternal principle as something which loves itself with an infinite love, which love is identified with the love of man to God, Spinoza comes close to raising it above the mere category of substance to that of subject (*Prolegomena to Hegel*, 257–8).

3.4.3 H.H. Joachim

Although not published until 1901 and, as such, belonging to a somewhat later phase of the movement, H.H. Joachim's *A Study of the Ethics of Spinoza* represents the culmination of the British Idealist view of Spinoza.[193] Joachim's idealist credentials were impeccable; having been an undergraduate at Balliol College (where he was a pupil of R.L. Nettleship) and a lecturer at St Andrews before returning in 1894 to Balliol (where he worked as a colleague to J.A. Smith, and under the mastership of Edward Caird) from whence he moved 1897 to Merton College (where he succeeded William Wallace, and was a colleague of F.H. Bradley's).[194] The idealist notions that had informed previous readings of Spinoza found their way into Joachim's book, but he was a rather different type of historical scholar from any we have yet considered. Unlike those who tended to look at the history of philosophy contextually with an eye to developments and general patterns, Joachim was a careful and painstaking textual exegete. But while he confined himself to the details of Spinoza's *Ethics* itself, it would be a mistake to suppose his work without input of his own or any general philosophical lessons to be learned.

Like the Cairds before him Joachim regards Spinoza's unity as an all-engulfing and ultimately empty abstraction. Undermining the diversity of the concrete world, he complains that, 'all the distinctive features of the worlds of Extension and Thought seem to vanish as "illusions" one by one, until you are left with the singleness of the attributes: *a singleness not concrete but abstract.*'[195] But where they adopt a straightforwardly subjective reading of the attributes, Joachim is more careful. The text, he sees, makes it clear that, for Spinoza, attribute is no 'ens rationis' or 'imaginationis'. Rather it constitutes the very essence of substance. The definition of attribute Spinoza employs as 'what intellect perceives as constituting the essence of substance' is, Joachim argues, not a mark of subjectivity but rather of Spinoza's (objective) idealism.

The conception of Attribute is Spinoza's way of expressing that the Real is what is known. Commentators have simply stepped outside this attempt to identify 'what is' and 'what is known,' and have said brutally 'Either Reality or what is known or knowable.' There are difficulties enough in Spinoza's conception: but it is no use to begin by postulating dogmatically the ultimate severance of that which he conceives as fundamentally one.[196]

3.5 Plato and Aristotle

One of the things which Muirhead says in his singular history of the British Idealist movement is that really it was not (as it is often dismissed) some kind of import from

---

[193] Although not the final piece of Spinoza scholarship; a commentary by Joachim on Spinoza's *Tractatus de intellectus emendatione* appeared posthumously in 1940.

[194] From 1919 to 1935 he was Wykeham Professorship of Logic.

[195] *Study of the Ethics*, 114.

[196] *Study of the Ethics*, 26–7.

Germany but that it sprang from a pre-existing native attachment to ancient philoso-phy; the seventeenth-century work of the Cambridge Platonists slow-burning until it re-ignited in a nineteenth-century revival of classical studies.[197] There is no evidence that any one apart from Muirhead ever thought the Cambridge Platonists a significant influence, but he is quite correct that the study of ancient philosophy played a very important role in the emergence of British Idealism. For the British Idealists were all deeply versed in ancient philosophy and use it frequently to construct or support their systems. It is, for them, as vital a reference point as Kant or Hegel; and we misunder-stand their philosophy unless we recognize this.

It must, of course, be added immediately that it is not an entirely *separate* reference point. They read Plato and Aristotle *through* Kant and, especially, Hegel. But we cannot simply relegate their classical studies to a branch of their Hegelianism. The ideas which the Idealists find in Plato and Aristotle may well be moving in the same direction as Hegel's, but this coincidence of view leaves it open whether they were just reprodu-cing what they had read in Hegel on this subject, or whether the identity of tempera-ment between Hegel and the British Idealists simply caused them both to interpret the classical Greek philosophers they had read in the same basic way. The latter is far from absurd, for in terms of personal biography they all came to the texts of Plato and Aristotle well *before* they met Hegel, and their interpretations are given with little or no reference to Hegel or use of his terminology. On the other hand, even if it was primarily of significance in confirmation of what they thought anyway, they certainly knew Hegel's *History of Philosophy*, so its role should not be discounted.[198]

In pointing out that the Idealists started from ancient philosophy, we must take care to avoid anachronism. For centuries, to possess knowledge of classical antiquity was just part of what it meant to be 'educated', and for centuries it has been believed that all philosophy begins with Plato and Aristotle. Indeed, it is really only in the second half of twentieth century that we find people doing philosophy with no knowledge of its ancient history.[199] Nonetheless there is a difference here. Although they were all classically educated, neither with their predecessors nor with their successors do we observe anything like the same amount, or kind, of use of ancient philosophy that we find with the Idealists.

Some context is useful here. In the mid-late nineteenth century (unlike today) practically all university students studied at least some classics. For a degree in the faculty of arts in Scotland, for example, the prescribed curriculum at this time was a broad one, of which compulsory Greek and Latin made up two-sevenths—only once this basic course had been passed was it possible to take additional subjects or to read for

---

[197] *The Platonic Tradition*, 13–15, 413.

[198] As Robbins asks in relation to Bosanquet and Plato (and we could widen both terms here) was this a case of Hegelianizing Plato or Platonizing Hegel? (*The British Hegelians*, 75).

[199] Indeed it is only comparatively recently that this branch of study acquired the name 'ancient philosophy' rather than just 'history of philosophy'.

Honours. Classics was particularly strong at Glasgow University (the *alma mater* of many idealists)[200] which saw a succession of eminent Greek scholars from Edmund Lushington, through Richard Jebb, to Gilbert Murray. At the same time in Oxford, classics—known locally as *Literae Humaniores* or 'Greats'—held even greater sway. The pre-eminent school in Oxford,[201] including modern as well as classical philosophy alongside ancient literature and history, it was the course of instruction through which an even larger number of the Idealists passed.[202] Jowett's role in this school has already been noted.

3.5.1 Plato's idealism

Jowett's interest in Plato was communicated to, and continued by, the next generation of Balliol philosophers. For example, Edward Caird's first published work was on Plato; written in 1865 while still in Oxford (having relocated by this time from Balliol to Merton) and long before he published anything on Kant or Hegel. Ostensibly a review of George Grote's *Plato and Other Companions of Socrates*, the piece is in fact a lengthy general essay on Plato's philosophy.[203]

Caird represents Plato first and foremost as a moral philosopher but one whom, having discovered that ethical questions lead on to metaphysical ones, is guided from his quest to understand the nature of goodness to investigate the Idea of the Good itself, in other words to move from the individual to the universal, from the mutable to the changeless.[204]

For Caird, as for Jowett, Plato's advocacy of the 'theory of Ideas' makes him an early champion of idealism, the doctrine 'that being and knowing, thought and existence, are one.'[205] To us, this might seem tenuous (even verbal) but, to Caird, taking a broad synoptic view of history, Plato began the great debate between realists and nominalists that has dominated philosophy ever since; and it is a shift of emphasis only that changes the question which asks whether the universal or the individual has greater reality into its more modern form that asks whether objective truth is to be reached through the activity of thought or found in the passivity of sensation; into the question that asks (in other words) how far intellect creates the world we know.[206] The comparison is important, for pushed to say in just what sense they were idealists, many of the British

---

[200] Glasgow idealists included John Caird, Edward Caird, Jones, Watson, Muirhead, and Mackenzie. Edinburgh produced Andrew Seth Pringle-Pattison, James Seth, Haldane, Sorley, and Ritchie. Wallace was educated at St Andrews.

[201] By 1870 the requirement to sit Literae Humaniores in order to gain any degree was dropped, but it continued for a long time to be by far the largest school in Oxford. Even in the early twentieth century nearly half of Oxford's graduates (48%) read Greats (Brock and Curthoys, *History of the University of Oxford*, 93, 612).

[202] Green, Caird, Nettleship, Bosanquet, Bradley, A.C. Bradley, Toynbee, Wallace, Ritchie, A.E. Taylor, Hoernlé, Rashdall, Webb. Several it should be noted were awarded scholarships which took them from Glasgow to Oxford.

[203] The piece contains many of Caird's characteristic ideas and in this connection its date is of interest, telling us how early these were fixed.

[204] 'Plato and Other Companions of Socrates', 356.

[205] 'Plato and Other Companions of Socrates', 369.

[206] 'Plato and Other Companions of Socrates', 364.

Idealists would reply (as Caird did) that they were using the term 'idea', not in its modern meaning, but with something of its older Platonic sense.[207] For them, as for Plato, the world was more truly universal than particular, more truly grasped in thought than sense, more truly one than many, and the ideas which underlay all things wholly objective in their being.

The impression of modernity increases as Caird considers how Plato would respond to the objection that the Ideas or Forms are really nothing but abstractions that we make from the individuals given to us in sensation. He suggests that Plato answers, as did Kant after him, that what we call sensation *already contains thought within it*[208] and that, without the organizing work of mind, sensations would give just a chaos of individual impressions; in other words, that the order of dependence in fact goes the other way around. Mere sensation is the abstraction. This may not sound very Platonic, admits Caird, but the only difference is that (unlike Kant) Plato did not express the thought 'scientifically', but rather in the form of a story—the myth of pre-existence or recollection.[209] For the upshot is the same; that we come to experience ready endowed with the non-sensory concepts necessary to structure and interpret it. With the right spectacles and sufficient generosity Plato's account of the origin of the a priori becomes an anticipation of Kant's doctrine of the categories.

For all that Plato advanced philosophy, Caird allows too that he left it with serious problems, the deepest of which was a kind of dualism. Platonism draws between the abstract static world of universals and the concrete changing world of individuals a contrast so sharp as to threaten to make the Forms or Ideas simply irrelevant to the world we know. But Caird does not leave the matter there. Already pursuing the sort of history of philosophy that would characterize his work on Kant and Hegel, he takes up Plato's problematic dualism and he attempts to show what would be needed to solve it. He then tries to argue that, in his later thought, Plato was himself beginning to take precisely these steps. He suggests that Plato modified his initial position which postulates a world of Ideas distinct from each other and distinct from the world, recognizing the relation of each Idea to others and especially to its contrary Ideas; what it *is* implies what it is *not*. In thus appreciating what he terms the 'relativity of thought',[210] Caird represents Plato as having moved well down the path from Platonism as commonly understood to Hegelianism, just as he saw Kant as having already moved beyond 'Kantianism' towards the same goal. The historical accuracy of this reading may be questioned, but that is perhaps to miss the point, for Caird quite admits that in the end Plato was unable to escape his basic dualism, the interpretive aim is rather to trace the logic of the ideas which Plato raises, to discern the 'drift of thought'

---

[207] 'Idealism and the Theory of Knowledge', 96. See also Chapter 4.3.1 below.

[208] 'Plato and Other Companions of Socrates', 365.

[209] 'Plato and Other Companions of Socrates', 366. For a similar lesson drawn from the doctrine of recollection see D.G. Ritchie, 'On Plato's *Phaedo*', 110–14.

[210] 'Plato and Other Companions of Socrates', 369.

that appears only with distance. And where Plato's thought ends up is, for Caird, quite clear; 'the hints he lets fall point, we think, to something very like the Hegelian Logic. "Either there Plato's dream is realised, or nowhere".'[211]

The details of this development in Plato's mature thought were worked out more fully in Caird's later book, *The Evolution of Theology in the Greek Philosophers* (1904) which, despite its title, is far from exclusively concerned with theology. The *Republic*, he argues there, puts the coping-stone upon the Ideal theory as, going beyond the mere existence of a collection of quite distinct Ideas, it asserts their systematic unity under the one supreme Idea of the Good.[212] Next stop: the Absolute Idea. The *Parmenides* famously raises the difficulty of how Ideas stand to their instances which, Caird insists, can never be solved so long as Ideas remain simply what is common to a number of individuals rather than a concrete or organic principle whose unity is displayed precisely in and through their diversity—a principle he suggests Plato is aiming at in both the *Thaetetus* and the *Sophist*.[213] Next stop: the concrete universal. Even more problematic is the relation between Ideas and the mind. If Ideas are utterly objective, they will be quite unknown to us, but if merely our thoughts they may be dismissed as subjective.[214] And since neither is acceptable, 'the only remaining alternative is that the distinction between thought and reality, subjective and objective, must be regarded as a relative difference—a distinction between factors in a unity, which imply each other and which cannot be separated.'[215] We would then have to regard the Platonic Idea as something realizable only in self-conscious mind, a point which Caird finds Plato to recognize in the *Sophist* when he declares that 'being in the full sense of the word cannot be conceived without motion and life, without soul and mind.'[216] Next stop: reality as subject rather than substance.

3.5.2 *Plato's* Republic

Caird was far from the last of the Balliol Platonists. Coming up to the College in 1865, Nettleship was taught by both Jowett and Green, who was only ten years his senior and whose teaching duties he took on after Green's premature demise in 1882—until his own early death climbing on Mont Blanc just ten years after that. In many ways Nettleship was a very different sort of Plato scholar than Caird. He offers no new interpretations of texts or history (unlike Caird, who continually advances new readings whilst positioning Plato in relation to other philosophers) and he offers no new

---

[211] 'Plato and Other Companions of Socrates', 374.
[212] *Evolution of Theology in the Greek Philosophers*, I:173.
[213] *Evolution of Theology in the Greek Philosophers*, I:186–7.
[214] *Evolution of Theology in the Greek Philosophers*, I:187.
[215] *Evolution of Theology in the Greek Philosophers*, I:189.
[216] *Evolution of Theology in the Greek Philosophers*, I:191. This is Caird's translation of *Sophist* 248E. Jowett translates as follows: 'Stranger: Can we ever be made to believe that motion and life and soul and thought are not present with perfect being? Can we imagine that being is devoid of life and mind, and exists in awful unmeaningness an everlasting fixture? Theaetetus: That would be a dreadful thing to admit, Stranger' (*Dialogues of Plato*, II:380).

metaphysical system (unlike Caird, where one gets the impression that history is really just a vehicle for advancing his own views). Instead he claimed simply to expound Plato. But the modesty of his work should not tempt us to pass him over, for really he drank as deeply from the same well as Caird, and if his idealism rests but lightly on his reading of Plato,[217] it is nonetheless there. It is to be seen most of all perhaps in his profound sympathy with the Platonic project; Plato is quietly endorsed, but only because he has first been turned into a mouthpiece for British Idealism.

Nettleship's first published work was a long article, 'The Theory of Education in the *Republic* of Plato.'[218] To apply Plato's educational plans to modern society in any detail is, admits Nettleship, simply impossible—a ten year course in science followed by a five year course in philosophy for all politicians would never wash. But he does believe that 'we might do a little towards carrying out some of its spirit.'[219] In particular, British education, with its sense of sharp division—even opposition—between scientific and literary education and its distrust of metaphysics, needs to recapture the unity of Plato's vision in which the study of science is seen as complementary to a previous training in literature and the arts, and in which the 'speculative spirit' is given due acknowledge-ment for the way in which it 'lets in the daylight through the mist of prejudice.'[220] Plato's analogy of the cave which Nettleship makes so much of here, and elsewhere,[221] was an image Muirhead too employed in the address he delivered at the opening of Birmingham University, urging on his audience an understanding of 'the function of education' as 'the opening of our eyes in order that we may be able to see things about us as real and living, full of interest and meaning, and not as the vague and shadowy forms they are to the uneducated and the unreflecting.'[222] Education takes us from phenomenal appearance to idealist reality.

In focusing on the *Republic* as a key text in the philosophy of education Nettleship started what was to become something of an Idealist hallmark.[223] Mackenzie too thought that the *Republic*, 'though ostensibly a treatise on political philosophy, is in reality concerned entirely with education.'[224] There is no either-or here but an identity. If society is a moral agent whose aim is to guide us to self-realization, then to investigate the State is to investigate education, and to study education is to study the State. That the State has such an educational mission was a point with which Henry

---

[217] As a result his writings continued to used and enjoyed long after Idealism had disappeared.

[218] During his lifetime, he only published two things. The other was a memoir of T.H. Green. His remains including 'Plato's conception of Goodness and the Good' (an abortive book, composed in 1881 or 1882) and 'Lectures on the Republic of Plato' (delivered between 1885 and 1888) were collected and published after his death, in his *Remains*.

[219] 'Theory of Education in the *Republic* of Plato', 169.

[220] 'Theory of Education in the *Republic* of Plato', 170.

[221] 'Theory of Education in the *Republic* of Plato', 152ff, *Remains* II:242–6, 257–63.

[222] 'Liberal Education', 141.

[223] Gordon and White claim that this emphasis on Plato's *Republic* contributed more to the pre-1900 growth of interest in educational theory than any 'original' efforts in this direction (*Philosophers as Educational Reformers*, 177).

[224] Mackenzie, *Introduction to Social Philosophy*, 351.

Jones, also, found himself in full agreement: 'even if the danger of State-interference were considerable,' he argued, 'I should still say, after Plato and Aristotle, that the first, the paramount care of the State, is to educate its citizens, and that the State itself is, in the last resort, an educational institution.'[225]

The educational significance of Plato's *Republic* impressed itself further on Bernard Bosanquet, a third Balliol Platonist who came up to the College only two years after Nettleship. In 1895, growing out of his university extension teaching,[226] he published *A Companion to Plato's Republic*, a full length commentary. He argues there that education for Plato involves a perfect unity between the inner and outer system, the nature of the mind itself determines the form of education which society gives it, an education which is at the same time 'the means by which the mind and character of society are realised in the individual.'[227] The part in the whole and the whole in the part, education is an expression of the organic relation of individual to state. In 1900, as part of a series for schools and training colleges, under the title *The Education of the young in Republic of Plato*, Bosanquet went on to publish a translation of books II–IV, together with commentary and an introductory essay on Greek education. In nineteenth-century Britain where education was intellectual, limited to the school or college environment, and something left behind on adulthood, what impressed him was the way in which Greek education was a moral process that took in the whole being of a person, and was a lifelong matter, fully integrated into the wider life of society. When we think how little instruction they received as against the vast amount that modern minds are forcibly crammed full of, and then compare the respective cultural results, the comparison is hardly favourable to us, laments Bosanquet.

The same theme can also be found taken up in an 1894 address, 'Plato's *Republic* as the Earliest Educational Treatise,' by Edward Caird, who stresses the holistic and embedded nature of education—education covers all aspects of life, lasts for all our lives and is possible only in and through the right social context.[228]

3.5.3 Plato's social conception of the individual

The importance of education was not the only idealist mark which Nettleship found in the *Republic*. Another insight for which Plato receives the commendation of his fellow idealist is his understanding of the relation between citizen and State. That might seem odd, for the ideal state which Plato sets out in his great dialogue is, of course, a totalitarian and a slave-owning one. But, at the same time, with its tri-part class-structure which mirrors the constitution of the mind and in which everyone's character

---

[225] 'Working Faith of the Social Reformer', 58.

[226] Helen Bosanquet, *Bernard Bosanquet, A Short Account of his Life*, 44.

[227] *A Companion to Plato's Republic*, 163. He says this holds for Aristotle as well as Plato.

[228] 'Plato's *Republic* as the Earliest Educational Treatise' 5–6, 16–17, 21. Caird, too, argues that, rather than a book of political theory, the *Republic* should be regarded primarily as a treatise on education, with this proviso: that it deals with the education of a social being through society itself (*Evolution of Theology in the Greek Philosophers*, I:140–1).

determines for them a place where they naturally best fit, his state is also a highly integrated functional unity orientated towards the good of society as a whole. Moreover, his communism, we might think, displays a recognition that our highest good is a common one. Nettleship notes that Plato is often accused by critics of sacrificing the rights of the individual to the community. But strictly, he responds,

> There is no such thing as an individual in the abstract, a human being literally independent of all others. Nor, conversely, is there such a thing as a community which is not a community of individuals, or a common life or interest which is not lived or shared by men and women. Nor is individuality, in the true sense of the word, diminished by participation in this common life or interest.... When a man so completely throws himself into the common interest that he can be said to live for others, he does not lose his individuality; rather his individuality becomes a greater one.[229]

Plato to his credit saw this, and what may seem an *attack* on individuality is, Nettleship urges upon us, really an attempt to raise it up to a higher level. For in so far as we throw ourselves into and behind the common lot, our individuality is not diminished but increased. No more than Plato do we think that an individual has an absolute right to do what he likes regardless of society, rather his rights are conditional on circumstances and depend upon the recognition of others. Plato understood that community may strengthen our power of action. His problem is just that he fails to grasp what might be regarded as the other half of the story (a point clearly made by Bradley in his *Ethical Studies*)—that life cannot be *wholly* social, and this explains his mistaken views about, for example, the family.[230]

In attributing to Plato such a social conception of the individual, Nettleship was reflecting the earlier views of both Jowett and Caird who represent Plato as arguing that it is only in and through society that man's higher nature may be developed.[231] As Caird later put it, the lesson of the *Republic*'s functionally integrated society is that man 'can find his good, only as he discovers his proper place in the social organism, i.e. the place for which his special tendencies and capacities fit him.' It is this way that we find our fulfilment, that each of us reveals ourselves to be essentially social, essentially a member of a State.[232] Moving forward a number of years, it should be noted also that this organic conception of Plato's state, in which everyone fits together in their different but interlocking roles becomes crucial in Bosanquet's development of his own social and political thought. He asserts in his *Philosophical Theory of the State* that, 'there is no sound political philosophy which is not an embodiment of Plato's conception.'[233]

---

[229] 'Lectures on the *Republic* of Plato', 177.
[230] 'Lectures on the *Republic* of Plato' 179. For Bradley see below pp.190–1.
[231] For Jowett see above[ms p.31]. Caird,'Plato and Other Companions of Socrates', 372.
[232] *Evolution of Theology in the Greek Philosophers*, I:161.
[233] *Philosophical Theory of the State*, 6. Bosanquet's political philosophy will be considered in more detail in Chapter 14.

3.5.4 Rejection of the 'two worlds' interpretation of Plato

Caird's disquiet at the seeming dualism of Plato has already been discussed, and in similar fashion Nettleship's reading of Plato's idealism is equally adamant in its rejection of any 'two-worlds' interpretation of the doctrine. In contrasting the 'visible triangle' with an 'intelligible triangle', he says, for example, we may be tempted to think of the intelligible triangle as if it were a far-distant second triangle of which the sensible triangle is a copy. But this is quite wrong. To speak of the intelligible triangle means simply that 'there is in the sensible triangle a property distinguishable from all its other properties, which makes it a triangle. The sensible triangle is the 'intelligible triangle' plus certain properties other than triangularity. These other properties the geometrician leaves out of account.'[234] This is, of course, a realism about universals not far removed from Aristotle's.

The 'two-worlds' reading of Plato rejected here is, it will be recognised, closely akin to 'two-worlds' reading of Hegel whose rejection by Bosanquet in his essay 'On the True Conception of Another World' was considered above; and in that essay he himself notes in passing that the same holds of Kant, St Paul, and Plato.[235] This last observation he developed explicitly some years later (1903) in an article on Plato's attitude towards death. Plato's claim in his *Phaedo* that the dead are at an advantage over the living might seem the height of other-wordliness, and modern minds may be tempted to put it aside as just puritanical ascetic cant. But the notion of 'dying to live', so popular among recent Idealists, encourages Bosanquet to set himself to re-consider the position and look for some grain of truth in Plato's uncongenial claim. He suggests that the germ of Plato's message of the mind's liberation from the body may be understood 'as an actual experience of human life'[236]—the denial of the body a rejection, not so much of a certain mode of *being*, as of a certain sub-set of *experiences* (sensory perceptions, pleasures, pains, and competitive desires, etc.) whose fragmentary and disconnected nature serve only to detract us from our pursuit of highest truth and highest good and to disturb the overall harmony of our experience. The man who makes the most and the best of his life will always keep at a distance those experiences he calls bodily, and in so far as he puts aside whatever keeps him from 'the important things of life', the progress of his experience that from one point of view might be called towards death, is from another perspective progress towards all that is most real; towards love and intelligence. In short, the simple contrast between the states of life and death Bosanquet recreates as a contrast between two sorts of condition within life

---

[234] 'Lectures on the *Republic* of Plato', 250–1.

[235] 'On the True Conception of Another World', xix,

[236] 'Plato's Conception of Death', 100. Though all the idealists were inclined to take Plato's doctrines of recollection, pre-existence, and transmigration as 'myth,' not all insisted on quite so immanentist an interpretation as Bosanquet. For example, Ritchie in an earlier paper ('On Plato's Phaedo') attempts to draw out of Plato's storytelling the basis for a functioning argument to the immortality of mind, not indeed as something intrinsic to it as to a kind of a metaphysical atom, but insofar as it knows the eternal Ideas.

itself. It should be noted that in their rejection of the 'other worldly', Caird, Nettleship, and Bosanquet were, of course, explicitly following Hegel's reading of Plato.[237]

3.5.5 Aristotle's idealism

There is a view that regards all philosophy at heart as either Platonist or Aristotelian, and placing it neatly in the first box, it might seem tempting to regard the rise of British Idealism as the rebirth of some sort of Hegelianized Platonism. But that would be too easy, for on close inspection the British Idealists display almost as high a regard for, and debt to, Aristotle.

For example, growing out of an abortive plan with Caird to publish an edition of Aristotle's *Nichomachean Ethics*, T.H. Green's first published piece was an article on 'The Philosophy of Aristotle'[238] which appeared in *The North British Review* in 1866, the year after Edward Caird's article on Plato.[239] From the start, following Jowett, Green opposes any simplistic version of history that would contrast Plato and Aristotle in deep theoretical terms. Differences in temperament there may have been, but it is quite wrong to see some great doctrinal gulf with Plato on the one side as the spokesperson for abstract metaphysics and Aristotle on the other as the champion of common-sense empiricism. Instead says Green, 'the great doctrine that the real is the intelligible and the intelligible the real, however imperfectly developed, is the foundation of both. If Plato is "idealist", Aristotle is more.'[240] Aristotle continues down Plato's path of investigation into the rational structure of universe. Both philosophies start from a basal belief that reality is such that rational investigation will gradually uncover its structure—his surface abandonment of the dialogue form should not mislead us into attributing to Aristotle some final or dogmatic rather than a discursive or exploratory stance.

Green's chief message in this paper is to insist that the proper movement of thought lies in the direction of the concrete rather than the abstract, a point he first illustrates by setting out the critique of modern empiricism that was explained above.[241] A 'popular'

---

[237] 'The Idea is nothing else than that which is known to us more familiarly by the name of the Universal, regarded, however, not as the formal Universal, which is only a property of things, but as implicitly and explicitly existent, as reality, as that which alone is true' (*Lectures on the History of Philosophy*, II:29). 'Through the presentation of his Ideas, Plato opened up the intellectual world, which, however, is not beyond reality, in heaven, in another place, but is the real world' (*Lectures on the History of Philosophy*, II:29). It is a misapprehension when, 'if these Ideas are not exactly made into things, they are made into a kind of transcendent existences which lie somewhere far from us in an understanding outside this world' (*Lectures on the History of Philosophy*, II:30).

[238] Looking back at it in 1912 Haldane assigned the highest importance to this particular article ('The Civic University', 83–4).

[239] From the point of view of tracing the development of Green's ideas, the essay is noteworthy for how many of the themes which we saw developed above in the 1874 critique of Hume, or the 1874–6 lectures on Kant, were already present. Similar profit may be had from study of the Caird essay.

[240] 'Philosophy of Aristotle', 47. Cf. William Wallace, 'The doctrine both of Plato and of Aristotle had been of a kind which, in modern times, we should term Idealism' (*Epicureanism*, 2).

[241] See above section 3.3.1.

or empiricist philosophy such as Locke's views the mind as directly acquainted with reality, in the form of many individual properties arranged in complexes, but this leaves no useful role for thought. It can work at nothing but the mere disassembling or recombining of such given realities which, the more they are distinguished from each other or from the subjects to which they belong, the more abstract they become—a process which takes us further away from reality not closer to it. But once (with Kant) we recognize the true role of the thinking self in knowledge, it is no longer possible to exclude thought as a factor in primary experience, to set up any simple contrast between passive experience which receives given reality and active thought which merely manipulates or rearranges it. Instead of taking concrete reality and abstracting from it in ever-increasing generality, the proper motion of thought must be under-stood as having precisely the opposite direction, moving from the most abstract to the most determinate, as thought itself makes, articulates, and develops known reality.

Green then attempts to demonstrate how these same thoughts play out in the way in which Plato's theory of ideas was subsequently developed by Aristotle.[242] The theory of ideas was Plato's attempt to solve the problem of how we could ever know objects, his conclusion being that such things are not properly sensible but intelligible; while sense is something fluid the object of knowledge may be stabilized in a definition graspable by thought. But such a theory of definitions, or Forms, was not the last word; it permitted development in two ways, one disastrous and one more profitable. Both of which we can find in Aristotle. It is our first encounter with things that suggests to us a name and grouping, but all too often such classes tend to be constructed on the basis of superficial and in the end unimportant points of commonality, even if behind them we might in time be able to find deeper and more significant connections. Almost as soon as it appeared, complains Green, instead of leaving just such lines of investigation open, the notion of Form became ossified in definitions of the first type, a fixed class instead of an open-ended relation. The universal looked like something empty and abstract set next to the living sensible individual, which then naturally came to seem the true object of knowledge. But there are other more fruitful ways to develop the initial Platonic insight, argues Green; we may recognize that our earliest knowledge of something is not our ultimate knowledge, the first manifestation not the final shape. On this view Form is not fixed but is capable of infinitely numerous determinations as it is fleshed out and brought into other relations—'the mere universal is a shell to be filled up by particular attributes'.[243] Both developments may be found in Aristotle, argues Green. It is the false abstract view of the universal that gives birth to the futile and barren theory of syllogism.[244] But if this is how we tend to think of Aristotle, it is because he has come down to us primarily through his *logic*. For his *metaphysics* presents (or at least hints at) a very different picture. Here the process of thought

---

[242] We might be tempted to complain that Green is reading back modern ideas into history, but he would insist the points are timeless.
[243] 'Philosophy of Aristotle', 56.   [244] 'Philosophy of Aristotle', 57.

appears, not as one of abstraction, but as concretion; a universality in virtue of which the object of knowledge may be brought into relation with all other things. In such a view thought is active in creating the *materials* of experience, not just their *arrangement*, and thus there is no simple distinction between a priori and a posteriori. Such a theory of the process of thought, argues Green, 'does away with the false antithesis between experience and reasoning, between induction and deduction, between relations of ideas and relations of things.'[245] The unified and timeless universal gradually actualizes itself through the successive details of empirical reality.

In this way Aristotle is seen to have had 'much the same doctrine' as Hegel,[246] although Green realizes that the leanings he identifies were never pursued to their terminus, and that he is to an extent saying for Aristotle what he did not say for himself.[247] Indeed, Aristotle's final failure is his inability to recognize the thorough identity of being and thought[248]—implicit in his workings—together with a retention of the contrast between 'contingent' and 'necessary' as two distinct sets, rather than a relative gap between the 'imperfectly' and the 'perfectly' known.[249] Moreover, as the creative work of our reason is excluded from the known world, so too God's formation of the world is restricted to that of its external first cause, and Aristotle is unable to arrive at the superior conception of deity as immanent in creation.[250]

This picture of Aristotle as a proto-idealist continuous with Plato was taken up by other Idealists, such as Ritchie who argues that, whatever difference, there is greater agreement between them—'almost every Aristotelian doctrine is to be found implicitly in Plato.'[251] Even more detail is to be found some time later in Edward Caird who, in his *Evolution of Theology in the Greek Philosophers*, boldly asserts that 'there are no two philosophers who are so closely akin in the general scheme of their thought', that is, 'in maintaining an idealistic or spiritualistic view of the ultimate principle of thought and reality.'[252] They might be thought opposed in so far as Plato champions universals and downplays individuals while Aristotle does the reverse, but Caird responds that, if at a lower level these are contrary notions, at a higher level they are seen to be reciprocal aspects of a single truth.[253] No viable metaphysics can afford to leave either behind; and in this regard, indeed, Aristotle may be thought to have a certain advantage, always keeping close to the details of the particulars that instantiate his forms where Plato was too keen to jump straight ahead to generalized abstractions.[254] Moreover, while he was no 'mere' empiricist, his interest in biological phenomena helps him to recognize the immanent teleological principle at work in all things in

---

[245] 'Philosophy of Aristotle', 64.

[246] This phrase comes from a set of notes taken by Bradley on lectures given by Green in 1867 (Green *Collected Works*, V:173/Bradley *Collected Works*, I:128).

[247] 'Philosophy of Aristotle', 83.   [248] 'Philosophy of Aristotle', 81.

[249] 'Philosophy of Aristotle', 88.   [250] 'Philosophy of Aristotle', 88.

[251] 'On Plato's Phaedo', 123.   [252] *Evolution of Theology in the Greek Philosophers*, I:261.

[253] *Evolution of Theology in the Greek Philosophers*, I:265–8.

[254] *Evolution of Theology in the Greek Philosophers*, I:272–3.

contrast to Plato who saw mind or soul as something fundamentally intellectual and only accidentally or externally connected to the material world.[255] For Aristotle there is form or soul everywhere.

But even if his ideas 'point towards a more complete idealism than Plato had ever imagined',[256] Caird complains, as had Green before him, that the journey is not completed; his final progress to full immanentism is barred by a deep-set dualism of form and matter. Aristotle wants to see form and matter, soul and body, as correlative aspects of reality but in the end keeps sliding back into a presentation of them as distinct, one more perfect and more real than the other.[257] In his near-contemporaneous *Chapters from Aristotle's Ethics*, Muirhead too worries about the form–matter structure, although in a slightly different fashion. Aristotle's form–matter conception of a person heads off any charge of substance dualism but, in stressing the necessity of mind's instantiation in body, he might seem to fall into materialism instead. Such danger is countered, however, by Aristotle's teleology in which (as Muirhead puts it) the instrument is fitted to the work not the work to the instrument. The origins of things may be material, but not the source of their meaning and value.[258] For to idealists, it must not be forgotten, a thing most really is where it is heading to, not where it has come from. And thus it is chiefly his teleological view of the universe that earns Aristotle a place in the idealist fold.

3.5.6 Aristotle's social holism

Jowett, Caird, and Nettleship all found in Plato the beginnings of a social holistic conception of the individual, and one of the things that drew the Idealists to Aristotle was the clear continuation of that orientation in his ethical and political thought. This was perhaps given its fullest early treatment by A.C. Bradley, younger brother of F.H. Bradley, and yet another Balliol philosopher. (He came up in 1869.) In his article, 'Aristotle's Conception of the State'—published in the same volume, *Hellenica* (1880) that saw Nettleship's essay—he draws out the significance of Aristotle's saying that man is a political animal.[259] Separated from Aristotle's world by Roman law, Christianity, hedonism, romanticism, the French revolution, and liberalism, he says, 'we must not expect to find in him our own ideas of the individual.'[260] Where we tend to look on man as having a nature of his own and society as an artificial coming together of distinct elements through accidental bonds of their own contriving, it is for Aristotle a natural process whose net result—though he does not use the precise term—is unity closely akin to organism. 'The State is said to precede the individual . . . as a whole precedes its

---

[255] *Evolution of Theology in the Greek Philosophers*, I:275.
[256] *Evolution of Theology in the Greek Philosophers*, I: 277.
[257] *Evolution of Theology in the Greek Philosophers*, I:280–1.
[258] *Chapters from Aristotle's Ethics*, 59–63.
[259] 'It is evident that the state is a creation of nature, and that man is by nature a political animal' (Aristotle, *Politics* I:2–1253a1).
[260] 'Aristotle's Conception', 189.

parts'.[261] The aim of the state is an ethical one, to help create a moral society and bring about the common good, while it is through the state alone, through citizenship, that we may become moral and realize our chief good.[262] Self development takes place in a social context towards a goal which is more than just individual pleasure. Though Bradley is not uncritical,[263] he holds up the prospect of modern life recapturing something of the Aristotelian political ideal, in which 'a man does not belong to himself, but to the State and to mankind', and 'to be free is not merely to do what one likes, but to like what one ought'.[264]

In view of their clear recognition of the social nature of the *telos* of the individual, Green (in his *Lectures on Principles of Political Obligation*) agrees that it is Aristotle and Plato to whom we must look for the true foundation of any theory of rights. In regarding humans as political by nature, Aristotle regards the state as arising out of and maintained by human life; an institution which imposes duties on them, but from which they derive their rights, that is, their ability, through education and protection, to discharge their various functions.[265]

Muirhead too picks up this theme and warmly recommends Aristotle for his insight into a point that has eluded more contemporary English ethical theorists.

It is as untrue now as it was in the time of Aristotle to claim that a man's life is his own. It belongs to him not as an individual but as a member of a community. The difference is that the community is no longer conceived of as bounded by a city wall or a neighbouring range of mountains, but as co-extensive with humanity.[266]

Man is a political animal whose happiness must be considered in social terms; and if once we separate the good of the individual from the good of the whole to which he belongs, their harmonious union becomes impossible. This is recognizably Aristotelian, but some of the conclusions Muirhead draws strike out more on their own. For example, he presents Aristotle as responding to the ancient dilemma of egoism and altruism by 'showing that the self which it is man's duty to love and seek to realize is the self which includes others, and in which therefore the prima facie opposition has disappeared',[267] in a system where human activity, 'just because it is human activity ... is not the activity of a mere individual. It has reference at every point to the larger whole in which the true life of the individual man is to be sought.'[268]

---

[261] 'Aristotle's Conception', 203.
[262] Aristotle's Conception', 202. The same point is made by Caird in *Evolution of Theology in the Greek Philosophers*, I:296.
[263] He condemns slavery ('Aristotle's Conception', 185) and the absence of political involvement of the working class ('Aristotle's Conception', 214).
[264] 'Aristotle's Conception', 241.
[265] *Lectures on the Principles of Political Obligation*, §39.
[266] *Chapters from Aristotle's Ethics*, 24. See also 8.
[267] *Chapters from Aristotle's Ethics*, 183.
[268] *Chapters from Aristotle's Ethics*, 206.

This discussion of Idealism and classical philosophy has concentrated on the early years of the school, but it should be noted idealist work in this area (unlike other parts of the history of philosophy) continued throughout its lifetime. If the Idealist movement was 'set off' by Jowett's rediscovery of Plato, this was swiftly followed by a re-invigorated interest in Aristotle. A crucial figure here was Ingram Bywater, who in 1885 set up an Oxford Aristotelian Society, though the philosophers to look at in this later period are R.B. Haldane, H.H. Joachim, J.A. Smith, A.E. Taylor, and G.R.G. Mure. In 1906 the Clarendon Press began a translation project of the entire Aristotelian corpus, with J.A. Smith and W.D. Ross as editors. But it was with Platonic studies that Idealism remained most closely associated, where later figures especially worthy of mention are D.G. Ritchie, H.W.B. Joseph, and A.E. Taylor.[269] Taylor was perhaps the most famous of all the Idealist classical scholars, however, he must be left out of our discussion; partly for reasons of space but more importantly because although he was an significant figure in the history of British Idealism,[270] he moved away from its doctrines to a sort of ethical theism by about 1908, and it is from this time onwards that most of his work on classical philosophy stems. Besides, his works of historical scholarship do not much draw on his own philosophical views, one consequence of which is that they have enjoyed a longer life than others; for he is still held in no small esteem.

---

[269] H.H. Joachim, *Aristotle: The Nicomachean Ethics* (Oxford, 1951); A.E. Taylor, *Aristotle* (1919); G.R.G. Mure, *Aristotle* (1932); *The Works of Aristotle*, edited by J.A. Smith and W.D. Ross (10 volumes, 1908); D.G. Ritchie, *Plato* (Edinburgh, 1902); H.W.B. Joseph, *Essays in Ancient and Modern Philosophy* (Oxford, 1935); A.E. Taylor, *Plato: The Man and His Work*, 1927.

[270] His critique of Green's ethics, and his representation of Bradley's metaphysics were especially influential. See pp.222, 528 below.

4

The Metaphysics of the Absolute

One of the most characteristic marks of British Idealist philosophy is the centrality it accords to issues of metaphysics. Unlike modern philosophers, who tend to suppose that their questions are best tackled on the level at which they arise without dragging in first principles, to the Idealists, the general nature of being so shapes everything that, probed with any seriousness, nearly all concerns resolve rapidly into metaphysical ones. It will already have been noted that it was metaphysics which interested them most in the history of philosophy, but the understanding was one to be applied generally. As they saw it, there could be no study of religion, the science of infinite or perfect being, without first considering *being itself*; while moral philosophy, the science of what *ought* to be, could hardly be pursued without understanding the relation between the ideal and the actual as well as the nature of moral agency; and it would be just absurd to investigate logic, the art of truthful thinking, without first understanding the relations that obtain between thought, reality, and mind.[1] Metaphysics was simply unavoidable—the sceptic who denied its possibility was, as Bradley put it, a 'brother metaphysician'[2]—and so the only question was whether it was entered upon clearly and self-consciously, or blindly and uncritically.

Metaphysics, as they viewed it, was not something to be approached cautiously or descriptively, but 'speculatively', with a bold and constructive attitude. If the name of 'metaphysics' has recovered somewhat from the opprobrium it suffered in the mid-twentieth century, it is still not done in this audacious spirit, and it is perhaps this difference in tone as much as anything else that distances the Idealists from modern philosophers. That it was *idealists* who felt emboldened to think in this way is, of course, no coincidence; for it was their idealism which told them, first, that reality

---

[1] Bradley wrote on both ethics and logic before attempting a treatise on metaphysics, but it should not be inferred from this fact that either of his first two works are free from metaphysical significance, or that they are not constantly straining against their own self-imposed directive to avoid it. And in the end he was compelled to spell out fully the implicit underlying metaphysic that had been guiding him thus far.

[2] *Appearance and Reality*, 1.

differs from appearance—no allegiance to common-sense or to ordinary language will reveal that truth which is other than it seems—and which assured them, second, that the universe is a fundamentally rational place. Mind and reality are in harmony, and so there is good ground to think that metaphysical speculation, rather than a kind of forlorn guesswork, might well be something with the power to hit, or at least advance us further towards, the target.

The British Idealists were not only distinctive in their view of the nature and significance of metaphysics, for the majority of them held also to a distinctive metaphysical world-view—the philosophy of the Absolute—with which the school became virtually synonymous. This chapter examines that system through the metaphysics of Green, Bradley, and Caird, noting the differences as well as the broad level of agreement between them. The order of treatment is chronological and therefore begins with Green.

4.1 T.H. Green

The range of differing readings it has met with testifies to the difficulties of finding a clear and unambiguous interpretation of Green's metaphysical system, but in its broadest outlines at least it is easy enough to grasp, and such a plan is useful to have in mind before focusing in on the details of the argument. For Green, reality is constituted by relations; the world is a single and eternal system of related elements. But relations are the work of the mind. So, Green infers, reality too must be something essentially mind-dependent. But, he continues, quite clearly none of us individually generate the world—there is more to it, for one thing, than simply whatever we are acquainted with—so our knowledge is best taken as but one moment in the wider experience of an all-encompassing eternal consciousness whose experience *does* make up the whole of reality.

4.1.1 Relations as the criterion of reality

That the fullest statement of Green's metaphysics is to be found in Book One of his *Prolegomena to Ethics* (1883), illustrates clearly the point made above about the centrality of metaphysics to British Idealist thinking. As he saw it, there could be no advance in moral philosophy without first getting straight on metaphysics. The discussion originally appeared in three articles in *Mind* 1882, which themselves drew on professorial lectures of 1880, but it is also a continuation of his 1878 discussion of Lewes, for the question with which Green opens the *Prolegomena* is precisely the one he had raised there, namely, whether there can be a natural science of man?[3] Can the methodology we employ in studying *things* be transferred across to the consideration of *conscious agents*? Are we who know and act on the world to be considered just one more element

---

[3] *Prolegomena*, §9. 'Can there be a Natural Science of Man?' For a listing of Green's Professorial lectures incorporated into *Prolegomena* see Nettleship's 'Memoir' cxxv. For an account of Green's discussion of Lewes see above §3.3.1.2.

in it? From one point of view the question seems foolish; for does there not already exist a science—empirical psychology—devoted to just this endeavour?

But Green is not so easily dealt with, for his question is whether when we treat thought or action this way, as natural events like any other, we are able to capture their proper nature as thought and action? Are the elements of empirical psychology that claim these titles—brain states, bodily movements, causal sequences, etc.—able to make good their claim to be the very things we experience as our own conscious life and deeds?

Green answers his own question negatively. Our knowledge of the things and processes of nature cannot result solely from those things and processes, for we experience them only ever as related together into one conscious whole; a unity which they themselves cannot explain, since 'as experienced' they are its product (and whatever it may be that makes matter in motion knowable cannot itself be the matter in motion known as its result) while 'in themselves' they are unknown (and nothing can be explained by the unknown). Our experience of nature must involve some further agency, presumably on our own part.[4] But is it then, we might worry, the experience of anything real or objective, for we tend to regard as 'real' only what is 'given' to us? In order to address this concern, says Green, we must ask ourselves what we mean when we say that something is real? Or, for that matter, unreal? Much is dismissed as unreal. Dreams, visions, stories, misperceptions, as well as (by their critics) unwelcome categories—such as phlogiston, causation, matter or 'the Absolute'—have all at one time or other, by some person or other, been denied their place in the ranks of fundamental or objective reality. But what does this mean?

To ask whether something is real or not is a potentially rather misleading thing to do, notes Green, in so far as it suggests perhaps that there is something else from which the real might be distinguished; the class (as it were) of unreal things. For of course there is no such class.[5] The object of some wholly false experience, such as a dream or an hallucination, presents itself to us as undeniably as does that of the most clearly veridical experience. To call something unreal is rather, suggests Green, to say that it does not 'fit' in with, that it does not bear the appropriate relations to, those other things already deemed to be 'real'. There is no room for such items in the world because they cannot, except on the most absurd and extravagant hypotheses, be reconciled with what we understand about everything else; they lack the permanence, stability, inter-subjective availability, or causal efficacy of what we paradigmatically consider to be objective or real. The contrast between real and unreal is not, as we sometimes and unreflectively suppose, the difference between what exists and what does not, but more properly the contrast between the permanent or unalterable order of things and their temporary or changeable order. Thus reality, for Green, is to be defined as 'a single and unalterable system of relations'.[6] A things is real precisely in so far as it can be fitted into the one

---

[4] *Prolegomena*, §9–10.
[5] *Prolegomena*, §22.
[6] *Prolegomena*, §21.

enduring systematic relational matrix—the more numerous, stable and fundamental its relations to everything else, the greater its claim to the title—and reality extends just as far as does that integrated and permanent complex of relations. Relationality then is the very foundation of reality. Without relations there would be no reality at all.[7]

This is a most significant definition. We usually suppose whatever is 'real' to be 'out there', and anything 'in here' to be 'unreal', that is, once something is recognized as being our own contribution to experience we tend, in virtue of that fact alone, to discount it. But, as Green notes, one important corollary of the definition he offers is that this attitude is justifiable only where that contribution is transient or otherwise irreconcilable with its context. Where our own constructions are equally (or more) stable than any external reality, they must be held to be equally (or more) real. The door is opened for idealism. Says Green, 'it is not the work of the mind, as such, that we instinctively oppose to the real, but the work of the mind as assumed to be arbitrary and irregularly changeable'.[8] A thing is called unreal because of its current relation to everything else, not in virtue of its historical or metaphysical origins.

The criterion of reality, then, is that of *system* which, understood as maximum possible extent, structure, and coherence of belief, must be to us but a goal of our thinking, not anything we currently possess. In contrast to such an 'ideal science', our own consciousness, partial and intermittent as it is, may be deemed 'merely ours' or 'subjective'. But if we think like this, we must bear in mind that the 'objective world' is not some sort of opposite or *contrast* to that which we know in our own consciousness, but rather its ideal *completion*.[9]

4.1.2 The mental nature of relations

If Green champions the reality of relations, he none the less finds them thoroughly mind-dependent, products of intellectual activity. While all reality lies in relations, 'it is not that first there are relations and then they are conceived,' he says, rather, 'Every relation is constituted by an act of conception'.[10] Relations are, as he elsewhere likes to express it, 'the work of the mind'. It is from this thesis that Green's idealism springs, for clearly if reality consists in relations, and those relations are judged ideal or mental, then reality as a whole must share the same fate. Nature properly understood, in order to be what it is, implies a principle which is not natural but spiritual,[11] he says. It is only through mind that there exist the relations which go to make up reality.

But why does Green think that relations are the work of the mind? Even Kant had only argued that *some* relations were ideal (such as those of space and time or causation),

---

[7] Though no debt is acknowledged, the origin of this view is most likely Lotze. The dictum that 'to be is to be related' is one which recurs throughout his metaphysics. See, e.g., *Metaphysics*, volume I, 38ff, 53; *Outlines of Metaphysic*, 18–19.

[8] *Prolegomena*, §21.

[9] Nettleship, 'Memoir', lxxviii; Nettleship, 'Lectures on Logic', 113–21.

[10] 'Lectures on Logic', 179.

[11] *Prolegomena*, §54.

not that they *all* were. Curiously enough, one of Green's major sources here seems to have been Locke. For the question of the reality of relations had been centre stage in British philosophy ever since Locke had argued that, unlike most other things of which we form ideas, relations are 'not contained in the real existence of Things, but something extraneous and superinduced.'[12] Locke's idea was that when we see, say, a low bush and a tall tree we have seen all we need to know that the bush is shorter than the tree. There are two objects, each with its own height, but no 'shorter than' which we must also perceive. 'Shorter than' just records our mental act of comparison, and has no independent being outside of that act.

Had relations some form of existence independent of the mind, the notion that we might perceive them ought, at least, to make sense. But not only do we *not* perceive relations, thinks Green, they are just not the sort of thing we really *could* perceive.[13] Our awareness of relations is something quite inexplicable in empirical terms, and hence it could only spring from the original work of mind, as something that we add to our own experience. The problem, as Green sees it, is that no mere series of perceptions could ever explain our consciousness of the series perceived, and thus that there can be no (Humean) impression from which we might derive the idea of a relation. For consciousness of events as related is not at all the same thing as a series of related events of consciousness.[14] As he says, 'Of two successive feelings, one over before the next begins, neither can be consciousness of time as a relation between the two.'[15] Even if the relation in question be one of succession, it will be no help for our ideas to succeed one another. 'In order to constitute the relation they must be present together'[16] he says. Yet that is impossible.[17] One of the key lessons Green drew from his long study of the empiricism of Locke, Berkeley, and Hume was precisely its inability to deal with relations; atomic in both metaphysics and epistemology, ultimately it leaves us with nothing but an aggregate of unrelated particulars. For the merely receptive consciousness of the empiricist, he urges, there are no relations between feelings, merely a series

---

[12] Locke, *Essay*, 322 (Bk.II ch.25 §8). We should not exaggerate the degree of consensus between Green and the empiricists over the mentality of relations. The empiricists acknowledge that it is mind which makes relations, but when we come to think about those relations themselves their position becomes rather more complicated. For considering such relations as identity, sequence, contiguity, cause, and the like, the empiricists tend to see these as elements which, if not actually given in experience, can nonetheless be pretty straight forwardly derived from it, through such simple procedures as comparison, union, abstraction. Green sees no possibility of this. For him, experience as a doctrine of passive sensations cannot account for our grasp of relations, since they are neither given in sensation, nor constructible solely out of what is given in sensation.

[13] See Chapter 4.1.3.3 below. The word 'perception' is here being used in the empiricist sense of a mental act *other than* conception. Used in the idealist sense of an action that *includes* conception Green would, of course, have no objection to saying that we perceive one thing to be related to another.

[14] *Prolegomena*, §16 (see also §§18, 35, 84) The problem as Green well knew was one that had defeated Mill, who had in the end found it inexplicable that mind 'which *ex hypothesi* is but a series of feelings should be aware of itself as a series' (*Examination of Sir William Hamilton's Philosophy*, ch. XII, 248).

[15] 'Lectures on Logic', 170.

[16] *Prolegomena*, §37.

[17] The doctrine of the specious present was introduced to overcome this problem. It did not.

of feelings. Conceived as an element of independent reality a relation is something that we could simply never come to know.

Though undoubtedly real, for Green, relations are something of a enigma, even an impossibility. Just how is it that two things get to stand in relation to one another?

Relation is to us such a familiar fact that we are apt to forget that it involves all the mystery, if it be a mystery, of the existence of many in one . . . a plurality of things cannot of themselves unite in one relation, nor can a single thing of itself bring itself into a multitude of relations. . . . There must, then, be something other than the manifold things themselves, which combines them without effacing their severalty . . . if it were not for the action of something which is not either of them or both together, there would be no alternative between their separateness and their fusion . . . we must recognise as the condition of this reality the action of some unifying principle analogous to that of our understanding.'[18]

What is Green trying to say here? A relational whole combines unity and diversity–though containing several components, it is yet one whole–but this is something strange that needs further explanation, for a single thing cannot on its own become many, nor many things become one. There must be something else that helps the relational structure to achieve this result, and the only thing which we know that is able to do this is *mind*. Our own minds, holding as they do, many ideas in one thought and many thoughts in one conscious experience, are examples of precisely such unity in diversity, claims Green. In consequence, he concludes, we need to recognize as the underlying condition that makes nature itself possible, the ground of its relationality, something analogous to our own mind.

Relations may be the work of the mind. But since quite clearly it is not yours, or mine, or any other finite mind that underlies the relations that constitute nature, Green postulates a higher experience to undertake the task—which, sharing in the unalterable character of the relations it grounds, he calls the 'Eternal Consciousness'.[19]

'Objective nature' must indeed be something else than ourselves and our states of consciousness as we are apt to understand these . . . but it does not follow that it is other than our states of consciousness in their full reality, i.e. in the fullness of those relations which presuppose relation to an eternal subject. I do not 'make nature' in the sense that nature = a succession of states of consciousness, beginning with my birth and ending with my death. If so, the 'objectivity' of nature would doubtless disappear; there would be as many 'natures' as men. But only by a false abstraction do we talk of such a succession of states. Their reality lies in eternal relations; relations which are there before what I call my 'birth,' and after my 'death,' if 'before' and 'after' had any proper application to them.[20]

---

[18] *Prolegomena*, §§28–9.
[19] *Prolegomena*, §67.
[20] 'Lectures on Kant', 32; See also his review of John Caird's *Introduction to the Philosophy of Religion*, 145; Green, 'Faith', 267–8.

As the underlying ground of all reality, including finite experiences such as our own, Green's eternal consciousness is clearly a relative of Hegel's Absolute, the world-mind which manifests itself through everything. However the argument by which he gets there, with its emphasis on the self that creates the relations that structure and make possible the experience of reality, is even more closely related to Kant's argument from the unity of apperception in his Transcendental Deduction. Green certainly saw it that way, as did many of his contemporaries. However, the two arguments are not exactly the same. While, both Green and Kant argue that experience is not a chaotic manifold, deriving its order and relation from an enduring transcendental subject, for Green there is no pre-existing manifold upon which it works its magic organizing power; mind is the author of terms as well as relations.

4.1.3 Objections to the eternal consciousness

Green's doctrine of the eternal consciousness was extremely influential. Post-Idealist thinking, however, has not been kind to it, and it has long been regarded as the Achilles' heel of his system; the arguments for it dismissed as weak, and its claims rejected as incoherent or inconsistent—either with each other or with the world at large they seek to account for.[21] Such opprobrium might seem to make baffling its previous success, and so to dispel the suggestion that our philosophical predecessors were just stupid—unable to spot a poor argument when they saw one—as well as to put a little more flesh on the bones of Green's case, it will be useful to rehearse some of the more frequent objections and their proper responses.

4.1.3.1 Failure to clearly explain The first and most fundamental problem which faces anyone trying to weigh up Green's doctrine of the eternal consciousness is simply that of finding any account of his meaning sufficiently clear and detailed to assess. For while the eternal consciousness is a creature which lurks continually in the background of all of his writings, only very rarely is it tempted out into the light.

This scarcity of detailed treatment is due in part to the fact that Green's principal interests lie elsewhere. He never wrote a purely metaphysical treatise, and the doctrine of the eternal consciousness as it occurs in the *Prolegomena* is really something of a staging post to further destinations; principally a theory of human willing and the subsequent development of an ethical doctrine based on a notion of the common good. It is not something argued, or significantly developed, for its own sake. Rather than stay to explore in more detail what he has uncovered, once the basic principle is established, Green moves smartly on to his next task.

If part of the difficulty stems from what Green has *failed* to say, what he *has* said is no less problematic, for Green has a marked tendency to express himself in vague, abstract, and idiomatic terms. As quoted above, his main statement of his conclusion is that we

---

[21] For a list of critics of the eternal consciousness see C. Tyler, *Thomas Hill Green and the Philosophical Foundations of Politics*, 26, note 25.

are required to posit the existence of 'some unifying principle analogous to that of our understanding', and this style of speaking continues throughout. The doctrine he tells us is that of 'a self-originating "mind" in the universe', simultaneously 'an end gradually realising itself' in the world and the 'condition' of that world being what it is. This mind, of which finite mind is but a 'limited mode' and to which all things are 'relative', 'constitutes' the world as a whole through being the 'medium or sustainer' of relations (which are themselves the 'work of the mind').[22] None of these expressions carry their meaning on their face, yet none are really explained. The case seems made out by metaphor as much as by argument. We find ourselves much in sympathy with William James who lamented, 'it is hard to tell just what this apostolic being but strenuously feeble writer means.'[23]

But before we join James and condemn Green for a failing indicative at best of poor writing style and at worst of poor thinking, we must consider the rejoinder that, far from being a *defect*, the way in which Green expresses himself is a mark of the thoroughgoing *consistency* of his thinking.[24] The general Kantianism which he adopts throws up a problem which is by no means lost on Green. For according to this scheme the eternal consciousness is understood as that which supplies the categories by which we unify and structure our experience, as that which makes it possible. But these concepts and structures apply only within experience and cannot legitimately be used outside or beyond it, not even to express the conditions which make possible that experience itself. As Green puts it, 'In speaking of this principle we can only use the terms we have got; and these, being all strictly appropriate to the relations, or objects determined by the relations, which this principle renders possible but under which it does not subsist, are strictly inappropriate to it.'[25] What makes thought possible cannot itself be thought.

Can we, then, say nothing about ultimate reality? Kant, who was at heart a metaphysical realist, could perhaps embrace this result, but the idea of a reality existing beyond the reach of our concepts is not something with which *Green* can sit contentedly. He wholly rejects the 'thing-in-itself'.[26] The role of philosophy is not to try to guess about what might or might not lie *behind* experience, but simply to analyse what falls *within* it.[27] Green's own solution to the puzzle is to argue that the eternal consciousness is something *immanent* in finite life and thought. It is not something wholly *beyond* or *different* from us, rather it is something *larger* or *wider* than us. The

---

[22] *Prolegomena*, §§29, 77, 68, 52, 51, 77, 50, 63, 24.

[23] *The Principles of Psychology*, 660.

[24] Although it also true that it stems in part from the tentative and exploratory nature of his own thought. His brother in law described him as someone who 'never possessed, even to his last days, a complete grasp of his own philosophical position' (*Memoirs of John Addington Symonds*, 119).

[25] *Prolegomena*, §75. 'As to what that consciousness in itself or in its completeness is, we can only make negative statements' (*Prolegomena*, §51).

[26] So opposed is he to the notion that, in his loyalty to Kant, he even doubts whether this really was Kant's view ('Review of J. Watson, *Kant and his English Critics*', 151).

[27] 'Mr Herbert Spencer and Mr G.H. Lewes', 449.

difficulty we experience in coming to know it is not that of one thing trying to apprehend another quite separate thing, but that of a part trying to grasp the greater whole to which it belongs. Rather than something too far away for us to see, the eternal consciousness is more like something too large for us to take in. The significant point here is that it is the eternal consciousness which makes us; we are its manifestations and only in virtue of its action are we self-conscious. To that extent we *are* acquainted with it, for we are acquainted with ourselves. But the acquaintance is only as *we* know it, with all the limitations of a partial view, not as *it* knows *itself*, in the complete totality of its being. This gives us a grasp of ultimate reality, but a limited one only. It makes talk about the eternal consciousness possible, but only of the thinnest and most metaphorical kind. If, in speaking about the eternal consciousness, Green says, we employ language which calls upon those categories and relations which only exist because of the eternal consciousness, 'it must only be on a clear understanding of its metaphorical character.'[28] Metaphor may point to what in literal terms could never be expressed. In this way it is seen that Green's (admittedly frustrating) mode of presentation, far from hindering understanding is, in truth, the only one that makes it at all possible.

4.1.3.2 Eternity The first of the two principal things which Green does tell us about his great unifying principle is, of course, that it is eternal. But in what sense did Green think the eternal consciousness was eternal? The great stress which he places on the unalterability of the relations which it grounds and which make up the real world might seem to suggest that its eternity is more properly a matter of permanence than atemporal existence.[29] However, it is clear enough from the texts that what Green meant was complete timelessness. Indeed no other interpretation can make sense of his key argument that a sequence of conscious events can never deliver consciousness of a sequence of events, for in effect what this amounts to is the claim that atomistic experience of succession is impossible. To experience the passing of time the successive states need to be brought together in one consciousness; past, present, and future held together in one experience itself falling outside of them altogether.[30]

The eternity of Green's unifying principle is one of the greatest obstacles to coherent understanding of it. The problem has two sides. First of all the very notion of timeless existence is hard to grasp for beings which are through and through temporal. If all of our experience is in time, the same would seem to be true for all of the things which we

---

[28] *Prolegomena*, §54.

[29] McGilvarey, 'The Eternal Consciousness' 481, 489–92. Sidgwick more modestly claims that Green equivocates between the two senses (*Lectures on philosophy of Kant*, 261). The notion of 'unalterability' is another of Green's metaphorical terms, for clearly I *can* alter many of the relations that go to make up the real world (Quinton, 'T.H. Green's 'Metaphysics of Knowledge', 30).

[30] 'a consciousness of events as a related series . . . cannot properly be said to be developed out of, a mere series of related events, of successive modifications of body and soul. . . . No one and no number of a series of related events can be the consciousness of the series as related' (*Prolegomena*, §16).

experience, which can make us doubt if it is ever legitimate to abstract off this condition as something inessential to existence itself. But perhaps the notion of timeless existence finds some small purchase when we think about abstract principles or mathematical objects, which seem not to exist in time.

The second aspect of the problem centres on the difficulty of relating any such timeless entity to the temporal world which we know. It is one thing to posit an ontologically separate realm of timeless being, but quite another to conceive how it stands to being in time. This second aspect of the problem becomes particularly acute with Green, for he understands the eternal consciousness as pre-eminently something which expresses itself over time through the life of the individual and the community. It is the 'essential influence' explaining, and the 'operative' force behind, a real history of human intellectual and moral progress.[31] But how can that which is eternal and changeless manifest itself in that which is essentially temporal and progressive?[32]

It may be argued, however, that there is a path through this most difficult of puzzles. Part of the way forwards is to realize that we have here, not one, but three different problems. First of all we can ask how, if reality is timeless, it can express itself in time? Would it not thereby automatically cease to be timeless? The key to solving this part of the mystery is to distinguish between *being temporal* or *having a temporal character*, and *being in time* or *taking time*. Something may easily *contain* time or *express itself in* time, without itself actually *enduring through* time. For example, if we take the *whole* history of the universe then it is not itself *in time*, in the same way that *space itself*, as a whole, is not anywhere *in space*. And we can find other parallels. There are, for example, certain states or conditions which hold changelessly through time but can be expressed only through changing events. Laws of nature explain and exist through the events that obey them but the laws of nature do not themselves take place. The case is similar with certain emotional and cognitive states. You cannot love someone without doing things for them, or believe something without it impacting on at least some of your actions, but the love or belief itself does not take time; it is simply expressed through or 'strung out over' a series of such temporal acts.

The second aspect of the problem is harder. In calling reality timeless, we seem to regard it as something complete or finished. Though perhaps 'strung out' across time in the manner just explained, from the timeless point of view it seems to be something whole and concluded, something which can be grasped fully in one eternal moment. Yet this character of its being seems to place it deeply at odds with the nature of time. For the very essence of time seems to be its incompleteness, its never-ending-ness, its perpetual on-going-ness. To be temporal is to be unfinished. It is to be a 'work in progress'. Thus understood, these two ways of viewing reality seem so opposed that it is hard to grasp how they could ever come together.

---

[31] *Prolegomena*, §173.

[32] It is worth remembering that this basic problem is not unique with Green, but found in all classical religious conceptions which posit a timeless God that knows or acts in an essentially temporal world.

Green himself is very sensitive to this dichotomy. Though it is 'an eternally complete consciousness', he is clear that his principle's expression in time is 'at once progressive and incapable of completion'.[33] To help elucidate this difficult relationship between the already complete and the 'work in progress', he offers us the example of reading a sentence; although we are conscious all the time that it has a meaning as a whole, only gradually or sequentially do we come to know what that meaning is. The two experiences co-exist.[34] But despite Green's illustration the tension remains throughout the *Prolegomena*. It is clearly visible, for example, among the three principal metaphors which he uses to characterize the relation between the eternal consciousness and the individual: reproduction, participation, and realization.[35] If 'realization' makes the eternal consciousness look future, something being gradually created, the other two metaphors—'reproduction' and 'participation'—make it look actual, something that is already achieved.

How then are we to reconcile the completeness of the eternal consciousness with the endlessness of human advance in time? Green's response to this problem is essentially Kantian in spirit. Like Kant who insisted that the Antinomies tell us nothing about reality in itself, Green holds that time is a form *we* bring to experience, and its essential unendingness a function of the structure which *we* have added, not of anything we may be attempting to express through it. That the infinite openness of time is just indefinite repetition or 'addibility' and quite different from the completed yet infinite eternity properly ascribable to God is a point Green makes quite clear in his criticism of Locke's unsuccessful attempt to move from the former to the latter idea.[36] At its root the contrast which is being alluded to here is, of course, the age-old dichotomy between a mathematical and a metaphysical conception of the infinite.

The third aspect of the problem about eternity and time is close to the second but not quite the same. It consists in the following worry. Does not the 'complete' or 'finished' nature of reality somehow rule out any genuine novelty, creation, or freedom? For part of what we understand in thinking of ourselves as existing in time is conceiving ourselves as having an open future. What we are and have been is fixed

---

[33] *Prolegomena*, §§67, 72.

[34] 'In reading [a] sentence we see the words successively, we attend to them successively, we recall their meaning successively. But throughout the succession there must be present continuously the consciousness that the sentence has a meaning as a whole; otherwise the successive vision, attention and recollection would not end in a comprehension of what the meaning is' (*Prolegomena*, §71). It must be confessed that Green's choice of metaphor here is not entirely a happy one, in so far as realizing that some sentence *has* a meaning and knowing what that meaning *is* are really two completely different states (you could know the first but have no idea about the second) not temporally different manifestations of the same state.

[35] Reproduction: *Prolegomena*, §§68, 71, 72, 99. It is in this context of reproduction, perhaps, that we ought to consider Green's even more obscure metaphor of a 'vehicle' (*Prolegomena*, §67) with its suggestion of distinction between the vehicle and what it conveys. Participation: 'Review of J. Caird, *Introduction to Philosophy of Religion*', 146; 'Value and Influence of Works of Fiction', 22; *Lectures on Logic*, 190. Another anomalous metaphor to note here is the suggestion that we '*co-operate*' (*Prolegomena*, §10) with the eternal consciousness in making the world. Realization: *Prolegomena* §§67, 68, 82.

[36] *Introduction*, §§140–2.

but what we may yet be is still undecided. However, if one is simply unpacking what is 'there already'—even if that process were endless—everything seems 'already settled'. If the Absolute is complete, it cannot at the same time be open-futured. There seems no room for any freedom or creativity. This argument is as straightforward as it is hard to resist.

However to see this as a problem for Green betrays a misunderstanding of his conception of freedom. Green's reason for writing Book I of the *Prolegomena*, his reason for enquiring if there can be a natural science of man, was to secure a place for human freedom, yet there is nothing in Green's notion of freedom which requires novelty.[37] Freedom consists, not in showing that certain actions are spontaneous or ungenerated rather than the result of causal law, but in finding a class of actions calling for explanation rationally or teleologically, rather than with reference to prior states, be that their presence or absence.[38] Nothing about teleology requires an open or undetermined future. Indeed it might even be suggested that the very opposite holds, for how can something be explained by its goal unless that goal is in some sense already real?

4.1.3.3 Are relations the work of the mind?

For Green, sense acquaints us with individuals but relations, the conceptual structures of experience, are work of the mind. However, this claim might be challenged. Why not say that relations too are simply experienced like everything else? An atomistic empiricism, such as that of Locke, Berkeley, or Hume, where all we are given is simple sensations, might well render relations the work of the mind, but why accept such an empiricism? Why not attempt a non-atomic empiricism, an empiricism where what is given in experience are relational wholes? Thus it has been objected that all Green has offered us here is an argument against an outdated and defunct psychology of atomic and unrelated sensations, and that were we to adopt some more holistic analysis of experience, then the entire argument would collapse.[39]

But the impossibility of such an answer stems from the very nature of empirical perception. Perception on any naturalistic account is simply a causal relation in which some mind is the passive recipient of an outside agency. But all causal transactions are between individual events; poisoning *in general* does not cause death *in general*, rather *this specific* poisoning causes *this specific* death. Whatever such perception acquainted us with would *from that very fact* be something particular. Relations are universals, however,

---

[37] It is at this point that he parts company with Martineau. Green's account of the relation between eternal completeness and freedom should also be compared with Edward Caird's. See Chapter 5.4.3 below.

[38] Human activity for Green is free (*Prolegomena*, §82), but this freedom is not acausal ('Lectures on the Philosophy of Kant', 95).

[39] Seth Pringle-Pattison, *The Idea of God*, 196. In a similar vein, Knox argues that William James' radical empiricism, in which we enjoy a direct experience of change, constitutes a way of refuting Green's argument for idealism. ('Has Green answered Locke?', 334–48). The objection has resurfaced too in modern times: Dimova-Cookson objects 'Green's mistake was to believe that all sensations come from "outside," all relations from the "inside"'. (*T.H. Green's Moral and Political Philosophy*, 29–30).

and thus if the mind is to know universals it must be through a quite different agency, thought.

4.1.3.4 What are their terms? Even conceding to Green that relation or synthesis is properly the work of mind, there remain further difficulties with his conception of relations. A particularly tricky problem emerges if we ask ourselves the apparently simple question: what is it that these reality-constituting relations relate? The answer to be found in his text is what Green variously calls feelings, sensations, or experiences.[40] But if mind is understood in terms of its relating or synthesizing activity, this is to bring in something irreducibly *other* than mind—whatever it is the mental relations bind together—introducing into the eternal consciousness system a kind of dualism wholly contrary to its professed idealistic character.[41] On the other hand, rigorously to exclude any such apparently non-mental element from the scheme, as his idealism appears to require, would seem to leave him with the absurdity of relations lacking any terms.[42] Either way he appears to be in trouble.

Green himself was sensitive to this challenge and goes to considerable effort to avoid it.[43] The main point of his reply is that, while we may characterize the difference between relations and the sensations they connect as one between the 'form' and the 'matter' of our experience, it is vital to recognize that this is only a *logical* or *conceptual distinction*, one we make in our intellect but which does not correspond to any similar division in reality itself. He insists again and again that there is, ultimately, neither pure feeling nor pure thought. 'It is as impossible to divide knowledge into elements, one contributed by feeling, the other by thought, as to analyse the life of an animal into so much resulting from the action of the lungs, so much from the action of the heart'.[44] Their only reality is as a pair of reciprocal abstractions we make from a more primitive whole. They emerge together, and their very meaning comes from opposition to each other. Together, as it were, they make up a picture, but neither is really capable of being considered in its own right for, says Green, 'it must not be supposed that the manifold has a nature of its own apart from the unifying principle, or this principle another nature of its own apart from what it does in relation to the manifold world.'[45]

---

[40]   *Prolegomena*, §§32, 48, 13, 20.

[41]   For a contemporary occurrence of this charge see Pringle-Pattison, *Hegelianism and Personality*, 74ff. It will not do to respond that feelings or sensations are mental too, for Green builds his idealism on a distinction between thought and feeling, rather than on one between the mental and the non-mental. For Green, the key claim is that reality is something thought not felt, and that is how he distinguishes his own objective Absolute idealism from any more subjective Berkeleyan idealism. 'We object intuitively to any idealism which is understood to imply an identification of the realities of the world with the feelings of men' (*Prolegomena*, §37).

[42]   For a list of earlier instances of this objection see Tyler, *Thomas Hill Green and the Philosophical Foundations of Politics*, 16, note 12. Curiously enough Green does refer at one point to his own position as that of 'the reduction of facts to relations' (*Prolegomena*, §37).

[43]   Green tackles the point at length in *Prolegomena*, §§ 42–51. See also 'Lectures on Logic', 181–2.

[44]   'Lectures on the Philosophy Kant', 6.

[45]   *Prolegomena*, §75.

It is his sense that neither is really possible on its own that lies behind Green's opposition to Kant's distinction between intuition and conception, which can easily be read as putting forward two independent sources which together combine to make up experience.

Yet this response is itself deeply puzzling, for it seems to cut right across Green's original argument for idealism. That argument used the pervasiveness of relations to argue for the ideality of all existence. But, as Hylton has argued, if thought is just one side of a distinction abstracted from experience, it cannot then constitute the whole of experience. For how can one half of an opposition drawn *within* the world then be used to ground the *whole* of that same world?[46] It is unclear that Green has an answer to this question, but Edward Caird's response to a very similar one will be considered below, and Green would likely have been in accord with that.[47]

4.1.3.5 The external world? The suggestion of a contrast between our reality—the reality we know—and reality itself—reality as a whole—brings to the fore another serious problem which has often been raised against Green's argument for idealism. Reality only exists for mind. But it does not simply exist for my mind; things do not simply come into being as and in virtue of, my knowing them. They are there already.[48] Hence, concludes Green, there must be a wider mind in which they exist all the time. Yet this argument simply invites the challenge: how do we know that nature covers more than just what we know? We all happily assume this, but by what right?

To see this as a problem for Green represents a fundamental misunderstanding of his whole approach. It raises the classical problem of scepticism about the external world, but Green was never really troubled by such subjective scepticism; his position was never that of the ego-centric inquirer beset by fears that reality, or at least knowledge, may stretch no further than his own awareness. Like Kant, whom he follows, he simply assumes that knowledge is possible and proceeds to analyse its nature and conditions. But whether or not we think he was justified in this attitude, the point tells us something of immense importance regarding the nature of his overall argument. Perhaps because he termed it the 'metaphysics of knowledge', at least some of Green's contemporaries interpreted his argument as epistemological and his idealism as subjective in the manner of Berkeley.[49] Yet this is wholly incorrect. Indeed, at the end of his review of John Caird's *Introduction to Philosophy of Religion* he takes issue with precisely such arguments for idealism. He criticizes the move from the epistemological anti-realism of reality-is-only-conceivable-by-thought to the ontological idealism of reality-only-exists-for-thought, arguing instead that in developing the case for idealism it is better directly to address the question of reality; to examine the very nature of what it

---

[46] *Russell Idealism and the Emergence of Analytic Philosophy*, 38.
[47] See 4.3.1 below.
[48] *Prolegomena*, §69; 'Mr Herbert Spencer and Mr G.H. Lewes', 487.
[49] This is the charge of Seth Pringle-Pattison in *The Idea of God*, 195–9.

is to be real and show that this involves ideas.[50] Such an idealism we might denote 'conceptual' as opposed to epistemological. What Green is offering us is an analysis of the concept of 'reality' and, whatever may be said about our *knowledge* of reality, our *conception* of reality is not one of something fenced in by our current awareness of it.

4.1.3.6 Causation If the eternal consciousness is hard to understand in its own right, it becomes even harder when we consider its relation to the finite world at large. As ever, Green offers us a number of different metaphors and phrases. The eternal consciousness 'renders' the relations of the world, nature 'results from' or 'exists through' its action, it 'constitutes' the world, understanding 'makes' nature, which is its 'product'.[51] But even at this level of metaphorical vagueness a problem emerges. For perhaps the most obvious thing about these expressions is that they are all causal terms. Yet causal talk in this context seems very problematic.

The problem is not hard to see. Indeed the three general difficulties considered above about language, time and consciousness each contribute to the obstacle. First, if causation is a relation and, as such, the work of the mind, we cannot speak of it as applying to ultimate reality or between ultimate reality and experience. The restriction is a Kantian one, although we should note that Kant, like Green, had a similarly unfortunate habit of speaking as though noumena somehow caused our experiences. The second problem concerns time. How can the eternal consciousness have a causal role, if causation is temporal, and it, as we have seen, is timeless? In the third place, Green's conception of the self as a Kantian unity of apperception makes it hard to find any distinction in this case between cause and effect. Although in some form it makes sense to distinguish between the agent or unifying principle and the manifold it unifies, from another point of view they are the same—the world has no character but that given to it by the unifying action of the agent, while the agent has no character but that which comes from its unifying action. If causation at all, it is an immanent self-causation for, as Green puts, 'there is no separate particularity in the agent, on the one side, and the determined world as a whole, on the other' but rather 'an indivisible whole which results from the activity of a single principle' Yet how can there be causation where there is no difference between cause and effect?[52]

Green is fully aware of these problems. Indeed he himself gives the example of 'cause' as a term which strictly speaking does not apply to ultimate reality but calls instead for metaphorical understanding.[53] What prevents this term from losing all meaning or appropriateness, he suggests, is the understanding we have of our own action in knowing the world. For, just as we make possible our own experience by

[50] 'Review of J. Caird, *Introduction to Philosophy of Religion*', 144–5.
[51] *Prolegomena*, §§52, 63, 46, 50, 38, 29.
[52] *Prolegomena*, §§76, 36. This criticism can be found in Sidgwick, *Lectures on the Philosophy of Kant*, 262.
[53] *Prolegomena*, §75.

rationally structuring and conceptualizing it, so the eternal consciousness makes the world by thinking it through an eternal system of relations.[54]

But even this picture is liable to misunderstanding. On hearing that relations are the work of the mind, the picture most naturally conjured up is of three elements: the terms to be related, the relations and the mind which creates them. However, with respect to Green's thinking this picture is misleading; for there is no self 'behind' the relations. Green operates with a conception of mind as a 'unifying principle'—indeed, this is a term he very often prefers to use instead.[55] Unification is not simply what consciousness *does*, it is what it *consists in*. Mind is thoroughly immanent in experience, it is not some agent *behind* the experience which *has* it and in consequence unifies it, but the very unity of the experience itself. This conception of mind or consciousness as merely a 'unifying principle' is a conception adopted by many of the British Idealists, and represents their understanding of what Kant meant by the transcendental unity of apperception.[56]

It might be charged that this is simply to explain the obscure by the even more obscure, but that would be unfair for, even if not a complete and fully luminous explanation, the comparison is nonetheless useful. Even if we cannot explain it, the relationship we have to our own thinking is something experienced by all. And it seems hard to deny that we are the authors of our thoughts; they do not simply come to us, rather they are our responsibility. In this sense the relationship is, or is like, causation. Yet our own causality *in thought* seems hardly to be of the same kind as that which we encounter within experience; we are not exactly the *efficient causes* of our thoughts. There is no prior act which we can find on the part of the agent which brings about the thought. Indeed we do not even seem clearly to be anything separate from our thoughts. Nor is it obvious that we stand temporally to our thoughts as more usual causes stand to their effects. Is a thought caused gradually as it is articulated in the mind, or must it be present in its entirety before we begin to express it? (Could one start a sentence without knowing how it is to finish?) To be sure, Green does not fully explain thought, but he points to a relation as undeniable in experience as it is creative in nature which *is* able to function as an effective metaphor for his meaning.

More understanding of the peculiar relation between eternal consciousness and the real world is had when we see that the former brings about the latter not just as its 'efficient cause' but equally as its 'final cause'. Green calls the eternal consciousness 'an

---

[54] *Prolegomena*, §77.

[55] *Prolegomena*, §§29, 32, 50, 75.

[56] Green explicitly identifies it with Kant's synthetic unity of apperception (*Prolegomena*, §33) arguing that its unity is correlative to that of the experience (*Prolegomena*, §32). Although Kant was rather vague about the metaphysical significance of the 'I' of the transcendental unity of apperception, the British Idealists were far more bold. For them this was the self and it was real, not just formal. However, there was not complete agreement. Pringle-Pattison in his *Hegelianism and Personality* (23–30) objected to this conception of self precisely on the grounds of its abstract thinness, a worry echoed by Dewey in 'On Some Current Conceptions of the Term "Self"' (73–4). But it was Bradley alone who saw that it is also—even just as much—the role of consciousness to divide as it is to unite.

end gradually realising itself', an already complete consciousness 'itself operative in the progress towards its attainment'.[57] In his moral philosophy it becomes the true good or *summum bonum* at which moral nature and human history aim. In other words, the world's development is not simply pushed from behind, but somehow drawn on from in front—it has a destiny or vocation to fulfil. The issue is complicated by the fact that due to the 'unending' nature of temporal progress the goal of the process of development cannot be identified with any actual temporal state, only an eternal ideal. This teleological component in Green (which draws our attention to the fact that he is often as indebted to Aristotle as he is to Kant or Hegel) is as uncomfortable to modern philosophers as it is central to his system, but it must be acknowledged that this is an element not simply in the metaphysics of the eternal consciousness but in his ethical and political thought as a whole, and it cannot easily be accepted in one place but rejected in another.

4.2 F.H. Bradley

Green's absolute idealist metaphysics was immensely influential, but it was not an isolated creation. Less than ten years later there appeared another system, destined perhaps even more to epitomize the metaphysics of the Absolute. This was the doctrine of Bradley's 1893 masterpiece *Appearance and Reality*.

A useful way to understand his system is to observe that for Bradley there are three distinct levels or orders of experience: immediate experience (which he also terms 'feeling'), relational experience, and absolute experience. It is his position that these three together form a developmental sequence in which immediate experience gives birth to relational experience which in turn gives birth to absolute experience; although whether this sequence is just notional or manifested in an actual chronological development, either in the life of the individual or of the species, is something he never took a clear position upon. From the point of view of philosophical understanding the best place to start to understand this sequence is not in fact at the beginning but in the middle, with relational experience, which as a state points beyond itself in two directions, both to its origin and its goal.

4.2.1 Relational experience

Bradley's philosophy begins with a critique of what he calls 'relational experience'.[58] At its simplest, this is any experience or thought about the world that employs relations in any way at all; which, of course, takes in *all* experience or thought in any everyday sense. To appreciate this we need simply to recognize the sheer pervasiveness of relations. Wherever we go, whatever we encounter, we meet with a myriad of

---

[57] *Prolegomena*, §§68, 70.
[58] For recent discussion of Bradley on relations see W. Mander, *An Introduction to Bradley's Metaphysics*; P. Basile, *Experience and Relations*.

relations, for they are what give structure to the world in which we live. Everything is related to the world around it, often in many different ways. Moreover we should note that relations hold, not just between things, but between their parts, between their temporal segments, between them and their properties, as well as between properties themselves.

We tend to think of a relation as something that *unifies* two or more distinct elements, as something that brings otherwise disparate items together into a single relational fact. However, for Bradley, relations are more than just unifiers, they also *divide*. Thus what he is considering here is as much the notion of division or separation, as that of union or togetherness. His topic is not just relations, but (as he puts it) the whole machinery of *terms and relations*. These come as one set. It is obvious that there could be no relations without distinct terms for them to relate, but Bradley finds it equally obvious that terms could not be distinct were it not for the relations which hold between them. And in this way distinction presupposes relation just as much as relation presupposes distinction.

What was Bradley's view of relations? A statement is easy enough to find. He says, 'The conclusion to which I am brought is that a relational way of thought—any one that moves by the machinery of terms and relations—must give appearance and not truth. It is a makeshift, a device, a mere practical compromise, most necessary but in the end, most indefensible.'[59] 'The very essence of these ideas is infected and contradicts itself'[60] he says, and the contradictions that he claims to find are famous. But before considering them more closely, a word of warning is due—no one should not expect to derive from relational statements some neat little *reductio* of the form 'P and not P'. The contradictions are less a matter of what is being *said*, than of the *practical implications* of what is being said, almost, we might put it, of what is being *done*; like using a pair of scissors to glue two things together, or trying to support both sides at a football match. The problem Bradley identifies is that the relational apparatus (the mechanism, that is, of terms and relations) is trying to describe a situation for which there is, as it were, no 'room' conceptually; like the concept of 'divorce' for certain strict Christians, or the difference between 'compromise' and 'defeat' to ultra hard-line political activists. Bradley's case against relations proceeds by considering a variety of ways in which we might try to understand them, each of which fails. These analyses achieved a certain fame, even notoriety, in their day, so it will be well to follow Bradley in his own presentation of the sorry tale.

What, we must ask ourselves, is a relation? The options, as Bradley sees it, are limited. Taking any two-term relation (and these are the only kind he recognizes) we can think of the relation either as some third sort of component placed somehow 'between' the other two, or else as some kind of property or quality 'attaching to' the

---

[59] *Appearance and Reality*, 28.
[60] *Appearance and Reality*, 21.

terms themselves. (Bradley does not distinguish between 'relation' and 'relational property'.)

The first is easily ruled out. We cannot take the relation to be any kind of extra element, for the question would then have to be asked how that element itself stood to the terms, introducing two new relations and so launching us on an infinite regress. It would, says Bradley, be like supposing that to attach two chains together, we need a further link, and then two more, and then another four, and so on . . . [61]

But if we turn to the second option, we fare no better; in the end, indeed, we seem to face the very same problem. For if the relation is but a feature of the objects related, then presumably it must set up within them a distinction between those of their features that enter into the relation and those that don't. To illustrate, being wiser than Socrates is, we may take it, a matter of one's intelligence or insight but not one's height or shoe size. But if we ask how the former set of features stands to the latter we can only be launching ourselves on yet another regress.[62] And it is hardly surprising that this should be so, for it would take a subtle logician to find other than a verbal distinction between the question of how a thing stands to its own relations and the question of how stands its non-relational to its relational nature.

The only remaining option we have for understanding relations is to say that they are indeed aspects or qualities of the terms that they relate, but that they are so fused with them, as to render impossible any separation between the term's relational and non-relational nature. But now either we have lost our relation altogether here and are left with simply a term (something we have already dismissed as absurd), or else what is being offered is nothing but a relation—there being no aspect of it that is not relational. Nothing can consist solely in its relation to others; the notion of a world of relations without any terms is, argues Bradley, even more absurd than that of a world of qualities without relations.[63] The options for making sense of them exhausted, Bradley concludes that relations are impossible.

4.2.2 Assessment of Bradley's case

It is only to be expected that so radical a line of argument was challenged, and one of its greatest critics was Bertrand Russell. Indeed the story of Russell's rise as a philosopher and of the emergence of analytic philosophy with which he is so closely associated was in large part the story of his break with Bradley's rejection of relations. One consequence of that triumph is the still widespread belief that Russell refuted Bradley's view of relations but, if we look at the details, the matter is less clear; for many of Russell's objections were based on fundamental confusions about or misrepresentations of Bradley's position.[64]

---

[61] *Appearance and Reality*, 28.
[62] *Appearance and Reality*, 26.
[63] *Appearance and Reality*, 27.
[64] For detailed discussions of the debate between Bradley and Russell see Hylton, *Russell, Idealism and the Emergence of Analytic Philosophy* and Candlish, *The Russell/Bradley Dispute*.

In his 1903 book *The Principles of Mathematics* Russell distinguishes between two theories of relations, the monadistic which he attributes to Leibniz and Lotze and the monistic which he attributes to Spinoza and Bradley.[65] In the first a relational proposition, aRb, is understood by analysing it down into two separate propositions, ar_1 and br_2, each attributing a different property to the two terms involved. In the second by contrast the relational proposition is understood by taking the two terms together and attributing a property to the pair, giving the schema *(ab)R*. Russell rejects both analyses on the grounds of their inability to deal with asymmetrical relations; on the monistic theory, for example, the distinct propositions 'a is greater than b' and 'b is greater than a' would both receive the same analysis, *(ab)Greater than*.

To a large extent this objection fails to touch its target for the monistic theory which Russell identifies as Bradley's is really a long way from his actual position. The analysis Bradley proposes is not merely a redistribution of the roles of subject and predicate within the proposition, but rather the translation of the entire propositional content into a predicate then referred to reality as a whole. Thus in the judgement 'S is P', instead of picking out S and saying that it is P, we say of reality as a whole that it is 'S-P ish', or as he later puts it 'Reality is such that S is P'.[66] *This* analysis can deal with asymmetry, for it takes up into its predication not only the relation itself ('greater than') but the asymmetry of actual instantiation ('a is greater than b' or 'b is greater than a').

Russell argues that the monadistic and monistic theories of relations are the only two options for someone who believes that all relations are subject–predicate in form.[67] But the accusation that Bradley holds all propositions to be of subject–predicate form is equally mistaken. For while he would admit that all judgements predicate or say something about reality, the question of what they do or how they function is different from any question concerning the logical structure of their content, and he certainly would not argue that we can reduce relational propositions to subject–predicate ones. Indeed quite the reverse; it was his view that subject–predicate ones are to be rejected precisely because they are relational—they involve a relation between subject and predicate—and on these grounds Bradley is as fierce a critic of subject–predicate logic as might be found anywhere.[68]

Russell's position is that in addition to subjects and predicates, relations constitute a third *sui generis* category, too basic to reduce to anything else. It is simply the business of relations to relate, and we cannot ask how. But this would not satisfy Bradley. For him relations are part of our conceptual structure, not something we may passively accept as immediate or given in experience and, as such, the problem is not merely that we don't understand them but that they are trying to do something which by Bradley's lights is impossible.

---

[65] Russell, *Principles of Mathematics*, §§212–16.
[66] *Essays on Truth and Reality*, 333; *Principles of Logic*, 630.
[67] Russell, *Principles of Mathematics*, §212.
[68] For further detail on Bradley's theory of judgement see Chapter 8.3.2 below.

Of Bradley's various arguments to demonstrate the unreality of relations perhaps the most attacked has been the 'chain argument'[69] but the majority of objections against it have been misplaced, failing to appreciate that it constitutes but one half of a broader case. The understanding of relation rejected here is not his own but one of a pair that might be suggested, and as critical as he is of thinking of a relation as a third something standing somehow 'between' its terms, he moves straight on to condemn in equal measure the opposite view that would seek somehow to bind up the relation inside the nature of its terms. More worthy of attention has been the response of those such as Cook Wilson who have argued that the chain regress is simply verbal and not a real one of genuinely new relations.[70] But if there is no need to bring in any further element to connect *a* and *R*, by the same token, it is hard to see what need there is to bring in *R* in the first place to connect *a* and *b*. Yet who could be satisfied with a world of just terms and no relations?

Perhaps Russell's most famous objection is that Bradley held what he calls 'the axiom or doctrine of internal relations', the view that all relations are internal.[71] The internal/external relations terminology here calls for explanation. Broadly speaking, the difference is that between thinking of a relation as either something more or less brought in from outside and placed between its terms, and thinking of it as something more or less bound up in the nature of those terms themselves. Thus what Russell's charge amounts to is a repeat of the accusation that Bradley held that all relations are grounded in or even reducible to the natures of their terms.

There are two levels at which one might respond to Russell's charge. At the most basic level it could be said, once again, that Russell has simply misunderstood Bradley's meaning. He accuses Bradley of thinking all relations are internal, when it is in fact his view that there are no relations at all. For Bradley argues that, considered neither internally nor externally, can relations be made to work. External relations stand outside, and make no real connection with, their terms, while internal relations lose themselves wholly in their terms leaving us either with a term that has swallowed its own relation or a relation that has swallowed its own term. Indeed, the terminology serves well to express Bradley's diagnosis of the fundamental problem. Internal and external are opposing notions. But a relation by its very nature strives to be *both* internal *and* external[72]—the relation in which things stand is no arbitrary accident but a function of their natures, and yet a relational fact is more than just a set of terms. Bradley laments the forced dichotomy—'the whole 'Either-or' between external and internal relations, to me seems unsound,'[73] he says—but he is stuck with it, for

---

[69] C.D. Broad said of it 'Charity bids us avert our eyes from the pitiable spectacle of a great philosopher using an argument that would disgrace a child or a savage' (*Examination of McTaggart's Philosophy*, I:85).

[70] Cook Wilson, *Statement and Inference*, II:692–5. See also Saxena, *Studies in the Metaphysics of F.H. Bradley*, 130–40; Tacelli, 'Cook Wilson as Critic of Bradley', 199–205.

[71] Russell, *Philosophical Essays*, 139; *Logic and Knowledge*, 335.

[72] *Collected Essays*, 677.

[73] *Essays on Truth and Reality*, 238.

concepts draw boundaries, obliging elements to fall either within or outside their range. The one and the many remain forever opposed in thought and cannot be unified, and this is the sense in which for Bradley relational statements are trying to do something for which there is in conceptual terms simply 'no room'. A relation tries but inevitably fails to unite the diverse, and because it fails, not as measured against some higher purer standard but simply in its own terms, as attempting something which its own nature undermines, Bradley thinks of it as self-contradictory. But note the direction of fit. Failure shows, not that things aren't the way thought is trying to tell us, but that thought just isn't up to the job of telling us how they really are.

But in an important sense it must be acknowledged that this is only half the answer. It cannot be the case that all relations are internal if all relations falsify reality, but Bradley does allow that some conceptions falsify more than others, and would agree that it is less inappropriate to view relations as internal than it is to view them as external.[74] To understand why he thinks so it is necessary to look to the stages of experience before and after the relational level but, before that, note should be taken of the consequences of Bradley's argument thus far.

4.2.3 Consequences of the relational argument

Relations are contradictory and cannot belong to reality, but relations are to be found everywhere, so anything which involves them will also be contradictory. To abandon relations is, Bradley readily admits, to condemn 'the great mass of phenomena'.[75] Not only are there no relations between things but we must reject too the very notion of a thing itself which, either as a possessor or a complex of properties is a thoroughly relational notion. A further immediate consequence is the unreality of space and time, for whether we take a reductionist or substantivalist view of them, these also are essentially relational. That space is not finally real is to be expected from an idealist, but to say existence is timeless,[76] that change however apparent is not ultimately real, while it aligns him with Green, separates him from several other British Idealists. Equally relational and therefore to be rejected are motion, change, and causation.

It is hard to appreciate just what it really means to dismiss in this way all the chief structures of the ordinary world. What becomes, for example, of physical nature? Bradley notes that the word 'nature' is ambiguous,[77] and defines nature for the physical sciences as the mind-independent world: 'Abstract from everything psychical, and then the remainder of existence will be Nature.'[78] Part of what he is trying to get at by the phrase 'abstract from everything psychical' is the scientific distinction between primary and secondary qualities, where all properties that are relative to a perceiving mind are

---

[74] *Essays on Truth and Reality*, 312. For more on degrees of truth and reality see Chapter 8.3.11 below.

[75] *Appearance and Reality*, 29.

[76] 'If time is not unreal, I admit that our Absolute is a delusion' (*Appearance and Reality*, 182). See also *Essays on Truth and Reality*, 336.

[77] *Appearance and Reality*, 434.

[78] *Appearance and Reality*, 231.

downgraded as appearance leaving only as really present in objects their invariant and quantifiable properties. But why, Bradley asks, should removing qualities, and especially ones relative to the mind, get us any closer to reality? To a well-rounded view removing the secondary qualities is just to remove the 'blood and flesh'[79] of reality. To a well-rounded view 'nature', as defined by the poet or artist, and full of qualities that depend on the mind, is more real than this abstracted skeleton of natural science.[80] In short, for Bradley, reality is found not by *removing* qualities or *narrowing* our point of view, but by *widening* it and *adding* them.

More specifically Bradley offers two arguments against any primary–secondary quality distinction. The first is taken directly from Berkeley and consists simply in pointing out that primary qualities are just as relative as secondary ones.[81] Bradley's second objection, however, is more interesting and can be put this way. According to the theory of primary and secondary qualities, objects with only primary qualities produce in us the experience of secondary qualities, as apparently residing in bodies alongside those primary qualities. But how does this miracle work? Why do qualities of a single kind sometimes produce in us accurate experiences of them, but at other times produce in us an experience of qualities of a wholly different kind? And in the latter case, why do they cause the precise experiences they in fact produce? Why for instance, does a given shape or texture (or the causal chain from these to a given brain state) cause us to experience one colour, rather than another, or rather than a smell? No one seems to know. A veil of ignorance, conveniently called 'misperception' or 'appearance', is drawn over the whole process. But such an empty theory should not satisfy anyone. It certainly did not satisfy Bradley, who objected that, 'The relation of the primary qualities to the secondary seems wholly unintelligible. For nothing is actually removed from existence by being labelled 'appearance'. What appears is there, and must be dealt with; but materialism has no rational way of dealing with appearance'.[82]

If physical nature considered apart from any relation to mind is to be dismissed, what is to be said of mind itself? Turning to another very important consequence of the relational argument, Bradley considers a variety of senses of 'self' but pronounces all flawed, because relational. Most significantly he argues that self-consciousness, the experience of subject and object in one self, is no exception to this. In self-awareness the mind becomes its own object and, in doing so, ceases to be identical with the knowing subject.[83] A relation is set up and the state thereby prevented from affording us any special key to the nature of reality. Again, Bradley distances himself from many of his Idealist colleagues.

---

[79] *Appearance and Reality*, 438.
[80] *Appearance and Reality*, 436.
[81] *Appearance and Reality*, 12–13. This argument repeats the traditional mistake of supposing that the distinction is one made on grounds of introspective epistemology. In truth an examination of its origins in Locke and Boyle clearly reveals it to be a hypothesis adopted on the basis of its explanatory power.
[82] *Appearance and Reality*, 12.
[83] *Appearance and Reality*, 94.

But if self is not ultimately real, that is not at all the same as to say it is no significance at all. Of all the ways in which reality may appear to us this is the highest, argues Bradley,[84] and if faced with a choice, it would be better to think of ultimate reality—the Absolute—as personal rather than impersonal.[85] Not a fictitious grafting on, but a failure clearly to see something much fuller, 'the Absolute is not personal, because it is personal and more,' argues Bradley; 'It is, in a word, super-personal.'[86] What this could possibly mean has left many puzzled,[87] but it is not unconnected with Lotze's view of limitless personality which was popular with the Personal Idealists.[88]

One final but nonetheless vital consequence of Bradley's anti-relationism is monism. The common-sense view of the universe as containing many distinct substances—pluralism—must be rejected. A non-relational world is a monistic world; 'Reality is one' he argues.[89] Relations unite, but they only unite what they first divide, and so their dismissal brings us to monism, not pluralism. But care is needed here, for what Bradley has in mind is not—as Russell once accused[90]—some sort of homogeneous unity like that of Parmenides. His Absolute is an Hegelian many-in-one or one-in-many. It does not exclude difference—though its differences are felt and not thought—but it is *one*.

4.2.4 Pre-relational experience

Bradley is a firm adherent of a principle that most would accept, the coherence of reality. 'Ultimate reality is such that it does not contradict itself,'[91] he says, and hence if contradiction is found in our experience—if the concepts we use to structure it refuse to sit alongside each other—that must be something we have introduced; the mind in trying to grasp reality must have distorted it. If this is so, then we get back nearer to something like the truth, if we discount all our troublesome contributions. In this way the contradictory realm of relational thought or experience points to something behind itself, to its origin in 'feeling' or 'immediate experience'. There is more than an echo of Kant here.

'Immediate Experience' or 'feeling' are the technical terms Bradley uses to designate the basic experiential state in which reality is given or encountered. 'The real' he says 'is that which is known in presentation or intuitive knowledge. It is what we encounter in feeling or perception.'[92] However exotic their flower may be, that the roots of Bradley's thinking on this score are to be found in the tradition of British empiricism is seen in his further insistence that such experience is our only handle on reality;

---

[84] *Appearance and Reality*, 103.
[85] *Appearance and Reality*, 472.
[86] *Appearance and Reality*, 471.
[87] For example, Henry Jones. See p.428 below.
[88] See below Chapter 10.
[89] *Appearance and Reality*, 463.
[90] *My Philosophical Development*, 290.
[91] *Appearance and Reality*, 120.
[92] *Principles of Logic*, 44.

'Nothing in the end is real but what is felt.'[93] However, what Bradley has in mind here is not simply the ordinary experience of everyday life, but rather something deeper which underlies that experience.

By calling it 'feeling' or 'experience', he wishes to protest against any more narrow or one-sided starting point, such as merely the experience of our senses. What Bradley intends with this term is a state that includes all types of sensation, emotion, will, and desire—in short, anything of which we are in any manner aware.[94] By calling it 'immediate', he wishes to stress that it is something presentational and pre-conceptual.[95] Although it contains diversity, it is 'seamless',[96] not yet broken up by our concepts and relations. 'It is all one blur with differences, that work and that are felt, but are not discriminated,' he says.[97] Notably, it is prior both to the distinction between self and not-self—it is a state as yet without either an object or a subject[98]—and to the distinction between knowing and being—the separation and downgrading of knowledge or concepts relative to existence or objects has yet to take place.[99] No doubt this is all very mysterious, and we might be tempted to cast about for examples that could help illustrate Bradley's meaning here; aesthetic or religious experiences, perhaps. However this is not a promising strategy, and such cases offer at best just analogies. For if feeling is given, it is not given in any experience which we as conscious selves could ever recognize and draw on, but has rather to be considered as something inferred from the kind of experiences we do enjoy, as their only possible basis and explanation. For purely logical reflection convicts ordinary experience, and so we are forced to postulate something more consistent and more coherent lying behind it.

Another important point to note about immediate experience is that it manifests itself filtered through what Bradley calls 'finite centres'.[100] These numerous[101] centres of experience are not to be thought of as objects existing in time or capable of standing in relation to one another; they are rather the raw data from which such objects and relations are built up as ideal constructions.[102] They are, we might say, the pre-conceptual experiential base from which we construct our entire conception of the world. Finite centres need also to be distinguished from selves. This is so in two respects. First, selves are objects that endure through time, and second, they are distinguished from their states. A finite centre, in contrast, has no duration and contains

---

[93] *Essays on Truth and Reality*, 190.

[94] *Essays on Truth and Reality*, 189.

[95] Qualification is in order here. Immediate experience need not be *wholly* free from concepts, for Bradley allows that it may become coloured or infused to a degree by previous thought or judgement (*Essays on Truth and Reality*, 177). See Ferreira, *Bradley and the Structure of Knowledge*, 158–9.

[96] Ferreira, *Bradley and the Structure of Knowledge*, 157.

[97] *Collected Essays*, 216; *Appearance and Reality*, 90.

[98] *Appearance and Reality*, 465.

[99] *Essays on Truth and Reality*, 159.

[100] *Essays on Truth and Reality*, 410.

[101] *Appearance and Reality*, 468.

[102] *Essays on Truth and Reality*, 411.

no subject–object distinction. For Bradley the self is something made out of, or abstracted from, a finite centre, and thus he allows that in so far as I think of myself as something developed out of a given finite centre, I may describe that centre as 'mine',[103] but it must always be remembered that I belong to the finite centre, not *vice versa*, and the self which is thus developed is but an ideal construction lacking any ultimate reality.[104] All experience we know is filtered in this fashion, but Bradley allows at least the possibility that there obtains within the Absolute some 'centreless' experience. He says, 'Why should there not be elements experienced in the total, and yet not experienced within any subordinate focus? . . . The abstraction of a finite centre does not lead visibly to self-contradiction. And hence I cannot refuse to regard its result as possible.'[105]

Worth noting is Bradley's description of these finite experiences as *centres*. What he wishes to convey with this word can be seen by examining the context in which finite centres make their first entrance. This is his discussion of indexical experience, what he calls the 'this' and the 'mine', in chapter 19 of *Appearance and Reality*. Just as we suppose there to be many finite centres,[106] he tells us that 'We are to assume that there does exist an indefinite number of 'this-mines'.[107] Just as all knowledge comes to us through finite centres,[108] we are informed that 'all our knowledge, in the first place, arises from the "this".'[109] And just as finite centres are immediate and pre-conceptual in nature,[110] we learn that 'the "this" is immediate . . . because it is at a level below distinctions'.[111] These parallels show us that he is here *identifying* finite centres with indexical experience, and indeed he says, 'the "this" and the "mine" express the immediate character of feeling, and the appearance of this character in a finite centre.'[112] The this-mine of indexical experience is something centred and the identification suggests that finite centres be thought of as centred in the very same way.

Equally noteworthy is Bradley's claim that they are *finite*. This refers not to their duration for, strictly speaking, they have no duration, but rather to their content, which is limited in its extent. They do not stretch out forever but have, as we might say, edges. They are bounded. This seems to be immediately and intuitively correct. For curiously, even if we ourselves can have no real grasp of what an infinite experience might be, we can be fairly certain that our own experience is finite in nature. As Bradley says, 'More or less of content may come from time to time within the man's feeling centre. But so long as that centre exists, there is a world within it which is

---

[103] *Essays on Truth and Reality*, 418.
[104] *Essays on Truth and Reality*, 248.
[105] *Appearance and Reality*, 467; cf. *Appearance and Reality*, 241–2, *Appearance and Reality*, 411 n.
[106] *Appearance and Reality*, 468; *Essays on Truth and Reality*, 412.
[107] *Appearance and Reality*, 197.
[108] *Appearance and Reality*, 416.
[109] *Appearance and Reality*, 198.
[110] *Essays on Truth and Reality*, 247–8, 415.
[111] *Appearance and Reality*, 199.
[112] *Appearance and Reality*, 198.

experienced immediately and a world without it which is not in this sense experienced at all.'[113]

It is important to note that immediate experience in and of itself is not essentially finite. It is only in so far as it is filtered through finite centres that it becomes so; a fact which plays an absolutely crucial role in Bradley's developmental scheme. Although in some sense nearer to the truth than relational experience, immediate experience is not fully harmonious. And its lack of harmony leads it to break up and develop into the relational consciousness. The transition from immediate experience to relational thought results from the clash between the finitude of its feeling centres and its immediacy. It presents itself as a harmonious state, something that is no more than what it appears to itself to be, a being and knowing in one. But in Bradley's eyes the finitude attributable to its manifestation through the 'this' and the 'mine' generates a tension which destabilizes that harmony.[114] Understanding the finite in Hegelian manner as that which is limited from outside, the centre in its finitude points beyond itself to a wider feeling of which it is but a portion and against which at the same time it is contrasted. Fully spelt out, its contents over-reach the limits of its own being, it feels wider than it is, and in this way enters in that distinction between subject and object which is the hallmark of thought, and which spells the demise of the immediacy of feeling.

Too much talk of change or development should not lead us astray, however, for Bradley is insistent that immediate experience is not left completely behind, but rather remains present in relational thought as a kind of foundation.[115] Immediate experience provides us with the very experiential content that is subsequently conceptualized in relational experience. Prior to the distinction between subject and object, it cannot for that reason become known to us as an object of awareness,[116] the focus of some act of introspection, but as the base from which all such awareness is drawn it *is* still known.

4.2.5 Supra-relational experience

If the contradictions of thought point backwards to immediate experience, they also point forwards beyond themselves to the Absolute. The developmental process which caused the breach, left to continue, heals itself again; for it is the nature of thought to aim at truth, and in uncovering its own defects it at the same time shows what would be necessary to rectify them. Specifically it is seen that error arises precisely from the separation of things one from another, from which it follows that the more they are reconnected, the more things are returned in understanding to the context from which they were abstracted, the more holistic our picture becomes, and the closer we will

---

[113] *Essays on Truth and Reality*, 173.
[114] *Appearance and Reality*, 407; *Essays on Truth and Reality*, 189.
[115] *Essays on Truth and Reality*, 160, 175, 178.
[116] *Essays on Truth and Reality*, 160.

approximate to truth. By putting the jigsaw back together, we replace the pluralistic vision with a holistic one.

Bradley recommends connected and holistic thinking over separated and pluralistic schemes, but he insists that more healthy patterns of thought can never give a complete solution to our problem. For however much we try to compensate for it, and however much we are aware of doing it, the very nature of thought is to differentiate—to separate one object from another, and all objects from the subject which thinks them. But to differentiate is to falsify. We divide *A* from *B* but then add that, of course, *A* and *B* must be taken together. Yet they are still separate in thought. In the end, argues Bradley, if the road to truth is the road of reconciliation, it must take us beyond thought, to an Absolute experience undifferentiated by concepts. It should thus be noted that Bradley has an importantly realist concept of the Absolute as something existing beyond (what he poetically describes as) thought's suicide.[117]

There are two kinds of things to know about any object: its character, and whether it exists, or as Bradley neatly puts it 'what it is' and 'that it is'. He attempts to use this distinction to explain the nature of thought itself, saying that thought consists essentially in a separation of the 'what' from the 'that'. His meaning here is that ideas and judgements concern themselves entirely with the nature of things, and are unable to assert their own instantiation or truth. Whatever they say, it is always a separate question whether they say something true. Another way of understanding this is to say that thought is general or universal in its nature, but reality is not—it is particular and individual. No thought—not even the very best there could be—is ever the same as that which is thought about; they are too different and too separate. The solution, as he sees it, is to attempt to reduce the generality of any thought by incorporating into the thought itself the wider context from which its object is taken, thus simultaneously increasing both its detail and the range of its application, or as he alternatively puts it, beginning to reunite the 'what' and the 'that'. But this is an unachievable task, in that its completion would result in the very undoing of thought itself, for which such separation is an essential condition. Bradley concludes that the search for ultimate truth is self-defeating, it is to embark on a process that carried through to its end can only result in thought's removal of itself from the picture—its 'suicide'.

For Bradley Absolute experience, experience driven by its own internal logic or engine to find a final consistency, contains all that is ultimately real. But what about all those elements of experience that get discarded along the way? Bradley designates these *appearance*, but what exactly does he mean when he says relations (and all those things that involve relations) are appearance, rather than reality? We might think this is to say they do not exist, to which we are likely to respond in a tone of common-sense indignation that surely such things *do* exist. But our indignation would be misplaced; Bradley does not, for a moment, want to deny that relations exist—nothing has been

---

[117] *Appearance and Reality*, 150. Realism here is to be taken in the sense of a belief in reality beyond the compass of thought, not in any sort of commitment to the correspondence of reality and thought.

spirited away. In this respect his position is comparable to the doctrine of secondary qualities, which says, not that objects don't really have colours, that colours don't exist, but rather that phenomenal colour is not a category applicable to ultimate reality. The reference to secondary qualities might suggest to us the metaphysical dualist's way of dealing with appearance, namely to think of it as mental representation (an idea or sense-datum) interposing between us and the world beyond, a kind of screen that gets in the way and prevents us from seeing things as they really are. However, Bradley's monism precludes any such move—his appearances are not in that sense appearances *of* anything.[118] For Bradley, the Absolute *is* its appearances. They are its content. To call something unreal or appearance is to deny that it possesses genuinely independent being which, of course, covers everything except the Absolute. Seen falsely and picked out one by one, aspects of the world present a misleading face and must be called appearance, but seen truly as participants in an integrated whole, they are transformed together to form reality, or the Absolute. As Bradley puts it, 'The Absolute, we may say in general, has no assets beyond appearances; and again, with appearances alone to its credit, the Absolute would be bankrupt. All these are worthless alike apart from transmutation.'[119] Ultimate reality is so far beyond conception that we could never think it, but at the same time it is all around us.

Appearance then for Bradley is a distorted vision or perspective on reality. It is a matter of taking something out of context and treating it as though it were fully and independently real. But distortion here is a matter of degree, hence Bradley believes that there is room for a theory of degrees of reality—where how much reality any given experience is accorded is a function of the amount of supplementation and transformation that would be required to turn it into Absolute experience. It is in this sense that statements of internal relations are truer than those of external ones.

To fill out this schema it is useful to consider in more detail what Bradley says about science. He attacks the specifically scientific approach to the world. Science is guided by the idea of generality. It is concerned not with particular things and events, but is rather a search for general laws and types. However, for Bradley this means that it can never be true of ultimate reality, for Reality is particular. Indeed the more general science becomes, the less true it is, and so in this sense science must be seen as aiming in an essentially falsifying direction. An illustration may help here. From the particular whole we abstract, for example, the notion of a body. We might formulate laws about bodies, but typically we do not, abstracting instead one aspect of them, for example, their motion. Again we might formulate laws about motion in general, but typically

---

[118] In historical terms, Collingwood has pointed out that Bradley is rejecting here a long-standing conception of 'appearance' which, taking its origin in Locke and Hume, reached a high pitch of development in the work of Bradley's more immediate predecessors, Hamilton and (especially) Mansel. For both thinkers human knowledge is limited to mind-relative phenomena cutting us off from an unknown ultimate reality. It is true that Mansel is rarely mentioned explicitly, but in Oxford at that time, the applicability would have been obvious ('The Metaphysics of F.H. Bradley', 232–8).

[119] *Appearance and Reality*, 433.

we do not, rather from that concept we abstract, say, the idea of rectilinear motion, making that the subject of our laws. There, at least for the moment we rest, but the point to note is that for Bradley each such division is a further falsifying move. It assumes that the thing or aspect we have carved off is independent from and unaffected by its context, or as the terminology puts it, that it is connected to it by a merely external relation. Thus Bradley says that, 'the external relations, which work, are summed up in the laws'.[120] But, though pragmatically justified, this assumption of externality is theoretically quite false, he claims.

In view of this fundamental criticism of the basic project of natural science, one might expect Bradley to counsel scientists to simply hang up their coats and call it a day. But this he does not do; indeed far from it. Despite these criticisms and within their framework, Bradley finds space to develop a sympathetic and intelligent positive philosophy of science. It is true that, for him, science is an irredeemably falsifying abstraction from the immediate whole that is reality. But paradoxically this should not be thought any special cause for concern. Since the perfection of knowledge is impossible, abstraction is a practical necessity of life which, so long as we appreciate its inevitable presence, need not be considered a fatal defect. It is no special problem because a degree of falsehood proportionate to the level of abstraction does not exclude a degree of truth proportionate to the same thing. What is important is to recognize and accept the level of abstraction involved in any intellectual activity. For natural science, what this means is that although its theories can never attain perfect truth, they may nonetheless be instrumentally or practically true. This thinks Bradley is their sole aim. 'The question is not whether the principles of physical science possess an absolute truth to which they make no claim. The question is whether the abstraction employed by that science, is legitimate and useful.'[121] Although ultimately unreal abstractions, the concepts of science are to be thought of as 'working ideas',[122] and as such, legitimate in so far as and only in so far as they do work. 'I do not object to *anything* that is offered, so long as and so far as it works, and so long as it is offered merely as something which works.'[123]

The task for which their instrumental or pragmatic success is to be judged is a purely phenomenalist one: 'To find and systematize the ways in which spatial phenomena are connected and happen—this is all the mark which these conceptions aim at.'[124] Bradley's most thorough defence of this phenomenalist viewpoint is given for psychology. In the course of that defence he defines phenomenalism as 'the confinement of one's attention to events with their laws of coexistence and sequence. It involves the complete abjuration of any attempt to ask . . . for ultimate truth or consistency, and it

---

[120] *Appearance and Reality*, 313.
[121] *Appearance and Reality*, 251.
[122] *Appearance and Reality*, 251.
[123] 'A Defence of Phenomenalism in Psychology', 373.
[124] *Appearance and Reality*, 251.

involves the adoption as relative truth of whatever serves best to explain the detailed course of facts or those particular ways in which things happen.'[125] Although he rejects phenomenalism as a method in metaphysics,[126] he thinks that in science it is the only possible way. For if science persisted in demanding absolute truth of its ideas, it would be wholly absorbed into metaphysics, and bogging itself down in unending contextual detail and disputes over first principles, become quite unable to advance in what everyone agrees to be one of its essential roles (even if they cannot agree that that is its *only* role), namely the systematization and prediction of phenomena.[127]

As an instrumentalist he naturally has to face the charge that mere phenomenal laws are insufficient to account for the explanatory role of science. It is certainly true that within this view of science Bradley cannot offer any deeper theoretical truths to serve as explanations of phenomena, however, he does not believe that this is necessary. Explanation for Bradley consists simply in the deduction of a statement about an event from some more general statement about the occurrence of such events, irrespective of its truth value. He claims that, 'You can only explain events . . . by the laws of their happening, and it does not matter for your purpose, so long as these laws work, whether they possess ultimate truth or are more or less fictitious and false.'[128] Explanation, in other words, is what has been called a 'pragmatic virtue'[129] quite unconnected with either truth or depth. 'What in short we want,' he says, 'are explanations that truly explain, and above all things we do not want true explanations.'[130]

It is crucial that calling Bradley an instrumentalist, or his own description of his position as phenomenalism, should not mislead us. For he does not, like some who have worn these titles, believe that the duty of a scientific theory is simply to give a true general description of the behaviour of observable things. He does not think this, because he does not believe in any realm of pure observation. 'The merely given facts are,' he says, 'the imaginary creatures of false theory. They are manufactured by a mind which abstracts one aspect of the concrete known whole, and sets this abstracted aspect out by itself as a real thing.'[131] Thus long before contemporary scientific realists took up the cry, Bradley was quite clear that no viable distinction could ever be made between the deliverances of our sense-perception and those of our theorizing. All perception is, he thinks, irredeemably laden with thinking.

4.2.6 Idealism

Bradley's three-step metaphysical scheme—which has the felt directness of immediate experience giving way to the plurality of relational experience, and then reconciling

---

[125] 'A Defence of Phenomenalism in Psychology', 364.
[126] *Appearance and Reality*, ch XI.
[127] 'A Defence of Phenomenalism in Psychology', 364.
[128] 'A Defence of Phenomenalism in Psychology', 375.
[129] Van Fraassen, *The Scientific Image*, 87–96.
[130] 'A Defence of Phenomenalism in Psychology', 375.
[131] *Essays on Truth and Reality*, 108.

itself in the diverse-unity of Absolute experience—picks out three kinds of *experience*. But is there not more to life than experience? Bradley insists that there is not. That is to say, he was an idealist. His argument for idealism is nothing like as developed as his argument for monism. It has even been suggested that he just assumes it,[132] but that is problematic, for the kind of idealism he offers cannot be simply assimilated to other known types available to take off the peg.

In many respects his might seem an Hegelian species of idealism, for it postulates something like an Absolute spirit in which we, together with everything else, are taken up. But for all Bradley was influenced by Hegel, it is clear that his idealism was not of this stripe; for Hegel's panlogicism repelled him. As he says of that view at the end of the *Principles of Logic*:

It may come from a failure in my metaphysics, or from a weakness of the flesh which continues to blind me, but the notion that existence could be the same as understanding strikes as cold and ghost-like as the dreariest materialism. That the glory of this world in the end is appearance leaves the world more glorious, if we feel it is a show of some fuller splendour; but the sensuous curtain is a deception and a cheat, if it hides some colourless movement of atoms, some spectral woof of impalpable abstractions, or unearthly ballet of bloodless categories. Though dragged to such conclusions, we can not embrace them.... They no more *make* that Whole which commands our devotion, than some shredded dissection of human tatters *is* that warm and breathing beauty of flesh which our hearts found delightful.[133]

Should we then think of him as offering an idealism more like that of Berkeley, who argues in anti-realist fashion that we can never pass outside the sphere of our own cognition, that we have no grounds for belief in anything beyond the ideas we encounter? The argument which he offers for this conclusion in *Appearance and Reality* might seem rather like Berkeley's famous 'one-step' argument. It is even, like that argument, put in the form of an instruction.

Find any piece of existence, take up anything that any one could possibly call a fact, or could in any sense assert to have being, and then judge if it does not consist in sentient experience. Try to discover any sense in which you can still continue to speak of it, when all perception and feeling have been removed; or point out any fragment of its matter, any aspect of its being, which is not derived from and is not still relative to this source. When the experiment is made strictly, I can myself conceive of nothing else than the experienced. Anything, in no sense felt or perceived, becomes to me quite unmeaning. And as I cannot try to think of it without realizing either that I am not thinking at all, or that I am thinking of it against my will as being experienced, I am driven to the conclusion that for me experience is the same as reality.[134]

But while superficially Bradley might seem to be arguing after Berkeley, in the end his case is very different. Where Berkeley's argument precludes the existence of anything

---

[132] Candlish, *The Russell/Bradley Dispute*, 45.
[133] *Principles of Logic*, 590–1.
[134] *Appearance and Reality*, 127–8.

lying outside our subjective grasp, Bradley is quite clear that reality transcends the subjective point of view. It is unfortunate that his argument here is put, like Berkeley's, in the first person form, for his thesis is that we are locked into *experience*, not that we are locked into *our own* experience.

Bradley holds that reality is composed of a species of mind which is fundamentally non-cognitive (i.e. neither perceptual nor conceptual) and supra-personal and in this respect the idealism with which it comes closest is in fact that of Schopenhauer whose doctrine of the Will proposes a comparable species of non-cognitive mentality as the underlying constitution of all reality, personal and impersonal.

4.3 Edward Caird

Bradley and Green offered largely original arguments for Absolute Idealism and, were theirs the only systems on offer, 'British Hegelianism' might be thought an odd epithet to locate the school, but other Idealists took their metaphysics more directly from Hegel. Chief among these was Edward Caird.

Because he developed his ideas historically, anyone who knows Caird's expositions of Plato, Aristotle, Spinoza, Kant, or Hegel will know already the main outlines of his metaphysics. Its chief claim is one of diversity reconciled in the embrace of a wider organic whole, whose work is not to obliterate difference (it is no 'facile monism')[135] but to manifest itself through such multiplicity. The unity is able to bring together any diversity, be it between sense and reason, form and matter, necessity and contingency, universal and particular; for all, argues Caird, are 'included within' that great dualism between subject and object which itself finds synthesis in the unity of self-consciousness.[136] And because this coming together is a force whose underlying character most fully shows itself in self-consciousness, the result (which he also sometimes refers to by its Hegelian name, 'the Absolute')[137] is fundamentally idealistic, as well as monistic. Says Caird, 'the world we live in is a spiritual world—a divine order, the source of which is akin to the principle of intelligence in our own souls'.[138] There are three elements to this widely adopted metaphysical system which come out more clearly in Caird's account than in any other, and these are worth bringing out in a little more detail.

4.3.1 Dialectic and progress

We learn more about Caird's metaphysics if we focus on something of a paradox that presents itself at first sight: very often we find in his writing what we might describe as a

---

[135] *Evolution of Theology in the Greek Philosophers*, II: 371.
[136] *Evolution of Religion*, I: 67.
[137] For example, *Evolution of Religion*, II:30; 'The Problem of Philosophy at the Present Time', 225.
[138] 'The Faith of Job', *Lay Sermons*, 304.

'direction of truth', but equally often he seems to tell us that the truth lies, not at the end of any given road, but in some kind of reconciliation between opposing paths.

To expand on this, again and again we find in Caird the claim that, over time, thought progresses in various directions towards the truth.[139] Note has already been made (in the context of his discussion of Kant) of his thesis that there takes place a development from the a posteriori to the a priori, and another example of the same sort of thing may be found in his essay, 'The Problem of Philosophy at the Present Time,' where he urges a similar progress in the direction of synthesis, a progress from multiplicity to unity. Against stoics, sceptics, and those who would follow Pope's injunction that 'the proper study of mankind is man', Caird argues that mind cannot shut itself up in its own sphere. We cannot know or realize ourselves without knowing the larger world or realizing its larger aims; for if we withdraw from the world we only reduce ourselves.[140] But our commitment is to more than just this synthesis; if we cannot keep separate subject and object, we cannot deny the rationality of reality itself, nor consequently maintain any absolute division in things. The urge for synthesis can stop nowhere short of absolute synthesis, the unity that embraces everything—God.[141] The path to philosophic truth is the path of fusion, the more we show that apparent differences or oppositions are really but one-sided abstractions from a higher organizational unity that embraces both, the closer we approach the truth. Nor are *a prioricity* and synthesis the only directions in which thought must properly travel. Caird further suggests that philosophical thought consists in rising from the particular to the universal,[142] and closely related to that, in an advance from the natural to the spiritual.[143] Equally importantly—although care must be taken to construe these terms correctly—truth is to be arrived at by moving in the direction of the concrete rather than the abstract. The path of increasing abstraction leads away from reality, the path of increasing concreteness towards it.[144] Taking all of these various directions together, a neat mechanism by which we could plot his final metaphysical position might seem to suggest itself. Is not the Absolute the culmination or zenith of all these tendencies? The point described by our highest concepts: a priori, unity, universality, spirituality, concretion, infinity.

But against this needs to be set another picture of Caird, as the great reconciler. His constant appeal to the doctrine of identity-in-difference, whereby all contrasts are held within and referred back to a higher unity that embraces both, makes him critical of the

---

[139] 'There is a certain trend or direction of progress from multiplicity to unity, from the natural to the spiritual, from the particular to the universal' (*Evolution of Religion*, I:62).

[140] 'The Problem of Philosophy at the Present Time', 202.

[141] 'The Problem of Philosophy at the Present Time', 203, 205.

[142] 'Religion is simply a higher form of that tendency which, in science, leads us to seek the universal beyond the particular, the one beyond the many' (*Evolution of Religion*, I:110–11).

[143] Caird speaks of 'the spiritual principle which urges him [man] forward in his unhasting, unresting course' (*Evolution of Religion*, I: 231).

[144] *Evolution of Religion*, I:150–1. 'the whole process of Hegel's philosophy is a movement from the abstract to the concrete' (*Evolution of Theology in the Greek Philosophers*, II: 247).

unswerving pursuit of any single idea or insight; for that can only lead to one-sidedness when the highest truth must give due acknowledgement to all points of view. Again and again he suggests that the reality is not to be found in any extreme position. Universal and particular, self and not-self, form and matter, analysis and synthesis—always, we need both of these.[145]

How are these opposing thoughts to be combined? The matter is very difficult and has vexed Caird's commentators; nowhere, perhaps, more so than with respect to that puzzling but ubiquitous term of his thinking, 'self-consciousness'. Is this something mental, or some sort of neutral mid-point which is neither subject nor object? The name itself suggests the former, and much of the time Caird speaks in that way. The lesson of Kant, which subsequent philosophies only develop not contradict, he tells us, is that in knowledge our mind meets not with something different but with itself:

in bringing more and more of the facts of the universe within his thought, man is not, so to speak, losing himself in the object, or taking into his mind an alien matter: he is only providing the appropriate nutriment for his growing intelligence. For the facts which he appropriates in knowledge are by the same process transmuted into the substance of the mind that grasps them, and so become the means to the development of the ideas which constitute it as a mind.[146]

But at times the result seems more symmetrical. In discovering the essential relation between self and object, we realize (argues Caird) that 'all our progress in knowledge of objects must deepen and widen our consciousness of the self; and all our knowledge of ourselves . . . must, in its turn, be an increase in our knowledge of the objective world.' We break down the alleged wall of division between them, and so stand on neither side.[147] Caird certainly did call himself an idealist, but complicates the point by adding that the idealism to which he is closest is that of Plato,[148] for whom ideas were 'primarily and emphatically objective' and whose idea of a thing was just 'the thing itself'.[149] But while it is clear how this distances Caird from any Berkleyean or psychological interpretation of idealism, it is unclear quite how if helps to relate him to the two poles of subject and object.

It will be recognized that the problem here is essentially the same as that which was raised above against Green, namely how if thought is just one side of a distinction abstracted from experience it can yet go on to constitute the whole of experience? But Caird's Hegelianism makes the solution to the puzzle somewhat easier to see. The key is to appreciate that dialectical transition from one point X to another Y, is much more than a simple movement from one element to its 'opposite' or 'negation'. Specifically it

---

[145]   See, for example, 'Metaphysic' (460–4) where he argues that during the early modern period religion became increasingly subjective while science became more and more objective, when what was needed was a fusion or synthesis between these one-sided extremes. This tendency to bring together seeming opposites was given even more prominence in the work of Caird's pupil, Henry Jones.

[146]   *Evolution of Religion*, I:158.

[147]   *Evolution of Religion*, I:136.

[148]   'Idealism and the Theory of Knowledge', 96.

[149]   'Idealism and the Theory of Knowledge', 95.

must be appreciated that Y has a nature of its own, that it is more than simply 'not X'. In this way while there is a genuine and permanent advance from X to Y, the starting point X is never wholly left behind and the movement is more like a synthesis than a lurch from one extreme to another. Thus, for example, the result of philosophical reflection is certainly universal, rather than particular, but it needs to be remembered that the genuinely universal is more than just the not-particular; it incorporates and relates itself to the particular. Likewise the ideal is not just the negation of the natural; it somehow includes it. It might almost seem as though there are two kinds of thought; thought as a part of reality and thought as constitutive of reality in its entirety. However, it is possible to view this not as a difference of kind but as one between the thought which constitutes our own reality and the thought which constitutes reality as a whole. As *our* thought grounds *our* reality, our thought perfected—that is, thought *itself*—may be supposed to ground reality *itself*. It is in just such terms that Green speaks. Our difficulty in seeing how ego and non-ego are both abstractions from thought stems from our confusing thought in itself (from which they stem) with the thought experienced by each of us, something which, as he puts it, 'is related to thought in its truth as the undeveloped to the full actuality'.[150]

4.3.2 The infinite

One of the tendencies of thought in which Caird believes most strongly is its drive to move from the finite to the infinite; experience starts with the finite but pushes on to the infinite, breaking down the barrier between them.[151] However, Caird's sense of the 'infinite' needs to be carefully understood.

Both we and the world as we encounter it present themselves to us as but limited islands of understanding set out against and conditioned by an unknown universe in space and time stretching out, without limits, on every side. But this consciousness of a limited world, argues Caird, presupposes a deeper consciousness of a world without limit, not in the trivial mathematical sense of not yet stopping—the mere endlessness of space and time—but in the true metaphysical sense of limiting itself. The finite object which points away from itself for its explanation shows that understanding cannot rest with anything but a self-bound self-determined whole.[152] The germ of this insight, that to recognize ourselves as finite we have first to have the idea of the infinite, Caird rightly attributes to Descartes[153]—although Descartes did not, of course, have quite the same Hegelian sense of the infinite that he endorses; a sense highly characteristic of British Idealism.

---

[150] Green, 'Herbert Spencer and G.H. Lewes', 432.

[151] *Evolution of Religion*, I:136.

[152] 'Metaphysic', 474–6. This argument from finite to infinite is very similar to one put forward by his brother John in his *Introduction to Philosophy of Religion* (112–22).

[153] 'Cartesianism', 280–4.

We get an even closer look at Caird's conception of the infinite in *The Evolution of Religion* where he compares it with that of two contemporaries, Max Müller and Herbert Spencer. For Max Müller the infinite is the negation of the finite. And as such, we can say nothing about this. For Spencer all thought is limitation or finitude and thus the infinite is what remains when all such limiting finitude is abstracted away. It is the underlying affirmative basis of the finite. But still the result is the same: we can say nothing about it. Caird argues that they both arrive at this common fate because, for all their difference, they make the same mistake. Setting the infinite *against* the finite, they limit it, and thereby turn it into another kind of finite.

What is needed instead is an alternative positive conception of the infinite. It is 'the unity of the differences of the finite,'[154] 'the all-embracing unity implied in all our consciousness of the finite'.[155] It must be conceived, 'not merely as that which the finite is not, but as that which includes and explains it; not merely as an indeterminate background of the finite but as a self-determining principle, which manifests itself in all the determinations of the finite without losing its unity with itself.'[156] There is, Caird insists, no ultimate distinction between the finite and the infinite[157]—although, as was noted above, this is not to say that the result is some neutral mid-point between the two.

4.3.3 *Individual psychology*

The discussion of Caird's interpretation of Kant drew attention to his opposition to any psychological or mentalist reading of the Critical Philosophy, and this point deserves to be emphasized. Although the temptation to do so, Caird appreciates, is strong to those brought up in the Lockean tradition, the relativity of all objects to the knowing self is *not* to be taken in a psychological sense.[158] Kant reaches a truth, which Aristotle too had grasped, in regarding mind as something universal in nature and the world it knows as something particular, namely that 'the intelligence is not one thing among others in the intelligible world, but the principle in reference to which alone that world exists'.[159] 'The world we know is a world which exists only as it exists *for us*, for the thinking subject; hence the thinking subject, the ego, cannot be taken as an object like other objects.'[160] As the source of space, time, and the categories that govern the world (especially causation), but not itself subject to them, the self is free—even if such a negative sense of liberty does not capture the whole depth of its freedom.[161]

---

[154] *Evolution of Religion*, I: 97.
[155] *Evolution of Religion*, I:102.
[156] *Evolution of Religion*, I:108.
[157] 'The Problem of Philosophy at the Present Time', 205.
[158] 'Metaphysic', 443.
[159] *Hegel*, 153.
[160] 'Metaphysic', 408; cf. *Hegel*, 117.
[161] *Hegel*, 118.

But, of course, it cannot be denied that we are *also* a part of that world and so it is vital, insists Caird, if confusion is to be avoided, that we learn to separate the conscious self or subject implied in all knowledge, from the empirical self which is one part of that known world, one object distinct from and alongside others. The former belongs to metaphysics, the latter to psychology.[162] But what is the relation between them, for they are not simply distinct or parallel points of view? On the contrary, the self-consciousness unity which grounds all reality is progressively realized or manifested in the life of the psychological individual.[163] As a natural being man is subject to external influence like any other, but as a simultaneously self-conscious being, he is also continually emancipating himself. An adequate understanding of human nature must find room for both of these points of view; 'it must conceive of man as at once both spiritual and natural; it must find a reconciliation between freedom and necessity'.[164] Caird, it would seem, wants to distinguish between a naturalistic psychology which treats man as just phenomena and a more adequate psychology that tries to take in his curious 'dual-standing'.

This does not exhaust all that Caird had to say on individual psychology. For looking more closely it may be wondered if he does not leave room, between the universal consciousness that grounds all reality and the experienced self of psychology, for a kind of individual self with metaphysical import. We catch a glimpse of this in writings such as his 1905 lay sermon on immortality. Using an argument that was to prove popular among Personal Idealists, he suggests that the spiritual experience of laying down one's life brings not moral death but growth,[165] and that 'if we think of the world as the manifestation of a rational and moral principle . . . we must regard it as existing for the realisation of that which is best and highest; and that best and highest we can hardly conceive as anything but the training and development of immortal spirits.'[166]

While this suggestion clearly has metaphysical implications, Caird never addressed how such immortality might be squared with his more universal Absolute. But certainly he did not think that the finite self could be the last or the final reality. Our minds stand out from the rest of the world as organically unified and, most importantly, self-conscious. But self-consciousness, which binds subject and object together in one whole cannot rest in mere finitude,

for no finite spirit is complete in itself. As finite, he is part of a greater whole, the member of a society which itself is but one phase of humanity, conditioned by all the other phases of it, and, indeed, by all the other elements that enter into the constitution of the universe. We can,

---

[162] 'Metaphysic', 447.
[163] 'Metaphysic', 448.
[164] 'Metaphysic', 451.
[165] *Lay Sermons*, 270–1; see also Chapter 6.3.5 below.
[166] *Lay Sermons*, 281; also, 276–7.

therefore, find that which is absolutely real or substantial only in a creative mind, from whom all things and beings must be conceived as deriving whatever reality or substantiality they possess.[167]

4.4 Comparison

The metaphysics of British Idealism is often dismissed as 'Absolute Theory' as though there existed a single doctrine to which they all ascribed. The three analyses just given should be enough to demonstrate that the actual situation was one of affinity rather than uniformity, but to fully establish the point it may be useful to make a few comparative remarks. But first of all it is worth noting something of the historical context.

Coming up to Balliol in 1855, Green was a Fellow there from 1860, and held the White's Chair in moral philosophy from 1877 until his death in 1882. His *Prolegomena to Ethics* was published posthumously in 1883, but the greater part had already been presented in lectures from at least 1878 onwards.[168] Coming as a senior student from Glasgow, Edward Caird entered Balliol in 1860 there striking up a life-long friendship with Green, who was a year younger than him. Following his degree he was for a while a junior fellow at Merton, before leaving Oxford in 1866 to become Professor of Moral Philosophy at Glasgow.[169] Bradley came up to Oxford in 1865 to University College. There is no record of his ever having met Caird (who left the next year) at that time, but it is known that he had contact with Green.[170] His *Ethical Studies* appeared in 1876, and his *Logic* in 1882, but full statement of his metaphysics had to wait until *Appearance and Reality* in 1893. Of course, in the task of helping to explain philosophical similarities and differences between them, these personal connections can only supplement and in no sense supplant the more fundamental philosophical ones.

4.4.1 Green and Caird

Clearly both Green and Caird espouse metaphysical systems in which the diversity of the universe is held together by an underlying 'principle of unity' which is more fundamentally spiritual or conscious than it is anything else. The world is for consciousnesses and cannot intelligibly be considered outside of this relation. Since both reject any hint of subjectivism and will not identify this consciousness with any finite mind, they need to say how it relates to finite minds, and here too they are very close. Caird's conception of the relation between consciousness itself and the individual

---

[167] *Evolution of Theology in the Greek Philosophers*, I:195.

[168] Nettleship, 'Memoir', cxxv.

[169] He eventually returned to Oxford as Master of Balliol College in 1893.

[170] Bradley attended some of Green's lectures, and what are undoubtedly his notes from these lectures have been reproduced in the collected works of both Bradley and Green (see note 10 to Chapter 3 above). Moreover a few of his undergraduate essays bear what appear to be comments by Green (Keene, 'The Interplay of Bradley's Social and Moral Philosophy', 87n.1) Of note also is a letter from 1872 or 1873 in which Bradley, along with some others, asked Green to join a philosophical essay society that they had formed, although it is not known whether Green did join (see *Collected Works*, 4:1–2).

psychological life, between freedom and natural law, is very similar to Green's understanding of the eternal mind as something which progressively realizes itself in finite consciousness.[171]

But despite these similarities it would be a mistake simply to identify their two positions, for there are also important differences. Caird voices two main criticisms of Green. He complains first of the remnant of Kantianism in Green's work which makes him suppose that our categories cannot apply to their source—the eternal consciousness. Green insists that we can only speak of it in negatives, that we can only know *that* it is not what it is,[172] but for Caird nothing can be beyond the grasp of reason. There seemed to him a contradiction between claiming both that reality is 'spiritual' and that we have no real or positive knowledge of its final nature;[173] although in his Preface to the memorial volume this is dressed up as a compliment—Green was one to work on the 'foundations' not the 'superstructure' and, feeling he had no right to views until he had subjected them to years of rigorous testing, his positions remained tentative.[174]

Of course (as was noted above and as Caird also observes) Green does not stick resolutely to his own restrictions and offers at least some 'metaphorical' hints as to the nature of the Absolute. But here too Caird voices a worry. He suggests that insofar as Green attempts to set out the idealist nature of the real, he has a tendency to subjectivism and psychologizing. To be sure, there occurs nothing so objectionable as Berkeley's 'mentalism' but Caird does detect overtones of something similar in Green.[175] His mind that makes relations has disconcerting similarities with Locke's.

From the other side, Green never lived long enough to criticize Caird's metaphysics, although his doubts about the over-enthusiastic and over-confident Hegelianism of his brother John (noted in Chapter 2)[176] would no doubt have been regarded as equally applicable to Edward. Where Green makes cautious suggestions, Caird ventures bold and sweeping assertions.

4.4.2 *Bradley and Caird*

As with Green and Caird, initial comparison of Bradley and Caird also presents a picture of similarity. Both philosophers develop systems of monistic idealism which, stressing the reconciling power of their Absolute, are more indebted to the Hegelian dialectic than is Green's. For both of them the Absolute is something which transcends

---

[171] Indeed, in explaining this point in his 1883 essay 'Metaphysics' (447) Caird appeals for support to Green's claim in his 1874 General Introduction to Hume's *Treatise* that that 'knowledge . . . is only possible as the progressive actualisation in us of a self-consciousness in itself complete, and which in its completeness includes the world as its object' (§152).

[172] 'Professor Green's Last Work', 560.

[173] Watson, 'Idealism of Edward Caird', 162.

[174] Seth Pringle-Pattison with Haldane, *Essays in Philosophical Criticism*, 5–6.

[175] 'Idealism and the Theory of Knowledge', 105. Caird's pupil, Mackenzie ('Edward Caird as Philosophical Teacher', 518) joins his teacher in thinking that Green's presentation of idealism tends towards such subjectivism as, somewhat later, did Seth Pringle-Pattison (*Idea of God*, 190–9).

[176] See above p.21.

the contradictions and differences of the world and, particularly, which transcends the distinction between subject and object.

But as before, closer inspection uncovers difference as well. There is no record of what Bradley thought about Caird, but his rejection of feeling or unconceptualized awareness as a source of knowledge must, for Bradley, have placed him among the rejected class of those who too closely assimilated thought and reality, those 'Hegelians' who would turn reality into a 'ballet of bloodless categories'.[177] Another difference between them concerns the reality of *time*. In some sense all three metaphysicians accept that time is but an appearance of an ultimately atemporal reality, but within that scheme there is room for difference, and it is Bradley who stresses most the ultimate unreality of time while Caird gives greatest emphasis to the essential temporality of all the Absolute's manifestations.

Certainly, if we look from the other side, these were grounds on which Caird was critical of Bradley. Here fortunately we have more material.[178] Caird's chief complaint was that Bradley used reason only to destroy and never positively; his thought was 'All blade and no handle'.[179] As critical as he was of Green's claims that the nature of the Absolute is inexpressible, Caird finds the same problem in Bradley's doctrine of thought's suicide, his picture of cognition as something which must develop until it ultimately destroys itself, its failure forlornly pointing towards something it was unable to achieve itself. Reason cannot be limited in this way. In short, Caird objected to Bradley's departure from the orthodox Hegelian fold; a point he well appreciated, describing himself in a letter to Bradley as 'an unregenerate Hegelian'.[180]

To Caird, Bradley's result is not just epistemically problematic—an attempt to reach behind thought—it is also metaphysically doubtful. He objects that in the great One beyond all discursive thought, everything just gets swamped together. Bradley's position was described earlier as 'monism' but this was a term Caird rejected for his own system. Monism for him, along with pantheism and mysticism, was the reduction of all diversity into featureless unity, and by contrast he strongly affirms the reality of diversity. He objects that Bradley's Absolute is too much like Spinoza's in which all differentiation is lost.[181] Of course, the objection is in a way unfair to Bradley, for he allows difference into his Absolute. But as merely felt and not discriminated by thought, or expressible in concepts, this concession is insufficient to appease Caird's rationalism.

---

[177] *Principles of Logic*, 591.

[178] As well as comments in Caird's published works, there are relevant letters to Henry Jones (see *Life and Philosophy of Edward Caird*, 188–95) and to F.H. Bradley himself (see Bradley *Collected Works*, 4: 9–10, 73–4, 76–7).

[179] Jones and Muirhead, *The Life and Philosophy of Edward Caird*, 206.

[180] 28 August 1893. In Bradley, *Collected Works*, 4:77.

[181] Jones and Muirhead, *The Life and Philosophy of Edward Caird*, 286–7, 298. Jones follows him in this objection, *Idealism as a Practical Creed*, 263–4.

4.4.3 Green and Bradley

The comparison between Green and Bradley yields the highest value of the three. The most startling similarity between their metaphysics is that both philosophers agree about the central place that must be given to *relations* in any attempt to understand our everyday experience, for both recognize the thoroughly relational character of that experience.[182] The world we know is saturated by a complex of relational linkages. Green finds relations at the heart of everything, while Bradley, in identifying what he calls the 'relational way of thought', brings out the manner in which all our basic categories are in one way or another relational. To condemn relations, he points out, is to condemn the entire world of ordinary experience.

But not only do they both consider relations utterly pervasive, they both take them very seriously. They are agreed that no attempt to understand reality could succeed in which relations were treated as somehow secondary or an afterthought. For both philosophers, unity is as important and basic as distinction. In this insight they join together in attacking the atomism of their empiricist predecessors. Nothing is wholly or ultimately separate from anything else, and the more you probe into experience the more relations you unearth. This resultant relational matrix uncovered is one source of their common monism.[183]

There is a second very important point of agreement between Green and Bradley. They concur, not just in the views they hold of their importance, but also in the accounts that they give of the origin of relations. Although their reasons for thinking this differ, and that difference will be considered below, both thinkers agree that relations come from us and not from external reality; they are our own mental creations not pre-existing realities awaiting discovery by us. Connected to this point, both philosophers hold also, not simply that it is thought which relates things together, but that it is the essence of thinking to generate such relations. That is the key function of mind. This stems, of course, from a common debt to Kant who emphasizes the distinctive work of the mind as one of synthesis.

If relations are integral to the world we experience, but nonetheless mental, it follows that that world is something through and through ideal, that is to say, something constructed by mind. This result is endorsed by both Green and Bradley, placing them squarely in that idealist tradition which sees the work of the mind in everything we experience; in which our concepts and categories are seen to flow, not from the world, but from us. This further Kantian debt is very clearly acknowledged in

---

[182] Instead of asking who influenced who here, arguably both owe their insight that relations provide the key to Lotze. And in this connection there exists an interesting exchange of letters between Jones and Bradley on Lotze (see Hetherington, *The Life and Letters of Sir Henry Jones*, 186–90; Bradley, *Collected Works*, 4:96–100.) An alternative possibility, worth exploring, is that their common interest in relations stems from their common interest in Herbart.

[183] See below (p.130) for an important qualification of this claim.

Green,[184] but remains rather more hidden in Bradley where the critical implications of the idea tend to shout much louder than its constructive significance.

But all is not agreement and it should be noted that these major similarities between Green and Bradley are partnered by some equally major dissimilarities. The most important of these can be very simply put: Green accepts relations while Bradley rejects them. For Green relations are real, for Bradley they are unreal. Green has no worries about the possibility or coherence of relations. Indeed, far from worrying about them, he holds up relationality as the very mark of reality itself. Reality is precisely the fixed and unalterable order of relations. Bradley, by contrast, worries deeply about relations and, looking at them from all angles, in the end judges them incoherent and impossible. Relationality, for Bradley, however permanent or pervasive it may be, far from being a badge of reality, is an incurable defect and a sign that we are dealing merely with appearance. For Bradley, in the last analysis, ultimate reality is something wholly non-relational (or as he prefers to put it, 'supra-relational'[185]).

Behind this ontological disagreement about ultimate reality lies a difference, not just in what is found acceptable, but also in the role that relations are seen to be playing. For Green relational thought unifies and binds together what would otherwise be distinct, it is the glue that holds the world together. Bradley, by contrast, sees relational thought as something disruptive and destructive, something that pulls apart what was originally together in a whole, the hammer that smashes the world apart. Bradley's point of view may seem perverse, but the idea behind it is not difficult. He does not want to deny that relations unify, but asks us to reflect more deeply on what that entails. You can only unify what is already disunified, he argues, and so relations, with their machinery of distinct terms and connecting links, are as much agents of disintegration as combination. They perversely offer to stitch back together what they at the same time pull apart.

This difference in their attitude towards relations connects interestingly with their relational holism noted above. At one level they are both monists because they believe that everything is related to everything else, and that nothing is so isolated as to be unaffected by its relations to its neighbours. But at a deeper level the picture changes. Green persists in thinking reality a unity because of its relational character. For Bradley, by contrast, at the deepest level, reality is a unity precisely *despite* its relations. Notwithstanding the attempts by our relational concepts to tear it asunder, it remains at bottom a non-relational unity.

Two qualifications are in order here. To say that Green accepts relations while Bradley rejects them is to draw the difference between them a little too sharply. Although he attacks the apparatus of terms and relations, Bradley accepts that beyond thought, in the Absolute, there does exist some kind of (non-relational) coming

---

[184] Kant's error for Green was simply that he did not go far enough in thinking through the consequences of the principles he established (*Prolegomena*, §41).
[185] *Appearance and Reality*, 494.

together of unity and diversity. Green, on the other hand, accepts that the unity-in-difference which relations claim to create for us is something mysterious, experienced in our own self-consciousness but not fully explained by it. In this way the contrast between the two philosophers closes slightly, and the issue becomes not whether differences can be brought together (which they both hold possible), nor whether this is mysterious (which they both accept it is), but whether this can in any sense be *thought* or not. Bradley thinks it a union forever beyond intelligible thought, something which we can see must be the case, but which we can never hope to grasp. Green, on the other hand, together with most of the other British Idealists, thinks it something we can intelligibly conceive because it is something uniquely revealed to us in our own self-consciousness. For Green, human self-consciousness, which he explicitly identifies with Kant's 'unity of apperception', provides the key to understanding the fundamental nature of reality; for Bradley, by contrast, it is just one more contradiction separating us from that reality.[186]

The second qualification concerns the use of relations as a criterion for reality. Whilst disagreeing, in the final analysis, with Green's idea that a thing's reality lies precisely in its relations, Bradley does see a limited role for this idea. His universe is a very democratic and full one offering at least a degree of reality to the worlds of myth, fiction, dreaming, and so forth. But how, within this crowd, can he pick out that subset which we commonly call the 'real world'? For this task he appeals, like Green, to relations, defining it as the universe of those things which are continuous in space with my body. It earns its place of pre-eminence because of its superior relational integrity; 'The order of things which I can construct from the basis of my waking body, is far more consistent and comprehensive than any other possible arrangement.'[187] Bradley and Green's methods of picking out 'reality' here are identical, the difference simply that the prize Bradley thinks he has captured in this net is smaller in scope and less fundamental in significance than that which Green claims to have caught.

Alongside that concerning relations, a further important contrast may be drawn between Green and Bradley's views regarding the relative roles of reason and experience in our investigation of reality. The explanation of Bradley's agreement with Green that relations are mental is that he finds them contradictory or impossible, and 'Reality is such that it does not contradict itself,' he tells us.[188] Thus, for him, their being mental is indicative of their *unreality*. But Green, it will be remembered, was trying to undermine precisely this traditional association of 'work of the mind' and 'that which is unreal'. Thus, far from following in his footsteps, Bradley is undoing all Green's efforts in this direction, and in a very real sense going back to Locke. 'Created

---

[186] Their differing attitudes towards self-consciousness have other consequences as well. Both philosophers reach idealist and monistic conclusions, in as much as Bradley's Absolute is parallel to Green's eternal consciousness. But Green (albeit tentatively) identifies his with God, something that Bradley's attitude toward the self absolutely precludes.

[187] *Essays on Truth and Reality*, 462.

[188] *Appearance and Reality*, 120.

by us' is once again contrasted with 'really there', and 'ultimate reality' to be thought of as the residue remaining once all input or contamination by 'us' has been removed.

As an anti-realist, Green accepts that we can know only what knowing itself has created, but he insists that what we know is none the less real for that. Moreover, as itself a product of our thought, the universe is rationally intelligible and may be uncovered through the use of our reason; for the world is relational and relations are something of which the knowing subject is conscious only because he *thinks*.[189] For Bradley, on the other hand, ultimate reality is unknowable or beyond thought, and intellect is consequently engaged on a hopeless quest, attempting to recover what it has already destroyed. With a gap opening up in this way between thought and reality, Bradley argues that our only true contact with uncontaminated being is in feeling or immediate experience, and hence that it is through feeling not reason that we come closest to knowing how things really are. Ultimate reality turns out to be a matter of feeling or experience, rather than thought. Green differs from Bradley, not so much by taking the opposite line, as by refusing to accept the sharp distinctions which Bradley here insists on. 'We deny that there is really such a thing as 'mere feeling' or 'mere thought,' he says, 'We hold that these phrases represent abstractions to which no reality corresponds.'[190] While, with respect to the Absolute, he holds that, 'It is one and the same living world of experience which, considered as the manifold object presented by a self-distinguishing subject to itself, may be called feeling, and, considered as the subject presenting such an object to itself, may be called thought.'[191] Looked at another way, the difference between Bradley and Green here could be put like this. While Bradley operates with a very strong nominalist intuition of reality as something particular, for Green universality is an eliminable aspect of what it is to be real.

Bradley's philosophical system is in many respects a development of Green's. He strengthens Green's admittedly sketchy arguments for the mind-dependence of relations, he realizes that the power of relations to unite presupposes a prior function of dissolution on their part, and he sees that if we are to criticize the data of experience for their conceptual or relational contamination we may not simply halt this critique where it suits us, but must press on to include the data of our own self-consciousness. But for each of these 'advances' there is a price to pay, and as a whole they tend to take his position in an anti-intellectualist, even a somewhat mystical, direction. Thus in the end it remains an open question whether we should view Bradley's philosophy as a legitimate and natural development of Green's or as its *reductio ad absurdum*. But certainly we see that it would be a great mistake to think of Bradley as belonging in any simple sense to 'the school of Green'.[192]

---

[189] 'Lectures on Logic', 171. 'Reason is self-consciousness' argues Green, and 'It is only as taken into our self-consciousness, and so presented to us as an object, that anything is known to us' ('Faith', 267).

[190] *Prolegomena*, §51.

[191] *Prolegomena*, §50.

[192] In this connection the fact that Bradley did not contribute to the memorial volume for T.H. Green is perhaps significant (although there exists no direct evidence bearing on the point either way).

4.5 The School of Absolute Idealism

Sketches completed of the three central systems of Absolute idealist metaphysics that came to dominate and define the British Idealist movement, it remains to show how these views were echoed in many other early Idealist philosophers, producing the effect of something close to a metaphysical orthodoxy. For if not doctrinal identity, undeniably there was close enough kinship between them to make it permissible to speak of a common metaphysical worldview—the philosophy of the Absolute.[193]

A very similar kind of monism may be observed, for example, in Nettleship. As early as 1889 in a short discussion of individuality we find him arguing that an individual is 'something that cannot be divided', that 'from which none can be taken away without the unity ceasing'. If the situation in which some object lies in any way shapes, affects, or colours it, such that to remove the context would alter or take away some part of the object's nature, then its individuality stands hostage to its surroundings. Strictly speaking, therefore, a complete individual could have no environment and would have to be all-embracing.[194] The monism of the Absolute.

Less strictly—'for everything except the absolute'—it may be allowed that individuality implies environment or limitation which, since that comes in degree, means that individuality also is a degree notion. Capable of being measured in two ways—by how much it takes within itself and by what it excludes against itself—'One might compare individuality to centre of gravity. Every material body has a centre of gravity. . . . On the other hand, each centre of gravity is determined by those about it.'[195] He envisions a fluidity in the scheme, both in terms of the framework chosen—one's centre of gravity may vary from one frame of reference to another; should we say, for example, that the poem lies in the poet or that the poet is to be found in the poem?—and in terms of the constantly shifting interplay between object and environment. 'The difficulty is to keep between the two extremes, as Aristotle might say, that of being nothing because one has only *one* centre, and that of being nothing because one has *no* centre; death by stagnation and death by dissipation.'[196]

For some, such as Bradley's colleague at Merton, William Wallace,[197] this general metaphysics of the Absolute emerged largely from their study of Hegel. Wallace never

---

[193] One name that might perhaps be expected to appear in this context is that of George Jamieson, whose 1895 *The Great Problem of Substance and its Attributes* puts forward a doctrine of the Absolute, as the all-comprehending and fundamental totality, the ground of all being and the source from which all particulars emanate. It is capable of being viewed, either objectively as Absolute Impersonal, out of which material reality is developed, or else in its subjective aspect as Absolute Personality, which he associates with Deity. Jamieson's idealistic Absolutism, however, is developed without use of—indeed in opposition to—the idealism of Kant and Hegel, which he regards as 'one of the most complicated and at the same time most mischievous structures ever built up by the perverted ingenuity of man' (*The Great Problem of Substance*, ix), and the main stream of British Idealism was quite uninfluenced by it.

[194] 'Individuality', 34.

[195] 'Individuality', 36.

[196] 'Individuality', 37–8.

[197] Wallace was elected in 1867. They overlapped from Bradley's election three years later until Wallace's untimely death in 1897.

made any attempt to set down systematically his own metaphysical position. Perhaps even more than Caird, he was content to develop his ideas by way of exposition and criticism of others—Epicurus, Lotze, Hegel, Kant, Schopenhauer—his accounts striving always to show forth their positive contributions, rather than attack their errors. But although in such accounts he rarely distinguishes with any explicitness between his own voice and that of whichever thinker he is expounding, no one can read his commentaries and be left in doubt about his philosophical standpoint. For example, almost as an aside, in the following (gentle) comments on the limitations of Kant's vision, we see his commitment to the broad principles of objective idealism.

Here and there, as in his aesthetic criticisms, there are glimpses vouchsafed to him of something within us and without us which proclaims the infinity in the finite and the universality in the individual. But the glimpses are distrusted under the prevailing sense that all is but an effect of the human position,—the inherent limitation of the human view.

'The great ideal realities of life' were acknowledged, Wallace continues, but only as ideas which human consciousness uses to regulate, round off, and unify the world, not as lying in the heart of the real itself.[198] And again, easy to miss as he expounds a point in Hegel's philosophy of nature, he lets slip that, 'We need hardly go to Hegel to be told that to know one thing thoroughly well is to know all things. The finite, which we inertly rest content with, would, if we were in full sympathy with it, open up its heart and show us the infinite.'[199] If the precise nature of that immanent infinity is left vague, that is deliberately so; for no more than any of the other Idealists would Wallace endorse the precise details of the Hegelian metaphysical system; each age must work these details afresh, he argues.[200] He is quite clear, however, that that system must be idealist; although ideas must not be hypostatized as some further mode of being, existing in abstraction from things as, in their different ways, both the realist and the subjective idealist are prone to do. Rather to have an idea of something is simply to know or think it. An idea is not given: it is a thing which is given in the idea. An idea is not an additional and intervening object of our knowledge or supposed knowledge. That a thing is our object of thought is another word for its being our idea, and that means we know it.'[201] Consequently truth must be understood not as a function of some comparison between an idea and something beyond, but as the result of growth in our knowledge, the successful bringing together of one idea with another.

A second figure to find himself under the general influence of Hegel was Bosanquet, who, in his contribution to the 1882 Green memorial volume, puts forward the view that there can be no sharp distinction between logic and metaphysics.[202] We can hardly

---

[198]   *Kant*, 218.
[199]   *Prolegomena*, 64.
[200]   *Prolegomena*, 12.
[201]   *Hegel's Philosophy of Mind*, Introductory Essay III, cv.
[202]   'Logic as the Science of Knowledge', 74.

say that the one deals with thought and the other with something beyond thought, for thought and reality imply each other. Nor can we see one as process and the other as product, the science of thinking versus the theories arrived at, for again these two depend on each other. The significance of this view, *for logic*, will be discussed at some length in Chapter 8, but it is worth noting too at this point its significance *for metaphysics*. On this view, suggests Bosanquet, 'ontological speculation will assume a less rigid form.'[203] Rather than treated in abstraction or in isolation, metaphysical matters must be settled by their overall ability to increase the coherence of experience.

Others followed Green more closely than they did Hegel. One enthusiastic supporter was D.G. Ritchie. In an 1890 essay on 'Natural Selection and the Spiritual World' Ritchie argues the need to recognize the existence of a spiritual principle, not in the exceptional, but everywhere as a condition of our knowing nature at all.[204] Defending the idealism that results, Ritchie argues that we may speak indifferently of 'Reality as such' or 'experience as a whole', since reality can have no meaning except insofar as it enters into some actual or possible experience. To suppose otherwise, that there is reality outside of all possible experience, is self-contradictory; for it is a claim to know that of which nothing may be known, since experience here is taken in the widest possible sense to include not just what we sense or feel, but what we think.[205] To object to such a wide use, to think reality given in sense but not thought, is unsustainable, for on the one hand what we are given in sense already involves judgement, while on the other, if reality is but what we think, it is not simply what you or I think, but what we would all think on the fullest information.[206] The echoes of Green here are strong.

To Green the eternal consciousness progressively manifests itself in the temporal expansion of human knowledge, which same growth Caird understands as the mind's gradual coming to full self-consciousness. In 1891 Henry Jones made interesting application of these ideas in relation to the poetry of Robert Browning, whose scepticism about human knowledge he takes exception to. The conciliatory nature of his idealism allows him to find a measure of truth in Browning's epistemic pessimism. Man, he admits, 'will never know reality, nor be able to hold up in his hand the very heart of the simplest thing in the world. For the world is an organic totality, and its simplest thing will not be seen, through and through, till everything is known, till every fact and event is related to every other under principles which are universal.'[207] But that is only half of the story.

---

[203] 'Logic as the Science of Knowledge', 75.
[204] 'Natural Selection and the Spiritual World', 115. See also his argument that 'a conception of the self as rational and universal . . . seems to be a necessary conclusion from the conditions of knowledge' in his *Natural Rights*, 96.
[205] *Cogitatio Metaphysica*, 85–8.
[206] 'What is Reality?', 81, 87, 91.
[207] *Browning as Philosophical and Religious Teacher*, 284–5.

The complete failure of knowledge is as impossible as its complete success. It is at no time severed from reality; it is never its mere adumbration, nor are its contents mere phenomena. On the contrary, it is reality partially revealed, the ideal incompletely actualized. Our very errors are the working of reality within us, and apart from it they would be impossible. The process towards truth by man is the process of truth *in* man; the movement of knowledge towards reality is the movement of reality into knowledge.[208]

Browning allows that God reveals himself to us in morality and in religion, but is it then reasonable to suppose that the matter is otherwise with knowledge?[209] If he sees in human love the manifestation of God's love, should he not take the same attitude towards human reason?[210] Though neither name is mentioned in the text, it is clear that this argument draws heavily on both Green and Caird. Of particular interest is the close connection Jones highlights here between knowledge and metaphysics, or we might even say the lack of connection, for in his argument epistemology is almost taken up bodily *into* metaphysics. Indeed only two years later we find him arguing that idealism neither contains nor needs an epistemology, because it recognizes no distinction between subject and object.[211]

Although always something of a maverick and an enigma at the same time, Bradley's metaphysics too exerted a strong influence. Some thirty years later in 1924 Mackenzie still felt it appropriate to describe *Appearance and Reality* as 'the most notable book, I suppose, in recent British Philosophy.'[212] Much adopted was his doctrine of degrees of truth and reality.[213]

---

[208] *Browning as Philosophical and Religious Teacher*, 285–6.

[209] *Browning as Philosophical and Religious Teacher*, 300.

[210] 'To be sure, no more than in morality, is completion or perfection ever attained in cognition, but since it lies in the very nature of such series to lack a final term, that is no mark against regarding them as manifestations of perfection' (*Browning as Philosophical and Religious Teacher*, 318).

[211] 'Idealism and Epistemology'. For further discussion of this essay see p.360.

[212] *Ultimate Value in the Light of Contemporary Thought*, 27.

[213] E.g. Bosanquet, 'Philosophy of Religion', 457; Seth Pringle-Pattison, *Idea of God*, 222; Illingworth, *Divine Immanence*, 187; Joachim, *The Nature of Truth*, §30ff; Mackenzie takes some issue with it ('The New Realism and the Old Idealism', 326–7).

5

Idealist Philosophy of Religion

5.1 The Victorian 'crisis of faith'

Looking back on the movement in which he himself had been a key player, John Henry Muirhead said that, 'British Idealism from the first has been in essence a philosophy of religion.'[1] And in this he seems correct; for of all the motivations for the emergence of idealistic philosophy and of all the reasons for its great success, by far the most important was its ability to respond to what has become known as 'the Victorian crisis of faith'.

By the 1860s what must then have seemed the easy faith of the early nineteenth century was straining under the onslaught of repeated intellectual challenges, and everywhere was felt to be under threat. Key aspects of this assault were biblical criticism, anthropology, the advance of natural science, and positivism. The Tübingen School of biblical criticism—the so-called 'higher criticism'—associated with F.C. Baur and his student D.F. Strauss had challenged traditional interpretations of scripture, casting doubt on the uniqueness of the Bible as an historical document and questioning the rationality of accepting any of its more supernatural claims. Combining such results with new anthropological insights into the myths and religions of other cultures could only further undermine the hitherto privileged position of Christianity. At the same time developments in natural science in the middle of the nineteenth century—geological discoveries of the age of the earth and the history of its development, Charles Darwin's theory of evolutionary biology,[2] and continual advances in physical understanding that, to many, seemed only to confirm materialism—produced a hitherto unimagined challenge to the reasonableness, not just of specific religious doctrines, but of the very belief in God itself. Giving to such advances themselves the status of scientific law, it is no surprise that many people were attracted to scientistic philosophy, most famously Positivism. The Positivist philosophy of Auguste Comte with its three-

---

[1] *The Platonic Tradition*, 197.
[2] *The Origin of Species* was published in 1859, *The Descent of Man* in 1871.

stage theory of human progress, from the theological (in which superstition reigns) through the metaphysical (in which humans resort to elaborate speculative explanations) to the 'positivist' (according to which everything is understood in terms of its true underlying causes and science itself comes to prominence as a kind of secular religion of humanity), offered to make historical sense of all these changes and exerted considerable influence on figures such as J.S. Mill, G.H. Lewes, and T.H. Huxley; all themselves influential voices in Britain. The retreat of superstition and metaphysical dreaming before the march of scientific reason was something that, in a certain light, many thought they could see happening all around them.

The crisis of faith which resulted from all this has been well-documented and is something that can be seen in many aspects of late Victorian culture. From the dogmatic atheism of figures such as G.J. Holyoake and Charles Bradlaugh, to the backwards-turning flight into traditional faith of the Oxford Movement, to the confused soul-searching of such figures as E.B. Pusey, F.D. Maurice, and the authors of the controversial, *Essays and Reviews* (1860), to the simple lament of Matthew Arnold's 'Dover Beach' (1867); everywhere we find the same sense that religious faith can no longer be taken for granted.

It was from this culture that Idealism rose, and directly to it that it spoke, for it was a crisis that exposed utterly the impotence of existing philosophies of religion. Empiricism, such as that set out in Mill's posthumous essays on religion, advanced a faith so tentative that the slightest challenge seemed able to reverse it, while the common-sense tradition of Hamilton and Mansel proved itself epistemically too weak to offer up anything more than the emptiness of Herbert Spencer's 'unknowable' or of Matthew Arnold's 'eternal *not ourselves* that makes for righteousness'.[3] By contrast, Idealism offered a path by which unassailable philosophical enquiry might contribute to the secure rebuilding of what had been lost. Not always explicit or orthodox, there ran a deep religious current through all of the idealist thinkers,[4] and a common conviction that human reason had the power not only to reach the transcendent but to give it sufficient content to ground human hopes. Idealism thus answered a pressing need of the age, seeming to many to offer a rational re-interpretation of religion which, at the same time as shedding itself of blind faith, was able to avoid agnosticism or atheism, and thereby hold on to the things of deeper value and significance in traditional belief. It was something that would satisfy both people's spiritual needs and the intellectual rigours of the new scientific way of thinking, and as such it revitalized philosophy of religion.[5] Nowhere perhaps is this more evident than with those who might be called the four 'founding fathers' of British Idealism: T.H. Green, John and Edward Caird, and F.H. Bradley whose philosophies of religion will form the subject of this chapter.

---

[3] Mill, *Three Essays on Religion*; Spencer, *First Principles*, Part I; Arnold, *Literature and Dogma*, 322.

[4] Even the atheism of McTaggart is no real contradiction to this claim. See Chapter 11.4.

[5] Interesting examples of that new life include Watson's *Christianity and Idealism* (1897) and D'Arcy's *Idealism and Theology* (1899).

As typifies their overall approach, and in contrast to contemporary philosophy of religion which is pursued in relative isolation from questions of general metaphysics, it will be seen that the Idealists made metaphysics central to their religious vision. So much so that the scope of this chapter may be felt to overlap considerably with the last. Hardly surprising, they would have replied, since to study God, the infinite, the foundational of everything, just is to study ultimate reality itself. Since all four were committed to the metaphysics of Absolute Idealism that equation might tempt us to expect a monolithic uniformity with respect to their philosophy of religion. In fact, however, as we shall see, the matter is quite otherwise, in that each of these philosophers fastened on to different aspects of the contemporary crisis of faith.

5.2 T.H. Green

The most important idealist voice in support of religion was that of T.H. Green. The son of a Yorkshire clergyman, religious questions were always central to his thinking, and upon graduation from Jowett's Balliol he considered a career as a dissenting preacher.[6] He opted instead for one in academia but, though probably the first layman to be made a Tutor at Balliol,[7] by his own confession his interest in philosophy was wholly religious, in the sense that all philosophy was for him 'but the reasoned intellectual expression of the effort to get to God',[8] and indeed much of his earliest work in that career was explicitly theological. Drawing on contemporary scholarship he lectured on biblical criticism,[9] and by the end of 1863 he was planning to translate Baur's *Geschite der Christliche Kirche*; a plan that never came to fruition, though the ideas which grew out of the project made their way into the important unpublished paper, 'An Essay on Christian Dogma'.[10] He also gave on two occasions seminal lay sermons in Balliol College; in 1870 he spoke on 'The witness of God' and in 1877 on 'Faith'.[11]

5.2.1 The search for a rational faith

The 'Essay on Christian Dogma' begins with a bold assertion that can leave no doubt where Green stands in relation to orthodox evangelical Christianity. At a time when the possibility of faith is the most pressing of all questions for any serious person, 'it is a pity,' he says, 'that the answer should be confused by the habit of identifying Christianity with the collection of propositions which constitute the written New

---

[6] Nettleship, 'Memoir', xxxv.

[7] 'Memoir', lxim.

[8] Letter to Henry Scott Holland 1872 (Printed in Green's *Collected Works*, V:442).

[9] 'Memoir', xci. Selections from these lectures may be found in his *Collected Works*, I:120–1, 124–5, 128–9, 227. Extracts from his lectures on the New Testament may be found his *Collected Works*, III:186–9, 190–206, 207–20, 221–9.

[10] 'Memoir', xxxvii–viii. Green had the highest opinion of Baur describing him as 'nearly the most instructive writer I ever met with' (ibid.). There is no date for composition of the essay but, read to the Old Mortality Essay Society (*Collected Works*, III:vi), it is likely an early piece.

[11] 'Memoir', xcii.

Testament.'[12] The kind of faith Green has in his sights here is one that might be termed 'traditional', one anchored in belief both in the literal truth of certain supernatural dogmas and in the actual historical occurrence of certain miraculous events, on the basis of the written evidence come down to us in the Christian Bible.

The 'pity' of such a viewpoint is two-fold; it not only 'imperils the faith by making it rest on an untenable dogma, but puts out of sight the vital essence of things necessary for salvation'.[13] There can be no question of dogmatically separating off some compartment of reality or region of belief, given by authority (either ecclesiastical or miraculous), and from which critical reflection is excluded—whatever presents itself as fact or truth must stand before the same court of human reason.[14] But if reason is let in, there can equally be no hope of escaping its corrosive power upon traditional beliefs. Interestingly for Green the resultant impossibility of belief in the supernatural is less an upshot of scientific advance or critical history, than of a specifically *idealist* reading of theism; 'for to me the philosophical condition of Theism is that there is nothing real apart from thought, whereas the doctrine of miracles implies that there is something real apart from thought, viz. "nature," but that thought has once or twice miraculously interfered with it.'[15] Miracles call for an unacceptable dualism. In consequence, argues Green (and here he is closely following Baur) rather than our experience of miraculous happenings giving birth and ground to our religious belief, it is those beliefs that lead us to see the miraculous in the world around us, to interpret the world in the light of our faith. Thus, although St Paul undoubtedly did regard the death and resurrection of Jesus as a real historical event, it was his daily personal experience of spiritual death and resurrection with that Christ 'that gave reality in his eyes to the supposed historical events', not *vice versa*.[16] Although he had never seen it, his inner experience of its effects, told him that Christ's resurrection must have happened. Dogma is the expression of faith.

But if traditional faith can no longer be maintained, more importantly urges Green, such a faith is not even *worth* maintaining,[17] for our best effort to settle abstruse and difficult questions of historical fact or theological dogma tells nothing about what really matters; the moral condition of our souls. 'It is not on any estimate of evidence, correct or incorrect, that our true holiness can depend. Neither if we believe certain documents to be genuine and authentic can we be the better, nor if we believe it not, the worse.'[18] The kingdom of heaven is not a university.

But in what, if not in such propositional assent, does true faith consist, if it is to exist at all? There are two parts to Green's answer, one looking backwards in time and the other looking forwards. To begin with, he urges that we need to recapture the original essence of faith as it existed in primitive Christianity. For propositional assent to dogma on the basis of belief in historical miracles was not at all the nature of the faith of Jesus,

---

[12] 'Christian Dogma', 161.   [13] 'Christian Dogma', 161.   [14] 'Faith', 266.
[15] Letter to Henry Scott Holland 1872 (Printed in Green's *Collected Works*, V:443).
[16] 'Faith', 258.   [17] 'Faith', 266.   [18] 'Faith', 260.

St Paul or the early church. For them faith was not an issue of intellectual assent, but a matter of personal experience, an 'immediate consciousness'[19] or intuitive certainty of the divine. As something given, as a lived experience not a theology, it was essentially unreasoning and felt no need to demonstrate its credentials or theorize about its own nature.[20] However, the further history passed from those small, inspired, and informal beginnings, the more faith become a sacred trust to be preserved and passed down the ages, taking on a distant, rigid and institutional character. In such a context it could no longer present itself simply as a kind life to be lived, but became instead a set of dogmas to be believed.[21] No longer 'the immediate expression of the highest possible spiritual life', it became 'a theology'[22] founded on new canonical writings. Yet this process of alienation from our faith could never completely separate us from God, and with Luther and the Reformation we see a return to something nearer that original sense of faith, in which 'the individual breaks loose from the outward constraint of alien ordinances, and places himself in a spiritual relation to God'.[23] And even now it remains true that for the spiritually alive, 'faith is a personal and conscious relation of the man to God, forming the principle of a new life, not perhaps observable by others, but which the man's own consciousness recognises.'[24] The 'practical Christian faith' neither essentially involves, nor ultimately depends on 'assent to propositions upon evidence',[25] but is rather a matter of the spirit with which we live. 'Its object is not past events, but a present reconciled and indwelling God'.[26] A life-changing transformation of consciousness, faith is 'a certain attitude or disposition which belongs distinctively to [the] 'inner man' and gives our worth as moral and spiritual beings'.[27] But, as such, it is also the beginning of God at work within us, and rather than an acceptance of revelation, 'it is the first stage of the revelation itself, of which love and knowledge are to be the completion'.[28]

The point of Green's historical analysis is not some evangelical or low church attempt to escape to or recreate the early Christian past, for he knows that that is impossible; we cannot simply forget two thousand years of intellectual advances. Rather we must look forwards and, if our intellect is ever to find satisfaction, if we are ever to reach a Christianity both living and defensible, we must discover a way to reconcile faith and reason. We need to 'penetrate behind the cloak of theological artifice' in order to discover 'a meaning true, permanently, and for us'.[29] Dogma has become untenable to us, but philosophy is the tool that can transmute its essential message, without loss of meaning, into a new coinage that we *can* hold; dogma must be transformed into philosophy.[30] It was Green's firm conviction that whatever was

---

[19] 'Christian Dogma', 164.   [20] 'Christian Dogma', 167.
[21] 'Christian Dogma', 169.   [22] 'Christian Dogma', 163.
[23] 'Christian Dogma', 179. For more on the great value and importance Green attached to the Protestant reformation and forms of life it engendered, see his 'Four Lectures on the English Revolution'.
[24] 'Faith', 260.   [25] 'Faith', 262.   [26] 'Faith', 263.
[27] 'Faith', 259–60.   [28] 'Faith', 256.   [29] 'The Witness of God', 232.
[30] 'Christian Dogma', 182. 'God is not wisely trusted when declared unintelligible . . . God is for ever reason; and his communication, his revelation, is reason' ('The Witness of God' 239). 'Christian dogma must be retained in its completeness, but it must be transformed into a philosophy. Other thinkers have assailed the

essential in Christianity could be restated in rationally acceptable terms. And this he urges is the task now before us. It will be feared, of course, that this is a proposal to *replace* religion with some alternative philosophical construction, but Green is clear that philosophy should not bring anything new into the world; its task is to 'but interpret, with full consciousness and in system, the powers already working in the spiritual life of mankind'.[31]

It will no doubt be asked how do these two answers fit together? Is Green saying that religion consists in immediate consciousness of a direct relation between us and God, or in the philosophical reconstruction of the underlying message behind ancient outworn myth and dogma? What have religious experience and philosophical theology to say to each other? They may seem opposed, but Green insists that any mindset which brings into conflict practical religious experience and its philosophical interpretation is itself flawed, for they are in truth but two manifestations of one and the same spirit and, as such, incapable of any real disagreement.[32] Their common source is, he argues, self-consciousness.[33] The argument here is precisely that of the metaphysics of knowledge which later appeared in his *Prolegomena to Ethics*, and which was examined in the previous chapter. Green's claim is that it is only for self-consciousness that the question of knowledge arises, but in its rational manifestation this search for knowledge, though it can never be completed,[34] presupposes that there is a reality, an ideal whole, 'one, complete, and absolute', to which it approximates; it presupposes (to put it another way) faith.[35] The springs of faith and reason may seem to differ, but in truth they have a common source and 'it is only a false abstraction of one from the other, reducing religion to an emotion and philosophy to a formula, that brings them into antagonism'.[36] In any one individual heart they may seem quite alien, but viewed in a wider context, 'in that fullness of their tendencies and relations which can be seen only in the history of thought' religion passes constantly into philosophy, while philosophy is but one manifestation of our spiritual life.[37]

5.2.2 God as the Absolute

What would it be to rethink religion using the tools of idealistic philosophy? The upshot of Green's programme may be looked at either from the widest angle or in some of its more specific applications. At its most basic the salvation of religion may be expressed in one word, 'idealism'. In his philosophical proof of a spiritual principle at

---

orthodox foundations of religion to overthrow it. Mr Green assailed it to save it' (Arnold Toynbee's Preface to his *The witness of God and Faith: two lay sermons*, 8).

[31] 'Popular Philosophy in its Relation to Life', 93.
[32] 'Faith', 264.
[33] 'Faith', 266–7.
[34] 'Nature remains to us an endless series in which the knowing of anything implies of itself something further to be known' ('Faith', 267).
[35] 'Faith', 267–8.
[36] 'Popular Philosophy in its Relation to Life', 120.
[37] 'Popular Philosophy in its Relation to Life', 121.

work in and behind all things—the ultimate metaphysical position he outlines in the *Prolegomena to Ethics*—Green in one stroke combats both atheism and agnosticism as, making place for meaning, value, purpose, and freedom in the universe, he challenges the rise of deterministic materialism. In the 'Metaphysics of Knowledge' we have a proof of the existence of God.

Green is not shy of identifying the eternal consciousness with God.[38] As an infinite and timeless consciousness expressing supreme moral goodness, Green's eternal consciousness has much in common with the traditional conception of God. But it must also be stressed that his supreme being is not something external to the world, but rather something thoroughly immanent in it. The relational world, if it is to have any reality beyond our knowing, presupposes 'the action of some unifying principle analogous to that of our understanding'.[39] Even more strongly he speaks of the 'consciousness which constitutes reality and makes the world one'.[40] Although a strand of thinking undeniably present within orthodox religious belief, not all traditionalists have felt comfortable placing this much emphasis on the immanence of God, for to do so smacks of pantheism.

5.2.3 A religion of moral and social duty

However, the immanence of God in the external world is not the immanence which interests Green the most, for, moving from the metaphysical to a more human perspectives, he argues that 'God is not to be sought in nature, nor in any beginning or end of nature, but in man himself.'[41] However much our conception of the world as a whole may presuppose God as the 'relational glue' holding it together, his is a presence even more manifest in the life of man. Green has two points here.

First, God is known, not as an external object through some act of intuition, but within, for 'the one divine mind gradually reproduces itself in the human soul',[42] and thus it is in ourselves that we will find God, if we are to find him at all; 'in being conscious of himself man is conscious of God, and thus knows that God is, but knows what he is only so far as he knows what he himself is.'[43] Man is not divine *simpliciter*, but does contain within himself seeds of divinity, seeds that may be cultivated and grown. In part this is an epistemic doctrine, the idea that in growing knowledge we gradually reproduce within ourselves the understanding of God, but in no small part too it is an appeal to traditional Protestant Christian ideas of God as the still small voice within.

This last point is important, for secondly, while it is true that God realizes himself in our knowledge, most importantly of all he realizes himself in the particularities of our moral life.[44] The work of faith 'which is at once God's and our own . . . is summed up in the one word, charity, or Christian love',[45] from which we may straightaway see

---

[38] He speaks of 'the complete self-consciousness, or God' (*Introduction to Hume*, §152) and describes God as 'the eternal spirit or self-conscious subject which communicates itself, in measure and under conditions, to beings which through that communication become spiritual' (*Prolegomena*, §184).
[39] *Prolegomena*, §29.   [40] *Prolegomena*, §51.   [41] 'Faith', 265.
[42] *Prolegomena*, §180.   [43] 'The World is Nigh Thee', 227.
[44] 'Christian Dogma', 184.   [45] 'Witness of God', 245.

that it is not simply in the individual, but in the *social* sphere, that God is revealed. God is active working through 'all the agencies of social life'.[46] For those used to thinking of God in more dramatic and external ways, 'our very familiarity with God's expression of himself in the institutions of society, in the moral law, in the language and inner life of Christians, in our own consciences',[47] and the very modesty of that idea, may blind us to its truth, but it takes only a little historical knowledge to see that this is the principle that lay from its inception at the very heart of Christianity. It was, argues Green, St John who first clearly explained the notion of 'an immanent god, a God present *in* the believing love of him and the brethren'[48] which 'needs no evidence of the presence of God, or the work of Christ the spirit, for it is that presence and work itself.'[49]

Green is very concerned to embed this moral and social manifestation of God in time, holding that the history of civilization may be seen as the progressive revelation of Christ. And he is certainly optimistic about human moral progress, believing that civilization marches forwards into more morally advanced forms; though he recognizes that progress is not brought about without reform or struggle. But while this historic revelation serves in one way to concretize the message of Christianity, in another it allows him to avoid pinning himself down. For he insists that Christianity cannot be captured in any one institution, or given form of words, or point in time; it is rather the expression of a 'common underlying spirit' gathering all of its many manifestations into one.[50] Its revelation is not made in a day, a generation, or even a century.[51] It is not even in fact a revelation that is ever finished; 'never complete' but 'constantly gaining in fullness',[52] it presents us in the form of history with an ever 'unexhausted series' of manifestations.[53]

Compared with traditional orthodox theologies Green's religion here is strongly non-supernatural, but should not be read in more naturalistic or reductionist a fashion than Green intends; for instance, as simply reducing religion to morality or citizenship, as saying that there is no more to religion than one's moral and civic duty. While it may be true for Green that religion is a vital social institution, and that citizenship becomes 'a form of divine service',[54] there is more to divine service than simple citizenship. Anything created on earth is but a finite and temporal appearance of a condition, in its true nature, both infinite and eternal.

In a similar fashion Green's God, immanent within us, is sometimes given an excessively naturalistic reading. He says that 'God is identical with the self of every man in the sense of being the realisation of its determinate possibilities, the completion of that which, as merely in it, is incomplete and therefore unreal.'[55] God is a being with whom the human spirit is identical 'in the sense that He *is* all which the human spirit is capable of becoming'.[56] But is such a divine being anything more than 'the best of us';

---

[46] 'The Witness of God', 240. [47] 'Faith', 270.
[48] 'The Witness of God', 244. [49] 'The Witness of God', 243.
[50] 'The Witness of God', 240–1. [51] 'The Witness of God', 239.
[52] 'The Witness of God', 237. [53] 'The Witness of God', 240.
[54] Boucher and Vincent, *British Idealism and Political Theory*, 37.
[55] 'The World is Nigh Thee', 227. [56] *Prolegomena*, §187.

'the good we might become'? Some interpreters have thought not. Colin Tyler, for example, sees such thoughts as signifying a thoroughgoing domestication of the divine and argues that Green's eternal consciousness is not some ontological over-being, but rather just an immanent potential within each of us. Each of us has, or better *is*, an eternal consciousness which progressively manifests itself through our temporal lives. On his interpretation, he insists, an atheist can happily believe in the eternal consciousness.[57] But again, and without denying its measure of truth, such an interpretation seems to push Green further in the naturalistic direction than he ever intended. Green seems clear that in appeal to the eternal consciousness we invoke a force greater than ourselves; a force whose activity 'is for us and may be in us, but it is not of us'.[58] It is true that God exists in us, but conversely it is equally true for Green that God is a being 'in whom we exist; with whom we are in principle one'.[59] In explicit rebuttal of such a reading, Green urges that we should not reject his view on the grounds that it makes God 'no more than a man'. For, appealing to the idealist doctrine that any assertion of identity 'not only admits of but implies difference or change',[60] he argues that we could not be identical to God unless God were also *more* than us. As oak to acorn, he is what we might become, but since that potential for growth is unlimited and we are only finite beings, he is also something radically other than us; the infinite over against the finite.

5.2.4 De-mythologizing religion

Whatever the precise details of its interpretation, an emphasis on the immanence of God in man allows Green to return to the miracles behind Christianity and reinterpret them in a philosophical fashion.

To take the incarnation, for example, any literal interpretation of this as an event in historical time in which divine nature took on human nature to form one person is simply impossible. For whatever Christ is, he is from all eternity, not momentarily.[61] While to give him two natures is to imply 'a double consciousness', something as unintelligible as it is miraculous.[62] Nor is a 'traditional' conception of Christ's nature just hard to maintain, it is positively harmful to do so, for, as Christ is 'externalised and mystified', the miraculous comes to overpower the moral and the spiritual, to the eventual corruption of our religious life.[63] And so the time has come to leave behind a belief in Christ as the physical manifestation of God in the life of one historical individual for belief in him as 'a person now spiritually present to us and in us'.[64] More specifically we should view Christ as the 'ideal man',[65] the model of life that would amount to full manifestation of God on earth, and the end to which all our moral striving points. Christ is the leader we all seek to follow,

---

[57] Tyler, *Thomas Hill Green and the Philosophical Foundations of Politics*, 26–31.
[58] 'The Witness of God', 234.   [59] *Prolegomena*, §187.
[60] 'The World is Nigh Thee', 225.   [61] 'The Incarnation', 207.
[62] 'Christian Dogma', 175.   [63] 'The Witness of God', 242.
[64] 'The Incarnation', 220.
[65] 'The Incarnation', 208; cf. Martineau on Christ above pp.32.

the perfect archetype we all try to reproduce, the supreme manifestation of the potential we all have within us. He is for us *a picture* of God. In Green's own words:

All religion . . . consists in the presentation of the objects of thought under the forms of imagina-tion . . . For religion to exist, we must in some mode imagine God, and the most nearly adequate imagination of him is as a man in whom that which seems to be the end of moral disciple and progress has been most fully attained.[66]

In other words, not merely Jesus, but all human beings, express divine incarnation; the only difference is one of *degree*. To be sure, this is not how the earliest Christians saw matters; to them the actual occurrence of the miracle of incarnation seemed an essential tenet of faith. But even for them, argues Green, and as we noted above for St Paul, their Christian faith was not derived from their understanding of the events that had occurred but rather was the precondition of their interpretation of those events. This point understood, presses Green, the highest faith can even dispense with any such belief.[67]

A similar de-mythologizing process can be seen at work in Green's analysis of the doctrine of the atonement. He argues that 'the primary Christian idea is that of a moral death into life, as wrought for us and in us by God',[68] a fact illustrated for us by the death–resurrection story, whose message is precisely that the regenerative power of self-sacrificial love should be understood as the supreme and central principle of the universe. From which we see that:

A death unto life, a life out of death, must, then, be in some way the essence of the divine nature—must be an act which, though exhibited once for all in the crucifixion and resurrection of Christ, was yet eternal—the act of God himself. For that very reason, however, it was one perpetually re-enacted, and to be re-enacted, by man. If Christ died for all, all died in him: all were buried in his grave to be all made alive in his resurrection. It is so far as [Christ] . . . thus lives and dies in us, that he becomes to us a wisdom of God, which is righteousness, sanctification, and redemption. In other words, he constitutes in us a new intellectual consciousness, which trans-forms the will and is the source of a new moral life.[69]

But if it is the heart of the Christian message, the fact of universal significance, the death–resurrection event cannot simply be isolated to one man or one place and time. There is no need to deny that it did historically occur, but the more important thing is to see is that it is something essentially eternal and continually re-enacted by man, whenever he dies to his lower self for the sake of others.[70] What Green is speaking of here is inner transformation. The appropriation of Christ's sacrifice is not the coming to believe in some historical fact, but the taking on of an identical spirit of self-sacrifice; 'Our mind must become Christ's, as Christ is God's. Our very self-consciousness, crucified with him, must cease to be our own. Only then can our works, as being of God that worketh

---

[66] 'The Incarnation', 219.   [67] 'The Incarnation', 219.
[68] 'Witness of God', 236.   [69] 'Witness of God', 233.
[70] It may be speculated that this was an influence on Collingwood's doctrine of history as re-enactment.

in us, work out the true salvation, the deliverance from the self-seeking self.'[71] A person and act originally tied to one time and place must become a principle or idea endlessly re-enacted. It seems odd, perhaps, to say that Christ is but 'an idea, or form of intellectual consciousness',[72] that what was first known as a concrete intuition must become an abstract idea of reason,[73] but it was Green's view that since in truth 'all moral action begins from ideas' to say so is in fact 'the very reverse of reducing him to an impotent abstraction'.[74] Ideas move the world. Nor should we make the mistake of thinking of ideas as trivial local creations. True, an idea may be our own invention, but equally, like this, the idea of Christ, it may be a communication from God himself.[75]

5.2.5 The influence of Green's philosophy of religion

Green's philosophy of religion was of immense importance. Initial influence was confined to Oxford and to his pupils, two of whom, Henry Scott Holland and Charles Gore, went on to become important theologians.[76] But shortly after his delivery of the second, both Lay Sermons were published (with a Preface by Arnold Toynbee) and, reproduced also in the 1888 *Collected Works*, they went a long way to disseminate Green's religious ideas beyond a merely Oxford-based circle.

We get a glimpse of their influence (and of his) in the novel *Robert Elsmere* (1888) by Mrs Humphry Ward, the wife of a Brasenose College don, who knew well the chief figures of contemporary Oxford life. It tells the story of a young man who, on coming up to Oxford, falls under the spell of his Tutor (Mr Grey) and who, subsequently influenced by the teachings of critical history, loses his faith, leaves the church he has only recently joined and takes up instead a life of social service in the East End of London. Grey is a thinly veiled portrait of Green—to whom the book is in fact dedicated—and Green's lay sermon itself even forms one important episode of the book, which quotes directly from the sermon.[77] But perhaps the most significant thing is the enormous success of the book; it was an immediate hit and final sales reached around a million copies.[78]

5.3 John Caird

At the same time as Green in Oxford was working out his ideas on religion, parallel processes were at work in Scotland, in the minds of the two brothers, John and Edward Caird. John Caird, the elder of the two, and senior by sixteen years to Green, came only late to academia, following a highly successful career in the Church of Scotland as a famous, if essentially orthodox, preacher. Suffering from the considerable stress of such success, he moved in 1849 to a quiet post at Errol, on the Firth of Tay. It was here that he

---

[71] 'Witness of God', 234.   [72] 'Witness of God', 235.   [73] 'Christian Dogma', 182.
[74] 'Witness of God', 235.   [75] 'Witness of God', 235.
[76] Green's influence is, for example, much in evidence in the 1889 collection of essays on the Incarnation which Gore edited, *Lux Mundi*.
[77] *Robert Elsmere*, 58–9, 330 and 536 (= 'Witness of God', 231–5, 238, and 246).
[78] Richter, *The Politics of Conscience*, 28, 379 n. 44.

found the leisure for serious reading and thought, and began to take on board the new thinking of the German Idealists and to question the ideas of the Scottish Common Sense school in which he had been educated. In 1863 he was persuaded by friends to apply for the Chair of Theology at his old university, Glasgow, to which he was duly appointed that same year; rising eleven years later to the position of Principal of the university, a post which he held until his death in 1898. In philosophical terms his most important piece of work was his 1878–9 Croall lectures which were published in 1880 in revised and enlarged form under the title, *An Introduction to the Philosophy of Religion*. His Gifford lectures, *The Fundamental Ideas of Christianity* (first given in 1892–3 and 1895–6) and three volumes of addresses and sermons were all published posthumously.

5.3.1 *The vindication of reason*

Like Green, Caird saw reason and more specifically idealism as the ship that would rescue Christianity out of the storm that was the Victorian crisis of faith. He wrote to a friend, of his own *Introduction to the Philosophy of Religion*, 'I shall be satisfied, if it leads some few who are in doubt on the highest matters, to see that Christianity and Christian ideas are not contrary to reason, but rather in deepest accordance with both the intellectual and moral needs of man.'[79] The path of thoughtful enquiry once started upon must be seen through to its end—'If you begin with reason and criticism you must go on with them . . . the wounds of reason can only be healed by reason.'[80] However, Caird was more explicitly indebted to Hegel than Green;[81] his *Introduction* is in effect a re-presentation in English of Hegel's *Lectures on the Philosophy of Religion*, while the guarantee that philosophy can never take us *away* from truth, however much it may seem to, for him derives from the very axiom of Hegelian rationalism—the conviction that what is real is rational and that what is rational is real.[82]

There is, in Caird's mind, no other viable approach to religious questions. It might be challenged that religion is a subject that lies altogether beyond the bounds of our limited cognitive capacities, and is hence something about which we ought to remain agnostic. But God then can only be for us the great unknown, or the 'unconditioned', to use Herbert Spencer's term, the philosopher that Caird singles out for special criticism in this regard. And such an attitude is simply absurd; we cannot simultaneously hold that God exists and yet that we know nothing about him. If our knowledge is truly limited to the finite world, then the correct conclusion to draw concerning the infinite is that no such thing exists, or that the assertion of its existence is meaningless.

---

[79] Quoted in Edward Caird 'Memoir' in *Fundamental Ideas of Christianity*, cxxxi. As Edward himself put it, 'Christianity and Idealism were the two poles of my brother's thinking, and the latter seemed to him the necessary means for interpreting the former' (cxli.).

[80] *University Addresses*, 189.

[81] Green in fact complained that 'he has been too much overpowered by Hegel' (Review of John Caird's *Introduction to Philosophy of Religion*, 146).

[82] *Introduction to Philosophy of Religion*, 2. A reference, of course, to Hegel's *Philosophy of Right*, Preface, xxviii.

Alternatively it might be argued that religious knowledge is more properly a matter for intuition than reason; a thought (as we have seen) not wholly alien to Green. But Caird is quite unpersuaded. He objects, 'the fact that I feel a certain way, or find in my mind a notion or impression of which I cannot get rid, is simply an empirical fact, a thing which happens and nothing more. It cannot be assumed without further reason that my moral and spiritual intuitions are, even for me, a revelation of infallible truth.'[83] Nor will we do much better if we try to rest our religious convictions on some divinely granted revelation. Caird is quite opposed to any naive literalist view of scripture. 'The Bible is not a book of scientific theology,' he notes, arguing that much of its language 'cannot be construed literally or taken as an immediate repertory of theological doctrine.'[84] And he strongly insists that we can never under any circumstances be forced to accept what is *opposed* to reason, or even that it makes any real sense to speak instead of what is *above* reason.[85] None of which is to say he was opposed to the notion of revelation itself—indeed he admits that 'a God who does not reveal Himself ceases to be God'[86]—but he does object to the isolation of something called revealed religion in contradistinction to the sphere of natural religion.[87] His point is that we must not regard human nature as 'a thing divided against itself',[88] and the true idea of revelation, that which is most ennobling both to God and to man, is of a disclosure addressed to the *whole* of our spiritual nature, which includes our reason as well as our emotion.[89] Man is unified and therefore it is with a unified voice that God speaks to him.

5.3.2 *The necessity of religion*

The heart of Caird's *Introduction to Philosophy of Religion* consists in, what effectively amounts to, a two-step proof of the existence of God. He first attempts to establish the falsity of materialism, and then goes on to demonstrate the necessity of a religious point of view. Materialism is false, argues Caird, because its starting point—the bare object or fact wholly independent of mind—is a false abstraction; for there exists nothing which does not have mind or thought as an inseparable factor of it. Whatever we encounter in experience or observation is always relative to mind. All our organs of sense can yield

---

[83] *Introduction to Philosophy of Religion*, 53.

[84] *Fundamental Ideas of Christianity*, II:173–4.

[85] To the former he says 'To try to convince me that I ought to distrust my natural reason and believe things that revolt it, involves the same practical paralogism as the attempt to prove to an insane man that he is insane' (*Introduction to Philosophy of Religion*, 64). While to the second he says 'Nothing that is absolutely inscrutable to reason can be made known to faith. It is only because the content of a revelation is implicitly rational that it can possess any self-evidencing power, or exert any moral influence over the human spirit' (*Introduction to Philosophy of Religion*, 73).

[86] *Introduction to Philosophy of Religion*, 60.

[87] 'There is...no such thing as a natural religion or religion of reason distinct from revealed religion' (*Fundamental Ideas of Christianity*, I: 23).

[88] *Introduction to Philosophy of Religion*, 64.

[89] *Introduction to Philosophy of Religion*, 61. It is interesting to note Illingworth's reversal of this argument in defence of the role of emotion in faith. See below p.366.

are 'simply isolated and transient sensations', 'an endless series of fugitive impressions'.[90] But, of course, that is not what we actually *experience*. We experience a stable and organized world. The extra unity and organization which gets added in to make this world is, argues Caird, the work of the mind; the self which is presupposed in all experience adds in the categories which structure and mould that experience. So far we are, of course, simply following Kant. But Caird goes on that to speak of how things are in and of themselves, apart from experience, is nonsensical, and so we must think of mind as providing not merely the form but also the very content of our experience. 'man . . . creates nature' he concludes,[91] and with this we leave behind the vestigial realism of the Kantian system and enter idealism proper.

The false starting point of materialism dismissed, Caird claims that 'when we begin at the real beginning . . . [thought] is forced onwards, from step to step, by an irresistible inward necessity, and cannot stop short till it has found its goal in the sphere of universal and absolute truth, or in that Infinite Mind which is at once the beginning and the end, the source and the final explanation of all thought and being.'[92] This general idea of thought working out its own natural progression from one limited perspective to a higher more inclusive point of view is, of course, an Hegelian one. However, the more detailed explanation of why and in what fashion this must be so may be attributed to Caird himself. Indeed, he uses a variety of arguments in this stage of his case—which he does not always carefully distinguish—but the heart of the contention is as follows.

Caird urges that it belongs to the very essence of mind to find itself in that which lies beyond it, to break down the barriers between it and its objects. It cannot be shut up in its own individuality.[93] What he means by this is that we are essentially knowing beings. The mind is plastic, able to take on the character of what it knows and able to know anything. But, if it is to know them, the things it takes on board, the natural and the social world, cannot be wholly external or foreign to it; looking at the world is, to a certain extent, like looking in a mirror.[94] Sometimes, rather than speaking of the mind finding itself in its objects, Caird employs a slightly different model, and says that subject and object presuppose a unity behind them that includes them both; they are one-sided abstractions from a deeper whole.[95] But the point is the same: either way we learn that the distinction between subject and object is neither absolute nor insurmountable, and that 'to be ourselves, we must be more than ourselves'.[96] The argument has one last step. As essentially finite beings, self-completion must always elude us; perfection 'is a goal that ever vanishes as we pursue it. We never are, but are ever only becoming, that which it is possible for us to be.'[97] But paradoxically argues Caird, this boundless possibility of advancement, both intellectual and moral, is itself a

[90] *Introduction to Philosophy of Religion*, 91.
[91] *University Sermons*, 314–15.
[92] *Introduction to Philosophy of Religion*, 87.
[93] *Introduction to Philosophy of Religion*, 114.
[94] *Introduction to Philosophy of Religion*, 115.
[95] *Introduction to Philosophy of Religion*, 122.
[96] *Introduction to Philosophy of Religion*, 124.
[97] *Introduction to Philosophy of Religion*, 117.

revelation of the Infinite and our essential relation to it. It tells us that God belongs to our very essence and that the infinite world to which we aspire is to our nature no more alien than the finite world we inhabit. The ultimate reality that grounds all things transcends not only the distinction between subject and object but also that between finite and infinite.

Caird moves on from his own argument for the necessity of a religious point of view to consider the traditional proofs of God's existence. He argues that they are all flawed, and the diagnoses which he offers of the cosmological, teleological, and ontological arguments are standard enough. But he goes on to claim that they retain a certain value if viewed as 'expressions of that impossibility of resting in the finite'.[98] The supposed core of insight which he uncovers in each case is hard to relate to the detailed arguments themselves, and one might be tempted to think here that it would have been better simply to say the arguments are invalid and then offer his own alternative, but to suggest this is to misunderstand something very central in his thinking. Like his brother Edward, he demonstrates immense generosity of spirit, finding it impossible to regard any thought as wholly worthless and always searching for some germ of truth that it might contain.

5.3.3 *The proper form of religious knowledge*

Emphasizing as he does the role of reason, it becomes necessary for Caird to address the question of the relation between philosophy and religion, and it is here perhaps that his Hegelian debt comes out most clearly. He argues that we must make a distinction between the content and the form of religious knowledge—there is only one truth, but it may be expressed in many and various modes. Religion and philosophy, he then goes on, say the same thing, they simply express it in a different way—they 'agree in substance and content, but differ in form'.[99] Religion expresses its message in a concrete and pictorial fashion, philosophy in an abstract and conceptual manner. The figurative or symbolic character of ordinary religious thought, in which spiritual ideas are represented by either material objects in space or events in time, makes it easy to grasp and gives it a power to speak directly to the emotions, rendering it suitable for the ordinary everyday consciousness. Thus Caird is able to say, for example, 'the Bible is no philosophy. Its glorious truths are to be apprehended not by the critical intellect but by the humble and loving heart.'[100]

---

[98]   *Introduction to Philosophy of Religion*, 125. For instance, though flawed as an attempt to argue from the contingency of the world to the existence of a necessary being which causes it, the cosmological argument has value as a recognition that the very instability and finitude of the world in itself already betrays a higher standard, while the true meaning of the ontological argument is said to be that 'as spiritual beings our whole conscious life is based on a universal self-consciousness, an Absolute Spiritual Life, which is not a mere subjective notion or conception, but which carries with it the proof of its necessary existence or reality' (*Introduction to Philosophy of Religion*, 126–9, 150). Edward Caird offers a very similar gloss on the meaning of the ontological argument (*Critical Philosophy of Immanuel Kant*, II: 128).

[99]   *Introduction to Philosophy of Religion*, 178.

[100]   *Essays for Sunday Reading*, 243.

Drawing a contrast between religion's core and its form, one notable consequence of this Hegelian perspective concerns other faiths. In the final chapter of his *Introduction to Philosophy of Religion* Caird argues that all of the world's religions can be seen as differing attempts to express the same truth, 'as the unconscious effort of the human spirit in various forms to express that elevation above ourselves and the world, that aspiration after and rest in an infinite unity of thought and being, in which the essence of religion has been shown to lie.'[101] His religious pluralism does not, however, regard all religions as on a par; there is, he claims, 'a rational order' in the 'apparently arbitrary succession'[102] of their histories, a continuous growth of understanding and spiritual awareness that culminates in Christianity. This (as will be seen below) was an idea more fully worked out by his brother, Edward.

The popular immediacy of pictorial religion is bought at a price and (even in its best forms) it suffers from a number of problems. Literally construed, of course, it is untrue,[103] it encourages us to substitute metaphors for real thoughts,[104] and it can even keep us from seeing the real facts of the matter. Philosophical representation is free from these defects. Because more abstract, it is able to separate out the message from the medium, and to deal with notions—such as self-consciousness or unity-in-difference—that defy all sensuous representation. It is thus a truer and higher medium. In consequence, ordinary thought, in so far as it is truth-seeking, must rise beyond the merely pictorial to be recast in a higher speculative system.[105] Indeed it is to precisely this task of rational reconstruction that Caird's entire philosophy of religion is devoted.

T.H. Green, as has already been noted, was of a similar opinion but, because he follows Hegel so closely, Caird's view of the relation between philosophy and religion is more open than Green's to the accusation that it is intellectualist and lacking in feeling; nothing less than an attempt to replace religion with philosophy. However, Caird has no intention of pleading guilty to this charge. He insists that philosophy does not seek to replace religion, and is in no sense a rival to it.[106] In what sense then is philosophical theology superior to religion? Only intellectually, and while religion has an intellectual component, that is not its main, its most important, or even an essential element. Although 'right views of himself and of divine and eternal things, is the most precious gift which God can bestow on the human spirit',[107] the real essence of religion lies in 'love and loyalty to Christ'[108] or 'the communion of the soul with God'.[109] The philosophical theologian is thus like one who takes up a practice (say, football) and becomes extremely adept at one part of it (say, free kicks), which although present and

---

[101]   *Introduction to Philosophy of Religion*, 312.
[102]   *Introduction to Philosophy of Religion*, 313.
[103]   *Introduction to Philosophy of Religion*, 178.
[104]   *Introduction to Philosophy of Religion*, 181.
[105]   *Introduction to Philosophy of Religion*, 205.
[106]   *Introduction to Philosophy of Religion*, 42.
[107]   *University Sermons*, 231.
[108]   *University Sermons*, 24.
[109]   *University Sermons*, 27.

perhaps very valuable, is not the main content or the main point of the game (you can still win matches with only a rudimentary skill at free kicks). As Caird himself puts it, you do not need a theory of music to appreciate it, nor a theory of love to feel it.[110] The superiority is in one sphere only.

5.3.4 The Christian view of God

Caird thought of his own worldview not simply as religious, but as specifically Christian, although, stressing the identity of man and God, he rejects any dualism and adopts instead what (in an 1880 volume of sermons) he calls a 'Christian pantheism'. Fully aware of how controversial that will sound he argues that this is both consistent with the individuality of man and the best way to secure it. Human individuality is not lost in divine unity for the deepest, most complete, unities are precisely those which bring together the greatest individual differences. (He contrasts the unity of a machine with that of a stone.[111]) Moreover, individual freedom may be preserved only if it turns out that the law and will of God are not something foreign to our true nature, for to bow to any external authority—even that of an almighty being—is (as Kant well understood) to submit to an outward law and give up our freedom.[112]

In his later and posthumously published Gifford Lectures, this view is recast but not fundamentally altered. There the Christian view of God which he advocates as 'infinite, self-revealing Spirit or mind'[113] is presented as a kind of *via media* between deism, which, in tracing everything back to the arbitrary will of God, ends up by explaining nothing at all, and pantheism, which he now construes in more extreme fashion as a doctrine which submerges all individuality, freedom, and value in a fatally abstract whole.[114] According to the Christian synthesis of these extremes, we, along with all things, participate in God as God participates in us; 'the true idea of [God's] relation to the world is that of a spirit which is ever revealing and realizing itself in all things and beings'.[115] The traditional Christian God is of course immanent in creation and so, to that extent, Caird is perhaps just drawing out under-represented elements of established belief, but the traditional Christian God is also a creator ontologically distinct from his creation, and in so far as Caird's God is certainly not in any sense a separate entity, but rather 'Him, of whom all other life is only the partial and imperfect manifestation',[116] this is still 'Christian pantheism' and as such his claim to be expounding orthodox doctrine must wash thin with many.

---

[110] *University Sermons*, 17.

[111] For more detail on the sense of unity that is being appealed to here see below Chapter 8.2, 8.3.5, 8.4.3.

[112] 'Union with God', 24, 25–6, 32.

[113] *Fundamental Ideas of Christianity*, I:143.

[114] Caird is here repeating the attack on pantheism made some years earlier in his *Spinoza* and already discussed in Chapter 3.

[115] *Fundamental Ideas of Christianity*, II: 141.

[116] *Fundamental Ideas of Christianity*, II: 65.

But even if 'God is all',[117] he is not for Caird *equally* manifested in everything. Indeed it is one of his principal objections to Spinozistic pantheism that God is thereby seen as equally near or far to everything when, in point of fact, some things are more truly revelatory than others; for God is seen more in mind than matter, more in the organic than the inorganic, and more in good than in evil.[118] Most of all for Caird, as for Green, God is most fully to be found 'in the life of individuals, in the order of society, in the events of history and the progress of the race'.[119] God is indeed the very ground of our lives, for on Caird's metaphysical system, finite consciousness is only possible in so far as it is thought of as a partial fragment of a wider infinite consciousness. 'All spiritual life is of God; all spiritual knowledge and activity are due to the operation of an infinite omnipotent agent on the human spirit',[120] he says; and again, 'all spiritual life rests upon the indwelling of the divine spirit in the human'.[121] But if God in this way thinks and acts through us does not that destroy our individuality? Caird insists not. Indeed, he urges to the contrary, that it is in the state of union with God that we most fully realize our true self.[122]

Caird's characterization of the synthesis between pantheism and deism as Christianity's distinctive contribution to the conception of God will grate with those who would be inclined to accord that title to Trinitarianism, the view of God as three-in-one. Caird, however, is unwilling to concede so much to something so opaque to reason. He argues that, 'it is scarcely conceivable that the new or distinctively Christian element should be, not light, but darkness'.[123] He does not reject outright the idea of the Trinity, and he certainly helps himself to the notions of God as the Father of all, as indwelling Spirit, and as Christ; but the relation between these three is something he touches little upon. The general drift of his thinking was in Hegelian fashion to regard it as some kind of figurative expression of identity-in-difference,[124] but it cannot be said that he got very far with this and, in the end, he had to admit to failure. He confessed to one of his pupils, 'I thought . . . that I should find in the formulae of the Hegelian philosophy a solution of the high mystery of the Trinity. I feel, I am bound to confess, that I have failed to satisfy my own mind.'[125]

---

[117] *Fundamental Ideas of Christianity*, I:140.

[118] *Fundamental Ideas of Christianity*, I:111–12.

[119] *Fundamental Ideas of Christianity*, II:141.

[120] *University Sermons*, 77.

[121] *Fundamental Ideas of Christianity*, II:158.

[122] *University Sermons*, 84.

[123] *Fundamental Ideas of Christianity*, I:58.

[124] He says in the Gifford lectures, after discussing the relation between Father and Son, 'perhaps in these images of things divine, we may discern the expression, under human analogies, of that principle of unity in difference, of that oneness of elements, distinguishable but indivisible, which we have seen to be the very essence of all intelligence' (*Fundamental Ideas of Christianity*, I:79).

[125] C.L. Warr, *Principal Caird*, 184. However, not everyone has shared this negative assessment of the value of Caird's limited discussion of the issue in his Gifford Lectures. J.S. Mackenzie described it as 'Probably the best interpretation of the Christian doctrine of the Trinity in recent times' (*Elements of Constructive Philosophy*, 463).

5.3.5 Jesus Christ

Turning to the doctrine of Jesus, Caird's general stance towards the founder of Christianity is thoroughly demythologizing in approach; we find in his life and person nothing miraculous and nothing supernatural. The taking up of such an attitude is placed by him in the context of the historical advance of human understanding.

Ignorance and superstition revel in the religion of magic and mystery, and find nothing to revolt them in the ascription to their divinities of the waywardness and capriciousness of arbitrary power. But, with the advancing spiritual life of the world, men are led more and more to seek their proofs of God and of divine action, not in sudden and unaccountable marvel or capricious displays of supernatural power, but in the manifestations of wisdom and beneficence in intelligible relations and sequences.[126]

Like Green, Caird sees Christ less as an historical figure and far more as a present reality. He is conceived of as a living spirit indwelling in individual Christians, in the Church, and in humanity at large; a spirit manifested in our achievements and progress, even in the natural world itself, and in our own communion with and response to these things. Caird says, 'the essence of the life of Christ is no more a thing of the past than the being and life of God is a thing of the past, or of any particular time or place. It is rather that eternal life which is for ever realizing itself in the spirit and life of humanity.'[127] Emphasizing this conception of Christ as something more 'visible' and immediate than any figure from the past could be, if it does not dismiss the historical question, certainly blunts its sense of urgency and, when Caird turns to consider that issue, the fundamental significance of the historical Christ is found to lie in his ability to serve for us as an *example*, both ethical and metaphysical.

In the first place Christ embodies the moral law for which God stands. In this respect Caird argues that 'the events of the life of Christ are for the Christian consciousness the outward representation of a spiritual content.'[128] He is for us a perfect concrete example of our moral ideal and, as such, his life provides us with an empirical handle on to what would otherwise be a wholly abstract rule or standard. Transformed from a cold impersonal principle into a living human individual, whom we may love and follow, God's power to bring about our moral and spiritual growth is vastly increased.[129]

In addition to his life, Christ's *being itself* may also be thought of as an example. In this case the principle illustrated is a metaphysical one. Caird insists that the doctrine of the incarnation must not be thought of as something inscrutable to reason.[130] He argues (as we have seen above) that union with God belongs to the very essence of humanity, it is the spring of our conscious being. However, such union may be realized, by being

---

[126] *University Sermons*, 72–3.
[127] *Fundamental Ideas of Christianity*, II:96. See also 94, 98, 247–8, and *Essays for Sunday Reading*, 99.
[128] *Introduction to Philosophy of Religion*, 170.
[129] *Fundamental Ideas of Christianity*, II:84–5.
[130] *Fundamental Ideas of Christianity*, II:100.

recognized, to a greater or lesser extent, its ultimate consummation taking the form of 'a spiritual life in which the very mind and will of God become identified with our own, in which it is God's thoughts our minds think, God's will that worketh in us, the very life of God in which we participate.'[131] A complete full and perfect union like this between God and man is, even for the most holy of people, a very distant ideal, and only once in history, viz. in life of Jesus Christ, has it ever occurred, thinks Caird. Jesus thus expresses, under the form of time, the fundamental principle of the union of human and divine.[132] He is an example of the higher metaphysical life that lies latent within us all, revealing to us our essential affinity with the divine. Caird does not intend to deny the uniqueness of the incarnation in Christ, and what is realized in full in Christ is realized only very imperfectly in our lives. But it is crucial that this is a difference of degree, not kind; for however unrivalled the union between God and man in the special case of Christ, Caird insists that 'it must yet be a union of which by its very structure and essence humanity is capable'.[133]

Behind the mistaken metaphorical pictures of the atonement, there lies, thinks Caird, an important truth. The elements of the atonement tell us that somehow God suffers because of our sins and that somehow we benefit from this. That invites two questions. First, how could a perfect person suffer for sin that is not even his? Caird suggests that we can make sense of this if we think of it as analogous to the case of an upright and loving a father suffering the disgrace into which his own family has fallen. 'Would he not be stung by an anguish, a borrowed humiliation, as bitter as if the sin had been his own?'[134] Secondly, we must ask, how could *we* benefit from *his* suffering, for guilt and merit are not transferable? The answer, argues Caird, is that in so far as we are brought into union with God, the distinction between who pays and who benefits is collapsed. 'It is not that the merit of the perfect righteousness and atoning sacrifice and death of Christ is, in some incomprehensible way, ascribed to us; but there is a profound sense in which they become actually our own—His sorrow our sorrow, His sacrifice our sacrifice, His perfect life, in all its ideal beauty and elevation, the very life we live.'[135] It is worth noting in this whole discussion of the atonement that Caird disregards all supernatural elements. He says nothing at all of the Cross and the resurrection events, which are for most Christians the essential vehicles of that atonement.

5.3.6 *Immortality*

The common understanding of, and interest, in the figure of Jesus that Caird and T.H. Green share is readily apparent, but one further matter which much exercised Caird,

---

though Green hardly touches on it,[136] was immortality. Caird offers three arguments for immortality. The first is simple enough and in effect no more than a corollary of his general position. He argues that the divine mind must be considered not only as infinite but also as something eternal, in the sense of being outside of time rather than simply possessing endless duration.[137] But we have already seen that human minds, though finite, partake essentially of the nature of the divine mind, and he infers that in so far as this is the case they too must be regarded as eternal.

Caird's second argument for immortality is based on the disproportion between what he describes as the 'greatness' of man's spiritual nature and the contrastingly brief duration and limited needs of his present life. What Caird means is that we have in us the capacity to develop knowledge and goodness without limit,[138] but that this would be a waste if we were not immortal. This argument is similar to that to be found later on in such figures as James Seth, Andrew Seth Pringle-Pattison, and Henry Jones.[139] But it would seem from what Caird says in expanding the point that the argument in fact hinges more on the notion of an undeceiving than an economizing, God. For how do we know that there is *not* such waste? Only, Caird admits, with the eyes of a prior faith in God; otherwise, 'the hopes and aspirations it encourages us to cherish [would be] but an elaborate and cruel deception'.[140]

Though typical of their genre, neither of these two arguments are especially striking, but it is also possible to find in Caird a third argument of greater interest—this time for a rather more demythologized species of immortality, that is neither personal nor timeless. Both in an early 1880 sermon and subsequently in his Gifford Lectures, he considers the notion of *Corporate Immortality*. This is the idea that each generation leaves its legacy to the next and that in so far as we do so we may be thought to live on in the progress of the race itself. He argues that Christianity encourages us to expect as the destiny of our race a time when the whole of humanity shall be permeated through and through with the spirit of Christ, as each individual fully participates in the moral and spiritual elevation of God. But what greater ambition could we have than to contribute towards this ultimate goal? Caird had a very strong sense of progress—'the history of human knowledge is a history, on the whole, of a continuous and ever accelerating-progress'[141]—and of our intellectual and

---

[136] *Prolegomena*, §185 hints at its possibility, but Green's only direct discussion of immortality is to be found in a brief note posthumously published in the third volume of his *Collected Works*, 159–60. Beyond the assurance that all thought finds a place in the timeless eternity of God, Green advances no specific opinions. Nettleship, however, remembers him as saying, 'I believe that when I die I shall see God.' On the other hand his brother-in-law reports the claim that, 'the Philosopher cannot be expected to know more for certain than the rest of men about such things as immortality' (both recollections preserved in notebooks in Balliol College Library; See Thomas, *The Moral Philosophy of T.H. Green*, 15, 376–8) and was himself of the opinion that Green did not believe in personal immortality (*Letters and Papers of John Addington Symonds*, 141). However, see also Craufurd's claim at Chapter 2 note 112.

[137] *Fundamental Ideas of Christianity*, II:258–9.

[138] *Fundamental Ideas of Christianity*, II:260–1; *Essays for Sunday Reading*, 33.

[139] See below Chapter 11.

[140] *Fundamental Ideas of Christianity*, II:296.

[141] *University Addresses*, 32.

moral indebtedness to the past—'that any of us attains to a high measure of intellectual and moral advancement and not merely to a stunted and arrested inward growth, is due to this, that we were born amidst the better Influences of the present rather than under the feeble light and in the depressing moral atmosphere of an earlier time.'[142] If it be objected that the continuation of one's higher values in the life of future generations is not really *personal* immortality, Caird admits it. But, he goes on, the Christian lives and works not for himself but for others; his dearest wish being for the redemption of the world from evil and the creation of heaven on earth.[143] And that is precisely what this is.[144] If it be objected that this state need not in any sense be thought of as *timeless*, Caird admits that too. Purify and ennoble the hearts of men, he says, and heaven could take place here and now. He claims that, 'The eternal world is not a world beyond time and the grave. It embraces time, it is ready to realize itself under all forms of temporal things.'[145]

5.3.7 The problem of evil

The history of the gradual manifestation of God is, in the teleological and essentially *practical* religion of Green, a history of the power of the creative spirit to bring good out of evil,[146] a history of the way in which Christianity in particular can turn around the human spirit and set it to work removing evil,[147] in a divine plan whose progress cannot be halted or reversed because in some timeless way it is already complete. We find a similar view of the practical meaning of evil in John Caird. Like Green, evil for him is notable for the possibility of moral regeneration it provides, and the momentous metaphysical significance which that implies. We have a higher spirit within us that can turn our lives around. Indeed, we have nothing less than God working within us. Christ has been at work behind history, and continues to be so, moving it along to its consummation.[148] Caird's understanding of evil merits further attention, however, for if in regarding the problem of evil as one of lived religion, Green leaves aside its more philosophical import, this is a challenge which the more theologically minded John Caird picks up.

He spends considerable time discussing the origin of evil. The Augustinian theory, that evil is the result of Adam's original sin, finds a surprising degree of favour. It might seem open to serious objection on the grounds that surely 'every man must bear his own burden'. But the moral history of humanity is not that of an aggregate of separate individuals, for 'the individual life is meaningless apart from other lives, and from that

---

[142] *University Sermons*, 381.

[143] We may detect here echoes of the controversy over quietism which took place in France in the closing years of the seventeenth century, occasioned by the ideas of François Fénelon who had argued that perfection involves getting rid of self-love altogether, even to the extent we should become indifferent to our own eternal fate.

[144] 'Corporate Immortality', 192; cf. *Fundamental Ideas of Christianity*, II:289–93.

[145] 'Corporate Immortality', 193.

[146] 'The Force of Circumstances', 6.

[147] 'The Force of Circumstances', 10.

[148] *Fundamental Ideas of Christianity*, II:96.

universal life of which all alike are only constituent elements or factors'.[149] We naturally think of society as made up of individuals, but 'It would be nearer the truth to say that it is society which creates the individual, rather than the individual society'[150] and the Augustinian view should therefore be applauded for 'its recognition of the organic unity of the race'.[151] There is in the end, thinks Caird, no escape from the claim that we, and not God, are the authors of evil.[152] But in idealist eyes even the free will defence takes on a new caste. Will necessarily realizes itself,[153] and it is the fundamental nature of the free willing creature to realize that in itself which is spiritual, universal, and infinite. Sin is the name for what occurs when it falls short from that call, and seeks satisfaction in objects that are not commensurate with it. 'It is not in the satisfaction of natural desires, but in the fact that it is an infinite nature that is seeking satisfaction in them, that the essence of sin lies.'[154]

Evil can be overcome, for we have within us the spirit of God, which is progressively revealing itself. But whereas Green stops at this point, Caird presses on to think about the metaphysical implications of such salvation. In prayer, for example, he thinks we attain to a perception that can see the unreality of evil.

the peculiar significance of prayer lies in this, that therein we rise above ourselves: we leave behind the interests which belong to us as creatures of time; we enter into that sphere in which all the discords and evils of the time world are but deceptive appearances and illusions, or possess no more reality than the passing shadows of clouds that lie here beneath our feet. The world in which we outwardly live is only the unreal and the evanescent making believe to be real; the true, the real, the world of unchangeable and eternal reality, is that in which we pray . . . even when we pray that evils may cease, it is, if our prayer be the prayer of faith, because in spirit we realise that they have already ceased, because we are in a sphere in which we discern the nothingness of all that is not of God.[155]

Care is needed, however. We cannot simply say that evil is unreal, some sort of illusion of finitude. This view Caird associates with pantheism and rejects. An adequate notion of sin (he argues) must see it as, 'the falling short of an attainable standard, the non-realization of the ideal of one's nature'; however for this to work, 'there must be a sense in which the infinite is not the contradiction, but the truth of the finite, the object or end in which alone man's nature can be perfectly realized'.[156] To put the point another way, nothing is ever purely negative. Negativity rather than mere nothingness has a positive aspect to it, and 'when we examine the process of thought by which any true idea is reached, we find that it includes a negative as well as a positive movement, and

[149] *Fundamental Ideas of Christianity*, I:226.
[150] *Fundamental Ideas of Christianity*, I:227.
[151] *Fundamental Ideas of Christianity*, I:232.
[152] *Fundamental Ideas of Christianity*, I:203.
[153] *Fundamental Ideas of Christianity*, II:55–7.
[154] *Fundamental Ideas of Christianity*, II:68.
[155] *Introduction to Philosophy of Religion*, 288.
[156] *Fundamental Ideas Of Christianity*, II:20.

that a spiritual truth cannot be grasped as a bare affirmation, but only as that which holds in it both negation and affirmation.'[157] Evil *is* unreal. But the perfect is not simply the *negation* of evil, the mere pushing it away, but rather the *conversion* of evil, that which overcomes the bad by triumphantly turning it to good.

5.4 Edward Caird

From 1860 to 1866 Edward Caird was in Oxford (first at Balliol and then at Merton) during which time he formed a close personal and intellectual bond with T.H. Green. In Green, he later recalled, 'I found one whose brotherly sympathy and inspiring example has stimulated me, more than any other single influence, in the prosecution of my philosophical work'.[158] He left Oxford to take up the Chair of Moral Philosophy in Glasgow, where he joined his elder brother John. And from then for nearly thirty years until Edward's recall to Oxford in 1893 to take up the Mastership of Balliol, and despite the fifteen years age difference between them, they enjoyed almost daily communication, helping to shape each other's views.[159] It is thus no surprise to find that Edward Caird's philosophy of religion is fundamentally of a piece with those of the two figures we have already examined.

The basic shape of his philosophical vision will be familiar enough from the previous two chapters, but its specific application to questions of religion merits further attention. Like both Green and John Caird, he turned to German idealism in his attempt to rescue religion; although perhaps even more explicitly than they, did he regard *Hegel* as the saviour of Christianity. According to Caird, the essence of Christianity is the doctrine that God is a Spirit, that is, a being whose whole life is self-determination and self-revelation, but this (he insists) is precisely the demonstrated result of Hegel's logic.[160] Again like them, he advocated an Absolute Idealism whose central principle is an infinite unity of self-consciousness underlying alike the subjective and the objective, as well as the finite and the infinite. The ground of everything, 'that in which we live and move and have our being,'[161] we may think of this as God.

The rationality of religion, then, rests on the possibility of an ultimate synthesis, in which man and nature are regarded as the manifestation of one spiritual principle. For religion involves a faith that, in our efforts to realise the good of humanity, we are not merely straining after an ideal beyond us, which may or may not be realised, but are animated by a principle which, within us and without us, is necessarily realising itself, because it is the ultimate principle by which all things are, and are known. This absolute certitude of religion, that man can work effectually because all

---

[157] *Introduction to Philosophy of Religion*, 194.
[158] Jones and Muirhead, *The Life and Philosophy of Edward Caird*, 370–1.
[159] E. Caird, 'Memoir', lxv. It is interesting that this Glasgow sibling union had its Edinburgh counterpart with the brothers James Seth (Chair of moral philosophy 1898–1924) and Andrew Seth Pringle-Pattison (Chair of logic and metaphysics 1891–1919).
[160] *Hegel*, 218. See above Chapter 3.1.2.
[161] *Evolution of Religion*, I:166–7. The Biblical reference is to Acts 17:28.

the universe is working with him, or, in other words, because God is working in him, can find its explanation and defence only in a philosophy for which 'the real is the rational, and the rational is the real.'[162]

There is here a strong emphasis on the presence of God in all things, since for Caird to call it transcendent is to imply that the ultimate ground of the universe is something beyond anything we know and hence unintelligible to us. Instead, 'we must think of God as essentially immanent in the world and accessible to our minds'.[163] Not that it is any simple matter to bring God into the world. There is danger on the one hand that the unifying principle of the world be simply reduced down to its contents—so that 'God' becomes just another synonym for 'world'[164]—and danger on the other that the world become swallowed up in God. Like his brother John, Caird is critical of any such Spinozistic pantheism in which the world of finite being is nothing and God all in all.[165] In Caird's system this latter risk is lessened by the fact that (again, like both his friend and his brother) it is in particular the *social* manifestation of God that really interests him. God may be immanent in everything, but he is most fully revealed in the moral life of man and society.

But Caird does not simply repeat the views of Green or of his brother; rather, something present in their works, but little developed, becomes the very key to his system. This is the idea of progress. For Caird, the finite world is a revelation of God, but it is not a static revelation. God does not reveal himself all at once. Instead the Absolute manifests itself in historical progress which, when we look around us, we may find everywhere.

5.4.1 Avoiding the lion's den

Evolution is such an important and pervasive concept in Caird's general philosophy that it is vital we understand the role it plays in his system; what leads him to push it to the fore. Evolution is for Caird the inevitable accompaniment of his belief in an underlying unity behind all things; the unity of self-consciousness, the unity of the finite and the infinite. So close are they in Caird's mind that they may even be regarded as two sides of a single principle.[166] The point is that the affirmation of an infinite identity-in-difference underlying the many diversities of the finite world leaves us with two very different realms—ultimate reality and its appearances—and to Caird, the key

---

[162] 'Metaphysic', 530.

[163] *Evolution of Theology in the Greek Philosophers*, I:257. Whether Caird always held such a non-supernatural understanding of religion might be questioned. In his 1866 paper 'Reform and reformation' he speaks at length, and without obvious metaphor, of *the Fall* (3–6). It should be noted, however, that this piece was part of his application for the Chair in Moral Philosophy at Glasgow.

[164] Schopenhauer, 'A few words on Pantheism', 99.

[165] *Critical account of the Philosophy of Kant*, 648. We have already considered this attack in Chapter 3.4.1 above.

[166] With reference to that unity insofar as it underlies all mankind, 'The concept of development is,' he argues, 'a corollary which cannot be disjoined from the principle of the unity of man itself' (*Evolution of Religion*, I:25).

advantage of evolution was that it allowed him to relate these two spheres together. Failure to do this was, he thought, the greatest weakness of previous idealisms.

In the first place it is necessary to relate the finite to the infinite. The generic Absolute Idealist position here is that the apparent diversity among finite things must be broken down, revealing their deeper unity in the infinite. But you cannot, responds Caird, arrive at any real unity between things by a simple removal of their differences, for the unity thus arrived at would be a bare identity, something utterly abstract and thin, a lowest common denominator—if, indeed, it could be found at all.[167] Rather, unity must be traced out through the evolution of a single principle. Historical development, in which we find a germ and follow it through the different stages of its growth, allows us to see the significant underlying unity in a highly complex pattern; it is, he claims, 'the most potent instrument for bringing back difference to identity which has ever been put into the hands of science'.[168] It allows us to find unity where it would otherwise go unnoticed; for, to use Caird's own example, without a notion of evolution to guide us, the task of showing that caterpillar, chrysalis, and butterfly are all the same creature would be just impossible.

But, of course, every relation has two sides, and besides relating the finite to the infinite, it is equally necessary to relate the infinite to the finite. The question that we need to answer here is, why does the infinite or perfect Absolute break up in the first place to produce the fragmentary and finite world of everyday experience? Caird insists that thought must be able to ascend both up to the universal and then down again to the particular. But from the Eleatics onwards he thinks too many Absolutes achieved only the first task.[169] They are, he says like the lion's den of Aesop's fable—all tracks point towards it but none away from it.[170] The terms he uses for such systems are 'mysticism' and 'pantheism',[171] and Bradley's is, he thinks, a perfect example; for Bradley frankly acknowledges that we don't know how or why the one infinite Absolute manifests itself in multiple finite particulars, only that it does.[172] Caird, on the other hand, believes that within his system he can answer this question, for he thinks that by building evolution into the heart of the Absolute itself, he is, in effect, saying that dynamic break-up—or, as Caird likes to put it, 'dying to live'—constitutes its very essence. It is no puzzle that the Absolute should embark upon the circle of self-

---

[167]   *Evolution of Religion*, I:24–5.

[168]   *Evolution of Religion*, I:26.

[169]   'Metaphysic', 393.

[170]   'Metaphysic', 515; *Hegel*, 60; *Evolution of Religion*, I:107; Jones and Muirhead, *Life and Philosophy of Edward Caird*, 196–7. The reference is to Aesop's fable of the fox and the sick lion. Various sources attribute the saying as Hegel's in relation to Spinoza, however, I have been unable to verify this in any Hegelian text. The earliest source for the analogy that I have found is Schwegler who employs it in discussion of Spinoza in his 1848 *Handbook of the History of Philosophy* (ch. XXVI).

[171]   *Evolution of Theology in the Greek Philosophers*, II:227, 234.

[172]   'We do not know how or why the Absolute divides itself into centres, or the way in which, so divided, it still remains one. The relation of the many experiences to the single experience, and so to one another, is, in the end, beyond us' (*Appearance and Reality*, 467).

recognition, for it *is* precisely that circle. The Absolute is not the thing that is evolving (as though this were the story of the Absolute); it is not even the final result of that evolution (as though we were striving to somehow reach or recreate the Absolute); rather the evolution is the Absolute. It is the Absolute realizing itself. It is the way in which the underlying divine unity-in-diversity is expressed. This answer, he thinks, amounts to more than just words; the full details of how and why the Absolute manifests itself in and through the particulars it does are precisely what he sets himself to explain in his several historical and evolutionary studies.

And Caird finds evolution everywhere, for human recognition of the underlying principle of reality as one of unity-in diversity is itself something that has only gradually been arrived at. Although it is not just knowledge that grows and evolves, for to the idealist Caird there can be no sharp distinction between knowledge and fact, and the evolutionary path traced out by the one must be matched in the other as both alike seek ever-fuller realization and manifestation of the unity-in-difference that grounds and underlies all reality. One example of such evolution has already been noted in his view of the development of philosophical understanding (Chapter 3). Another will be encountered in his view of the development of ethical understanding (Chapter 6). Even the idea of development itself has developed, he argues; only recently achieving its current position of prominence as an intellectual tool.[173]

5.4.2 *The evolution of religion*

Caird then finds evolution everywhere. However, his main worked example is that of religion, as set out in his Gifford Lectures, *The Evolution of Religion* (delivered 1890–92.) For Caird, all religions despite their seeming differences are expressions of a single insight. But the attempt to understand this form of life must proceed not by seeking what is *common* to all religions, but rather what *underlies* them all.[174] It is seen more specifically in what lies behind the unfolding story of their growth, for, instead of thinking of religion as a timeless truth, he sees it as an evolving human perspective. The essence however is revealed, not in the origin, but rather in the end state of this story; 'we must read development *backwards* and not *forward*, we must find the key to the meaning of the first stage in the last.'[175] The story is not necessarily, it should be noted, one that would be recognized by religious practitioners themselves, for Caird at the same time draws an important distinction between what a religion means to its adherents and what it really means in the wider picture of history; for, as he puts it, 'Though man is essentially self-conscious, he always *is* more than he *thinks* or *knows*; and his thinking and

---

[173] *Evolution of Religion*, I:21–4.
[174] *Evolution of Religion*, I:51.
[175] *Evolution of Religion*, I:45. This (as we shall see) is something of a trademark idealist doctrine. At much the same point in time we find Henry Jones arguing that a thing's essence lies in its end or ideal, that 'the real nature of anything is that which it has in it to become, rather than that which it already is' ('Is the Distinction between 'Is' and 'Ought' Ultimate and Irreducible?', 94).

knowing are ruled by ideas of which he is at first unaware, but which, nevertheless, affect everything he says or does.' This is recognizably Hegel's 'cunning of reason'.[176]

He argues that an examination of the history of religion reveals three basic stages to this evolution; objective religion, subjective religion, and Absolute religion. And here it must be pointed out he is largely following Hegel's three-fold division of 'the religion of nature', 'the religion of spiritual individuality', and 'the Absolute (revealed) religion' in his *Lectures on the Philosophy of Religion*.[177] But the details are Caird's own. In objective religion a person looks outward, and God is represented as an object among other objects. It begins in fetish worship, but the universalizing force that drives evolution onwards pushes it ultimately to pantheism. Its downfall lies in its inability to capture our inner religious life. In subjective religion our attention turns inward and the true voice of God is thought of as something within us. Above the demands of outward life now are set those of our own heart or conscience. Examples of subjective religion include Buddhism and Stoicism, although the most typical and highest exemplar, thinks Caird, is Judaism. But any such religion is ultimately defective because it detaches God from the natural world of his creation, and thus we are forced to move on to Absolute, or spiritual, religion, which is represented by Christianity. Christianity, according to Caird, with its theory of a spiritual principle at work in both subject and object alike, is the culmination 'beyond which religion cannot go',[178] It is, of course, a synthesis of the best in objective and subjective religion. Though Christianity is the highest form of religion, Caird never supposes that we have now reached the end of history. Indeed, it was his view that the Absolute is infinite, and so the process of its self-realization could never be finished.[179] For all it achieves the highest kind of insight, he argues, the religion brought in by Christ needed and still needs much development.[180]

The view of Christianity arrived at is, as might be expected, in line with those already discussed. Christianity's 'first and last word is the unity or reconciliation of the human and the divine.'[181] This leads Caird on to a non-supernatural view of Christ. 'Christ is divine *just because* he is the most human of men, the man in whom the

---

[176]   *Evolution of Religion*, I:74. Hegel, *Philosophy of History*, 34.
[177]   It is worth noting that in Caird's supposed comprehensive account of religion (as in Hegel's) Islam is not mentioned once.
[178]   *Evolution of Religion*, II:321.
[179]   He speaks of Christianity as 'a living and growing spirit . . . *ever* manifesting new powers and leading us to new truths' (*Lay Sermons*, 67, emphasis added). However, it is worth noting that one of his own pupils took his position to imply that time must be conceived as a closed and *finite* circle (J.S. Mackenzie, 'Edward Caird as a Philosophical Teacher', 522).
[180]   'Christianity, if it is the only religion that corresponds to the idea of religion, is just for that reason the most complex of all religions; and it therefore needs for its explication the longest and most painful process of development' (*Evolution of Religion*, II:260). 'It is indeed the principle underlying all religion which in it comes to self-consciousness. Yet, on the other hand, it has to be admitted that this principle was as yet only stated in the most general way, and not worked out to its consequences' (*Evolution of Religion*, II:263). 'Truth, and especially the truth of Christianity, is a complex thing, and its meaning could only be unfolded part by part in the long process of history' (*Lay Sermons*, 64).
[181]   *Evolution of Religion*, II:291.

universal spirit of humanity has found its fullest expression . . . the ideal or typical man . . . the purest revelation of God in man.'[182] Christ's claim that he came to fulfil the law not to abolish it is taken as meaning that he saw himself as continuing revelation already given, deepening it and widening it, but not offering anything radically new.[183]

Some ten years later Caird was honoured by an invitation to give the Gifford lectures again. His second set concentrates on a more specific element in the story only touched on in the first set. It is more restricted in two respects. Rather than religion as a whole it focuses on reflective thought about religion, that is theology, and rather than world history as a whole it focuses on the classical period—for that, argues Caird, is where theology began.[184] Covering the entire period from the Presocratics to the Neo-Platonists, *The Evolution of Theology in the Greek Philosophers* (delivered 1900–2) reads history backwards through a neo-Hegelian lens to see one continuous story of how reason's attempt to understand reality led to dualism. Plato and Aristotle in their attempts to make sense of what would otherwise be chaos instituted a division of form and matter, which in turn generated dualism between thought and sense, and even between the pure spiritual intelligence which is God and the material world. This severance of higher from lower, or spiritual from material, was taken even further in post-Aristotelian thought which, unable to find unity by comprehension, looked to find it by abstraction. It sought to systematize reality, 'not by binding all the different elements and aspects of the universe into one whole, but by isolating one of these elements, treating it alone as absolutely real.'[185] It might well be thought that the scepticism-generating conflict between Stoics and Epicureans, or the mysticism of the neo-Platonists, which resulted from this shift should have stretched more than they do Caird's confidence in the triumphant march of reason; but, notwithstanding this diminution in speculative achievement, Caird is undaunted:

we cannot admit that this new movement of thought is to be regarded as a retrograde one, still less that it shows a failure of the human intelligence in the face of the problem of the universe. It is quite possible that a system of philosophy may be less rich and comprehensive, as well as less stringent in its method, and yet that it may indicate a relative advance in human thought. There may be a dialectical value in the absence of dialectic.[186]

---

[182] *Evolution of Religion*, II:233. Says Caird, the 'Sonship Jesus, as the Messiah, claims for himself, that he may claim it for man' (*Evolution of Religion*, II:139).

[183] *Lay Sermons*, 162.

[184] *Evolution of Theology in the Greek Philosophers*, I:29. Caird finds there to be three distinct stages in the evolution of theology: the period of Greek and Roman antiquity in which thought was marked by freedom from any constraint by popular religious experience or authority (resulting in an excessively abstract intellectualism), the period from the Christian era down to the Reformation in which matters were almost wholly reversed and philosophical activity was thoroughly subordinated to the authority of the Church (resulting in a tendency towards fixed and fossilized dogma), and the modern period in which we find a reassertion of the ancient freedoms of Greek speculation, but this time made with due cognizance of the existing facts of Christian life and thought (*Evolution of Theology in the Greek Philosophers*, I:43–57).

[185] *Evolution of Theology in the Greek Philosophers*, I:38.

[186] *Evolution of Theology in the Greek Philosophers*, II:40.

While of interest in itself the greatest import of Caird's account of classical theology is for Christianity. The core message of Christianity is of the unity of God and man, and as the Absolute Religion it was self-conscious from the first, that is to say, possessed of a theology. Turning to its only source, it used Greek ideas to construct that theology, but given the character of those ideas, it must be appreciated that ancient philosophy was not simply the germ from which Christianity grew but also a force against which it had to fight.[187] The Christian revelation of unity was constantly pushed in a dualistic direction. For example, its response to Christ's failure to return to earth gave it an 'other-worldly' character, its inability to address the whole man in his social context led to monasticism, while the final unity of Christ's divine and human nature was bought at the price of making him unique, opening up a new gulf between him and other men. But the fight with ancient theology was one that made Christianity all the stronger, and Caird generously allows that, 'we must regard as a friend in disguise the enemy which again and again has forced the church and the world to recognise, how imperfectly the spiritual object of Christianity has been obtained.'[188]

5.4.3 Three problems in Edward Caird's philosophy of religion

Caird's developmental Absolutism raises many questions—for himself, for his contemporaries, as well as for current readers—and further insight may be had by isolating three of them here. In the first place his system may seem to be almost a contradiction in terms, in so far as the ideas of the Absolute and of time appear wholly opposed one to another. For the Absolute is precisely the whole of reality, conceived of as unitary, complete, and perfect, and this in itself seems to rule out any idea of evolution or growth. It is the changeless as opposed to the changing. Moreover, in so far as he endorses Kant's Aesthetic,[189] Caird would seem committed to the view that time is appearance, something we add to experience. How then can it apply to the Absolute? The problem raised here is, of course, the same as that which was raised against Green: how can the one consciousness that grounds all relations be both eternal and manifest itself in time?

Caird himself saw that it was no easy task to harmonize these two differing aspects of his thought. Indeed, in a private letter to a friend he confessed that reconciling the completeness of God with the essentially changing universe was 'the greatest of all difficulties in the whole theory'.[190] It is far from clear that he ever finally solved this problem to his own satisfaction.

---

[187] *Evolution of Theology in the Greek Philosophers*, II:369.
[188] *Evolution of Theology in the Greek Philosophers*, II:371.
[189] See above p.54.
[190] Letter to Mary Sarah Talbot, 1893. 'The greatest of all difficulties in the whole theory . . . is . . . the union of the conception of God as a self-determining principle manifested in a development which includes nature and man, with the conception of Him, as in a sense eternally complete in Himself. . . . A clearer conception of the idea that 'God is love' going beyond Himself to be Himself, would probably contain the solution of such difficulties, if one could get it realised and stated' (Jones and Muirhead, *The Life and Philosophy of Edward Caird*, 185).

Caird freely admits that the Absolute *itself* does not evolve. Time and change hold only *within* it. It may contain nothing but change, yet it itself does not change. The way Caird expresses this idea is to argue that, however much it may seem to the contrary, evolution is not genuinely *creative*. Time cannot add anything but only unfold or unpack what is already there.[191] Progress, for Caird, involves no new elements, but is always the working out of what is latent within; this is why, if looked at one way, everything is changing, looked at another, it is all static.[192] A triad of notions—self, not-self, and God—he insists, 'mark the circle from which thought can never escape'.[193]

In the end Caird wants to say that the opposition between time and eternity is itself a false one. The distinction is often thought of as that between change and changeless-ness, but Caird wants to challenge this; for him the eternity of the Absolute is dynamic as well as static. It has within it both variation and stability. Thinking forces these apart and opposes them, but that separation is to be resisted, and for Caird the concepts of bare change and bare permanence are both equally unacceptable.[194] Philosophy requires the overcoming of all distinctions and dualisms, including that between transience and intransience. Thus, he urges, 'Objects can be recognised as real only if, and so far as they have that unity in difference, *that permanence in change*, that intelligible individuality, which are the essential characteristics of mind.'[195] The unity of permanence and change is a variety of the more generic unity that holds between identity and diversity.

As with Green's eternal consciousness, we may feel tempted to ask of Caird's Absolute, is it something timelessly complete, or something future—even if that future be an open-ended one? Like Green, Caird appears to equivocate. On the one hand he insists that the Absolute is always with us—its development just an unfolding of what was present in latent form all along—and not to be thought of as something future. Yet at the same time, he allows that the Absolute becomes more fully self-known as time progresses which, since self-knowledge is its very essence, would imply it becomes also more fully real. But the deeper answer, it would seem, must be that we have here a dichotomy that Caird would wish to see dissolved, namely that between becoming and what we become, between process and product. The Absolute is both the end of the story and the story itself.

If Caird did not think of the *Absolute* as itself taking time, he had no doubt that the *dialectic* did, that is, he conceived it as a real process of evolution with its own discernible

---

Mackenzie ('Edward Caird as Philosophical Teacher', 522) says that for Caird time is both real and uneal. He himself takes a similarly ambivalent attitude (*Lectures on Humanism*, 223–8).

[191] 'The essential characteristic of development is that nothing arises in it *de novo*, which is not in some way preformed and anticipated from the beginning' (*Evolution of Religion*, I:182); see also 164–5, 201–2. The natural contrast to this position is that of Bergson's *Creative Evolution*.

[192] *Evolution of Religion*, I:171, 204.

[193] *Evolution of Religion*, I:164.

[194] *Evolution of Religion*, I:172.

[195] *Evolution of Theology in the Greek Philosophers*, I:193, emphasis added.

duration. However this creates a second kind of difficulty for his system, for in so far as a synthesis brings together a thesis and its opposing antithesis this claim to the historical actuality of dialectic seems to amount to an assertion of the ontological reality of contradiction. And, even if it must be also admitted that, in practice, the examples Caird puts forward turn out more often to be tensions and conflicting forces than genuinely logical incompatibilities, such was his view. Contradiction for him was 'the living pulse of reality'.[196] Philosophers like Pringle-Pattison, Bradley, and McTaggart could make no sense of this; they took the dialectic as something holding not between things and events but among our concepts of them and, as such, to be an eternal and timeless relation.[197]

Caird will have nothing to do with any attempt to re-house the dialectical process within thought. For one thing, he argues, such relocation undercuts any solution to the problem of evil. From an Hegelian perspective evil can have no final reality—the Manichean notion of an evil absolutely opposed to good is a dualism that cannot survive. But it will not do to say that the obstacle or contradiction on the path to perfection that we call evil is simply an appearance in the mind, for undoubtedly evil is real. It can have no place in that timeless perfection which the world manifests and to which history points, but neither is it nothing. It is in this vein that he speaks of 'the optimism of Jesus', the principle 'that evil exists in order to be overcome and in order to develop the power of good by the very process of overcoming it'.[198] The over-coming is not simply one in thought.

The third difficulty to consider is less metaphysical in character. One of the hardest things for contemporary readers to accept in Caird's evolutionary scheme is his endlessly optimistic talk of 'progress'. He seems to typify the worst complacency, of the age in general, to be sure, but perhaps also more specifically of the British Idealist movement. Looking backwards from his own age he sees only advance. He talks without embarrassment of 'the religion of savages'[199] or 'the primitive conscious-ness'[200] and describes evolution as a 'bridge over the gulf between ourselves and the men of an earlier and simpler stage of culture.'[201] Yet in this modern age, most people will be inclined to judge the sort of optimistic, hierarchical progressiveness that Caird preaches not just intellectually naive and untenable, but morally repugnant and intolerable.

While in many respects Caird must be found guilty as charged, two points may be mentioned to show that his view is not as crude as it might first seem. First, it should be noted that the development Caird proposes is not simply successive, like that of bud, flower, and fruit. Rather, he says, all three forms of consciousness (that is, objective

---

[196]   The phrase is Muirhead's (Jones and Muirhead, *Life and Philosophy of Edward Caird*, 353).

[197]   See Chapter 3.1.4.

[198]   *Evolution of Religion*, II:114.

[199]   *Evolution of Religion*, I:200.

[200]   *Evolution of Religion*, I:220.

[201]   *Evolution of Religion*, I:25.

consciousness, subjective consciousness, and self-consciousness) coexist, and at no time do we find one without the others;[202] however they are not always equally emphasized and 'in successive periods each of these elements in turn determines the form of our conscious life, and so becomes the mould in which all our ideas and ideals are cast'.[203] No view of the world is so primitive as to lack all grasp of the highest principles, and no view so sophisticated as to be free of all naivety. Second, although he sees development all around him, we cannot simply accuse him (like some) of being unaware of the interpretive bias he brings to bear. He is the first to admit that any developmental story has to be drawn out from the facts; that progress is a conceptual key for understanding what would be otherwise mysterious, and not a brute fact writ large on the face of the world. It is an idea that can widen our view and enlarge our sympathies, allowing us to see the underlying identity between peoples and religions that we would otherwise miss. Indeed, it is precisely this ability to draw out the deeper identity that we know must be the case, which in Caird's eyes legitimates it as an interpretive tool. Evolution may be a conceptual key rather than an empirical fact, but for all that, it is, Caird would insist, the correct key, and here two questions need to be separated: whether we should admit that the universe, as a whole, does not simply change but in some sense progresses, and whether we should allow *Caird's version* of that progress. Acceptance of the first is no commitment to acceptance of the second.

5.4.4 The influence of Edward Caird's philosophy of religion

Like T.H. Green, Edward Caird had many pupils through whom he came to exercise a great deal of philosophical influence. In general philosophical terms these will be considered elsewhere, but in the specifically religious domain mention should be made of Henry Jones, his Glasgow pupil who went on to develop his own significant philosophy of religion,[204] and of William Temple who came under his sway at Balliol and who went on to become Archbishop of Canterbury.[205]

5.5 F.H. Bradley

It is sometimes thought that Bradley was either unfriendly to or uninterested in religion, but this could not be further from the truth. In the widest sense of the term he was an extremely religious man. He believed that reality possessed an underlying spiritual or divine significance, which humankind could only become the poorer for losing its appreciation of, and in the words of one who knew him well, 'His whole life and thought was permeated by a conviction of the reality of the unseen things and a supreme devotion to them.'[206]

---

[202] *Evolution of Religion*, I:77.   [203] *Evolution of Religion*, I:188.   [204] See Chapter 11.
[205] Temple described himself as 'a loyal pupil of Edward Caird' (*Nature, Man and God*, 58).
[206] A.E. Taylor, 'F.H. Bradley', 9.

Taken in any more specific sense, however, religion remained for him a fraught and difficult topic. Although he believed in the Absolute, he declined to identify it with God, and although he saw a close connection between religion and morality, he showed himself on occasion markedly hostile to Christian morality. Moreover, traditional religious commitments to matters such as the miraculous or the promise of life after death were either rejected or ignored. Like Green he was the son of a clergyman, but in his case the religious household of his evangelical father, Charles Bradley, a prominent member of the Clapham Sect, had a more negative effect on him,[207] and often his attitude towards the church itself seems highly critical, if not frankly hostile.

Thus while Green and both of the Caird brothers thought of themselves as unequivocally Christian, Bradley's own relationship to Christianity is more ambiguous. Many, no doubt, thought his views sufficient to place him outside the fold of orthodox religious belief,[208] but he himself was in no hurry to accede to their charge; 'if allowed to remain in the church in which I was born' he said 'I see no advantage in moving.' Adding, perhaps a little disingenuously, 'being no theologian I am not even aware that any opinion which I hold is heretical.'[209]

5.5.1 Religion and philosophy

The metaphysical scheme which Bradley advances, in which the fundamental nature of reality is both mental and unified, and in which 'higher, truer, more beautiful, better and more real—these, on the whole, count in the universe as they count for us',[210] is one of manifest religious significance. It may be philosophical, but Bradley believed that it was possible in some cases for philosophy, and more especially metaphysics, to fulfil our religious or mystical needs (where these are understood in a broad sense.) He warns that 'Philosophy will always be hard.... But its certain reward is a continual evidence and heightened apprehension of the ineffable mystery of life, of life in all its complexity and all its unity and worth',[211] and he even thinks that 'with certain persons, the intellectual effort to understand the universe is a principal way of experiencing the Deity'.[212] It is not unlikely that Bradley is speaking of himself here.

So at first sight, then, it might seem appropriate to place Bradley in close affinity with the other three British Idealists considered, all of whom developed similar metaphysical schemes, and all of whom equated their Absolute with the God of religion. But such an identification would be over-hasty. Like them, he acknowledges a very strong and intimate connection between religion and philosophy, but for Bradley, that some

---

[207]   He wrote to his sister Marian in January 1922, 'Of course, as to the religion in which we were brought up, my feeling was and is and always will be one of loathing—with regret for certain persons so far as they accepted it' (*Collected Works*, V:256).

[208]   For instance, he withdrew *Appearance and Reality* prior to its consideration by the Clarendon Press because he had been informed that it would be rejected as controversial, almost certainly because of its religious implications (Candlish, 'Scepticism, Ideal Experiment, and Priorities', 264).

[209]   'Note on Christian Morality', 182.   [210]   *Appearance and Reality*, 488.

[211]   *Essays on Truth and Reality*, 106.   [212]   *Appearance and Reality*, 5.

people find it possible to derive religious satisfaction from metaphysics, no more turns philosophy into theology, than does the fact that people derive aesthetic satisfaction from nature turn natural history into art. It does not in itself establish any deep or essential connection between these two subjects, and he has no wish to follow his idealist colleagues in claiming that there is any such connection. Bradley is far more of a common-sense philosopher than is usually credited, and for all his monistic tendencies he has too great a respect for the genuine diversity of the given world to ignore patent differences and distinctions as though they did not exist. He thinks that to follow Hegel and suppose that religion is superseded by philosophy can only turn religion into some kind of failed philosophy, which is as gross an error as treating it as some kind of primitive and unsuccessful science, and does justice neither to religion nor to philosophy. Moreover, to identify God with the Absolute is inevitably to sacrifice one concept or the other, since it is simply false to suppose that the Absolute corresponds to the God of ordinary religious consciousness. It is at least part of our ordinary conception of the divine that God is a being set over against the finite individual, while it makes no sense whatever to think of the Absolute as set over against anything; and God is traditionally regarded as personal, while Bradley was quite certain that personhood was no ultimately real factor in the universe. To insist on calling the Absolute 'God' is merely to enter into a disingenuous play with words that empties both terms of all their original significance. By such a move, he says, 'You will only make a fog, were you can cry out you are on both sides at once. And toward increasing this fog I decline to contribute.'[213]

Thus we see that Bradley breaks with those we might call the orthodox Hegelian theists, such as Green and the Cairds. It will be shown in a later chapter that he was not the only one to do so—the Personal Idealists also tried to loosen the connection between the God of theism and the Absolute of philosophy—but what makes Bradley's rebellion especially interesting, is that he rejects not just this metaphysical identification but the underlying conception of the relation between philosophy and theology. He argued, against this model, that while philosophy is a *theoretical* discipline, religion is essentially *practical* in nature. Religion is not primarily an attempt to describe or even to picture the world.[214] It is something active rather than passive, something volitional rather than cognitive. He says, 'religion is essentially a doing'[215] and a little later on, 'In order to be, religion must do.'[216]

Matters are complicated by the fact that in the final analysis Bradley does not believe it is possible to make anything other than an operational contrast between the practical

---

[213] *Appearance and Reality*, 472. 'If you identify the Absolute with God, that is not the God of religion' (*Appearance and Reality*, 395).

[214] 'Religion is not the mere knowing or contemplation of any object, however high. It is not mere philosophy nor art, because it is not mere seeing' (*Ethical Studies*, 315).

[215] *Ethical Studies*, 315.

[216] *Ethical Studies*, 333; cf. *Essays on Truth and Reality*, 124.

and the non-practical.[217] And since volition and cognition are impossible in complete isolation from one another, he therefore allows that religion must contain at least some dogma.[218] There is thus a sense in which religious faith brings together theory and practice.[219] But Bradley clearly states that insofar as the religious attitude *does* involve cognition, the theories which it employs are merely 'working ideas',[220] and only insofar as it is taken to be something fundamentally practical that its true nature, purpose, and value appear.

5.5.2 Religion and morality

Thus conceiving it something practical rather than theoretical, in his treatments of the subject, Bradley approaches religion though a discussion of morality. He sees religion as a solution to the inconsistencies that he finds in ethical life and consequently as something which supersedes it.

In the final chapter of his *Ethical Studies* Bradley argues that it is the very nature of morality to aim at an end which can not completely be realized. The concept of the good, or how things *ought* to be, makes sense only so long as they are in fact *not* quite that way.[221] But as such morality is contradictory, because it 'aims at the cessation of that which makes it possible';[222] for 'No one ever was or could be perfectly moral; and, if he were, he would be moral no longer. Where there is no imperfection there is no ought, where there is no ought there is no morality.'[223] He concludes that, since its postulated ideal can never be achieved, morality can never fully satisfy us, and that, unable to satisfy us, it cannot be the last word on matters.

To the Hegelian-minded Bradley, as something contradictory, morality calls out for solution. He says, 'Reflection on morality leads us beyond it. It leads us, in short, to see the necessity of a religious point of view. . . . Morality issues in religion.'[224] The relation here, we must hasten to add, is logical rather than temporal; Bradley has no wish to deny that man has been religious from the beginning. It should be noted that religion, as the solution to the paradox of morality, is thought of as something necessary and inevitable. But it should also be noted that the logical relations go *both* ways. Religion succeeds only because it gives what morality sought, but (as one commentator has put it) 'morality is intelligible when and only when it is transcended by religion'.[225] This is so because of Bradley's Hegelian belief that all contradiction is produced by illegitimate abstraction from a higher unity and thus presupposes that fuller picture in which it is solved. Hence we can also say that were it not for religion there would be no morality.

---

[217] *Essays on Truth and Reality*, 101–6.   [218] *Ethical Studies*, 338; *Appearance and Reality*, 399.
[219] *Principles of Logic*, 724.   [220] *Appearance and Reality*, 399.   [221] See below Chapter 6.1.7.
[222] *Ethical Studies*, 234.   [223] *Ethical Studies*, 234.
[224] *Ethical Studies*, 314; cf. *Appearance and Reality*, 393.   [225] Wollheim, *F.H. Bradley*, 265.

What allows religion to give us the satisfaction that morality cannot is its affirmation of an ethical ideal that is actually fulfilled.[226] It is the staggering assertion that our dearest hopes are not merely aimed at or wished for, but realized. Bradley claims that the ideal of morality and that of religion are the same, the only difference being that, for morality it is something which ought to be but is not, while for religion it is something that not only ought to be but somehow actually is. In the more Hegelian idiom favoured by *Ethical Studies*, as the dialectical successor to morality, religion is a synthesis of the conflicting elements at work at the lower level of ethical reasoning. But if religion is a 'solution' to the 'contradiction' of morality, the Hegelian construction of this step should warn us off any expectation that it is a *final* solution. It may mark the end of the book, but as will be observed both below and in the next chapter, puzzles remain. And this is inevitable, for as has already been shown, Bradley did not believe the contradictions of the universe such as to be finally solvable by any purely intellectual manoeuvring.

It should be noted that although religion transcends morality, it does not negate, but incorporates it. 'Morality . . . survives within religion. It is only as mere morality that it vanishes',[227] says Bradley. Since it originates from morality, religion has important similarities with it. For Bradley, religion's practical aim is the same as that of morality. Like morality it aims to realize the ideal, both in ourselves and in the world, and thus they provide us with the very same duties, 'as all moral duties are also religious, so all religious duties are also moral'.[228] The significance of this is two-fold. First, there is no possibility of these two spheres differing or coming into conflict with each other. Secondly, if we take religion away from the real world, the world of nation, society, art, or science, it has nothing left to do and so vanishes. Consequently, just as Bradley argues that there could be no merely 'private' morality, he concludes that there can be no merely 'private' religion; as morality requires the wider social community, so religion only makes sense within a wider, but invisible, community of believers.

But religion is not simply the same thing as morality. The main difference between them is that in religion the objective is no mere idea but something actual. Religion is more than simply pious hoping. It is not just morality, not even morality 'touched by emotion' to use Matthew Arnold's phrase,[229] and it is not just a name for our deepest hopes and desires. Its great value and importance to humankind stem precisely from its assurance of success. In this fashion, we might say, Bradley stresses *realism* or *truth* as a crucial component of the religious consciousness; and here we may see him as opposing the views of contemporary thinkers such as Arnold, although his criticisms would apply equally to any more modern anti-realist or non-cognitivist view of religion. Once

---

[226] How this perfection of the universe sits with the existence of evil will be considered in the next chapter.
[227] *Ethical Studies*, 333, cf. *Appearance and Reality*, 390.
[228] *Ethical Studies*, 333.   [229] *Literature and Dogma*, 21.

again, we find that Bradley takes his stand with common sense against theological sophistication.

5.5.3 The contradiction of religion

Having seen how he extols its virtues, it may come as a surprise to observe (as hinted above) that religion, for Bradley, is nonetheless something inherently contradictory. But this is a conclusion which cannot be avoided for, as we have seen, religion is only one part of life, and it was Bradley's firm belief, applied throughout his philosophy, that anything less than the whole, as an abstraction from that, is irredeemably flawed. As something contradictory it must be judged but another form of appearance.

Although there is essentially just one contradiction, it manifests itself in several different fields. Religion turns out to be contradictory in its experience, in its theories, and in its practices; and these may be considered in turn. To even the casual observer religious psychology appears as a confused and contradictory subject. It is characterized by conflicting feelings; admiration, approval, and devotion on the one hand, fear, resignation, and estrangement on the other. But, for Bradley, that is symptomatic of an even deeper incoherence. The religious consciousness presents itself, not just as an actually existing reality—the saved soul—but also as something which needs to be brought about in ourselves. The good in us is both realized and to be realized. 'The self at once struggles to be perfect, and knows at the same time that its consummation is already worked out.'[230] On the one hand, whether we think the kingdom of heaven future or present, 'what is done is approached, not with the knowledge of a doubtful success, but with the fore-felt certainty of an already accomplished victory.'[231] But on the other hand, the work of perfecting ourselves, the work of combating evil, is always something still to be done. Both of these elements are given to one and the same consciousness, and that forces it into a perpetual 'oscillation in sentiment'.[232] For Bradley, the experience of religion is the experience of that which is evolving yet already evolved. This paradox is, of course, both a version of that met with above in Green and Caird, and one which even orthodox Christian theology would recognize.

Any attempt to express the religious consciousness in theory is equally contradictory. What religion asserts is the 'inseparable unity of human and divine',[233] but such a unity threatens to submerge its two terms one into another. In consequence, religion also involves an assertion of their separateness, yet to speak of man and God as distinct and joined by a relation is, in view of Bradley's monistic denial of the reality of all relations, equally disastrous. It is a direct and inevitable consequence of Bradley's general philosophical position that any relations between man and God, or within the divine itself, are immediately fatal to its claim to describe ultimate reality. There is a tension between on the one hand, pantheism or immanence, and, on the other, separateness or transcendence. Bradley strongly criticizes any emphasis on individuality (either human

---

[230] *Appearance and Reality*, 390–1.   [231] *Ethical Studies*, 334.
[232] *Appearance and Reality*, 392.   [233] *Ethical Studies*, 330.

or divine) when it is pushed to such an extreme that it prevents us from recognizing the immanence of God. He considers this particularly destructive in the case of orthodox Christianity; to keep God outside nature is to impoverish him,[234] while only if God and man are considered to be identical in a subject can we make any sense of the Atonement.[235] But he also insists that to press unity too far is to court disaster in precisely the opposite direction; for complete suppression of the relation between God and humankind, can only lead to the invisibility, and subsequent disappearance, of religion and the good. Pantheism is not consistent with an individual creator God.

Rather in the manner that he proposes a theory of judgement which, although it cannot escape contradiction, does bypass the worst defects of subject–predicate thought, despite his belief that incoherence was unavoidable in matters of theology, Bradley speculates on the possibility of constructing a belief system in which the level of incoherence might be reduced.

There is, I should say a need, and there is even a certain demand, for a new religion. We want a creed to recognize and justify in due proportion all human interests and at the same time supply the intellect with that to which it can hold with confidence. Whether we shall get this new religion, and, if so, how, whether by modification of what exists or in some other way, I am unable to surmise.[236]

It might be suggested that what Bradley seeks and calls for here might be met by some eastern religions, but it seems likely Bradley himself had in mind nothing more than a strongly immanentist version of Christianity.

It is not surprising that the contradictions which infect religious consciousness and theory should make their way into religious practice. On the one hand, if religion finds everything in the world to be already good, 'it may cease to be moral at all, and become at once, therefore, irreligious.'[237] For if everything is already good, every action becomes indifferent, and religion esteems any practice, however worthless, by an empty spirit of devotion. On the other hand, if it overemphasizes discord, then 'it is threatened with a lapse into mere morality'.[238] For then the religious believer forgoes the perfection and peace of the spiritual life, becoming nothing more than a particularly zealous worker in the cause of the good. Bradley argues that the ceremonies of religion are all marked by a kind of double-think,[239] for instance, we must pray as though everything depended on God, but act as though it depended on us.

The net result of all this contradiction is that religion turns out to be a matter of what Bradley calls, 'self-deception', 'compromise', and 'mythology.' Given the contradictory nature of religion, we might wonder how it can possibly be something so satisfying to us. This brings to the fore the question of faith, for, in Bradley's mind, it is faith that

---

[234] 'Unless the Maker and Sustainer become also the indwelling Life and Mind and inspiring Love, how much of the universe is impoverished!' (*Essays on Truth and Reality*, 436).

[235] *Ethical Studies*, 323. Bosanquet and both Caird brothers take the same view. (See below p.431 note and above pp.156, 164–5).

[236] *Essays on Truth and Reality*, 446.   [237] *Appearance and Reality*, 393.

[238] *Appearance and Reality*, 393.   [239] *Appearance and Reality*, 392.

turns these contradictions into productive lived realities. In this we see his debt to Protestant Christianity.[240] He defines religious faith as 'the identification of my will with a certain object,'[241] arguing that it is an essentially practical affair (although he is not prepared to take this as a definition of faith in general.) Bradley stresses the fact that faith is more than just a cognitive state; it is a volitional one. But so, it might be said, is practical reasoning. And here he brings in a second virtue of faith. Unlike practical reason, it can deal with the contradictory, for faith too is contradictory; it is a making believe, which implies that one simultaneously does and does not believe. Putting the same point another way, faith, though the active identification of myself with the religious object, at the same time presuppose an existing separation to be overcome between myself and that object. Bradley argues that the only legitimating role of private or public religious ceremony is that of strengthening faith.[242]

5.5.4 The truth of religions

The contradictions of religion should not lead us to think that it is worthless, for it is a consequence of Bradley's general views that *all* thought is contradictory, but he does not regard this as incompatible with its also possessing a degree of truth. That the truth of any given idea or ideas is a matter of degree is a Bradlean idea we have already met with in the previous chapter, and something measured by 'the relative importance of the purpose which the ideas serve, and how well, viewed from all sides, they aid and express its satisfaction'.[243]

What in the case of religion is that purpose? In *Appearance and Reality* Bradley writes as though he did not really know what it is, suggesting that we need to initiate an enquiry into the matter, and offering some preliminary methodological hints.[244] He even indicates that there may be no single simple answer, 'I have come to the conclusion that it is impossible to answer this question [what is religion?], unless we recognize that religion, in the end, has more meanings than one.'[245] However, at other times he is more positive. He says 'Religion is the attempt to express the complete reality of goodness through every aspect of our being',[246] and again that it is the attempt 'to realize in the fullest sense in my will the supremacy of goodness'.[247]

Whatever uncertainty may attach to the precise aim of religion, what is more certain is that in whatever way we understand its purpose, religion scores very highly indeed, and thus possesses a very great degree of truth. Bradley says, 'there is nothing more real than what comes in religion'[248] and, 'The man, who demands a reality more solid than that of the religious consciousness, seeks he does not know what.'[249] Indeed at one

---

[240] *Ethical Studies*, 325.   [241] *Essays on Truth and Reality*, 24.   [242] *Ethical Studies*, 339.
[243] *Essays on Truth and Reality*, 431.   [244] *Appearance and Reality*, 399–401.
[245] *Appearance and Reality*, 388 note.   [246] *Appearance and Reality*, 401.
[247] *Essays on Truth and Reality*, 431.   [248] *Ethical Studies*, 398.   [249] *Ethical Studies*, 398.

point he seems to suggest that *anything* which fulfilled our deepest religious needs would thereby be true.[250]

There is one last aspect of his theory of degrees of truth and reality which is worth drawing out. We perhaps feel a lingering sense of dissatisfaction that God is not to be associated with the Absolute. But here a comparison with metaphysics is instructive. Bradley argues that the axioms of metaphysics though not true are the truest possible; they are as close as we can approach cognitively to the Absolute.[251] And the same seems to hold of religious beliefs. From the practical side to life, God is as real and important as one can get. Thus there is no sense in which we are being asked to make do with second best. The Absolute is no more the last step which religion might but is forbidden to take, than death is the last event in life we might but never do experience.

5.5.5 Critical history

Bradley's very first philosophical work was a short pamphlet entitled *The Presuppositions of Critical History*, published in 1874, which deals with the problem of evidence in historical research. There is much of general epistemic interest in this work,[252] but its significance to us here—and at the time—is otherwise; for although he discusses in the book only general questions of the philosophy of history, avoiding all talk of religion, the underlying significance of his topic would not have been lost on any of Bradley's contemporaries. In a Europe that was still reeling from the blow it had been struck by the biblical criticism of the Tübingen school—and still further in the background we can also sense Hume's famous discussion of miracles—the unstated issue under consideration was the rationality of belief in the biblical miracles.

Philosophically, Bradley tries to steer a middle course, arguing that history is not the simple recording of bare facts, but neither must it be subjectivist or generally sceptical. In short it is critical. The position he finally comes down to is that historical investigation rests crucially upon the use of analogy; we are entitled to believe about the past only that which bares some analogy to what we know in our own experience. Of course, the implications of this conclusion for the possibility of miracles and the quest for the historical Jesus are sceptical. Since they are clearly not analogous to anything today, miracles must be considered as unlikely. Via a discussion of three classical, rather than biblical, examples, Bradley notes that a historian's decision can never be final, since later experience may provide us with suitable analogies.[253] But even this concession is not promising, for in effect it would simply show that some event was not miraculous after all. Turning to the question of recovering the historical Jesus, though his illustration of the difficulties facing an artist attempting to restore an old and badly corrupted fresco, Bradley suggests that it may be that the historical people we want to

---

[250] *Essays on Truth and Reality*, 431.   [251] See below Chapter 8.3.11.
[252] For discussion see Holdcroft, 'Bradley Collingwood and *The Presuppositions of Crtical History*'.
[253] *Presuppositions of Critical History*, 63–4.

seek just cannot be retrieved.[254] Thus, in keeping with the other British Idealists he argues for a naturalistic interpretation of the Bible that excludes miracles.

Nevertheless it must be said that all this was a subject which Bradley found extremely difficult, and to which he returned on more than one occasion. His views on the matter were always tentative, and he warns that, 'the extent and general nature of the influence, which a modification of history must influence on religious belief is a subject on which it is remarkable easy to come to a conclusion, and extremely hard to come to the right one.'[255]

5.5.6 Christian morality

During his middle years Bradley wrote some extremely hostile papers on Christian morality. He said, 'if by Christianity is meant the moral doctrine of the New Testament and of the early Christians, I have certainly urged that this is defective. Viewed as a supreme guide in life I do not hesitate to call it detestable.'[256] His criticisms of New Testament and early Christian ethics stem from the same worry that produced his general criticism of over-emphasis on individuality in ethics.[257] In sharp contrast to, for example, Green or Edward Caird, he regarded early Christianity as the one-sided view of a millennial cult who saw little need for the notion of an enduring society. Bradley considers their resulting morality to be so absurd that no modern Christian ever held it honestly. He objects that it is simply unable to cope in any realistic way with contemporary social institutions and with such socialized concepts as private property and patriotism. In this opposition to Christian morality we find a strong point of contrast between Bradley and the other three Idealists considered in this chapter, for they in questioning orthodox religious dogma held all the more firmly to orthodox Christian values.

Although he calls for 'a return to a non-Christian and perhaps Hellenic ideal',[258] Bradley's opposition to Christian morality should not be over-stressed, however, for when he attempts later to put forward an alternative morality, he admits there is a sense in which it might be called Christian.[259] In line with his criticisms above, and the position outlined in the pre-religious stage of *Ethical Studies*, this ethic emphasizes the social whole. It consists in the immanent realization of the divine in the finite world and the assertion of the good as the self-realization of the world as a whole, implying both autonomy: no external authority, and autocracy: no limits to the rights of the whole over its constituent members.

Is this a Christian ethic? It may sound unfamiliar, but we should surely have much sympathy with Bradley when he argues that any sharp stress on the individuality of persons is at odds with genuinely Christian ethics, claiming that 'Unless there is a real identity in men, the "inasmuch as ye did it to the least of these" becomes an absurdity.'[260] Even if his emphasis is on nation or state, this marks but a practical limitation of

---

[254] *Presuppositions of Critical History*, 58–9.   [255] *Presuppositions of Critical History*, 3.
[256] 'Note on Christian Morality', 177.   [257] See Chapter 6.   [258] *Collected Essays*, 149.
[259] 'Note on Christian Morality', 182.
[260] *Ethical Studies*, 334–5 note. The Biblical reference is to Matthew 25:40.

focus, for Bradley admits that in the end any nation must aim at the good and the harmony of all mankind.[261]

5.5.7 *Personal immortality*

Unlike Idealists such as Caird and Jones, but in line with others such as Green and Bosanquet, Bradley was not very concerned about the doctrine of personal immortality. In general he finds it difficult to square with his scepticism as to the ultimate coherence of selves. And although he is not prepared to deny it, in so far as we lack an adequate theory of personal identity, and hence of survival, he is not keen to say much either way.

He is extremely sceptical about spiritualistic evidence for personal immortality, and on the whole seems to think it unlikely to be true, but more importantly than that, he questions the very need for and significance of the doctrine. He notes with approval the desire to be reunited with those we have loved, but of other motives he is more damning. The fear of death he finds quite nonsensical. And in general he argues that our requirement is for a qualitative difference, not simply a quantitative one. Rather than mere extension, what is needed is an assurance 'that what we call this life with its before and after is not the main reality'.[262] In calling for a qualitative over a quantitative enhancement to life Bradley emphasizes the mystical element of religion; even if we cannot say what it is we seek we know that it is something very different from our present reality.

In sum, such matters cannot be known one way or the other, but as they stand are probably not very important anyway. About such things the philosopher cannot be expected to know more for certain than the rest of men, but it is not in such beliefs that the essence of religion consists.

5.6 Concluding remarks

Reviewing the philosophies of religion of Green, the Cairds, and F.H. Bradley we find a complex pattern of both similarity and difference. There is common commitment to the power of reason to vouchsafe for us a metaphysic of Absolute Idealism which in its assertions of the primacy of the spiritual and the immanence of the infinite within the finite grounds our religious aspirations. Philosophy saves us from the crisis of faith. But looking in more detail, we find that each approaches that crisis differently. Green's concern is to preserve the significance of religious life. If traditional dogma is untenable, philosophy may offer an alternative, but must we nonetheless say that the history of the Christian worldview has been the history of a misapprehension, that the personal faith of millions is an exercise in self-delusion? By taking the notion of the Holy Spirit at work within the life of the believer, of the Church, or of history itself, and making that

---

[261] *Collected Essays*, 175.   [262] *Appearance and Reality*, 438.

the very centre of his system, Green develops a perspective from which he can hold fast to traditional religious attitudes and values without traditional religious dogmas. He suggests that philosophy can reconstruct the metaphysical truth behind religion's discredited theology, but offers little himself by way of detailed thought towards that project. For John Caird, by contrast, this becomes the central work to be undertaken in support of religion, as he deploys the full resources of Hegelian philosophy to shore up, not simply theism, but Christianity itself. To the uncritical believer his faith is the God-given centre of his world and one of the chief elements that contributed to the Victorian crisis of faith was the disquieting attainment of sufficient *perspective* to seriously undermine that comfortable parochialism, the clear recognition of the existence of other faiths and even other (past) Christianities. The vital point in Edward Caird's eyes was to find a grand narrative within which all this variety and change could be understood as development and direction, a teleological scheme in which even the religious perturbations of the current age could be seen to have their place and purpose. John and Edward Caird together with Green presented perspectives which, if different, could be easily combined, and the resultant system was one that claimed the allegiance of a great many of the Idealists. Bradley, by contrast, was more idiosyncratic. He was less willing than they to reinterpret ordinary or established belief, and from his refusal to regard the Absolute as either personal or divine, through his doubts about dogma, to his uncomfortable admission that his ethics was in many respects more Hellenic than Christian, all too often his philosophy articulates Victorian religious doubts rather than solving them. But what he has to say does speak also to their resolution. For if religion is contradictory, the contradiction is an Hegelian one; resolved in a higher level that re-packages its valid insights while purging itself of its flaws.

6

The Idealist Ethic of Social Self-Realization

In addition to and, indeed, connected with its fresh metaphysics and philosophy of religion, the British neo-Hegelian school put forward a radically new kind of moral theory; one which we might call the idealist ethic of social self-realization. Prior to this decisive point, moral philosophy in Britain was a contested domain with no one mode of thought achieving dominance. In the mid-nineteenth century, it had been characterized, in the main, by hedonistic utilitarianism (such as that of Bentham or J.S. Mill) which tended to be 'radical' and, balancing it, by various brands of intuitionism (such as that of William Whewell or Henry Calderwood) which in their appeal to 'moral sense' or 'conscience' were more conservative. To that mix had gradually been added the influence of Kant's moral thought (transmitted through, for example, Martineau) and of evolutionary naturalism (pressed, for example, by Herbert Spencer, Francis Galton, and Leslie Stephen). But for all these new forces had begun to make themselves felt, the basic understanding of moral philosophy, as an ahistorical search for first principles of right action, had continued essentially unchanged. Idealism shattered this. Rapidly gaining popularity, its re-construal of the moral problem came to be the dominant mode of thought in ethics for twenty years, and a major force for twenty more after that. Indeed for many people, less interested perhaps to follow them into other more speculative areas, it was *the* philosophical doctrine that defined British Idealism. This chapter will examine that system of ethics, through the theories of Bradley, Green, and Caird, as well as (more briefly) those who popularized and developed them.

6.1 F.H. Bradley

In 1876, setting out a moral philosophy quite unlike anything that had gone before, F.H. Bradley burst onto the philosophical scene. Without simply appealing to an outmoded religious conception of the universe, his *Ethical Studies*[1] nonetheless claimed to overturn

---

[1] For many years Bradley declined to republish *Ethical Studies*. This was due as much as anything to its highly polemical nature and 'the decay of those superstitions against which largely it was directed' (*Ethical*

the narrow orthodoxies of the scientific world picture and offer a view of mankind as something transcending any analysis simply in terms of matter endowed with instinct. Perhaps more than any other, it was the book that made people really take notice of the new idealistic wave—in retrospect Bernard Bosanquet described it as 'epoch-making'.[2]

One of the most distinctive things about the book was its *style*, which is bold, lively, and picturesque. It still makes a great read.[3] But while that may commend it to us, *as literature*, it must be confessed that, *as philosophy*, and especially to modern reading tastes, it can make its import hard to follow. Bradley's ideas and terminology are often alien and unfamiliar, his arguments are often compressed, while his aims—even at times his conclusions—are often left implicit. Moreover the book is highly polemical and, while this makes for writing that is smart and full of memorable turns of phrase it makes at the same time for writing which is often far from lucid; too frequently he descends into ridicule of opponents when what is really wanted is argument or explanation.

But what made the book truly radical when it was first published was its use of Hegel. It has often been noted that *Ethical Studies* was in fact the most Hegelian of all Bradley's writings. This is so in two respects. First, there is the Hegelian pedigree of many of its concepts and themes; for example, its central claim that neither individuals nor their ethical duties can be understood except in the context of the wider social whole in which they occur is a clear, and acknowledged,[4] reworking of the Hegelian notions of *Sittlichkeit* and concrete universality. But secondly, the Hegelian influence extends beyond the book's content to its very structure. It has an explicitly dialectical form in which positions are advanced, criticized, and then modified in an ever advancing (and ascending) sequence, which is why Bradley insisted that 'the essays must be read in the order in which they stand'.[5] He was right to stress the point. The book must indeed be read from one end to the other, not selectively taking particular chapters out of context (as has often happened), for it is constructed as a continuous argument with the earlier essays preparing the way for those that follow, the later ones amplifying or qualifying those that come before it. Its style is dialectic in the sense that many of its claims are but provisional, asserted at one point only to be modified later on. But the debt to Hegel should not be allowed to obscure all others; the book also drew heavily on Aristotle in its emphasis on the development of character and the fundamentally social or political make-up of human nature. Bradley concludes his discussion of the position of the utilitarians with the recommendation that they need to

---

Studies, 356n); the need for such a book had simply passed. But in the year of his death he began preparing additional material towards a new edition. Although the task was unfinished, and consequently we cannot assume that these are the only changes he would have made, the revisions which were subsequently incorporated into the second edition of 1928, were neither very serious nor very numerous. They concern for the most part psychological matters (reflecting the growing emphasis that psychology came to play in his thinking).

[2] Bosanquet, 'Life and Philosophy', 58. 'A page of it dilutes into a hundred of any other' he claimed (59).
[3] The poet T.S. Eliot was a great admirer. See below p.347.
[4] See below p.188.
[5] *Ethical Studies*, viii.

read—not Hegel—but Aristotle; for his own theory of self-realization is not he thinks fundamentally at variance with that of Aristotle (and Plato) that we should seek happiness or well-being.[6]

A recurring difficulty in understanding and assessing Bradley's *Ethical Studies* lies in the fact that much of what he assumes is left unsaid. His aim was to write a book of moral philosophy only, without trespassing into matters of logic, metaphysics, or psychology, but he is handicapped in this ambition by the very fact that he himself did not believe that there were any sharp or final divisions between questions in ethics and deeper questions about the nature of ultimate reality. In consequence we find him constantly touching on more fundamental issues which underlie and explain his meaning, but from which he draws himself back, or at which he merely hints. Many of these he went on to develop in later works, and a full understanding of his position requires a grasp of the rest of his thought (which is one reason why, reversing chronology, this study has looked first at his metaphysics), but the reader of *Ethical Studies* alone does not have available that material.

6.1.1 Free will

The book opens with a discussion of free will and responsibility. Bradley tries to capture the common-sense, or 'vulgar', notion of responsibility—for a person to be responsible for an act it must be one which they did, it must have issued from their will without compulsion, and it must have been chosen in understanding (especially moral understanding) of the situation; we cannot be responsible where we do not understand what we do. But neither the indeterministic nor the deterministic philosophies of action standardly advanced can really capture this picture, he complains. Indeterminism in its suggestion that certain actions can escape from the causal nexus altogether, reduces liberty to unpredictable and inexplicable chance which, far from saving freedom, 'annihilates the very conditions of it.'[7] Determinism, on the other hand, by resolving everything into sequences of causally connected states, commits itself to a psychology concerned with nothing besides collections of sensations held together by necessitating laws of association; a psychology that renders the enduring objects in which we believe but fictions of the mind, and hence even 'the mind itself . . . a fiction of the mind'.[8] In other words, it loses sight of the underlying continuous agent without which responsibility is nonsense. Neither way is philosophy able to do justice to our ordinary viewpoint.

This discussion highlights a notable feature of the book, namely its great respect for everyday moral thinking. As his thought went out of fashion in later years Bradley's philosophy acquired a reputation for being both abstract and absurd, faults which twentieth-century approaches grounded in science and common sense were supposed to have corrected, but we see here that this reputation was undeserved. However, we

---

[6] *Ethical Studies*, 129, 140.   [7] *Ethical Studies*, 12.   [8] *Ethical Studies*, 38.

should not make the opposite mistake of supposing that he was simply a slave to everyday intellectual habit or prejudice; if we respect common sense we need not do so uncritically and what is needed, he argues, is to find 'a philosophy which *thinks* what the vulgar *believe*'.[9] The rest of *Ethical Studies* itself may be read as his attempt to do just that.

On the basis of this chapter's support for the common-sense understanding of moral responsibility, it has sometimes been thought that Bradley held a retributivist view of punishment. But the true picture is more complex. Neither straightforwardly endorsed, nor quite rejected and left behind, the view of the vulgar is rather 'carried forward' somehow to find its place in a higher synthesis. We get a sense of what that place might be when, revisiting the question some years later, Bradley argues that there is value in each of the three 'traditional' theories of punishment—education, deterrence, and retribution—but that each must be superseded or held subordinate to a higher law, 'what we may call the principle of social surgery'.[10] Bringing together Darwinism and idealist social holism, this justifies punishment in terms of its value to the social body *as a whole*.

6.1.2 Self-realization

After this initial discussion, the substance of the book proper begins with a consideration of the question, 'Why should I be moral?' which Bradley rejects as senseless. Morality is precisely the assertion of some end valuable in itself, so that were we to seek it for some other ulterior reason our action would not be moral at all. Yet taking it as an end in itself, there can be no categorical imperative, no value or rule a man may be compelled to recognize regardless of his own personal feelings and desires. If he will not acknowledge some particular value, or others which entail it, including that of consistency itself, if at the extreme he asserts complete scepticism and just does whatever he feels prompted to do, then argument ceases.

Thus we cannot prove that there is anything good in itself, we can only assume that there is and ask what it might be. That, of course, is not something to be expressed in simply a sentence—it is the topic of the whole book—but there is, thinks Bradley, merit in offering as a place to start from 'the most general expression' possible of that goal.[11] In its very broadest terms Bradley suggests that we may find the end of all action in *self-realization*. The fundamental issue of ethics is not what we do but what we are. He does not offer to prove the appropriateness of this 'formula',[12] in part because that would require a completed metaphysical system, but also because it is to some extent

---

[9] *Ethical Studies*, 41.

[10] *Collected Essays*, 152.

[11] *Ethical Studies*, 64. This strategy opens up the possibility of a certain species of justification for morality after all. Although it may not be defended as instrumental to some further goal, we can say more than just that it is to be pursued for its own sake, for in so far as morality is a part and not the whole end of human life, it may be shown to be an integral element in a wider human end pursued for its own sake (Irwin, *Development of Ethics*, 546).

[12] *Ethical Studies*, 65.

simply a blank schema, something to be filled in and rendered plausible in the essays that follow. But if not proved, the claim may be explained. Were the psychological egoist correct that people aim only at pleasure, that is, at pleasurable states of their own being, it would follow immediately that all action aims at self-realization. Bradley rejects that doctrine, but his own position is not very distant from it, for he holds that we only aim at what we desire, that 'what we desire must be in our minds',[13] and hence that all deliberate action is a species of self-fulfilment. In wanting a given state to obtain our very identity becomes bound up with it—it 'belongs to' us and is 'made part of' us as we 'feel ourselves one with it'—making its realization a realization also of our own self. Our identity lies in the realization of our goals.

However, Bradley goes on, what we aim to realize is not simply *a state* of the self but rather *the self as a whole*. For the self is more than simply a sum of its parts. What is needed instead is 'some concrete whole that we can realize in our acts, and carry out in our life',[14] something with a persistent overall cohesive pattern and not simply a haphazard series of disconnected individual elements. The good life is not that which jumps from whatever is best at one moment to whatever is best at another, like an investor who somehow manages always to buy stock which is rising which he sells before it falls, or like a politician who manages to switch sides just as public opinion changes, or like the fashionable dresser who somehow manages always to keep up with whatever look is in vogue. No, the good life is a life good as a whole, one springing from a unity of vision, a life which manifests a single aim and overall coherence—whatever the vicissitudes of the world around us. It is a life of integrity. We seek to realize ourselves as what he calls an 'infinite whole.'[15] This Bradley understands, not in the mathematical sense of being without end, but in the Hegelian sense (already encountered) of being self-contained; the finite is that which is limited from outside, the infinite that which is limited from within.[16] Understood in this way Bradley's demand that the moral life be infinite has clear parallels with Kant's demand that it be autonomous rather than heteronomous. It must, of course, be asked how, if human beings are finite and inevitably affected from outside, they could ever become an infinite whole of the kind that is suggested here. Bradley's reply is this: 'You can not be a whole, unless you join a whole.'[17] In other words, only as an integral member of some unity with which we are fully identified, can we enjoy anything like the autonomy of existence which is recommended here. It is worth stressing that at this stage the notion of 'self-realization' remains an entirely formal one—an immoral man realizes himself as much as a moral one—and thus 'the question in morals is to find the true whole, realizing which will practically realize the true self.'[18] It is to this question

---

[13] *Ethical Studies,* 82.   [14] *Ethical Studies,* 95.
[15] *Ethical Studies,* 74. see also *Mr Sidgwick's Hedonism,* 85.
[16] Bradley's discussion of this point was very influential. Among other places, we find it repeated in Bosanquet, *Life and Finite Individuality,* 181, and Jones, *Principles of Citizenship,* 82–4.
[17] *Ethical Studies,* 79.
[18] *Ethical Studies,* 69.

Bradley now turns, considering two standard ethical positions, both of which could be thought of as ways of fleshing out this bare pattern: hedonism or 'pleasure for pleasure's sake, and Kantianism or 'duty for duty's sake'.

6.1.3 Hedonism

To begin with he objects that the doctrine of hedonism fails to accord with our ordinary moral beliefs; 'if there be any one thing that well-nigh the whole voice of the world, from all ages, nations, and sorts of men, has agreed to declare is *not* happiness, that thing is pleasure, and the search for it.'[19] But the position is theoretically flawed too. In his eyes the fundamental problem is its inability to provide us with any solid or realizable goal for our lives. In conceiving of pleasures as mental states isolated from the means by which they are arrived at, it fixes on merely subjective and transitory feelings and reduces the good life to nothing but a series of such 'perishing particulars'.[20] The 'self' to be realized evaporates into a heterogeneous sequence of instantaneous 'satisfactions'. The hedonist attempts to give more unity and coherence to his postulated ideal by suggesting we aim at a 'sum' of pleasures, but the pleasures *of a lifetime* cannot be summed until we are dead and past enjoying them. We might seek instead to maximize the pleasures *of the moment*, but if our target here is as much pleasure as possible, we must all inevitably fail to reach it since no one can experience an infinity of pleasures, while if we aim for as much pleasure as we can get, trivially everyone all of the time achieves that, at least by the lights of the hedonist psychology that underlies this theory in the first place.[21] But if these are the problems of egoistic hedonism, it is clear that they cannot be overcome by 'modern utilitarianism' which seeks not the pleasure of one but that of all. For if there can be no greatest happiness for an individual, the sum of happiness for many is just as much of a 'wild and impossible fiction'.[22] Nor thinks Bradley is hedonism even practical. John Stuart Mill would have us believe that the rules of morality lay down our gathered knowledge of what produces pleasure, a kind of 'moral Almanac',[23] but it is always possible to imagine cases where following these rules would not produce the greatest happiness. In such cases, if we keep to the rule it is unequal to its professed end, but if we break it then it seems to show itself unnecessary. Bradley's attack on hedonism has become justly famous, and in it his invective reaches great heights.

At the time of his writing this chapter the principal statement of hedonistic theory was still John Stuart Mill's *Utilitarianism*, but just before the book went to press, Henry Sidgwick brought out his important *Methods of Ethics* (1874), which also advanced a utilitarian view and with much greater sophistication and detail than Mill. Bradley added a short note to the end of his chapter in response to Sidgwick's book, but, feeling he had not done the matter justice, he also published a pamphlet the following year. Entitled *Mr Sidgwick's Hedonism*, this detailed critique adds little new with regard to

---

[19] *Ethical Studies*, 86–7.   [20] *Ethical Studies*, 96.   [21] *Ethical Studies*, 97–8.
[22] *Ethical Studies*, 103.   [23] *Ethical Studies*, 105.

Bradley's views on hedonism in general, but holding that any consistent hedonism must be egoistic, he argues that Sidgwick's universalist objectivist version fails to make its case to the contrary. Were the egoistic to claim (as Sidgwick thinks he does) objective desirability for his own goals whilst denying it to those of others he could be convicted of inconsistency, but in fact he makes no such claim. He holds not that his are the only desirable ends, but rather that his are the only desirable ends *to him*. The egoistic position is in effect the denial that *anything* is *objectively* desirable, and as such immune to logical critique.[24]

6.1.4 *Kantianism*

Turning his attention to hedonism's main rival, Bradley objects that Kantianism is no more able to face the court of common sense than it, for the ethic that urges 'duty for duty's sake' insists that laws are exceptionless, but ordinary morality does not suppose this at all. There can be no absolute universal principles of moral action, for inevitably laws conflict and there is no rule which in some circumstances might not be broken. Nor again is Kantianism without deeper theoretical defect. It weakness lies, Bradley urges, in the excessively abstract or formal character of its conception; in concentrating exclusively on its rational side it fails to realize the self as a whole.[25] The problem is that no act can be the mere carrying out of an abstract principle of duty, and we cannot will without willing something definite, but there is no way of passing from the mere form of duty to any particular duties themselves, or what comes to the same thing, any act whatsoever can be shown to be in accordance with such abstract principles. In short, it tells us to do the right thing for the sake of the right, but it does nothing towards telling us what that thing is. Bradley was not, of course, the first to raise these objections, and he makes explicit his debt to Hegel in this critique.[26]

Hedonism was found excessively particular, Kantianism excessively universal. Both errors, argues Bradley, arise out of a false abstraction, in the one case of pleasure itself apart from pleasant acts, and in the other of the general form of duty apart from individual duties themselves. What is needed is a middle path between these two extremes, a combination of the particular and the universal, a reconciliation which can at the same time hold on to their other valid insights. This is precisely what Bradley offers in the next chapter entitled 'My Station and its Duties'.

6.1.5 *'My Station and its Duties'*

Progress is made once we see that previous theories, especially hedonism (but to an extent Kantianism also), operate with a mistaken conception of individuality. They treat individuals as distinct elements that can be added up to form an aggregate. But that is wrong. Humans are social creatures. They do not live alone (like, say, polar bears) but in communities. Moreover this is essential to their being. Although the actual forms of

---

[24] *Mr Sidgwick's Hedonism*, 98–104. [25] Irwin, *Development of Ethics*, 561–2.
[26] *Ethical Studies*, 148 note 1.

association which we find among people are conventional (which explains their diversity) we can have strong grounds for saying that social life itself is both natural to and constitutive of our being.

Now, this idea is hardly original. Many of the Idealists (as has already been noted) were wont to trace it back to Aristotle, and even Plato. Bradley's immediate source was more contemporary however, for his position owes much to Hegel's conception of the self; indeed the case is advanced in part through extensive quotation from Hegel.[27] For Hegel any individual self is *what* it is only because of *where* it is—it owes its nature to the social context in which it finds itself—with the consequence that what is most truly individual is, in reality, the community as a whole.[28] Still at the time unfamiliar in Britain, Bradley develops this notion with new vigour and intensity, for he is reacting against the strong individualism of prevailing British philosophy. The key figure he wishes to take issue with here is Mill who asserts the metaphysical autonomy of the individual; people combine together in societies like collections of atoms in physics, Mill insists, not fusions of substances in chemistry.[29]

The falsity of such individualism can be seen in many different ways, responds Bradley. Socialization begins with our birth. We are not born a blank slate, but come into the world already bearing the characteristics of our family, our nation or race, and our species. Although the second is in this day more controversial, the first and third of these must be allowed. Much of the character with which we are born we share with our family and species, from whom we inherit it. But what nature starts nurture only confirms, because from the moment it is born the child is educated and socialized by and into its community. Our very life with others is a constant schooling that inevitably shapes us profoundly, a unremitting formative pressure that not even the wisest or most stubborn among us can resist. Which of our beliefs, attitudes or characteristics have we come to quite by ourselves wholly unaided? In explicating this process of socialization Bradley particularly calls attention to language, for language is far less our servant than we imagine. It shapes our very thoughts and characters, but at the same time carries with it the ideas and sentiments of society. One need only think, for example, of the way in which the language of the Bible has dug itself deep into the consciousness of Western civilization. Bradley emphasizes too that the socially determined development of our self is not a process of our youth only. Once we reach adulthood, we take up a position in life, and our identity is largely formed by that station and role in society, he urges. A person may be, say, an office worker, a parent and a member of the local football club, and probably most of his weekly activities can be explained under one or other of those three headings. We like to think that we make our place in life, but in truth matters are reversed and it is our place in life that

[27] *Ethical Studies*, 172–3, 185–7. The citations are from Hegel's *Philosophische Abhandlungen* and his *Phenomenology of Spirit*, §§349–52.
[28] See for example *Phenomenology of Spirit*, §§306, 447, 461.
[29] *A System of Logic*, Bk VI, ch. VII.

makes us. As a last but no less vital element of the picture, our identity is massively shaped by our relations to others, our family, friends, colleagues, and acquaintances. 'I am who I am because of everyone', a recent advertising slogan for a mobile phone company (Orange), could well have been Bradley's own here, for he holds that social relations make for personhood. We define who we are, we become who we are, through our interrelations with others.

Where do all these points take us? What Bradley is arguing here is that the mere individual, the unit out of which Mill wished to build society, is a non-existent 'fiction'.[30] The individual apart from the community is an unreal 'abstraction',[31] not even comprehensible except as a member of a society. The idea that society is assembled out of distinct units, Bradley dismisses as a 'fable'.[32] Not even marriage, he says, the seemingly most obvious and simple such social composition, is really like this; the marriage unit shapes its two members as much as the other way round. Society, Bradley is suggesting, is an organic whole[33] in which we are but members; like ants in a colony. On our own apart from the wider whole we are really incomplete beings. The agent must not be abstracted out of this context and considered apart from his social relations, for it is they that work to constitute his very identity. 'To know what a man is . . . you must not take him in isolation. He is one of a people, he was born into a family, he lives in a certain society, in a certain state.'[34]

This essentially metaphysical account of self and society has an ethical dimension too. Because we are social in nature, our happiness is social in nature. Fulfilment lies in my station and its duties: 'What [a man] has to do depends on what his place is, what his function is, and all that comes from his station in the organism.'[35] To be moral is to be a good member of one's society, loyally discharging the various responsibilities which membership involves. To some extent this is something which can be demonstrated empirically, for doubtless one of the most satisfying of human joys is that of friendship and community, that of belonging, that of playing a useful role. But more deeply the point is a philosophical one. Because the self we realize is social, so necessarily its happiness is social. A happy father is one whose family is well and content, a happy ruler is one whose subjects thrive under his reign, a happy teacher is one whose students are learning, a happy shopkeeper is one whose customers are satisfied. Whatever his private feelings, in his social role, his content or discontent is social in nature. But it is our social self, Bradley argues, that is our true self, who we are as opposed to who we may take ourselves to be. Since we are social, it is only within a society that we can properly realize ourselves. To make the same point in deontological rather than teleological terms, the moral imperative which I experience as a binding and coercive force capable of standing over and against my individual choice or

---

[30] *Ethical Studies*, 168.   [31] *Ethical Studies*, 173.   [32] *Ethical Studies*, 174.
[33] For more on the notion of an 'organic whole' see Chapter 7.3 below.
[34] *Ethical Studies*, 173.
[35] *Ethical Studies*, 173.

opinion is cashed out as the will of the society in which I find myself, something which in leaving behind my apparent and private self for my more genuine and social identity I come to recognize and embrace as in fact my own true will, the voice of my more authentic identity. Ethics is not about private individuals, not even about the relations between such private individuals, but a matter of the communal life in which we all share, and therefore continuous with political philosophy. This politicizing of moral philosophy, whose other side is precisely a moral underpinning of political philosophy, which we here find in Bradley is as typical of idealist thought as it is unfamiliar today where the disciplines tend to be kept apart.

The goal sought was a combination of the universal and the particular. The ideal of 'My Station and its Duties', as a unified aim for a whole life rather than just a disparate set of targets and as something pertaining not simply to the individual but to the wider social whole, is certainly 'universal'; yet it is in no way formal or abstract, existing as it does only through the concrete details of the actual duties of any given station. It is thus what Bradley calls a 'concrete universal',[36] in the earliest application of this Hegelian notion, later picked up by many of the Idealists. Although the term itself falls out of use in his later writings, the basic notion of a whole which incorporates diversity, 'a perfect unity of homogeneity and specification',[37] remains a very central one throughout his philosophy.

6.1.6 Ideal morality

Presented as a dialectical solution to hedonism and Kantianism, many have thought that 'My Station and its Duties' was Bradley's final position. Moreover widely reported and anthologized (sometimes only in part) the doctrine has often been taken as crude conservatism ('accepting and keeping to your position in the social hierarchy') or relativism ('our moral duty is set by whatever community or age to which we happen to belong to'). But the material to avoid these errors may be found in the last few pages of the chapter as Bradley himself lists a series of 'very serious objections'[38] to his theory. We hope to leave our bad self behind and find our higher truer self in our social station, but a self may become so corrupted or encrusted by bad habits as to be unable to take up its station, and even the best of us can claim the benefits of service only for that period of time in which we are fully engaged in the satisfying work which it gives us. Moreover, even so far as we succeed in placing ourselves in society, we can have no guarantee of self-fulfilment in doing so. For the social whole in which an agent finds himself may demand of him self-sacrifice, or itself 'may be in a confused or rotten condition.'[39] For although there can be no absolute timeless morality, and what is thought right in one age may come to seem wrong in another, such relativism is mitigated through the idea

---

[36] *Ethical Studies*, 162. See Chapter 8.3.5 below.
[37] *Ethical Studies*, 188. Bradley's terminology here is Kantian (*Critique of Pure Reason* A568/B686).
[38] *Ethical Studies*, 202.
[39] *Ethical Studies*, 203.

of evolution, the understanding of history as 'the working out of the true human nature through various incomplete stages'.[40] Nor may a man take his morality *simply* from the society in which he lives. For that is something in a state of historical transition, and as a rational creature he cannot give up the capacity to stand outside his society, reflect upon it, and work to make it better. Nor finally is quite everything that we are given us by society; there are some aspects of self-development which do not involve others at all. Says Bradley, 'the content of the ideal self does not fall wholly within any community, is in short *not* merely the ideal of a perfect social being'.[41]

In other words, there is more to ethics than just my station and its duties. Precisely what more emerges as we move on to consider the next stage of the journey, which Bradley designates 'ideal morality'. Evolving out of the previous stage by retaining its genuine advances at the same time as correcting its flaws, the content of the good self to be realized at this level can be placed under three different heads. The first and still most important (in the sense of providing the largest part of our duties) is our station and its responsbilities, but to this is added a second element which, although still social, covers our aspirations 'beyond what the world expects of us, a will for good beyond what we see to be realized anywhere'.[42] Many people have no moral ideal beyond the station in which they live, but there are others capable of rising to a point of view from which to see a better morality for society. They are, of course, its critics and reformers. The third region concerns duty which, although a recognizable moral imperative, such as the pursuit of beauty or of truth, 'in its essence does not involve direct relation to other men'.[43] Although neither science nor art could ever have arisen without society, and both undoubtedly benefit society, they may be pursued as ends in themselves without appeal to any social organism. It is vital that we notice these two further elements of Bradley's moral system, for they serve to clear him of charges all too often made, that his thought is overly conservative and that he wholly subordinates or even reduces the needs of the individual to those of society. Individuals may, indeed must when necessary, criticize their society, nor are they merely its pawns; they have a life of their own not given to them by their context. But for all that, individuals cannot be understood apart from society.

6.1.7 *The value of the Absolute*

Although the most plausible and complete account of morality that can be given— there is no better system of morality to follow it—ideal morality is, thinks Bradley, no

---

[40] *Ethical Studies*, 192. 'We hold…that the true nature of man, the oneness of homogeneity and specification, is being wrought out in history; in short we believe in evolution. The process of evolution is the humanizing of the bestial foundation of man's nature by carrying out in it the true idea of man' (*Ethical Studies*, 190). In individual terms Bradley sets out in some detail the evolution of the good and bad moral selves in man (*Ethical Studies*, 276ff), while the book's own passage from Hedonism, through Kantianism and Hegelianism, to a new system of 'ideal morality' follows a clearly recognizable path through the history of Western moral philosophy.

[41] *Ethical Studies*, 205.   [42] *Ethical Studies*, 220.   [43] *Ethical Studies*, 222.

more dialectically stable than its predecessors and it too must give way to a higher state. 'Reflection on morality leads us beyond it. It leads us, in short, to see the necessity of a religious point of view.'[44] This transition and Bradley's general view of religion have already been examined, but bringing together metaphysics, religion, and ethics there is one last matter for us to consider; the *value* of the Absolute. Although not to be equated with God, Bradley regards the Absolute to be something of very great value indeed. 'In every sense it is perfect',[45] he tells us. Reality itself, he claims, is so arranged that it meets our own highest evaluative standards—intellectual, emotional and spiritual—in a truly fortuitous and satisfying way; 'Higher, truer, more beautiful, better and more real—these, on the whole, count in the universe as they count for us.'[46] But this claim, for all we might hope it true, will hardly reassure until we have addressed the many questions it throws up.

If the Absolute is perfect, the only possible solution to the problem of evil is that it is some sort of appearance. But, argues Bradley, the price of this solution is that so also must goodness be, for the two are an opposing pair. The Absolute as a whole, he concludes, can be called properly neither good nor evil. However applicable we may find them to its parts, these are contradictory and relational terms which cannot apply to the ultimate reality itself. He says, 'Evil and good are not illusions, but they are most certainly appearances. They are one-sided appearances, each overruled and transmuted in the whole.'[47]

Why does Bradley believe this? The problem he locates is the same as that which powered the transition from ethics to religion discussed in the previous chapter. The basic dilemma can be set out simply enough. To say that ultimate reality is evil is to say that it ought not to be as it is, but, in view of the holism inherent in Bradley's conception of ultimate reality, this presupposes an unacceptable and contradictory separation between idea and existence. The better reality is taken to be, the closer we would get towards healing this unsatisfactory schism (for what is and what ought to be are being brought closer into line with one another) and one would naturally expect that if ultimate reality were to achieve the culmination of this process that it would therefore be in a state of complete goodness. But Bradley argues that it would be no less contradictory to suppose that ultimate reality be good, for, to put it paradoxically, if it truly is as it ought to be then there is no longer any way that it *ought* to be, and thus no content to calling it good. The nub of Bradley's point is this. As standards, good and bad separate what is and what ought to be, demanding as he puts it 'resolution of this difference between idea and existence',[48] but this is a contradictory demand that could

[44] *Ethical Studies*, 314.
[45] *Appearance and Reality*, 213.
[46] *Appearance and Reality*, 488.
[47] *Appearance and Reality*, 355. He says, 'the good is not the Whole, and the Whole, as such, is not good. And, viewed thus in relation to the Absolute, there is nothing either bad or good, there is not anything better or worse' (*Appearance and Reality*, 363).
[48] *Appearance and Reality*, 363.

only be met at the expense of these notions themselves, which presuppose the separation. This contradiction is most clearly seen in that form of the good that we call satisfied desire. Bradley says, 'A satisfied desire is, in short, inconsistent with itself. For, so far as it is quite satisfied, it is not a desire; and, so far as it is a desire, it must remain at least partly unsatisfied.'[49]

The Absolute, then, is something quite beyond good and evil. But does this not leave it in an evaluative vacuum? Bradley thinks not. The Absolute which transcends good and evil is, he thinks, from the evaluative point of view, something perfect. What he means by this claim can be seen by noting that the reason why good and evil do not apply to reality is different in each case. What stops reality being bad is the impossibility of an unsatisfied standard—the divorce between ideal and actual can never be quite complete—what stops it being good is that a satisfied standard is no standard at all. This means that, although the Absolute transcends both good and bad, the transcendence has a definite direction from bad to good rather than good to bad, and that allows us to give some sense to the claim that reality is perfect. Though we cannot really grasp the value of the Absolute, it being beyond our ethical concepts, the passage from bad to good and beyond functions as a kind of arrow towards what we mean.

A comparison may be useful here. Suppose I want to emigrate somewhere safe, and am told of a country that contains neither outlaws nor police. Is this a useful piece of information for me? Perhaps not, for it could be that the country has no laws and thus that these categories do not apply, in which case the information would tell me nothing about how safe it was. But the information might be very relevant, for it could be that the country does have laws, and that the police, being so successful, have caught all the outlaws and, finding themselves without work, have all retired, in which case this would be a very safe place. The sense in which Bradley's Absolute is neither good nor bad is akin to the second rather than the first scenario. Though reality is neither good nor bad, the way in which these concepts fail to apply, allow and give at least some sense to the claim that it is nonetheless perfect. The ascent to perfection has been completed and, in being so, left behind.

There is an exact parallel between Bradley's approach here and that which we found in his metaphysics. In both cases our ordinary concepts do not apply to the Absolute, but the standard against which they fail, allows us to plot a higher sense, and thus give meaning to the idea that reality nonetheless possesses a perfection that transcends our concepts and our comprehension.

Reference to the metaphysical case makes it easier to avoid one potential misunderstanding. Although perfection is for Bradley something that lies at the end of a scale of increasing goodness, it differs from any notion that could be arrived at by merely reflecting upon such a scale and extending its upper ranges without limit. This can be seen in his final definition of perfection. He defines perfection as 'a state of harmony

---

[49] *Appearance and Reality*, 363.

with pleasure', 'a balance of pleasure over pain'.[50] At first sight this might seem to be a return to the discredited world of finite evaluations, but that this is not the case can be seen from the fact that he goes on to add that this has nothing whatsoever to do with quantity. He says, 'If the perfect is the concordant, then no growth of its area or increase of its perfections could make it more complete.'[51] What matters is not how far good outstrips evil, but the simple fact that it does. For evil is the separation of what is and what ought to be, and if that has been removed then good has been removed as well and perfection attained.

But even if we find meaning in the claim that the Absolute is perfect, what licenses us to say that it actually is? It may lie at the end of a dialectical chain of evaluative concepts, but why should it be instantiated? Again in metaphysical terms it may be the most coherent and most real of all possible entities. But why should the culmination of logic and metaphysics be also the culmination of value theory? Is not this just too convenient? Can it be proved? Bradley considers a method that would make this task very easy. In theoretical matters we have a standard (the absence of contradiction) and we assume that this standard is met. We can hardly do otherwise. But is there not also a standard for practical matters, and why can we not assume that this too is met? If we have the right to presume that reality meets the logical criteria of our theoretical thinking, have we not the same right to assume that it meets the practical criteria of our evaluative thinking?

Was this Bradley's reason for believing in the perfection of the Absolute? At first sight it might seem as though it was, for in his discussion of religion he comes close to endorsing something very like this line of thought. He argues that religion evolves of dialectical necessity out of morality.[52] But, for Bradley, the main difference between them is that in religion, unlike morality, the objective is seen not merely as a goal or ideal but as something actual and already realized in the universe. Thus in saying that morality leads to religion, Bradley is giving us a kind of ontological argument, for what, in effect, he is claiming is that, at the end of the day, we cannot think of ultimate goodness as possible only.

However, while not denying that there is some necessity to this passage of thought, Bradley does not in the end consider this to be a genuine argument for the existence of God. He objects that morality and religion are practical matters, whereas the claims that reality is perfect or that God exists are metaphysical or theoretical ones. But, he urges, practical concerns are not in the business of giving descriptions, and we cannot derive descriptions from them. The ethical or religious postulation of perfection remains a moral or practical conclusion rather than a theoretical one. As a description of how things are, he therefore rejects it, concluding that the desired result 'cannot be drawn directly from the practical criterion'.[53] He says, 'If I am theoretically not satisfied, then

---

[50] *Appearance and Reality*, 136, 213.   [51] *Appearance and Reality*, 216.
[52] See above Chapter 5.5.2.   [53] *Appearance and Reality*, 131, cf. 136.

what appears must in reality be otherwise; but, if I am dissatisfied practically, the same conclusion does not hold.'[54]

But how then does Bradley attempt to solve this problem of moving from fact to value? Although there is no direct transition to be made from logically complete to evaluatively perfect, there are, thinks Bradley, a couple of indirect transitions that can be attempted. The first is a straightforward empirical appeal. Bradley claims that, 'In the world, which we observe, an impartial scrutiny will discover more pleasure than pain.' He does not undertake to really justify this optimism, merely hinting that he thinks a weighting of the psychological arguments on either side would be fatal to pessimism. This idea is not explained, but presumably he believes that psychology does, or will, reveal us to be basically optimistic creatures. It would be impossible here to assess whether or not Bradley is correct in his optimism, but it is worth noting that, while he thinks that there is a balance of pleasure, he acknowledges that 'it is difficult to estimate, and easy to exaggerate, the amount of the balance.'[55] The second kind of indirect transition from fact to value is a priori. It consists in arguing that satisfaction of the theoretical or cognitive part of our being which necessarily accompanies metaphysical truth would be impossible without an accompanying satisfaction of the practical or feeling part, that 'A true philosophy must accept and must justify every side of human nature.'[56] In more detail he argues that knowledge finds rest only in that vision of reality as an harmonious whole that philosophers call the Absolute and in which there can exist no unresolved conflict or discord, but pain causes and is caused by precisely such conflict, and thus we may infer that the Absolute cannot contain an excess of pain; 'we are forced to assume theoretical satisfaction; and to suppose that existing one-sidedly, and together with practical discomfort, appears inadmissible'.[57]

6.2 T.H. Green

Just as influential as Bradley in the spreading of idealist ethics was the figure of T.H. Green. It is true that his ethical system did not appear in print until 1883, several years after Bradley's, but for many years prior to that it had been making an impact in Oxford (and beyond), especially after his election to the Whyte's Professorship of Moral

---

[54] *Appearance and Reality*, 135.
[55] *Appearance and Reality*, 175. [56] *Essays on Truth and Reality*, 14.
[57] *Appearance and Reality*, 139–40. Bradley himself felt this indirect argument from the absence of contradiction to the absence of pain to be less than perfect, and in the last chapter of *Appearance and Reality* entitled 'Final Doubts' he admits that, 'The idea of a painful universe, in the end, seems to be neither quite meaningless nor yet visibly self-contradictory. And I am compelled to allow that, speaking strictly, we must call it possible' (*Appearance and Reality*, 474). His reason for conceding this is strange. He admits that so far as we have experienced it, pain seems to be linked to conflict, but is reluctant to state with finality that this belongs to its essence. Perhaps they only seem to require each other because of our partial and limited view, such that there might somewhere in the universe be a kind of pain which could exist in the absence of conflict.

Philosophy in December 1877.[58] Certainly once Green's *Prolegomena* was in print, alongside *Ethical Studies*, these two books became the twin pillars of idealist ethics.

6.2.1 Motivation

As was discussed in Chapter 4, the First Book of Green's *Prolegomena* deals with what he calls the 'metaphysics of knowledge' in which he argues that nature could only be known if consciousness stood 'outside' it, functioning autonomously and free from its limitations. Moving on to Book Two, the essential role of this preliminary exercise in metaphysics becomes clear as this result is employed to build up his ethical system, for he argues that what holds of knowledge is paralleled by what holds of action; just as naturalism is unable to explain conscious knowledge, it is also unable to explain conscious purposive action.[59] In so far as we are conscious we are free. Classical empiricism and reductionist systems of ethics, such as utilitarianism, become bound together as the twin targets of Idealism.

Green has a distinctive conception of what it is for an action to be free. He opposes any notion of freedom as indeterminism; nothing happens without a reason. The only legitimate question is what sort of reason? A free action is one brought about from within rather than imposed from without, and brought about, moreover, through conscious choice rather than blind impulse, instinct, or desire. Unmotivated willing of the later kind would make action but 'an arbitrary freak of some unaccountable power' and nothing to be proud or ashamed of[60]—'far from free action being *unmotivated*, it is rather determination by motives, properly understood, that constitutes freedom'.[61]

But if what we choose is a function of our character and circumstances how can it be free? It all depends, argues Green,[62] on how we understand the terms 'character and circumstances'. If these are understood to mere natural phenomena (such as animal desires, instincts, and surrounding causal contexts), events with the power to bring about behaviour, then their action must indeed destroy freedom. But the introduction of consciousness into the picture changes everything, and the threat to freedom vanishes if character and circumstance are understood instead on the idealist model. Internalized by self-consciousness, desires or appetites are transformed into 'motives' while the circumstances of action are those things only which are taken in by reflexive awareness and understood as the possibilities for action.[63]

The key point about this transition from desires and circumstances to conscious motives is that it is a transition from efficient to final causation. On the idealist model, with the introduction of self-consciousness, action is explained not by prior factors

---

[58]   The origination of many of Green's ideas may be traced back even earlier than this to the late 1860s at which point they were undoubtedly a key impetus to Bradley (who attended Green's lectures) in the development of his ethical thought (see note 170 to Chapter 4 above).

[59]   With the case of knowledge the theory in his sights was the evolutionary understanding of mind, here it is explicitly identified as evolutionary ethics (*Prolegomena*, §§5–7).

[60]   *Prolegomena*, §110.   [61]   'Lectures on Kant', 95.

[62]   *Prolegomena*, §106.   [63]   *Prolegomena*, §120.

which push from behind but by a future ideal which calls it forth. Desire in so far as it is conceived in consciousness becomes motive, as the self posits some object which would satisfy its want; but to explain something by motive or reasons is to understand it teleologically, in terms of its final as opposed to its efficient cause. And so the issues of whether or not there is a prior cause or of what kind it may be, fall away as beside the point—we move out of the realm of casual explanation altogether—and the only issue is whether or not the factors which explain the action may themselves be explained naturalistically.[64] If not, whatever the underlying causal story, we can say that a person 'exerts a free activity,—an activity which is not in time, not a link in the natural chain of becoming, which has no antecedents other than itself but is self-originated.'[65] Reasoned or motivated action is only possible because we are not parts of the natural rank. Conscious desire is of a radically different order to animal desire, for in consciousness we can stand over our wants and gauge them. Ethical life is explained not historically by the forces that make us what we are but teleologically by the potential we have to become something more. In this way Green opposed any kind of view of morality as but the progressive articulation of animal instincts or sympathy, rejecting the programme of figures such as Spencer or Hume for whom to account for the moral consciousness it is enough to give a naturalistic historical description of its origins and growth.

6.2.2 Self-satisfaction

Human agency then, is to be explained in terms of motive rather than desire. Unlike the mere animal pushed from behind by some want, desire, or impulse, because they are self-conscious, human beings have the capacity in thought to transcend both the present and the actual and look forward to possible future states, thereby creating for themselves ends which they then endeavour to bring about.

Green goes on to argue that the motive determining an agent's will is always an idealized future state of his own self, a conception of himself as satisfied—whatever it may be that he seeks. For this reason, argues Green, moral action is 'an expression at once of conscious contrast between an actual and possible self, and of an impulse to make that possible self real; or, as it is sometimes put, it is a process of self-realisation, i.e. of making a possible self real.'[66] This position is clearly in line with that of Bradley—indeed it is Bradley who more commonly uses the term 'self-realisation'; Green tends to prefer 'self-satisfaction'[67]—and in historical terms their arrival at this

---

[64] *Prolegomena*, §87. Idealism takes Green by a shorter route to Kant's conclusion that freedom is not a property of human beings as existing in nature, space and time, but really belongs to them as atemporal subjects (Irwin, *Development of Ethics*, 583).

[65] *Prolegomena*, §82.

[66] 'The World is nigh thee', 224. Nettleship dates this fragment as prior to 1871 (*Collected Works*, III, Preface vi) so we should not see the term 'self-realisation' here as a reference to Bradley.

[67] If our concern is with exact chronology, that Bradley probably received the notion from Green, whose lectures he attended in the late 1860s, is confirmed by his own admission—'Self realization as the ethical end. I do not remember who first introduced it into English ethics (perhaps Green)' *Collected Works*, III: 255—but

common formula represents an important shift in ethical thinking. Instead of asking with the utilitarian, intuitionist, and even Kantian philosophers of the day, 'what ought I to do?' they—and the many Idealists that followed them—re-construed ethical inquiry in the mould of an older question 'what kind of person ought I to be?'; for this understanding of the moral ideal as a matter of developing our capacity for reason and will (where this has a social element to it as well) is highly reminiscent of the eudaimonistic tradition of Plato and Aristotle—in which both were, of course, thoroughly grounded.

The claim that all conscious purposive action seeks self-satisfaction may seem like the most ruthless psychological egoism, and in places Green appears to speak in such a fashion. Self-reflection he suggests will tell us that 'to every action morally imputable, or of which a man can recognise himself as the author, the motive is always some idea of the man's personal good'.[68] But on closer reflection we see his view is quite otherwise. Rather the derivation flows from the very definition of conscious action itself. Whatever we want, in wanting it we necessarily want also a state in which our own wanting is satisfied. There is nothing necessarily self-directed in the content of the want. This is important, for only such a derivation can explain the categorical nature of demand; the call to self-realization is universal and exceptionless. But now the formula begins to look trivial. Whatever we want, it is self-satisfaction, just because we want it. Or to put the same point another way, it is useless to say we should aim at self-realization, for there are a great number of selves we might realize—many of which might far better be left unrealized!

Content is provided, however, if we reflect further about the nature of satisfaction. Presented at first with just a sequence of wants, the self cannot be satisfied with a piecemeal approach, and 'there arises the idea of a satisfaction on the whole'.[69] The generic notion of the good is that 'it satisfies some desire'[70] but, as the idea that we might become 'better' than we are inevitably leads on to the idea that we might become 'the best' we can possibly be, so the generic notion of the good begets that of the true or unconditional good, as 'an end in which the effort of a moral agent can really find rest'.[71] It is that which fulfils the agent's desire for 'an abiding satisfaction of an abiding self',[72] an idea clearly related to Bradley's injunction to be an 'infinite whole'. Nor can satisfaction of the self simply be restricted to the satisfaction of desires, it calls for the realization of capacities. Morality demands that through right action we realize our potential. But any given act realizes our capacity only in part, a fact which

---

credit for published priority, however, should be given to Wallace, who, in the *Prolegomena* to the 1874 edition of *Hegel's Logic* (clx, clxxxiv) first introduced the term into Idealist circles. Much more is made of the notion in the expanded 1894 edition.

[68] *Prolegomena*, §95, cf §91.
[69] *Prolegomena*, §85.
[70] *Prolegomena*, §171.
[71] *Prolegomena*, §171.
[72] *Prolegomena*, §234.

itself gives birth to the idea of our complete realization.[73] We thus arrive at the conclusion that the ultimate goal must be the complete development of our potentiality; human perfection.[74]

If, as Green tells us, the moral ideal resides in the complete realization or perfection of human capacities, it is only natural that we should ask just what this amounts to. But here we meet an obstacle. Since our potential never yet has been perfectly realized, we cannot properly say quite what that would imply. Green's moral theory is a species of ideal or perfectionist ethics, but since our moral understanding lies in need of development just as much as our moral nature itself, a measure of ignorance is, he concludes, unavoidable. The utilitarian is content to take us as we are and uses current values to define the ideal, but as we mature so do our ideals, and hence our conception of the goal itself also must grow and develop. We cannot know now what we would want if we were better people.

Fortunately, even if it may not yet be known in full, the moral ideal may be known in part for we are not left entirely without help; we may turn to history, we may criticize prior theories and we know at least that the true good is a common good. Each of these three points will now be considered.

6.2.3 Moral development

Some of what is needed Green thought we could learn by looking at actual historical moral developments. Ethical codes change over history and, although there is no chance for us to stand outside of time and anticipate the ideal from which they all fall short, relativism is not our only alternative, for we may yet regard this history as the gradual unfolding of the divine spirit within us. Green believes that 'the history of human character has been one in which the [eternal] consciousness has throughout been operative upon wants of animal origin, giving rise through its actions upon them to the specific quality of that history.'[75] Though our potential cannot yet be known, 'to a certain extent it has shown by actual achievement what it has in it to become, and by reflection on the so far developed activity we can form at least some negative conclusions in regard to its complete realisation'.[76] A 'subjective' history of the moral thoughts and feelings of mankind would be hard to write, but these also exist 'objectively' in the norms, practices, and institutions of society,[77] and when Green speaks of the historical development 'through which human life has been so far bettered' it is primarily these 'institutions and useages' he has in mind.[78] History shows us 'an actual progressive realisation of human capacities in knowledge, in art

---

[73] Compare: It is popularly believed that humans use only 10% of their brain power; a thought which can only lead us to wonder what we could achieve if we used it all.

[74] See, e.g., *Prolegomena*, §§178–9, 181, 195, 205, 247.

[75] *Prolegomena*, §95.

[76] *Prolegomena*, §172.

[77] Colin Tyler, *Thomas Hill Green and the Philosophical Foundations of Politics*, 93.

[78] *Prolegomena*, §180.

and in social life'.[79] We are bound within moral worldviews that inevitably change over time, but if we understand this as a process of evolution, perspective enough is found for the present to pass judgement on the past. Green claims, for example, that a higher moral standard is possible for the Christian than for the Greek,[80] while more specifically, the 1865 abolition of slavery in the United States—about fifteen years before he wrote—would surely have stood out as another clear marker of human moral progress. History may even enable us to say something more: with the insight afforded by where we have got to so far, while we cannot tell what would be 'best', we can see what personal and institutional changes would make life 'better'.

The relationship is reciprocal. Not only does history give some content to the moral ideal, but the notion of an operating moral ideal is (thinks Green) the only plausible way we have of explaining the actual facts of human moral effort.

It represents a conception to which no perceivable or imaginable object can possibly correspond, but one that affords the only means by which, reflecting on our moral and intellectual experience conjointly, taking the world and ourselves into account, we can put the whole thing together and understand how (not *why*, but *how*) we are and do what we consciously are and do. Given this conception, and not without it, we can at any rate express that which it cannot be denied demands expression, the nature of man's reason and man's will, of human progress and human short-coming, of the effort after good and the failure to gain it, of virtue and vice, in their connection and in their distinction, in their essential opposition and no less essential unity.[81]

Thus for Green the idea of the supreme good is not just an ideal, something potential, but also something at work in the world, an idea which 'has been the essential influence in the process by which man has so far bettered himself' and which 'is the condition of character and conduct being morally good'.[82] For where does the idea originate that we might become better than we are, that we might even become perfect, except from the eternal consciousness within us, from the better self we already implicitly are?

At this point vital parallels emerge between Green's moral, metaphysical, and religious views. As current knowledge and the possibility of future knowledge are both explicable only on their being gradual reproductions in us of a complete vision already realized in the understanding of an eternal consciousness, likewise actual moral progress and the possibility of future development is ultimately explicable only as the self-reproduction in us of a divine life already enjoying the perfection after which we strive. Both of these stories may in their turn be understood from a religious point of view, for in both cases the historical development may be seen as the progressive realization in the temporal realm of the eternal spirit of God. As knowledge advances we come more and more to think the thoughts of God, while through moral progress we gradually bring about the kingdom of heaven. It could be complained that Green

---

[79] *Prolegomena*, §257.   [80] *Prolegomena*, §253.   [81] *Prolegomena*, §174.
[82] *Prolegomena*, §173.

replaced religion with science and ethics, but looking at it the other way it could just as well be approved that on his system one's intellectual and ethical contribution to society becomes elevated to a form of divine service.[83]

6.2.4 Intuitionism, utilitarianism, and Kantianism

We get some further idea of what Green thought the true good would consist in by considering his criticisms of some alternative theories. Green rejects as false and unnecessary the intuitionist assumption of any special moral sense or faculty. The way in which we discover ethical truth—what *ought* to be—is the same as that in which we discover metaphysical truth—what ultimately *is*—namely, reason (where this is understood in a broad sense to cover the full range of human cognitive powers, not simply the narrow and formal manipulation of concepts). To suppose otherwise that we have some special ability (intuition) to make moral judgements without deriving them deductively or inductively from others is to undermine the unity of knowledge and of the moral agent. It is not some part of our mind or part of ourselves that feels and acts morally. An act of will is an expression of the whole person.[84]

Utilitarianism, the main contemporary rival, fares no better. Green objects that we seek many goals quite other than pleasure and often we seek that which will give us no pleasure at all.[85] Nor can the mere pursuit of pleasure explain the imperative we feel, instead of seeking satisfaction in whatever currently attracts us the most, to try to become better human beings with more worthy desires.[86] The standard rejoinder to points like these—that the attainment of any such goal is still a pleasure to us—rests on a confusion exploded long ago by Butler, argues Green.[87] The fact that satisfaction or pleasure inevitably accompany the achieving of any end does not imply that pleasure is the original object of desire. To be sure, attainment of what is good gives pleasure, but it yields pleasure because we think it good, not *vice versa*.[88] It is not that first we want pleasure and so seek a source, for something is only a source of pleasure because we first want that thing itself. To a degree Mill understood this, but the changes he introduced to accommodate it (the notion of higher pleasure, and the notion of pleasure as a complex whole with many diverse parts) amount to the 'virtual surrender' of utilitarianism.[89]

Moreover, the ideal proposed by hedonism is an impossible one. We are pleasure seekers and so ought to maximize pleasure, we are told, but 'a sum of pleasures is not a pleasure'.[90] It is not something we could ever enjoy, or coherently aim at as a goal. Echoing Bradley's objection,[91] Green complains that pleasures follow one another in a

---

[83] Boucher and Vincent, *British Idealism and Political Theory*, 37.
[84] *Prolegomena*, §153. 'No desire which forms part of our moral experience would be what it is, if it were not the desire of a subject which also understands: no act of our intelligence would be what it is, if it were not the act of a subject which also desires' (*Prolegomena*, §130).
[85] *Prolegomena*, §159.   [86] *Prolegomena*, §223.   [87] *Prolegomena*, §161.
[88] *Prolegomena*, §171.   [89] *Prolegomena*, §167.   [90] *Prolegomena*, §221.
[91] See above p.186.

series and, even if they may be added in thought, there is no means in reality of accumulating and experiencing them as a whole. A.E. Taylor objected to this argument suggesting that no experience ever really perishes—everything that we feel as well as everything that we think and do leaves a residue or deposit that enters into all subsequent experience[92]—but even if no experience is ever done with, it is still never enjoyed as a whole. The sum of its pleasure is still always spread out across time.

Henry Sidgwick's *Methods of Ethics* offers a very different species of utilitarianism to that of Mill, but appeared too late for Bradley in his *Ethical Studies* to engage in any detailed criticism.[93] Green is not so handicapped, and tackles Sidgwick head on in the final chapter of the *Prolegomena*.[94] He admits that universalistic hedonism cannot be charged with confusing the object of the desire and the pleasure we anticipate from attaining it, that it is a doctrine of the disinterested pursuit of pleasure, but he argues that in practical terms it is weaker than the theory of human perfection. For where we are thinking of departing from common practice or resisting personal inclination, it is hard to estimate whether this would increase or decrease universal pleasure, and the goal of promoting happiness cannot be translated into any specific claim to be or do anything in particular, a difficulty that is much less where the promotion of human excellences and virtues is taken as an end in itself.[95]

In his Preface to the 1906 edition of the *Prolegomena* Edward Caird describes Green's position as a modification of Kant's,[96] and certainly Green's ethics is in many ways close to that of the Critical Philosophy. Like Kant, Green regards ethical obligation as flowing from the very nature of conscious action and independent of our particular desires, as something categorical or applicable to all rational beings.

But Green also finds problems with Kant's ethics. The difficulties (it must be allowed) lie not so much in the system itself as in his statement of it[97]—'though his doctrine is essentially true, his way of putting it' is defective[98]—but they are nonetheless serious. He rejects what he describes as Kant's view than man has a two-fold nature and a two-fold causality; a moral self and a sensuous self; a self on the one hand intelligible, noumenal, and free, and a self on the other hand sensible, phenomenal, and determined. Since all we are acquainted with is the latter, complains Green, Kant's doctrine amounts to an admission of utter ignorance about the true self and its connection with the world. In knowing actions as they present themselves to us, we known them as 'they really are not.'[99] Moreover, in ruling out desire as a motive he rules out just what makes actions valuable, as well as rendering

---

[92] *Problem of Conduct*, 323.
[93] Although, as was noted, he did subsequently write a pamphlet.
[94] It is worth noting that the two had been at school together, at Rugby, and remained on friendly terms in later life (See letters in Green, *Collected Works*, V: 422–4, 458–9).
[95] *Prolegomena*, §374, §380.
[96] Preface to fifth edition (v).
[97] Irwin, 'Morality and Personality: Kant and Green', 32.
[98] 'Lectures on Kant', 124. A claim that could so easily have been made by Caird.
[99] 'Lectures on Kant', 104.

them psychologically impossible.[100] For Green, duty need not be independent of *all* desire, only of natural pre-conscious pre-deliberative desire. Insofar as desire is rational and conscious it has a place in ethics. Kant's mistake is to assume there is no alternative between determination by natural desire for pleasure, and determination by abstract contemplation of the moral law; for we often in all consciousness desire things other than pleasure.[101] Green's case against Kant's 'two-worlds' view is strong, but of course, he faces his own (not so very different) problem of how to relate together his two 'worlds' of *cause* and of *motive*; and just as he struggles to explain exactly how the eternal consciousness relates to historical knowledge, a deep puzzle remains as to how his world of 'free' action relates to the causal world which underlies and indeed expresses it.

As did Bradley, Green complains also that in refusing any appeal to experience, the Kantian idea of duty is but an 'empty abstraction, an idea of nothing in particular to be done'.[102] Kant focuses solely on the *form* of the motive—to do our duty—without regard to its *content*—whatever object it is that we will. Taken strictly this would lead to the complete 'paralysis of the will'.[103] And what can be meant by calling such an abstraction a 'law', where it is neither enforced by some superior power nor describes the actual course of phenomena?[104]

As a further criticism, Green objects that in concentrating wholly on motive, Kant makes the error of too much ignoring the consequences of action.[105] Ascertaining the right course for action is certainly more than a calculus of possible outcomes, but neither should they be utterly ignored. For as long as we take a full view of the matter, 'There is no real reason to doubt that the good or evil in the motive of an action is exactly measured by the good or evil in its consequences.' Appearance to the contrary—appearance, that is, of good action resulting from bad intentions or vice versa—is but the result of the limited view we take of both motive and consequences.[106] A wider view may show us to be more instruments than agents, and the value of what we may do may change with our perspective.

Comments such as these have encouraged some to think of Green, while certainly not a hedonist, as perhaps still a consequentialist.[107] And in specifying a goal of action—human perfection—Green would seem to be putting forward a variety of teleological ethics. But if so, the teleology is Aristotelian not consequentialist. Though they are our goals, self-realization and the common good are not things to be aggregated or maximized; that *everyone* has absolute value as an end never a means

---

[100] 'Lectures on Kant', 155.   [101] 'Lectures on Kant', 139–40.

[102] 'Lectures on Kant', 154.   [103] *Prolegomena*, §247.

[104] 'Lectures on Kant', 155.   [105] 'Lectures on Kant', 154.

[106] *Prolegomena*, §295. 'From the difficulty of presenting to ourselves in any positive form what a society, perfected in this sense, would be, we may take refuge in describing the object of the devotion, which our consciences demand, as the greatest happiness of the greatest number; and until we puzzle ourselves with analysis, such an account may be sufficient for practical purposes' (*Prolegomena*, §286).

[107] For this case see Weinstein, *Utilitarianism and the New Liberalism*, ch. 2. For the case against see Simhony, 'T.H. Green was no Consequentialist of any Kind'.

acts as a prior moral constraint on any goal,[108] and the failing of utilitarianism is that it cannot absolutely rule out the oppression of the weak by the strong or the few by the many.[109] Moreover, like Kant, Green stresses the absolute importance of motives. This is vital, not just for freedom, but also for the very value of an action. Ethics is founded on the distinction between the good and bad will;[110] it consists in 'the imposition . . . of rules requiring something to be done irrespectively of any inclination to do it, irrespectively of any desired end'.[111] 'The one unconditional good is the good will',[112] he allows, for the motive not merely determines the act, it '*is* the act on its inner side.'[113] Two actions alike in moral effects (consequences) could nonetheless differ in the moral character they represent.[114]

But is this not contradictory? In measuring value must we not choose between assessing intentions or assessing outcomes, between the deontology of Kant and the teleology of Hegel? Surely value cannot (without ambiguity) indiscriminately reflect both of these? Green however rejects this forced choice between an ethics of agency and an ethics of result. To insist on a choice between them implies a clear separation between the will to achieve and the goal to be achieved, but where the goal itself is human perfection that can never quite be the case; 'when we are giving an account of an agent whose development is governed by an idea of his own perfection, we cannot avoid speaking of one and the same condition of will alternately as means and as end'.[115] Our effort to realize the good is itself also part of the good we try to realize, so that in circular fashion right effort is that aimed at perfection, while perfection is what right effort aims at. The good we seek is precisely to do or be good. But rather than 'an illogical procedure', this is, suggests Green, 'the only procedure suited to the matter in hand'. 'It means that such an ideal, not yet realised but operating as a motive, already constitutes in man an inchoate form of that life, that perfect development of himself, of which the completion would be the realised ideal itself.'[116]

6.2.5 The common good

The last point which helps Green to define more substantively his moral ideal—providing content to what would otherwise remain a merely formal notion—is perhaps the most important of all. Transforming the seemingly individualistic doctrine of self-satisfaction into something almost directly its opposite, Green argues that while it is indeed true that the moral ideal is one of personal development, it needs to be recognized that people are fundamentally social creatures, and hence that our true personal good properly understood turns out to be a common or social good. 'Finding

---

[108] *Prolegomena*, §217.
[109] *Prolegomena*, §214.   [110] *Prolegomena*, §155.
[111] *Prolegomena*, §193.   [112] *Prolegomena*, §292.
[113] *Prolegomena*, §105. 'the only true good is the good will' (*Prolegomena*, §240), 'the actions which ought to be done . . . are actions expressive of a good will' (*Prolegomena*, §293).
[114] *Prolegomena*, §294.   [115] *Prolegomena*, §195.   [116] *Prolegomena*, §196.

our own pleasures and pains dependent on the pleasures and pains of others, we form the idea of a satisfaction of self which includes the satisfaction of others, not simply as a means to our own pleasure, but as ends in themselves deserving their own satisfaction',[117] for 'man cannot contemplate himself as in a better state, or on the way to the best, without contemplating others, not merely as a means to that better state, but as sharing it with him'.[118] Our goal—'the perfection of human character'—spelled out, is seen to be 'a perfection of individuals which is also that of society, and of society which is also that of individuals'.[119] In addition to—indeed as part of—our interests in ourselves we have interests in other persons, such that our own good is really part of something wider than us; 'the idea of an absolute and a common good; a good common to the person conceiving it with others, and good for him and them, whether at any moment it answers their likings or no.'[120]

This doctrine that the true good is a common one (the common good) does away with the age-old distinction and conflict between egoism and altruism. It is an idea which 'does not admit of the distinction between good for self and good for others'.[121] It renders the distinction between benevolence and reasonable self-love 'a fiction of philosophers'.[122] To pursue a selfish life is to misunderstand one's own true nature and hence where one's own true happiness lies.

Unpacking this idea further we may note three senses in which the common good is 'common'. It is thought (for example, by some relativists) that there are as many different conceptions of the good as there are individuals who seek it, with no way to choose between them. But this (to introduce our first sense) was not Green's view. He believes, whatever the differences in what we seem to seek—the result of our varying times, cultures, and temperaments—and whatever the differences in the degree to which we recognize it, that at bottom we are all led by a shared ideal standard of the good; a mutual sense of what is needed to bring about ultimate human satisfaction: 'the true good is a good for all men, and good for them all in virtue of the same nature and capacity'.[123] But even if all people have the same ultimate ends, these may be incompatible. If we both want to win, or if we both want great power and influence, we may find ourselves in competition. And here we find a second thing Green means to deny. The common good 'is common to all men in the proper sense,—in the sense, namely, that there can be no competition for its attainment between man and man'.[124] Distinguishing between the 'good things of the soul' and the 'good things of the body',[125] we see at once that what we seek must be a spiritual good, since material goods will always be scarce and so potential sources of conflict. The good (as we noted above) is something to be or do, not something to possess. But even if we all have the same harmonious goals, these may only run in parallel. There is, for example, no conflict in knowledge—your knowing something in no way prevents my doing so—

---

[117] *Prolegomena*, §201.   [118] *Prolegomena*, §199.   [119] *Prolegomena*, §247.
[120] *Prolegomena*, §202.   [121] *Prolegomena*, §235.   [122] *Prolegomena*, §232.
[123] *Prolegomena*, §244.   [124] *Prolegomena*, §281.   [125] *Prolegomena*, §243.

but the pursuit of knowledge may be a solitary affair. This kind of value too Green wishes to reject, bringing us to the third and strongest sense of common good; that of a unique goal for all members of society, a single project in which we are all involved. Isaiah Berlin famously argued that there can be no one good but only a plurality of conflicting ones,[126] and many have thought him correct. But it should be remembered that Green's identical task upon which all are embarked need not prescribe identical roles for all—the case may be more like an orchestra where the aim is to combine many different activities harmoniously together into one whole.[127] This is how Green would regard that joint venture to which we are all committed, a multi-stranded creation which we could regard either as the perfection of human nature or the realization of God.

It will be asked what Green thinks entitles him to make this astounding claim? At times he seems to present the matter as a straightforwardly empirical truth. A little reflection on human nature or history will reveal to us that we just are creatures who need each other to flourish. We are all possessed of what Hume called 'sympathy'. Green's argument here needs to be carefully understood, as he himself is very aware. 'It may seem unphilosophical now-a-days to accept this distinctive social interest on our part as a *primary fact*, without attempting to account for it by any process of evolution',[128] he admits; and he does not even wish to deny—indeed he thinks it most likely—that this associative tendency has an instinctive base, or as he puts it an 'animal origin'.[129] But, he insists, no causal account of our behaviour could explain its moral status, for animals, however cooperative their behaviour, are not moral. The point is rather that such feelings, 'through their presence in a self-conscious soul',[130] become transformed into a conscious goal. We are not bound to our animal past, but it is a plain fact that when we take serious review of our goals, we see that not only do we need the help of others to be happy, we need the happiness of others to be happy.

In a slightly different line of thought, Green suggests that it is our desire for a more permanent or stable kind of satisfaction that calls us to pursue a common good. Man pursues his desires, but as Schopenhauer noted, there is a certain futility in seeking to meet a desire which as soon as it is met morphs either into boredom or the desire for something else. If thus reflecting on the transitory nature of our pleasures and desires, we ask ourselves 'what can satisfy the self which abides throughout and survives those desires',[131] the thought of ourselves as permanent gives rise the 'idea of a social good—of a good not private to the man himself, but good for him as a member of a community'.[132] Rather as short strands of wool fibre are spun together into a

---

[126] 'Two Concepts of Liberty', 212–17.
[127] This analogy is explored in Dworkin, 'Liberal Community', 225–7.
[128] *Prolegomena*, §200, italics added.
[129] *Prolegomena*, §200.   [130] *Prolegomena*, §201.
[131] *Prolegomena*, §229.   [132] *Prolegomena*, §232.

continuous thread, the ever-changing and short-lived self, by interweaving its own with other equally transient contributors, becomes part of something larger that is both constant and enduring—at first perhaps the family line, but then spreading out to the wider school or college tradition, the community, the nation, the religion, or the species. The idea of ourselves as permanent is always the idea of ourselves as social. As private individuals we change all the time. Our appearance, our knowledge, our feelings, our desires, none of it is constant; not least because the world is always changing around us. Only in so far as our self is defined by a wider framework—in so far as we stand as a member of some family, profession, nation, or religion—is there any constancy in us. And of course such wholes continue after our death. Our identity is given in part by our interests, but insofar as our interests are identified with those of a wider body to which we belong, their pursuit and thus our identity continues after death. 'It is this association,' argues Green, 'that neutralises the effect which the anticipation of death must otherwise have on the demand for permanent good.'[133] This idea we have already encountered in John Caird's notion of 'corporate immortality'.[134]

But perhaps Green's strongest argument for the common good is one about psychological development. We may set the good as self-development, but it must be recognized that selfhood or personality can only develop in a social setting. 'Society is the condition of the development of a personality'.[135] In ourselves we are only potential people. That potentiality is never realized until we live in society. Sociality is the precondition for even being a person.

Social life is to personality what language is to thought. Language presupposes thought as a capacity, but in us the capacity of thought is only actualised in language. So human society presupposes persons in capacity—subjects capable each of conceiving himself and the bettering of his life as an end to himself—but it is only in the intercourse of men, each recognised by each as an end, not merely a means, and thus as having reciprocal claims, that the capacity is actualised and that we really live as persons.[136]

Green's claim here is that of the fundamentally social nature of the self, the same thesis Bradley urged in 'My Station and its Duties'. Each of us, from the first, argues Green, finds ourselves 'existing in manifold relations to nature and other persons', and 'these relations form the reality of the self'.[137] The individual in whom we are interested 'is not an empty or abstract self' but one affected 'by manifold interests, among which are interests in other people'.[138] Indicative of this is Green's notion of conscience; however individual to us it may seem, it is in reality a social voice.[139] But (to return to the common good) if people only come to exist in concert with others, the same must be

---

[133] *Prolegomena*, §231.   [134] See Chapter 5.3.6.   [135] *Prolegomena*, §191.
[136] *Prolegomena*, §183.   [137] 'Lectures on Kant', 146.   [138] *Prolegomena*, §199.
[139] 'No individual can make a conscience for himself. He always needs a society to make it for him' (*Prolegomena*, §321).

said of their satisfaction. If our very being is not some private possession, but a joint stock, its fulfilment too must be judged something public rather than something exclusive.

The individualism or selfishness of great figures like Napoleon or Caesar might be thought to count against Green's argument here, but even characters such as these, he argues, rather than counterexamples, are a reflection of their times—for 'what we call egoistic motives do not act without direction from an involuntary reference to social good'.[140] For example, the personal glory they seek cannot be understood wholly without reference to what those they rule consider to advance the nation; no one ever became celebrated for running a country into the ground.

Reciprocity is the chief characteristic of the relationship between men and the society 'which is at once constituted by them and makes them what they are';[141] and therefore, set alongside this holistic vision developed above, it is important to note also Green's strong insistence that the 'ultimate standard of worth is an ideal of *personal* worth'.[142] For Green, apart from embodiment in individual personalities, larger notions such as 'nation' or 'humanity' are mere abstractions. Likewise the notion of 'spiritual progress' means nothing unless manifested in individual lives.[143] The goal is one that must be realized in *persons*, and no goal could ever be accepted requiring their 'extinction'—even by absorption into something greater.[144] This last point would seem to rule out any understanding of the Absolute or eternal consciousness as something in which finite minds are lost or absorbed.

6.3 Edward Caird

Insofar as it is known today, the idealist ethic of social self-realization is associated with the names of T.H. Green and F.H. Bradley. However, to these two figures needs to be added a third, contemporaneous with them, and equally important as one of the 'founding fathers' of this style of ethics. This was Edward Caird. Though every bit as important as Green and Bradley, Caird's role in this story has been eclipsed—his name now remembered mainly in connection with philosophy of religion and philosophy of literature. But much of his earliest and most original work was in Moral Philosophy—of which subject, indeed, he was the professor at Glasgow University.

As was noted in the first chapter, the rise of British Idealism coincided with the rise of professionalism in academia, one aspect of which was the creation of a new class of

---

[140] *Lectures on Principles of Political Obligation*, §128. This point is echoed precisely by Edward Caird, who argues that the careers of great individuals (selfish kings or idiosyncratic radicals, and such like) are only an apparent exception to this rule since in reality they too express their own time ('Reform and the Reformation', 9).

[141] *Prolegomena*, §110. The self must be regarded 'as at once individual and universal' ('Popular Philosophy', 99).

[142] *Prolegomena*, §184.   [143] *Prolegomena*, §§184–5.   [144] *Prolegomena*, §189.

university teacher. This change provides a useful yardstick against which to compare our three philosophers. For, from this point of view, Bradley belongs squarely to the old world. After graduation, he was awarded a fellowship at Merton College without any teaching duties whatsoever, and even within Oxford became something of a recluse. It was through *his writing* that he became widely known and influential. Green straddled the age; his *Prolegomena* and his two lay sermons were publications as celebrated and influential as Bradley's, but he was equally important as a teacher, profoundly influencing a generation of Oxford men. Caird by contrast belonged to the new world: his influence was almost entirely as a *teacher*. As such it was real, but not of the kind to remain visible in later years. For unlike Bradley or Green, he left no single ethical monograph.[145] Other than buried deep within a series of reviews and in his discussions of other philosophers, his ethical ideas lived only through his students.[146]

So what were Caird's ethical views? Although he never produced a book on moral philosophy, careful examination of the works which he did publish in the 1860s, 1870s and early 1880s, together with previously unpublished materials, allow us to form a clear enough picture of his position. We may begin with a very early essay 'Reform and the Reformation' most probably submitted in 1866 as part of his application for the Glasgow Chair.

6.3.1 The evolution of ethical understanding

Caird's worldview emphasizes to an extreme something present to a degree in all British Idealist thought, indeed, in late nineteenth-century thought generally, the notion of change. The world in which we find ourselves is not fixed or static but in constant flux; its dynamic, moreover, not formless and random, but marked by distinctive and intelligible laws and productive of a developmental progress or evolution. Like it or not, recognize it or not (and more often we do not, for, as much as anything else, our vision is a product of the context in which it occurs), everything is caught up in streams larger than itself, making its own contribution in the forward movement of the wider whole. Only through the lens of history can the pattern be discerned, and only as the servants of history can we ever achieve anything: 'man cannot create; all his success is dependent upon his striking in with mighty agencies already at work. His highest effort is to place himself directly in the path of some irresistible law, and then let himself be borne forward by it to the certain execution of his purpose.'[147]

---

[145] A forthcoming work by Caird on ethics was advertised in the Muirhead Library of Philosophy between 1893 and 1907, but failed ever to materialize. See Tyler, *Unpublished Manuscripts*, II:x; Tyler, *Idealist Political Philosophy*, 128 note 4.

[146] See Mackenzie, 'Edward Caird as a Philosophical Teacher', 511–12. Such influence, it should be added, was not utterly ephemeral, for he inspired important textbooks. See 6.4.3 and 6.4.4 below.

[147] 'Reform and the Reformation', 2.

This idea has already been explored with regard to religion and to the history of philosophy, and it may be found no less at work in ethics, argues Caird, for history reveals a continued development of what he variously calls 'moral experience', 'moral life', the 'spiritual consciousness of the race', the 'great consciousness of humanity', the 'moral progress of humanity', or 'the moral world which is built up by the actions of men'.[148] Our first question must be to ask just what he means by this miscellany of vague terms, for their import is hardly clear. He is not thinking here, at least not primarily, of moral codes—don't kill, don't lie, don't steal, etc.—for Caird admits that these have remained relatively static, the common possession of all nations and times. However, he presses, 'Morality is not exhausted by such vague abstractions: but consists rather in the manner in which these are united with life'.[149] This is not much clearer, but it includes at least two things between which he slides a little too easily for comfort. In part he is talking about moral understanding, about that which would be considered in a history of moral philosophy. For our understanding of the meaning, nature, and significance of our moral codes may change over time even if the codes themselves do not. But the separation between these two is not complete, and he is talking also about our actual values and attitudes themselves. For any given time or culture will have its own ethical flavour or perspective, from the Greek worldview through medievalism or the Restoration to *fin de siècle* Europe or the Swinging Sixties. The primary evidence for such shifts in moral outlook lies in the organization of society and its institutions, and in the general behaviour of individuals. And this too would seem to be an important element of Caird's meaning.

History moves for Caird in a broadly dialectical sequence; that is to say his historical reconstructions all take the form of one position whose flaws give way to its opposite, whose reciprocal flaws generate a kind of synthesis of whatever is of enduring value in each of them. To tell any story in this way carries a sense of completion, but Caird insists that the end point of any one sequence can only be the start of a new one. One might object then that nothing is achieved, that history only moves in circles, but Caird insists that the movement is better viewed as a spiral; we pass again and again over the same ground but each time we do so it is at a higher level.[150] Dialectical completion does not entail the completion of history.

As has already been noted, for Green ethics is a matter of the eternal consciousness' gradual reproduction or realization of itself in the life of the individual and in the history of humanity, and Bradley too presents an explicitly developmental ethics; in cultural-historical, in individual, and in philosophical terms. Caird's view is in

---

[148] 'Professor Green's Last Work', 559; *The Social Philosophy of Comte*, xv; 'Reform and the Reformation', 7, 8, 27; *Evolution of Theology in the Greek Philosophers*, II:3.

[149] 'Reform and the Reformation', 28.

[150] 'Reform and the Reformation', 16, 24–6. As well as by Caird, the illustration is one offered too by William Wallace (*Prolegomena to the Study of Hegel's Philosophy*, 3). But both, of course, are drawing on the observation made first by Hegel that what seems circular may also appear progressive. See *Lectures on the Philosophy of History*, I:27, 346.

fundamental harmony with these, but while in both Green and Bradley the moves are cautious—we find only tentative historical interpretations and an unwillingness to say what 'complete self-development' or 'ideal morality' might amount to—by contrast, Caird is not so shy, arguing that we can use the idea of progress, 'not only as a key to the history of the past, but also to determine, in outline at least, the idea of moral perfection'.[151] Such boldness, of course, lays him least open of the three to charges of relativism, but conversely most susceptible to charges of complacency and conservatism; for too often he writes as though liberal rational Christianity or the discrete nation state represent the very culmination of human intellectual and social development.

6.3.2 The dialectic of freedom

If ethical life evolves, what drives it to do so, and in what direction does it proceed? For Caird the answer to these two connected questions lies in the fact that human nature—at least as it is given to us—is something divided, an antagonism of opposing forces in which we cannot rest and which continually drives us on until we can overcome it. We are creatures out of kilter with ourselves, pushed onwards until we can find—which is for Caird but to restore—the harmony of our true selves.[152] What is this dualism that afflicts us? Again Caird is hard to pin down and one is tempted to complain that the fluidity of his thought gets the better of him. He describes the division as one between the actual and the ideal, between our lower and higher nature, between the flesh and the spirit, between what we are and what we could or ought to be—all phrases too general to bite. But even where Caird is more specific than that, we find that he runs together several dualisms that philosophers today would feel happier to keep separate. In his writings it possible to pull out what seem to be really three different versions of the story.

   In one of its earliest versions, in his 1866 lecture 'Ethical Philosophy', the story gets played in explicitly historical terms as the long search for 'the true idea of freedom'.[153] In this, of course, Caird is following Hegel who, in his introduction to the *Philosophy of History*, says that world history is nothing but the progressive development of the self-awareness of freedom.[154] Caird argues that, because the ancient Greeks had no concept of universal human nature in general, they were unable to grasp the true significance of freedom; for them it was simply a privilege that law gave to some and not to others. Only with the emergence of Christianity could the real problem of ethics be grasped:

---

[151] 'Professor Green's Last Work', 561.

[152] Eternally we always are that which temporally we are not but hope to bring about. Whether Caird also believed that at some earlier stage of either human cultural history or individual psychological development people enjoyed a more harmonious conscious life is unclear. Relevant here is his discussion of the Fall ('Reform and Reformation', 3–6).

[153] *Ethical Philosophy*, 13.

[154] 'The History of the world is none other than the progress of the consciousness of Freedom' (*Lectures on the Philosophy of History*, Introduction, 19–20).

with all men created by, and equal before, God, it became possible to see clearly the gap between what we all ideally are and what we actually find ourselves to be, and in consequence to appreciate the real significance of freedom—to appreciate that man must be free because he has a moral destiny to fulfil. The need to be free from the determining influence of the external world led some to withdraw from it, for example, into the cloister,[155] but most were not so quiescent. Luther, in setting individual faith against Church authority, was one of the first to really fight for freedom, but it was a principle he took only so far, and what the German reformation whispered the French Revolution shouted. Raising us above consciousness of self as merely a natural being, a bundle of desires and powers, the development of self-understanding in terms of 'the rights of man' was a necessary step in the development of morality, but not the final step. For in replacing external authority with unfettered internal licence, with all the horrors that led to, what the French Revolution failed to see was 'that the true freedom is not freedom from law, but from ourselves'.[156] The lesson that must be learned, says Caird, is to take the obstacles to freedom, and neither running from them nor blindly opposing them, to learn how to use and transform them into agencies for our own moral growth. How can this be done? We need to learn to re-envision our relations to the world, and especially to the people, around us. 'If we regard ourselves as mere atoms, having an existence and a happiness apart from all relations with men and things into which we have been brought, these relations will seem to us so many fetters upon our liberty.'[157] But this atomic conception of self is unreal; we do not exist except through these relations and have no worth without them. We realize our freedom precisely by developing our relations with others; and what seems a barrier is in fact an opportunity for growth and liberty. From family, to society, to race, to the greatest whole of them all, God, we cannot escape our part in the larger organic unity to which we belong; but, accepting it, recognizing that it is in us as much as it is outside us, it ceases to be a yoke and becomes the very liberty we seek. 'The freedom that struggles against social necessity, must ultimately discover that it is only in the social organism that the individual can be really free.'[158] True liberty is not unconstrained *carte blanche*, but neither does it consist in slavish obedience to the rules or norms of the society in which we find ourselves; the best life combines 'social unity with independence'.[159]

Caird's analysis here was influential, and explicitly followed by, for example, Henry Jones in his *Idealism as a Practical Creed*.[160] But it is also interesting to compare the conception of freedom developed in this essay with that of Green and Bradley. Green

---

[155] *Evolution of Religion*, II:284ff.   [156] *Ethical Philosophy*, 19.   [157] *Ethical Philosophy*, 21.
[158] *Critical Philosophy of Immanuel Kant*, II:561. 'True independence for a being like man, who is essentially part of a greater whole, is not to be reached by shutting others out of his life—for he who shuts others out, shuts himself in—but by that widening of sympathy which makes the life and interests of others part of his own' (*Lay Sermons*, 10–11).
[159] *Lay Sermons*, 6.
[160] Henry Jones, *Idealism as a Practical Creed*, Chapters II to IV, trace Caird's story exactly.

too distinguishes between freedom, understood as simply the exemption from compulsion by others, and a higher, real, or positive sense of freedom, the ability to find an abiding satisfaction of our true selves—a process which Green argues is necessarily social.[161] In a similar vein Bradley argues that since nothing could be wholly free from external influence, the freedom we seek, rather than a mere absence, is something positive, the power of self-assertion. But even the glutton or drunkard expresses themselves and so we must add that it is only in so far as we express our *true* self that we are free.[162] And our true self Bradley tells us is our social self.[163] Other people, rather than a curb on freedom, are our great chance to acquire it.

6.3.3 The dialectic of egoism and altruism

The dialectic between 'external constraints' and 'infinite caprice'[164] is not the only way to recount 'the moral significance of history'.[165] Another popular way would be in terms of the distinction between egoism and altruism, for it is tempting to see moral advance as the progressive triumph of altruism over egoism. Such we might think is the message of the Kantian philosophy in its insistence that we replace action motivated by natural desire (which, Kant thinks, is necessarily always self-interested) with that done in accordance with duty (whose essence is universalizability). Something similar may be found in Comte who argues that the natural development of human nature is one in which egoism is transcended by altruism. And even a philosopher like Sidgwick thinks that reason leads us to pass from an unacceptable ethical hedonism to a doctrine of universal benevolence.

There are, thinks Caird, two flaws with this picture. In the first place, altruism, for all its importance, cannot in itself provide us with a coherent ethical goal. Unbridled egoism may lead to a 'war of all against all', but if altruism is the giving up of our happiness in order to secure the happiness of others, the reign of universal altruism would simply replace one struggle with another; 'a struggle of all and each to surrender to each other the finite goods of life, instead of a struggle to retain them.'[166] The familiar and embarrassing struggle in a restaurant when each person insists on paying for the meal.

The mistake stems from a second flaw, from a failure to properly think through just what is involved in the overcoming of egoism. This we can see, argues Caird, in the case of each philosopher mentioned above. Since Comte (like Hume) sharply separates

---

[161] 'On the Different Senses of Freedom', §§1,18; 'Liberal Legislation and Freedom of Contract', 372, 384.
[162] *Ethical Studies*, 56–7.
[163] The mere individual, the unit out of which Mill wished to build society, is a non-existent 'fiction' (*Ethical Studies*, 168). The individual apart from the community is an unreal 'abstraction' (*Ethical Studies*, 173). The idea that society is assembled out of distinct units, Bradley dismisses as a 'fable' (*Ethical Studies*, 174).
[164] *Ethical Philosophy*, 17, 19.
[165] *The Social Philosophy of Comte*, 171.
[166] *Critical Philosophy of Immanuel Kant*, II:401.

desire and reason, for him the transition from egoism to altruism is one brought about by natural evolution, not through the intervention of reason. But, argues Caird, in his extended critique of the positivist system first published in a series of papers in 1879, such a transition makes no sense without reason or self-consciousness,[167] for where there is no explicit sense of ego or non-ego, there can be neither egoism nor altruism in the first place.[168] We must distinguish between appetite in its natural state existing in an animal not conscious of itself which, however it is directed, cannot really be either selfish or unselfish, and the same impulse which in the light of reason appears to us as conscious desire or motivation. Our impulses, says Caird, 'in becoming combined with self-consciousness . . . are changed as by a chemical solvent, which dissolves and renews them'.[169] Thus only through reason may egoism be over-thrown, but the same reason will never allow us to settle for so simplistic and confrontational a picture. Thus taken up and utterly transmuted by conscious thought, reason can no longer let egoism and altruism stand as bare unanalysed impulses, they are entered on a process of analysis that ends in their dissolution. 'The progressive triumph of altruism over egoism, which constitutes the moral significance of history, is only the result of the fact that an individual, who is also a conscious self, cannot find his happiness in his own individual life, but only in the life of the whole to which he belongs. A selfish life is for such a being a contradiction.'[170] In other words, taken up into reason itself, we see that neither motive can thrive without the other, that self and not-self are two different sides of our single self-conscious nature, which must be developed reciprocally. The individual self-fulfilment we seek is not something set against the good of others, but something to be found only by submerging oneself in the life of others.

Sidgwick is more willing to allow that the process which brings about the switch from egoism to altruism might be a rational one, but even he has not properly understood that process complains Caird, in an 1875 review of *The Methods of Ethics*. Sidgwick suggests that reason must prompt a universalization of desire, a recognition that what we seek for ourselves we should seek for all beings, but really this is to make the very same mistake as Comte, for Sidgwick fails to see that the determination of our desires by the rational conscious self 'must entirely change the character of these desires'. The mere generalization of natural desire would produce nothing more than Carlyle's universal 'Paradise of Pigwash' but in fact the process is one in which these natural impulses are determined 'first by the idea of self, and then by the idea of a self that is social, that finds itself in losing itself in the life of others'.[171] In other words, reason, in coming to recognize both the self and the not-self, cannot then rest with any

---

[167] Caird seems not to find any clear distinction between these.

[168] *The Social Philosophy of Comte*, 169–70.

[169] *The Social Philosophy of Comte*, 170. The echoes of Green's discussion of desire and motive are strong here.

[170] *The Social Philosophy of Comte*, 171.

[171] Review of Sidgwick's *The Methods of Ethics*, 614.

partial conception of this dichotomy, but must press on to see their essential relativity and the impossibility of any ultimate opposition between them.

The answer to the problem of egoism does not lie in 'altruism', for sacrifice of one's self to another 'offers no real deliverance from the prison of individuality' says Caird in his second book on the philosophy of Kant;[172] 'it would not take us beyond the negation of our immediate selves to the conception of a higher common self in which we are really united.'[173] Instead we must sacrifice the individual to the wider social whole. And yet (laments Caird) this 'higher altruism' remains unavailable to Kant for whom selves are permanently external to one another.

Once again, what Caird is arguing here is closely comparable with what Green and Bradley say on the same subject. As was shown above, to Green, one's own true good is a common good which simply does not divide up into good-for-self and good-for-others, undermining the very contrast between egoism and altruism. Bradley opposes the doctrine of psychological egoism or 'universal selfishness',[174] but at a deeper level he too rejects (as 'mere reckless theorizing'[175]) any simple view of the struggle to become moral—the war between the 'bad self' and the 'good self'—as just a conflict between our egoistic and altruistic tendencies; for all such desires can be steered in either healthy or unhealthy directions,[176] and it is certainly not true that the good self is just the social self. It was necessary to pass, it should be recalled, from the unqualified sociality of 'My Station and its Duties' to the more nuanced stance of 'Ideal Morality'. Instead, he presents a reconstruction of the psychological and moral development of self according to which the 'egoistic' grows seamlessly into the 'altruistic'. The child first finds affirmation in its own sensations, then in external objects, then in other people.[177] The development of the 'bad self' occurs through a kind of disruption to this process whereby the agent seeks to affirm itself in aims and objects both disharmonious and opposed to the good.[178]

6.3.4 The dialectic of naturalism and rationalism

A third framework which Caird uses to tell basically the same tale, sets out the dichotomy as one between what we might call empirical naturalism and transcendent rationalism. On one telling of it, the story of the eighteenth and nineteenth centuries is that of the growth of materialistic naturalism; a rise which, with its attendant determinism, was rapidly felt to be the gravest threat to ethics. If human beings are nothing more than animals with desires which fall under natural law then value—what *ought* to

---

[172] *Critical Philosophy of Immanuel Kant*, II:402.
[173] *Critical Philosophy of Immanuel Kant*, II:401.
[174] *Ethical Studies*, 250–6. It is either trivial or just plain false, he argues (*Ethical Studies*, 255).
[175] *Ethical Studies*, 278.
[176] *Ethical Studies*, 278–9.
[177] *Ethical Studies*, 279–93.
[178] *Ethical Studies*, 293ff. For a detailed discussion of this process of moral self-development see Don MacNiven, *Bradley's Moral Psychology*, and Keene 'The Interplay of Bradley's Social and Moral Philosophy', 100–5.

be as against what *is*—seems as impossible as the free will necessary to bring it about. If Green's target in this regard was Hume, Caird zeros in on Comte; for Comte too contrasts our heart and our head, our instinct and our intellect, and sees the former as the real force behind human action; something which he consequently regards as wholly determined by natural forces.

Against this naturalism Caird sets the Kantian position. Kant agrees that desire as a natural force leaves no scope for freedom but, opposing reason to desire, argues that we are not merely natural creatures, and that human action may in fact be determined by reason. Rejecting the liberty of indifference in favour of a conception of freedom as self-determination, Kant identifies the willing self with the reasoning self, which allows him to see action occasioned by reason as autonomous and free in contrast to that occasioned by desire which is heteronomous and unfree.

But this is not the happy solution to our troubles it first might seem. For in lifting the rational self-conscious subject right out of the world of objects, in not allowing it to be determined by the sensitive side of human nature, Kant renders mysterious its supposed capacity to bring about action. Surely pure intelligence cannot motivate at all. To deal with this problem, Kant talks as though our passion supplies the maxims for action which reason then tests for adequacy. But, as he himself has set up the terms of the problem, such a taking up of natural desires as maxims by rational self-consciousness looks like some sort of a relapse into heteronomy of the will,[179] for 'when [the self] admits into its motives the determination of its sensitive being, it is submitting to a foreign yoke, and by its own activity making itself a slave'.[180]

Caird proceeds to offer a diagnosis and solution to Kant's problem; a third step in this dialectical opposition between naturalism and rationalism. He presents it as something implicit in Kantianism, a continuation of its underlying direction and something Kant himself was close to saying. We might prefer to regard it as Caird's own positive contribution to ethical philosophy. But to insist on a choice between these two is to misunderstand his own way of working, which was always historical.[181]

Central to Kant's system is the sharp dualism he draws between the rational and the non-rational sides of our nature. And in so far as it permits him to see that naturalism is inadequate to express our full nature, that separation, allows Caird, is a strength in his system. But the strength becomes a weakness when he draws the contrast so sharply that it prevents him from seeing that the distinction is one which in the end, at the highest levels, must be dissolved.[182] Although consciousness of self as active is distinguished from consciousness of self as determined by natural desires, it at the same time

---

[179] *Critical Philosophy of Immanuel Kant*, II:184.

[180] *Critical Philosophy of Immanuel Kant*, II:185.

[181] Here we may make an aside. While it is certainly a shame that Caird never wrote the full length ethical treatise he apparently intended to (see note 145 above) the pity is mitigated by the fact that, had he done so, it would probably not have looked very different from the material we do in fact have. It would certainly have been historical.

[182] *Critical Philosophy of Immanuel Kant*, II:196, 2:226.

implies it.[183] Consciousness cannot be absolutely alien to its desires any more than the knowing self can be absolutely alien to the things it knows. The antagonism of desire and duty can only be understood in relation to a unity which combines them both.[184] The rational self is not determined *by* its desires, but neither is it determined in plain *opposition* to them, rather (recognizing that they are not in the last analysis foreign to it) it realizes itself *through* them. The key to understanding this lies in the distinction, already looked at in connection with altruism and egoism, between appetite and desire. Rendered conscious appetite becomes desire, and there are two important points to note about this transition.

Kant was suspicious of natural drives and urges as a kind of heteronomy, some sort of external imposition on the rational will, but where those forces are rendered conscious, this danger disappears. In so far as we are reflexively aware of it, the animal impulse becomes a motive of self-realization; we identify ourselves with the object of desire. Rather than simply desiring a given thing we desire to be a person whose life is qualified by that thing. This is very clearly set out in the 1875 review of Sidgwick: 'desire, so far as it is determined by the rational nature of man, implies a sense of defect of that to which, at the same time, the self is regarded as necessarily related, and without which its existence is incomplete; it implies, in short, self-identification with an object.'[185] In this way, rather than some heteronomous imposition on the self, our desire becomes an expression of free self-realization.

The second point to note concerns the content of such desire. Contra Kant, Caird argues that reason is in fact able to generate a goal for itself that is not merely formal. He suggests that, paralleling the way in which in the Transcendental Deduction the self finds its own unity in the phenomenal world, from the practical side of things the self may find itself in the notion of *how the world ought to be*. As in creating the phenomenal world it is simultaneously creating itself, so in realizing the moral world it is realizing its own true self.[186] If we ask what this amounts to, again Caird (generously) thinks that Kant was nearly there; this time in his doctrine of the Kingdom of Ends. In its first appearance, the self-conscious self-determining individual may seem a merely formal universality, nothing but the *negation* of the particular. But on deeper investigation this abstraction from particularity turns out to be 'the transition from the individual to the social self-consciousness'.[187] The desired universality is found not by simple negation of the individual, but by its immersion in a wider whole. We abstract from our own particularity, not into some empty formalism, but into the truer universality of a community to which our particular existence is subordinate. Such a universality, argues Caird, is concrete and gives content to the moral life.

---

[183] *Critical Philosophy of Immanuel Kant*, II:205.
[184] *Critical Philosophy of Immanuel Kant*, II:206. This is a specific instance of a more general point in logic, for Caird, that all difference implies a wider embracing unity. See Chapter 8.2 below.
[185] Review of Sidgwick's *The Methods of Ethics*, 612.
[186] *Critical Philosophy of Immanuel Kant*, II:191–2.
[187] *Critical Philosophy of Immanuel Kant*, II:238.

This picture of a social self as the synthesis able to mediate between the directionless particularity of hedonism, and the barren universalism of Kant, is clearly one that closely parallels both Bradley and Green's presentation of the matter. 'My Station and its Duties' is quite explicitly a synthesis between the excessive particularism of 'Pleasure for Pleasure's sake' and the excessive universalism of 'Duty for Duty's sake'. While Green too, we saw, works to find a path between these two. In the end, for all his disagreement, Green remains close to Kant—closer than Bradley—but not even Green goes so far as does Caird to suggest that the answer is present all along in Kant. Nor (it should be said) is this the most plausible element of Caird's case.

6.3.5 Social holism

It will not, of course, have escaped attention that in all three versions of the dichotomy which Caird finds to beset human nature, the story of dialectical salvation is one that propels us towards a form of social holism, towards a recognition that human nature, and thus human fulfilment, must be understood in fundamentally social terms. For Caird, as (of course) for Green and Bradley, the life of the individual set against the whole must give way to the life of the individual for and in the whole.[188] The phrase Caird most commonly uses to characterize this phenomena is 'die to live', and it is so important—he claims, for example, that it gathers up the Hegelian philosophy in a sentence[189]—that we should stop a moment to consider it. It comes of course from Christianity, from the promise of Christ that he who loses his life will in fact find it.[190] Caird seems to use it in at least three different ways. For him, it means death to sin, to flesh, to the world, and it also means death to selfishness, the end of self-concern, the step of giving one's life to God. These two are 'ethical' points, but there is a third deeper 'metaphysical' issue about identity; for Caird reads it also as saying that we must give up our superficial or apparent self to find our deeper or real self. If we hold on to the atomic self we cannot progress, but if we can let it go, we find not its destruction but an altogether higher level of being within the social whole. Adapting Tillich's 'God beyond God' notion we might speak here of 'the self beyond self'.[191]

---

[188] We may note here, as an aside (though hardly a surprising one given their contact) that John Caird, as early as 1880, expresses very similar views. No one is or can be independent of others, he argues, 'whether you will or no, there is a sense in which other minds and wills are part of you. . . . From the very dawn of your existence your spiritual nature is steeped in the life of the past, in the spirit of the age and society into which you are born, and in the unconscious influences that emanate from other minds. . . . Each soul does not make a new start to shape its independent career. For good or ill, it is part of an organic whole.' However, 'Union with other minds and lives is not the suppression but the evolution and realisation of our own individual nature' ('Union with God', 28–9, 28).

[189] *Hegel*, 44.

[190] Mark 8:34–5, Luke 9:23–4, Luke 14:25–33, John 12:24. The phrase came to idealism filtered also through Goethe whose celebrated poem 'Selige Sehnsucht' ('Blessed Longing') addressed to a moth, includes in its final stanza the exhortation, 'stirb und werde!' ('Die and become!').

[191] Paul Tillich, *The Courage to Be*, 182, 186–90.

6.4 The popularization of idealist ethics

That together the systems of Bradley, Green, and Caird exerted a profound influence on moral philosophy can be seen in much of the ethical literature that appeared during the 1880s and 1890s. Some philosophers were content simply to recommend their foundational writings to others,[192] while some expounded them in textbooks of their own, and even in cases where independent argument was advanced the marks of influence were still very strong.

6.4.1 *W.R. Sorley* The Ethics of Naturalism

Deriving from a set of lectures given as part of his Shaw Fellowship in Edinburgh, and submitted too for his Fellowship at Trinity College Cambridge, Sorley's *On the Ethics of Naturalism* was published in 1885; a new (and significantly revised) edition appearing some twenty years later in 1904. The bulk of the book consists in an attack on naturalism which, though broadly in line with the views of Bradley, Green, and Caird, is developed with some originality.[193] However, the book's positive alternative, which he sets out in its final chapter, is a virtual paraphrase of Green.[194]

   The fundamental problem, says Sorley in that chapter, is that all any naturalistic approach (such as that of evolutionary theory) can tell us is the direction in which things tend, but what ethical philosophy asks for is the direction in which things *ought* to tend. Efficient causation cannot yield teleology, while no account of the origin of social action can tell us its proper end or goal.[195] The mistake, he suggests, is linked to that of trying to find a naturalistic explanation of the origin of consciousness. Self-consciousness is not something we may derive from the world of unconscious objects, however complex their form or function may become. 'It is, on the contrary, the supreme condition of the world of objects having any existence whatever. It is only through objects being brought into relation with the identical and permanent subject of knowledge, that there is unity in nature, or, in other words, that there is a known world of nature or experience at all.'[196] In a connected fashion, genuinely ethical or purposive action calls for self-consciousness, in this case 'not an apprehension of the manifold of impression into the unity of consciousness' but rather 'the externalisation

---

[192] Bosanquet, for example, in his pre-1891 address on 'The Kingdom of God on Earth' (116) acknowledges that the ethical code he is putting forward is an attempt to 'popularise' that advanced by Bradley in 'My Station and its Duties', while in his 'Working Faith of the Social Reformer' (49–50) Jones advances his case for the determination of individual character by social context through extensive quotation from the same.

[193] Part One of the book deals with traditional theories (psychological hedonism, utilitarianism, and the moral sentiment' theory of Shaftesbury and Hutcheson) while Part Two of the book considers the theory of evolution (Spencer and Leslie Stephen). Failing to establish any connection between survival and pleasure, he argues that evolutionary theory may not assimilate its goal to that of hedonism, but neither is it able to supply its own alternative end (*Ethics of Naturalism*, 257–61).

[194] In the second edition this chapter was completely rewritten, and the explicit following of Green dropped. See below for more on Sorley's later ethics.

[195] *Ethics of Naturalism*, 264–71.

[196] *Ethics of Naturalism*, 282.

of self-consciousness in realising a conceived end or idea.'[197] Only a conscious being can be deliberative or purposive. An agent must choose an end as his own, but 'an end can only be made our own when conceived as necessary for realising or completing our idea of self',[198] and in this fashion the goal of all conscious action may be thought of as self-realization. (Although Sorley points out that Green's own term 'self-satisfaction' must not be misread as 'the pleasure of self-satisfaction'.)[199] What is the nature of the true self that must be realized? Sorley is more tentative than Green, but he does argue that we must recognize in others not merely a 'similar consciousness' but an identical one, calling alike for realization in us both.[200] This does not do away with all conflict, but it 'establishes the principle that the realisation of one's own nature involves the realisation of that of others'[201]—Green's common good.

6.4.2 S. Alexander Moral Order and Progress

In 1877, after two years at the University of Melborne, Samuel Alexander came to the Balliol College of Jowett, Green, Nettleship, and A.C. Bradley, and in 1882, following a degree in *Literae Humaniores*, he was elected to a fellowship at Lincoln College, the first professing Jew to be so recognized by an Oxbridge college. Winning the newly instituted Green Moral Philosophy Prize in 1887,[202] his first book, *Moral Order and Progress* (which appeared in 1889), had strong idealist credentials.[203] Alexander says that it was A.C. Bradley whose teaching inspired him to study ethics[204] and F.H. Bradley, his tutor's brother, who went through the proofs of the entire book with him, but more perhaps than either of these—and as Alexander himself acknowledges—are his very great obligations to Green.

He is, for example, fully signed up to the idealist notion that there exists an organic relation between individual and society; man is known to us only as a social being whose moral life grows out of his social upbringing, so it is idle to start inquiry from a position of individualism.[205] Instead we must recognize the social nature of the moral ideal; 'Every good act, every part of the moral order, is...thus a common good in virtue of the tie it creates between all the members of the order.' In consequence Alexander denies any fundamental distinction between egoism and altruism[206] and emphasizes the importance of self-sacrifice and service.[207] Other followings of Green

---

[197] *Ethics of Naturalism*, 284.   [198] *Ethics of Naturalism*, 287.
[199] *Ethics of Naturalism*, 287–8.   [200] *Ethics of Naturalism*, 289.
[201] *Ethics of Naturalism*, 290.
[202] The Green Moral Philosophy Prize was originally established in 1884 to give immediate effect to a decree in the will of T.H. Green by which on the death of Mrs T.H. Green the sum of £1,000 was to be bequeathed to the University of Oxford for the purpose of funding a triennial prize 'on a dissertation on some subject relating to moral philosophy'.
[203] *Moral Order and Progress* was successful enough to go into a third edition by 1899, but in later life Alexander moved away from this position and allowed the book to go out of print.
[204] The book is dedicated to A.C. Bradley.
[205] *Moral Order and Progress*, 113.
[206] *Moral Order and Progress*, 175.
[207] *Moral Order and Progress*, 176.

include a stress on the presence of consciousness as the key differentia of voluntary or moral action,[208] a distinction between negative and positive freedom—the contrast between the removal of restraints and responsibility for right action[209]—and advocacy of the progressive nature of the moral ideal.

But endorsement of such Greenian themes is not incompatible with Alexander's expressing also 'dissent from his fundamental principles'. Like Sorley, Alexander is much concerned with the new 'evolutionary ethics' which was at the time an important force. But while Sorley is almost wholly critical, Alexander finds much more to approve. He finds a convergence between idealist and evolutionary ethics, something which can be seen 'by comparing the idealist doctrine, that morality is a common good realised in individual wills, with the view...that conduct is moral according to its contribution to social vitality'. In both we see individualism replaced by the recognition of an organic connection between the individual and his society.

That Alexander can see the naturalistic and post-Kantian traditions pointing to a single result reveals some crucial differences between him and Green. To begin with he opposes Green's intrusion of metaphysics into ethics, although the claim is not pushed as far as it might be: while complaining that Green's metaphysical and timeless self 'is both for psychology and for ethics an unnecessary idea',[210] he does allow 'that ethical inquiries really stand very near to metaphysics', so in the end his criticism is simply that 'ethics is not a part of metaphysics because it happens to stand, so to speak, next door'.[211] More fundamentally he takes issue with Green's ethic of perfection or self-realization. There is no single standard of perfection and every act is an act of self-realization so that rather than use these notions to determine the content of morality, we must appeal to morality itself to fill out their meaning.[212] This is an uncharitable objection, for Green would admit that the self-realization formula by itself is insufficient to determine action, while Alexander's alternative (Platonic) suggestion of 'equilibrium' is not obviously more useful. (He suggests that the idea of good or right signifies an adjustment of parts in an orderly whole, which in the individual represents an equilibrium of different powers, and in the society an equilibrium of different persons.) Alexander takes issue too with Green's key objection to Hedonism, that there is no such thing as the sum of pleasures. The objection forms part of Green's general critique of psychological atomism, which is a fair one; a mere succession of mental events has no unity. But once conscious unity has been accounted for (and it is, argues Alexander, unnecessary to bring in some metaphysically transcendent self for this purpose) no reason remains to deny that pleasures can be added. In Alexander's mind, Green, although right in rejecting individualism, gives the wrong reason for rejecting hedonism. The problem is not that pleasures cannot be *added*, but that, differing in quality and not just in quantity, they cannot be *compared*.[213]

[208] *Moral Order and Progress*, 75. [209] *Moral Order and Progress*, 8.
[210] *Moral Order and Progress*, 76. [211] *Moral Order and Progress*, 78.
[212] *Moral Order and Progress*, 187–8. [213] *Moral Order and Progress*, 197–202.

Alexander's *Moral Order and Progress* is usefully compared to a second expanded version of an essay which won the Green Moral Philosophy Prize, this time in 1899— A.E. Taylor's *The Problem of Conduct* (1901). At the same time as holding on to a monistic idealism much indebted to Bradley, and drawing heavily on various elements of idealistic ethics, as with Alexander, Taylor's debts sit alongside much opposition to the school, and to Green in particular. Indeed going further than Alexander and finding nothing but a gap between Green's ethics and metaphysics, the book commits idealist heresy in arguing for a general disassociation of ethics from metaphysics, insisting that the former needs to be treated empirically. Ethics, if it is to be any use must be based not on general principles of metaphysics, but on the study of human nature in its concrete empirical entirety, as it is revealed in the sciences of psychology, sociology, and anthropology. 'It is for empirical psychology to say what qualities are and what are not of "absolute" worth for human beings' Taylor insists.[214]

6.4.3 *J.H. Muirhead* The Elements of Ethics

Sorley, Alexander, and Taylor all wrote independent essays, but this was not the only kind of writing to be found in the moral philosophy literature at this time; and one of the most interesting measures of Idealism's influence is the appearance of a number of textbooks, condensing and presenting the new ethics for the use of students.[215] The emergence of such books, paralleled in many other academic disciplines, reflects the changes in university teaching at this point in history, but it also demonstrates the contemporary strength and hegemony of the idealist position. Students needed text-books to help them with what was then 'state of the art'. And that was Idealism.

The first of these books to appear was John Henry Muirhead's The Elements of Ethics (1892). His idealist grounding was thorough; Glasgow university, where he studied under Edward Caird,[216] Balliol College, where Jowett, Green, A.C. Bradley, and Nettleship all taught, and Manchester New College (at that time in London) where James Martineau was Principal. What most interested Muirhead was developing the ethical implications of the idealist vision. Lecturing at both Royal Holloway and Bedford Colleges, he was one of the founders of the London Ethical Society in 1886,[217] and involved too in the London Society for the Extension of University Teaching. It was lectures for the latter that formed the basis of *The Elements of Ethics*, which appeared as one of a series of University Extension Manuals. The book was phenomenally successful, bringing his name to a very wide audience. The volume

---

[214] *Problem of Conduct*, 169.

[215] Since the concern here is with British Idealism, there is space only to mention Dewey's *Outlines of a Critical Theory of Ethics* (1891) which it has been argued 'could almost be read as a corrected, revised edition of Bradley's *Ethical Studies* for the American undergraduate student of ethics' (Welchman, *Dewey's Ethical Thought*, 75). Its preface expresses its great indebtedness to Caird, Bradley, and Green.

[216] As well as acknowledging his debt in the Preface, Muirhead dedicated the later editions (from the third edition (1910) onwards) to his former teacher.

[217] den Otter, *British Idealism and Social Explanation*, 84.

recognized the growing ascendancy of idealist ethical thought, and with no pretence of originality, presents to students the thoughts of Green, Bradley, and Caird. In this Muirhead met a real need; for these ideas were still not readily available to a wider audience. Green's *Prolegomena* was a hard book,[218] while Bradley deliberately kept his *Ethical Studies* out of print, and Caird's views could be found only in obscure articles or buried under his various historical studies.

The book introduces nearly all the key themes of idealist ethics from the holistic nature of explanation—'A phenomenon is...only fully explained when enough is known of the particular system in question to permit us to apprehend the phenomenon in light of the known relations of the other parts, and therefore as a coherent member of the whole'[219]—to the close dependence of ethics on metaphysics—'the nature of the world at large and man's relation to it are of the utmost importance to ethics'.[220] Emphasizing that human desires are always conscious and directed at more or less definitely conceived objects (which distinguishes them from mere appetites which we share with animals), Muirhead urges that all are related to the self, in the sense that it is their realization *for a self*, some form of self-satisfaction, that is desired. To desire some object is to desire to become the possessor of that object, to desire to do something is to desire to be a person who has done that thing.[221] He stresses, though, that this is not the same as saying that desire is always self-interested; personal good is not the same as personal advantage.[222]

He rejects both Hedonism and Kantianism, locating their most fundamental flaw in a common and mistaken understanding of the difference between feeling and reason. For the Hedonist the fundamental nature of the self is to feel, its goal given by mere sensation, reasoning contributing simply the means. But the self is more than just feeling and cannot be satisfied with just that.[223] For the Kantian the fundamental self is the reasoning self, its goal given by mere thought, and desire something to be excluded from ethics at all cost. But this is to condemn our natural moral sentiments, the ordinary affections of love and pity, hope and fear. Contra both parties, Muirhead insists that we must break down the division between feeling and reason; 'there can be no object of desire, in the proper sense of the word, which is not constituted such by reason itself'.[224] To fail to see this is to confuse appetite, which we share with the animals, and desire, which calls for a consciously conceived object. Appetite is the raw material of desire as sensation is the raw material of perception. As there can be no desire without the conscious activity of thought or reason, so there can be no activity in a thinking or rational self without desire. The rational life is not one without desire, but instead one regulated by our higher rather than our lower desires.[225]

---

[218] In this connection mention should be made of W.H. Fairbrother's *The Philosophy of Thomas Hill Green* (1896) A summary for students, this testifies both to fact that Green was taught and that students found it hard.

[219] *Elements*, 21. [220] *Elements*, 31–2. [221] *Elements*, 49–50.
[222] *Elements*, 80. [223] *Elements*, 108. [224] *Elements*, 121.
[225] *Elements*, 122.

The more recent evolutionary utilitarianism of Spencer and Stephen is found equally unable to provide a goal, although it is credited for revealing that the self is no isolated atom, but rather something essentially social. This point Muirhead establishes at some considerable length. 'It is the function it performs in virtue of its special place in the organism which makes the hand a hand and the foot a foot. In the same way it is his place and function in society that makes the individual what he is.'[226] Because our nature is social so must be the standard of moral judgement; the good is a common good, undermining the traditional distinction between altruism and egoism.[227] Man 'can only realise his own life in so far as he realises the life of the society of which he is a member. To maintain himself in isolated independence, to refuse to be compromised by social relations, is the surest way to fail to realise the good he seeks. To seek life in this sense is to lose it. On the other hand, a man finds salvation in the duties of family, profession, city, country. To lose his life in these is to find it.'[228] From this he draws, among other things, a clear prohibition on suicide: 'no man has a right to take his own life, because no man has a life of his own to take'.[229] Such social holism is not of course without metaphysical significance, but in general it is notable that, while not dissenting from that system, the introductory nature of his task leads Muirhead to set out the ethics of Idealism wholly without its associated metaphysics of the Absolute.[230]

Perhaps the most interesting discussion of the book is found in the final section which tackles head on issues of moral progress and relativism, left somewhat implicit in the writings of Green, Bradley, and Caird. Reflection on differing moral codes of different times and countries reveals the fact that the moral standard is relative.[231] But 'the actual standard of any particular period, while undoubtedly relative to the special circumstances of the time and country, is not on that account an isolated and accidental phenomenon, but takes its place as a stage in the evolution of a universal moral order.'[232] Moral perspectives are time and culture bound, but their historical sequence is nevertheless one of increasing depth and adequacy.

---

[226] *Elements*, 162.   [227] *Elements*, 153.   [228] *Elements*, 160.

[229] *Elements*, 164. As the self-destruction of will itself, Green in his Lectures on Moral and Political Philosophy regards suicide as among the class of things which, though 'ludicrously wrong', utilitarianism is powerless to forbid (*Collected Works*, V:159–60). In similar fashion James Seth argued that 'Suicide, being self-destruction, so far as that is possible to us, must always contradict the fundamental ethical principle of self-development' (*Study of Ethical Principles*, 262). Although recognizing that some suicides, for example, to save others, might fall into a different category (*Ethical Studies*, 158), Bradley seems to have been similarly opposed to suicide. He puts it thus in his *Aphorisms*: 'One said of suicide, "As long as one has brains one should not blow them out." And another answered, "But when one has ceased to have them, too often one cannot"' (#48). This comment is, however, cryptic and admits of more than one reading. Caird's view on the question is unrecorded.

[230] He does briefly digress to endorse a Green-like argument that the knowing subject must be more than just a passive recipient of sensations (*Elements*, 216–18), but the line of thought is taken no further than this.

[231] *Elements*, 193.

[232] *Elements*, 211.

6.4.4 J.S. *Mackenzie* Manual of Ethics

Muirhead was not the only one of Caird's Glasgow students to write such a volume. One year later in 1893, J.S. Mackenzie published his *Manual of Ethics*, part of the University Corresponding College Tutorial Series for students taking external degrees such as those for the University of London.[233] Similarly popular and finding its way 'into the remotest corners of the globe', the book 'made his name familiar almost wherever ethics was taught and English spoken'.[234] Though offering rather more contributions of its own, the *Manual* does fundamentally the same work as Muirhead's (indeed, Mackenzie says that had the *Elements* appeared before he started work, his book would probably not have been written at all),[235] that is, a presentation of the idealist ethical viewpoint as found in the writings of Green, Bradley, and Caird; from which it borrows freely.

Kant is dismissed as offering a merely formal principle, from which no definite matter or guidance can be derived.[236] He is moreover too strict in ruling out all action which springs from feeling rather than the direct application of reason, for many such actions we value highly. The real problem is that Kant's perspective is too narrow. With a view to itself alone or its immediate consequences the universalization of a given action may be unproblematic, but if we look more widely and consider 'its bearing on the whole scheme of life', this is something we could never will. It is not enough that a principle of action is consistent with itself. It must also be 'consistent with *the self*—i.e. with the unity of our lives as a systematic whole'.[237]

Drawing on a detailed critique first put forward in his 1890 *Introduction to Social Philosophy*,[238] Mackenzie repeats Green's complaint against hedonism: 'If pleasure is the one thing that is desirable, it is clear that a sum of pleasures cannot be desirable; for a sum of pleasures is not pleasure. We are apt to think that a sum of pleasures is pleasure, just as a sum of numbers is a number. But this is evidently not the case. A sum of pleasures is not pleasure, any more than a sum of men is a man.'[239] But again a deeper fault is found. Treating desires separately, each with an equal right to satisfaction as long as they yield the same length or intensity of feeling, hedonism ignores the fact that what we seek to satisfy is not our *desires* but *ourselves*.[240] What is important is that we will, not the greatest sum of happiness, but the best kind of happiness, that is, one belonging to the highest type of character.[241]

Again repeating his earlier view,[242] Mackenzie argues that in this way both doctrines point towards the moral ideal as some form of self-realization or the development of character; perfection rather than either duty or happiness. He follows Green in stressing

---

[233] Like Muirhead's book, he acknowledges his debt to Caird. Mackenzie by this point, after a period at Trinity College Cambridge, was working as assistant to Robert Adamson at Manchester.

[234] *John Stuart Mackenzie*, 164; J.W. Scott, 'John Stuart MacKenzie'.

[235] *Manual*, Preface vi.   [236] *Manual*, 57–8.   [237] *Manual*, 66.

[238] *Introduction to Social Philosophy*, 200–26.   [239] *Manual*, 113.

[240] *Manual*, 114.   [241] *Manual*, 115.

[242] *Introduction to Social Philosophy*, 228–36.

that we are driven by conscious desire rather than mere appetite, that action is to be explained teleologically rather than causally. It follows, Mackenzie argues, that 'moral life consists in the constant endeavour to make . . . more and more explicit—to bring out more and more completely our rational self-conscious, spiritual nature'.[243] Thus, via an elision of concepts that is worrying but typifies the school, he moves from the deliberate and conscious nature of action to the conclusion that the true self is the rational self.[244] Although, lest we fall back into some sort of Kantianism, he is quick to point out that, 'to occupy the point of view of reason . . . therefore, is not to withdraw from all our desires, and occupy the point of view of mere formal self-consistency; it is rather to place all our desires in their right relations to one another'.[245] Thus the imperative of morality is not an imperative imposed from without, but 'simply the voice of the true self within us'; conscience is the voice which says 'to thine own self be true'.[246] Related to this, to be free means that one is determined by oneself,[247] but the fact that one's truest self may be something somewhat hidden awaiting to be discovered means, rather than that we *are* free, that it is better to say we are *developing towards freedom*.[248]

The true self is the rational self, but it is also the social self, for every individual belongs to a social system and is inconceivable without it. Society is an organic unity— 'The parts of it are necessary to each other, as the parts of an animal organism are'[249]— and so the ideal self is something that may be embodied only in the life of a society. Undermining the opposition between egoism and altruism, we can realize our true self only by pursuing social ends. We must sacrifice ourselves, negating the merely individual self (which is merely the apparent self) and rising by stages to 'a universal point of view—i.e. a point of view from which our own private good is no more to us than the good of anyone else'.[250] Interestingly, as with Muirhead's book, although Mackenzie charts the transition from the individual to the social, the next move up to the metaphysical (to God or the eternal consciousness) is not pursued.

6.4.5 J. Seth Study of Ethical Principles

The last of the textbooks to consider, James Seth's, *Study of Ethical Principles* (1894) has a slightly different pedigree and nature. Rather than at Glasgow, Seth's training was at Edinburgh University where his teachers were Alexander Campbell Fraser and Henry Calderwood. In 1886 he accepted an invitation to succeed Jacob Gould Schurman as Professor of Metaphysics and Ethics at Dalhousie College, Halifax, Nova Scotia, moving from there in 1892 to Brown University as Professor of Natural Theology.[251] His introduction was thus written in part for a different student market, but the great

---

[243] *Manual*, 135.   [244] *Manual*, 137.   [245] *Manual*, 138.
[246] *Manual*, 138.   [247] *Manual*, 142.   [248] *Manual*, 147.
[249] *Manual*, 154.   [250] *Manual*, 156.
[251] In 1896 Seth moved briefly to Cornell, before he returned to Edinburgh in 1898 to take up the Chair in Moral Philosophy.

success it enjoyed—equal to either Muirhead's or Mackenzie's—was certainly not confined to North America.

He follows the idealist pattern of finding deficient and one-sided both the claims of hedonism and 'rigorism' (or 'rationalism' as he terms it in later editions); both sides make legitimate claims, but neither may be granted sole control of ethical thought. Self-realization is fine as an alternative formula, but Seth warns it is something of a truism to say that the end of human life is self-realization: 'every ethical theory might claim the term "Self-realisation," as each might claim the term "Happiness." The question is, What *is* the "Self"? or *Which* self is to be realised?'[252] There can be no useful ideal of self-realization without an adequate definition of selfhood or personality. Much of what Seth says in this regard is familiar. Rejecting the merely sentient self of hedonism, and the merely rational self of rigorism, his own position—which he names 'Eudaemonism' or 'the ethics of personality'—seeks to realize the *complete* or *total* self, rational and sentient. Rejecting too the social atom, it is a call to self-sacrifice, to the deep truth of the Christian principle 'Die to live'. 'The subjection of the individual, impulsive, sentient self to the order of reason is a Herculean task' he admits, but 'The higher or personal self can be realised only through the death of the lower or individual self, as lower and merely individual'.[253]

However it must be noted that Seth's basic position was that of ethical theism and, as such, more Kantian than Hegelian; with Caird, Bradley, and Green all playing relatively minor roles. And not all of Seth's points were so supportive. In particular he voices fundamental concerns around freedom and personality.[254] Although it is true that service to others is the way to perfect self-realization, forming 'a bridge from the individual to the social virtues, the essential identity of altruism with the higher egoism',[255] society is not an organism. That he warns is only a metaphor and 'the individual can never wholly identify himself with the society, simply because he remains, to the last, an individual'.[256] To move even further out, into the metaphysics of the Absolute, he cautions 'sacrifices, with the freedom of man, the reality of his moral life. If I am but the vehicle of the divine self-manifestation, if my personality is not real but only seeming—the mask that hides the sole activity of God—my freedom and my moral life dissolve together'.[257]

---

[252] *Study of Ethical Principles*, 204.
[253] *Study of Ethical Principles*, 213.
[254] These had been evident from his first book *Freedom as Ethical Postulate* (1891).
[255] *Study of Ethical Principles*, 278.
[256] *Study of Ethical Principles*, 142.
[257] *Study of Ethical Principles*, 384.

7

Idealist Political and Social Philosophy

Of all its contributions to the discipline, it is the political and social philosophy of British Idealism that has enjoyed the longest life. While their doctrines in metaphysics, religion, and logic were swiftly forgotten once the movement's heyday had passed, their social thought continued to attract consideration and, even to this day, can boast a small band of scholars dedicated to its examination. A great deal of this attention, it must be allowed, has been negative. Often their positions have been criticized as *statist*, subordinating the interests, value, and agency of the individual to those of the state itself, but even if more careful consideration of those views is able to rebut such accusations, the general *tone* of their work remains at great remove from anything which is currently popular. As well as being unfashionably grounded in the metaphysics of the Absolute, their doctrines flow seamlessly from their religious and moral thought; two contentious subjects modern multi-culturalist approaches are keen to exclude from the discipline, but which for the idealists were its essential lifespring. Not all attention has been critical, however, and for philosophers seeking a ground to community which transcends the merely pragmatic, egoistic, or utilitarian, the social philosophy of Idealism continues to offer valuable insights.

7.1 T.H. Green

7.1.1 Political obligation

As with many of the domains treated so far, consideration properly begins with the figure of T.H. Green whose 1879–80 *Lectures on the Principles of Political Obligation*, first published in the posthumous *Collected Works* of 1885–8, were the inspiration for the mass of what came afterwards. Both chronologically and thematically, this work followed on immediately from that completed in ethics, the transition from moral to political philosophy marked by the transition from talk about individuals and their social relations to talk about the *state*. This Green defines as 'a body of persons, recognised by each other as having rights, and possessing certain institutions for the maintenance of those rights'.[1] There is no mention of geographical extent and the emphasis on recognition is perhaps unusual[2] but, these points aside, there is nothing very remarkable in Green's definition here. Common enough too is Green's choice of the state itself as the appropriate unit in terms of which to conduct his discussion. In addition to establishing continuity with the traditional literature in political philosophy, focus on the state reflected, as Green well saw, the political reality of his day. He by no means intends to deny that there exist many other smaller social units—family, tribe, church, club, and such like—but the state must be regarded as superseding them; for, however precedent and separate their origin, these lesser wholes are taken up into the state as organic parts, strengthening its bonds as it harmonizes and strengthens theirs, making it for its members, 'the society of societies, the society in which all their claims upon each other are mutually adjusted'.[3] Nor does he think there any a priori prohibition on units larger than the state. Indeed, the claim that every human ought to be free amounts, he admits, to a recognition of 'the idea of the universal brotherhood of men, of mankind as forming one society with a common good'. But in actual fact we pay no more than lip service to this ultimate moral community, and there currently exist neither the institutional mechanisms necessary to bring about any such wider harmonization, nor the desire to create them.[4]

Green's interest in the state revolves around the notion of political obligation, those things which the state may *force* us to do (either for itself or for each other). We are familiar enough with the notion of moral obligation; there are many things we *ought* to do. But with the state comes a new dimension to obligation; there appears a range of things which we may be *compelled* to do, whether we like it or not. What kind of things can we be coerced into doing, or punished if we refuse to do? And what possible justification can there be for such force?[5]

To answer these questions we must inquire into the nature of the state. There are various approaches one might take; one might look at it genetically (in terms of its origin), structurally (in terms of its form) or phenomenologically (in terms of what it is like to live in a state), but rather than any of these, Green argues that we need to look at it teleologically (in terms of its purpose). To really understand the state we need to ask what it is *for*, what it is *aiming at*. Assuming for the moment that we allow the very idea that a state could have a goal, what kind of a goal might it have? Once more various answers are possible; the state might exist to win power and renown, to create wealth, to foster culture, or to spread the glory of God. But again Green takes a quite different line, and at this point we see very clearly how his political philosophy builds directly on his moral philosophy, for Green adopts a fundamentally *moral* conception of the state.

---

[1] *Lectures on the Principles of Political Obligation*, §132.
[2] On this see below pp.235–7.
[3] *Lectures on the Principles of Political Obligation*, §141.
[4] *Lectures on the Principles of Political Obligation*, §§154–5.
[5] Green does not always distinguish these terms as clearly as he might. See Harris 'Green's Theory of Political Obligation and Disobedience', 128.

The state is an instrument for the moralization of man. The aim and whole rationale of the state is to make us *good*; not happy, healthy, safe, or prosperous, but *good* (although attainment along the way of these further benefits is by no means excluded). This is the sphere of political obligation. Political structures concern whatever is required for our moral development.[6]

Lest this sound more contentious than it is, a number of points in its defence should be made. First of all, it should be added that 'good' here must be understood, not in any narrow moralistic sense, but in the broader Greek tradition of the cultivation of human 'excellence' (*aretae*). It is the ambition of the state that the character of each individual should grow to become the best it can possibly be.

Furthermore, since right inner disposition or motivation is an essential element of genuine goodness, and inner or spiritual life is essentially free, no one can be *forced* to become virtuous. The state's coercive licence extends to external or outward acts only, and even here it must be allowed that interference is more likely to work in the opposite direction; for example, the attempt to enforce religious observance tends to weaken it, while disproportionate regulation of behaviour undermines the development of one's own autonomous moral sense, and the ready availability of state aid can take away the need to exercise prudence and self-restraint. For this reason constraints should be as few as possible and state action limited to the creation and maintenance of the conditions necessary for moral growth. The state cannot itself make happen individual self-development, merely encourage and help us in it, removing some of the obstacles that stand in our way.[7] As we shall see below, that the state should assist but not undermine individual effort was a theoretical point on which all of the Idealists followed Green, although where practically they drew that line was something which allowed for much difference.[8]

The notion of a state concerned with our virtue rather than our happiness or our welfare little attracts modern readers, however it must be remembered that Green operates with an equivalence between 'the moralization of man' and 'the common good', and thus another way to make the same point would be to say that in place of managing the various pleasure-seeking activities of distinct and egoistic individuals— the traditional object of political theory—Green proposes a new goal for society, that of seeking the common good. To suggest that the purpose of the state is to promote the good of all its members is a far more attractive notion, but the point to remember is that (for Green) our *common good* lies precisely in our *being good*.

A moral conception of the purpose of the state clearly presupposes a prior theory of morality, and this too is something that will make some more modern and liberally minded thinkers uneasy. To an age which has largely lost confidence in the possibility of sure (or even shared) ethical belief, Green's starting point seems utterly alien and

---

[6] *Lectures on the Principles of Political Obligation*, §21.
[7] *Lectures on the Principles of Political Obligation*, §§14–17.
[8] For example, we may contrast Ritchie (7.6.3 below) and Bosanquet (14.1.6 below).

contentious. But before we allow his 'moral' approach to political thought to condemn his position as hopelessly Victorian with nothing useful to say to any contemporary multi-cultural audience, it is vital that we understand it correctly. His 'moral absolutism' is not that of one self-appointed group in society who 'know best' what all the others should be doing. For as we have already seen in the previous chapter, full knowledge of the common good is beyond the grasp of any one, while partial grasp in so far as it is obtained is the distributed possession of all. Green champions a collective moral purpose, the common goal of a common good, but there is nothing monolithic about this. The state does not and cannot identify this goal for us, because it—together with all its institutions, laws, duties, freedoms, and rights—is but a device to help us in the great endeavour of collectively identifying our mutual good, a good to which each citizen must both contribute and adjust himself.

7.1.2 Sovereignty and the General Will

Having established the scope of political obligation—the range of things we may be obliged to do—our next question must be as to its authority. What justification may be given by those who claim the licence to make us act in these ways? Green arrives at a response to this question through consideration of the inadequacies of previous answers. Beginning not in classical but in early modern times, Green considers at some length the *social contract* tradition of Spinoza, Hobbes, Locke, and Rousseau.[9] According to this theory the state may be thought of as the result of a contract (perhaps historical, but perhaps merely hypothetical) made by individuals in a 'state of nature' prior to all civilization, a voluntary agreement in which they pool their power for the mutual advantage of all but at the same time give up their natural right to sovereign autonomy and submit to the higher power they have created. Green wholly rejects this view—and in this, of course, he is following both Hegel and Carlyle.[10] His objections are of two kinds. His first complaint that the theory presents human beings as the possessors of 'natural rights' prior to the existence of any society will be considered in more detail in the section below. But secondly he objects that even if, *per impossibile*, we were to allow the idea of a contract it would be quite unable to explain obligation. If all there is at the outset is power and enmity (the 'war of all against all') then the pooling of resources for mutual benefit will not produce genuine obligation, just a new and stronger form of coercion. Only where we can see a common good in acting a certain way will we feel an obligation that is more than mere compulsion to do so, but in that case, it is our perception of mutual interest not the contract that binds us to act. The whole contract theory confuses mere coercive power with morally grounded duty

---

[9] 'Popular philosophy', 113–17, 122–4, *Lectures on the Principles of Political Obligation*, §§36, 46, 54, 55, 77.

[10] Hegel, *Philosophy of Right*, §§75, 100, 258; For Carlyle the contract was a myth—sadly Rousseau forgot to tell us its date, he joked (Ritchie, *Darwin and Hegel*, 187, 214)—because 'if all men were such that a mere spoken or sworn Contract would bind them, all men were then true men, and Government a superfluity' (Carlyle, *The French Revolution*, Part II, Book I, Chapter VII).

or obligation. There is no path from one to the other. If all there is at the start is mere power, the right of the state to our obedience at the end will be one of mere power also.

For Green the contemporary alternative to social contract theory was utilitarianism which justified political obligation by means of a hedonic calculus; the state is entitled to demand certain forms of behaviour on account either of the great happiness to be won or the great pain to be avoided by doing so. As we have already seen in the previous chapter, Green does not dismiss utilitarianism as worthless; he concedes that it has considerable practical application[11] and also—of special note here—that it shares his opposition to natural rights.[12] But nonetheless he thought it deficient as a theory of personal morality, and neither did he feel it could give an adequate account of political obligation. For although, like his own teleological defence, it justifies compulsion by reference to common well-being, this is not the well-being of *all* but only of the *majority*, and even if for most practical purposes its upshot is the same as that of the Categorical Imperative, for the sake of the many, it sanctions treating as a means rather than as an end, the unfortunate few—its victims, who as a result are coerced rather than genuinely obligated to obey.[13]

As so often with the British Idealists, Green approaches his own more positive account of obligation historically, in this case through closer consideration of the ideas of Rousseau. Although he opposes Rousseau's appeal to the idea of a contract, he approves of his suggestion that the state's foundation lies in the *General Will*; the idea that a state is legitimate insofar as it embodies or articulates the real underlying wishes of its members. This, argues Green, is 'the permanently valuable thing in Rousseau'[14] and the theory of the social contract may even be regarded as a confused recognition of its basic truth.[15] To be sure, Green finds problems with the expression of this doctrine, complaining that Rousseau's emphasis on democratic voting in effect reduces the unified General Will (*volonté générale*) to something more like a sum of desires that he himself dismisses as the Will of All (*volonté de tous*),[16] and for this reason (connecting the theory of obligation with his own ethics of self-realization) Green prefers his own understanding of it as 'an impartial and disinterested will for the common good',[17] which allows that a minority might better see than the mass where the true interests of their society lie. But overall, the theory finds his support. That the basis of political obligation lies in *will* counters the more common view that it resides in *force*; that fear or mere expediency is what grounds our

---

[11] See Chapter 6.2.4. This rapprochement especially impressed D.G. Ritchie. See below pp.257–8.

[12] Bentham famously called natural rights 'nonsense on stilts' ('Anarchical Fallacies', p.501). For an idealist discussion of that critique see MacCunn, *Ethics of Citizenship*, ch.III.

[13] *Prolegomena*, §214.

[14] *Lectures on the Principles of Political Obligation*, §77.

[15] *Lectures on the Principles of Political Obligation*, §116.

[16] *Lectures on the Principles of Political Obligation*, §§75, 73, 98.

[17] *Lectures on the Principles of Political Obligation*, §69.

obedience to the state. But Green objects that even where a sovereign authority continues to hold coercive force it is not generally that power, but recognition of the state's *de facto* alignment to the common good, which determines people's habitual obedience to it.[18] He admits that this sense of shared enterprise or interest is not often conscious or fully articulated, and endorses various ways in which it might be strengthened.[19]

A key point to note about Green's positive theory of obligation is that it makes the concept an essentially *social* one. Our obedience is called for, not as one side of some mutual adjustment of distinct wills, but as our contribution to a shared quest for a common goal, higher than the aspiration of any individual. The state to which we are obligated is precisely 'an institution for the promotion of a common good'.[20] In consequence of this, the obligation is a *moral*, rather than a merely civil, legal, or pragmatic affair. Moral duty and political duty are not simply equated—the former demands more of us than the latter, for one thing—but they do have a common source; the recognition of a communal well-being, conceived also as our own well-being, whether, at any given moment, we feel inclined to it or not.[21] We see here the breadth of Green's conception of 'the state'. The state is a sovereign body, but we go wrong if we suppose that supreme coercive power is all that is essential to a state, if we think of it as but the governing part of society, for we must include too the legitimating ground of that authority which lies in the will of society itself, the governed, turning the state into something wider than society instead of something narrower than it. As thus social and moral, the obligation which results is a duty to *serve* and not simply a duty to *obey*. The state may legitimately call from us a contribution to the common weal every bit as much as conformity to its rules and regulations. Here Green's notion of the coincidence of religious and ethical service, already noted, is further extended into the political sphere. What I give to my fellows or to my state I give at the same time to God.

7.1.3 Rights

So much for *obligation*, for what we owe to the state, it may be said, but does not the state also owe certain things to us? Do not we have certain rights which it is the state's job to secure and protect for us? This is something with which Green would most certainly agree. Although (as noted above) he opposes any doctrine of *natural* rights, he nevertheless held that the principal way to provide people with the opportunity to achieve the common good, to remove the obstacles to their self-realization, is precisely through a system of rights and obligations. But what for Green are rights, and which rights does he think we have?

---

[18] *Lectures on the Principles of Political Obligation*, §92.
[19] *Lectures on the Principles of Political Obligation*, §§120–3.
[20] *Lectures on the Principles of Political Obligation*, §124.
[21] *Lectures on the Principles of Political Obligation*, §117.

'A right is a power claimed and recognised as contributory to a common good',[22] asserts Green. This claim has a number of significant implications, the first of which is that it renders rights neither universal nor inalienable. What contributes to the common good at one time or in one context may not do so at or in another and therefore rights are not necessarily permanent, but may change as conditions or as society itself changes; old rights may be swept away or new ones created.[23] Nor are our rights to be thought of as unlimited, for something contributory to the common good in certain amounts or contexts might be harmful in different measures or situations. Such might be said, for example, of private property. In both these respects Green's conditional teleological conception of rights is quite different from the more common absolutist understanding of them. This might be regarded as a weakness, as it often is against utilitarianism which also subordinates individual rights to a higher social standard. However, the 'common good' is not at all the same as the 'greatest good for the greatest number' insofar as it holds fast, Green insists, to the absolute value of each individual person.[24] In the common good, no one gets left behind or forgotten.

Since the common good is a social good it follows that rights too must be social. Rights may attach to individuals, and they may be for an individual's own benefit, but both of these points must be qualified. They attach to individuals only in so far as they are members of a society.[25] The isolated individual on a desert island could have no rights, and thus if I assert a right, my claim is not *qua* individual, but always with my corporate hat on. Moreover any benefit derived, though it may accrue to the individual, is given ultimately for the good of all. I may be granted the private use of something, but only because it is better for society as a whole that I should be; part of our common prosperity consisting precisely in the prosperity of each. The fact that rights are social means also that there are no purely natural rights; no rights attaching to individuals prior to the formation of society. Green does allow an alternative sense in which we may think of natural rights as 'ideal', the sort a perfect society ought to accord us,[26] but in its traditional form, the doctrine, for all its long pedigree, fails at several points: its picture of human individuals existing in the absence of all society is as historically fictitious as it is metaphysically absurd, and even were we to allow such an impossibility, it would merely *assert* not *justify* the rights it maintains, rights which

---

[22] *Lectures on the Principles of Political Obligation*, §99.

[23] *Lectures on the Principles of Political Obligation*, §142.

[24] *Prolegomena*, §214.

[25] *Lectures on the Principles of Political Obligation*, §138. 'No one ... can have a right except as a member of a society ...' (*Lectures on the Principles of Political Obligation*, §25). Green's view is in this regard comparable to that of Wallace who argues that 'the mere individual has no rights as such; he has rights only as a person, i.e. as member of a society, as embodying in himself, at least partially, the larger aggregate of which he is a unit' (*Lectures and Essays*, 258). Since the state is for all practical purposes the larger society in question, it follows that the state is 'the ultimate creator, guardian and guarantee of all right in this world' (*Lectures and Essays*, 262).

[26] *Lectures on the Principles of Political Obligation*, §9.

would be egoistic ones of private self-interest, existing without correlative duties, something Green thinks illogical.[27] One of the most significant consequences of the sociality of rights is that people can have no right to anything which is not in the common good. The mere fact that we would like to do something, however important it may be to us, is no basis for a right. Since 'every right is derived from some social relation',[28] the notion of a right to act against society, or even just unsocially, is a plain contradiction.[29] The fact that we have no right against the state does not mean that we have no rights against the *misuse* of state power, for example, the right not to be arrested without charge. Indeed, the state may well give us just such rights, for they contribute greatly to the common good. Rights against state oppression are some of the most important ones we have. Nor does it rule out our right to rebel against any state which, failing to express the general will, destroys the basis of its own purpose.[30] Promotion of the common good is the very root of political obedience, and therefore where a corrupt authority no longer promotes the common good, we may legitimately resist.[31] Our rebellion may be thought of as the assertion of the rights of a better or truer state against an imperfect or corrupt one, suggests Muirhead, expounding Green.[32] Not simply our right, it may even be our *duty* to rebel for, as Mackenzie points out, 'we can often serve our state best by attacking its faults and resisting its aims'.[33] However, since the rule of law itself is one of the greatest components of the common good, deciding to do this is no light matter. Nor, given the complexities involved, is it a simple one for which clear criteria may be set out in advance; although generally Green thinks that obedience coupled with work for reform is a better option than open revolt, especially in a democratic country.

A further crucial component of the definition of rights which we are considering is that they must be recognized by society; we have a right to all and only what society recognizes as necessary for our moral development.[34] In this claim we see again just how far Green stands from the natural rights tradition which holds us to possess certain basic rights regardless of whether we or anyone else suppose that we do—for in the state of nature, by definition, there can be no social recognition. By contrast, for Green,

---

[27] See, for example, *Lectures on the Principles of Political Obligation*, §§38, 116.

[28] *Lectures on the Principles of Political Obligation*, §141.

[29] *Lectures on the Principles of Political Obligation*, §138.

[30] *Lectures on the Principles of Political Obligation*, §§100, 107–9, 142–4.

[31] 'So far as the laws anywhere or at any time in force fulfil the idea of a state, there can be no right to disobey them' but that 'does not carry with it an obligation under all conditions to conform to the law of his state, since those laws may be inconsistent with the true end of the state, as the sustainer and harmoniser of social relations' (*Lectures on the Principles of Political Obligation*, §142–3).

[32] *Service of the State*, 72–3.

[33] 'Use of Moral Ideas in Politics', 22.

[34] 'There can be no right without a consciousness of common interest on the part of members of a society' (*Lectures on the Principles of Political Obligation*, §31) 'Rights have no being except in a society of men recognising each other as *isoi kai homoioi* [equals]. They are constituted by that mutual recognition' (*Lectures on the Principles of Political Obligation*, §139). For further discussion see Gaus, 'The Rights Recognition Thesis'.

only insofar as they are recognized, do our rights come into being.[35] Why does he say this? Green derives his rights recognition thesis from the co-relativity of rights and duties. At its simplest his point is just that I can't really or effectively be said to have a right unless others recognize a corresponding duty to me. This is true, but Green's point runs even deeper than that. The insight is not so much that my right entails another's duty (to me), but rather that my having a right means that others must have it too and thus that I have duties (to them). I can't have the right without recognizing it in others as well. The point is not just the pragmatic calculating one that I ought to recognize others' claims if I want them to recognize mine. It is a deeper acknowledgement that our common human nature means anything I claim for myself must apply equally for them. In the end a right exists only because society agrees that a certain power or other should be defended or prohibited. But without 'consciousness of common interests' there could be no agreement on which to base these decisions. In the end rights are indicators not (as Marx thought) of egoism and atomism, but rather (as Kant and Hegel believed) of our common humanity and mutual society.[36]

The rights recognition thesis has not been popular, and so we may consider some objections that might be raised against it. It might be objected that social recognition places an unwelcome cognitive hurdle in the way of rights possession. Green explicitly states that animals have no rights, because they cannot meet the recognition criterion,[37] while the level of rights granted to the mentally infirm will involve a complex triangulation of the strength of their incapacity, whether or not it is curable and the kind of contribution they may be able to make to society.[38] Some may find such results unpalatable, but we should not make the mistake of regarding the absence of right as itself some sort of licence to ill-treatment (any more than its presence is some kind of trump card ever-available to be played against the same). It might be objected that Green is making the outrageous claim that people have only those rights which the state says they have. But that is mistaken, for Green distinguishes between legal rights, which require *state* recognition, and moral rights which require only *social* recognition. People can still have rights although a state—or even all states—refuse to recognize them, so long as society at large allows that they do.[39] Even this might seem refuted by historical cases, such as that of slavery, where (surely) we want to say that there was a right to freedom even though neither states nor individuals admitted it. But Green replies that recognition can be either explicit or implicit, and even where there is no conscious acknowledgement of something, the logic of our action and attachments may say otherwise. In his dealings with the slave, argues Green, however unfair they may be, the owner recognizes him as a person capable of living in community with

---

[35] In this sense he allows that a right is an ideal entity (*Lectures on the Principles of Political Obligation*, §§38, 136).

[36] Simhony, 'Rights that Bind', 238, 248–9.

[37] *Lectures on the Principles of Political Obligation*, §139.

[38] *Lectures on the Principles of Political Obligation*, §154.

[39] *Lectures on the Principles of Political Obligation*, §144.

others, and this is enough to ground his rights as a member of society. Only if we saw him as irredeemably sub-human, and in all our dealings treated him as such, would we be justified in denying him such rights.

7.1.4 Property, punishment, and family

These general comments concerning state, individual, obligation, and rights may be given further substance if we consider their application in three more concrete dimensions; private property, punishment, and the family.

Green supports the right to private property, for he thinks it contributes to the common good by allowing us to express our *will*. It is a mode of self-realization, a vehicle by which we give reality to our ideas and wishes, a way of manifesting and developing ourselves as persons.[40] As thus contributory to the common good, we must respect also the property claims of others, and without such recognition of ownership, of course, there simply is no property. Given its value in this regard, it might be wondered if the state ought not to grant everyone some allocation of this good, but Green rejects any such communist distribution on the grounds that it would defeat precisely the moral development it seeks to bring about; for the very acquiring and looking after property is a large part of its good for us. Green thinks of private property as the institution that has allowed us to develop morally beyond primitive or feudal life, but part of this system is free transfer, and so he accepts too that it brings with it a certain inevitable inequality.

Green allows that this case for private property holds only within certain limits. Where the struggle is simply to survive, or where a person has more wealth than they can use, property is unable to serve the self-realizational function which justifies its existence, but rather than reject as inherently flawed the capitalist system which produces such inequalities Green seeks to modify it, regarding its defects as ones which stem from historical abuses that can be corrected. He looks to increase property owning among the poorest classes, and his arguments support state intervention to secure at least minimal living conditions. For the job of the state is to remove the obstacles to self-improvement, but 'until life has been so organised as to afford some regular relief from the pressure of animal wants' no possibility can emerge for '"living well" or "well-being" as distinct from merely "living"'.[41] He looked also to promote the redistribution of wealth among the already better off; especially to encourage—he does not go so far as to say *enforce*—equal inheritance of property among all children rather than primogeniture. Generally, everyone has a right to enough, but no one has the right to more than they need, and always it must be remembered that the right to property is not absolute or unconditional. We have a right to own property only in so far as doing so contributes to the social good; that's what property is *for*.

---

[40] *Lectures on the Principles of Political Obligation*, §§213–14. He is here following Hegel, *Philosophy of Right*, §41ff.
   [41] *Prolegomena*, §240. See also §243.

The reverse side of our duty or obligation to the state is its right to compel our compliance or punish our disobedience, but punishment too is an institution subordinated to the common good.[42] Green insists that it is not the business of state punishment either to ascertain and chastise wickedness per se, or to impose moral virtue. It must respect the right to free life, for that is its very justification. The state has the right, however, 'to prevent such action as interferes with the possibility of free action contributory to social good'.[43] Within this ground, Green sees aspects working together of each of the three traditional theories of punishment; retributive, deterrent, and reformatory.[44]

He rejects any derivation of punishment as the state regulated continuation of private vengeance,[45] but he allows for an element of desert. A criminal may be punished only where they have knowingly and avoidably violated some right, and in such a case,

> the person punished himself recognizes it as just, as his due or desert .... The criminal, being susceptible to the idea of public good, and through it of rights, though this idea has not been strong enough to regulate his actions, sees in the punishment its natural expression. He sees that the punishment is his own act returning on himself, in the sense that it is the necessary outcome of his act in a society governed by the conception of rights, a conception which he appreciates and to which he does involuntary reverence.[46]

Of course, such punishment cannot be just unless the system of rights it reflects is just.[47] Punishment may also be preventative, so long as we remember that what is being prevented is violation of rights and so long as it is proportionate. This allows Green to suggest—controversially—that penalties may vary according to the deterrent needed. Though a burglar and fraudulent banker may transgress to the same degree, the threat of imprisonment with hard labour by which we try to deter the first is more than what is needed to deter the second.[48] Similarly in criminal negligence cases the level of punishment is set by the importance of the right violated and the degree of terror needed to deter such negligence, not any assessment of the degree of moral shortcoming involved. (The train driver who fails to observe a signal has made no greater mistake than we are all of us constantly guilty of in less dangerous circumstances.)[49] Punishment may also be reformatory but, if so, its aim is not the moral good of the criminal

---

[42] For further discussion see Brooks, 'T.H. Green's Theory of Punishment'.
[43] *Lectures on the Principles of Political Obligation*, §176.
[44] For discussion of whether it is really possible for Green (and Bosanquet, who attempts something similar) consistently to combine these three very different justifications see Crossley, 'The Unified Theory of Punishment of Green and Bosanquet'.
[45] *Lectures on the Principles of Political Obligation*, §178.
[46] *Lectures on the Principles of Political Obligation*, §186.
[47] *Lectures on the Principles of Political Obligation*, §189.
[48] *Lectures on the Principles of Political Obligation*, §193.
[49] *Lectures on the Principles of Political Obligation*, §198.

himself—that is a matter with which the state has no direct business—but only his recovery from such criminal habits as impede the common good.[50]

Green's attitudes towards the family have a radical edge but are also, inevitably, rooted in their time. He applauds family life as a kind of anticipation of the common good. 'The formation of family life supposes that in the conception of his own good to which a man seeks to give reality there is included a conception of the well-being of others, connected with him by sexual relations or by relations which arise out of these. He must conceive of the well-being of these others as a permanent object bound up with his own, and the interest in it as thus conceived must be a motive to him over and above any succession of passing desires to obtain pleasure from, or give pleasure to, the others.'[51] Since the conditions of family life shape the possibilities of our moral development, they are matters of public right, and not just personal morality.[52] It is quite appropriate, therefore, that the state should intervene to ensure a fair and open opportunity for all, for example, by excluding the imbalance of rights that inevitably accompanies polygamy, by divorce laws in which no one should be bound to an unfaithful or abusive partner, by compulsory education, or by protection or removal of children at risk. But at the same time there should be no interference in purely private life (so, for example, the state should not take it upon itself to prosecute or punish marital infidelity)[53] nor any action that might undermine self-reliance or morality (for example, Green regards marriage as a life-long commitment and fears that to hold out the possibility of divorce on the grounds of incompatibility would itself generate such incompatibility).[54] Although more restrictive than today, given the very unequal nature of sex relations in late Victorian Britain, Green's views on marriage, together with his support for women's education, make it appropriate to regard him as what we would now call a feminist.[55]

7.1.5 Freedom

In this discussion of rights we have not yet touched upon what many would regard as the most important right of all, the right to freedom, and it is to this that we must now turn, for Green's view of freedom represents one of his most important contributions to political thought. In an 1879 lecture 'On the Different Senses of Freedom' Green distinguishes three senses of the term. First there is *free will*. Exercised by each individual without aid or impediment from anyone else, this is what marks the difference between action and mere behaviour, and has already been discussed at some length in the chapters on metaphysics and on ethics. Second, there is *juristic freedom*, the liberty accorded us by the law. While this needs a society to grant it, once granted, it too may

---

[50] *Lectures on the Principles of Political Obligation*, §204.
[51] *Lectures on the Principles of Political Obligation*, §236.
[52] *Lectures on the Principles of Political Obligation*, §242.
[53] *Lectures on the Principles of Political Obligation*, §§243–4.
[54] *Lectures on the Principles of Political Obligation*, §246.
[55] Anderson, 'The Feminism of T.H. Green'; Leighton *The Greenian Moment*, 302–9.

be enjoyed by individuals in isolation. Third, there is *real freedom*. Unlike the first two senses, which can apply indifferently to good or evil actions, real freedom contains an evaluative component. It is 'a positive power or capacity of doing or enjoying something *worth* doing or enjoying',[56] the ability to realize oneself, the capacity to do good. Green's second and third senses are often contrasted as negative and positive freedom, and correlated with talk of negative and positive rights; we have rights not merely to non-interference but also to other positive advantages (and duties not merely to let others alone but also to help them). But in another sense real freedom may be thought of as a continuation of the juristic sense of freedom; as the latter liberates us from the constraining incursions of others, so the former liberates our better nature from the equally constraining influence of our weakness and irrationality. Real freedom is also, again unlike the other two kinds, necessarily social. That might seem odd; no one is more free, we might suppose, than the solitary wandering child of nature. However, freedom of that sort is 'not strength but weakness' insists Green.

> The actual powers of the noblest savage do not admit of comparison with those of the humblest citizen of a law-abiding state. He is not the slave of man, but he is the slave of nature. Of compulsion by natural necessity he has plenty of experience, though of restraint by society none at all. Nor can he deliver himself from that compulsion except by submitting himself to this restraint. So to submit is the first step in true freedom.[57]

In other words, the only way to be free from the contingencies of nature (either external nature or one's own) is to submit oneself to the common goals of society which in return grants one both strength and purpose.[58] Freedom is a social good; we find our freedom in service to the common weal. Human nature is such that unrestricted negative or individual liberty means in practice the freedom to pursue selfish, short-sighted, and materialistic advantage; something which tends to result in social structures and hierarchies that effectively bar most people from enjoying the goods or powers that it renders their more fortunate or adroit brethren 'free' to enjoy; and something which by lowering the moral quality of society as a whole, effectively blocks everyone from enjoying the higher benefits of a cooperative, far-sighted and profound community. Where negative freedom is the bluntest of tools, positive freedom is more focused—a freedom to access the things that really matter on the part of those who are usually denied them.

Green is sometimes thought of as advocating real freedom only. But in fact he thinks that we need all three kinds. There can be no real freedom without juristic freedom,

---

[56] 'Liberal Legislation and Freedom of Contract', 370–1. Italics added.

[57] 'Liberal Legislation and Freedom of Contract', 371. Compare D.G. Ritchie 'The savage, roaming solitary like a wild beast in search of prey, is more a mere part of nature and less a free individual than the citizen who lives along with others in a complicated political society whose ends are rational and the development of which it is possible to trace' ('Rationality of History', 135).

[58] Green's line of argument here is recognizably the same as that of Edward Caird, which was considered in the previous chapter (see above pp.211–12).

and no juristic freedom without free will. He is not *opposed* to the juristic or negative power to do what one wills free from compulsion by others, but insists that there is *more* to freedom than this; that negative liberty is but a first crude step towards a higher and wider positive sense of freedom in which people have the effective ability to bring about something worthwhile. Because higher, the latter has the authority to limit or trump the former, and this was something Green argued at length in his 1881 essay 'Liberal Legislation and Freedom of Contract'. He urged there that the state's work of encouraging and removing the barriers to moral growth should result in a great deal of positive action, much of which may limit traditional negative freedoms. For example, although in general he accepted the idea that the free market was the best way to benefit the whole society, he saw clearly how its mechanisms could disadvantage the poor, leaving them little or no chance at a decent life, and he advocated extension of the power of the state over working conditions, education, health, housing and town planning, and the relief of unemployment. As to the corrosive effects of such intervention, self-help is a deep and ultimately essential virtue, he allowed, but he realized too that it is one not equally possible for all people in all circumstances. Green's argument was influential in changing liberal attitudes in a more interventionist and welfare orientated direction, although in this advocacy of state intervention, his followers such as Ritchie, Jones, and Haldane tended to go further than he did.[59]

'Positive freedom' has been the subject of severe criticism in the twentieth century, most famously in an essay by Isaiah Berlin, 'Two Concepts of Liberty' which, if not directed specifically at Green, was aimed at his tradition and the implications of his thought.[60] In his essay Berlin distinguishes between two understandings of liberty, the negative, which consists in freedom from interference, and the positive, which consists in self-mastery. As initially set out, he admits, the difference seems small but the ideas may be developed so as to become almost opposite. Self-mastery becomes the triumph of the higher, ideal, or true self over the lower self, which in turn becomes the triumph of the social over the private self, which develops into the anti-democratic coercing of others for their own good.[61] This is the very opposite of negative liberty, or freedom from interference, which Berlin regards as the genuine or original sense. The notion here of a 'real' or 'true' meaning of liberty is an odd one, but of course what lies beneath Berlin's encomium is a claim about which is the more important or more valuable form of freedom.

Berlin's essay has produced a library of response, but in this context it will suffice merely to argue both that he misinterprets Green and that Green's view has within it built-in safeguards to prevent its ever being developed in the direction Berlin fears.[62]

---

[59] Boucher, *The British Idealists*, xxiii.

[60] 'Two Concepts of Liberty', 180n, 196.

[61] 'Two Concepts of Liberty', 179.

[62] At least one commentator (Richter, *Politics of Conscience*, 202–4) has found Berlin plausible, but the majority have been less persuaded. Strong rebuttals of Berlin may be found in Nicholson, *The Political Philosophy of the British Idealists*, 124–6 and Simhony, 'T.H. Green's Theory of Positive Freedom'.

For all its influence, the model that Berlin uses to explain positive freedom is seriously flawed. To begin with, he mischaracterizes the nature of the higher social self by identifying it with the state. Although a perfect state would indeed embody it, the higher self must not be identified with the state in which we just happen to live, for it is an *ideal* which draws us forward, as likely to speak with the voice of our own conscience as with that of our current laws and institutions. There is in Berlin's interpretation an assumption that others—those representing this higher self—know better than we do what is our own best interests,[63] but while Green admits that people are not always best judge of their own true good, he is equally clear that no one has privileged access to the content of the common good. It is something whose full appreciation we all collectively inch towards. Worst of all, Berlin imagines that on this scheme a higher form of life will be somehow *forced* upon those currently pursuing something lower. But nothing could be further from the truth. Green is absolutely clear that no one can be forced to be free; 'of course there can be no freedom among men who act not willingly but under compulsion'[64] he says. The root problem is that Berlin's metaphysical picture of 'two selves' is really something of a misrepresentation of Green. Children are not pushed aside or taken over by the adults they become (in the way that red squirrels are ousted by grey ones) rather they develop into those adults, and in the same way what Green describes is not the imposition of one self on another, but the emergence of new values and ideas. As we grow we seek higher forms of satisfaction, forms which are increasingly social rather than selfish, but these are sought from within not imposed from outside. We need not deny that *in a sense* there are two selves, but the matter is perhaps easier to comprehend insofar as we identify the higher self with the divine rather than the social self, for here we have to hand a widely accepted model for the process, namely the indwelling of God. To the religious mind, the divine may realize itself in us, but in no sense does this undermine the fact that self-realization is something that we do *for ourselves*.

Part of Berlin's reason for doubting that Green has the true or right sense of freedom is that he thinks Green has over-inflated its worth conflating it with that of other goods, such as 'justice' and 'equality'. We should simply accept, he thinks, that valuable freedom may co-exist with, even lead to, much that is evil. For Green, by contrast, only understood as positive freedom can sense be made of the importance and value we attach to this notion in the first place; for surely individual freedom has value only to the extent that it leads to the good. In itself, or misused, it has no value. Autonomy is a precondition for, but not itself a component of, the good will.

Berlin is a pluralist and objects to any attempt to set up one value as supreme or binding on all. Individuals must simply be left to choose as they please from among life's many and conflicting goals. However, it is important to keep these last two ideas

---

[63] Berlin, 'Two Concepts of Liberty', 179. To make quite fair assessment of Berlin due note must, of course, be taken of the historical context in which his essay was first written.

[64] 'Liberal Legislation and Freedom of Contract', 371.

separate. To say that all must seek self-realization or the common good might seem like an oppressive monism, but it needs to be recognized that Green has a very pluralistic understanding of the common good. Beneath the terminological appearance of uniformity, it is in truth a wide and multi-faceted thing.[65] Yet Green insists that it is also a harmonious and integrated thing; 'There is no such thing really as a conflict of duties'[66] he says. This is where Green and Berlin differ most fundamentally; Green asserts diversity of ends but without conflict, whereas for Berlin conflict (or at least its possibility) directly follows from diversity.

7.2 Edward Caird

The political and social philosophy of Green dominated the Idealist movement; however, the writings of those thinkers who followed him into this domain contain not simply repetition and allegiance, but a complex pattern of development and difference, making them individually worthy of attention. Consideration may begin with Edward Caird and with a comparison between his and Green's attitudes towards Rousseau; for in 1877—two years before Green gave his *Lectures on Political Obligation*— Caird himself wrote an important paper on Rousseau. As might be expected from the other similarities we find between them there is considerable continuity in their treatments. Like Green, Caird objects to Rousseau's postulation and exaltation of a natural pre-social state of human life, his adherence to the idea of contract, his theory of education and his account of religion. But Green and Caird do not simply repeat each other. For example, where Green finds in the General Will a point of promise, Caird is struck only by its utter inaccessibility; either we seek without success to find it in some element of agreement among the many wills of all citizens or, recognizing that the General Will differs from the will of all, it reveals itself as some kind of despotic device whereby the latter may be suppressed and the state 'force individuals to be free'.[67]

Caird's own social holistic understanding of the individual emerges through his consideration of two units, the family and the state. Green himself had suggested that we might regard the state as 'an organisation of a people to whom the individual feels himself bound by ties analogous to those which bind him to his family',[68] but in Caird this idea of the family as a microcosm of the state is developed even further. In both we find 'an organization—i.e. a self-maintaining, self-developing unity—in which in the movement of life a multiplicity of parts are continually subordinated to the whole.'[69]

---

[65] The function of society being the development of persons 'It does not follow from this that all persons must be developed in the same way' (*Prolegomena*, §191) for the common good 'may be pursued in many different forms by persons quite unconscious of any community in their pursuits' (*Prolegomena*, §283).

[66] *Prolegomena*, §324.

[67] 'Rousseau', 128, 141.

[68] *Lectures on the Principles of Political Obligation*, §123.

[69] *Lectures on Moral Philosophy*, 42. Caird's account of the family closely follows that of Hegel's *Philosophy of Right*, §§160–80.

Thus, for example, in the family the independence of the separate individuals is dissolved so the whole may be thought of as a single moral personality. The family is that in which we come to be what we are, that without which we have no value or dignity. It is only in its other members that we find ourselves, only out of their unity that we grow to a sense of our own independence. We may speak of a person's *duty* to their family, or think of family commitments as *fetters* on their natural scope or capacity, but this is to take a false abstraction of the individual, for the family—like the state—is precisely the arena in which we develop and exercise our own being, so that 'in the state and the family the man is truly not bound but freed'.[70] Both family and state are teleological units, whose moral purpose dictates their structure. The reciprocal rights and duties of parents and children 'are only expressions of the fact that it, the family life, has for its end the education of the children to moral freedom and therefore whatever is necessary to that end is to be granted on both sides.'[71] At the heart of family life is, of course, marriage, which in essence Caird regards, not as a natural or legal relation, but as a moral one; 'it is a contract of two independent Persons—whereby they cease to be independent Persons and become *one Person*'.[72] Like Green's, his views on marriage are advanced for his time. It is a partnership between equal but complementary individuals, and must be monogamous—'polygamy is and involves the slavery of women' and is anyway contrary to the nature of marital affection.[73] Caird in his own life worked tirelessly to enhance the position of women, especially in education, but also in the workplace. Nonetheless, his views about the complementary nature of men and women show his attitudes still to be very much of his time; he tells us that men think generally and women intuitively, that men need combat and independence while women seek unity, and that man's true sphere is in the outside world as against woman's natural place in the bosom of her family.[74]

For all its great value the family suffers two limitations. It comes to a natural end, and it is a unity of *feeling*. As a permanent and rational unity, the state is higher than the family.[75] Caird regards it, however, in a similarly holistic fashion; 'A nation is not a mere aggregate of men . . . it is a unity at once real and ideal, a spiritual body'. The unity is an organic one; that of a association of people, however numerous and diverse, all of whom 'can feel the throb of one emotion and one impulse of life', born out of a common history (especially of struggle) and, more importantly, some common goal, mission or object of pursuit 'which may often be sought almost unconsciously'.[76]

---

[70] *Lectures on Moral Philosophy*, 43.
[71] *Lectures on Moral Philosophy*, 61.
[72] *Lectures on Moral Philosophy*, 50.
[73] *Lectures on Moral Philosophy*, 55; Green also insists on monogamy.
[74] *Lectures on Moral Philosophy*, 52–4.
[75] *Lectures on Moral Philosophy*, 48–9, 61.
[76] *Lay Sermons*, 100–2.

It is from this union that the greater part of our moral lives flow, it is the chief source of our obligations ('the duties of man are still to us mainly the duties of the good citizen') and the chief arena in which we may act ('it is in the main by acting with and upon [the national state] that we can serve humanity').[77] Caird is well aware of the possibilities of misinterpretation that attend such statements and sees that the horizons of morality do and must extend beyond national boundaries. A nation cannot live for itself alone but is continually influencing and influenced by other nations, and the worlds of science, art, and literature or of economic, social, and political community have much wider compass. Moreover, Christianity itself has taught us to regard national life as part of something universal; God's interest is in humanity as a whole.[78] But, however that may be, the actual fact of the matter is that today the highest really organized whole is still the nation state.[79] Green said as much, but behind what is *de facto* the case, Caird senses a deeper point of principle; for while it was the emergence of Christianity that taught us the universal brotherhood of men, something that seemed in the Early Christian and Medieval eras to point towards a single theocratic world state, it was precisely the later development of Christianity (in the form of the Protestant reformation) that urged individual nations to demand the freedom to mould their own religious destiny.[80]

As well as *demanding*, service to one's state is a *high* calling, the more so if the state served is a noble one like Britain. And there can be no doubt that Caird is prepared to sing the praises of Victorian Britain as loudly as anyone. Both in granting individual liberty and in developing the power of civic association Britons have been a nation of originators as well as leaders. But he is not complacent. 'No one can think,' he insists, 'without grave misgiving of the evil and wretchedness that lurk in our crowded cities, of the hardship and destitution that still survive alongside of the greatest wealth which any people has ever accumulated, or of the vulgar ambition and greed that darken our political and social life.'[81]

As a way of manifesting the eternal consciousness Green sees service to the state as a kind of religious service, yet religion was one of his primary examples where the state could not successfully interfere. We find a similar tension in Caird when he explores the relation between church and state. Initially one might think these are separate; the one dealing with what is inner and eternal, the other with what is outer and temporal. But such a thought soon breaks down. Unless state gives way to church, man's higher calling is subordinated to his lower, yet if church marks certain domains—family and individual life—beyond the reach of politics, they in turn may block the state's pursuit of its proper goal. In truth, the division cannot be maintained, for history shows us that the growth of religion and the growth of society are two sides of the same coin. 'In this way it would seem that . . . religion is of the very essence of the state and that its highest task must be to preserve the religious life of which it is the very embodiment.'[82] Where for Comte an adequate social philosophy must pass beyond the stages of theology and metaphysics to a religion of positivism, for Caird, 'there can be no religion of Humanity, which is not also a religion of God'.[83] To deepen and develop our social life and feeling is precisely to deepen and develop our religious life and feeling, and *vice versa*. But paradoxically (and as we noted just above) one part of the development of religion (especially in its Protestant Christian context) has been to realize precisely that in religion there can be no compulsion, resulting in a species of separation between state and the religion which nonetheless constitutes its very heart. That the state is something of profound spiritual significance in Caird is a point on which there can be no doubt, but two qualifications are in order. First, 'that *Religion* is greater than the state does not necessarily imply that the church is',[84] for church and clergy are but one social institution and class among many. Second, it must be remembered that a religious attitude is not one that looks down upon or disregards the temporal world. It is not an 'other-worldly' point of view but one that 'spiritualizes' the everyday world.[85]

In raising the issue of state intervention in religious life, we broach the more general question of state interference in societal life at large. Green's view of the role of the state was an uneasy combination between standing-back and getting-involved; he insists that it can do no more than remove obstacles but at the same time advocates the provision for all of positive freedom, the real chance at a life worth living, something which could only be achieved by transgressing many traditional 'rights' and 'liberties'. We find the same two-sided ambivalence in Caird. He demands that, whatever the state does, it must never act in a way that will undermine individual freedom, independence, or creative energy; indeed, more strongly, he insists that no state action can ever really be of any help to people 'unless it be such as to call out and stimulate their individual energy . . . our methods must always be those in which we help men to help themselves'.[86] The watch-word is self-help.[87] He uses an analogy to make his point; 'Men are like trees in the forest which can only grow at a certain distance from each other, which allows them to stretch out their boughs and show their full proportions'.[88] With such thoughts we might expect Caird to advocate a very light-touch. But far from it. He objects that the *laissez-faire* hidden hand theory of social

---

[82]   *Lectures on Moral Philosophy*, 104.

[83]   *The Social Philosophy and Religion of Comte*, xvii.

[84]   *Lectures on Moral Philosophy*, 106.

[85]   *Lectures on Moral Philosophy*, 107; see also *Lay Sermons*, 111–12; this common idealist attitude may also be seen, for example, in John Caird's discussion of immortality, or in Bosanquet's 'On the True Conception of Another World'.

[86]   *Moral Aspect of the Economical Problem*, 14.

[87]   In this Caird (and the British Idealists generally) taps into a strong Victorian value, most clearly illustrated perhaps in Samuel Smiles' fantastically popular book, *Self-Help* (1859) which used numerous examples to exhort its readers to set to the work of improving themselves, to develop their own character.

[88]   *Moral Aspect of the Economical Problem*, 16.

development only works in so far as people are already moral.[89] The state's moral ambitions means that it must take into its own hands certain of our key interests, that it must place limits on the permissible range of people's freedoms, and even make positive demands from individuals for specific services.[90] It is not easy to say exactly what work should be done by the state, but enough should be done 'to secure to each citizen what is absolutely necessary for his retaining or recovering the position of a citizen, and to protect against dangers that might be fatal to the common weal.' More specifically Caird suggests that 'experience seems to prove that while special interests— the interests of classes—can take good care of themselves—that the great general interests of the community—health, education, and pauper relief—must inevitably suffer in the long run if left without the active assistance and direction as well as the control of government.'[91] But we should not cast Caird a greater socialist than he really was. Henry Jones may have reported that he once said that class distinctions had become artificial and in need of breaking down,[92] but the evidence is that he simply wanted to help the poor and disadvantaged not do away with class altogether. Likewise, while he seeks to remove the worst forms of human competition, war, and the exploitation of the weak by the strong,[93] and allows that in certain cases monopoly may be preferable to competition,[94] he nonetheless insists it would be a mistake to abolish all competition—'because competition is as necessary to human development as association', because it could only be prevented by a kind of social regulation, akin to slavery,[95] and because it is 'the natural process whereby the individual is pressed up or down, till he finds his proper place—the place in which he can best serve the community'.[96]

In the end we can only judge on a case by case basis. But if with Green, this piecemeal approach sounds somewhat tentative and ad hoc, with Caird, it is more principled. Looking back on the history of the debate he holds that initial views were extreme; that first appeared unfettered freedom and *laissez faire* capitalism which led to 'anarchism', against which rose up an equally abstract socialism, attempting to impose a fixed and fair order on society, but becoming in the end a 'social despotism' which reduced the individual to a mere instrument of the community.[97] However, intellectual life evolves and no one anymore holds such polarized views; indeed we are moving in a side-to-side fashion from abstract extremes towards a mid position that draws from both perspectives. Moreover, this is the only way we can proceed; progress has to be gradual, not

---

[89] *Lectures on Moral Philosophy*, 88.
[90] *Lectures on Moral Philosophy*, 90. For instance, taking control of policing or municipal government, imposing labour law, and demanding from individuals jury service.
[91] *Lectures on Moral Philosophy*, 97.
[92] *The Life and Philosophy of Edward Caird*, 149 note.
[93] 'Individualism and Socialism', 187.
[94] 'Lecture on Political Economy', 160.
[95] *Moral Aspect of the Economical Problem*, 15.
[96] 'Individualism and Socialism', 187.
[97] 'Individualism and Socialism', 177.

revolutionary,[98] and where and how far it is best to intervene are questions 'which can only be settled by slow experiment'.[99] With particularly economics in mind—though the point applies to all the sciences of man: ethics, politics, and history—he opposes any attempt to work from purely a priori abstract principles, because 'as man is a progressive being—so all the sciences that analyse his life must be progressive—must be constantly accumulating new facts and evolving new principles'.[100]

7.3 J.S. Mackenzie

The fresh focus that the Idealists gave to social questions was drawn out and underlined in the work of one of Caird's pupils, John Stuart Mackenzie, who sought to carve out a new and distinct branch of study which he called 'social philosophy'. From 1895 Professor at University College Cardiff, he wrote two introductory textbooks out-lining this sub-discipline[101] and it was his great hope that it would come to be taught in universities.[102] 'Concerned with the relations of men to each other, with their relations to the material world, and with the development of individual character in so far as that is affected by these relations',[103] the subject was to have three main departments: political philosophy, economic philosophy, and philosophy of education. Methodo-logically contrasted with any empirical approach which looks to the natural history or the mechanics of society, this application of philosophy to social questions—'the systematic effort to deduce the laws of social life from certain primary princi-ples'[104]—Mackenzie thought must focus on the metaphysics of society and on its 'logic' (by which he means the normative question of its goal or ideal).[105] The result was a branch of study closely connected to, but distinct from, ethics.[106]

In metaphysical terms, Bradley, Green, and Caird had all argued that the individual is in a sense incomplete and cannot be understood in abstraction from its social context, implying that the real whole is society itself. Mackenzie, following this lead, takes up the matter from the other end (so to speak) and looking at society itself asks whether we may really regard it as a unity, and if so, what sort of a unity? If the British Idealists are sometimes said to be loose in their handling of this term, that could not be said of Mackenzie here. He distinguishes between three types of unity; monism, which views

---

[98] 'Individualism and Socialism', 190–1.
[99] 'Lecture on Political Economy', 160.
[100] 'Lecture on Political Economy', 161.
[101] The first was published in 1890, the second in 1919.
[102] *Introduction to Social Philosophy*, 357; *Outlines of Social Philosophy*, 102.
[103] *Introduction to Social Philosophy*, 62.
[104] *Introduction to Social Philosophy*, 12.
[105] *Introduction to Social Philosophy*, 28–32.
[106] *Introduction to Social Philosophy*, 46–8. In a similar vein, in his 1882 inaugural lecture on taking up the White's Chair at Oxford, vacated by the death of Green, William Wallace argued that while any account of the origin and contents of morality must draw on the results of sociology and make reference to the social context from which it springs, this can never account for its authority, which depends on its recognition by reason as essential to bring about the ideal ('Ethics and Sociology', 241).

a unity as a single system in which the nature of every part is predetermined by the nature of the whole (e.g. a single crystal); monadism, which views unity as a collection of mutually independent parts, each possessing a separate nature of its own (e.g. a heap of stones); and a third intermediate kind of unity in which neither parts are independent of their whole, nor the whole independent of its parts—a real unity which expresses itself through difference. Within this third class he distinguishes between mechanical unity (e.g. the solar system), chemical unity (e.g. a compound which completely transforms the nature of its original parts), and organic unity (e.g. a single plant).[107] The last is the kind which he thinks holds of society.

He admits that the notion of 'organic unity' gains some of its force from the biological analogy it invokes, but insists that as a mode of union it may be given independent content, listing three defining characteristics, each of which he argues may be said to hold of society. In the first place an organic unity is one in which the parts are intrinsically related to the whole. Mackenzie follows his idealist predecessors finding it 'clear' that the individual nature of a human being is formed and coloured by their society. Indeed, so great is the dependence of individual on nation or culture that one might well be tempted to regard the relation as monistic. He lays particular stress on common language.[108]

Secondly, an organic unity is one that grows from within. Mackenzie argues that (in the same way as human character cannot be changed overnight by external fiat, but only by the accumulated effect of many individual acts of will) societies cannot be made, altered, or changed externally or from the top by, for example, change of government or conquering powers, but only gradually through the development of individual lives. In this sense they too may be said to grow from within.[109] Yet to say that society grows from within invites misunderstanding. A plant grows from within, but only in a prescribed way. Its development path is fixed by nature, whereas that of society, being self-reflective, is unconstrained. Returning to the subject nearly thirty years later Mackenzie emphasizes this point: 'A natural organism cannot add a cubit to its stature, nor can it make any radical change in the disposition of its parts. A society may transform itself out of all knowledge. . . . It is indeed alive, but it is alive with thought. It "distinguishes, chooses, and judges," and shapes its future by reflection on its past and criticism of its present.'[110] This leads him to prefer the notion of a 'spiritual unity'—a unity of spiritual beings conscious of themselves as pursuing some common good.[111]

Lastly, an organic unity is one with its own internal end. It strives to bring about, not something separate from it, but some state of its own being. That this applies to social

---

[107] *Introduction to Social Philosophy*, 128–36; This careful taxonomy of types of unity is further developed in *Elements of Constructive Philosophy*, Book II, chapter V.

[108] *Introduction to Social Philosophy*, 150–4. He is here following Green, *Lectures on the Principles of Political Obligation*, §123.

[109] *Introduction to Social Philosophy*, 155–8.

[110] *Outlines of Social Philosophy*, 50.

[111] *Outlines of Social Philosophy*, 58.

life, Mackenzie admits, is something that might well be questioned. It might be objected that, no more than individual ethical life, has social life any goal or purpose at all—internal or external. These are simply modes of behaviour to which evolutionary development has led us, contingent upon whatever given circumstance favours 'survival', and hence utterly variable across different cultures and eras. Mackenzie responds that in such comparisons superficial variations tend to attract far more attention than fundamental agreements, and in so far as it amounts to a claim that the moral life of humanity cannot be rationally explained, this species of objection is best refuted by providing just such an explanatory account.[112]

If society has an aim, if there is some good it pursues, what might that be? It must, Mackenzie argues, be a function of the human goal itself which is self-realization; the fulfilment of our rational conscious nature as a whole. Such satisfaction is inevitably social, for 'it is only in the lives of other human beings that we find a world in which we can be at home'.[113] Mackenzie's argument for this conclusion has already been considered in the last chapter,[114] but what is new for us to note here is its application to society. What kind of a social ideal does this ethic entail? Three varieties of social ideal—emphasizing individual liberty, socialist intervention, and aristocratic hierarchy respectively—he finds each one-sided; and linking their partiality with three similarly one-sided social metaphysics, he suggests that an organically unified society must aim at a synthesis of all three.[115]

In terms of real content this must be confessed thin, but Mackenzie does appreciate that synthesis can only be achieved through the recognition and careful balance of many elements, calling for our own moral growth both individually and collectively, and also that it cannot be achieved immediately or mapped out before the start. It is necessarily progressive, rendering the social ideal itself an essentially progressive one.[116] Not that Mackenzie is naive or simplistic about progress. In an age where, in all departments—historical, cultural, material, even metaphysical—'progress' and 'evolution' were as widely used as concepts as they were assumed as facts, Mackenzie urges caution. Is the progress we so fondly believe in real? Can it be continued? We must not look to biology to guarantee that it can (as the work of some thinkers like Spencer might suggest), for biological advance is not moral advance; more complex developed and integrated lives are not necessarily happier or better ones.[117] Nor can we rest in a mere empirical appeal, as Mackenzie feels that Green and Bosanquet were content to do, since one observation can so easily be overturned by others.[118] But if progress is

---

[112] *Introduction to Social Philosophy*, 187.
[113] *Introduction to Social Philosophy*, 233.
[114] See above p.226. It should be noted that the argument for self-realization (with its detailed attack on hedonism) that we find here (*Introduction to Social Philosophy*, ch. IV) was in fact published three years before that of his *Manual of Ethics*.
[115] *Introduction to Social Philosophy*, ch. V.
[116] *Introduction to Social Philosophy*, 295.
[117] 'The Idea of Progress', 204–5.
[118] 'The Idea of Progress', 202–3.

illusory or impossible, we must ask what prevents it. Mackenzie suggests two possible obstacles. It might be feared that development of the baser elements in life undermines progress in its higher aspects, for example, that the richer our material lives grow the poorer our spiritual lives become. Mackenzie responds that while this may on occasion be so, it is predominantly a feature of the earliest phases of development. The narrowing of interest which results from the great effort to wrest from wayward nature technical and commercial control of life passes as material prosperity is won, and time and effort are released for life itself. Again it might be feared that the good of the individual and that of society are opposite so that advance in one must mean decline in the other. But any 'opposition between the good of the individual and the good of society seems on the whole to be superficial',[119] Mackenzie responds, for in the end no one can find realization or happiness solely within himself, and our own deepest interests are inseparable from those of our society. It is hardly surprising that for an absolute idealist the two great obstacles to human progress should come out as materialism and individualism, but it is a testament to the breadth of Mackenzie's vision that he can further see how, in a different light, these two may also be thought of as the solutions to our problems.[120]

Although setting out a new field, 'social philosophy', Mackenzie is ready to admit that there is no sharp dividing line between it and the more theoretical aspects of adjacent disciplines, and one of the most interesting and valuable aspects of the work is to observe its intersection with them. To take political philosophy, for example, Mackenzie is a democrat but sufficiently in thrall to Ruskin and Carlyle to worry about democracy. Against the charge that it is government by a uniform mediocrity, which pulls us all down to the lowest common denominator, Mackenzie responds that a true democracy must be aristocratic; we all contribute and we all count, but that does not mean that we should all try to steer the ship. If all are members of a living whole, there is no need for everyone to do everything; rather each must seek out the role for which he is best fitted. Against the charge that the combined self-interest of everyone is not the same thing as the common interest of all, that the Real Will must be distinguished from the will of all, Mackenzie argues that for a successful democracy its members need to be animated by a higher spirit of service. To be effective democracy requires the cultivation of citizenship.[121]

Mackenzie's appreciation of economic questions was also advanced for the time. Much concerned with the poor social conditions of modern industrial countries, he advocated a high degree of social intervention,[122] although he certainly wanted to

---

[119] 'The Idea of Progress', 212.
[120] *Introduction to Social Philosophy*, ch. II.
[121] 'The Dangers Of Democracy', *passim*.
[122] 'the remedy for the most prominent of the evils which accompany a highly developed industrial state, is to be found in a certain measure of what may, in a somewhat loose sense, be described as Socialism' (*Introduction to Social Philosophy*, 313). 'The cultivation of good citizenship in its various aspects is so essential to the life of a community that it can hardly be left exclusively to the efforts of private individuals. It needs a

defend private property[123] and the traditional rights of gift and inheritance.[124] The British Idealist philosopher most interested in economic questions, however, was Arnold Toynbee. Toynbee came up to Pembroke College, Oxford in 1873 but was forced to withdraw due to ill-health, re-matriculating two years later, this time at Balliol, where he was taught by both Jowett and Green. Upon graduating he was employed as a tutor and lecturer at Balliol, but as much as to academic matters he devoted himself to social reform, working with the poor in both London and Oxford, and supporting adult education, not least through public lectures. His early death in 1883, aged only thirty, robbed Idealism of one its most energetic reformers. The focus of his interest was political economy; his only book, the posthumously published *The Industrial Revolution in England* (1884) which popularized the term 'industrial revolution', is an exploration both of economic history and the fundamental principles of economics. Though by no means opposed to traditional liberal values, his experience of the realities of social deprivation persuaded him that they needed to be supplemented by a greater measure of state intervention, and just like Green in his 1881 address, 'Liberal Legislation and the Freedom of Contract', Toynbee sought to inch his way forward carefully. He said in a speech the following year:

We have not abandoned our old belief in liberty, justice, and self-help, but we say that under certain conditions the people cannot help themselves, and that then they should be helped by the State representing directly the whole people. In giving this State help, we make three conditions: first, the matter must be one of primary social importance; next, it must be proved to be practicable; thirdly, the State interference must not diminish self-reliance. Even if the chance should arise of removing a great social evil, nothing must be done to weaken those habits of individual self-reliance and voluntary association which have built up the greatness of the English people.[125]

This was a sacred obligation of the privileged class to serve the poor. In one of his last speeches, addressing the working-class members of his audience, he admitted that 'we [the middle classes] have neglected you. Instead of justice we have offered you charity, and instead of sympathy we have offered you hard unreal advice . . . you have to forgive us, for we have wronged you; we have sinned against you grievously—not knowingly always, but still we have sinned, and let us confess it; but if you will forgive us—nay, whether you will forgive us or not—we will serve you, we will devote our lives to

---

well-planned organisation; and it is naturally regarded as one of the functions of the State to provide this' (*Outlines of Social Philosophy*, 107).

[123] Following Green he argues that it 'is essential to the very idea of personality. A man does not become completely human until he possesses something which he can call his own, on which he may in some measure impress his character' (*Introduction to Social Philosophy*, 270).

[124] Not only is the desire to provide enduring support for one's family an important inducement to work, but the relief from work that inheritance can provide gives space for society to develop a culture and 'A great deal of culpable idleness and misused wealth may be tolerated for the sake of even a few men of culture' (*Introduction to Social Philosophy*, 273).

[125] 'Are Radicals Socialists?', 219.

your service.'[126] If the tone and language here seem religious that simply locates the true source of Toynbee's practical and intellectual effort; 'without religion a man were better dead,' he wrote.[127] We should add, however, that, much influenced by Green, this was a religion of liberal creed and active citizenship. Rejecting too any distinction that would place the church in charge of man's spiritual needs and restrict the state to his material requirements, Toynbee held that the State has the same end as the Church, viz. the promotion of the highest form of life. Indeed, he thought that 'the ideal Church is the State'.[128]

7.4 Henry Jones

The notion of society as an organic whole emerges as something of a leitmotiv in Idealism. We have seen it now in Green, Caird, Bradley, and Mackenzie. But before we note its appearance in the thought of yet another of Caird's pupils—Henry Jones— a certain amount of context is useful. Although highly characteristic of their thought, we should not make the mistake of thinking that the idea of society as an organism was either the exclusive preserve or the original creation of the British Idealists. As well as through earlier encounters with the suggestion in the philosophies of Plato, Hobbes, Hegel, and Coleridge,[129] the idea also entered nineteenth-century British conscious- ness through the evolutionary-minded system of Herbert Spencer. His 1860 essay on 'The Social Organism' argued that, just like natural organisms, from small beginnings involving simple configurations of largely independent parts, societies gradually grow in mass, structural complexity and mutual dependence of their parts until at last, 'the activity and life of each part is made possible only by the activity and life of the rest'. A society has a kind of life which, unlike the lives of any of its component members which come and go, survives from generation to generation.[130]

Spencer's conception was not the same as that of the Idealists, however, and in the 1883 memorial volume for T.H. Green (which appeared some seven years before Mackenzie's *Introduction*) Jones sought to attack it—giving to his paper the very same title Spencer had chosen for his.[131] Though promising, he argued, Spencer's concep-

---

[126] *Progress and Poverty*, 53.

[127] 'The Church and the People', xxviii.

[128] 'The Ideal Relation of Church and State', 238.

[129] Plato's *Republic* treats the state as a structure whose parts work together like an organism (Bk IV); Hobbes opens his *Leviathan* with a comparison between society and the human body (Introduction); Hegel, *Philosophy of Right*, §§267, 269, 271, 286; Coleridge, *On the Constitution of the Church and State*, 78–9, 95.

[130] 'The Social Organism', 272. See also his *Principles of Sociology*, vol.I, part II, ch.II. For discussion see D. Boucher, 'Evolution and politics', 89–91. Another evolutionary minded ethicist to take the same approach was Leslie Stephen who argued 'that society is not a mere aggregate but an organic growth, that it forms a whole, the laws of whose growth can be studied apart from those of the individual atom' (*Science of Ethics*, 31).

[131] See also his 'The Working Faith of the Social Reformer', 39–41. Essentially similar objections to Spencer's so-called 'social organism' are also repeated in D.G. Ritchie, *Principles of State Interference*, 13–22. Another similar idealist discussion of the 'social organism' from the same year may be found in Wallace's 'Ethics and Sociology', 242–6.

tion was vitiated by his individualistic presuppositions. For Spencer is careful to insist that he speaks only analogically, and his organism is ultimately an aggregate composed of many distinct individuals each of whom seeks his own good. Spencer maintains that, 'society exists for the benefit of its members; not its members for the benefit of society',[132] but even to raise the issue of which serves as means to the other's end, complains Jones, implies that we may form an independent conception of their aims, which is false.[133] Society has no ends which are not those of individuals, but equally individuals must find their ends in society. Says Jones, 'it seems to me that the first and last duty of man is to know and to do those things which the social community of which he is a member calls upon him to do. His mission is prescribed to him by the position in society into which he is born and educated, and his welfare depends upon its performance.'[134] Without common enterprise or goal there is no organism, just an aggregate. Spencer tries to court organicism without giving up his individualist credentials but, in truth, it is an all-or-nothing affair; 'whatever the difficulties may be in finding the unity of the social organism, if we hold by the doctrine and make it more than a metaphor, we must recognise that society and individuals actually form such a whole, and that apart from each other they are both nothing but names; and we must cease to speak of individuals as if they ever could exist apart from society.'[135]

The biological metaphor is in fact somewhat misleading, thinks Jones, for it mis-construes the real nature of the unity. Indeed, since the various parts of natural life forms are all in point of fact connected together mechanically, its tendency is to make us regard components as rather too separate and distinct.[136] Unlike the constitution of some plant or animal, the complexity of human beings is that of a living creature endowed with self-consciousness and freedom, and no theory which denies or short-sells that could ever be accepted.[137] At first sight this point might seem to take us away from social unity, but on deeper reflection it does the very opposite, for our spirituality and freedom are precisely the glue that binds society together.[138] Society gives us our freedom and in our freedom we come together as a society; we find ourselves in our social duties and through that contribution together create our community. The closeness of the bond lies precisely in the consciousness or spirituality of the relation between part and whole. Behind this argument we have, of course, the (by now) familiar idealist conception of freedom as service. Jones admits that there exists also an individualistic and capricious understanding of 'freedom' that would splinter people

---

[132] *Principles of Sociology*, 479.
[133] Cf. D.G. Ritchie, *Principles of State Interference*, 100–4.
[134] 'Social Organism', 193.
[135] 'Social Organism', 193.
[136] 'Social Organism', 208; 'Working Faith', 40–1.
[137] 'Social Organism', 200.
[138] 'The bond of the social organism . . . is freedom' ('Social Organism', 200).

apart, but to the Idealist such subjective liberty is not real freedom—it yields only inertia, caprice, or the fatal path of hedonism.[139]

7.5 J.M.E. McTaggart

Notwithstanding its popularity, it should be noted that the conception of society as organic was not accepted by all Idealists. In an important article in 1897 the Cambridge Idealist, McTaggart, argued against the view, taking as his template Mackenzie's three-part conception. The second element, that an organism grows from within rather than by accretion from without, McTaggart regards as but an implication of the first, that it manifests an intrinsic relation of parts; and while he does not dispute that individual and society are thus inter-related, the same holds, he argues, between *any* two things in the universe and therefore picks out nothing distinctive to the *organic*.[140] Mackenzie's condition excludes any theory which holds that individuals are completely unaffected by living in society, but surely no one ever thought *that*?

The heart of the issue, for McTaggart, lies with Mackenzie's third criterion, whether the end to which the system works forms an essential element in its own nature—whether it is an end in itself—or whether the system is a means to some end beyond or outside it. To allow the title 'organic' to unities of the latter kind, would be to open the door to things whose goals were potentially indifferent or even hostile to that which was seeking to bring them about—a property possible enough in itself, but surely not for anything we want to call an 'organism'.

McTaggart allows that Absolute Reality as Hegel conceives it would be an end in itself, and even that it can be thought of as a kind of society.[141] But (he argues) it does not follow from this ultimate 'theological' truth that any actual 'earthly' society does, or ever could have, the same status. Even if it is true that our ideal is some state of society which is an end in itself, and true also that the only path to realize this is through our present society, it still does not follow that we ought to regard our present society as an end in itself.

What makes McTaggart's opposition especially significant here is not simply that he strikes a note so different from other Idealists, but that he explicitly draws this opposition *from Hegel himself*. Since he defines for us an ideal of perfection towards which we must always strive, surely 'the true lesson to be learned from the philosophy of Hegel,' insists McTaggart, 'is that earthly society can never be an adequate end for man.'[142] Moreover, although it is often said that Hegel sees the nature of society as 'organic', he

---

[139] 'Social Organism', 201–4.

[140] 'The Conception of Society as Organism', 81. See also *Nature of Existence*, §§109–13, 137–43. In this fashion 'The fall of a sand-castle on the English coast changes the nature of the Great Pyramid' (*Nature of Existence*, II §309, 11–12).

[141] His own metaphysical views incline him to this. See 'Further Determination of the Absolute'.

[142] 'The Conception of Society as Organism', 193. For further discussion of McTaggart's suspicion of social holism see Chapter 13.1.1 below.

does not himself use this term. Nor is it very suitable. For self-conscious persons are *more individual* than a hand or foot and, on Hegelian principles, the more individual things are, the deeper needs to be their unity, calling for society to express a unity more profound than the simply organic.[143]

7.6 D.G. Ritchie

If Mackenzie and Jones owed most to Caird, the next figure to be considered, D.G. Ritchie, was primarily indebted to Green. A student of his at Balliol, Ritchie described Green as 'the philosophical teacher from whom I learnt most'.[144] But Ritchie goes back to the details of Hegel far more than does Green, insisting on the coincidence of the real and the rational—even if he admits that Hegel was often too ready to find such an equation reflected in the current state of science or social institutions.[145]

7.6.1 The social nature of the individual

Ritchie is fully signed up to the social conception of individuality that was typical of nearly all of the British Idealists.

The individual is thought of, at least spoken of, as if he had a meaning and significance apart from his surroundings and apart from his relations to the community of which he is a member. It may be quite true that the significance of the individual is not exhausted by his relations to any given set of surroundings; but apart from all these he is a mere abstraction—a logical ghost, a metaphysical spectre, which haunts the habitations of those who have derided metaphysics. The individual, apart from all relations to a community, is a negation...personality is a conception meaningless apart from society.[146]

Where Green, Bradley, and Caird all argue a priori, Ritchie is particularly keen to employ results from modern science in support of this position; recent biological advances, he suggests, have been vital in the process whereby ideas of organism and evolution have largely replaced older conceptions of mechanical aggregation. In welcoming support from contemporary science his thought is allied to Samuel Alexander's, though his welcome, like Henry Jones', is tinged with caution, and he objects to the still-individualistic character of thinkers such as Herbert Spencer. Moreover, for all he embraces empirical allies, the view they are called to support remains a metaphysical one; the claim that our particular self or *ego* is really but the imperfect

---

[143] 'The Conception of Society as Organism', 178. Here McTaggart is perhaps not so far from Henry Jones above (see pp.253–5). For further discussion of McTaggart's own conception of that 'deeper' unity see Chapter 10.1.3 below.

[144] Quoted in P.P. Nicholson's Introduction to the *Collected Works of D.G.Ritchie*, xvii. Upon graduation Ritchie was awarded a Fellowship at Jesus College, for whom he tutored until in 1894 he was elected Professor of Logic and Metaphysics at the University of St Andrews.

[145] 'Darwin and Hegel', 70–2.

[146] *State Interference*, 11; *Natural Rights*, 102.

realization of a more universal self quite clearly one that owes its ultimate source to Green's 'metaphysics of knowledge'.[147]

Ritchie's social conception of individuals leads him to a correspondingly social conception of their satisfaction, that is, to the idealist doctrine of the common good—an end for the whole community which is at the same time an end for each of its members. The state has as its goal the best possible life for each individual, but since that best life is literally inconceivable in the absence of organized society, the state is not simply a means to its achievement, but is at the same time, in some fashion, 'an end to itself'.[148] Even more than this, and meeting again the same triad we found in Green, the ideal self to be realized is understood so universally as to become not simply the realization of society but the realization of God himself.[149]

However, in spelling out the *content* of the common good, distance opens up between Ritchie and other Idealists; for while they were very dismissive of utilitarianism, he is more sympathetic.[150] He sees idealism as a tool which offers the possibility of 'reforming Utilitarianism' into something more serviceable.[151] The Idealist in holding that 'the ultimate end is the wellbeing of all mankind' means essentially same thing as the utilitarian when he speaks of the greatest happiness of the greatest number, suggests Ritchie, 'but it is put in a less misleading way'.[152] It is less misleading because utilitarianism in its traditional form suffers two defects. On the one hand, 'The difficulties of the utilitarian theory arise from its individualistic basis, from its assumption that a society is only an aggregate of individuals'.[153] While on the other, it is hampered by its undue emphasis on transient feeling (pleasure and pain). There is no harm in calling the final goal 'happiness' or designating 'right conduct' as that which leads to it. The lesson Idealism teaches is just that this needs to be unpacked, not as transient and individualistic pleasure, but rather in terms of social self-realization; the development and enduring welfare of the social organism as a whole. How far Ritchie's proposal takes him either from Idealism or towards utilitarianism are not easy matters to judge—nor helped by Ritchie's own lack of detail. The resultant position must certainly be distinguished from orthodox utilitarianism. His conception

---

[147] See above Chapter 4.1.

[148] *State Interference*, 102. Some critics have found such claims uncomfortable. John Morrow, for example, argues that 'while Green shared the liberal concern with the individual ... Ritchie and Bosanquet. ... cannot be regarded as liberals at all, since they regarded individuals as of secondary importance' ('Liberalism and British Idealist Political Philosophy', 93). But this is mistaken; focus on the true aims of the state in no way trumps or excludes focus on the true aims of the individual, since the two are exactly the same.

[149] *Philosophical Studies*, 237.

[150] For more on this see Weinstein, *Utilitarianism and the New Liberalism*, ch.5. For criticism of Weinstein's interpretation see Tyler, 'Vindicating British Idealism: D.G. Ritchie contra David Weinstein'.

[151] *Natural Rights*, 97.

[152] *Philosophical Studies*, 299. In Ritchie's eyes Green had been saying much the same, *State Interference*, 142–5.

[153] 'Ethical Democracy', 81.

of the moral goal both qualifies and goes beyond theirs,[154] while utilitarianism's willingness to sacrifice the few for the many is quite at odds with his metaphysically grounded commitment to the intrinsic value of each individual.[155] In general Ritchie seems confused about the relation between self-realization and the utilitarian end, his suggestion that they be combined one that is itself poorly developed. He foresees an advance in clarity and precision. In appealing to social utility, he thinks, we are appealing to something that can be *tested*—albeit by reference to past experience[156]—but that is not the same thing as a decision procedure, and the measure of any given action's contribution to the common good, for him, even if it involves that, cannot be reduced down to any simple enumeration of various of its causal outcomes.

7.6.2 *Natural rights*

Ritchie's most important book, *Natural Rights*, completed while he was still at Oxford and published during his first year as professor at St Andrews, takes up another theme of great importance to Green. Contrasting them with legal rights (those recognized by the state) and moral rights (those recognized by society, irrespective of their recognition by the state) Ritchie defines his subject, 'natural rights', as those which their proponents think *ought to be* recognized and, especially, those which are most fundamental; the ones which act as the base from which the others may be deduced.[157] But such a definition is minimal and only invites the question, how are we to determine what rights an ideal society would sanction? Ritchie recognizes three traditional categories of answer to this: authority, nature, and utility.[158] But each is found wanting.

Simplest would be to base rights in some authority external to the mind of the individual, such as a god or king; but such a derivation renders the source of our evaluative standards immune from evaluation itself and ultimately as arbitrary as it is unaccountable.[159] It is no help to change the appeal to some historical contract or tradition, since there exists no reason to respect such agreement which is not already a reason to respect rights more generally.[160] Dissatisfied with looking outside of ourselves we might turn inwards and look to individual conscience or sentiment, our own natural feelings; but this varies so much by individual, class, cultural environment and

---

[154] 'Happiness or contentment is rather a means to the good life than the end of it [for] much of the best work in the world comes from (or at least with) unhappiness; because much happiness comes from ignorance and Indolence' (1886 letter, *Philosophical Studies*, 237n).

[155] 'Each can claim to be an end-in-himself without inconsistency or necessity of conflict, only because none is an end-in-himself, except as partaking of the one "Reason" or "Nature" which is what all the higher religions have meant by God' (*Natural Rights*, 97).

[156] 'History is the laboratory of politics.' (*Natural Rights*, 103). For example, appealing to historical examples, Ritchie argues that our judgements on the legitimacy of past wars owe more to their actual results than to abstract principle ('War and Peace', 145–50).

[157] *Natural Rights*, 78–80.

[158] *Natural Rights*, 81.

[159] For example, if what makes things valuable or right is just that they are commanded by God, there is no room to ask if God's commands are themselves good (*Natural Rights*, 83).

[160] 'Contributions to the History of the Social Contract Theory', 224.

historical era that it offers no stable criterion. Finally, to make some advance we might appeal to something more objective, such as the evident security and welfare of the society we inhabit; but utilitarianism, in so far as it treats individuals as atoms and looks only to their feelings of pleasure and pain cannot suffice. It cannot, for example, explain our preference for an equal distribution over a grossly unequal one where the total happiness is slightly greater.[161]

Once we recognize the social nature of the individual, however, the basis for rights becomes clearer; we see that the question of *which rights ought to be recognized* must be considered from a much broader perspective. 'The person with rights and duties is the product of a society, and the rights of the individual must therefore be judged from the point of view of a society as a whole, and not the society from the point of view of the individual'.[162] 'The appeal to natural rights, which has filled a noble place in history, is only a safe form of appeal if it be interpreted . . . as an appeal to what is socially useful'—useful not simply for the existing members of a given society, but for its future members, and for humanity at large.[163] Although attaching to individuals, rights are not themselves individual in nature, but social. They depend for their existence on membership of a society, and depend for their legitimacy on the contribution they make to the good of society.[164]

There are several things to bring out here. For Ritchie (like Green) rights require recognition. But (again like Green) he distinguishes between legal rights, which require *state* recognition, and moral rights which require only *social* recognition.[165] Since rights are the creation of society, there can be no right of the individual against the society of which they are members. Talk of 'rights' in this context must be read as an appeal to those rights which an ideal, or at least a better, society *ought* to grant us.[166] Rights are accorded on the basis of their contribution to social utility. But Ritchie points out that utility *varies historically*, such that what was useful or necessary at one time may not be so at another. Thus any satisfactory theory of rights must be historically conditioned.[167] He cites the institution of slavery which was 'a necessary step in the progress of humanity'[168] and universally accepted in its day, but which, now it has outgrown its use, strikes us as quite horrible and contrary to natural right. Indeed, he suggests there

---

[161] *Natural Rights*, 96.

[162] *Natural Rights*, 101–2.

[163] *Natural Rights*, 103.

[164] For this reason they do not belong to animals (*Natural Rights*, 107); cf. Green above p.236.

[165] The position of Green and Ritchie here should be contrasted with that of Bosanquet, for whom recognition must always be by the state within its laws and institutions, even if only implicitly (Boucher and Vincent, *British Idealism and Political Theory*, 138–40).

[166] 'The Rights of Minorities', 282. 'When people seriously appeal to justice against society, what they really mean is that a higher form of society should supersede a lower. But it would be much better to say so directly, and not to talk about natural rights or abstract justice at all' (*Natural Rights*, 106–7).

[167] *Natural Rights*, 286.

[168] *Natural Rights*, 103. Also 'Rationality of History', 142–3. Ritchie here follows Hegel's historical justification of Greek slavery as a necessary condition for the development of 'aesthetic democracy' (*Philosophy of History*, Part II, section II, chapter III, 265).

are probably many things we do now that one day will seem terrible but to us today seem natural.[169]

7.6.3 State interference

Those who press the case for charity over state action tend to rest on the separation of morality and religion as 'private' from the 'public' domain of politics, arguing that social and moral regeneration call for individual responsibility and can never be brought about by direct government edict. Ritchie acknowledges that there is truth in this case—in Greenian fashion he thinks that 'the direct legal enforcement of morality cannot be considered expedient or inexpedient: it is *impossible*. The morality of an act depends upon the state of the will of the agent, and therefore the act done under compulsion ceases to have the character of a moral act'.[170] But in focusing on only half a truth this view creates a falsehood, ignoring the possibility that intervention might have *indirect* as well as direct effects, and attributing greater significance than is due to free will. Far more than we care to recognize, both the virtue of the respectable as well as the vice of the disreputable are a result of the conditions in which we find ourselves, responsibility for which is communal.[171] Within the realms of possible and appropriate intervention, again like Green, Ritchie thinks there are no 'natural rights' or general a priori limits that may be placed *ab initio* on permissible state interference in private life.

Instead the proper limits of state action must be determined 'simply and entirely by "Utilitarian" considerations'[172] and each proposed intervention must be looked at experientially on a case by case basis. And here perhaps we find more difference with Green. While unlike Green, Ritchie was not especially involved in active politics, he paradoxically had even greater enthusiasm for social and political reform by the state. And as Freeden has pointed out, whereas Green had warned that 'to attempt a restraining law in advance of the social sentiment necessary to give real effect to it, is always a mistake', Ritchie thought that in fact new laws themselves 'may produce those opinions and sentiments which go to the furtherance of morality'; that 'the economic change must come before the moral'.[173] Institutional change may encourage and not simply reflect social change. For example, although there is no distance between them on the basic principles behind private property (that its only justification lies in its contribution to the common good), in contrast to Green's somewhat cautious attitude,

---

[169] *Natural Rights*, 104.
[170] *State Interference*, 147.
[171] *The Moral Function of the State*, 4–5.
[172] *State Interference*, 167.
[173] Freeden, *The New Liberalism*, 58; Green 'Liberal Legislation and Freedom of Contract', 384; Ritchie, *The Moral Function of the State*, 8; Ritchie 1890 letter in Robert Latta's Memoir in *Philosophical Studies*, 48. In general Freeden sees Green as much less important than Ritchie, and Idealism as much less important than has commonly been supposed, in the turn of the century transformation of liberal thought (*The New Liberalism*, 16–7, 55–60). These are of course historical claims.

Ritchie is more prepared if he sees the need to ride roughshod over existing claims of natural or historical right to land or property.[174]

7.7 Idealism and evolution

Darwin's theory of evolution by natural selection has been touched upon several times in the discussion so far, but its significance to idealist social and political thought is a matter of sufficient importance to merit consideration as a separate topic. Idealists were not the only ones, of course, to explore the connections between evolutionary and social theory, and there were many naturalistically minded thinkers who also took up the theme. Generally the social philosophy of these people was more sympathetic towards evolution than that of the Idealists, but the 'evolutionary school' against which Idealism tended to position itself was far from monolithic, and consideration of their views needs to bear in mind the various differences between such 'evolutionists' as Charles Darwin, Alfred Russel Wallace, Herbert Spencer, G.H. Lewes, Leslie Stephen, Benjamin Kidd, and Thomas Henry Huxley.

7.7.1 A.S. Pringle-Pattison

For all the importance they gave to ideas of development and evolution, Green and Caird were unwelcoming to the theory of natural selection. Green's insistence that there could be no science of man ruled out its application to social, ethical, or political questions,[175] while Caird's principle that developmental explanation should be of the higher by the lower and not the other way round cut right across its basic methodological assumption.[176]

In this they influenced many subsequent Idealists. We find the same negative attitude taken up, for example, in the work of Andrew Seth Pringle-Pattison. In 'Man's Place in the Cosmos' he discusses the views of Huxley, whose 1893 Romanes lecture, 'Evolution and Ethics', had caused quite a stir. For all that he supported Darwinism extending even to the common ancestry of man and apes, in criticism of the ethics of evolution, Huxley had argued that an ethical life calls us to act in a way quite opposed to that which leads to success in the cosmic struggle for existence. In place of self-assertion, competition and the survival of the fittest it calls for self-restraint, co-operation, and the fitting of as many as possible for survival. To progress ethically man should resist, not imitate, cosmic processes and, through the use of his intelligence

---

[174] 'Origin and Validity'. 29; 'Locke's Theory of Property', 192. Collini describes him as the most radical of the Idealists (*Liberalism and Sociology*, 38n).

[175] In January 1875 J.A. Symonds, his wife's brother, described a conversation with Green saying 'he seems bent upon attacking evolution from the idealist point of view' (*Letters and Papers of John Addington Symonds*, 69–70).

[176] *Evolution of Religion*, I:45. In Caird's account of the evolution of the idea of evolution Darwin earns but one cursory mention (*Evolution of Religion*, I:24).

and will set himself apart from them.[177] In a paper published later the same year Seth Pringle-Pattison finds himself largely in agreement with this position, praising the uncompromising stand taken on ethical life and the resulting distance set between human and non-human nature. Huxley, he applauds, has called us back to the view of 'human life as an *imperium in imperio*—a realm which, though it rises out of nature, and remains exposed to the shock of natural forces, requires for its laws no foreign sanction, but bases them solely on the perfection of human nature itself'.[178] Ethical feelings and institutions may evolve, but that process cannot account either for their content or their validity.

However, Pringle-Pattison's idealism causes him to dissent from Huxley in two places. Huxley's stance works only by dividing the cosmos in two, he complains, by treating spiritual life as alien to the rest of nature. But this is to give up one of the greatest benefits of the theory of evolution, namely, its profound insight into the unity of nature. Yet how can we throw out our bath water without losing our baby? Only, answers Pringle-Pattison, if in place of a causal unity building up from lowest to highest, we think instead in terms of a teleological unity reaching back from highest to lowest. In this way rather than reduce the moral into its non-moral building blocks, we may regard the earliest stages of life as the first awakenings of a greater capacity inherent in reality from the start.[179] His second complaint is that Huxley, for all that he endorses the call to ethical life, is agnostic about the final value of the universe. His is, in the end, a stoical and defiant stand on behalf of value in the face of a quite possibly hostile or indifferent universe. By contrast, reassured of the fundamental unity of the cosmos, Pringle-Pattison regards an affirmation of the ultimate and binding value of ethical life as entailing in its turn a full scale metaphysical assertion of the value of reality as a whole.[180]

7.7.2 D.G. Ritchie

Not all Idealists were so hostile to evolutionary theory, however. Bosanquet, for example, shows a degree of sympathy with it,[181] but the Idealist who felt himself

---

[177] 'Evolution and Ethics', 82–3.

[178] 'Man's Place in the Cosmos', 11–12.

[179] 'Man's Place in the Cosmos', 17.

[180] 'Man's Place in the Cosmos', 31–2. The following year Henry Jones in his Glasgow inaugural address voiced similar objections to Huxley's dualistic claim that the moral order is antagonistic to the natural, partly on the grounds that since one is unconscious and the other intelligent there is no point at which they could meet and conflict, but mainly on the grounds that, both being products of the same process, they must be understood as partners not enemies in the great cosmic enterprise. Nature in itself is neither moral nor immoral, but as a necessary precondition of both moral and conscious life, 'the moral achievements of man are also nature's' ('Is The Order of Nature Opposed to the Moral Life?', 20, 28).

[181] Where Huxley both divides and opposes the natural and moral spheres, Bosanquet stresses their continuity, and the necessity of the struggle for existence to the positive development of human character ('Socialism and Natural Selection'). Given this coincidence, in terms of what really matters, viz. its harmony with human cognition and value, he regards the hypothesis of a naturally evolved universe as but minimally different from that of an intelligently designed one ('Old Problems Under New Names', 108–11).

most in line with Darwinian evolution was D.G. Ritchie. Ritchie attempts to argue that evolution by natural selection and Hegelian idealism are wholly compatible with, and even supportive of, each other—labelling the resultant position 'idealist evolutionism'.[182] Not only do they both tell a dynamic developmental story in which the world grows without external influence from simple to complex but, suggests Ritchie, evolutionary theory agrees with Hegel in asserting the fundamentally rational character of history.[183] Indeed it is even possible to regard *heredity*, *variation*, and *elimination of the least fit* as just new forms of the Hegelian categories of *identity*, *difference*, and *negativity*.[184] Ritchie stresses the resolving power of both theories. Just as Hegelian dialectic can synthesize opposed thesis and antithesis, evolution has helped modern thought to overcome 'sophistical' and falsely dichotomized thinking.[185]

In taking this line, Ritchie set himself against the majority of Idealists who saw these schools as opposed—thinking that to trace development from the bottom could lead only to materialism, hedonism, utilitarianism, and individualism—and he therefore attempts to dispel this alleged opposition. Natural selection and Hegelian dialectic might seem to work in opposite directions, he says, one looking to origins the other to ends, but it needs to be remembered that they are wholly different *kinds* of explanation. And since they are quite different, there is no reason why they may not run simultaneously. Darwin's approach is temporal and causal. By contrast, Hegel's underlying principle is a timeless and logical relation. He is explaining a thought-process. This tends to get presented historically, but that is in fact misleading,[186] and there is often as much value in 'reading Hegel backwards' as a criticism of categories.[187] A nice illustration of the complete failure to appreciate this difference can be found, notes Ritchie, in Lewes and Spencer's plan to appeal to heredity in explanation of the a priori. This is just confusion, for the a priori (at least in so far as it appears in Kant) is not something psychological, but rather logical or conceptual.[188]

Of course, the fact they are totally different types of explanation will not remove conflict between them if each claims to be *complete*, the only one that we need, but that too Ritchie challenges. Spencer insists that evolution by natural selection is simply a question of explanation of the lower by the higher, but Ritchie insists that we must think of it as *also* containing an element of teleology.[189] To understand what anything really is, we must look to the final and most perfect form of it that we can find. Crude origins 'only have their value for the scientific investigator because he looks at them in the light of what they come to be'.[190] 'We only understand a part of anything when we

---

[182] *Darwin and Hegel*, Preface (vii).   [183] 'Darwin and Hegel', 58.

[184] 'Darwin and Hegel', 56.

[185] *Natural Rights*, 24. In this, of course, his thinking echoes Caird's. See e.g. *Evolution of Religion*, I:26.

[186] 'Darwin and Hegel', 50.

[187] 'Darwin and Hegel', 47–9.

[188] 'Note on Heredity as a Factor in Knowledge', 36–7.

[189] *State Interference*, 44–5.   [190] 'Rationality of History', 131.

can look at it as a part of a whole, and we only understand the elementary stages when we know them as the elementary stages of something more highly developed'.[191] 'Looking back on the whole process, we may say that nature "intends" the fittest'.[192] In this way, suggests Ritchie, 'Darwin restores "final causes" to their proper place in science'.[193] Although it is true that we can never divest ourselves of the knowledge of where evolution has taken us, we must be wary of falsely reflecting that future back onto the past, and Ritchie's case for teleology is barely more than asserted here. More plausible is his argument, from the other side, that neither is Hegelian explanation complete in itself. Validity is a logical not a temporal relation but inferences can only be drawn by people in time, and in the same way dialectic, even if in essence a pattern of thought, must still be manifested in time. But this can only be through causal historical processes.[194]

What was most radical about Darwin's theory of natural selection was, of course, its application to human life. It is therefore no surprise to find Ritchie further investigating this matter. How far into the human sphere can Darwinian ideas be applied? He considers two areas—intellect and ethical life—and his conclusions are generally positive about each. Contra both Idealists like Green and evolutionists like Alfred Russel Wallace,[195] he thinks that evolution might explain the origin of our intellectual faculties. Consciousness, reflection, and language are all useful for survival, and it is simpler to explain their origin by natural selection than by some mysterious intrusion from outside;[196] although it is also noteworthy that, once originated, they can be further adapted to purposes which seem to have no direct survival advantage either to the individual or the species.[197] Our systems of belief too he thinks may be explained in the same way, arguing that the process by which we come to think what we do is not merely *analogous* to natural selection, but in fact the very same process at work in the cognitive sphere.[198] The functional survival value of true belief is rather clearer to see than that of consciousness, and modern philosophy of mind, if sharing Ritchie's confidence with respect to the natural origin of the latter, has still offered but little to substantiate it.

---

[191] 'Darwin and Hegel', 47; *Natural Rights,* 27–8.

[192] 'Ethical Democracy', 73.

[193] 'Darwin and Hegel', 60–1.

[194] 'Darwin and Hegel', 51.

[195] Although as we have seen he has grave doubts about the evolutionary epistemology of Spencer and Lewes, interestingly Green does not completely rule it out 'To deny categorically . . . that the distinctive intelligence of man, his intelligence as knowing, can be developed from that of "lower" animals would . . . be more than we should be warranted in doing' (*Prolegomena*, §84). We must distinguish here the *metaphysical* question of the explanation of consciousness, from the *historical* question of its origin within the human vehicle. Alfred Russel Wallace by contrast was certain that natural selection could not in any way account for the origin of life, consciousness, or the higher human faculties, arguing that these called for some kind of spiritual intervention from outside ('The Limits of Natural Selection as Applied to Man').

[196] *Darwinism and Politics*, 93, 101; also Essay II, §3.

[197] 'Social Evolution', 10.

[198] 'Ethical Democracy', 74–5.

Ritchie also broadly endorses the attempts of philosophers such as Clifford, Stephen, and Alexander to account for *ethics* in evolutionary terms.[199] He even suggests that Hegel agrees with the evolutionists in denying any ultimate distinction between 'is' and 'ought'[200] as well as in repudiating individualism.[201] Attempting to hold a middle ground between those who would simply reduce ethical to natural life and those who would keep them forever distinct, Ritchie finds a significant 'convergence of results'[202] between evolutionary theory and Idealism. Specifically he holds that natural selection is able to assist Idealism in its work of vindicating the essential truth and correcting the errors of utilitarianism.[203] Rescuing us 'from the arbitrary and subjective standards of intuitionism'[204] and shifting our thinking to the level of organisms, the theory of natural selection tells us only the fittest society or race survives, and that the customs and ideas of the fittest society are precisely those most advantageous to its stability and endurance.[205] In this way natural selection may be used to explain the origin and development both of our social and political institutions,[206] and of our moral intuitions which result from them.

Keen as Ritchie was to extend evolution by natural selection into the human sphere, he thought this needed to be done with care and he attacked the previous misuse of Darwinian ideas in these areas. He argues that evolutionary theory has in the past been poorly and uncritically applied.[207] Although 'the phrases "social organism" and "evolution" are on everybody's lips' he says 'those who use them most frequently have often grasped their significance the least.'[208]

He insists that (rightly understood) they do not give sanction to *laissez faire* economic thinking.[209] It may be that unbridled competition has brought our society considerable advance, but it is also hideously wasteful, and there is no reason to think we could not do as well or better at less cost.[210] He is similarly sceptical of those who would cite social evolution in support of democracy. He has no quarrel with the notion that society *is* developing in an increasingly democratic direction and he doubts it will ever return to feudalism or aristocracy.[211] Nor is he *opposed* to the development— less worried than Mill, Carlyle, or even Mackenzie, he urges that even if others know better than we what we should aim for, they must still make us want what they recommend, and so the only right of a minority is to try to become a majority if they can.[212] However, he insists that the future of society is not fated but up to us, and that progress achieved is no ground for the conclusion that continuation along the current path is necessarily advantageous. Indeed, he sounds a warning. Even if wisdom

---

[199] *Darwinism and Politics*, Essay II, §2. [200] 'Darwin and Hegel', 68.
[201] 'Darwin and Hegel', 72. [202] *State Interference*, 168.
[203] 'Darwin and Hegel', 62. The result he calls 'evolutionist utilitarianism' (*State Interference*, 169).
[204] 'Ethical Democracy', 80. [205] 'Ethical Democracy', 82.
[206] *Darwinism and Politics*, 106. [207] 'Darwin and Hegel', 41.
[208] *Natural Rights*, 277. [209] *Darwinism and Politics*, Essay I §5; *State Interference*, 108.
[210] *Darwinism and Politics*, 30. [211] 'Ethical Democracy', 88.
[212] 'The Rights of Minorities', 270–3, 281.

does not confer a right to rule, he argues we must distinguish between means and ends, for there is such a thing as scientific expertise in administration, and to simply hand over the running of the factory, town, or country to all of its workers, inhabitants, or citizens would only undermine prosperity.[213] He also argues that, in the same way as democracy among children would be a cruelty not a kindness, so it should be withheld from 'lower races'.[214] The key point he suggests is to distinguish between democracy itself and the democratic spirit (of 'liberty, equality, fraternity') for the two are not necessarily coincident.[215]

Ritchie is very aware of the potentially conservative implications of evolutionary functionalism but he seeks to mitigate them by pointing out, even if social institutions which have survived must once have served some useful function, there is no need to admit that they still do so today.[216] Indeed, he urges the work of reform can just as well be construed as helping evolution along. Rules tend to ossify and so only societies which reform survive, in which case we may regard an 'intelligent and far-sighted utilitarian policy' as itself 'a system of rational artificial selection'.[217]

Beyond this, Ritchie makes two more theoretical points. First, even if it can explain how we have come to hold the ethical beliefs we do, no more than Pringle-Pattison does he think that natural selection can explain the nature of morality *itself*. The fittest to survive are not necessarily the best in any other sense.[218] Progress is not the same as evolution,[219] since natural selection may produce degeneration just as much as it may produce advance. 'The ultimate question' of good and bad 'belongs to the metaphysic of ethics. But for the practical discussion of what is better or worse in social conduct and institutions' natural selection may help, he allows.[220]

The second theoretical point is that to Ritchie's thinking the introduction of *consciousness* (that by which man becomes free from the tyranny of nature) introduces a vast difference into the workings of natural evolution.[221] He claims that the role of consciousness and of social institutions, over and against heredity, have been underestimated in evolutionary theory. Natural selection no longer means the same things for humans as for animals. He suggests a three-stage story in which 'natural evolution' gives way to 'imitative evolution' (the half-conscious process of conjecture and refutation through which societies develop their beliefs, convictions and structures) which in turn gives way to 'rational evolution' in which the process is taken up in consciousness.[222] Conscious reform of habitual rules is part of the natural evolutionary process, not a violation of it.[223] Ritchie was not simply claiming that consciousness added a new thrust to natural selection; rather, it changed its workings so totally that Darwinism, originally a system expressing the primacy of impulse, became an almost

---

[213] 'Ethical Democracy', 89.
[214] 'Ethical Democracy', 92.   [215] 'Ethical Democracy', 91–2.
[216] *Natural Rights*, 16–18.   [217] 'Ethical Democracy', 81–2.
[218] *Darwinism and Politics*, 13.   [219] *Natural Rights*, 111.
[220] 'Ethical Democracy', 80–1.   [221] *Darwinism and Politics*, 24.
[222] 'What are economic laws?', 170.   [223] *Darwinism and Politics*, 32–3.

completely conscious and reasoned process. Rational selection takes over from natural selection. For example, evolution explains our broadly welfare-related intuitions. But

when reflection appears, however, a higher form of morality becomes possible; the useful—*i.e.*, what conduces to the welfare of the social organism, is not recognised merely by the failure of those societies in which it is not pursued, but by deliberate reflection on the part of the more thoughtful members of the society. The utilitarian reformer reflects for his society, and anticipates and obviates the cruel process of natural selection by the more peaceful methods of legislative change. The theory of natural selection thus gives a new meaning to Utilitarianism.[224]

Whether Ritchie's proposal here is really a continuation of evolutionary thinking or the rejection of it for a quite different alternative, is not easy to settle, nor can the critic be confident that the position Ritchie wishes to outline is even a consistent one. And in purely historical reputational terms he was right to fear that his reconciling efforts to bring Idealism and evolution together would just make *both* sides look on him as a heretic.[225]

7.8 John MacCunn

Before ending this discussion of idealist social philosophy, there is one last name which deserves briefly to be noted: John MacCunn; from 1881 Professor of Philosophy University College Liverpool[226] and before that a pupil of Caird's in Glasgow and Green's at Balliol. MacCunn's principal work *The Ethics of Citizenship* was published in 1894 and is a typical piece of idealist political thought. He argues there that equality should be understood as a recognition of the fact that man is a being with a moral worth that distinguishes him from a mere animal or chattel, and that respect for this worth means he must be accorded equality of civil and also political rights (for to develop morally we need a public life).[227] In itself this recognition is consistent with much other inequality, for worth itself is unequally distributed, and in so far as other inequalities result from that fact it would be inconsistent not to admit them.[228] But the same principle also limits how great those inequalities may become, for no inequality should be allowed that holds back human worth, that prevents people from receiving a fair chance in life. Redistribution beyond this point, however, is of doubtful value.[229]

As to the nature of political and civil rights more generally, MacCunn's view is much like Green's. He is opposed to natural rights, but finds Bentham's insistence that our only rights are legal ones equally implausible. Instead we must think of our rights as *those which ought to be granted us*. This is a social matter. 'Rights are not mysteries; not gifts from a higher Source, of which we can tell no more than that we have them' he

---

[224] *Darwinism and Politics*, 105.   [225] *Darwin and Hegel*, Preface (vi).
[226] Which afterwards in 1903 became the University of Liverpool, and where from 1882 to 1890 he was a colleague of A.C. Bradley.
[227] *Ethics of Citizenship*, 4–12.   [228] *Ethics of Citizenship*, 16–18.   [229] *Ethics of Citizenship*, 20–6.

argues, rather they are 'certain advantageous conditions of social well-being indispensable for the true development of the citizen, enjoyable by all members of the community, and of which we are prepared to say that respect for them ought (in one way or another) to be enforced'.[230] It cannot be assumed that the rights it would be expedient and practical to grant at one time and place would hold for all other times and places.

To speak without qualification of rights as *granted* sends a potentially wrong signal. It is true that there are various modes of *civic* life (employment, health, family, public life, religion, education, and the like) that need to be in place, if men are to become citizens not merely in name but in reality. But citizenship is no passive gift. 'Men become citizens in truth and in substance, only when they use their rights.'[231] Rights are but an opportunity to do our duty, their real value rises and falls with the use to which they are put. For example, what value freedom of speech without thought to the worth of what we say, or freedom of worship to those who can no longer be bothered to worship anything?[232] And we can only rely on democracy if we play our part and become responsible voters, one aspect of which must be to stand out against majority opinion when necessary. 'Reasonable trust in the majority there can never be where there is not a readiness, if need be, to withstand the majority to the face; for it is only out of men prepared so to do that a reasonable majority can be made.'[233] Our right to suffrage is not given but earned by its responsible exercise.

7.9 Practical applications

There is one final topic to consider before concluding this chapter, and that is the high level of involvement in practical politics on the part of the British Idealists. Of course, they were not the first philosophers ever to take seriously ethical or political questions—a whole history of philosophy can be cited to counter that claim. Nor were they the first to apply their ideas practically—we may think of Plato's unsuccessful attempts to persuade Dionysius II of Sicily to adopt his political scheme or Bentham's famous Panopticon. And it is also true that late Victorian culture generally placed great emphasis on involvement in social works.[234] But none of these qualifications take away from what is a distinctive point about British Idealism—that it was at its very heart a philosophy about the transformation of, not just laws and public institutions, but society itself; a philosophy which therefore could not and did not remain aloof from praxis.

---

[230] *Ethics of Citizenship*, 55–6.   [231] *Ethics of Citizenship*, 69.
[232] *Ethics of Citizenship*, 71.   [233] *Ethics of Citizenship*, 116–17.
[234] An important figure in this regard was John Ruskin. He exerted influence through his writings and, from 1869 onwards, as Oxford's first Slade Professor of Fine Art, by his presence in the University. His famous Hinksey road-building project of 1874, saw the participation of the Idealist Arnold Toynbee, as well as Oscar Wilde, Alfred Milner, and H.D. Rawnsley.

A certain modesty prevailed. 'All philosophy has to do' argues Bradley 'is "to understand what is," and moral philosophy has to understand morals which exist, not to make them or give directions for making them.' It should not be thought, says T.H. Green in a similar vein, that any moral theory could make anyone 'a better man' or bring about in people 'a more lively sense of their duty to others'.[235]

But this was not perhaps entirely honest. The Idealists 'taught' philosophy as a church 'teaches' religion—as an opening of eyes and a call to service. John MacCunn, a former pupil of Green, saw clearly that his tutor's interest was not simply academic.

No reader of his *Prolegomena to Ethics*, can fail to feel the repressed fervour of its pages, and those who knew the man can never forget the unobtrusive passion for righteousness that shone through a character which shrank from easy expression of itself. It was ethical temperament, habitual moral aspiration, religious fervour. Doubtless. But was it not also, in part, the fruit of a life-long, determined, reasoning reflection upon the moral possibilities and destiny of man?[236]

This practical focus continued throughout the movement's history, so that even Collingwood, who came up to Oxford in 1908, was able to recall how the school of Green saw philosophy as 'a training for public life' and sent out 'a stream of ex-pupils who carried with them the conviction that philosophy, and in particular the philosophy they had learned in Oxford, was an important thing and that their vocation was to put it into practice'.[237] In this Balliol was pre-eminent, but the other centres of Idealism were equally committed to praxis. A.D. Lindsay paid tribute as follows to the influence of Caird and Jones in Glasgow, equally tireless campaigners, and both of whom he had known:

The influence of their personalities and their teaching fitted generation after generation of their pupils to face all the thronging problems which multiplied in the second half of the nineteenth century. They were not either of them mere academic teachers. They trained a great school of teachers of philosophy, but they were also the inspiration of teachers and preachers, of administrators and statesmen, of men who through them did better service to their day and generation in all manners of ways.[238]

---

[235] *Ethical Studies*, 193; *Prolegomena*, §331. Bosanquet too holds that moral philosophy cannot give guidance for conduct. Its function is to understand good and evil conduct, not to take command of individual lives. Philosophy has to understand, not to dictate (*Some Suggestions in Ethics*, 161), For each of us our task is 'original, unique, creative' (*Some Suggestions in Ethics*, 149), 'Ethical Theory cannot either lay down the rules for conduct or pronounce judgment on particular actions' ('The Practical Value of Moral Philosophy', 144). That the task was more than just intellectual was equally clear to Mackenzie who concluded his *Introduction to Social Philosophy* by suggesting that 'a philosophic understanding of our social problems is not even the chief want of our time. We need prophets as well as teachers, men like Carlyle or Ruskin or Tolstoi, who are able to add for us a new severity to conscience or a new breadth to duty. Perhaps we want a new Christ. We want at least an accession of the Christlike spirit—the spirit of self-devotion to ideal ends—applying itself persistently in all the departments of life' (376–7). For more detailed discussion of the relation between description and prescription in Green's ethics see A. Vincent, 'Ethics and Metaphysics in the Philosophy of T.H. Green'.

[236] *Making of Character*, 237.

[237] Collingwood, *Autobiography*, 17.

[238] 'Idealism', 1.

It is this practical import of British Idealism that stands out, making it a movement as interesting to social historians as to historians of philosophy. The present work is not a social history, and others have written extensively about this side of things,[239] but it is worth stopping to summarize a few main points because idealism is subject to the perennial objection that it is a kind of retreat from reality, some sort of refuge in a world of dreams. But whatever may be true of other idealisms, nothing could be further from the truth here. We have seen how in metaphysics the British Idealists went out of their way to stress that the Absolute was not something 'other-worldly' and similarly with ethics and political theory—even if their later enemies were wont to criticize them as just sermonizing—their concern for the ideal in no way meant lack of concern for the actual. Indeed, with an idealism so immanentist, the inconsistency would be if they had *not* been active to such a degree in practical affairs.

In a few cases the engagement was through traditional politics. Haldane entered parliament (1885) and T.H. Green was the first University member ever to be elected to the Oxford city council (1876), while less successfully, after Green's death in 1882 Toynbee also stood for election to Oxford city council and in 1918 Millicent Mackenzie stood for parliament seeking to represent the University of Wales.[240]

But generally their efforts were more immediate than political. Much of their energy was directed towards improving the lot of the most disadvantaged in society. One manifestation of this was the Charity Organisation Society (COS). Set up in 1869 to distribute poor relief on a more 'scientific' basis, it attempted to distinguish between the 'deserving' and 'undeserving' poor, between cases in which assistance would encourage and those in which it would only undermine efforts at self-improvement.[241] This was (as we have seen) a distinction many Idealists stressed and the Organisation's members included C.S.Loch, Arnold Toynbee, Canon Samuel Barnett, Helen Bosanquet, and notably, Bernard Bosanquet, who on coming into an inheritance, in 1881 resigned his Oxford Fellowship and moved to London, in order to devote himself to social work and writing.[242]

Another important initiative was the University Settlement Movement. In 1883 COS member Samuel Barnett (himself an alumnus of Wadham College) gave a lecture at St John's College entitled 'Settlements of University Men in Great Towns' in which he suggested that by living among the people they sought to help, those with a university education could more effectively channel their work for the disadvantaged. Central to the scheme was education (though the provision of libraries and lectures) the

---

[239] See for example Carter, *T.H. Green and the Development of Ethical Socialism*; den Otter, *British Idealism and Social Explanation*; Gordon and White, *Philosophers as Educational Reformers*; Leighton, *The Greenian Moment*; Vincent and Plant, *Philosophy, Politics and Citizenship*.

[240] *John Stuart Mackenzie*, 116.

[241] For further detail see den Otter, 'The Restoration of a Citizen Mind: British Idealism, Poor Relief and Charity Organisation Society'; Sprigge, *God of Metaphyics*, 347–51.

[242] He was tempted back into Academia to take the Chair in Moral Philosophy at St Andrews from 1903 to 1908.

aim being to offer spiritual improvement as much as practical. Barnett's initiative culminated in the establishment of a settlement in 1884 in East London, named Toynbee Hall, after Arnold Toynbee who had died the previous year.[243] Within a very short time there were many other such settlements,[244] significant not just for the way in which they reflected idealist principles, but for the heavy involvement of the Idealists themselves (who offered lectures) and their pupils in this work. Initially support for the movement was strong, but gradually it fell away. For example, the COS who affirmed in its journal in 1884 that 'there must be many like us who share our conviction that this is an experiment which of all others at this time is most hopeful and most worth trying', by 1895 was complaining that those who still thought this a viable model for social improvement 'must have been sleeping for twenty years'.[245] Bosanquet warned against 'the glorification of the settlement life' and feared the potential harm that might be done where groups of inexperienced young men or young women came together, burning 'to do good' but without proper knowledge, training, or resources.[246]

At the same time there grew up a number of other related organizations which (while not exclusive to) both involved Idealists and expressed principles of idealist spirit.[247] These included the Christian Social Union, particularly associated with Green's former pupil, Henry Scott Holland, and the London Ethical Society, set up by J.H. Muirhead and James Bonar.[248] For general support and especially lectures the LES drew on such figures as Edward Caird, J.S. Mackenzie, William Wallace, Henry Jones, D.G. Ritchie, and Bosanquet, making it an important source for many subsequent Idealist writings. Notwithstanding his close involvement with it, Bosanquet came somewhat to disagree with the direction taken by the LES; disapproving of their aim to become some sort of alterative 'ethical' church and insisting on the need to keep separate 'teaching' and 'preaching'.[249]

The Idealists were great campaigners too on many more specific matters, urging a range of social changes that would benefit the worst off in society. They supported

---

[243] In memorial of a different kind, like Green, Toynbee also appears in a novel by Mrs Humphry Ward. He was the inspiration for the character Edward Hallin in her *Marcella* (1894).

[244] Oxford House in east London (Founded in 1884 by Green's pupil, Henry Scott Holland), Mansfield House in Canning Town (1890), University Hall (founded in 1890 by Mary (Mrs Humphry) Ward, re-established in 1896 as the Passmore Edwards Settlement, and finally renamed in 1920 as the 'Mary Ward Centre'). The Women's University Settlement in south London (1897), Bermondsey University Settlement (1891), Cambridge House (1894), and Lady Margaret Hall Settlement (1897). Outside London we may note the Glasgow Settlement (founded in 1889 and with which the Caird brothers were much involved), the Manchester University Settlement (1895), Liverpool University Settlement (1906), and Bristol University Settlement (1911).

[245] Harrow, 'The English University Settlements 1884–1939', 3.

[246] 'The Duties of Citizenship', 25–6.

[247] For further detail see Ian MacKillop, *The British Ethical Societies*.

[248] den Otter, *British Idealism and Social Explanation*, 118; Gordon and White, *Philosophers as Educational Reformers*, 114–21.

[249] Helen Bosanquet, *Bernard Bosanquet, A Short Account of his Life*, 44; Muirhead, *Bernard Bosanquet and his Friends*, 49.

labour reform, such as the factory acts (Edward Caird was especially concerned to help the situation of women workers[250]) and were keen advocates also of electoral reform. (Both Edward and John Caird worked for women's suffrage, although Green it seems was not a supporter.[251])

One such cause, which now seems dated, but which Green in particular thought vitally important was temperance.[252] Teetotal himself, it was Green's belief that drink was a more potent source of social harm than almost any other, and he supported the power of local authorities to reduce the number of licences, restrict opening hours, or even close down pubs altogether. Given that none of the other Idealists followed him in this cause, it is tempting to bring in personal reasons: his brother was an alcoholic. But this temptation should be resisted, for the argument is logical. He rightly points out that alcohol dependency is a bar to moral progress—obviously so for the alcoholic, but equally so for his family and for the neighbourhood—and as such idealist principles clearly sanction its removal. It might be objected that outside agencies should not attempt to impose personal habits, and that here is a perfect opportunity for self-discipline. But Green would respond that in this case, as often as not, people are unable to help themselves. Again, it might be objected that people have a right both to drink and to sell alcohol. But Green would simply not agree that we have any such unconditional right. Indeed, the restriction of alcohol is one of the examples he discusses in 'Liberal Legislation and Freedom of Contract' describing drunkenness as a 'wide-spreading social evil, of which society may, if it will, by a restraining law, to a great extent, rid itself, to the infinite enhancement of the positive freedom enjoyed by its members'.[253]

Holding a metaphysics in which reality consists in the progressive completion of rational thought, especially through the medium of human culture, holding an ethics in which the human ideal consists in self-realization, and holding a political theory centred around the duties of citizenship in pursuit of the common good, it was inevitable that education—the system whereby we develop intellectually and socially—should take on special importance to the British Idealists. But they recognized too a practical imperative here, rightly seeing this as the key from which nearly all other positive social change would follow. In consequence, the one cause which exercised their attention more than any other was education. Indeed, so important a theme is this that a division in its treatment is appropriate here, considering the early years at this juncture, and leaving later developments for a subsequent chapter.

Green was especially active in this regard. Comparing a lack of basic education in modern society to physical handicap[254] he advocated free compulsory state-provided

[250] Jones and Muirhead, *Life and Philosophy of Edward Caird*, 118–25.
[251] Jones and Muirhead, *Life and Philosophy of Edward Caird*, 96–101, 150–2; Anderson, 'The Feminism of T.H. Green', 683–4.
[252] For further detail see Nicholson, 'T.H. Green and State Action: Liquor Legislation'.
[253] 'Liberal Legislation and Freedom of Contract', 384.
[254] 'Liberal Legislation and Freedom of Contract', 374–5.

primary education (something achieved during his lifetime in 1880). Himself from 1865–6 a School Inspector on behalf of the Taunton Commission,[255] he was also a moving force behind the establishment in 1881 of the Oxford High School for boys,[256] the city's first secondary school, giving concrete expression to his allegiance to the notion of a 'ladder of learning' all the way up from elementary to university education. Committed to widening University access, he supported the Association for the Higher Education of Women in Oxford, and he took charge of Balliol Hall, a lodging house on Oxford's St Giles, set up as part of an extension scheme to make available more places for deserving scholars at Balliol.[257]

It has been said that if the Idealists did not write at great length on educational theory, this was because they had no need for a separate philosophy of education, the *raison d'etre* of their entire philosophy being an educational one.[258] Certainly it is true that one might read the systems of Green, Bradley, or Caird as extended discussions of self-realization or socialization, plausible candidates for the aim of education; but it should not be thought that the Idealists eschewed altogether writing *specifically* on philosophy of education. We have already noted the advocacy and analysis of Plato's *Republic* as a treatise on education by Nettleship, Bosanquet, and Caird, and moving away from classical studies the work of two further writers, Mackenzie and MacCunn, deserves special attention.

Mackenzie locates three elements to social progress, the economic and industrial subjugation of nature, the perfection of social machinery, and personal development; but it is the third—the work of education—he thinks the most important.[259] As the training that develops our character and brings us into harmony with others and with the universe at large, education, more than any other social ideal, is a good 'common to all', communicable and undiminished in sharing,[260] and it 'may even be said to be the chief end of life'.[261] Education is a broader process than simply formal institutions—Mackenzie insists, for example, 'that all citizens should have sufficient leisure to be able to give some cultivation to their whole nature as human beings, and not sink into the slavish position of being merely machines for the performance of particular services'[262]—it is also 'so essential to the life of a community that it can hardly be left exclusively to the efforts of private individuals. It needs a well-planned organisation; and it is naturally regarded as one of the functions of the State to provide this'.[263] Holding thus that 'a nation is bound to provide for its children the possibility of becoming good citizens', he argues that the aim is to develop intelligence rather than to

---

[255] Gordon and White, *Philosophers as Educational Reformers*, 73–4.
[256] Nettleship, 'Memoir', cxix. See also Green's lecture on 'The Work to be Done by the New Oxford High School', in his *Collected Works*, III.
[257] Gordon and White, *Philosophers as Educational Reformers*, 83–4.
[258] Gordon and White, *Philosophers as Educational Reformers*, 48.
[259] *Introduction to Social Philosophy*, 351.   [260] *Introduction to Social Philosophy*, 366.
[261] *Outlines of Social Philosophy*, 94.   [262] *Outlines of Social Philosophy*, 106–7.
[263] *Outlines of Social Philosophy*, 107.

impart specific information and skills, and that the elements of general culture should be easily accessible to all.[264]

John MacCunn's *The Making of Character*, subtitled 'Some Educational Aspects of Ethics', was published in 1900 in the Cambridge Series for Schools and Training Colleges (the same series that included Bosanquet's *Education of the Young in the Republic of Plato*) and enjoyed considerable success.[265] It is an extended discussion of the many factors—from heredity, to natural environment, to family, and society at large—that contribute to the formation of moral character. Indeed one aspect of the book is the relatively minor place given to institutions of formal instruction, such as schools, relative to the overall moral environment of our society. Opposing the view of individuals as 'mutually hostile human atoms'[266] which would leave our concern for one another inexplicable, MacCunn follows Caird in thinking that the unit from which development starts is the family member, whose concern may naturally be extended further outwards.

---

[264] *Introduction to Social Philosophy*, 354.
[265] It was reprinted eight further times until 1931, later impressions containing new material.
[266] *The Making of Character*, 106.

8

Idealist Logic

The investigation now turns to logic and although it has taken some time to reach this point in no way should that be thought to suggest that the subject was anything less than absolutely central to British Idealist thinking. There can be no understanding of the idealist movement as a whole which does not come to grips with their distinctive doctrines of logic, and very often where concepts or arguments appear problematic or implausible, the problem turns out to be a lack of proper understanding on our part of their underlying logic. It was argued earlier, of course, that the foundation to idealist philosophy lay in metaphysics, but if a good case can be made for saying the same thing about logic the two points should not be thought contradictory for, as will be seen, the Idealists did not distinguish sharply between these fields. Indeed, at a certain level they did not distinguish between them *at all*.

Nevertheless, a proper grasp of idealist logic is one of the hardest things for modern philosophers to attain. In large part this is due to the great success of twentieth-century logic, whose triumph has all but obscured the possibility of any other kind of logic. As a dominant religion tends to regard any other belief system as mere 'superstition' and not religion at all, modern logicians have difficulty even recognizing other approaches, doubtful whether they really qualify as 'logic'. The antidote to such myopia is an understanding of the history of logic which reveals a kaleidoscope of different ways to think about reasoning, a diversity of understandings of the very nature and purpose of 'logic' itself. Specifically one way to ease this problem of recognition is to appreciate that, just as in the early twentieth century modern symbolic logic burst onto the scene with a new method which ousted its predecessors, so too Idealism instituted its own 'logical revolution' overturning previous patterns of thought.

The story of British logic in the mid-nineteenth century is as little known as that of the idealistic logic which supplanted it, but may briefly be set out as follows.[1] It begins with Richard Whately, whose 1826 textbook, *The Elements of Logic*, did much to restore the subject from the neglect into which it had fallen. Separating it out from

---

[1] For greater depth see Gabbay and Woods, *Handbook of the History of Logic*, volume IV.

other extraneous topics such as method and psychology with which it had become entwined, Whately's conception of logic was a purely abstract one, though the syllogistic system he outlined was wholly traditional and Aristotelian. Continuing Whately's view of logic as a purely formal discipline unaffected by considerations of subject matter, more innovative was the logical system of Sir William Hamilton appended to his 1846 edition of the works of Thomas Reid. Popularized in contemporary textbooks and further developed by Thomas Spencer Baynes, Hamilton's formal system (which covered both inductive and deductive logic) is best known for its doctrine that predicates as well subjects may be quantified, according to which, for example, 'All As are B' can be read as either 'All As are all Bs' or 'All As are some Bs'. This approach had, however, a rival in Mill's *System of Logic* first published in 1843. Taking a much broader conception of the subject, Mill attempts to defend empiricism as the only possible source of knowledge outlining and defending the inductive method, not simply for the physical sciences, but also for the 'moral' (human) and 'formal' (logic, mathematics) sciences. As an investigation into our knowledge, Mill's conception of logic goes beyond the merely formal, but his key effort went into the attempt to show how supposed necessary truths—the central concern of the intuitionist or a priori view of human knowledge—may be accounted for by appeal to experience and association alone.

It was against this background that the Idealists put forward their innovative understanding of logic. Following initial explorations on the part of T.H. Green and Edward Caird, systematic development of the topic was first made by Bradley, whose *Principles of Logic* raised discussion of the subject to a new and higher level, but his was far from the last word, giving as it did the opportunity for Bosanquet to develop his own parallel system of logic, in harmony with Bradley's but at the same time critical of it and extending beyond its compass. In this chapter I examine these developments, leaving further growth in the discipline after 1900 to a subsequent chapter.

8.1 T.H. Green

The earliest example of idealist logic, a set of lectures given by Green[2] in 1874–5, present a critical commentary on the chief approaches of his own time, allowing us to see from the very start how the Idealists distanced themselves from their contemporaries. He divides existing logicians into two groups, those who regarded the subject as a study of the 'forms of thought' and those who regarded it as 'the science of knowledge'—but with neither is he able wholly to agree.

The first conception, that of logic as a purely formal science, as the investigation of what can be said of arguments without regard to their content, Green dismisses as an outmoded understanding which reached its height in the medieval world but which modern thought has now moved beyond. The barrenness of Aristotelian syllogistic

---

[2] For further details see J. Allard, 'Logic as Metaphysics'; P. Ferreira, 'Green's Attack on Formal Logic'.

was, it will be remembered, a point he had already pressed in his earlier essay on Aristotle.[3] With well-articulated principles and a venerable history, scholastic thinking is not, of course, *entirely* useless and Green admits that it has a certain practical value in analysing what is already known—for this reason it was useful to the Catholic Church in theological argument where the aim is to convict opponents of inconsistency—but it is of no use in trying to discover new truths about the world and for this reason, he argues, it has now been discarded by rationalists as well as by empiricists.

From this vantage point Green comes down hard on those, in his own day, whom he thought had failed to learn the lessons of the age and were attempting to re-establish formal logic as a *speculative* science, as an account that tries to describe the way in which we actually think and learn about the world. As typical of this tendency he focuses on the work of Hamilton and Mansel. According to their view, by abstracting from what is given to it in sense experience, the human mind has the capacity to construct concepts or (as Green terms them) 'attributes' which then, solely from their own definitions and without appeal to anything else, have the power to represent all objects of a given class. Given two such attributes, judgement is then understood as the claim that one is either contained in or excluded by the other, while reasoning explores more complicated inter-relationships between several such judgements. For instance, an individual may be thought of as contained in or excluded from a class because contained in or excluded from another class which itself contains or excludes the first.

Green raises various objections. In the first place, he questions whether the merely formal manipulation of fixed class definitions in this fashion really constitutes a *process* of thinking at all? Is not the 'result' of such thinking the same as its beginning?[4] The formal logician can hardly refute the charge of vacuity; indeed some of his analyses positively invite it. The inference from 'All men are mortal' to 'Some mortals are men', if not far, seems at least to travel *some* distance, but if on Hamilton's scheme we quantify the predicate so that our starting point reads 'All men = some mortals' even this minimal act of thought vanishes.[5] It might be suggested that there is at least process in so far as implicit contradictions or containments may, by this method, be made explicit, however Green objects that such transitions if they occur are not explained by any merely formal workings, but by something further and experiential. The demand that real thought must progress is one we shall meet again in Bradley.

The deeper source of this defect lies in the understanding taken of the relation between intuition or perception and conception. It is supposed that objects are first given in sense and only then 'taken up' in thought, but that is quite mistaken. For if we attempt to identify any such object, making sure to filter or abstract out anything in it that may be put down to later conceptualization, we find that it quite disappears in our hands. A book, to take a simple example, might seem an object of intuition, but 'all

---

[3] 'Philosophy of Aristotle', 56–9. See above p.83.
[4] 'Lectures on Logic', 163.
[5] 'Lectures on Logic', 164.

qualities in virtue of which I recognise the object as a book depend on its relations to objects not now presented in intuition at all',[6] and for Green (as we have already had occasion to discuss) the knowledge of relations is conceptual not intuitive. In the absence of such conceptually constituted relations nothing at all remains as presented, for even demonstrative notions like 'this', 'here', or 'now' indicate something within a field of experience related to, yet distinct from, its enduring subject of experience, matters which go beyond anything given in mere presentation. The key point is that a thing's reality, its individuality, lies in its universality, in its relation to all other things.[7] In holding individuality not incompatible with but vitally dependent on universality, Green puts forward here, not just a new sense of what it is to be an 'individual', but also transformation in the idea of the 'universal' which becomes that which brings together diversity within one whole, the many-in-one.[8]

Implicit in this conception of reality is a critique of the very notion of formal definition. It is a 'great mistake' to take a thought as something defined by a given 'bundle of attributes', as though that could give it a fixed and self-sufficient meaning without need to call on any wider background of concepts and experiences, for 'neither the thing as we at any time conceive it, nor the thing as we feel it, is the thing in the *fullness* of its reality,' urges Green.[9] Reality consists in relations, but the relational matrix around anything expands outwards indefinitely, with the result that our concept of it—if it is to be the concept of a real thing—must do so as well. Thought leads always beyond itself. Of course, there is a role for fixed definitions, allows Green, but these are of use 'only for rhetorical purposes' as expressing a temporary agreement or in *reductio ad absurdum* of an opponent's position.[10]

As well as attack its understanding of definition Green wishes also to reject the understanding of thought from which the theory starts. The notion that thought works by selection, by taking away from what is given in sensation, simultaneously increasing in both generality and abstraction, until in the end we are left with nothing but the notion of pure being in general, cannot but favour perception over thinking in the attempt to know reality. 'If the function of thought is abstraction, the highest idea (as that on which the function of thought has been most exercised) will have least reality: in short, the more we think, the less we shall know.'[11] But, suggests Green, a different understanding of thought, as a process that takes us from the abstract to the concrete, would reverse that ranking. It might be objected that surely knowledge begins in the sensory experience of real objects—the most concrete state of all. But although it is true that knowledge begins with experience of objects that are real, it is only

---

[6] 'Lectures on Logic', 168.
[7] 'Lectures on Logic', 189.
[8] These notions are further developed in the idea of the Concrete Universal. See Section 8.4.3 below.
[9] 'Lectures on Logic', 190.
[10] 'Lectures on Logic', 190.
[11] 'Lectures on Logic', 193.

in themselves that they are so. *For us*, the knowing subjects, in our first attempt to come up with a generic account of the knowing relation, they start as just 'something', 'the thing known', or 'mere being'—the most abstract condition of all.

In contrast to the formal line of Hamilton and Mansel, Mill's 'scientific' approach to logic concerns itself with the actual processes whereby we arrive at knowledge, with what today we would call scientific method. But while this for Green is the right overall line to take, the details of Mill's approach he finds quite wrong. Green's general criticisms of Mill flow from his attack on the empiricist tradition to which he belonged, while many of the more specific points he makes were picked up in greater detail by Bradley, but there is one central aspect of Mill's logic which Green criticizes—his account of necessary truth—that is worth our stopping to consider in more detail for the light it sheds on idealist logic.

As a dyed-in-the-wool empiricist, Mill attempts to understand alleged a priori truths such as mathematics and geometry as in fact very highly generalized descriptions of experience. This presents Green with an awkward dilemma, for insofar as Mill holds all judgements of one class and denies any great distinction between the a priori and the a posteriori he has Green's sympathy, but his attempt to explain such truths as the result of constantly repeated experience leaves Green unpersuaded. Where we simply universalize from past experience, necessity wholly eludes us, for however psychologically reinforced the result may be, it remains at root but a habit of expectation which might yet be disappointed. However, there is no need to seek refuge in some completely separate class of intuitive judgement, if we recognize that the process by which we establish such logically necessary maxims is no different really from the process by which we establish any other natural necessity, viz. passing beyond mere uniformity to ascertainment of the full range of conditions upon which the phenomena in question depends. All general truths are necessary in the same way, the only difference being that some depend on a smaller range of conditions than others—a geometrical figure may be circular without having any other properties, while for a physical body to be circular depends on the fulfilment of innumerable other conditions—making some negations appear more inconceivable than others. Whether any proposition is contingent or not, whether its negation is conceivable, is hardly to be answered by considering it in isolation, but rather by thinking about it in the situation in which it is known. Yet clearly a proposition relatively unconnected to its background can be overturned with little consequence, something which becomes harder and harder the more it is tied into the context known to condition it. In this way to say that a general proposition is wholly true, *unconditioned from outside*, and to say that its contradictory is inconceivable are, for Green, in the end one and the same thing, even if that is an ideal met only by the whole of knowledge itself.[12]

---

[12] 'Lectures on Logic', 264–5.

8.2 Edward Caird

Edward Caird's understanding of logic follows Kant's in drawing a contrast between transcendental and general logic, where the former studies the broad nature of thought insofar as it applies to known objects, while the latter treats it wholly formally without regard to *any* specific content. He is, however, more critical of purely formal schemes than Kant. Kant, he suggests, was only ever able to use these as a 'clue' to discovering the Categories because the logic he appealed to was not in fact completely formal, and subsequent developments have made very clear that, pursued rigorously, this approach culminates in wholly empty tautology, something which has no place in any actual judgement or inference.[13]

But if for its *rationale* he looked to Kant, for the *content* of any such 'transcendental logic' Caird's eyes turned to Hegel. Indeed, probably no one did more in the early years than he to establish in people's mind the connection between 'Idealist logic' and 'Hegelian logic'. Without worrying too much about the *details* of the Hegelian scheme, Caird tried to press on contemporary logical thought what he took to be the two key lessons from Hegel; the doctrine of *relative identity*, and the *relation between logic and metaphysics*.

At the very centre of the logic that Caird took from Hegel is his advocacy of *relative identity* or *identity-in-difference*, and a corresponding opposition to what he terms *abstract identity*. There is probably no concept more central to idealist thought, or more alien to modern philosophy. We shall meet with it in some detail as a relatively autonomous principle in the discussion of Bradley, but here we may note it in its first more Hegelian entrance, where it may be regarded as a combination of two different ideas: that *nothing is absolutely isolated* and that *all opposition implies unity*.

To take the first thought, it is tempting to suppose (with Bishop Butler) that everything is what it is and that's all there is to it. But Caird disagrees; what a thing is cannot be properly understood except in terms of what it is not. Not only must every predicate divide reality into two, its range and its complement, but even more profoundly, like day and night or male and female, the one could not have the nature it does had not its opposite the character it has. Caird's point here is, discernibly, a more Hegelian rendering of Green's thesis that everything is what it is through its relationality to that which is other than it.

Isolate a thing from all its relations, and try to assert it by itself; at once you find that you have negated it, as well as its relations. The thing in itself is nothing. The absolute or pure affirmation, just because it is absolute or pure, is its own negation. Referred to itself and itself only, it ceases to be itself; for its definition, that which made it itself, was its relation to that which was not itself.[14]

---

[13] *Critical Philosophy of Immanuel Kant*, I:335–8.
[14] *Hegel*, 162.

But (moving to the second thought) neither can we say that in order to understand the world all we need to grasp are the sum of its various contrasts and distinctions. For Caird denies that difference is even possible except against a backdrop of identity or union. There can be no sense in thinking things different from one another unless they can be brought together and compared. There can be no pure separation, opposition, or antagonism, for

a thing which has nothing to distinguish it is unthinkable, but equally unthinkable is a thing which is so separated from all others things as to have no community with them. . . . An *absolute* distinction by its very nature would be self-contradictory, for it would cut off all connection between things it distinguished. It would annihilate the relation implied in the distinction, and so it would annihilate the distinction itself. . . . All difference presupposes a unity, and is itself, indeed, an expression of that unity.[15]

In accepting these two ideas, Caird endorses the Hegelian principle that all thought proceeds dialectically. Every thought moves naturally towards its opposite, and every opposition points to a higher unity. But ascending to that unity, our new thought too must give rise to its opposite, setting the whole process off again in ever higher and more complex cycles. It is a process that can end only with 'the full analysis or differentiation of all the contents of the idea of self-consciousness, and their integration in that idea, as the unity of them all'.[16] It should be noted that not all Idealists found quite so close a connection between relative identity and dialectic; for example, Bradley accepts the former and largely rejects the latter, while McTaggart accepts the latter but rejects the former.

The conception of logic which holds today, and which held too when British Idealism emerged was that logic was a science sharply separated from metaphysics. Thought is something other than whatever is thought about, and so any study of its forms or developments tells us only about our thinking and not about reality itself. Caird rejects this view. The apparent separation of thought from its object is a natural characteristic of our first consciousness of things, he allows,[17] but in more developed mentality we can no longer regard thought and being as separate from each other.[18] Knowledge cannot be regarded as a one-sided affair, in which our thinking is moulded to bring itself into conformity with objects, but must instead be treated as a reciprocal business, in which it is just as necessary for the objects of thought to be changed in order to bring them into conformity with the principles of their apprehension.[19] But if the processes of cognition affects the very objects of knowledge, then its study (that is, logic) can no longer be regarded as something purely formal or analytic. Logic is as concerned with the content of judgement as any other science, focused on what we think and not just how we think it. Its interest in the world is, admittedly, more general than that of other sciences, but this is a difference in degree not in kind.

---

[15] *Hegel*, 135–6.   [16] *Hegel*, 164.   [17] 'Metaphysics', 486.
[18] *Hegel*, 15.   [19] 'Metaphysics', 487.

The claim that there is no ultimate distinction between logic and metaphysics is, of course, an Hegelian one. And ever since Hegel made it there have been those who have wanted to reject it as an absurd confusion between knowledge and reality. There were even (as we shall see a little later on) Idealists who wanted to reject it on these grounds. But in this connection it is important to note that Caird goes to great lengths to acquit Hegel (and himself) of charges of 'panlogicism', at least, in their most extreme forms. There may be no ultimate *distinction* between logic and metaphysics, but that is not at all the same thing as *reducing* reality to mere thought, or *deducing* it from thought. Against any such panlogicist attempt to turn the world into nothing but thought, Caird protests that, 'A thoroughgoing idealism will not fear to admit the reality of that which is other than mind and even, in a sense, diametrically opposed to it.'[20] While against the deductivist charge he urges that to suggest, 'Hegel tries "to spin the world out of his brain" . . . is against his own account of his method and also of his own practice,'[21] for he clearly acknowledges that 'nature is essentially different from pure self-consciousness, and that therefore logic can never by direct evolution of its categories anticipate the investigations of science'.[22]

The unity of knowing and being is the inevitable consequence of idealism, and there is no denying how alien a conception of logic it seems to modern philosophical understanding, but it must be remembered that neither the knowledge nor the being referred to are those familiar to us in ordinary experience—these are certainly quite different from each other—but rather the full and complete development of each. In this sense, subject and object are like paths which for all they might seem to go in opposite directions, in fact arrive at the very same destination.

8.3 F.H. Bradley

8.3.1 Bradley's conception of logic

If Green and Caird's contributions to the development of idealist logic have not received the attention they deserved, it is because they were overshadowed by the work of F.H. Bradley, whose 1883 masterpiece *The Principles of Logic* gave idealism a thorough and detailed treatment of all key aspects of the subject, securing the revolution in thought that Green and Caird had merely announced. And so it is to Bradley that we must now turn our attention.

Logic is a normative science and traditionally that has meant that it is characterized by a fixed *partition* between what it deems legitimate and what it deems illegitimate ways of thinking. By contrast, for Hegel, the various modes of thought form a *scale*, a ranking of forms from the barest and least adequate at one end up to the fullest and

---

[20] *Evolution of Theology in Greek Philosophers*, II:27.

[21] Jones and Muirhead, *Life and Philosophy of Edward Caird*, 168.

[22] 'Metaphysics', 439. For his attempts to avoid misconceptions of Hegel's philosophy of nature see *Hegel*, 195–202.

most true at the other. This scale is, moreover, something *teleological*, a fundamentally dynamic structure with each moment leading to and even bringing about the next, for thought needs to be understood as itself seeking something, even as possessing its own inner drive towards truth, consistency, and completeness; a drive that leads it onwards from unsatisfactory expressions to ever more satisfactory ones. In so far as it adopts a similarly hierarchical and dynamic understanding of the topic, Bradley's conception of logic was broadly Hegelian, although the pressing question of whether that developmental structure was a notional one or a real historical process was generally left unanswered.

This observation helps us to understand his conception of the *purpose* of logic which is, he claims, 'to set out the general essence and the main types of inference and judgment, and, with regard to each of these, to explain its nature and special merits and defects' for the 'degree in which the various types each succeed and fail in reaching their common end, gives to each of them its respective place and its rank in the whole body'.[23] The thought that it is the business of logic to classify and analyse types of thinking is familiar, less so that it should be given an evaluative role, scoring patterns of thinking for their relative effectiveness. But the point is important in so far as it highlights that for Bradley (as it had been for Green and Caird) logic is the science of *knowledge*; it is concerned with determining how adequate various forms of thought are to express and convey *truth*, something determined in part by the practice of thinking itself—thought in its very nature sets its own goals and critical standards—but something determined equally by the nature of reality.

There can be no dispute that Hegel exercised an absolutely central influence on Bradley's thinking about logic. In addition to the 'teleology of knowledge', this can be seen in such points as his advocacy of identity-in-difference, of concrete universals, of the view that association involves universals, of the distinction between genuine and spurious infinity, and of holistic coherentism as a standard for truth. On the other hand, however, *The Principles of Logic* is certainly not in any obvious sense an 'Hegelian' logic; its admission of inherent conceptual development does not take it so far as an a priori attempt to determine a hierarchical scheme of categories for thought, nor does it contain explicitly dialectical triads of reasoning. Indeed, in anticipation of the charge of discipleship Bradley announces in the book's Preface: 'Assuredly I think him a great philosopher; but I never could have called myself an Hegelian, partly because I cannot say that I have mastered his system, and partly because I could not accept what seems his main principle, or at least part of that principle. I have no wish to conceal how much I owe to his writings; but I will leave it to those who can judge better than myself, to fix the limits within which I have followed him.'[24]

Perhaps the greatest difference between Bradley's approach and that of the modern discipline, which virtually defines logic as a concern with the structural properties of

---

[23] *Principles of Logic*, 620.
[24] *Principles of Logic*, Preface, x. The 'main principle' here is Hegel's identification of thought and reality, the rejection of which we considered in Chapter 4.2.

thoughts, is that he had no interest in merely formal questions. Drawing out the message of Green and Caird, Bradley regards it as impossible to model logic on mathematics, and his use of symbols is as sparing as it is lacking in system. To his mind, little of logical interest depends on solely on form—for the ultimate test is always one of the adequacy of our scientific or philosophical thinking to fact or reality itself.

8.3.2 The general nature of judgement

The Principles of Logic begins with the topic of judgement. Though unfamiliar today, this starting point is quite deliberate and chosen in contrast, not only to the *sentence*— which as an essentially grammatical unit often fails radically to capture the underlying logical structure of the thoughts behind it—but also to the *proposition*. Propositions are rejected as illegitimate abstractions, too far removed from the realities of belief and knowledge to which they are supposed to contribute; for it is a key element of Bradley's view that judgement cannot be understood in isolation from the actual context in which it is made. Unlike a proposition, a judgement is an *act*, specifically a mental one.

Bradley describes judgement in the following way: 'Judgment proper is the act which refers an ideal content ... to a reality beyond the act.'[25] His thought is that in judgement we abstract out some aspect or feature of the world we encounter and assign it objective reference to some part or parts of reality; we characterize some object or other by predicating our ideas of it.

The word 'ideal' in the phrase 'ideal content' indicates to us that judgement involves the manipulation of ideas. But what are ideas? It is crucial to understand Bradley correctly on this matter. He distinguishes between two senses of 'idea'; between, as we might variously put it, the symbol and the symbolized, the image and its meaning, the psychological and the logical idea.[26] As individual psychical occurrences, ideas 'are facts unique with definite qualities ... the same in all points with none other in the world'.[27] They are particular existences which occur at specific times, determinate yet fleeting events in the ceaseless flux that is our inner mental history. But, Bradley goes on, these private mental events can have a meaning as well as a nature, the psychological ideas can come to be logical ideas also. This occurs when they are treated as *symbols*, as signs of an existence other than themselves. Indeed, he insists that, in the logical sense, 'Ideas are not ideas until they are symbols.'[28] Ideas for logic have meaning, they refer beyond themselves. They do not properly 'exist', in the manner of some event having a location in space and time, they are facts no more inside our heads than outside them,[29] rather they are universals such that more than one mind may without

---

[25] *Principles of Logic*, 10.
[26] *Principles of Logic*, 6; cf. Nettleship, 'Lectures on Logic', I:127.
[27] *Principles of Logic*, 4.
[28] *Principles of Logic*, 2.
[29] *Principles of Logic*, 7.

contradiction think one and the same thought. Making the point in a slightly different way Bradley distinguishes within any psychological idea between its nature or content and its actual existence—its 'what' and its 'that' as he calls them.[30] In becoming an idea for logic the content is separated notionally from its existence and referred to some other reality. In this way an idea, considered in its logical aspect, is, he thinks, a kind of 'parasite cut loose'.[31] It does not exist in its own right.

Bradley's purpose in drawing this distinction is to insist that logic is interested in ideas only as meanings and not as mental events, and in so claiming he is placing himself in sharp opposition to the British empiricist tradition. For that school, from Locke and Hume through to John Stuart Mill and Alexander Bain, regards ideas—the subject matter of logic—precisely as those things which psychological introspection reveals to us, the dated mental events which make up our private stream of consciousness. Yet Bradley sets himself against all this, urging that, 'In England at all events we have lived too long in the psychological attitude.'[32] This is a radical attack, and immediately, we can draw at least two corollaries distancing him from his psychologistic predecessors.

First of all, it follows that an idea is not, as traditional empiricism has often thought, some sort of a *copy* or *image* of what it represents. Ideas do not possess meaning by copying the objects or impressions which they signify, for they do not possess meaning *in their own right* at all. Rather they are *given* meaning by being made to stand for something else. This relation of representation is one of artificial custom, as can clearly be seen from one of the examples which Bradley uses to illustrate it, viz. the signification of flowers.[33] That some flowers stand for love and others for hope is clearly a matter of convention, not resemblance. Of course, images may come before the mind when we think or understand, and they may even resemble the object of our thought, but that is not what gives them their meaning.

A second corollary concerns our ideas of universals. For the traditional empiricist, who believes that our ideas copy our impressions, and that all of our impressions are of particular existences, our acquisition of universal concepts is a puzzle. The struggles of Locke and Berkeley on this issue are famous. Bradley, however, insists that it is simply a 'false assertion, that merely individual ideas are the early furniture of the primitive mind',[34] and so for him the problem is non-existent. Unlike mental images, logical ideas are not particular, either in their being or in their signification, but rather universal from the start.

Given that judgements are made up of ideas referred away to reality it might be wondered why Bradley's logic has only two main divisions (judgements and inferences), instead of the traditional three (terms, propositions, and inferences.) But this is quite deliberate and, in fact, even to speak of ideas in this way as the 'components' of a judgement is potentially misleading. For on Bradley's view judgements are prior to ideas. As logical entities, as things possessing truth or falsity rather than just

---

[30] *Appearance and Reality*, 143.   [31] *Principles of Logic*, 8.   [32] *Principles of Logic*, 2.
[33] *Principles of Logic*, 3.   [34] *Principles of Logic*, 35.

psychological existence, there can be ideas only in so far as they are signs, but ideas can be signs only in so far as actually used to refer to things, that is to say, in so far as they figure in the context of judgement. Thus although we may consider their nature, ideas have no independent reality, and there exists only a conceptual difference between them and the judgements in which they occur. In this way Bradley anticipates another widely accepted tenet of modern logic, the 'context principle'—the doctrine that a word has meaning only in the context of a proposition. Often attributed to Frege, this principle has in fact been held by others before him, including many of the British Idealists.[35]

If ideas are universals, it must be asked how we ever come to connect them with reality itself for that, to Bradley's mind, is something quite individual and particular. The answer to this question is: through sense perception. Bradley is insistent that it is in present, waking awareness, and in that alone, that we encounter reality. It is our sole point of cognitive connection with reality.[36] In consequence, our judgements, to be judgements of reality, must all of them be judgements of perception. Bradley insists that 'all judgements predicate their ideal content as an attribute of the real which appears in presentation'.[37] Sometimes this occurs directly, and we simply describe what is perceptually given to us. But, of course, Reality vastly exceeds our limited perception of it; it is never fully given, and often hardly given at all. And thus in most cases our judgements refer only *indirectly* to perceptually given reality. The qualitative content of our judgement 'is not attributed to the given as such; but by establishing its connection with what is presented; it is attributed to the real which appears in that given.'[38] Through a continuity with what is given, we attach it to one and the same world as that which we encounter in perception.

Perception plays two roles in Bradley's theory of judgement. Not only does it provide us (as we have just seen) with the reality to which our ideas are referred, but it serves too as the source from which those ideas are drawn. For all his insistence on their logical character, it is significant that Bradley never uses the term 'concept' to characterize the tools of our thinking. Just as at the next level up he rejects 'propositions' in favour of actual judgements, his ideas are not abstract Platonic entities, but retain a residual tie to the psychological, for the mental contents we abstract and refer away are precisely those given to us in actual perception. A logical idea or sign, he says, consists of a part or aspect of the content of some state, 'cut off, fixed by the mind and considered apart from the existence' of that state.[39]

---

[35] It can, for example be found in T.H. Green ('Lectures on Logic', 190), Nettleship ('Lectures on Logic', I:127), and Bernard Bosanquet (*Logic*, 9). See also Manser, *Bradley's Logic*, 60–4.
[36] 'We seem to find contact with reality and to touch the ground nowhere, so to speak, outside the presented' (*Principles of Logic*, 72).
[37] *Principles of Logic*, 50.
[38] *Principles of Logic*, 72.
[39] *Principles of Logic*, 4.

Because it typically involves numerous ideas, judgement is usually thought to possess a structure, and prior to the twentieth century this was usually thought to be sub-ject–predicate in form. That is to say, all judgements were held to attribute some predicate to some subject. However, Bradley rejects this account of the structure of judgement. He has two points of difference with it. First of all he argues that it is better to regard the whole judgement as a *single* ideal content attributed to the subject of the judgement. For a single judgement like 'The wolf eats the lamb' can be divided up in many different ways and, depending on the fineness of the divisions, be thought to contain any number of different ideas.[40] It makes more sense, thinks Bradley, to hold that 'any content whatever which the mind takes as a whole, however large or however small, however simple or however complex, is one idea, and its manifold relations are embraced in an unity'.[41] He rejects the received view that judgemental complexity may always be resolved into the same one subject–predicate scheme: 'S is P'. That is, says Bradley, a mere 'superstition'.[42] One strategy which he employs to make this point is simply to list types of propositions which it is very hard to analyse in this way, such as 'A and B are equal' or 'The soul exists'.[43] But he has a deeper, more theoretical, argument as well. Thinking about links, such as conjunction or the copula, which, it might seem, we use to combine our ideas or to link predicates to subjects, it needs to be remembered that these 'relations between the ideas are themselves ideal. They are not the psychical relations of mental facts. They do not exist between the symbols, but hold in the symbolized. They are part of the meaning and not of the existence.'[44] In the judgement 'The wolf is eating the lamb', the idea of 'eating' does not simply connect the two ideas, 'wolf' and 'lamb'. It is rather a third idea which along with them we refer to the situation itself. And the same holds with such words as 'and' and 'is'. They are not ancillary to our thoughts, but part of what we are thinking.

Bradley's second point of difference with the subject–predicate form of judgement follows from the first. Subject–predicate judgements can be regarded as attributing some idea or predicate to their subject. But if, as Bradley thinks, the whole judgement forms one single idea, of what subject is this idea being predicated? Instead of each picking out different subjects, Bradley suggests that all judgements should be read as having the same subject—reality as a whole, to which they attribute their entire content. Thus in the judgement 'S is P', instead of picking out S and saying that it is P, we say of reality as a whole that it is 'S–P ish', or as he later puts it 'Reality is such that S is P'.[45]

---

[40] *Principles of Logic*, 11.

[41] *Principles of Logic*, 12. The notion of 'one idea' here is, unlike the 'simple idea' of empiricism, the notion of something which, though unified, may be characterized also by internal complexity.

[42] *Principles of Logic*, 13, 21, 50.

[43] *Principles of Logic*, 13.

[44] *Principles of Logic*, 11.

[45] *Principles of Logic*, 630. Thus, in a sense, it turns out that all judgements are subject–predicate after all, but this must be understood as an external account of their *function*, not any sort of analysis of their *content* or *structure*.

In this sense all judgements have denotation and all are existential,[46] for they all refer to something that cannot fail to be present, namely, reality itself.

8.3.3 The dialectic between categorical and hypothetical judgements

It is natural to make a distinction between categorical and hypothetical judgements, between those which assert something unconditionally and those which make a claim subject to other factors. Bradley argues, however, that at a deeper level this distinction breaks down. Rather than mutually exclusive classes, it is the case at one and the same time both that all judgements are conditional and that all are categorical.

Given what we have seen so far, the second of these is easy enough to show. All judgements are categorical, for they all affirm something about reality. Each takes reality as a whole as its subject and asserts some quality of it.[47] Even hypothetical judgements are in a sense categorical; there must be something about reality itself that grounds the hypothesis made and, even if not explicitly so, this is yet as genuinely asserted as any other quality.[48]

But why should it be thought that all judgements are hypothetical? Bradley argues that even the most apparently categorical judgements, subjected to further analysis, turn out to be really conditional. Universal categorical judgements, for example, such as 'All animals are mortal' speak not simply of animals *now* but of past and future animals too, indeed, of all possible animals. 'We *mean*, "Whatever is an animal will die," but that is the same as *If* anything is an animal *then* it is mortal. The assertion really is about a mere hypothesis: it is not about fact.'[49] Similarly Bradley suggests that the assertion 'Equilateral triangles are equiangular' simply affirms that with one quality you inevitably get the other; it says nothing about where, when, or if such things are anywhere to be found.[50] Rather than a categorical assertion about a determinate set of referents, what the statement offers is simply a connection between ideas. This analysis of universal judgements will, of course, seem both familiar and natural to any one acquainted with modern logic.[51] It should be noted, however, that Bradley's position is not exactly the same as that adopted today. For he draws a sharp distinction between true universal statements and mere collective statements, restricting the hypothetical analysis to the former. Modern logic by contrast is unable to distinguish formally between nomic universals and accidentally true generalizations, but uses the same hypothetical analysis for both.

---

[46]   *Essays on Truth and Reality*, 426n.
[47]   *Principles of Logic*, 106.
[48]   *Principles of Logic*, 86–9.
[49]   *Principles of Logic*, 47.
[50]   *Principles of Logic*, 82.
[51]   Russell did acknowledge Bradley as a source of this idea (see 'On Denoting', 481), although on other occasions he credited Frege and Peano (*Our Knowledge of the External World*, 50) which rather annoyed Bradley (*Collected Works*, 5:207).

And a similar conclusion follows if we turn to apparently singular categorical judgements. Here Bradley offers two arguments. The first is one from what we might call the distorting incompleteness of perceptual selection. In this argument Bradley takes what might be considered the paradigm example of a singular categorical judgement, one in which we ascribe some character to presently given sensation, and objects that its claim to be categorical is undermined by the fact that it takes up only a fragment of the reality given in ordinary experience. Such judgements latch upon one part of what we perceive and characterize that, ignoring the rest. They give hostage to fortune in assuming they are entitled to make this selection, and their claim remains conditional on what they have done. The problem is that what they have done is far from neutral and as a consequence of their restricted attention they suffer from the twin defects of *incompleteness* and *distortion*. They are incomplete because they leave out the context, but nothing can exist without context, and so the judgement 'must always presuppose a further content which falls outside the fraction it offers. What it says is true, if true at all, because of something else. The fact it states is really fact only in relation to the rest of the context. It is not true except under that condition.'[52] But worse than this, by selecting something out of its context we distort it; just as a colour considered on its own in isolation can look quite different from how it does *in situ* alongside others. 'It was in the fact and we have taken it out. It was of the fact and we have given it independence. We have separated, divided, abridged, dissected, we have mutilated the given. And we have done this arbitrarily; we have selected what we choose. But if this is so, and if every analytic judgment must inevitably so alter the fact, how can it any longer lay claim to truth?'[53] Clearly what lies behind both of these arguments is a committed holism, such that everything is connected to everything else and everything depends on everything else.

Bradley's second main argument for the conclusion that singular judgements are conditional is quite different and working from the alleged impossibility of direct reference urges, in effect, that such judgements are not really singular at all. For if we can only speak in generalities, if we can only refer to properties and not individuals, then we can only speak about how things would be were they in fact instantiated, that is hypothetically. Of course, no one would deny that *many* ideas are general, but most philosophers have held that we have the power of singular thought in at least some cases. But this is something Bradley denies. For him *all* ideas are universal. 'Nothing in the world that you can do to ideas, no possible torture will get out of them an assertion that is not universal.'[54]

Bradley considers four classes of putatively singular expression, but finds none able to secure genuinely individual reference. Definite descriptions, such as 'the man wearing a pork-pie hat', or 'the third turning on the left' might seem to pick out unique individuals. But on reflection we see that they always could apply to other possible

---

[52] *Principles of Logic*, 97.   [53] *Principles of Logic*, 94.   [54] *Principles of Logic*, 63.

individuals as well. 'The event you describe is a single occurrence, but what you say of it will do just as well for any number of events, imaginary or real.'[55] We might think that time and space could come to our aid here. If 'the man wearing a pork-pie hat' could pick out more than one such individual, surely a further specification of the form, 'at place x and time t' can make good this gap? Bradley disagrees. He says, 'We must get rid of the erroneous notion . . . that space and time are "principles of individuation," in the sense that a temporal or spatial exclusion will confer uniqueness on any content.'[56] For in themselves points of space and time are utterly indistinguishable. It is only when 'the series is taken as one continuous whole, and the relations between its members are . . . fixed by the unity of the series'[57] that exclusion makes its appearance. A given item may be located *in* or *by* its context but cannot be picked out *from* its context. Moving to a third suggestion, it will be remembered that Mill, among others, thought that proper names were mere marks for individuals, that they had denotation but no connotation. But these Bradley rejects too as really universals.[58] A person would not get a name unless he were first recognized as distinct, continuing though change, and this is a matter of his nature or attributes.[59] But can we not at least pick out unique individuals using pure demonstratives, like 'this' or 'that'? Again Bradley disagrees. Demonstratives, he argues, rather than specific references are really the most general words of all, for anything whatever may be called 'this' or 'that'. He draws a distinction between what he calls 'this' and 'thisness'. The former is the felt unique encounter with reality—'unique, not because it has a certain character, but because it is *given*'[60]—the latter what we are left with when we try to think or express this fact, the generic property of being a unique individual, which applies to everything. A thing's 'stamp of uniqueness and singularity comes to it from the former and not from the latter,'[61] but all we can ever express is the latter.

These two main arguments (from the conditioned nature of perceptual abstraction and the impossibility of singular reference) together with his preferred analysis of general statements, Bradley takes to establish that *all* judgement is really hypothetical. The result is an important one, for it highlights a sense for him in which all judgement is limited and false, in which all falls short of the richer, seamless, unfenced whole that is given in feeling.[62] For if judgement is conditional reality most certainly is not.

8.3.4 The dialectic between identity and difference

As was noted above, although one ideal content referred to reality as a whole, a judgement need not be thought of as *without* internal structure or differentiation, and a question therefore arises over how its various pieces relate together to mean what they do. In answer to this, the notion of identity-in-difference which we met above in Caird was further developed by Bradley who argues that, as well as union between the hypothetical and the categorical, every judgement also expresses a combination of

---

[55] *Principles of Logic*, 63.   [56] *Principles of Logic*, 63.   [57] *Principles of Logic*, 63–4.
[58] *Principles of Logic*, 59–63.   [59] *Principles of Logic*, 61.   [60] *Principles of Logic*, 64.
[61] *Principles of Logic*, 65.   [62] See Chapter 4.2.4 above.

identity and difference; an identity-in-difference. As with Caird, Bradley arrives at this doctrine via the rejection of two extremes. It is represented as the only possible middle ground between the two poles that judgements may not occupy: complete identity and complete difference. To take the first, Bradley rejects as impossible the notion that there might be no difference whatsoever between the terms of a given judgement, a relation which he variously calls 'simple identity',[63] 'abstract identity',[64] or 'mere identity'[65] and symbolizes with an equals sign.[66] Nothing is just itself. As already noted, the idea here comes from Hegel, and Bradley is quite explicit in acknowledging the debt,[67] but it is probably more familiar to contemporary logicians from Wittgenstein who in his *Tractatus* argues that a perfect language would have no use for the identity sign, since an identity statement does not tell us anything either about the world or about our language.[68] However, we should not be misled into thinking that Bradley's claim is simply one about the sign of *identity*. Rather it is a point about the identity and/or difference between the elements of a judgement, however the judgement itself may choose to join them. For if '$A = A$' is vacuous, the same holds of such judgements as 'A and A', 'A or A', 'If A then A', 'A only if A', or 'A is a-ish'. At times Bradley seems to imply that such abstract identities are false, but his deeper meaning seems to be that they are simply nonsense. $A = A$, he says, 'sins against the very form of judgment'.[69] In any judgement there must be a movement of thought or else nothing is *said*.[70] Bare identity, he thinks, could never satisfy the intellect's demand that something at least must be asserted.[71]

But not only does Bradley reject judgements of abstract identity, he equally—and much more controversially—rejects any judgement of what he calls 'mere difference'.[72] Any attempt to combine in thought elements with nothing in common is ruled out as impossible. Why? This doctrine might be thought to come from Hegel also, for certainly Hegel says something very much like it (as the antithesis for which his discussion of identity forms the thesis).[73] But, unlike the case of abstract identity, Bradley never acknowledges such a debt, nor is it especially helpful to see Hegel as his source.

---

[63] *Principles of Logic*, 374.

[64] *Principles of Logic*, 146.

[65] *Principles of Logic*, 373.

[66] *Principles of Logic*, 25.

[67] *Principles of Logic*, 14. See Hegel, *The Science of Logic*, II:37–43 and *Hegel's Logic*, 165–8.

[68] *Tractatus Logico-Philosophicus*, §5.33.

[69] *Principles of Logic*, 141.

[70] 'Thought most certainly does not demand mere sameness, which to it would be nothing . . . if the law of contradiction forbade diversity, it would forbid thinking altogether' (*Principles of Logic*, 50); cf. *Appearance and Reality*, 508; *Principles of Logic*, 25, 371–2.

[71] The most common response to the suggestion that statements of identity have no place in logic is, of course, that taken by Frege in his distinction between the sense and reference of a term: shared reference need not be trivial if there exists also a difference in sense. Bradley rejects this distinction, however (*Principles of Logic*, 642–3).

[72] *Principles of Logic*, 373.   [73] See Hegel, *The Science of Logic*, II:43–58 and *Hegel's Logic*, 168–75.

One crucial element for this view (which will be considered below) revolves around his theory of negative judgement but another (which may be considered here) stems from his understanding of what we might call the *powers* of thought. Thought itself (he says) can never make a conjunction between distinct elements—it has not the resources to do so—it merely reports the conjunctions it finds. Matters would be fine, he suggests, 'if thought in its own nature possessed a "together," a "between," and an "all at once."'[74] but 'thought can of itself supply no internal bond by which to hold them together'.[75] 'The intellect has in its nature no principle of mere togetherness.'[76] Where we are faced with a conjunction of complete differences, a purely external connection, there seems no scope in reality to *think* such a union. All we can apprehend is brute combination, without basis or explanation. An external 'and' says Bradley 'does but conjoin aliens inexplicably . . . there is in the end neither self-evidence nor any "because" except that brutally things come so.'[77] He compares it to the mechanical view of the world, and objects that such a union is 'groundless' or 'without reason'.[78] At times this looks like some sort of appeal to sufficient reason, and certainly that accusation has been made,[79] but Bradley also presents it as some sort of law of thought. Unless there is some ground or point of union, he seems to be saying, thought cannot bring anything together. It cannot be *satisfied*. That, he tells us, is just how thought works: 'you are left in short with brute conjunctions where you seek for connexions, and where this need for connexions seems part of your nature'.[80] Just thinking of A and thinking of B is not the same as thinking of A and B, but the only way we can significantly think 'and', the only way we can give that thought any content, is to find a point in common, and that is why 'an identity must underlie every judgment'.[81]

Combining, then, the impossibility of abstract identity with the impossibility of mere difference, Bradley takes himself to have shown that all judgement must express an identity-in-difference. But what does it really *mean* to say that all judgements must occupy a middle ground between identity and diversity, that all must assert a *point* of identity between differences? It is possible to distinguish between a number of different senses in which this thesis might be taken.

It can be read as the harmless enough point that a thing cannot be self-identical without being different from other things; being oneself and being distinct from others are but two sides of the same notion. Another way to read Bradley's thesis here is to see

---

[74] *Appearance and Reality*, 504.

[75] *Appearance and Reality*, 504.

[76] *Appearance and Reality*, 511.

[77] *Appearance and Reality*, 502.

[78] *Appearance and Reality*, 501. 'I understand by an external relation to mean a mere conjunction for which in the quality there exists no reason whatever' (Bradley, *Collected Works*, 4:216).

[79] For example by Russell, *Philosophical Essays*, 143.

[80] *Essays on Truth and Reality*, 115. 'Thought demands to go *proprio motu*, or, what is the same thing with a ground and reason' (*Appearance and Reality*, 501), 'to be satisfied my intellect must understand . . . my intellect can not simply unite a diversity' (*Appearance and Reality*, 509).

[81] *Principles of Logic*, 28.

it as one about the unity of a *judgement*. There must exist something which binds many ideas into one thought. There can be no thought without parts or multiple contents, but they only function as contents at all in the space of one judgement. Much of what Bradley says seems best understood in a third sense: the coming together of *things* into union or association with each other. Thus he says, 'Every judgement makes a double affirmation, or a single affirmation which has two sides. It asserts a connection of different attributes, with an indirect reference to an identical subject; or it directly asserts the identity of the subject, with an implication of the difference of its attributes.'[82] For example, the statement 'Dogs are mammals' he thinks should be read as saying that any subject which has the property of being a dog has also the property of being a mammal.[83] Another reading would distinguish between qualitative and numerical identity, to take the thesis as telling us that qualitative identity is compatible with numerical diversity (i.e. many different things can all have the same property) and that numerical identity is compatible with qualitative diversity (i.e. one and the same thing may possess many different attributes). These four interpretations of Bradley's identity-in-diversity thesis each break it down into some species or other of ambiguity—judgements are held identical in one respect, but different in another. However, it is unclear in the end that this is correct. For we can identify a fifth sense of the thesis—as a claim that things must be in the same respect and at the same time, both identical and diverse—which however puzzling and seemingly contradictory, has textual support. Bradley insists that, 'Identity and difference . . . are inseparable aspects of one complex whole. They are not even 'discernible', if this means you can separate them in idea, so as to treat one as remaining itself when the other is excluded. And the whole is emphatically not a 'synthesis', if that means it can be mentally divided.'[84] Statements such as this or the paradoxical claim that, 'It takes two to make the same',[85] tempt us to understand him in this fifth stronger sense.

If the doctrine of identity-in-difference is hard to interpret precisely, it is hard also to locate its proper sphere of application. Although we have considered it in connection with *judgement*, in Bradley's mind it is a thesis which can just as easily be applied to other fields. For example, since he finds no sharp distinction between judgement and inference, the result can be extended outwards to *inference*—inference requires a point of identity, but also a genuine difference.[86] It can also be contracted inwards to units smaller than whole judgements, viz. individual *ideas*. Ideas too express identity-in-difference. Here it is helpful to remember Bradley's claim that there is no simple answer to the question whether any content held in mind—'wolf-eating-lamb' was the example he used—constitutes one idea or several.[87] Thirdly the doctrine finds its way into the issue of universals, to which we now turn. A true universal—what Bradley calls a 'concrete universal'—is also, he argues, a species of identity-in-difference.

---

[82] *Principles of Logic*, 174. [83] *Principles of Logic*, 178. [84] *Collected Essays*, 295–6.
[85] *Principles of Logic*, 141. [86] *Principles of Logic*, 288, 460. [87] *Principles of Logic*, 11.

8.3.5 The concrete universal

The notion of a concrete universal was not, of course, new to Bradley. It had its origins in the philosophy of Hegel, and found its way into his philosophy via the thought of several of Hegel's successors.[88] The first explicit introduction of the idea in Bradley's writing occurs through a consideration of the traditional doctrine of the inverse variance of extension and intension. According to this doctrine, the wider any term's extension, the narrower its intension. For example, as we move from dachshund to dog to mammal to animal we pick out larger and larger classes, but say something less and less specific.

Bradley rejects wholly this understanding. He describes it as either 'false or frivolous'.[89] It is frivolous in so far as it describes merely a psychological accident about how we may visualize things. As a matter of psychological fact about human mental images, it may be that the more universal they become the more detail we find that we have to drop from them, or, as he puts it elsewhere, the more 'schematic' they become. But this paucity, belonging as it does to the psychology of images, does not make ideas logically any the thinner. It is simply beside the point. The doctrine is frivolous too, in so far as it reports the uninteresting fact that *if* you arrange ideas pyramidically, subtracting from each layer below to form the layer above, then of course as you rise you will find yourself saying less and less.[90] But the more important question is whether our ideas really *are* arranged in this way. And Bradley is perfectly certain they are not, making the doctrine in fact quite false. The properties used to differentiate species are never so distinct from the property that characterizes their genus itself, which rather collects and sums them. Were universals formed by mere subtraction, the doctrine of inverse relation would be correct. But in fact genuine universals are *concrete*; for content increases rather than decreases the more universal our ideas become.

Bradley's paradigm example of a concrete universal is the individual.[91] A particular object, and especially a living individual, is universal, thinks Bradley, in the sense that it is spread out in the world, that it brings together under one label a host of elements that from another point of view seem to be different or distinct. The union could be either of diversity at a time (what unites all an individual's properties together as his or hers) or of diversity over a time (the reason why properties held or acts performed at different times are still properties or acts of the very same person), but either way it is a bringing of many diverse elements together into one unified whole. Such a union of diverse predicates is to be contrasted with one formed by abstraction. For in the latter case we pull out what is

---

[88] *Hegel's Logic*, §163; Lotze, *System of Philosophy: Logic*, Bk I, ch.1, §§15, 31; Sigwart, *Logic*, §42 (268–70). The importance of the notion to Hegel was stressed by both Stirling, *Secret*, xxii; and Wallace, *Prolegomena*, 221. For a discussion of the extent to which the idea may genuinely be found in Hegel see Stern, 'Hegel, British Idealism and the Curious Case of the Concrete Universal'.

[89] *Principles of Logic*, 170.

[90] *Principles of Logic*, 172–4.

[91] *Principles of Logic*, 187–8.

held in common by many different individuals, bringing these shared features under one label. We end up with a union of similar predications rather than of differing ones.

The idea that universals are abstract, no doubt gains much of its support from contrasting them with bare particulars, and it is not unconnected that Bradley attacks these also. Experience is not, as the empiricists think, an encounter with bare particulars which we then overlay with concepts. Atomic particulars are as unreal an abstraction from surrounding context as are universals—a 'that' without a 'what' is as impossible as a 'what' without a 'that'. On Bradley's account both particulars and universals arise simultaneously from the application of thought to immediate experience; an inevitable pair, neither ultimately valid nor capable of working on its own. His thought here runs close to that of Green.

8.3.6 Negative judgement

All that has been said thus far concerns judgement in general, but there are a great many points that can be made about specific varieties of judgement to which Bradley turns after his initial more general discussion. One of the most important types (in the sense that what he says here affects many other issues) is that with which he begins, namely negative judgement.[92] There are two main components to his view.

First of all he argues that negative judgements stand 'at a different level of reflection'[93] from affirmative ones. In affirmative judgement we attribute content to reality directly, but for negation there must first be 'the suggestion of an affirmative relation'[94] which we go on to deny. If I maintain that the tree is not yellow, this must be understood as rejecting the suggestion that it is. What is repelled is 'the suggested synthesis, not the real judgment'[95] so Bradley is not maintaining that there must be or have been some actual proposal or belief which is then denied; his point is a logical rather than a psychological or historical one.[96] In this thesis Bradley is quite at odds with most modern logicians who see positive and negative propositions as standing at the same level. A negation sign reverses the truth value of any proposition, but since not-not-P is equivalent to P, any negative may be rewritten as positive or any positive as a negative.[97]

Secondly, Bradley argues that negative judgements presuppose a positive ground.[98] For there exist no negative facts and, in consequence, there can be no 'mere' or 'bare' denial.

If not-A were solely the negation of A, it would be an assertion without a quality, and would be a denial without anything positive to serve as its ground. A something that is only not something

---

[92] For more details see Stock, 'Negation: Bradley and Wittgenstein'.
[93] *Principles of Logic*, 114.
[94] *Principles of Logic*, 114.
[95] *Principles of Logic*, 116.
[96] A.J. Ayer misinterprets Bradley in precisely this way ('Negation', 798).
[97] See Ayer, 'Negation', 804–8.
[98] *Principles of Logic*, 114.

else, is a relation that terminates in an impalpable void, a reflection thrown upon empty space. It is a mere nonentity which cannot be real.[99]

Instead negation must be understood as working on the basis of something positive. If a negative judgement is true of some reality it must be because that reality has some positive feature incompatible with whatever it is that is being denied. The tree is not yellow because it is some other colour instead. Although this ground is not made explicit—it is 'undetermined',[100] 'unknown' to us,[101] even 'occult'[102]—negation makes sense only if we think of it as in this way grounded in the assertion of some such positive contrary. In this way Bradley reconciles negative judgement with his overall conception of judgement in general as always referring some content to reality. The thought that there could be no negative facts has met with wider approval in modern logical thinking, though fewer have followed precisely Bradley's way of securing this.

It might be thought here that Bradley has simply confused the contradictory and the contrary. But that would be unfair. The distinction remains. Insofar as logic needs to distinguish between the contrary and the contradictory, Bradley describes the contradictory as 'the general idea of the contrary. Not-A for example is any and every possible contrary of A.'[103] Not-A 'is a general name for any quality which, when you make it a predicate of A, or joint predicate with A, removes A from existence. The contradictory idea is the universal idea of the discrepant or contrary.'[104] But although possible in this way to distinguish them, for the most part Bradley does not bother to do so, finding the contrast of little moment.[105]

The reduction of negation to positive contrariety is of great significance in Bradley's thinking. It is, for example, a crucial plank in explaining the rejection of bare conjunction that we encountered above. For Bradley urges that the bringing together in judgement of mere difference is something that may be dismissed as contradictory. Indeed, it is not simply as a species or example of contradiction but, Bradley suggests, the very essence of contradiction itself. Contradiction is precisely the attempt to bring together two things with nothing in common.[106]

The suggestion that difference and contradiction are identical is a strange one—for *prima facie* they do not seem to be the same at all—and in order to properly understand it we must appreciate that Bradley is exploiting a distinction between appearance and reality. For Bradley, at the level of ultimate reality there are no genuinely contradictory, that is, genuinely different, predicates. Contradiction is a theoretically limiting case that never in fact happens.[107] This might seem obvious, something we could all agree on, nothing more than the principle of non-contradiction. But we need to see that

---

[99] *Principles of Logic*, 123.   [100] *Principles of Logic*, 110.   [101] *Principles of Logic*, 117.
[102] *Principles of Logic*, 120.   [103] *Principles of Logic*, 146.   [104] *Principles of Logic*, 123.
[105] *Appearance and Reality*, 500.
[106] 'If you merely conjoin it with something outside that is different and not itself, this in principle is contradiction' (*Essays on Truth and Reality*, 227n).
[107] 'Nothing in itself is opposite and refuses to unite.... There are no native contraries' (*Appearance and Reality*, 510–11). 'In the end nothing is contrary nor is there any insoluble contradiction' (*Appearance and Reality*, 505).

Bradley's understanding of the matter is more radical than our own. Our view would be that while there are many predicates which *might* contradict, nowhere are they instantiated in any way such that they *do* so, nowhere are they co-instantiated. Bradley's view by contrast is that there simply are no contradictory predicates. Nowhere, even in possibility, can we find two utterly different, or contrary, predications. This then is a far more radical reading of the principle of non-contradiction, but Bradley's fundamental idealism precludes any deep separation between what might be and what actually is, between the ideal and the real.

Faced with apparent opposites, rather than take the milder course of denying that they really are united, Bradley pursues the more radical option of denying that they really are opposite.[108] But, of course, there certainly *seem* to be such predicates, a fact which Bradley must explain. He suggests that the appearance of contradiction arises where we take an incomplete or insufficiently developed view of the predicates or the subject in which they are supposed to be united. In general, predicates merely seem to be contrary when, 'we have abstracted from them and from the subject every condition of union'.[109] We seem faced with an insoluble contradiction because the things appear incapable of further analysis.[110] But in fact, suggests Bradley, on spelling out their full conditions, apparent contraries or discrepants may turn out to be after all just different and perfectly concordant. 'If one arrangement has made them opposite, a wider arrangement may perhaps unmake their opposition, and may include them all at once and harmoniously.'[111] The so-called 'opposites' turn out to be not really opposite at all, but rather complementary.[112] Some examples may help us here. Bradley himself observes that if we narrow the existence of a thing down to one moment in time then it cannot be in two places, or that if we regard the soul as some sort of indivisible unity then it cannot affirm and deny at the same time. But why insist on such limitations?[113] Alternatively we might consider the fact that a painting can be beautiful (in daylight) and ugly (in artificial light), or the fact that dynamite is combustible (when dry) and non-combustible (when wet).[114] Similarly on a simple (timeless) conception of an object colour predicates are incompatible, but once we widen our perspective to include duration they become compatible.[115]

---

[108] '"Opposites will not unite, and their apparent union is mere appearance." But the mere appearance really perhaps only lies in their intrinsic opposition' (*Appearance and Reality*, 500).

[109] *Essays on Truth and Reality*, 271.

[110] *Appearance and Reality*, 505.

[111] *Appearance and Reality*, 500.

[112] They are 'moments which would be incompatible if they really were separate, but, conjoined together, have been subdued into something within the character of the whole' (*Principles of Logic*, 149). Bosanquet's view on this matter is identical to Bradley's. He says 'no predicates are intrinsically contrary to one another. They only become so by the conditions under which they are drawn together' (*Principle of Individuality and Value*, 223).

[113] *Appearance and Reality*, 506.

[114] Ferreira, *Bradley and the Structure of Knowledge*, 102–4.

[115] Wollheim, *F.H.Bradley*, 147.

Apparent contrariety is thus resolved into difference, but this should not be thought the end of the matter. For (to Bradley) *complete* difference is no more acceptable than, indeed, no different from, contradiction. And so Bradley argues that where predicates seem to be quite different—whether they strike as explicitly contradictory or not—this too must be regarded as but an appearance; something which occurs only because we have ignored some wider context or point of union and which, on closer examination, can be removed. Bradley insists that wherever things seem completely different there will always be in fact a point in common. Again, an example may help: black and cold are different, but it may well be that a thing's blackness and coldness are found to come from a common source. It is in the merely apparent nature of contrariety and difference that we find the key to understanding Bradley's view of Hegel's dialectic. Dialectic is not in Bradley's thinking, as certain critics have taken it to be, some sort of denial of the law of contradiction, it is rather an exploitation of the point that elements which seem at first irreconcilable may in a wider perspective in fact be combined.[116]

Thus armed with this understanding of the distinction between appearance and reality, Bradley is able to hold that while, at the level of ultimate reality as a limiting case nowhere in fact realized, contradiction is the same as complete difference, at the level of appearance, we may yet distinguish between apparent contradiction and apparent difference.[117] Which of these we meet with is a function of the kind and degree of abstraction we make. Roughly, the narrower our view of a subject the more pairings of predicates will seem contrary, but as we widen our view the more they will seem to be merely different.

8.3.7 The nature of inference

The second great topic of Bradley's logic, to which he turns in the second half of the *Principles*, is the question of inference. However, it must be noted from the start that Bradley finds no great gulf between judgement and inference, for judgement itself he regards as an inferential process. Within every judgement there are deeper levels of meaning and implication. Sometimes (as we have already seen in the cases of judgements of sense or negative judgements) the analyses which Bradley offers make this latent structure quite explicit, but it is something that holds true, in some measure, for all judgements; since all judgements are made subject to conditions.

Perhaps nowhere more than in his discussion of inference does it become manifest that Bradley is not a formal logician. It is common to distinguish between formal and material inferences—between inferences which do not depend on the particular subject matter of what their propositions describe and those which do—and to hold that logic considers only the former. However, Bradley places no such restriction on himself. He includes under the heading of inference any extension beyond what is

---

[116] *Principles of Logic*, 149, 410.

[117] It is at this level of appearance that Bradley insists that 'differents and discrepants should never be confused' (*Principles of Logic*, 146).

simply given to us in perception, whether formal or material in character. Inferences such as 'Charles I was a king, he was beheaded, so a king may be beheaded' or 'Today is Monday so tomorrow is Tuesday', or scientific inferences, cannot in any straightforward way be rendered formal but are not for that reason excluded from consideration; for the subject matter of logic is simply *true reasoning* and therefore includes any systematic movement in thought from one truth to another. Of course we may not go *outside* of our premises to establish any conclusion, for the activity then would simply not be *inference*—which is essentially the derivation of a result from a source.[118] But inference is a matter of developing connections and relations to ideas beyond that source. And these, though internal to our initial content, may lie hidden or implicit within it; outside our explicit cognitive apprehension. For this reason valid inferences cannot be captured in merely formal structures. It is not possible to draw anything except a relative distinction between form and content,[119] while the possibilities of useful inference exhaust any fixed list of schemata.[120] This is not to exclude absolutely considerations of form. Bradley freely admits that inferences fall into *types*; we cannot reason from mere particulars, and so any inference must in principle be applicable in other imaginable cases.[121] But no distinction which we might draw between form and matter could ever be anything other than relative, such that on a different framework what was material could be presented as formal.[122] Moreover, thinks Bradley, such distinctions are in the end rather useless for, even if we were to make and stick with them, they can never provide us with a hard and fast set of forms or models adequate to cover all valid inferences. 'It is impossible that there should be fixed models for reasoning; you can not draw out exhaustive schemata of valid inference.'[123] That there could be such a fixed schedule is, he says, simply not possible because in the end we must always be defeated by 'the endlessness of the field'.[124] Rather than distinguish different types of inference, or separate out correct from incorrect inferences, as many logicians have sought to do, Bradley's real concern in the *Principles* is to establish the general nature of inference.

Bradley begins his discussion of inference with three adequacy conditions on any acceptable theory, although perhaps rather than three distinct points they may better be regarded as three aspects of a single idea. First of all he notes that there is a difference between reasoning and mere observation; reasoning is something active that we *do*, not something passive that happens to us. If a truth is inferred, it is more than simply seen.[125] Inference is more than one thought prompted or followed by another, with the conclusion coming to us irresistibly from without. But although we *make* inferences, neither is this some arbitrary or capricious act on our part, rather we are led or constrained in doing so by reality itself; we *discover* rather than invent the result of our inference. Secondly, he notes that in inference we pass from one truth already possessed

[118] *Principles of Logic*, 521.   [119] *Principles of Logic*, 524, 532.   [120] *Principles of Logic*, 521.
[121] *Principles of Logic*, 522.   [122] *Principles of Logic*, 532.   [123] *Principles of Logic*, 268.
[124] *Principles of Logic*, 268.   [125] *Principles of Logic*, 245.

to a further truth. The conclusion is thus not self-existent but in an important sense dependent on its premise or premises.[126] Thirdly, inference must convey some new piece of information.[127] It must do more than repeat a part or the whole of the premises. Thus 'A therefore A' or 'A and B therefore A' do not count as inferences. This demand for some *movement* on thought's part, found also in his view of judgement and in Green's logic, is a requirement not repeated in modern logic which would regard patterns such as these as valid inferences, albeit dull and pointless ones.

On the basis of these conditions, Bradley then proposes a general model of inference. 'Every inference combines two elements; it is in the first place a process, and in the second a result. The process is an operation of synthesis; it takes its data and by ideal construction combines them into a whole. The result is a perception of a new relation within that unity.'[128]

Although there can be produced no list that would exhaust every possible inference, there are, Bradley holds, two general conditions which may be laid down to hold on them all. First there is the necessity of an identical point. He says, 'It is impossible to reason except on the basis of an identity.'[129] Bradley's idea is that premises can only be combined where there is a 'common point'[130] or 'centre of identity'[131] between them. And he means here an numerical identity, not merely some similarity or likeness.[132] There must, of course, exist also difference between them—mere repetition would be pointless—but were the premises wholly different it would simply not be possible to think them together in one construction.[133] In large part Bradley is repeating here thoughts we considered above when we looked at the impossibility of judgements of bare conjunction; what holds of two elements in a judgement holds equally of two premises in an inference. Bradley's second condition—the necessity of at least one universal premise,[134] when one reflects upon its basis, is really not much more than a reapplication of the first. For he defends it on the grounds that if there must be a term common to the premises, a single content in multiple different contexts, that is universal, and this must figure in at least one of the premises.[135]

Bradley first attempt provides him with a good initial account of inference, but when he returns to the subject in Book III of the *Principles* he finds a number of deficiencies with this basic model. He notes that inference does not always result in a new relation, that sometimes what we perceive as the conclusion is instead a new quality. In this connection he uses the example of sailing around some land and, realizing that one has arrived back at one's starting point, concluding that the land is in fact an island.[136] He worries too about mathematical inferences. Arithmetical operations 'produce new results; they are ideal operations which give conclusions, and justify what they give', and so 'they are palpable inferences'.[137] But a calculation

[126] *Principles of Logic*, 245.
[127] *Principles of Logic*, 246.
[128] *Principles of Logic*, 256.
[129] *Principles of Logic*, 285.
[130] *Principles of Logic*, 285.
[131] *Principles of Logic*, 389.
[132] *Principles of Logic*, 286.
[133] *Principles of Logic*, 288.
[134] *Principles of Logic*, 285.
[135] *Principles of Logic*, 294.
[136] *Principles of Logic*, 396.
[137] *Principles of Logic*, 401.

like $5 + 5 = 10$ 'establishes no relation between the terms of the premises. On the contrary the relation, which appears in the conclusion, has one terminal point which never appeared in the data at all.'[138] A third type of inference to slip the net is, he suggests, inference with only one premise.[139] For example, we may infer, 'If A then C'. This might be shorthand for, 'If anything is B it is C, but here A is B, and therefore it is C', but no such premises need ever come before the mind. Dialectical inference too seems to escape the model.[140] This he describes as a passage of thought in which one idea is felt insufficient and supplemented by a contrary one. In allowing both sides of dialectical scheme here to be positive, Bradley disagrees with more standard interpretations of dialectic, which emphasize negation and call for a unity of opposites.[141] But, however understood, it is a pattern of inference that cannot be accommodated on the original model. Last of all Bradley also rethinks the crucial role of identity in the operation of inference. Where before he had insisted there must always be a common centre, his account is modified to accommodate inferences with no explicit centre. He continues to hold that a centre can be found for every inference, but he now allows that instead of being explicitly stated the centre of identity may be implicit, something we have to extract by a process of analysis or synthesis. For example, in the case of comparison we can only say that A is like B by extracting from A and B some property x which they both share.[142]

Reflecting on these deficiencies in his first account Bradley proposes both a new criterion for inference and a new model of how it works. The criterion is *necessity*. He suggests that 'wherever we have necessary truth there is reasoning and inference'.[143] The thought behind this criterion is that in inference we are always given some 'because' to our 'why?', some reason why what is the case must be the case, explanation constituting the underlying significance of necessity.

Bradley develops his improved model of what happens in inference in terms of what he calls *ideal experiment*. He loosens his initial specification suggesting that in inference, 'no matter what the operation may be, there is always some operation. This operation is an ideal experiment upon something which is given, and the result of this process is invariably ascribed to the original *datum*'.[144] The term 'ideal experiment' conjures up the more modern term 'thought experiment', with which it has indeed much in common. It is a mental operation in which we take thoughts or ideas and let them evolve under their own logic. It differs from mere imagination in that the result is determined not by us but by the way things are. It is even somewhat unpredictable. Yet unlike a concrete experiment in the world that involves particular things, 'This process is ideal, in the sense that it advances on the strength of a connection between universals.'[145]

---

[138] *Principles of Logic*, 404.   [139] *Principles of Logic*, 407.   [140] *Principles of Logic*, 408ff.
[141] *Principles of Logic*, 410.   [142] *Principles of Logic*, 461.
[143] *Principles of Logic*, 394; cf. *Principles of Logic*, 531.   [144] *Principles of Logic*, 431.
[145] *Principles of Logic*, 441.

8.3.8 Mistaken views of inference

If in its positive presentation Bradley's theory of inference can begin to seem a bit vague, more teeth are found if we consider those elements in what other writers have said about inference which he *opposes*. We may begin with his critique of traditional syllogistic logic. He strongly rejects the claim that all valid arguments can be put in syllogistic form, together with the related notion that in all inference we find a major and a minor premise. Bradley has a two-fold strategy. In the first place he simply points out that there exist valid inferences falling outside this scheme.[146] But he has deeper worries too. He complains that the principle of class inclusion (upon which syllogism is based) commits a *Petitio Principii*. For the statement 'All men are mortal', read as a statement about a collection, already contains the conclusion we go on to draw from it, that 'John is mortal'. It therefore yields no new knowledge, violating the third criterion on the adequacy of inference.[147] The problem is avoided if we read the statement as a connection of attributes.[148] But if this preserves the validity of the inference, it can no longer be regarded as syllogistic in form.

Later on Bradley takes the case further. He admits that, with some contrivance, it is possible to force, or as he puts it to 'torture', most inferences into some sort of syllogistic pattern.[149] But to oblige them to lie in such a 'bed of Procrustes'[150] can only distort how they work, producing the most unnatural results. For example, you can try to turn the general principle of any inference, the basic type to which it belongs, into a premise and proceed to run the argument from that point. But this is not really what is going on when we make that inference; for such a major premise will be nothing but an abstracted repetition of the inference itself.[151] The rule or type according to which an inference proceeds is not itself required as a further premise of the inference.[152]

Not all of Bradley's readers were wholly impressed by his critique of syllogism, but turning from traditional 'deductive' logic to the logic of 'induction', Bradley's arguments became considerably stronger and more influential. Indeed, he himself regarded his differences with the syllogism as minor compared next to those he has with empiricist logicians, such as John Stuart Mill. He attacks both Mill's doctrine of the association of ideas and his inductive canons. The theory of the *association of ideas* (pioneered by Locke and developed into a scheme of sophisticated orthodoxy by subsequent figures such as Hume, Hartley, and Mill) is an empiricist attempt to account for the causal principles that lead one idea to follow upon another.[153] According to the doctrine all human thought, however complex, may be derived from conditioned

---

[146] *Principles of Logic*, 248.   [147] *Principles of Logic*, 248.   [148] *Principles of Logic*, 249.
[149] *Principles of Logic*, 526.   [150] *Principles of Logic*, 267.   [151] *Principles of Logic*, 525–6.
[152] Bradley's point here is similar to that made by Lewis Carroll in his famous paper, 'What the Tortoise said to Achilles'.
[153] Ferreira, *Bradley and the Structure of Knowledge*, 236–9; Ferreira, 'Bradley's Attack on Associationism'; F. Wilson, 'Bradley's Critique of Associationism'.

connections between simple sensory elements, based on similarity and/or repeated juxtaposition in space and time. Where things A and B, similar or contiguous with one another, are repeatedly experienced together this creates in the mind a habit or tendency such that whenever we next experience or think of A, even without B, B nonetheless is recalled in our mind. Perhaps the best known example of this way of thinking is Hume's use of 'constant conjunction' to explain our idea of causation or necessary connection, but for the associationists theirs was an entirely general theory, able to account for all of our thinking, even inference. Mill for instance argues that in syllogism, 'the minor premise always affirms a resemblance between a new case and some cases previously known; while the major premise asserts something which, having been found true of those known cases, we consider ourselves warranted in holding true of any other case resembling the former in certain given particulars.'[154]

Bradley does not attempt to deny that association *occurs*[155]—for whether or not it does is a matter of empirical fact—what he disputes is the empiricists' *explanation* of it. Ideas, on their view, are unable to bear any 'real connection' between each other, and the resulting 'trains of thought' amount to nothing more than chance or fate.[156] The fundamental problem is that the images or ideas of which the theory speaks are all particulars, individual dateable private psychological events. But such items can never be associated, for by their nature they are fleeting and can never recur. 'There is no Hades where they wait in disconsolate exile, till associationism announces resurrection and recall.'[157] Talk of recalling a connected idea is only plausible to the degree that we forget this, for any new occurrence will always be in fact a different idea. Bradley's point is that where such associative chains of thought occur the connections must be, not between particular ideas, but between *universals*. Far from explaining the origin of our general ideas, association would not even be possible unless we first had them. 'I maintain that all association is between universals' he insists 'and that no other association exists.'[158] At least the classical logic recognized this fact, although the debt he explicitly acknowledges for this view is to Hegel.[159]

Bradley follows these objections to associationism with an extensive critique of Mill's account of inductive inference. As well as the less familiar thought that inference may be from particular to particular, Bradley attacks the notion that inference may go from particulars to *universal truths*; that is to say, the principle of induction, as most famously formalized in Mill's canons of inductive inference. Bradley has no sympathy at all with these formulations and insists that their methods, although professing to start from mere particulars, in fact imply universals.[160] He further argues that, rather than properly inductive they can all be seen as examples of a single quite different pattern of reasoning, inference by elimination; 'they fix a relation between certain wholes, and then, by removal of parts of each, establish this relation between the remaining

---

[154] Mill, *System of Logic*, Bk II, ch. IV.   [155] *Principles of Logic*, 299.
[156] *Principles of Logic*, 302.   [157] *Principles of Logic*, 306.   [158] *Principles of Logic*, 307.
[159] *Principles of Logic*, 346; a debt repeated at *Principles of Logic*, 515 n.1.   [160] *Principles of Logic*, 359.

elements'.[161] Running through each of the five cannons in turn in order to diagnose their individual faults, Bradley does admit that there is a sense in which all of them work if, that is, you add to them some proviso of the sort, 'in this particular case', but thus to rescue them is he complains utterly to destroy their generalizing power as types of inference.

8.3.9 *The validity of inference*

In the final chapter of the *Principles* Bradley addresses the question of the validity of inference. That he should even ask about this shows how different his conception is from that of the modern logician who, for all his efforts to define formally in just what it consists, takes the validity of inference in general as unproblematic. As Bradley sees it, the question can be asked at two levels, logical and metaphysical.[162]

At a logical level we ask whether premises really do prove their conclusions. The problem—which he later refers to as 'the essential puzzle of inference'[163]—is that inference must yield new knowledge. But in that case it seems, through the mind's operation on its starting material, that we have altered it. If we *make* the conclusion we cannot also claim to have *found* it. And so we face a dilemma: 'If nothing was altered, then there was no inference; but if we altered aught then the inference is vicious.'[164] In other words, inference must yield new knowledge but the requirement of validity seems to prevent that.

He suggests that, in part, the solution we need is 'to regard our reasoning as simply a change in our way of knowing'. The change is not in the object, but in ourselves. 'If, by altering *myself*, I am so able to perceive a connection which before was not visible, then my act conditions, not the consequence itself, but my knowledge of that consequence.'[165] Every inference modifies its own starting point. But I play no part in that. 'My vision is affected, but the object is left to its own development.'[166] Yet such a breach between the psychological process of inference and the objective validity of the inference can give only half the answer we seek. For the mere correction in our vision, a mere shift in attention, hardly amount to an inference—as Bradley notes in the second edition.[167] Even if we play no part in it, and are thus freed from blame, the fact that the premises themselves evolve under an internal logic challenges our belief in the validity of the inference. For the conclusion becomes different from the premises. It is this second aspect of the puzzle which comes to the fore in the extended discussion of inference which Bradley added to the second edition of the *Principles*. He suggests there that the basic solution to our puzzle lies in 'the double nature of the object'.[168] The inference starts with a special object, but that object is more than itself. An element in a wider whole, it has an identity that points beyond itself, and which develops along its own natural lines through the process of inference. What we uncover in the inference

---

[161] *Principles of Logic*, 363. [162] *Principles of Logic*, 551. [163] *Principles of Logic*, 599.

[164] *Principles of Logic*, 554. [165] *Principles of Logic*, 554. [166] *Principles of Logic*, 555.

[167] *Principles of Logic*, 573 n7. [168] *Principles of Logic*, 599.

is not something new smuggled in from outside our starting point; it is 'nothing beyond the intrinsic development of its proper being'.[169] In other words, the conclusion is not asserted in the premises (as Mill had said), but it is thinks Bradley implicit in them. If conclusions are contained in premises it is, to use a phrase from Frege, 'as plants are contained in their seeds, not as beams are contained in a house'.[170] This is what Bradley means by the term 'self-development'. There must be *development* or else there is no new knowledge, but it must be *self*-development or else the inference would be invalid.

In this way the key to the validity of inference lies in *coherence*.[171] As the premises unpack their latent connect, they connect themselves with the rest of our beliefs and thus inferences (like judgements, as we shall see below) are judged by the overall coherence and comprehensiveness they are able to generate in our system of beliefs. The ideal standard here is that of perfected or complete knowledge, where everything connects to everything else. In Bradley's own words, 'Our actual criterion is the body of our knowledge, made both as wide and as coherent as is possible. . . . And the measure of the truth and importance of any one judgment or conclusion lies in its contribution to, and its place in, our intelligible system.'[172] Although this allows us to give an affirmative reply to our first question of the validity of inference, it is a reply that must be qualified. In the second edition, he insists that every inference is fallible.[173] The reason for this is that each inference is individual and if, from some perspective one given inference may seem to increase coherence and comprehensiveness more than another, from an even wider perspective our judgement may be reversed.

In the second part of the chapter Bradley turns from this concern with the logical validity of inference, to the more metaphysical question of whether what takes place in the ideal realms of inference in fact corresponds to how things are in reality. Do our thought processes correspond to actual processes in the world? If there is evolution in our datum, is there a corresponding development *in rerum natura*?[174]

Even as he began his account of inference, stating the requirement for a point of identity in all inference, Bradley noted already that the validity of inference depends on the 'enormous' metaphysical assumption 'that what is the same ideally is really the same'.[175] So this is a question that has lain in the background throughout the discussion. But now that he comes to address it directly, the implications of an affirmative answer are ones which Bradley finds it hard to accept. He is struck by the overwhelming difference between thought and sensuous reality. Their natures and modes of connection are so fundamentally unlike one another that can we really be sure that what happens in one is matched by the other? Were we to affirm, with Hegel, that the Real just is the rational, matters would be easy. But can we really say this? Bradley's doubts come to the fore, and the *Principles* ends with his deeply felt denunciation of panlogicism and its 'unearthly

---

[169] *Principles of Logic*, 600.   [170] Frege, *The Foundations of Arithmetic*, §88.
[171] Sievers, 'Inference and the Criterion of System'.   [172] *Principles of Logic*, 620, cf.489.
[173] *Principles of Logic*, 619–21.   [174] *Principles of Logic*, 580.   [175] *Principles of Logic*, 292.

ballet of bloodless categories' that we noted in Chapter 4.[176] These anti-Hegelian sentiments and their commitment to the inescapability of some form or other of realism separated Bradley from a great many of his idealist companions. Thought, he agrees, is not wholly separate from the real which is given in experience—he is no dualist—but neither is it simply identical to reality, as someone like Caird would allow. Rather it must be regarded as unreal abstraction from presentation pointing, though its own deficiencies, beyond itself to a deeper reality. In the historical sequence of Bradley's philosophical development the working out of this stance led to the metaphysics of *Appearance and Reality* we have already considered.

8.3.10 Truth

Given his understanding of logic as the search for truth, it seems appropriate to conclude our consideration of Bradley's logical views with a discussion of his conception of truth. We can begin with the most common theory of truth, the correspondence theory, according to which a judgement is said to be true if it copies, mirrors, or corresponds to the facts. At times in the *Principles* it might seem as though Bradley held a correspondence theory of truth, for there are many references in that work to copying or corresponding or fitting the facts.[177] However, it is quite clear that the correspondence theory was not in fact one which he endorsed, and in the second edition of the *Principles*, he explains that he employed it there as a simplifying assumption only.[178]

But, in truth, only the most cursory of readings could ever have suggested that this was his view. For even in the first edition, he strongly attacks the theory. 'The common-sense view of facts outside us passing over into the form of truth within us, or copying themselves into a faithful mirror, is shaken and perplexed by the simplest enquiries',[179] he complains. His objections to the theory are two-fold. In the first place, he believes that thought and reality are so fundamentally different, that any talk of correspondence between them is quite ridiculous. Thought is abstract and general where reality is concrete and particular, the felt here and now of sensuous reality. But how can something essentially general and hypothetical ever correspond to something essentially individual and categorical? How can what is thought ever mirror what is felt? Secondly, Bradley attacks the idea of bare unconceptualized facts to which truths are supposed on this account to correspond. For as we saw, perception and judgement emerge together and there can be no intelligible encounter with reality that is not at the same time thought or conceptualized. If we have focused on what is given in

---

[176] *Principles of Logic*, 590. See above p.119.

[177] *Principles of Logic*, 41–2, 579–80, 583; cf. *Essays on Truth and Reality*, 109 n.

[178] *Principles of Logic*, 591 n. Although as late as 1904 we find him making an equally misleading statement 'If my idea is to work it must correspond to a determinate being which it cannot be said to make. And in this correspondence, I must hold, consists from the very first the essence of truth' (*Essays on Truth and Reality*, 76). But this too he retracts as merely a necessarily one-sided corrective point (*Essays on Truth and Reality*, 120 and note).

[179] *Principles of Logic*, 46.

perception enough to pick it out and describe it, we have already categorized and interpreted it. Nowhere do we encounter bare reality against which to measure our beliefs as the correspondence theory calls upon us to do. 'The merely given facts are,' Bradley says, 'the imaginary creatures of false theory. They are manufactured by a mind which abstracts one aspect of the concrete known whole, and sets this abstracted aspect out by itself as a real thing'.[180]

If not a correspondence theory of truth, may we attribute a coherence theory to him? According to this theory, truth consists in the coherence and comprehensiveness of propositions among each other. By far the greatest number of commentators have thought that Bradley held a coherence theory of truth, but the real situation is quite otherwise. Nowhere does he say that truth *consists* in coherence. For Bradley this is the *criterion*, not the nature, of truth.[181] On the other hand, it must be admitted that statements to the effect that the more coherent something is, the more true it is, are ambiguous and not hard to misinterpret. So it must be confessed that a careless reading might well give this impression.

Bradley's actual theory of truth is unusual and rather perplexing. But notwithstanding these facts, there is no excuse for misinterpreting him, for there can be no doubt as to what he actually says.[182] Although it is repeated in numerous other places, the theory is most clearly expressed in his *Essays on Truth and Reality*, where he says,

> The division of reality from knowledge and of knowledge from truth must in any form be abandoned. And the only way of exit from the maze is to accept the remaining alternative. Our one hope lies in taking courage to embrace the result that reality is not outside truth. The identity of truth knowledge and reality, whatever difficulty that may bring, must be taken as necessary and fundamental.[183]

The position has been identified as what we might call an identity theory of truth. For a judgement to be true, we must remove all difference between it and its subject, such that in the end it does not simply correspond to reality, but is identical with it. To understand this, more needs to be said about Bradley's understanding of the relationship between thought, feeling, and reality. As Bradley sees it, reality comes first in feeling, undifferentiated by thought. From this emerges thought. But thought distorts reality, for it treats as hard and fast distinction what is really a fluid identity-in-diversity. This is the source of all its errors. The process of removing distortion, repairing the damage, is one that in the end must take us beyond thought itself, as Bradley puts it, to thought's suicide. Since it works precisely by division, to rise above division, is to rise above thought. It must be transcended into a higher experience that is reality itself. The goal of our thinking is an identity with reality that would take us beyond thought itself.

---

[180] *Essays on Truth and Reality*, 108.
[181] *Essays on Truth and Reality*, 202. See also Chapter 12.1.3 below.
[182] Correct accounts of his theory of truth may be found in Candlish, 'The Truth about F.H. Bradley' and Baldwin, 'The Identity Theory of Truth'.
[183] *Essays on Truth and Reality*, 112–13.

We see here how we have transcended logic for metaphysics—this strictly metaphysical view is of no use for logic, since truth on this understanding is not even a property of judgements.[184]

8.3.11 Degrees of truth

We may return from such far-off metaphysical regions to consider one further important implication of Bradley's general conception of judgement for his theory of truth. All judgement is made subject to conditions, facts outside its explicit statement which nonetheless bear upon it. Were these conditions all to be included within the body of the judgement it would express a truth, but so long as they are ignored the judgement must be regarded as strictly false. It is clear that, between these two extremes, there exist a myriad of degrees as more or less of these conditioning factors are explicitly acknowledged in the judgement itself, and one of the most notable aspects of Bradley's theory of judgement is his exploitation of this possibility in the form of a doctrine of degrees of truth.[185] Bradley accepts, of course, that for the most part we act as though truth and falsity were absolute but none the less, he thinks, when we assess judgements in anything more than a pragmatic way degrees of truth force themselves on us. We see, argues Bradley, that no judgement is wholly true and no judgement wholly false, but rather that all lie somewhere in between.

No judgement is wholly true because any judgement is always subject to unstated conditions, which as long as they are left out vitiate the judgement. Some may be acknowledged, but in the end it would be impossible wholly to correct this failing, for the presence of such conditions is a consequence of the very action of thought to abstract, separate, and divide what is given in experience as a single sensuous whole. So long as we think, we must divide and abstract and our thought must of consequence be incomplete and distorted; but partial truth.

And yet on the other hand, it must always remain partially true. Because whatever we say is referred to reality as a whole, our judgements can never fail to contain some measure of truth. They may so distort and abstract that putting right their failings would change them almost beyond recognition, but it cannot be that nothing in what they say, not even when 'redistributed and dissolved'[186] is able to find a point of reference in reality. For this reason, says Bradley, 'Error *is* truth, it is partial truth, that is false only because partial and incomplete.'[187] We abstract a content and attempt to refer it to a reality with which it seems discrepant, but reality owns both of these elements and in a wider view, 'this jarring character is swallowed up and is dissolved in fuller harmony'.[188]

---

[184] Walker, *The Coherence Theory of Truth*, 97.

[185] While there can be no doubt that this is his view in *Appearance and Reality*, it is to be noted that he denied it in the first edition of the *Principles* (*Principles of Logic*, 197). Allard reads this as saying simply that something cannot be more or less affirmed ('Degrees of Truth in F.H. Bradley', 141).

[186] *Appearance and Reality*, 323.

[187] *Appearance and Reality*, 169.

[188] *Appearance and Reality*, 170.

But what, it will be demanded, *are* degrees of truth? The idea is a very alien one to those brought up to believe in only two truth-values. Bradley suggests that they may be understood as a measure of *transformation* that would be required to turn something into a complete truth. To add in those factors that have been ignored is to modify the judgement and 'the amount of survival in each case,' he suggests, 'gives the degree of reality and truth' of the original judgement.[189] While it is unclear how this could result in any sort of measure, the idea finds intuitive purchase.

It might be wondered how one could truly state the theory that all truth is partial. But Bradley has within his resources a way to solve this challenge. He makes a relative distinction between absolute and finite truth. Both are conditioned and depend for their truth upon factors not included within the judgement, but the former, which include the truths of metaphysics, are as general as judgements can possibly be, and thus unconditioned by anything which it would be possible for us to recognize and add. He says, 'Absolute truth is corrected only by passing outside the intellect. It is modified only by taking in the remaining aspects of experience. But in this passage the proper nature of truth is, of course, transformed and perishes.'[190] In this way they are as true as any judgements could ever be. If corrigible, they are not *intellectually* corrigible. 'There is no intellectual alteration which could possibly, as general truth, bring it nearer ultimate Reality.'[191] And so while it might be worrying to think that the doctrine that there is no absolute truth was incomplete, if that meant that it might later be completed and modified (perhaps into something very different), if it is as complete as any judgement could be, we need have no such worry.

8.4 Bernard Bosanquet

8.4.1 *Comparison between Bosanquet and Bradley on logic*

Another idealist philosopher who wrote extensively on logic was Bosanquet. The position he presents is in many ways very similar to Bradley's—their fellow idealist Mackenzie even suggested 'Bradley and Bosanquet have almost to be regarded as one person'[192]—and with

---

[189] *Appearance and Reality*, 323.
[190] *Appearance and Reality*, 483.
[191] *Appearance and Reality*, 483.
[192] 'Review of *Ethical Studies*', 235–6. Notwithstanding all these similarities, the logical views of Bradley and Bosanquet must not simply be assimilated. For one thing Bosanquet was an important critic of Bradley. After Bradley published *Principles of Logic* in 1883, Bosanquet published a critical account of it, *Knowledge and Reality*, in 1885. In particular, Bradley's closing rejection of any view that existence might be the same as reality (*Principles of Logic*, 590, see above Chapter 4.2.6) seemed to Bosanquet suspiciously close to a reassertion of that dualism between the constructive work of thought and the given reality of perception that it had been the effort of the great German idealists to discredit (*Knowledge and Reality*, 16–26). But in truth they were closer than this over-reaction suggests; Bosanquet in saying that everything fell within intellect was using 'intellect' in a wide sense that included perception or feeling, while Bradley's talk of a world 'more glorious' that that of mere thought—he later wrote to Bosanquet—was never the attempt to step outside of experience that Bosanquet feared (*Bernard Bosanquet and his Friends*, 49–55).

clear affinity also to the logical ideas of Green, Caird, and Nettleship, his multiple writings helped considerably to create the sense of something like an 'Idealist school of logic'. Indeed, Bosanquet's *The Essentials of Logic* (1895) could well be regarded as the first *popular* exposition of this logic.

For Bosanquet, as for Bradley, logic is the science of *knowledge*, the science of what is required to make our beliefs *true*. Thus with judgement we find him attempting to assess, for example, *how well* its particular forms express any given reality. (For example, comparative judgements are treated as a kind of half-way house or stepping-stone towards the superior class of quantitative judgements.)[193] Similarly with inference we find him trying to determine, not simply whether any given example is valid or not, but *how well* it captures the reality of its situation, which, since adequacy is a function of completeness, is a matter of looking beyond the inference itself into its surrounding context. (For example, analogical is found superior to merely enumerative inference, because it begins to explore a possible basis for the connections it asserts.)[194] In consequence, Bosanquet wholly avoids what he dismisses as 'the trivialities of formal Logic'.[195] Mere symbols he holds are inadequate to represent either judgement or inference—since all form is influenced by its individual subject matter—and of value only for use in passing illustration.[196] It is not to be denied that logic constitutes a separate discipline. It is more general than any of the special sciences. But it is never so general as to render it wholly formal. Its subject matter is knowledge *qua* knowledge, but since different kinds of things are known in different ways, it can not be wholly blind as to content.[197] The formal conception of logic is both wider and narrower than Bosanquet's own. Focused only on what is consistent as opposed to what is actually the case, it is wider because it is equally happy dealing with false beliefs as true ones. At the same time it is narrower in scope, ignoring anything implied or suggested and restricting itself only to what is actually said.

For Bosanquet, logic is the science of knowledge rather than, more generally, of thought. Its proper unit is thus the *judgement* as opposed to the proposition. (A proposition is something whose existence is quite independent of whether or not it is known.) Judgements essentially involve minds; they are made or asserted. Bosanquet may be an idealist, but he is quite emphatic both that there exists no 'third realm' of abstract ideal entities and that there exist no 'floating ideas'; no ideas which are simply entertained and not judged. Objective reference (meaning) is distinguishable from reference to reality (affirmation) only by an artificial act of abstraction.[198] What seems to be merely entertained is in reality asserted subject to unknown conditions, while what we might think of as mere consciousness is in fact a complex of judgements.

Like Bradley, Bosanquet holds that in judgement we predicate an ideal content of reality as a whole.[199] This result can be displayed as the solution to a paradox. On the

[193] *Logic*, I:108ff.   [194] *Logic*, II:107.   [195] *Essentials of Logic*, v.
[196] *Essentials of Logic*, 49.   [197] *Essentials of Logic*, 44.   [198] *Logic*, I:5.
[199] Judgement 'always refers to a Reality which goes beyond and is independent of the act itself' (*Logic*, I:97).

one hand, ruling out as impossible pure difference or bare negation without any basis in positive reality, judgement must be regarded as wholly affirmative or existential. On the other hand, ruling out the possibility of direct individual reference, all thought must be regarded as attributive, its entire content passing over onto the predicative side. Reconciliation is found in the thought that the entirety of each judgement forms one great predicate referred to the real world as a whole. Although the complete content of the judgement is indeed universal, anchored to reality it remains individual or concrete also. Mill claimed and it is commonly thought that individuals cannot be defined but only designated, yet if mute pointing or bare naming fail in their task, only through such complete predication attributed to reality as a whole will reference be possible at all, making it truer to say individuals cannot be designated but only defined.[200]

It is vital to remember here that both the content of the judgement and the reality judged are much larger than might first be thought. On the one side, there is far more implied by any judgement than just what we actually say. Every judgement implies a whole host of others, and only a very small part of this knowledge is in the focus of our attention when we judge. Indeed, in the end, suggests Bosanquet, as link leads on to link all of our knowledge is implicated; the whole of London, even the judgement that the Antipodes are real, are part of the determining background for the present perception of this room, he writes.[201] On the other side, although we only meet in our perception with a very small piece of reality, we know that it is part of something much larger, and so the subject of which we judge too extends far beyond the limited sphere of our acquaintance with it.

If the subject of reference lies outside a judgement then its entire content becomes one vast predicate, but in that case what must we say about its internal structure, its apparently complex construction out of many distinct terms? Bosanquet adheres to the same context principle as other Idealists, and holds that these are really abstractions, since, 'A name has meaning only in a sentence or by suggesting a sentence.'[202] Distinct ideas are not meaning-elements in their own right. The dogma that all judgements have a subject–predicate structure, he likewise rejects. It is, he says, 'a mere superstition'.[203] Although reality is one and extends beyond the content of the judgement, we meet with only a portion of it in perception. And admittedly, it is impossible to judge without explaining how and where reality accepts the qualification we attach to it, so that in every judgement there must be some starting point, some locus of contact with ultimate reality. For this reason subject and predicate remain 'essential elements' within the judgement, but it must be appreciated, they do so only as differences within a larger whole of predication, not as representative of the true structure of the judgement.[204] The genuine subject of the judgement—reality—is never one of its terms.

---

[200] *Logic*, II:261–2.   [201] *Essentials of Logic*, 33–5.
[202] *Logic*, I:37. His point here is that judgements are expressed in sentences.
[203] *Logic*, II:260.   [204] *Logic*, I:78.

For Bosanquet, as for Bradley and other Idealists, all judgement asserts an identity-in-difference. According to this doctrine no statement of the form A = A is ever true (because it does not say anything), while every statement of the form A = B is false (because it states what is patently not the case). The 'laws of thought' which modern logic is able to see as unproblematically true tautologies, Bosanquet finds in this their barest form to be quite hopeless.[205] What is needed instead he concludes is an understanding, not just that things similar in some points may be dissimilar in others, but that their very similarities themselves must also somehow and at the same time be differences. It is this doctrine that forms the substance of Bosanquet's 1888 *Mind* paper, 'The Philosophical Importance of a True Theory of Identity', and the point is emphasized again in his slightly later *Logic*. Attacking the law of identity he complains that, 'If it means that A is A and no more, or is *mere* A, then it is aggressively untrue, for it denies the synthesis of differences which alone can make a judgement. . . . In an absolute tautology which excludes or omits difference, identity itself disappears and the judgement vanishes with it.'[206] Identity is a matter neither of bare sameness nor of bare difference, but rather of a true synthesis or unity of differences.[207] Elsewhere he gives the example of the judgement 7 + 5 = 12. The significance of the equals sign can hardly be denied, but equally clearly the right hand side of the equation does not simply repeat the left hand side; 'If 12 were not the same as 7 + 5, the judgement would not be true. If it were not different, the judgement would not be a judgement.'[208]

Like Bradley, Bosanquet finds an important continuity between judgement and inference. A judgement is really a conclusion, an inference not yet made explicit, while inference is defined as judgement which has *mediate* reference to reality.[209] For this reason there is no deep difference either between truth and validity. An inference (to be found valid) is simply a judgement (to be found true) whose ground or reason is explicitly set forth. Necessity is a mark of them both, not just of inference; for in any conscious judgement there is present a general sense of necessity—that something *makes* it true—but in the higher phases of thought this sense of necessity is explicitly referred to some ideal content within the judgement, turning it into inference.

---

[205] *Logic*, II:210–15. If they are not to be taken in their 'barest' form, the range of potential 'postulates of knowledge' may be widened from those traditionally put forward and, in addition to the laws of identity, contradiction, and excluded middle, Bosanquet includes the law of sufficient reason (*Logic*, II:215); opening the way to solution of the problem of induction, there being no fundamental difference in kind between inductive and deductive inference. For more on this see Ferreira, 'Bosanquet, Idealism and the Justificatiion of Induction'.

[206] *Logic*, II:210.

[207] It is to be noted that Bosanquet's understanding here causes him to use 'identity' and 'unity' pretty much interchangeably.

[208] *Meeting of Extremes in Contemporary Philosophy*, 103.

[209] *Logic*, II:1.

8.4.2 *Logic and metaphysics*

The many similarities noted above between Bosanquet's and Bradley's Logics mask one fundamental divergence between them about the relation between logic and metaphysics. We noted, briefly at the end of Chapter 4, Bosanquet's view that Logic—'the science of knowledge'—cannot ultimately be distinguished from Meta-physics—'the general science of reality'—any more than one can separate a result from the process which produces it. This for him was a fundamental consequence of his idealism.

I entertain no doubt that in content Logic is one with Metaphysics, and differs if at all simply in mode of treatment—in tracing the evolution of knowledge in the light of its value and import, instead of attempting to summarise its value and import apart from the details of its evolution.[210]

But as we have seen, this was something with which Bradley could not agree. Tentatively at first in the *Principles of Logic*, then more firmly in *Appearance and Reality*, he put forward an idealism that rejected the identity of thought and reality. Thought is irredeemably defective and partial and, even in its highest form, there can be no direct reading off from the nature of one to the other.

This difference manifests itself among other places in their respective theories of truth. Both agree in rejecting correspondence as the test of truth in favour of a standard internal to thought itself, that of systematic coherence and comprehensiveness. But while a criterion for the best that thought may achieve, holding even the best thought inadequate to capture reality, Bradley is unable to find in coherence the nature of truth itself. Bosanquet's by contrast is most accurately described as holding a coherence theory of the nature of truth. For him, no proposition is true in itself; its truth can be determined only by its logical relations to other propositions in a system. Specifically, a proposition is true when its assertion produces a greater organization or coherence in knowledge than its denial.[211]

8.4.3 *Concrete universals*

We saw above how, in connection with the notions of extension and intension that Bradley introduced the idea of the concrete universal. He does not, however, make very great use of it. But in the philosophy of Bosanquet it rises to great prominence. From there it came to be used extensively throughout idealist thought, appearing in many places as a kind of leitmotiv. It therefore merits our stopping to examine in detail.

For Bosanquet, as for Bradley, the issue of the concrete universal was a logical or metaphysical, and not a psychological one. His approach to the matter was thus in sharp contrast to that of the British empiricist tradition of Berkeley and Hume. For those two philosophers the question of whether universal ideas were abstract was one to be settled

---

[210] *Logic*, I:232; cf II:271.   [211] See also Chapter 12.1.3.

by introspective psychology, and their opposition to them was based in large part on their belief in the crucial role in thought of *images*, which it would seem cannot be abstract. But for Bosanquet all of this is just irrelevant. He argues that the term 'idea' has two senses. It can stand for a momentary mental state of some individual, something particular, in which sense it is impossible to speak of two people having the same idea, or one person having the same idea twice. Alternatively it can stand for the meaning of a word, something that can be grasped by more than one person and repeated on more than one occasion; in short, something universal. Logic concerns itself only with the latter sense; with the logical import of an idea, not its psychological face. 'Mere mental facts, occurrences in my mental history, taken as such, cannot enter into judgment'[212] says Bosanquet.

It has been noted in the literature[213] that Bosanquet seems to operate with at least three different notions of what it is to be a concrete universal. The question of how, if at all, these are related one to another must be addressed in due course, but for the moment, simply to note the details of what he says, they may be set out in turn.

1. The self-identity of an individual   With Bosanquet's first sense of 'concrete universal' the strangeness (we might even say, the perversity) of the doctrine stands out sharply, for he uses it to refer to what we would normally, that is to say, on the traditional view, think of as a concrete particular. This sense of concrete universal of course corresponds to Bradley's usage and almost certainly derives from it. Bosanquet first introduces this sense in his early (1888) paper, 'The Philosophical Importance of a True Theory of Identity', where he suggests that 'the individual as designated by a proper name' is the very best example of such a universal.[214]

A particular object, and especially a living individual, is universal, thinks Bosanquet, in the sense of being spread out in the world, of combining together under one label a host of elements that from another point of view seem to be different or distinct. The key point is that rather than bringing together many abstracted instances of the same property, as with the traditional view, we are thinking here of a coming together (either synchronic or diachronic) of many dissimilar properties under one unified scheme.

2. A reciprocally determining system   However, this is not the only sense in which Bosanquet speaks of concrete universals. The second way in which he uses the notion is to stand for what he calls a 'system'; that is to say, a group of distinct but mutually

---

[212] *Essentials of Logic*, 78–9.

[213] Foster, 'The Concrete Universal', 7–8. Similar distinctions are made by both Kemp Smith, 'The Nature of Universals' and Acton, 'The Theory of Concrete Universals'.

[214] 'Philosophical importance of a true theory of identity', 359. In a similar vein see also: 'The test of individuality which it [the concrete universal] imposes is not the number of subjects which share a common predicate, but rather than this, the number of predicates that can be attached to a single subject' (*Principle of Individuality and Value*, 39–40) and: 'the individual is the highest and only true form of the universal' (*Logic*, II:257).

interconnecting elements so arranged as to make them into some sort of a unified structure, rather than just a disparate conglomeration. This use of the term is best approached by reflecting further upon his view of inference. Bosanquet's line of thought here can perhaps be explained as follows. Holding first, that inference requires universals, and second, that inference requires system, he is encouraged to identify universality with system. And since systems are concrete entities, he thus comes up with another kind of concrete universal.

It is worth looking at both of the premises of this informal argument, viz. that inference requires universals and that inference requires system. To take the first, the difference between particulars and universals with respect to inference—the fact that universals have entailments between them while particulars do not[215]—has been recognized since the time of Plato.[216] Thus Bosanquet is making no especially controversial point when he claims that, 'Inference cannot take place except through the medium of an identity or universal which acts as a bridge from one case or relation to another. If each particular was shut up within itself...you could never get from one which is given to another which is not given.'[217] And here too he is of course following both Hegel and Bradley. The second claim, that all inference involves system, is less obvious, but Bosanquet is no less certain that it is so. 'Ultimately the condition of inference is always a system'[218] he says. In the broadest possible terms, Bosanquet's point is that only where you have items arranged such that the state of one is non-arbitrarily connected to the state of another, will it be possible to infer anything about one from something about another. But this is precisely for them to be in a system. Wherever items are thus arranged, inference will be possible; the more the connections the stronger the inference. In an atomic world where everything was radically distinct from everything else, both in existence and nature, there could be no inferences, for there would be no system whatsoever on which to draw.

Combining these two requirements for inference together we get the notion of a universal as itself a system. Other more or less equivalent terms that Bosanquet uses for such systematic arrangements are 'organism', 'world', and 'cosmos'.[219] He describes two of them in the following way. 'A world or cosmos is a system of members, such that every member, being *ex hypothesi* distinct, nevertheless contributes to the unity of the whole in virtue of the peculiarities which constitute its distinctness...such a diversity recognised as a unity, a macrocosm constituted by microcosm, is the type of

---

[215] Or rather that they have them only in so far as they are described by universal terms.

[216] Mill is the notable exception to this claim (*System of Logic*, Bk II, ch. III, §3).

[217] *Essentials of Logic*, 139. In a similar vein, it is possible Bosanquet tells us 'because the world as known consists of universals exhibited in differences, and the contents from which and to which we proceed are not shut up within their respective selves, but depend on a pervading identical character or universal of which they are the differences' (*Logic*, I:2).

[218] *Essentials of Logic*, 140. For futher details see Allard, 'Bosanquet and the Problem of Inference'.

[219] That these are only 'more or less' equivalent is not to be denied and a rather typical weakness in Bosanquet's thought.

the concrete universal.'[220] The point about such systems most crucial for our purposes here is that they are concrete; they are made up of actual members in actual relations to one another. This is perhaps most clearly shown by contrasting them, as Bosanquet does, with classes. 'It takes all sorts to make a world; a class is of essentially one sort only,' he says.[221] His point is this. A class works by ranging across objects and selecting out some as in certain respects similar—for example, the class of dentists or of herrings. But by thus taking them out of their actual context and ignoring their *dissimilarities* what we classify together are really abstractions—nothing is *just* a dentist or *just* a herring. A system, on the other hand, such as the National Health Service or a marine ecosystem, binds together contextualized and functioning elements of reality, and is thus itself something concrete.

3. Generic or complex universals The third sense in which Bosanquet uses the term concrete universal is to denote a complex generic category or natural kind (such as 'man', 'animal', or 'orchid') as opposed to a simple common quality, type, or relation (such as 'red', 'fast', or 'to the left of'). Once again following Bradley, on more than one occasion Bosanquet introduces this use of the term via a critique of the traditional doctrine of the inverse ratio between intension and extension.[222] According to that doctrine, which has of course a very long pedigree, the more specific content or meaning (intension) a term possesses the fewer objects to which it applies (extension). Thus in calling something a bird we say more than were we simply to call it an animal but not as much as were we to call it an ostrich, yet there are more animals and fewer ostriches than there are birds. In this way it is often thought that general terms may be arranged in a kind of pyramid structure; the few with little content but large extensions at the top, and the many with great content but small extensions at the bottom.

Bosanquet has but little sympathy for this view. 'It remains doubtful whether the doctrine of inverse relation is important in any sense in which it is true' he says.[223] What he means by this is that, although ideas *could* in principle be arranged in this way, that is not how in actual fact they *are* arranged. He urges that the natural genus-species classification with which we are all so familiar is not in fact the pyramidal system which it seems, or which the adherents of the traditional doctrine claim it to be.

---

[220] *Principle of Individuality and Value*, 37–8. In a similar vein, starting from the example of the number system, he says, 'Alter the value of any combination, and some correlatives, and ultimately the whole system, must be altered. If 1 is 5, 2 is 10. All is relevant to all. There is something in each which runs through every point in the system, and makes each of them, though apparently unique and peculiar, respond to every other, and vary, though in its own individual manner, yet correspondingly to the variations of other points or traits. Complexes, in so far as they present this character, are true "wholes" or "universals"' (*Implication and Linear Inference*, 8).

[221] *Principle of Individuality and Value*, 37.

[222] *Logic*, I:55f; *Essentials of Logic*, 94f.

[223] *Logic*, I:56. He is here echoing the words of Lotze, 'it seems to me to be untrue where its truth would be important, and comparatively unimportant where it is true' (*System of Philosophy*, I:39) also Bradley, *The Principles of Logic*, I:170 and 174.

In the first place, all too often when we look at groups of things placed together under a single kind, we can see no common core, no property or properties which they all share. This is most obvious with the case of colour. What is the common core between, for example, red, blue, and yellow? That is to say, if we took away what differentiates them, what would we be left with? Nor is the matter any clearer with such things as tastes, smells, sounds, emotions, or mental phenomena in general. What can we point to that all members of each of these categories share? 'The meaning of a genus-name does not *omit* the properties in which the species differ,' concludes Bosanquet; 'If it did, it would omit nearly all properties.'[224]

Although plausible in places it might still be questioned how generally persuasive this point is. Surely, it might be urged, we can subtract, for example, possession of teeth from dolphins to recognize the common cetacean nature they share with other biological whales, or subtract rationality from humans to see the common animality they share with other creatures, and so on. But Bosanquet now brings in a second line of attack, and objects that to proceed in this way is to treat species and genus as externally related to each other, when in fact they are far more intimately connected than that. The traditional pyramid system treats each level of classification as separate, as, to be sure, in a pyramid each layer is distinct and separable. But real qualities cannot come apart like this, they all affect one another. Each quality is what it is only in its context, not just 'horizontally', but 'vertically' also; not just in relation to the qualities that surround it, but in relation to the higher level genus they belong to.

That our actual system is not a pyramid system is clear to see if we remember that, according to that method, we could use *any* qualities we like in constructing the different levels of the pyramid—we could sub-divide triangles by, say, colour, further sub-dividing the colour types by, say, size, and so on—and the inverse relation would still hold. But not only do we not do this, it is clear that it is no accident that we do not. For 'right angled' and 'red' bear utterly different relations to the 'triangle' that we designate their genus; 'to be right angled is a way of being a triangle, to be red is not'.[225] The sub-classifications of the species are chosen precisely because of their unique and special relation to the character of the genus; they are *ways* of realizing that genus.

Bosanquet thinks that in reality all properties affect one another; you cannot separate them. Humans are rational animals. But this distinctive feature of human animals, their rationality, means that they are animals in a different way to that in which, say, lions or tigers are animals. Their animality is of a modified type. He says, 'the animality of men is quite different from the animality of beasts, and is not an attribute common to both

---

[224] *Essentials of Logic*, 95. As Nettleship, another believer in concrete universals, puts it, a propos triangles, 'we cannot absolutely *leave out* the particular properties of equilateral, isosceles, and scalene triangles; for if we did we should be left not with triangularity, but with nothing at all' (*Lectures on Logic*, 155). The standard model has it that by abstraction or omission of difference we should be left with what is common, but in fact the very reverse seems to be the case and if there is anything that makes them all triangles that is lost as well.

[225] B. Blanshard, *The Nature of Thought*, I:586.

in the sense in which a tree-trunk is the common support of two of its branches'.[226] Similarly isosceles, scalene, and equilateral are all different ways of being a triangle; blue, red, and green different ways of being coloured; loud and soft different ways of being a noise. It is not *wrong* to think of animality as common to humans and other species, or triangularity as common to all triangles, or colour as common to all colours, we need simply to remember that in each sub-type it is *modified*. Men and lions do have a partial resemblance—that is not being denied—as do different kinds of triangle or colour, but this is not to be broken up into what they share completely and what they do not share at all.[227]

How then does Bosanquet think we should view species terms? Although increased extension requires us to take with it not just what is common, but the differences as well, clearly he does not want to go so far as to simply *identify* intension with extension. His preferred way of explaining things is to say that a term of wider application, though not lesser in meaning, is 'more schematic'. What does this mean? The idea was perhaps most clearly explained by Lotze, from whom Bosanquet derives it, and who puts it in the following way: 'the universal is produced, not by simply leaving out the different marks *p1* and *p2*, *q1* and *q2*, which occur in the individuals compared, but by substituting for those left out the universal marks *P* and *Q*, of which *p1*, *p2*, and *q1 q2* are particular kinds.'[228] The kind, as Bosanquet puts it, is characterized not by a fixed mark but by a 'scheme of modifiable relations'.[229] Thus, for example, animality is not a fixed residual core, but a universal mark or pattern that varies according to its context. Bosanquet even admits that this universal mark may on occasion have a null value, for example, we may pick out a species of flower with the scheme, 'petals, three or four, sometimes none'.[230] But that, he insists, is not the same thing as omission.[231]

Bosanquet's view of species and genus, terms, then is clearly contrasted with the view which thinks of them as formed by abstraction. Were classification simply a matter of abstracting out features held in common by different individuals or groups, it would introduce many irrelevant or arbitrary groupings while at the same time be simply blind to other genuine ones (such as colours). A genus thinks Bosanquet is not a bringing together of similarities but an interrelated system of differences.

Bosanquet speaks of 'concrete universals' in at least three different senses, then. Certainly each picks out something of note in our ways of talking about the world but, looking at the three new conceptions together with the traditional one, the key question to ask is, in what sense (if any) are all of these *universals*? Indeed, what *is* a universal? We can begin to think about this by considering just what Bosanquet meant by the term. His understanding of the word 'universal' is a very generous one; any connection which brings together some sort of multiplicity under one heading, any

---

[226] *Logic*, I:58.   [227] *Logic*, I:210.   [228] Lotze, *System of Philosophy*, I:31.
[229] *Logic*, I:59.   [230] *Essentials of Logic*, 95.
[231] Bosanquet's account here should be compared with that of Nettleship in his *Lectures on Logic*, 155.

mechanism that allows for some kind of general talk, any union or connection or identity, in his thinking, is a universal.[232] A universal is 'what many properties or individuals have in common' or 'that which is found to be one among many', and only if (*per impossibile*) every difference whatsoever were marked by a different proper name could we say that there would exist no universals at all. Traditionally the question of universals has often been put by asking how, despite its numerous instances, can a property or relation still be one? But if this question goes to the heart of the matter, if singularity in multiplicity is the essence of what it is to be a universal, then what Bosanquet is doing is simply extending this idea such that *any* union of differences, *any* identity through diversity, *any* many-in-one (or one-in-many) can be regarded as a universal. If we take the standard account of universals, together with each of his three types of concrete universal, they can all be seen in their own different ways to determine universals in this generous sense, that is, to combine a many under one. Thus: what all these objects have in common is that they are all blue (Abstract universal). What all these properties have in common is that they are all Caesar's, they all belong to the same individual subject (Concrete universal–sense 1). What all these individuals have in common is that they all belong to the same system, world, or cosmos (Concrete universal—sense 2). What all these individuals (or species) have in common is that they all belong to the same species (or genus) (Concrete universal—sense 3).

But even if we agree to allow this rather loose idea of union as the root idea at work behind the notion of a universal, might it not be objected the four senses we have before us are all so very different that we have in effect four completely separate kinds of such 'universal'? With specific regard to the different senses of 'concrete universal' introduced by Bosanquet he might be accused of simply conflating under a single term three quite unrelated types of case. But this charge would be unfair. While it cannot be denied that living beings, systems, and species are all different, and that Bosanquet papers over some important dissimilarities with his vague and eulogizing use of the word 'individual', it must be allowed that there is an important point of commonality here, one clear feature which these three concepts have in common, but which traditional universals lack. This is that they are all unions of *differences* while a traditional universal collects under it a group of elements which are each the *same*. With traditional universals we ignore all differences and focus on what is the same in a class; we isolate out a single property in various different instances, or the common members of a class, or the residue left after discarding the differences between species. By contrast the three new types of universality embrace difference rather than exclude it; an individual has many diverse properties, a system is made up of many distinct kinds of elements, while

---

[232] Early on he takes it as synonymous with 'a meeting point of differences' ('Philosophical importance of a true theory of identity', 358). While in his *Logic* he says he takes it as any 'synthesis of difference' (*Logic*, I:59). For the world to contain universals is for it to be synthetic (*Distinction between Mind and its Objects*, 35).

we arrive at a genus not by ignoring the underlying species-differences but by explaining them as modifications of a single schematic pattern.

It is for this reason, moreover, that Bosanquet characterizes the contrast between his own and the traditional understanding as one between *concrete* and *abstract* senses. The term 'abstract' is, in Bosanquet's hands, not so simple or familiar as might be thought. To understand his use of it, we should focus less on the standard modern dictionary sense of being ethereal, intangible, or non spatio-temporal, as on the root verb from which the adjective derives: to abstract. To abstract is to remove one thing from out of its context, leaving it both thinner and incomplete.[233] In abstraction we take out all the differences, and are left with a bare uniformity, 'a whole of repetition'.[234] The elements brought together or unified in the universal are all exactly the same. Concrete universals, on the other hand, incorporate difference within themselves. Concrete is in this respect the opposite of abstract. It is a matter, not of spatio-temporality, materiality, or observability, but of contextual fullness of character, of completeness.

Suppose it be granted that there is a genuine and common respect in which the three new senses may all be thought of as universals, an objector from the camp of the traditionalist understanding will no doubt remain unconvinced. 'Do we not just have two senses of universal now,' he may ask; 'those that embrace and those that exclude diversity?' (adding, perhaps, that really it might just be simpler to think up a new name for the first class). Bosanquet, however, would protest. He allowed that the concrete and the abstract were very different conceptions of what it is to be a universal. But he never regarded them as equal claimants. For him this was a difference not between two senses, but between two *rivals* for the true sense, of universality. In other words, a large part of the case for concrete universals lies in their ambition to *replace* the traditional view of universals. Bosanquet insists that once we see properly what universals are we will come to understand that only those that combine difference are truly universal, and those of the traditional repeating kind barely so at all. The inclusion of diversity he describes as 'the true type of universality',[235] its elimination by contrast a disastrous step that can only take us away from truth and reality. 'It is important,' he warns, 'that we should dismiss the notion that the higher degrees of knowledge are necessarily and in the nature of intelligence framed out of abstractions that omit whatever has interest and peculiarity in the real world. *Nothing has been more fatal to the truth and vitality of ideas than this prejudice.*'[236]

But why did Bosanquet think more highly of universals based on the inclusion of diversity than of those based on its elimination? There were perhaps three elements to this view. To begin with the preference is in part simply a reflection of his distaste for

---

[233] Bosanquet distinguishes his from the more usual understanding in his *Logic*, I:214. He argues that in the sense in which it is contrasted with sense-perception all thought is abstract, but that there is another sense of abstract which pertains rather to the content of thoughts, and in this sense only some thoughts are abstract. It is this latter sense that concerns us here.

[234] *Principle of Individuality and Value*, 35.

[235] *Principle of Individuality and Value*, 40.

[236] *Logic*, I:60–1, my italics.

abstraction itself, of his desire to remain close to the level of actual concrete experience. He has an almost nominalist or empiricist reluctance to move away from what is actually given in experience, and a desire to find the explanations he seeks in concrete reality rather than in the artificial creations of intellect. Locating the explanatory force of the world in concrete universals, or individuals, allows him to do just that. But Bosanquet's suspicion of abstraction is not simply a matter of epistemic caution—How can I be sure of anything other than what is given in experience?—it is based also on an objection of principle. He subscribes to a strong form of holism, according to which all of the world's content exists but as elements within one overarching being, the Absolute, which determines their own nature just as much as they together go to make up its. In view of this holistic commitment, to abstract is inevitably to distort or falsify in the sense that nothing taken out of context appears in quite the same way as it does in context. The universal instantiated and in context appears quite different from how it seems when abstracted and held in isolation—for instance, the genus type is modified in each species in which it is found. If we consider things simply in so far as they are members of type or class, we abstract them out of their context, producing as an inevitable result distorted fragments rather than full existences. Since universals based on the inclusion of context and difference bypass or minimize this distortion they are, thinks Bosanquet, to be preferred. While these two points go some way towards explaining Bosanquet's preference for universals of difference over those of sameness, there is also a third and deeper, if rather more puzzling, idea at work here. Bosanquet thinks that universals of the first kind are superior *qua universals* to those of the second, for universals hold things together, but the greater the differences combined the more 'work' they do, the greater the 'glue' required. Bosanquet argues that the traditional method of constructing universals gives what he calls mere 'generality' not 'universality', and contrasting these two, he says, 'the difference is that the ultimate principle of unity or community is fully exemplified in the former, but only superficially in the latter. The ultimate principle, we may say, is sameness in the other; generality is sameness in spite of the other; universality is sameness by means of the other.'[237] This was a point recognized too by McTaggart in his discussion of Hegel, whom he takes to argue that the more individual things are the deeper needs to be the principle of their unity.[238]

---

[237] *Principle of Individuality and Value*, 37.
[238] 'The Conception of Society as Organism', 178. See above p.256.

Edward Caird

T.H. Green

John Caird

F.H. Bradley

R.B. Haldane

R.L. Nettleship

A.S. Pringle-Pattison

William Wallace

Henry Jones

James Seth

A.C. Bradley

Bernard Bosanquet

H.J.W. Hetherington

A.E. Taylor

W.R. Sorley

J.M.E. McTaggart

H.H. Joachim

D.G. Ritchie

JOHN STUART AND MILLICENT MACKENZIE IN 1928.

John Stuart Mackenzie and Millicent Mackenzie

J.H. Muirhead

Sarvepalli Radhakrishnan

R.F.A. Hoernlé

James Ward

9

Aesthetics and Literature

One of the features which most distinguishes British Idealism from any philosophy today was that it offered a comprehensive *weltanschauung*, or worldview; a universal scheme capable of application to any sphere upon which the human mind might latch. This point may be illustrated by considering its implications for a field unlike any of those yet examined—the domain of aesthetics. British philosophy has never been drawn strongly to the subject of aesthetics, and it would be wrong to suggest that the Idealists stand out as any great exception to this tendency, but in the few cases where it did attract their attention, the characteristic traits of idealist thinking were as discernible in the results as they were in any other area. In this chapter I shall examine the aesthetic views of Edward Caird and Bernard Bosanquet, before considering in detail the important relation that obtained between Idealism and poetry.

9.1 Edward Caird

One of the most typical marks of idealist thinking is, as we have seen, the tendency to approach subjects historically, to identify current debate as but the latest phase in an ongoing sequence, and thus it is no surprise to find Edward Caird—the most historically minded of all the Idealists—interpreting aesthetic ideas in this fashion. Caird never made any systematic attempt to trace the development of aesthetic sensibility, but buried within his other writings, we are offered two interesting glimpses of his idealist interpretation of that process.

The first occurs as part of the discussion of Greek religion in his *Evolution of Religion*. He claims that Greek religion was a kind of half-way house between objective and subjective religion, between a religion in which attention is focused externally and God found in the material world, and one in which it is turned within and God discovered in ourselves. For although the Greeks still looked out into the external world to find deity, the object they lighted on was *man*—their God's were so thoroughly *humanized* that at times it seems only the accident of mortality which distinguished us from them—placing them on the very doorstep of the conception of God as something manifested within human consciousness. This ambiguous threshold nature of Greek religion, thinks Caird, gave birth to and was reflected in its *art*.[1]

In ancient Greek consciousness we have the beginnings of a recognition that the sphere of reality cannot be restricted to just material nature, but while yet there is no *explicit* discovery of the spiritual as separated from and opposed to the natural, this insight finds no rational outlet in religion, philosophy, or science; its only means of expression is in *art*. Thus it was, argues Caird, revealing his fundamentally cognitive conception of the aesthetic, that true art first emerges in Greece; prior to that we find only mysterious symbolism, or the crude exaggeration of size and colour. The advance from natural to spiritual religion is expressed in 'the way in which the poetic imagination gradually fills up the objects worshipped . . . with a higher spiritual meaning,' he says, 'even while they are still conceived as mere objective beings which take their place among other objects'.[2] Most particularly, in implicit recognition of the fact that *man himself* is the key to understanding reality, the Greek artist breaks free from the bonds of convention which hitherto dictated artificial or symbolic representation of the natural to give centre stage to the expression of humanity, 'to give to his figures that plastic individuality and moving grace which makes the human form the living expression of human thought and passion'.[3] Religion and value, for Caird and for Idealism generally, are expressed through the developing spirit of humanity; Greek art as a celebration of humanity makes implicit recognition of this.

But, from an idealist point of view, the aesthetic activity of ancient Greece provides a lesson in the limitations as well as the potentialities of art, for Caird insists that this is still only a half-way stage. It seeks to express humanity as standing out against the rest of the natural world, but there is no sense yet of any kind of reality that transcends nature, of a realm that could never be captured but only hinted at or symbolized by the sensuous medium of art. The Greek artist 'has only discovered that which lifts man above nature, but not yet that which lifts him above himself'.[4] Art may be a vital step along the road that leads to the discovery of spirit, but it can never make that whole journey for us.

A second glimpse of the development of aesthetic understanding that Caird offers comes from his discussion of Kantian aesthetics in *The Critical Philosophy of Immanuel Kant*. Unsurprisingly, this too turns out to be a sort of transition point or half-way house for, on Caird's reading, whatever Kant *takes himself* to be saying, really he is well on the way to saying something more. Despite himself, he is already stating and moving onto the next stage. Thus we see here (as, indeed, we saw before) that it would be quite wrong to dismiss Caird's account as simply an exposition of Kant, for his modifications and clarifications amount in effect to a complete rewriting—even inverting—of Kant's position. What especially interests Caird is the way in which Kant's aesthetics, the product of his later thinking, seems to pull down or move beyond the dualisms which infect his earlier more basic position. We can draw out a variety of such threads.

---

[1] *Evolution of Religion*, I:271. [2] *Evolution of Religion*, I:287.
[3] *Evolution of Religion*, I:273. [4] *Evolution of Religion*, I:274.

First of all Caird detects the earliest hints of a kind of thought able to transcend the great chasm between the phenomenal and the noumenal that so contaminates the Kantian design. That scheme sharply contrasts the pleasant, that which is external and heteronomous to self and which we desire, with the good, that which is internal and autonomous to self and which we will. And between these two there might seem to be no middle position; until we reflect upon the notion of beauty. Aesthetic satisfaction is satisfaction in what is external. In the appreciation of beauty, we delight not simply in our selves, but in the outside world. However, since our enjoyment is *disinterested*—we feel no desire to possess that which we value—the experience cannot be a heteronomous one, the taking on of some foreign or alien value. Instead, love of beauty must be a case of self-expression, self-realization: 'We find our self realised in it, or we find in it an existence in which we can rest, because it is not alien to the consciousness of self.'[5] But if that is so, it is not tied to our will in the same way as is moral fulfilment. It seems to be an object of satisfaction simultaneously external and internal.

We find the self realized in that which is not-self. But to begin to break down this division is to begin to break down one of Kant's most fundamental dualisms, for if what is referred to self is appearance and what is referred to not-self ultimate reality, then 'what can this mean except that we find the noumenal in the phenomenal . . . ?'[6] Aesthetics may be a lower form than philosophy, but imagination comes before full insight, and it has much to teach us. In aesthetic sensibility we get a foretaste of the union of self and not-self. Art is like a mirror to ourselves, revealing to us at the deepest levels our unity with the wider whole in which we belong. Linked to the contrast between phenomena and nounmena (and just as axiomatic, it might seem, to the Kant of the first *Critique*) is the contrast between intuition and understanding, whose respective contributions, though they come together to produce experience, are radically other than each other—one individual and passive, the other universal and active. As we saw, Caird wholly rejects this contrast from the start but, he suggests, Kant's development of the notion of aesthetic experience is an indicator that he too came in time to see its flaws. Aesthetic appreciation for Kant is fundamentally singular or intuitive—we *sense* beauty we don't *reason it out*—and yet, despite the fact that it does not proceed by subsuming objects under concepts, it nonetheless claims universal a priori validity, that is, we may pronounce something beautiful without first making some sort of empirical check on whether others respond in the same way to it. In this understanding of aesthetic sensibility, suggests Caird, we find a coming apart of the apparent opposition between sense and understanding. It is unfortunate, he continues, that Kant disguises from himself the true significance of his position with talk of the 'harmonious working' of distinct faculties, for really what we have here is 'union'; a 'third something' or 'common root', a 'perceptive understanding'.[7] Again aesthetics

---

[5] *Critical Philosophy of Immanuel Kant*, II:455.
[6] *Critical Philosophy of Immanuel Kant*, II:455.
[7] *Critical Philosophy of Immanuel Kant*, II:458.

serves as the fore-runner of a vital philosophical advance. Picking up its lead, idealism preaches the presence of the ideal at the heart of the real, a union which is the very lifeblood of art—essentially meaningful, but essentially embodied. It is the function of art and poetry, urges Caird, to serve in this way 'the higher education of man, by teaching us to see the universal in the form of the particular'.[8]

On Kant's aesthetic scheme, although judgements of beauty are not produced in the understanding by subsumption under concepts, pleasure in the beautiful nonetheless results from a 'free play' of the sensory imagination with the understanding which is akin to but less rigid and constrained than subsumption, and hence a source of enjoyment. And here Caird finds another point in the system to challenge, for he regards this as too lowly a combination to have such an effect. Understanding merely brings distinct objects together under one heading, but there is no aesthetic joy in that. Aesthetic pleasure consists rather in 'a consciousness that takes the individual object out of the limits of the context of experience, in which it is only a partial existence essentially related to other partial existences, and makes it into a complete whole by itself: an object conceived apart from its limitation or determination by other objects as a kind of microcosm or little world in itself.'[9] But this is possible only insofar as understanding turns into pure reason, whose ideas point beyond possible experience to truths of the noumenal world that knowledge itself cannot reach. Kant's own system implicitly recognizes this, for he characterizes beauty as 'purposiveness without purpose' and while the highest category understanding can produce is that of law or necessary connection, it is to reason that we must turn for the idea of design or purpose.[10]

For Kant aesthetic experience is, albeit shared, thoroughly subjective. A function of the disinterested pleasure we feel in things, it is non-cognitive and gives no insight into the world. The purposiveness we find in beautiful things does not correspond to any objective purpose *in rerum natura*. Caird finds a measure of truth in this thought, insofar as the beautiful object does indeed present itself as self-contained and self-harmonious, unconnected to the world around it.[11] But the point is not one that can take us very far, for strictly speaking, since all finite objects are dependent and essentially related to others around them, any such appearance must be judged on further reflection a limited and misleading one. Yet subjectivity and illusion cannot be the last word on aesthetic experience, for as we have already seen, Caird finds in it the beginnings of an insight with the power to overcome the dualisms that so beset Kant's thought. And sure enough, on Caird's reading, Kant's aesthetics hint too at an overcoming of the contrast between subjective appearance and objective truth. Beauty *is* truth. Caird argues that art must be regarded as 'an anticipative grasp of a truth which is beyond ordinary knowledge, and of which philosophy is a continual but never completed

---

[8] *Evolution of Religion*, I:234.   [9] *Critical Philosophy of Immanuel Kant*, II:459.
[10] *Critical Philosophy of Immanuel Kant*, II:461.
[11] Bosanquet also suggests that works of art may be in this way self-contained; 'infinite' in the Hegelian sense of that term ('On the True Conception of Another World', xxvi).

verification'.[12] 'Science is a fiction which looks like truth, while Art is a truth that looks like fiction'.[13] Properly understood,

> the Beautiful will be simply the revelation to sense and in a particular object, of that which is the inmost reality or meaning of things. It will be partly an illusion: for that meaning can be seen in its fullness only in the *whole* world as it exists for an intelligence which apprehends the universal as such and sees the particular through it.... But, on the other hand, in so far as the world is organic ... the illusion will lift us to a higher level of truth than that science which regards the part merely as a part, or a finite thing externally related to other finite things.[14]

While there is legitimate doubt whether any of these ideas are really present in Kant's aesthetics, unsurprisingly, there is no doubt how close they bring us to Hegel's position.[15] According to Hegel's philosophy, the third and final stage of Spirit's triadic path from Subjective to Objective to Absolute is itself characterized by the triad—art, religion, philosophy—implying that each of these three subjects express the same basic message, albeit in progressively superior fashion. The Idea that philosophy states in explicitly rational form, religion can only express in a lesser pictorial guise, while art cannot utter it at all, but simply presents it to us in concrete, material, sensory form. Hegel stresses the idealizing tendency of art; what is represented in art may be taken from nature, but it is the role of the artist to bring out its universal meaning. Although up to this point he has been kept in the background, it is with this explicitly Hegelian position that Caird concludes, arguing that art should be compared only with those other forms of consciousness which reveal the ultimate unity of man's life in all its differences, that is, with religion and philosophy.[16]

9.2 Bernard Bosanquet

9.2.1 The evolution of the aesthetic consciousness

The British Idealist who wrote most extensively about aesthetics was Bernard Bosanquet.[17] Like Caird, his first approach to the subject was historical, but his efforts were much more detailed and systematic. In 1892 he published *A History of Aesthetic*, which runs to over five hundred pages and was the first such work ever to be written in English. Aesthetics, he tells us, means 'the philosophy of the beautiful' and so the history of aesthetics must be 'the history of the philosophy of the beautiful',[18] but this could suggest something more narrow that Bosanquet intends for he offers not merely

---

[12] *Critical Philosophy of Immanuel Kant*, II:466.
[13] *Critical Philosophy of Immanuel Kant*, II:466.
[14] *Critical Philosophy of Immanuel Kant*, II:469–70.
[15] *Hegel's Philosophy of Fine Art*. For more detail on Hegel's theory of art see Desmond, *Art and the Absolute*.
[16] *Critical Philosophy of Immanuel Kant*, II:476.
[17] For a general discussion of Bosanquet's aesthetics see Lang, 'Bosanquet's Aesthetic: A History and Philosophy of the Symbol'.
[18] *History of Aesthetic*, 1.

a history of various philosophical systems, but an evolution of what he calls 'the aesthetic consciousness', the 'sense of beauty, which is itself determined by conditions that lie deep in the life of successive ages'.[19] Hard to pinpoint precisely, but at once intellectual and cultural, the idea is in many ways an aesthetic parallel of Edward Caird's similarly wide-ranging notion of 'ethical life'.[20]

It will be no surprise to learn that the story Bosanquet tells is much influenced by Hegel. His first foray into aesthetics was in fact a translation in 1886 of the introduction to *Hegel's Philosophy of Fine Art*,[21] the concluding section of which is reproduced as an Appendix to his *History*, and in some respects he follows Hegel to the letter. For example, arguing that as Absolute Spirit takes us beyond either Subjective or Objective Spirit so the products of art are aesthetically superior to those of nature, Hegel took art rather than natural beauty as his primary concern.[22] Endorsing this thought, Bosanquet argues that there is no beauty independent of human perception or imagination—it is not an intrinsic property like mass or shape—in which case it seems mistaken to focus on its everyday appearances to the ordinary consciousness rather than its more refined grasp by the educated mind. Just as the facts of physical nature do not give themselves up readily to the ordinary untrained observer, but require the penetrative insight and mathematical abstraction of the scientist to reveal them, so we should allow the artist to show us what is truly beautiful.[23] This is not to say that nature cannot be beautiful, but where with a work of art we have at hand the artist's intention to guide us in appreciating it, with unmodified nature 'the artist's work has to be done by the spectator himself'.[24] It is thus no surprise that our appreciation of natural beauty is shaped by the art of great painters, for in a way, 'natural beauty is that beauty in respect of which every man is his own artist'.[25]

Bosanquet is being equally Hegelian in reading the evolution of aesthetic concepts as a steady development from the abstract to the concrete,[26] but the precise details of the story sketched, on the other hand, are his own. The ancients, he claims, understood beauty as rhythm, harmony, regularity, repose, symmetry—abstract relations of system and order that Bosanquet classifies under the general heading unity-in-variety. But the romantic sense of life and the craving for free expression that were hallmarks of the modern world destroyed the satisfaction which had once been found in such a view, and led to a more advanced sense of beauty as significance, expressiveness, the utterance of all that life contains, the conception of the characteristic.[27] Yet, since the correction of any one-sided view must fall into its own one-sided-ness, the story

---

[19] *History of Aesthetic*, xii.

[20] See above Chapter 6.3.1.

[21] His own introduction to this volume, the essay 'On the True Conception of Another World' was itself an important early discussion of Hegel, that we have already noted on several occasions above.

[22] *Introduction to Hegel's Aesthetik or Philosophy of Fine Art*, 38–9, 90–3.

[23] *History of Aesthetic*, 3.

[24] 'The Part Played by Aesthetic in the Development of Modern Philosophy', 382.

[25] 'The Part Played by Aesthetic in the Development of Modern Philosophy', 383.

[26] *History of Aesthetic*, 8.   [27] *History of Aesthetic*, 4–5.

cannot end here but must point in the end towards a 'reunion of content and expression',[28] something Bosanquet thought he detected in modern times, and which informs his own proposed definition of beauty as, 'that which has characteristic or individual expressiveness for sense-perception or imagination, subject to the conditions of general or abstract expressiveness in the same medium'.[29]

To highlight some key steps in this story, we may begin with the ancient Greeks, of whose productions Bosanquet takes a somewhat less elevated view than Caird. At this stage in history, he claims, art was regarded as simply imitative or image-making. But gradually and repeatedly, he argues, for example in the aesthetic ideas of Plotinus, Erigena, Dante, and Aquinas, art was able to break free from the straight-jacket of imitation to arrive at a conception of itself as symbolic—the symbolism, at first, of spiritual things but then, later, in principle, of anything.[30] The next crucial step was the romantic movement, which emphasized the expression of feeling and emotion in art, expanding the range of beauty beyond its earlier more limited scope to include material such as the ugly and the sublime; a key text here being Burke's *On the Sublime and the Beautiful* (1756). The problem thrown up by this transition from narrow, formal, and surface beauty to its symbolism for, and expression of, deeper realities was first voiced in general form by Kant whose problematic Bosanquet puts in the form of the question, 'How can the sensuous and the ideal world be reconciled?' or more specifically, 'How can a pleasurable feeling partake of the character of reason?'[31] Bosanquet thus locates the crucial moment in the development of aesthetics at the same juncture as did Caird only a few years before, but he is less generous to Kant than was Caird. To Bosanquet's mind, for all that it attempts to keep apart universally valid aesthetic judgement from merely individual judgement of taste, Kant's answer to this question remains too subjective,[32] and it is Hegel's correction of this alone that provides 'the greatest single step that has ever been made in aesthetic'.[33] For to Hegel, beauty is the expression in sensuous form of the Idea—to a degree in nature, but even more so in art. It is the manifestation in concrete reality of ideas, functioning at its very heart like a word or symbol.[34] Art reconciles form and content, reason and feeling, the ideal and the real. It reveals to us the spiritual world, or one had better say the spiritual character of *this* world for, if 'it takes us into a new world', it is not 'another world', but our own world

---

[28] *History of Aesthetic*, title to ch.XV.

[29] *History of Aesthetic*, 5.

[30] *History of Aesthetic*, 4, 112, 114, 131, 143, 148, 158. 'Imitation is only a rule of art, and prima facie can make nothing beautiful which is not given as beautiful. Symbolism is a mode of interpretation; and . . . has the one advantage of absolute universality. If all that has a meaning may be beautiful, then there is nothing in which we may not chance to detect an element of beauty' (*History of Aesthetic*, 143).

[31] *History of Aesthetic*, 173, 187.

[32] *History of Aesthetic*, 266.

[33] *History of Aesthetic*, 342.

[34] 'That the world of the mind, or the world above sense, exists as an actual and organized whole, is a truth most easily realized in the study of the beautiful. And to grasp this principle as Hegel applies it is nothing less than to acquire a new contact with spiritual life' ('On the True Conception of Another World', xvi).

'twice-born' revealed in its profoundest and truest self.[35] As well as to Hegel's account, Bosanquet's final view is also close to theories that locate the distinctive nature of art in the expression and communication of feelings or emotions. The book concludes with a discussion of recent aesthetic advances in England, considering how Ruskin's emphasis on the beauty of nature and Morris' emphasis on workmanship sharpened this result, by bringing it back from the over-refined and formal to the more lowly and everyday.[36]

The story told here is, of course, the idealist one. But not only does the evolution of aesthetic ideas fit in with the general evolution of philosophical ideas, Bosanquet even argues that it was the former which gave birth to the latter. Aesthetics, he claims, was a crucial factor in the birth of idealism; reason enough, were there not others, why philosophers should not neglect it as a subject. According to Bosanquet, Kant's pioneering, but formal and abstract, recognition that ultimate reality consists in a kind of union of sense and reason, neither of which alone can claim to be truly real, was turned into Hegel's concrete self-manifesting Absolute Idea at once real and ideal, precisely through the aesthetic insights of Wincklemann, Goethe, Schiller, and Schelling; for it is to them that we owe the appreciation of art as a union of sense and thought and a revelation of whatever is highest in man, which insight Hegel uses as a model for his philosophical system in general and enshrines by giving art a place of honour in the culminating dialectical triad of Absolute Spirit.[37]

On the Hegelian scheme Absolute Spirit manifests itself progressively through the three stages of Art, Religion, and Philosophy. Art gives way to Religion which in turn gives way to Philosophy, as one and the same message expresses itself first materially, then pictorially, and only at the last in explicit rational form. Read as an historical thesis, one implication which might be drawn from this story—associated with Benedetto Croce—is that, at some point in the future, art will cease, to be taken over by a higher religious form of consciousness. Bosanquet vigorously rejects this interpretation. He objects that, 'The phases of experience which reveal relative approximations to completeness are not successive in time nor vanishing in logic. . . . As factors implying the whole system and implied in it they are grades of the spirit in the fullest sense. The absolute is the whole which they constitute, and if any of them were eliminated would be the absolute no longer.' The phrase, 'the death of art', he complains, nowhere occurs in Hegel; his term 'Ausflösung' indicates not the *death* but the *dissolution* of art, in the sense of resolving a contradiction or transforming its significance.[38]

---

[35] 'Life and Philosophy', 56. In this late essay (1924) we see the very same ideas as in the early Hegel essay 'On the True Conception of another World' (1886).

[36] *History of Aesthetic*, ch. XV. See also 'Individual and Social Reform', 30–1.

[37] 'The Part Played by Aesthetic in the Development of Modern Philosophy'. See also *History of Aesthetic*, 441; *Bernard Bosanquet and his Friends*, 259.

[38] 'Croce's Aesthetic', 430–1. See also Iiritano, 'Death or Dissolution? Croce and Bosanquet on the Auflösung der Kunst'. That the stages of Hegelian dialectic are co-existent rather than sequential was also much emphasized by Edward Caird (*Evolution of Religion*, I:77) though Bosanquet here refers back to Hegel himself (*Hegel's Logic*, §237).

Bosanquet continued to think about aesthetics and, nearly a quarter of a century after his *History*, returned to the subject in a short book, *Three Lectures on Aesthetics*. There without worrying about 'the historical order of things' he tries to reconstruct the same conceptual development of aesthetics, this time with reference to the difficulties that it has to overcome.[39] At its simplest the artistic impulse is one of mere expressiveness,[40] but a whole new dimension enters in when its products and patterns are taken also as *representations*, for representation is non-aesthetic—its concern is with truth and knowledge. The problem is how the aesthetic can be extended into the representational,[41] the representation serving the expression rather than the expression becoming subordinate to the knowledge.[42] This is an opportunity as well as a challenge,[43] for in moving beyond simple lines, shapes, and patterns, a whole new range of material becomes available to us. Of course, the exact balance struck varies from art to art, and to some extent these two always remain in competition and struggle,[44] but Bosanquet concludes that a synthesis is possible,[45] that our knowledge can aid our expressiveness, and even take on an expressiveness of its own.[46]

He also revisited his ideas about beauty and ugliness. In the *History*, the story Bosanquet tells is one of the gradual expansion of the beautiful, and at the last his view that beauty is expression combined with his Hegelian belief that all of reality is an expression result in the conclusion that there is no such thing as ugliness. By the time of *Three Lectures*, however, he came to see that this was too simplistic. Without denying that nature contains no true ugliness, he insists that not all beauty is 'easy' and that we must admit too a class of 'difficult beauty', accessible only to those with 'aesthetic insight',[47] and including such things as the sublime, the tragic, the grotesque, the comic, objects marked by intricacy or internal tension, or themes from across the full range of human response—at least some of which we would be inclined in more colloquial or conventional terms to call 'ugly'. These differ, however, from 'true ugliness'. True ugliness is always a failure of expression, which never occurs. Although it may to some extent be found in the duplicitous expression of 'insincere and affected art'[48] or art with a decorative element inconsistent with its purpose,[49] in the end there is no 'invincible ugliness, such as no sane imagination can see as beautiful',[50] for all art expresses to some degree and thus has beauty—if only we can see it—while nature itself, since it does not express at all, is never ugly in this sense.[51]

[39] *Three Lectures on Aesthetic*, 38.   [40] *Three Lectures on Aesthetic*, 40.
[41] *Three Lectures on Aesthetic*, 44.   [42] *Three Lectures on Aesthetic*, 46.
[43] *Three Lectures on Aesthetic*, 43, 52.   [44] *Three Lectures on Aesthetic*, 56.
[45] *Three Lectures on Aesthetic*, 57.   [46] *Three Lectures on Aesthetic*, 47.
[47] *Three Lectures on Aesthetic*, 85.   [48] *Three Lectures on Aesthetic*, 106.
[49] *Three Lectures on Aesthetic*, 108.   [50] *Three Lectures on Aesthetic*, 97.
[51] See J.S. Mackenzie, *Ultimate Values*, 142; Jacquette, 'Bosanquet's Concept of Difficult Beauty', 79–88; Raters, 'Unbeautiful Beauty in Hegel and Bosanquet', 162–76.

9.2.2 Aesthetic appreciation and production

As well as discussing the content and evolution of our aesthetic sense—which things we find beautiful—Bosanquet also considers what might be regarded as the more psychological aspects of the question—just what is going on in our being when we appreciate or create beauty.

At its simplest aesthetic experience is 'a pleasant feeling',[52] but of course there are many pleasant feelings, not all of them aesthetic, so further conditions on the state must be specified. Bosanquet lists five. First, it is *stable*. Unlike the pleasures of eating and drinking which are impermanent and diminish as they are satisfied, pleasure in beauty persists. Secondly, it is *relevant* or annexed to some particular object which evokes it. Thirdly, it is *common*, you can appeal to others to share it. It is not relative or just-a-matter-of-taste. 'To like and dislike rightly is the goal of all culture worth the name,' he suggests.[53] Fourthly, it is *contemplative*. Unlike either practice or theory, where with hands or minds we work on something, in looking on the object we make no attempt to alter it. We simply take it as it is. Yet it should not be supposed that this is a wholly passive state, for a crucial element in that contemplation is the *imagination* as we explore in mind the possibilities it suggests.[54] Fifthly, and all-importantly, it is a feeling which becomes 'organized', 'plastic', or 'incarnate'.[55] A feeling or idea in becoming expressed in material reality, in being given 'imaginative shape', is transformed. It must submit to the laws which govern physical objects,[56] and in so doing becomes something deeper, more significant, and more universal. 'A work of art, or any object regarded as beautiful, makes an appeal to feeling; which, as just such an appeal, must be immediate, although the feeling to which it appeals is moralized and spiritualised.'[57]

So much for the subject of experience, but what of the person 'most to be considered in aesthetic,'[58] the creative artist? The feeling involved in aesthetic production is, argues Bosanquet, the same as that involved in aesthetic appreciation, which is a weaker form of it—he takes 'the spectator's attitude . . . to be merely a faint analogue of the creative rapture of the artist'.[59] In this way we come very close to what is called the expressivist view of art, which regards aesthetic creativity as a process whereby a feeling on the part of the artist is externalized in some medium in order that it may then be recognized and absorbed by the person appreciating the resulting work.[60] As Tolstoy put it, 'Art is a human activity, consisting in this, that one man consciously, by means of certain external signs, hands on to others feelings he has lived through, and that other people are infected by these feelings, and also experience them.'[61] Bosanquet allows that the aesthetic attitude may be described as 'feeling expressed for expression's

---

[52] *Three Lectures on Aesthetic*, 3.   [53] *Three Lectures on Aesthetic*, 5.
[54] *Three Lectures on Aesthetic*, 26ff.   [55] *Three Lectures on Aesthetic*, 7.
[56] *Three Lectures on Aesthetic*, 8.   [57] *Logic*, II:233–4.
[58] *Three Lectures on Aesthetic*, 30.   [59] *Three Lectures on Aesthetic*, 35.
[60] See Apata, 'Feeling and Emotion in Bosanquet's Aesthetics', 177–96.
[61] *What is Art?*, 50.

sake',[62] although he insists that it is vital too that we distinguish between emotion 'merely discharged' and emotion 'expressed'—between, for example, a jump for joy and a dance.[63]

But if allowed that Bosanquet's view is similar to expressivism, it must not be too closely identified with that position. In Croce, to take its key representative,[64] what gets expressed in physical form is some wholly internal state. Bosanquet allows that art is more than just physical—'Expression after all is an empty name, unless there is something to be expressed,' he admits[65]—but he a strongly objects to any dualism, protesting that the idea cannot be separated from its physical expression. Art is a fusion of body and soul. He calls Croce's view, in which beauty can be wholly internal, a 'false idealism',[66] insisting that 'The point of the aesthetic attitude lies in the adequate fusion of body and soul, where the soul is a feeling, and the body its expression, without residue on either side.'[67] For fear of taking away the intrinsic value to art, of turning it simply into a vehicle for the expression of something else, Croce rejects as inessential its external manifestation—indeed he doubts external reality altogether. But this in Bosanquet's eyes is a profound mistake, for without sacrificing its unity or primacy, 'Art is in truth the perpetual union of body and spirit, and to refuse to study the body in which it clothes itself betrays a bias which indicates a one-sided philosophy.'[68] At least one commentator has found more than simply aesthetic significance in such thoughts, describing Bosanquet's position here as a kind of synthesis of naturalism and idealism; beauty is the fusion of body and soul.[69]

For Bosanquet, embodiment is essential and the different arts are distinguished by their different media. This leads him to disagree with Hegel on the subject of poetry. Poetry, for Hegel, occupies a quite specific place in the pantheon of arts. The general forwards movement of ideas which culminates in the triad art–religion–philosophy, works also within art itself, which (Hegel argues) displays a progressive development of its ideas; beginning with its most concrete forms, such as architecture and sculpture, and progressing through the range as spirit gradually withdraws itself from the sensuous finally to become religion. To sketch the culminating triad of this movement, music is more inward and subjective than painting as time supersedes space, while poetry, synthesizing painting and music, constitutes the final idealization of the sensuous. In poetry the message becomes wholly internal; the sounded word becomes merely a symbol for the unsounded thought or mental picture. Bosanquet disagrees. He insists,

---

[62] *Three Lectures on Aesthetic*, 37.
[63] 'On the Nature of Aesthetic Emotion', 395–6.
[64] The view is also associated with R.G. Collingwood.
[65] 'Croce's Aesthetic', 414.
[66] *Three Lectures on Aesthetic*, 73.
[67] *Three Lectures on Aesthetic*, 75; also v–vi, 7.
[68] 'Croce's Aesthetic', 415.
[69] MacEwen, 'Bosanquet, Santayana, and Aesthetics', 127–44.

contra Hegel, that poetry has a proper medium which is *sound*.[70] It is hard to disagree, and tempting to infer that Hegel probably *read* more poetry than he ever *listened to*.

It has already been noted how Bosanquet was as interested in aesthetic production as in consumption, and also as interested in craft as in fine arts. Putting these two ideas together encouraged him to advocate craft in schools as a way of developing our aesthetic and even our moral sense.[71] In the process of trying to *make* beauty (he gives the example of learning to carve wood) we discover how to *see* it all around; 'a certain change is produced in [the] mind; a new perception is awakened new interest is acquired. [A man] sees things to which he was blind before, and enjoys things to which he was insensible before.'[72] Moreover, since aesthetic values are at root one with all others, this enlargement of sensibility is a form of training which is ultimately moral, which serves to 'intensify the sense of the value of life,' to heighten which 'is to make life more worth living, and therefore more worth developing'.[73] The debt to Ruskin and Morris so approved in his *History* stands out clearly here, as he argues that 'The perception of beauty implies, above all things, an awakened mind.'[74] Where we see beauty, can we be wholly blind to goodness?

9.3 Poetry

9.3.1 The affinity of poetry and philosophy

Edward Caird and Bernard Bosanquet were the only British Idealists who wrote or thought at any length on philosophical aesthetics.[75] There was, however, one specific issue in aesthetics which captured the attention, and influenced the philosophy, of nearly all of them. This was the topic of poetry. There can be no understanding of British Idealist philosophy (in any of its varieties) without an appreciation of what kind of activity they thought they were undertaking; their own conception of philosophy. But there can be no understanding of their conception of philosophy without an appreciation of their view of its relation to poetry. For they saw these as correlated pursuits.[76] Of course, there are two terms here and to say that they viewed them in

---

[70] *History of Aesthetic*, 460–62; *Three Lectures on Aesthetic*, 64–7.

[71] See Trott, 'Bosanquet, Aesthetics, and Education: Warding Off Stupidity with Art', 113–26; Vincent, 'Bosanquet and Social Aesthetics', 54–62.

[72] 'Individual and Social Reform', 26.

[73] 'Artistic Handwork in Education', 78.

[74] 'The Home Arts and Industries Association: Aims and Objects', 135–7. See also Vincent, 'Bosanquet and Social Aesthetics', 54–62.

[75] There are two possible exceptions to this statement. J.A. Smith wrote on aesthetics, but most his work remained unpublished. R.G. Collingwood published on the subject (*Outlines of a Philosophy of Art*, *The Principles of Art*) but although a figure continuous with aspects of the idealist tradition, his thought differed in many respects from theirs, and this much later body of work is not helpfully understood in the same framework.

[76] There are three possible objections to this claim, all fair, to a degree. (i) Everybody took poetry seriously at that time. Victorian society held poetry in an esteem we no longer do today, quoting it in all types of writing. This is true, however the Idealists took that interest to new heights. (ii) The British Idealists were not

close relation tells us as much about their notion of poetry as it does about their conceptualization of philosophy, but the latter is especially worth stopping to note, for in an age where philosophers rarely regard themselves as partners with poets, examining this earlier view may help us challenge some of the more simple-minded criticisms that have been raised against their affinity.

Few philosophers today would define their work in relation to poetry,[77] but to the Idealists this was a natural and important relation for, as they saw it, there exists a deep coincidence of *aim* between the ends pursued by these two endeavours. Both poetry and philosophy seek understanding; they are in the business of knowledge.[78] They seek, moreover, the same kind of truth; to lay bare the most hidden, most profound and most universal principles at work behind both thought and reality. Notwithstanding their many and undeniable differences, at bottom, poets and philosophers are searchers and spokesmen for the same things.[79] If we look to the sources for such a conception, then immediately we find ourselves in one of the areas where the label 'Anglo-Hegelian' is most readily applicable, for in no small degree the model at work here is that of Hegel's philosophy of art as it figures in his more general account of the development of consciousness (or Geist). For, as we have already seen, to Hegel, poetry is the highest phase of art, one step below religion; art and religion themselves forming the first two triads of the last stage of the Absolute Idea. It is the least pictorial of those pictorial forms whose aim is the same as philosophy itself. Even if (like Bosanquet) some thought poetry a mode of expression *more embodied* that Hegel had supposed, this basic account of its role and position was wholeheartedly taken up.

The claim that the British Idealists saw poetry as an expression of the very same kind of truth as philosophy, can be fleshed out in a little more detail, for there are several aspects to it. To begin with, the knowledge that they both seek to reveal is of a kind that lies hidden beneath the surface of things. There can perhaps be no more important distinction in idealist thought than that between appearance and reality; things we

---

the only intellectuals who believed there was a close relation between poetry and philosophy; Coleridge, Carlyle, John Stuart Mill, and Leslie Stephen to name but four all saw important connections. This also is true, but again it may be argued that the Idealists explored this link more thoroughly than others. (iii) Not all the Idealists give the same elevated significance to poetry. This too can be admitted. Although all the Idealists display great knowledge of and love for poetry, it was especially Edward Caird, and his followers, Jones, Mackenzie, Pringle-Pattison, and Haldane who discuss it in detail. Green, McTaggart, and Muirhead, on the other hand, seem relatively immune to its charms.

[77] I mean, of course, in the Anglo-Saxon world where, as it has recently been put, the barricades between the two are vigilantly maintained. (Eagleton, *The Meaning of Life*, 5).

[78] From such a perspective the career of A.C. Bradley, who taught both philosophy and literature, loses some of the strangeness with which modern academics would regard it. For further detail see below p.415.

[79] 'The poet, like the philosopher, is a seeker for truth, and we may even say for the same kind of truth' (Caird, 'Goethe and Philosophy', 55); 'In the end philosophy is at one with poetry. . . . Their goal is the same.' (Jones, *Idealism as a Practical Creed*, 10); 'The higher kinds of poetry . . . may, then, be said to aim at the same kind of insight as that which philosophy seeks to gain' (Mackenzie, *Elements of Constructive Philosophy*, 16); 'the highest truth of philosophy is a rational and self-conscious poetry, as the highest poetry may be described as an irrational and unconscious philosophy' (Caird, 'Plato and the Other Companions of Socrates', 352).

think real (like matter, space, and time) turn out not to be and divisions we think absolute (like that between subject and object, between different subjects, between finite and infinite) turn out to be fluid. Common sense and ordinary language are no guide to ultimate reality. But in the same way there can be no everyday common-sense poetry—at least not among what they designate 'the higher poetry'. Anything merely common or vulgar 'by its presence at once turns poetry into prose' says Caird. Though it may present to us immediate sensuous reality, poetry only does so in order to reveal deeper things, for 'poetic truth does not lie on the surface'. Although, like the scientist, he may trade in empirical life, he is not taken in by it, and 'the poet, like the philosopher, is in search of a deeper truth in things than that which is the object of science.'[80] The poet may *use* the sensuous and the everyday, but only to allow us to see *beyond* it.

One of the most characteristic aspects of the Idealists' conception of philosophy is that it is universal in vision. For them philosophy has the widest scope of all subjects; it is 'the attempt to comprehend the universe not simply piecemeal or by fragments but somehow as a whole.'[81] As Ritchie puts it, 'Philosophy is the endeavour to speak not merely the truth, but the whole truth.'[82] Here it might seem different from poetry, for surely poetry presents what is specific and concrete. But on deeper reflection the matter is otherwise. For poetry never focuses on the individual object or event for its own sake, its presentation of the particular is only of value in so far as it allows us to recognize the universal in it. We value most the poems that show us universal truths, which is what we value most in philosophy.[83] As we saw, this point was key in Caird's account of Kant's aesthetics.

If a slogan was wanted to capture the spirit of British Idealist philosophy, it would perhaps be hard to do better than 'relative identity' or 'unity-in-diversity'. This (as we have already seen) is a ubiquitous, difficult, and multi-faceted concept. It suffices here simply to note that the Idealists saw this as the notion which poetry *also* expresses best. It unites the sensuous and the abstract; many particulars, parts, images, or feelings all held together by a single idea. It combines; always seeking life, organism, unity, and purpose, where science (by contrast) pursues analysis down into lifeless mechanism. It speaks to the whole person.[84] Both philosophy and poetry aim, in Caird's words, to restore the 'broken harmony' of life. Reflecting upon the way in which Wordsworth brings a variety of ideas and images together, Caird argues that it is in precisely this synthetic role that he 'makes poetry the counterpart and coadjutor of philosophy'.[85]

---

[80] Caird, 'Goethe and Philosophy', 58, 59.

[81] Bradley, *Appearance and Reality*, 1.

[82] Ritchie, 'What is Reality?' 94.

[83] Philosophy tries to 'enable us by reflection to recognise as the universal principle of reality that ideal which poetry exhibits to us in special creations' (Caird, 'Goethe and Philosophy', 63).

[84] Caird, 'The Problem of Philosophy at the Present Time', 191.

[85] Caird, 'Wordsworth', 153.

Appearance and reality, universality, unity-in-diversity—the poet is saying the same thing as the philosopher; or, it might reasonably be objected, the same thing as the *Idealist* philosopher. And *that* is precisely the conclusion which they draw. The Idealists felt that they themselves were saying just what the preceding generation of poets had said. They saw the best poetry as giving an idealist message that coincided with their own. The chief figure to cite here is Henry Jones who argued (in *A Faith that Enquires*) that 'Idealism received its inspiration from Wordsworth and Coleridge and their fellow-poets, no less than it received its specific problem from Kant',[86] while his *Idealism as a Practical Creed* has a chapter titled 'The Idealism of Wordsworth and Browning', which explains in detail precisely how poetry gave birth to philosophical idealism. But Jones was not alone in this view. Green too says that the reconstruction of moral ideas in England came, not from a new and sounder philosophy, but from the deeper views of life of the contemplative poets, especially Wordsworth.[87] We find Mackenzie also in his 1890 *Introduction to Social Philosophy* arguing how recent poetry has taught idealism,[88] while Bosanquet in his *The Principle of Individuality and Value* suggests that the conception of nature or the universe in space and time 'interpreted as a living system'—that is, the Idealist view—is precisely 'the meaning which lies at the root of all art and poetry'.[89] And if we may move away from the strictly poetic to the literary for a moment the influence of Carlyle—whose radical idealist message is indissolubly linked to his radical expostulatory prose style—can hardly be over-stressed. Hilda Oakeley, a lesser Idealist whose work has been little read, sees no accident in all this anticipation. She speculates that the world-spirit needs must be filtered through national character and that perhaps it was inevitable that the spirit which on the continent produced philosophy, in Britain produced poetry; Wordsworth was Britain's Spinoza.[90]

9.3.2 *Differences between Hegel and the Idealists*

Before the British Idealists are simply written off as just reproducing Hegel's theory of poetry, two differences should be noted. Both concern relative orderings. In line with Hegel, many of the Idealists see the pairing of poetry and philosophy as joined by a third term, religion.[91] They agree that all three are in the same business. But whereas Hegel sees the order: poetry, religion, philosophy, at times they seem to reverse the ranking of the first two. There is an important historical point here. By the late nineteenth century, religion in many people's eyes had failed. One aspect of this we see in figures like Green and the Caird brothers who, it might be argued, sought to

---

[86] Jones, *Faith that Enquires*, 194–5.
[87] 'Popular Philosophy', 118.
[88] Mackenzie, *Introduction to Social Philosophy*, 376–7.
[89] Bosanquet, *Principle of Individuality and Value*, 358.
[90] Oakley, 'Poetry and Freedom', 93–5.
[91] 'there is no difference whatsoever between the interpretation given by science and that of poetry, or religion, or philosophy' (Jones, *Browning as a Philosophical and Religious Teacher*, 175).

replace theology by philosophy, but in another aspect, says Henry Jones, poetry can be seen as taking over where theology has failed. In his *Browning as a Philosophical and Religious Teacher*—note the title—he claims that,

In our day, almost above all others, we need the poets for . . . ethical and religious purposes. For the utterances of the dogmatic teacher of religion have been divested of much of their ancient authority, and the moral philosopher is often regarded either as a vendor of commonplaces or as the votary of a discredited science. . . . There are not a few educated Englishmen who find in the poets, and in the poets alone, the expression of their deepest convictions concerning the profoundest interests of life.[92]

Not only might art be higher than religion, it might even (some of the Idealists wondered) be higher than philosophy. Reflecting on the way in which poets have taught us to see the divine in *nature*, Mackenzie concludes his *Introduction to Social Philosophy* with the call for a new poetry that can teach us to see it in *humanity* and in society. Now this is something that idealist philosophy thinks itself to have already uncovered, but his point is that the philosopher, as such, cannot become either a prophet or a poet.[93] He cannot make this discovery *live* for us. Seth Pringle-Pattison agrees, arguing that 'both religion and the higher poetry—just because they give up the pretence of an impossible exactitude—carry us, I cannot doubt, nearer to the meaning of the world than the formulae of an abstract metaphysic'.[94] Philosophy in its ruthless abstraction, cannot satisfy our full life.

Some later reflections of Bradley's may help us to understand this. For Bradley too certainly casts doubt on the supreme position Hegel gives to philosophy. 'Philosophy aims at intellectual satisfaction,' he says, 'It seeks to gain possession of Reality, but only in an ideal form. And hence it is realization of but one side of our being.'[95] And so it is with the rest of our various pursuits. Pleasure, morality, beauty, knowledge, love—none we may view as the one supreme good that sums and includes the rest. But poetry, it might be argued, insofar as it can hold together the aesthetic, the intellectual, the moral, and the spiritual is truer to the whole of life than many other more one-sided abstractions.

9.3.3 *The old quarrel between poetry and philosophy*

If turning to one historical forerunner allowed the British Idealists to see poetry and philosophy as important allies, not all the signs pointed in the same direction. For the classically educated scholars they were, they all knew that perhaps the greatest idealist of them all—Plato—had been of a quite different view. And it is interesting to note their responses to that, for nearly all of them—at one point or another—feel called explicitly to take on Plato's contrary position.

---

[92] Jones, *Browning as a Philosophical and Religious Teacher*, 4.
[93] Mackenzie, *Introduction to Social Philosophy*, 376–8.
[94] Seth Pringle-Pattison, 'A New Theory of the Absolute', 220.
[95] Bradley, *Essays on Truth and Reality*, 11–12.

To set the scene, in the first half of Book X of his *Republic* Plato argues that the poets will be banned from his ideal city, since 'there is from old a quarrel between philosophy and poetry'.[96] There are two bones of contention. First, poetry is an imitative art, but imitative art can only represent things as they look from the outside. Indeed, given the already difficult relation between forms and objects, it must be confessed that art supplies merely the copy of a copy. It is but a source of falsehood. Secondly, poetry encourages unworthy emotions. It appeals to feelings rather than reason, and encourages sentiments that otherwise we would be ashamed of and suppress. Art should only portray worthy things. Interestingly, Plato ends with a suggestion that poetry might be reprieved, if she can plead her case.

There is no single 'British Idealist response to Plato'—his outburst of hostility to poetry evokes a variety of different reactions, although all are much embarrassed by the display. Not only does it contradict their own view, but it smacks of hypocrisy for, as Nettleship notes, 'Plato himself is something very like a great poet.'[97] At one extreme, Mackenzie suggests that Plato, in putting forward such an absurd view, is being deliberately ironic and humorous.[98] And in a somewhat similar vein, Bosanquet suggests that, rather than condemning art for being merely imitative and superficial, we should read Plato as offering a *reductio* of such a view; something along the lines of '*If* poetry is just imitation then it is worthless and to be dismissed from the ideal society.'[99] A.E. Taylor, by contrast, warns us off such easy answers insisting that Plato's is a serious proposal, and that 'we shall not appreciate his position unless we understand quite clearly that he is in downright earnest'.[100]

The two Idealists who come most closely to accepting Plato here are Edward Caird and Henry Jones. Caird says that the old quarrel between poets and philosophers of which Plato speaks is as far from reconciliation as ever. Nor would we wish them wholly reconciled, for (despite their close relation to one another) each does best service by keeping within its own limits;[101] a sentiment echoed by Jones who urges that 'the feud of which Plato speaks, between these 'two civilising inspirations' will last through all time.[102] Nettleship, by contrast, holds that talk of any real difference between them is spurious; 'there is no reason why a poet should not really in his own way be animated by the same spirit as a philosopher,' he insists, for 'there is a point, as Wordsworth indicated, where philosophy and poetry, imagination and science, meet. . . . The greatest philosophers and the greatest poets have not as a rule felt themselves to be at enmity.'[103] And between these two extremes of hostile difference and harmonious identity lies the perfect idealist synthesis of J.S. Mackenzie who argues that 'just because poetry, religion, and philosophy, in their highest

---

[96] Plato, *Republic*, 607b.   [97] Nettleship, 'Lectures on the "Republic" of Plato', 354.
[98] Mackenzie, *Manual of Ethics*, 293.   [99] *History of Aesthetic*, 30.   [100] Taylor, *Plato*, 280.
[101] Caird, 'Goethe and Philosophy', 54.
[102] Jones, *Browning as a Philosophical and Religious Teacher*, 3.
[103] Nettleship, 'Lectures on the "Republic" of Plato', 354. See also 'Lectures on Logic', 118.

expressions, are essentially aiming at the same thing in different ways, they are rather apt to come into conflict with one another.'[104] And perhaps he has a point, for it is true that siblings or co-religionists quarrel more frequently and fiercely than complete strangers.

James Seth latches on to the fact that Plato dismisses from his state the poets, not poetry itself, and that the exclusion is not necessarily final; a point also stressed by Bernard Bosanquet, who says that Plato's suggestion of a possible reprieve should not be dismissed as mere irony.[105] There are perhaps two lines of thought here. One strictly localizes Plato's focus here and sees him as attacking the literature of his day—which must have been at a very low ebb, suggests Seth—and the superstitious regard in which it was held. Several of the Idealists take this route, for of course it leaves us in a position from where we could—albeit with a certain aesthetic snobbery—continue to endorse the presence of art in society. Nettleship (for example) thinks that *in their lower phases* poetry and philosophy do indeed strike one another as antagonistic, and ventures that we all recognize a certain shame in the enjoyment we get from reading novels.[106] Again it is A.E. Taylor who calls the lie to this sort of response. 'We are only throwing dust in our own eyes if we suppose that Socrates wants merely to repress the cheap music-hall and the garish melodrama,' he says. By contrast, 'he is seriously proposing to censure just what we consider to be the imperishable contribution of Athens to the art and literature of the world'.[107]

The second, and perhaps more typically Idealist line of response, comes from Bosanquet who sees Plato's position as an early, and perhaps, inevitable step in the growth of aesthetic understanding. The Greeks were bound to an imitative conception of art, according to which representation of immoral content can only 'double the examples of immorality',[108] and there is no doubt that this conception led to a subordination of art to moral purposes that much encumbered Plato; and Aristotle too.[109] But it is axiomatic to idealism that we do not reach truth in one bound; we must start with first steps and mistaken ones. Insofar as he offers criticisms that allow us to move beyond this first simplistic conception, and insofar as his own philosophy itself expresses a belief in Ideas behind, and of greater reality than, their appearances, Plato points us forward to the truth.[110] He may have been quite wrong to suppose that poetry is simply the imitation of visible appearances, for in truth it seeks to uncover the hidden structure of reality itself. But his mistake put us on the right path, making it

---

[104] Mackenzie, *Elements of Constructive Philosophy*, 17.
[105] Seth, 'The Relation of the Ethical to the Aesthetic Element in Literature', 171; Bosanquet, *Companion to Plato's Republic*, 402.
[106] Nettleship, 'Lectures on the "Republic" of Plato', 354, 352.
[107] Taylor, *Plato*, 279.
[108] *History of Aesthetic*, 17.
[109] *History of Aesthetic*, 18.
[110] Bosanquet, *Companion to Plato's Republic*, 400–1.

almost a step in the right direction. In classic idealist style, those who in the past opposed me, thereby in fact spurring me on, may now be credited as my helpers.

9.3.4 Literary style and the new philosophy

It might perhaps be complained that everything which has been said so far has been at the meta-level; abstract discussions about the nature of poetry and philosophy, but the crucial thing to note is that these views had a real effect on the way the Idealists worked and wrote about philosophy. No one who has read British Idealist philosophy can have failed to observe the distinctive literary character of their efforts.

There are perhaps two things to note here. First, we have their frequent quotation of poetry. Flick through any book, or look in the index, and you find constant appeal to poetry. We should add here also their frequent use of biblical language (Jones and Caird in particular) and their regular citation of writers like Carlyle. And all this is not simply decoration, but crucial to the argument. Poetry is used to *make* points, not simply to *illustrate* them. Secondly, there is the very way in which they write themselves, the highly 'poetical' and literary nature of their own language. Of the many possible examples, every reader will have their favourites, but by way of illustration one might instance, for example, the metaphors of Bradley's 'bloodless categories', Pringle-Pattison's 'impervious' self, or Jones' 'gardener' state, or one might point to the paradoxes of John Caird's assertion that 'to be ourselves, we must be more than ourselves' or Joachim's claim that as no roads in themselves lead us to lose our way, so no judgements themselves are in error.[111] Connected to this they were all very expansive writers, often taking pages to gradually make and develop what we might call a single point. Ideas are first introduced, then repeated, expanded, and developed over many paragraphs, the writers more concerned to capture the cast of mind at work behind the thought or theory that offer any neat simple formulation of the idea itself.

Many of the Idealists produced work of great literary merit; still a delight to read. But, of course, not everyone was impressed. As the new century grew, a rival philosophy emerged with a new style of writing: clear, precise, simple, and short. Using either ordinary language or precisely defined technical terms it was modelled on the language of mathematical and empirical science. It was suggested in Chapter 1 that the Idealists contributed towards the professionalization of philosophy, distinguishing it from other disciplines. But if so, in time they themselves began to look 'amateur' as the discipline became professionalized in an even narrower 'specialist' sense. No longer a subject just anyone could write or read, it became (like science) the select preserve only of a 'trained' few.[112] The short science-style article replaced the multi-volume Gifford-lecture-style book. Not surprisingly the new writers took a dim view of their

---

[111] Bradley, *Principles of Logic*, 590–1 see above p.119; A.S. Pringle-Pattison, *Hegelianism and Personality*, 216 see p.358 below; Henry Jones, *The Principles of Citizenship*; 137 see p.509 below; J. Caird, *Introduction to the Philosophy of Religion*, 124 see p.150 above; H.H. Joachim, *The Nature of Truth,* 143 see p.443 below.

[112] Collingwood, *Autobiography*, 50.

predecessors. At the extreme, of course, the logical positivists regarded their writing as literally nonsense. Ayer in his *Language, Truth and Logic* notoriously attacks a sentence 'taken at random' from Bradley's *Appearance and Reality*, while Carnap regarded metaphysics as no more than poetry; a comment which led Ayer famously to gibe that the utterances of many philosophers should have been published in the *London Mercury* rather than in *Mind*.[113] But even if not nonsense, a great many of the new generation of analytic philosophers regarded the Idealists' writing as uneasy, loose, woolly, and rhetorical. And these are views that persist to this day.

We may let Geoffrey Warnock speak for his generation. 'It is not surprising' he allows 'that a philosophy of this variety—so ambitious, so deliberately un-ordinary, so determinedly grave—should have found expression in a characteristic manner of writing', but a modern philosopher, he continues, would find their style 'almost unbearable'. Bradley, he admits, was capable of 'impressive rhetoric, and conveys in his extraordinary sentences a sense of explosive energy'. On the other hand, 'Bosanquet's manner was less idiosyncratic but more literary, and closer to bombast. He wrote sometimes with an air of vague seriousness, in which the serious intent was almost completely muffled by the vagueness. And in the writings of the lesser men solemnity and unclarity seem to rise not seldom to the pitch of actual fraud.' Even Bradley's arguments, Warnock suggests, depended 'mainly upon the persuasive force and artifice of their presentation', such that 'to strip off the highly coloured rhetorical dress would be to harm substantially the doctrine itself, or even to find that one arrived, as with an onion, at nothing in the end'.[114]

Warnock's comments are as deeply unfair as they are mistaken. As the analytic philosophers came forwards with a changed conception of philosophy so they advanced a new literary style in which to present it; clarity and precision became the order of the day. As Candlish has put it 'even if idealism's subject matter is timeless, its style quickly became hopelessly dated'.[115] But it was disingenuous of the new philosophers then to turn back upon the Idealists and berate them for their manner of writing for, in truth, the older philosophers' style was just as well fitted to *their* conception of philosophy. As T.S. Eliot said of Bradley's prose, it was 'for his purposes . . . a perfect style'.[116] Both the Idealists and the new analytic philosophers shared a belief that one's conception of the proper nature and task of philosophy and one's conception of its

---

[113] Ayer, *Language Truth and Logic*, 49. Carnap, 'The Elimination of Metaphysics through the Logical Analysis of Language'. Ayer's gibe is reported in Mace, 'Representation and Expression' (38). The comparison between metaphysics and poetry is, of course, deliciously ironic in that the British Idealists' high esteem of poetry would have made them delighted by such an attempt to disparage their metaphysical efforts.

[114] Warnock, *English Philosophy since 1900*, 6–7. 'Too many fine phrases; too little argument'—Green, he complains elsewhere, had 'no firm grasp of what philosophy was about', the clear statement and clear resolution of problems. ('A Sage for a Time', 606).

[115] *The Russell/Bradley Dispute*, 181.

[116] Eliot, 'Francis Herbert Bradley', 197. Eliot came to Oxford to write a thesis on Bradley (*Knowledge and Experience in the Philosophy of F.H. Bradley*). For further details see Jane Mallinson, *T.S. Eliot's Interpretation of F.H. Bradley*.

proper method or literary style were two things that went hand in hand, and to attack the second was but a shabby and ineffective way to disagree with the first. A consideration of some of the key objections, and the underlying differences between their philosophical approaches, will make this clear.

To begin with it was objected that their writing was just *too broad and general*. With so wide a compass, it was thought, if one managed to say anything true at all, it could only be the thinnest of platitudes. It was believed that the lesson of the verification principle was that to work, words need to be tied down to precisely defined empirical applications.

But the Idealists did not write the way they did by accident. In contrast to the analytic philosopher's limited horizons, the correct philosophical view for them was the *global* view; philosophy being precisely the attempt to look at the universe, if not as a whole, then from the widest angle possible. To take an artistic analogy, the Idealists were trying to paint vast tableaux while their analytic cousins preferred to work on small canvases. And hence they chose literary tools to match.

These were outlooks distinguished by temperament—with a pessimistic assessment of our ability, the analytic ambition is modest and its vision small—but also by an underlying theory of language. For the notion that the more general your terms the less they manage to say is the widely-held view that intention varies in inverse proportion to extension. Almost an analytic dogma, this was (as we have already seen) a view openly dismissed by figures such as Bradley and Bosanquet as either false or trivial. Universality for them was not abstract, but concrete, and on their logic the wider your reach, the more you manage to say.

A second closely connected, but slightly different, objection is that the Idealists' writing was *slippery*. Their arguments moved rapidly across seemingly diverse issues, failing to respect distinctions and reaching grand conclusions on what can seem spurious identities, or vague hunches as to 'the general drift of things'. Instead of inching forwards by slow small steps, they move too fast and jump too far, weaving arguments that are suggestive but hard to pin down. There is, for example, a splendid passage in which Haldane simply lumps together Plato, Aristotle, Spinoza, Kant, Hegel, and Hume as propounding a single idealist message![117] Any modern philosopher would find it hard not to protest, pointing out many significant and fundamental differences between these figures, but all too often idealism seems almost blind to such details, shrugging them off as besides the point. 'There is far less discrepancy amongst the conclusions of the philosophers themselves than at first appears,' Jones tells us, 'for it is the way of philosophers, as it is of theologians and politicians, to make much of their differences.'[118]

There is no need to deny the fluidity of idealist thought and writing, but again the difference of style reflects a deeper difference in the very conception of what it is to do

---

[117] *Education and Empire*, 167.   [118] *Idealism as a Practical Creed*, 14.

philosophy. The analytic philosophers advocated a *piecemeal* approach; looking at concepts, problems, and arguments separately one by one. By contrast, the Idealists were *holistic*; they sought always to connect disparate ideas, to find the points of similarity, to reach out from their starting point to other fields. Like the poet who illuminates by bringing together incongruent and unusual images that help us see what familiarity has blinded us to, the philosopher seeks always to broaden our vision and show how all truth connects together in one integrated and comprehensive system. Scepticism certainly has its place and we should not just buy *any* system, but, urged Seth Pringle-Pattison, 'It is important to remember that despair of system is despair of philosophy, for philosophy just *is* system.'[119]

A third common charge against their writing is vagueness and imprecision. The analytic philosophers set immense store by clarity and exactness, bemoaning the nebulous and indistinct style of their idealist predecessors. G.E. Moore was particularly pained and exasperated by their lack of precision, and many of his papers from the early years of the century revolve around his uncovering of multiple ambiguities in stock idealists terms.[120]

But once again what is presented as infelicity of style is in fact the result of deep and considered philosophical opinion, in this case about the very nature of meaning itself. For few of the Idealists believed that words *had* precise meanings. Rather they should be thought of as containing great depths and levels of sense and implication; riches that we might find in them, or even that they might unfold for us, but which certainly stretch out of sight beyond the horizon of our immediate vision. Concepts are not self-contained; rather, as Nettleship puts it, 'every one of my ideas is in a context which it colours and by which it is coloured'.[121] 'Definitions are dangerous tools to handle,' says Jones, making a similar point, 'They are never entirely or permanently true of the facts of mind or of the world of spirit, for these do not have fixed boundaries: they do not shut out one another, and none of them is static or can bear being "fastened down".'[122] The notion that there might be such a thing as *the* analysis of a term struck them as crude; any non-trivial expression should be expected to contain *many* levels of analysis passing one into another and passing in the end even beyond the term itself. Bradley in particular explains how any term or judgement cuts off a content from a wider

---

[119] *Scottish Philosophy*, 196.

[120] See for example 'The Refutation of Idealism', *Principia Ethica*, §§18–22, 'External and Internal Relations' and 'The Conception of Reality'. C.D. Broad was similar: 'I have an extreme dislike for vague, and oracular writing; and I have very little patience with authors who express themselves in this style. I believe that what can be said at all can be said simply and clearly in any civilized language or in a suitable system of symbols, and that verbal obscurity is almost always a sign of mental confusion' ('Critical and Speculative Philosophy', 81).

[121] *Lectures on Logic*, 146.

[122] Jones, 'Education of the Citizen', 225. As J.E. Turner put it, 'All living ideas have jagged edges' (quoted in A.S. Nash, *The University and the Modern World*, Preface. Arnold Samuel Nash was a pupil of Turner's in Liverpool in the 1920s). Collingwood made a similar point with his notion of 'the overlap of classes' (*Essay on Philosophical Method*, ch.II).

presented whole, by which it is then conditioned, and to which it inevitably points for its complete significance. But the point was shared by all.

Calling up a new accusation, it was objected that the Idealists had a very odd way of speaking, that they used words in mysterious ways. For the new philosophy, by contrast, reality was something to be described in ordinary language; the watchword was 'common sense'.[123] For example, Moore has immense difficulty understanding what Bradley means when he says that time is unreal because he is using words in the 'wrong' way. He does not mean (and Moore comes over as quite the authoritarian here) 'what he *ought* to mean—just what anyone else would mean if he said that Time was unreal, and what any ordinary person would understand to be meant, if he heard those words'; rather he is using words 'in some highly unusual and special sense'.[124]

But this charge is every bit as superficial as the others. The Idealists did not use the kind of ordinary language that Moore thought they should, not out of some perverse desire to confuse, but because they simply did not believe that reality could ever be accessed in that way. In the first place ordinary language comes from ordinary experience and, as has already been noted, for Idealists, reality was something hidden, something quite other than ordinary experience. But the point goes deeper than that, for they held that reality was not simply beyond experience, but also beyond language and thought itself. Their philosophy precludes literalism. This is an important point and worth explaining more fully via a couple of illustrative figures. First we can take T.H. Green. Green is basically a Kantian—his eternal consciousness is understood as that which supplies the categories by which we unify and structure our experience, as that which makes it possible. But just like Kant before him, this puts Green in an impossible dilemma, for if what he says is true then he cannot say it. The problem is that the concepts and structures apply only within experience, and cannot legitimately be used outside or beyond it, not even to express the conditions which make possible that experience itself. What makes thought possible cannot itself be thought.[125] We find a similar problem in F.H. Bradley. The relational mode of thought is contradictory and points beyond itself. But all thinking is inevitably relational, and so we must conclude that it too points beyond itself—thought's 'happy suicide'—to an Absolute reality in some fashion felt but never said.[126] Not everyone perhaps was quite as pessimistic on this score as Green and Bradley, but even figures like Caird and Bosanquet, who would be reluctant to place any final limit on the grasp of reason in its most perfect form, would certainly allow that reality outstrips our current capacity to grasp it in thought or language.

---

[123] To be sure, it was necessary on occasion to draw a distinction between surface grammar and logical grammar, but that was only because we had been beguiled away from the patent facts of the matter by the sophistical illusions of language.

[124] Moore, *Philosophical Studies*, 208.

[125] Green, *Prolegomena* §75. For further discussion see Chapter 4.1.3.1 above.

[126] Bradley, *Appearance and Reality*, 152. For further discussion see Chapter 4.2 above.

Words are thus limited and philosophy is working at the verge of meaning, at the very edge of language. In this respect it is much like poetry, for in a poem too words are altered from their commonplace meaning. This is why the Idealists make such frequent use of poetry; the poet can take us beyond the limits of abstract terminology and help us appreciate things which cannot be said literally. But not only can the poet be philosophical, the true philosopher must also be (in some measure) a poet,[127] and so the same point explains why the Idealists themselves write so 'poetically'. Their exploitation of the power of words to suggest as well as to describe is quite deliberate. 'Philosophy cannot dispense with metaphor,' argued Ritchie, the only requirement is that it do so in as full consciousness as possible, for 'it is metaphors which escape notice that are dangerous'.[128]

In this context we should also note here Bradley's *Aphorisms* which, though privately printed at the Clarendon Press after his death in 1930 according to his wishes, stem from the period around *Appearance and Reality*.[129] Sometimes funny, sometimes beautiful, with an eye to the broader themes of life, these have been ignored by philosophers as just literature. But they are more than just idle witticisms. He describes them as 'attempt[s] to fix my passing moods',[130] and many express in stark literary form some of Bradley's philosophical ideas—including the one lifted to appear in the Preface to *Appearance and Reality* itself: 'Metaphysics is the finding of bad reasons for what we believe upon instinct, but to find these reasons is no less an instinct.'[131] Where a page of text is dead, an aphorism may offer a living glimpse. He says, 'An aphorism is true where it has fixed the impression of a genuine experience.'[132] But tragically the difference is only one of degree, since in the end, of course, for Bradley no idea can ever really capture reality and 'Our live experiences, fixed in aphorisms stiffen into cold epigram. Our heart's blood, as we write with it, turns to mere dull ink.'[133]

It is such picturesque use of language, of course, that leads the Idealists to be accused of *rhetoric*, and it has been thought by many since that their writing is really too coloured and expressive for serious philosophy. At times ponderous and solemn, at times preachy and moralizing, at times Sunday-sermon inspiring, its tone off-put a great many Edwardian readers. C.D. Broad, for example, contemptuously dismisses Green as offering nothing but a 'comforting aroma of ethical "uplift"' that turned undergraduates into prigs rather than philosophers.[134] Nor was this always just a matter

---

[127] In this connection we may note May Sinclair's 'Guyon: a Philosophical Dialogue', a lengthy poem setting out the case for Absolute Idealism.

[128] 'On Plato's Phaedo', 123.

[129] See G.R.G. Mure, 'F.H. Bradley: Towards a Portait', 32–3; Broomfield, 'Getting Real: In Praise of Bradley's Aphorisms'.

[130] *Essays on Truth and Reality*, 14 n.

[131] *Appearance and Reality*, xiv.

[132] Aphorism, #41.

[133] Aphorism, #25.

[134] Broad, *Five Types of Ethical Theory*, 144.

of *tone*, for with the writing of lay sermons (employed by Green and both Caird brothers) it became a matter of explicit literary *form*.[135]

The underlying suggestion is that there is something disreputable and unprofessional about such ways of writing. For the analytic school took science as their model; they aimed to be wholly rational and expunge all value and emotion from their discourse. Such things had no place in physics and they had no place in philosophy either. But while philosophers who model themselves on science may feel embarrassed by expressive language, the Idealists took no such view of philosophy, finding appeal to emotional, moral, and spiritual values wholly in order. For them these were the highest levels of mind and so it was entirely appropriate that they should be present alongside the highest levels of reasoning. The new intellectual perspective held that such values had a rightful place only in art and not in philosophy, but for the Idealists the contrast between philosophy and art was not that between reason and emotion, but rather that between reason and imagination—the sensory. In passing from art to philosophy we leave behind what is sensual or pictorial, but not what is moral, emotional, or spiritual.

We come lastly to perhaps the most serious objection of all, which is that in the writings of the British Idealists, poetry, metaphor, and literary art usurp the place of argument. Take away the rhetoric, says Warnock, and there is nothing left. This is perhaps a more awkward objection than the others for, often enough, this is the difference *they themselves* stress between philosophy and poetry. Poetry they say is direct and intuitive, whereas philosophy is mediate and argumentative. That is almost, one might say, what is so good about it; its cuts out all the contentious wrangling![136] But even here the situation is more complex than it first appears, as can be seen if we look at the work of Henry Jones on Robert Browning.

9.3.5 Jones on Browning and the role of argument

The case of Browning is interesting. In the decades after his death in 1889 he was held up as a great thinker and philosopher. The contemporary literature abounds with such titles as 'Robert Browning as a Religious Poet', 'Browning's Philosophy', 'Browning's Theism', 'Robert Browning as Religious Teacher', 'The Poetry and Philosophy of Browning', 'Robert Browning; Poet and Philosopher'.[137] Of course, times changed

---

[135] J. Caird, *University Addresses, University Sermons*; E. Caird, *Lay Sermons and Addresses*; Green, *The witness of God and Faith: two lay sermons*.

[136] Poetry is distinguished from philosophy by 'its spontaneous and even unconscious character' (Caird, 'Goethe and Philosophy', 59). 'Poetry reaches the results of philosophy by short cuts and without the endless argumentation' (Jones, *Introduction to A History of the Problems of Philosophy*, vii) The criticism is also one they were not above using against each other. Pringle-Pattison thought this something the neo-Hegelians were guilty of (*Hegelianism and Personality*, 102, 107, 120, 123, 128, 188) a charge in which Haldane felt there was at least some justice ('Hegel and his Recent Critics', 587).

[137] A.W. Symons, 'Robert Browning as a Religious Poet', *The Wesleyan-Methodist Magazine*, December 1882, 943–7; John Bury, 'Browning's Philosophy', *Browning Studies*, London 1895; Josiah Royce, 'Browning's Theism' Boston Browning Society Papers, New York 1897, 18–25; A.C. Pigou, *Robert Browning as Religious Teacher*, London 1901; E.H. Griggs, *The Poetry and Philosophy of Browning*, New York 1905; F.M. Sim, *Robert Browning: Poet and Philosopher*, London 1923.

and that reputation was reversed and in modern times his standing as a serious thinker is almost completely sunk.

In the middle of this story, in 1891, we find Henry Jones' book, *Browning as a Philosophical and Religious Teacher*. From its title we might think this is just another Browning-as-philosopher book, but in fact the case is more complex. Jones does think Browning a voice of great philosophical significance, a spokesman for what might be called 'optimistic idealism'. But, he insists, when we do him the honour of treating him as a *philosopher*, he falls far short of the mark. For in truth he was a poor philosopher, subscribing to a kind of scepticism about human cognitive powers, which Jones considers destructive of his optimism and his idealism alike. There was much in this criticism and so, paradoxically for all his high opinion of Browning's philosophical message, Jones became a key early figure in the subsequent eclipse of the poet's reputation as a thinker.

However, as Jones developed, his understanding of the difference between Browning's poetical message and his philosophical skills softened, and he saw a rapprochement. In the book he presents the matter as one of a direct clash of head *vs.* heart, reason *vs.* intuition, but in time he began to appreciate that reason is a more holistic thing. It involves our entire conception of the world as human beings. In this sense Jones' conception of the proper method of philosophy and poetry came closer into line. A key text here is his 1905 lecture on *The Immortality of the Soul in the Poems of Tennyson and Browning*.

With liberal use of quotation he makes the case that both Browning and Tennyson believe in the immortality of the soul, and that both take themselves to do so as a matter, not of argument, but intuition. But in fact, claims Jones, they are wrong about themselves and they stand on stronger ground than they know. Far from ousting reason they have employed it fully. They seem simply to rest on strong convictions which are deeply felt, and we might suppose the strength of conviction arises from the depth of feeling. But in truth matters are reversed. The power of feeling comes from the strength of the beliefs, and their strength 'from the fact that they have been made one with our rational life by a thousand judgments and practical experiences. The feeling of their vital strength is the result of a satisfied intelligence, and the intelligence is satisfied only when experience seems to be a congruous whole.' What tells the poet that what he has to say is true? His heart, the romantic may reply. And there is no need for us to disagree says Jones, for 'what is "the heart" in such a context, except the whole rational experience of the man chastened and purified and enlightened by observation up and down the broad order of things and the ways of men, and made wise by much reflection?'[138] Only on that assumption can any purpose, patterns, meaning or value be found in life. The issue, we must remember, is not the *validity* of any such case, but simply the fact that it *is* a case, that what we are presented with here is indeed an

---

[138] Jones, *Immortality of the Soul in the Poems of Tennyson and Browning*, 31, 37.

argument, in the sense of 'an hypothesis making sense of life and experience as a whole'.

Of course we need not say that *all* feeling is like this, that every feeling is the assimilated argument of experience, for as Edward Caird puts it, 'Whether the phrase "I feel it" means little or much, depends on the individual who utters it. It may be the concentrated expression of a long life of culture and discipline, or it may be the loud but empty voice of untrained passion and prejudice.'[139] But that poetry at its best is no mere assertion is something Caird would certainly endorse. In his essay on Goethe he argues that, although poetry neither describes a world exhausted by, nor itself falls under, the dead hand of necessitating laws of nature, it should certainly not be supposed that 'any great poetic creation is produced by an imagination which merely follows its own dreams and does not bend to any objective law'.[140] Nettleship makes the same point. It may be hard to draw any exact line between individual caprice and the sense of rightness or necessary connection that makes for great art, but of a line, note or word in the latter we may ask, just as we do of a step in reasoning, 'Is it exactly right?'[141] Poetry is subject to its own kind of law; caught by a deeper metaphysical necessity; the spirit of truth speaks through the poet and makes him write what he does. There is an inevitability and unavoidability in his words.

The point is more completely grasped if we look to the idealist theory of inference itself, as developed most fully by Bradley and Bosanquet. Philosophy may be abstract but in its search for truth it is drawn back to the concrete and the individual—'Truth lies not in abstraction but in concretion,' says Caird.[142] What holds of judgement and truth holds equally of inference and validity; the final criterion of the validity of inference lies not in pre-determined abstract formal schema, but in the full complexity of individual reality—'system' in Bosanquet's terms, 'the ideal self-development of an object' in Bradley's.[143] Our attention is drawn here to something very important about the Idealists' notion of reason. Again and again they assert the centrality of reason, upholding that 'the real is the rational'. But what on the idealist scheme is 'reason'? It has already been noted that they have a broad, non-formal conception of logic but it should be recognized that their 'use' of reason is really even wider than that. It signifies something like 'the proper working of the whole person'. In place of the Humean notion of 'reason' as the deduction of sure conclusions from indubitable premises, they go back to an older tradition that embraces the full employment of all our intellectual powers. How much does this include? Clearly coherence and connectedness are vital—it is about building a picture of reality as a whole. But equally important are articulatedness and the ability to express things in words—which is why brute

---

[139] Caird, *The Social Philosophy of Comte*, 160–1.
[140] Caird, 'Goethe and Philosophy', 58–9.
[141] 'Lectures on logic', 119.
[142] Caird, *Evolution of Religion*, I:151.
[143] Bosanquet, *Essentials of Logic*, 40; Bradley, *Principles of Logic*, 598.

intuitions do not count as part of reason and why, also, in the right context, emotion or imagination may properly contribute to it. But the scope of the term may be broadened out even further than this, for 'reason' takes in more than simply the workings of any one individual mind. At its most powerful it is something collective, social, and historical. Drawing on Hegel's idea of the 'cunning of reason', Caird makes much of the way in which an intellectual evolution larger than any one of us may steer our individual thinking in one direction or another, while Ritchie draws attention to the fact that this process in which we ourselves are unaware of the collective intellectual development driving our ideas may to us seem the very opposite of deliberation. 'The Universal Reason works unconsciously, and in some cases immediately. That is inspiration.'[144] Such often enough is the reason of the poet.

---

[144] *Philosophical Studies*, 261. For Caird see Chapter 5.4.2 above.

10

Developments in Idealist Metaphysics

10.1 Personal Idealism

10.1.1 A.S. Pringle-Pattison

It has been examined how, from the 1870s onwards, and speaking by and large with a common voice, Idealists were enthusiastic in advancing a constructive absolutism which, if not entirely Hegelian, was very much in that mould. But soon this consensus within the fold was broken, and the call broadcast for a different kind of idealism.[1] Although he was quickly followed by others, the first and chief voice in this regard was that of Andrew Seth Pringle-Pattison. His earliest writings were orthodox. As well as historical pieces on Kant and Hegel (which we have already noted), in 1882, together with Richard Burdon Haldane (with whom he had been a student at Edinburgh), he edited the collection, *Essays in Philosophical Criticism.* Dedicated to the memory of T.H. Green, who had died the year before, this volume of essays by, as yet, little-known figures all influenced by German philosophy may be seen as a kind of manifesto for the fledgling Idealist school.[2] Four of its papers we have already noted including Pringle-Pattison's own contribution, the opening essay of the collection, an Hegelian exposition of Kant's errors entitled 'Philosophy as a System of Categories'.[3]

But shortly afterwards Pringle-Pattison's thinking began to move in a new and more controversial direction. His 1885 book, *Scottish Philosophy; a comparison of the Scottish and German answers to Hume*, in addition to setting Reid and Kant side-by-side as responses to the challenge of scepticism (somewhat to the latter's disadvantage) concludes with a chapter in assessment of Hegelian absolutism which, while applauding Hegel's logic

---

[1] For further details on both Personal Idealism and its historical context see Bengtsson, *The Worldview of Personalism.*

[2] The volume was born out of an abortive attempt by a group including Seth Pringle-Pattison, Haldane, and Robert Adamson (at that point still an idealist) to set up a new journal to rival *Mind*, which they felt was too focused on traditional empiricism at the expense of metaphysics (Barbour, 'Memoir of Andrew Seth Pringle-Patton', 37–8; Muirhead, *Platonic Tradition*, 174 n.2).

[3] See above pp.46, 59, 134–5, 253–5.

based upon difference rather than abstract identity, questions his system's claim to completeness and its adequacy to deal with the fact of human individuality.

Two years later, in a book titled *Hegelianism and Personality*, these first questionings developed into a fully fledged critique. He acknowledges as well-taken the basic lesson of Kant; that knowledge can never arise from atomistic sensation alone, since everything is indissolubly connected with everything else through the forms of space and time together with the other categories, necessarily involved in knowledge on account of the need for a permanent subject of experience. But beyond this root, he objects that the idealism of Green and his followers errs grievously in turning Kant's *theory of knowledge* into a *metaphysic of existence*.[4] Specifically, disregarding the fact that it is supposed be a transcendental result, part of a wholly immanent analysis of experience, they take Kant's 'unity of consciousness' or 'consciousness in general' and convert it into 'a universal or divine consciousness',[5] an external theory of precisely the kind Kant was seeking to exclude. The principal cause of this error, continues Pringle-Pattison, is the Hegelian lens through which they read Kant. He allows that 'there is much in Hegel of the highest philosophical importance and truth'[6]—such as the centrality given to self-consciousness,[7] the stress on teleology,[8] and the rejection of Kant's unhelpful defence of categories in terms of their origin in favour of an immanent criticism of concepts each by another[9]—but he finds much more to worry him. Clearly influenced by his early encounter with Lotze,[10] the principal objection voiced is that Hegel offers, as a *metaphysic*, what is really only valid as a *logic*.[11] Forgetting that existence is one thing and knowledge quite another,[12] he tries to construct the world itself out of abstract thought,[13] reversing their true order of dependence; real things are not the shadows of thoughts, but *vice versa*.[14]

Pringle-Pattison allows that to a degree Hegel has been misunderstood. Rather than the purely a priori synthetic construction it purports to be, building up reality from the most basic category of Being itself to the ultimate pinnacle of the Absolute, Hegel's system he argues is best 'read backwards' as offering an analysis of the ordinary processes of common experience (even if its author does tend rather to suppress this aspect of his thought).[15] Moving beyond any simple contrast between a priori and a posteriori, his transitions are all 'empirically conditioned'.[16] But he cannot be absolved from all fault, for if not *a prioristic*, his account certainly is necessitarian. Pringle-Pattison complains that contingency itself is treated as a category, as just one more form alongside others through which the Absolute Idea must be realized. The offer thus to bring it within the range of our rational comprehension is tempting, but to be resisted; for 'to say that a thing is contingent or accidental, is to say, in so many words, that we can give no rational account of why it is as it is, and not otherwise',[17] and surely the most striking

---

[4] *Hegelianism and Personality*, 21.   [5] *Hegelianism and Personality*, 29.
[6] *Hegelianism and Personality*, 229, also 83.   [7] *Hegelianism and Personality*, 98.
[8] *Hegelianism and Personality*, 83.   [9] *Hegelianism and Personality*, 84–8.
[10] See Chapter 2.5 above.   [11] *Hegelianism and Personality*, 104.
[12] *Hegelianism and Personality*, 126.   [13] *Hegelianism and Personality*, 111.
[14] *Hegelianism and Personality*, 147.   [15] *Hegelianism and Personality*, 95, 107.
[16] *Hegelianism and Personality*, 91.   [17] *Hegelianism and Personality*, 137.

thing about nature, as contrasted with any logical system, *is* precisely its lack of explicable connection. In the end some things just lie side-by-side, or succeed one another, in pure matter-of-factness.[18]

Worst of all, Pringle-Pattison objects, Hegel speaks throughout his writings of self-consciousness, spirit, or intelligence *in general* without, apparently, appreciating that these are just abstractions, and that only *individual* spirits or intelligences are real.[19] 'Spirit' was intended by Hegel as a device to designate the ultimate union between man and God which would avoid the blank identity of Schellingian pantheism, but in the end this supposedly 'concrete idea' is exposed as nothing more than the abstract notion of what is held in common, 'intelligence as such', uniting its terms 'only by eviscerating the real content of both'.[20] Unless that which we designate the ground of reality can truly be called personal, our position ceases to be idealist, at least in the historic use of that term,[21] but whenever we try to spell out the idea of union we find ourselves falling down on one or other side; 'when we have hold of the divine end we have lost our grasp of the human end, and *vice versa*'.[22] Nor is this accidental, for the notion which Hegel is trying to capture, that of one mind existing as a proper *part* of another, is itself an impossibility.

> though selfhood . . . involves a duality in unity, and is describable as subject-object, it is none the less true that each Self is a unique existence, which is perfectly *impervious*, if I may so speak, to other selves—impervious in a fashion of which the impenetrability of matter is a faint analogue. The self, accordingly, resists invasion; in its character of self it refuses to admit another self within itself, and thus be made, as it were, a mere retainer of something else.[23]

Expanding on a point that would become notorious, he went on, 'I have a centre of my own—a will of my own—which no one shares with me or can share—a centre which I maintain even in my dealings with God Himself.'[24]

'*Et tu, Brute!*' begins Ritchie's 1888 review of Pringle-Pattison's book,[25] reacting to it as an attack from within the ranks of Idealism on what might be regarded as some its most central tenets, and an attack which needed repelling. Ritchie was prepared to admit that Hegel's identification of development in thought with development in time is unhelpful and that often he is indeed best 'read backwards', and to admit also that the philosophy of nature is one of the weakest parts of the whole system, but Ritchie nonetheless seeks to defend Hegel (and Green) against the charge of reifying (indeed, deifying) what is found to hold within thought; against the accusation of converting a logic into a metaphysics.

What, it must be asked, is this 'reality' which is set up over against knowledge itself? Pringle-Pattison asserts again and again that the real is the concrete individual as opposed to the abstract universal, but Ritchie retorts we cannot know any individual

---

[18] *Hegelianism and Personality*, 132.
[19] *Hegelianism and Personality*, 151.
[20] *Hegelianism and Personality*, 155.
[21] *Hegelianism and Personality*, 193.
[22] *Hegelianism and Personality*, 156.
[23] *Hegelianism and Personality*, 216.
[24] *Hegelianism and Personality*, 217.
[25] Ritchie, Review of *Hegelianism and Personality*, 256.

except in its universal aspect.[26] On Kant's theory of knowledge there is simply no room for any metaphysics distinct from that of the theory of knowledge itself and thus, for Hegel or Green, Nature is really what it is for reason. Pringle-Pattison wants to deny any such identity, holding that a full statement of our knowledge of a thing is not equivalent to the existent thing itself, but even this point may be allowed without calling into doubt their ultimate coincidence, once we recall that *our* knowledge, however full, can never be complete.[27]

Turning to the question of contingency, Ritchie rounds, not just on Pringle-Pattison for extending its sway in nature, but on Hegel himself for allowing it any foothold at all. It is, he argues, quite false to idealism to allow that anything at all in reality is brute or irrational.[28] For Pringle-Pattison, in the realm of nature, things just lie side-by-side with no logical passage between them[29] while in the realm of spirit each person has a distinct will of their own,[30] but Ritchie finds the later dangerously close to arbitrary libertarianism[31] and the former unduly defeatist; we may not know the connections which hold between things in nature, but need we despair of ever finding them out? Indeed (as we saw above) one of the things that attracted him to Darwinism was the promise it offered of linking what might otherwise seem disconnected phenomena.[32]

Ritchie takes exception also to the kind of individual Pringle-Pattison wants to set up as a bulwark to the all-engulfing Hegelian Absolute. It is, he complains, just another false abstraction. Logic and ethics tell us alike that we can neither think of the world nor live in it as though the whole of reality were centred around us—however tempting that might be—for 'the real individual is not the individual in isolation from all other individuals, but is the synthesis of the universal and particular self'.[33] In metaphysics as much as in ethics, we must give up the isolated or atomic self, for the contextual self.

Ritchie and Pringle-Pattison went on to trade objections in a series of articles in the *Philosophical Review*, but rather than follow the minutiae of that debate we may turn to look at the objections, published the same year, of a second critic, Pringle-Pattison's former collaborator, R.B. Haldane. Unlike Ritchie, Haldane is prepared to admit that both Green and Hegel have an unfortunate tendency to slide from epistemology into metaphysics, the transcendental self—something that in truth has no meaning except for experience—becoming hypostatized first into an absolute subject and then into an

---

[26] Ritchie, Review, 257.   [27] Ritchie, Review, 261.   [28] Ritchie, Review, 261.

[29] *Hegelianism and Personality*, 132–3.

[30] *Hegelianism and Personality*, 217, 218.

[31] Ritchie, Review, 260.

[32] Ritchie, Review, 262. By way of example, he cites Darwin's suggestion of a connection between cats and clover. Darwin hypothesized (*Origin of Species*, ch.III, 74) that the frequency of red clover flowers in a district is determined by the population of bees which pollinate them which is determined by the population of field mice who destroy the bees' nests which is dependent on the number of cats (See also 'Darwin and Hegel', 57–9).

[33] 'Darwin and Hegel', 73.

absolute cause.[34] He thus concedes a large part of Pringle-Pattison's attack on the metaphysical basis of Neo-Kantianism, but overall the finds the book 'misleading'[35] and complains that Pringle-Pattison has paid insufficient care to that which is of real value in Hegel; 'what will remain . . . after the world has ceased to dispute about his metaphysics and theology', namely, 'the new method which he elaborated for the investigation of the contents of consciousness'.[36] The key point of that method is that we not only cannot get outside of consciousness, but need not do so; that (contra Pringle-Pattison) were we to fully think through and understand the universe, however much the result might differ from how we currently think of it, the process would not require us to bring in any element foreign to thought itself. Nothing about ultimate reality escapes the fullest development of rationality, because the two are not in the last resort different from each other.

In a series of subsequent papers, Pringle-Pattison developed the implications of his objection that metaphysics must not be confused with epistemology. At the root of philosophy, he suggests, there lies a problem. 'Epistemologically there is a union of subject and object: the knower and what he knows are in a sense . . . one. But ontologically, or as a matter of existence, they remain distinct—the one here and the other there—and nothing avails to bridge this chasm.'[37] As we shall see below, Pringle-Pattison was not in the end a sceptic, but even this way of conceptualizing the problem drew strong criticism from more orthodox Hegelian idealists. For example, in an important paper of 1893, 'Idealism and Epistemology', Henry Jones vigorously rebutted Pringle-Pattison, insisting that for idealism there can be no final separation between thought and reality, no world of objects distinct from the best thought about them. The whole notion of epistemology as a subject is misguided and alien to idealism.[38] Epistemology treats of the relation between thought and reality, between ideas and things, but true idealists do not recognize the existence of any such 'world of ideas' requiring relation to a sphere of 'things', and are thus as little troubled with epistemology as the naive-est of materialists.[39] Pringle-Pattison had accused Green of turning a theory of knowledge into one of metaphysics, but in truth he himself has done the very reverse; he has taken a metaphysical theory of known reality and abstracted from it some entirely fictitious world of ideas within which he then insists his knowledge is confined.[40] He would agree that Berkeyanism is as false as materialism, but has failed to notice that his own epistemology is really just subjective idealism in disguise.[41]

---

[34] 'Hegel and his Recent Critics', 587.

[35] 'Hegel and his Recent Critics', 589.

[36] 'Hegel and his Recent Critics', 588.

[37] 'The Problem of Epistemology', 513.

[38] Bosanquet makes the same point in the second edition of his *Logic*, 'I entirely disclaim the epithet "epistemological". . . . For I understand it to imply a theory of cognition in which truth and reality are treated as external to one another, in fact, some form of correspondence theory' (263 note).

[39] 'Idealism and Epistemology', 302.

[40] 'Idealism and Epistemology', 457.

[41] 'Idealism and Epistemology', 471. See also 'Epistemology and Ontology', 570.

Pringle-Pattison's opposition to Hegelianism—his insistence that individual reality is quite different from universal knowledge—might well put us in mind of Bradley; his complaint that Hegelianism when we ask for bread puts us off with a logical stone[42] seems to echo the same concern as Bradley's protest that it offers us lifeless tatters in place of warm flesh.[43] In fact, however, the two philosophers are far from closely allied, and in 1894 Pringle-Pattison (who by this time had risen to the Chair of Logic and Metaphysics at Edinburgh) published a lengthy article, 'A New Theory of the Absolute', criticizing the doctrine set out in Bradley's *Appearance and Reality*. Bradley's thesis that all finite things are fragmentary, pointing beyond themselves ultimately to the whole universe meets with his approval, and he agrees that there cannot in the end exist 'a plurality of independent reals'.[44] But the further thesis that all such phenomena are 'unreal' or 'illusory', because diverse or relational, he regards 'the very acme of logical perversity'.[45] It is to rest in an abstract identity which, while it might apply to formal concepts, is quite inappropriate to the reality we experience whose very essence (as Hegel has shown) is to be a unity-in-diversity.[46] Most visibly this is so in the fact of our own existence, whose given nature we must simply accept. If we cannot understand our own selves, what can we ever hope to understand? If water chokes us, what shall we drink?[47] In the second constructive half of his book Bradley argues that the puzzles insoluble in relational thought may somehow be solved in a inexpressible supra-relational experience. But (complains Pringle-Pattison) such a mystical union excludes all contradiction only because, like Spinoza's and Schelling's before, it excludes all variety and difference.[48] Bradley's imagination abounds in metaphors to illustrate how the finite loses itself in the Absolute, but moving beyond metaphor we must wonder, for example, what can possibly be meant by a '*self*-fruition' in which the self disappears?[49] To say we know that reality is *experience*, when it is not like any experience that we know, is no help at all.[50] When in some hands Hegelianism would reduce the development of the Absolute to the history of humanity,[51] Pringle-Pattison applauds Bradley's sense of the vastness of the universe—he well recognizes that, 'Life is more than logic, and God is more than man'[52]—but for all that, reality is not something to be sought behind or beyond appearances but something revealed

---

[42] *Hegelianism and Personality*, 118–19 (cf. Matthew 7:9).

[43] *Principles of Logic*, 591. Indeed, Pringle-Pattison approvingly cites this passage at *Scottish Philosophy*, 203.

[44] 'New Theory of the Absolute', 150.

[45] 'New Theory of the Absolute', 156.

[46] 'New Theory of the Absolute', 160. For more on Pringle-Pattison's understanding of abstraction see pp.387–8 below.

[47] 'New Theory of the Absolute', 164.

[48] 'New Theory of the Absolute', 168.

[49] 'New Theory of the Absolute', 177; *Appearance and Reality*, 161.

[50] 'New Theory of the Absolute', 199.

[51] 'New Theory of the Absolute', 202.

[52] 'New Theory of the Absolute', 204.

through them[53] and, 'as water cannot rise higher than its source', neither may our speculative grasp hope to transcend our experience.[54]

Pringle-Pattison's critique of Hegel, while probably unfair to the best of his previous idealist commentators, left a mark on subsequent scholarship,[55] but beneath his apostasy lay a deeper point of dissention concerning just what it means to be real—the absolutist's charge that his 'individual self' is an unreal abstraction runs headlong into his insistence that it is a datum given in *consciousness*—and beneath that an even more fundamental difference about where true value lies. His humanistic outlook repudiates utterly any abstraction of race or world-spirit that, on its way to greatness, like Moloch, passes through, swallows up, or otherwise tramples over, the lives of individual conscious beings.[56] The finite self has an unconditional value, not to be sacrificed on the alter of the Absolute.

Publishing little else of note in the intervening years, in 1917 Pringle-Pattison brought out *The Idea of God in the Light of Recent Philosophy*, an elaboration of his Gifford lectures of 1912–13. Drawing together the reflections of many years, it is in this work that we find the most developed and final account of his philosophical system—although it must be admitted that, always sceptical of claims to completeness and often developing his views through criticism and opposition to those of others, even here his work retains its characteristically tentative and exploratory style.

Jones had accused Pringle-Pattison of attempting to prove idealism through purely epistemological reasoning, but *The Idea of God* rejects all such arguments, singling out for special criticism, Berkeley, Ferrier, and T.H. Green.[57] Rejecting the inference to a universal knower to ground the reality of those things which fall outside our own awareness,[58] he sees Green's case, no less than Berkeley's, as ending in an 'ego-centric' predicament. But the root difficulty, he thinks, lies in the way Green sets up his problematic. He works from a conception of awareness as the receipt of atomistic and unrelated sensations—without this his argument for the further aid of a 'combining consciousness' does not even get off the ground—but, while this might have been admissible in relation to the old psychology of Locke and Hume which he was criticizing, from the perspective of a more modern approach such as William James' 'radical empiricism' which treats experience is a unified whole rather than a multiplicity of different elements it is simply irrelevant.[59]

The alternative argument he offers is one based on emergent levels or orders of nature. He begins by drawing on recent developments in biology, instancing the work of J.S. Haldane and Henri Bergson, which, he claims, demonstrates the falsity of

---

[53] 'New Theory of the Absolute', 216.
[54] 'New Theory of the Absolute', 207.
[55] McTaggart's 1896 *Studies in the Hegelian Dialectic* shows clear traces of its influence (55–6, 59–72).
[56] 'Man's place in the Cosmos', 61–2.
[57] *Idea of God*, 190–9.
[58] Not all Personal Idealists rejected this inference. Rashdall endorsed it. see Chapter 11.1.3
[59] *Idea of God*, 196. How Green could respond to such a worry is considered at Chapter 4.1.3.3 above.

mechanistic reductionism. '"A self-stoking, self-repairing, self-preservative, self-adjusting, self-increasing, self-reproducing machine" is only by an abuse of language spoken of as a machine at all' he urges.[60] In passing from the physical to the chemical, the organic to the inorganic, or the merely animal to the human, though nothing external is introduced that would breach the continuity of nature,[61] there nonetheless emerge new and irreducible categories of being. In this way (and linking in to his earlier criticisms of evolutionary theory)[62] he opposes what he describes as 'the lower naturalism', which explains by 'levelling down' or by interpreting the more developed by the less developed, in favour of what he calls 'the higher naturalism', which acknowledges the emergence of real differences when it finds them and looks for understanding not to the beginning but to the end of things, in the confidence that reality is the continuous manifestation of a single power whose character is best revealed in the final rather than the initial stage of its evolutionary process, and whose full nature can be learned only from the course of that process as a whole.[63]

As one further step in this progression, the development of conscious beings must be thought of as the evolution of something organic to nature, a natural expansion of it, and not something external to or standing over against it. But this is idealism, the theory of an essential and constitutive bond between knower and known, for 'if we keep steadily in view the fact that man is from beginning to end, even *qua* knower, a member and, as it were, an organ of the universe, knowledge will appear to us in a more natural light, and we shall not be tempted to open this miraculous chasm between the knower and the realities which he knows.'[64] Neither separate from it, nor creating it for himself, but inside and continuous with the world that he knows, the knowing subject develops in correlativity with the known object.[65] One consequence of this idealism, this outgrowth of life and consciousness from nature, is that there can be no fundamental disharmony or mismatch between them. Not of course in every detail, but largely and on the whole, our experience must be true to the reality which gives it birth. Pringle-Pattison argues this first with respect to so-called secondary qualities and then, extending the case, for our aesthetic and moral appreciation. It is not our most rudimentary, but our highest, faculties that must be judged most revelatory of the nature of things and so it is not to sense experience but to ethics and religion that we must look for the most adequate account of the true nature of things.

---

[60] *Idea of God*, 77.

[61] It is, he thinks, illegitimate to appeal to any supplementary 'vital principle' (*Idea of God*, 70–1).

[62] See above Chapter 7.7.1.

[63] *Idea of God*, 90–1.

[64] *Idea of God*, 112.

[65] *Idea of God*, 129. Although undoubtedly idealistic, Pringle-Pattison aims to give full justice to the independence of reality. Mind certainly does not *create* nature, indeed it depends as much on nature as nature does on it. 'It is sufficient for the purposes of idealism that nature as a whole should be recognized as complementary to mind, and possessing therefore no absolute existence of its own apart from its spiritual completion; just as mind in turn would be intellectually and ethically void without a world to furnish it with the materials of knowledge and of duty. Both are necessary elements of a single system' (*Idea of God*, 189).

The book ends with a discussion of time, a pressing topic given the importance Pringle-Pattison accords to the notion of development. A large part of the reaction against the Absolute Idealism of such figures as Green, Bradley, and Bosanquet was a reaction against the eternal or timeless character of their systems. We find this, for example, in the worries of Belfort Bax and C.B. Upton, as well as the more famous critiques of William James, who coined the term 'block universe', and Henri Bergson, whose *durée réelle* represents the precisely antithetical position.[66] But most of the idealists, however sympathetic they felt to that viewpoint in which free personal development takes centre stage, were sufficiently Kantian to balk at taking time as something real in its own right. Thus Pringle-Pattison is typical here when he rejects the James–Bergson view that temporality brings genuine novelty or progress into the system and thinks instead of time as something present *within* the whole. He speculates that the eternal view of the Absolute may both include and transcend time in a fashion analogous to that suggested in recent psychology by the idea of the specious present.[67]

With respect to the place of finite individuals in the system as a whole, Pringle-Pattison continued to speak out for the position which, by this point, had acquired the name 'Personal Idealism'. The divisions which exist between selves remain important, and selves are not the kind of things which can be 'blended' or 'merged', either with each other or with God. Each individual has a unique nature, 'a little world of content which is nowhere exactly repeated',[68] and our contribution to the Absolute is precisely ourselves as such a unique and particular individual. The ultimate basis of this stance remains experience, which speculative theory is powerless to override. No theoretic difficulty in conceiving how we can be free, for example, should prevent us from recognizing that we are.[69]

However, sensitive to the views of his opponents and seeking compromise wherever possible, *The Idea of God* weakens somewhat the earlier stance of *Hegelianism and Personality*. Acknowledging that earlier statements of his (and in particular the word 'impervious' which he has 'many times regretted')[70] might perhaps have implied the contrary, he is now clear in condemning as a fiction the mere individual as exclusive self-contained unity or 'metaphysical atom'.[71] The views of McTaggart and Howison, for example, come in for sharp criticism. The Absolute is certainly no 'republic' of distinct selves.[72]

---

[66] Bax complains that their Absolute is 'something statically complete in which, as such, there is no development, no becoming' (Belfort Bax, *The Real, the Rational and the Alogical*, 245) while Upton complains that development and growth become but 'an endless series of timeless illusions' (*Lectures on the Bases of Religious Belief*, 306). See also William James, *Pluralistic Universe* and Henri Bergson, *Creative Evolution*.

[67] *Idea of God*, 354.

[68] *Idea of God*, 267.

[69] *Idea of God*, 292–3.

[70] *Idea of God*, 389 note.

[71] *Idea of God*, 257–8.

[72] *Idea of God*, 316–18.

10.1.2 Further Personal Idealists

Pringle-Pattison's defiance of the all-engulfing Absolute in the name of individual personality was well received in several quarters and there quickly developed after him, within the idealist movement as a whole, a distinct sub-group of Personal Idealists. But if this was a school he had done much to originate and as whose leading figure he was still regarded, his own position was not always typical of theirs. For that reason it is worth noting several other Personal Idealists, not only for the way they added to and elaborated his initial worries, but also for the various differences that began to emerge among them.

One of the earliest to follow Pringle-Pattison's lead was his own brother, James Seth who in his first publication, a small pamphlet published in 1891 and entitled *Freedom as Ethical Postulate*, strikes what is perhaps the key note of Personal Idealism. Asserting that no philosophy can command our attention unless it does justice to the notion of human freedom, he opposes any naturalism (such as that Henry Sidgwick or Leslie Stephen) or any compatibilism (such as that of Shadworth Hodgson) which would deny or diminish our liberty. He is equally dismissive of Kant's thought that it may be secured through relocation to some noumenal realm, but his strongest opposition on this score is to any Hegelian monism. Green's claim that autonomous moral life can no more be resolved into the empirical than can our conscious intellectual life is welcomed, but the subsequent theory of the Absolute realizing itself through finite selves, he complains, 'deprives us of freedom just when it seems within our grasp';[73] if our true freedom lies in God it is something found only at the cost of losing ourselves. Absolute Idealism, as he put it three years later in his *Study of Ethical Principles*, 'sacrifices, with the freedom of man, the reality of his moral life. If I am but the vehicle of the divine self-manifestation, if my personality is not real but only seeming—the mask that hides the sole activity of God—my freedom and my moral life dissolve together.'[74] There can be, Seth asserts, no genuine solution to the puzzle of free will which does not accord full reality to the finite individual; though for himself he offers no positive account of freedom, instead taking it as a basic axiom, something incapable of further analysis.

Another very early follower in whom we find the same immediate sense of freedom and morality deployed as argument for the non-negotiable reality of personhood was R.J. Illingworth, but in his hands the argument is widened out both epistemologically and metaphysically. Personality is our necessary experiential staring point, 'the gateway through which all knowledge must inevitably pass'.[75] It cannot be analysed or defined because everything else we know presupposes it, or is abstracted from it, but it gives us 'our canon of reality, the most real thing we know, and by comparison with which we estimate the amount of reality in other things'.[76] Key to the notion of a person is self-consciousness—Illingworth explicitly endorses Green's argument from the *Prolegomena*

---

[73] *Freedom as Ethical Postulate*, 21.   [74] *Study of Ethical Principles*, 393.
[75] *Personality Human and Divine*, 25.   [76] *Personality Human and Divine*, 43.

that conscious experience requires a subject which stands outside and unifies the known object[77]—but crucial too are desire and will, and this broadened conception comes to the fore as he advances a holistic theory of knowledge. Against the charge that he rests illegitimately in mere *feelings*, he responds that any 'sharp distinction between feeling and understanding, the emotions and the intellect, is wholly artificial, and untrue to fact. Knowledge starts neither with mere understanding, nor with mere feeling, both of which are abstractions, but with personal experience.'[78] Just as we confront not a part of our environment but the whole, we do so not with a part of ourselves—some rational subset of our faculties—but with our total unified personality. Things can be understood correctly only by our whole self, with its complex interaction of emotion, intellect, and will.

The sense that there came to obtain something akin to a *school* of like-minded philosophers gained prominence in 1902 with the publication of a volume of essays by several contributors entitled *Personal Idealism*. The collection highlighted, its editor Henry Sturt claimed, a growing sense in philosophy of the need to vindicate the notion of personhood against two-sided attack, from naturalism and from Absolutism. The first of these (it should be noted) had never quite gone away, while the second— though they shared its broad idealist perspective—was rejected by the various contributors for its adoption of an impossible extra-human standpoint and for its inability adequately to recognize human volition and all that entails.[79] Sturt went on to develop this case in his more ambitious 1906 work, *Idola Theatri: A Criticism of Oxford Thought and Thinkers from the Standpoint of Personal Idealism*. Via detailed case studies of Green, Bradley, and Bosanquet he charts how idealism has drawn on four characteristic fallacies, Intellectualism, Absolutism, Subjectivism, and what he calls 'the Passive Fallacy'—the failure to recognize the kinetic and dynamic character of experience. All he regards as German imports, 'uncongenial to our national habit of mind'.[80]

Two contributors from the 1902 volume are especially deserving of mention. Rather undermining Sturt's last point, one—Boyce Gibson—had for a while studied under Rudolf Eucken at Jena, and it is to Eucken must be credited the pragmatic strand which we find in his thinking. Experience for Boyce Gibson is essentially 'action' or 'deed'; not mere reflection upon life, but part of it, shaping, deepening, and developing it, always opening up new possibilities. It is only in and through endeavour, he argues, that we come to realize our own spiritual unity.[81] In his essay Boyce Gibson asserts that there are two quite separate approaches to psychology, the external and the internal. The inductive experimental methodology is a legitimate one, but it is not the only or necessarily the best line of attack, for unlike 'the inner, vital, truly causal point of view' it is unable to recognize the fact of free agency.[82] Picking up the epistemological concerns about Personal Idealism of Henry Jones, another of his teachers, he tried to

---

[77] *Divine Immanence*, 174–8.   [78] *Divine Immanence*, 57.   [79] *Personal Idealism*, Intro vi, viii.
[80] *Idola Theatri*, 7.   [81] 'A Peace Policy for the Idealists', 410–1.
[82] 'Problem of Freedom in its Relation to Psychology', 169.

argue that starting from the personal point of view need not forever imprison one inside it, proposing in one subsequent paper a 'peace policy' in which personal and absolute idealism might come together.[83] However, the union is effected only sketchily and with much vagueness, arguably another less welcome debt to Eucken.[84]

At one level Hastings Rashdall in his contribution endorses the epistemic dichotomy that Boyce Gibson finds, distinguishing between the being of *things* (which exist *for others*) and the being of *persons* (which exist *for themselves*).[85] But another perspective emerges at the same time. Picking out the key features that go to make up personality, he admits that in rudimentary form these characteristics may be found in many animals too, such that it is impossible to say just where the phenomenon begins; 'Personality in short is a matter of degree'.[86] Something capable of varying degrees of presence, its reality becomes an altogether more complex affair. With Bradley in his sights, he argues that if 'real' means 'out of all relation to anything else' then obviously selves are not real (and we hardly need five hundred pages to prove it!) But that is not the normal sense of 'real', and employing a more regular understanding of the term, what Bradley complains of as 'paradoxes' begin to look like mere 'platitudes'.[87] Displaying in extreme form a tendency more or less present in many of the Personal Idealists,[88] the argument for idealism Rashdall understands in fundamentally Berkelyan terms.[89] To be sure, he allows that Kant's contribution was needed properly to bring out the distinction between sensation and thought that Berkeley underplayed, and to the familiar Berkeleyan arguments for the mind-invoking nature of sensation he adds an argument from his former tutor, Green, to the effect that all relation too calls upon mind,[90] but where more Hegelian thinkers see Berkeley as mired in a subjectivism the removal of which was the *raison d'etre* of the idealist programme, for Rashdall, Berkeley is the very father of idealism. Rashdall is atypical of Personal Idealists, however, in his separation of personality from the issue of indeterminism or contingency, which he regards as of no help to freedom.[91]

[83] 'Peace', 416–24.

[84] 'There is in Eucken's immense literary output,' Bosanquet complained 'no really precise and serious contribution to philosophical science. Free cognition has . . . been submerged by moralist rhetoric' ('Philosophy of Eucken', 378).

[85] 'Personality: Human and Divine', 383.

[86] 'Personality: Human and Divine', 374. As we shall see in the next chapter, if there are degrees below there may also be degrees above. Socrates may be more of a person than the savage, but God more of a person than Socrates. This idea, originating in Lotze, is found in several of the Personal Idealists.

[87] 'Personality: Human and Divine', 385.

[88] Except, as we saw, Pringle-Pattison.

[89] In a 1909 article in *Mind*, he assimilates his own position to that of other 'genuinely Idealist writers' such as Lotze, Bradley, Ward, Taylor, and McTaggart, as opposed to the 'soft idealism' of the school of Watson (i.e. Caird and Bosanquet) which having defeated materialism, then meets realism by unsaying everything it has just said ('Professor Watson on Personal Idealism', 114–15).

[90] *Philosophy and Religion*, 15.

[91] *Theory of Good and Evil*, Bk.III,Ch.III. In this matter he stands with McTaggart (see Chapter 13.1.5 below).

A somewhat different species of Personal Idealism was that of the Cambridge philosopher, James Ward. A Fellow of Trinity College, he first made his name as the author of important criticisms of the associationist psychology of Mill and Bain,[92] but Ward's was an unusual idealism in at least two respects. Unlike most other idealists he possessed a deep knowledge of and interest in natural science, and especially the new discipline of psychology. Even more distinctive was the fact that although like the other Personal Idealists he challenged the dominance of the Absolute Idealist scheme, he did so by retreating from Hegel, not to Kant, but further back to Leibniz; for the system he defended was a species of monadism, although unlike Leibniz he allows his monads to interact.[93] There are clear points of contact between this philosophy and that of the other Personal Idealists—stressing the harmonious order that binds monads together into one progressively evolving universe Ward's vision culminates in an ontologically distinct God who draws the universe towards him—but the metaphysical root of his position is really quite removed from the ultimate basis of theirs—he does not share the epistemological primacy they give to the first personal viewpoint of moral agency.

Returning to the mainstream, the high point of the Personal Idealist tide is found perhaps with the work of W.R. Sorley. His philosophy received its fullest exposition in lectures given first at Manchester College Oxford in 1913–14, expanded as Gifford lectures delivered at Aberdeen in 1914–15, and finally published under the title *Moral Values and the Idea of God*. For Sorley ethical experience is undeniable. Attempts to explain it, such as the Cartesian, Hegelian, or Spencerian programmes to derive value from some physical or metaphysical basis, all fail, while attempts to explain it away, such as moral subjectivism, a position he associates especially with naturalism, fare no better; values are not constituted by feeling or desire, but belong to the fabric of reality itself.[94] Ethics stands on its own, then, a genuine element of the Real, and consequently any satisfactory view of ultimate reality must leave room for it and account for its foundational place in the overall scheme. 'Our metaphysics must be founded on ethics,' urges Sorley, finding in our idea of the 'ought' guidance towards a true idea of the 'is'.[95]

Value does not simply stand on its own, he admits, but attaches to specific items. It is found not in universal abstractions but in concrete individuals.[96] Such particulars may

---

[92] The attack, which is to be found in his entry on 'Psychology' in the ninth (1886) edition of the Encyclopaedia Britannica, is comparable to and contemporaneous with that of Bradley's 1883 *Principle of Logic*.

[93] His system is set out in his two sets of Gifford lectures, *Naturalism and Agnosticism* (1899) and *The Realm of Ends* (1911). A comparable figure to note in this context is Herbert Wildon Carr, in that he too defended a species of Leibnizian idealism. See his *A Theory of Monads* (1922).

[94] Although, as an idealist, Sorley allows some sense in which values are relative to mind, the same holds for all facts, he thinks, and there are no grounds for denying objectivity to morality that would not equally be grounds for denying the objectivity of knowledge in general.

[95] *Moral Values*, 6.

[96] *Moral Values*, 91.

be either things or persons, but any value the former may possess is instrumental only with respect to the latter,[97] leaving persons as the sole possible location for the realization of intrinsic value. But if we admit selves, Sorley argues, we must admit also freedom.

We must recognise that the self which is the origin of the action, and in which we distinguish both the idea of goodness and the desire for an object inconsistent with the good, is the real cause of the action and exercises a real choice. It is the nature of the self to act and thus, in certain circumstances, to choose or select between possible alternatives. This is neither a freak of unmotived willing nor an irruption of a pure ego into the realm of time. It is simply the real choice of a real self.[98]

Acknowledgement of these facts helps with our subsequent choice of a metaphysical system. The monist's emphasis on unity is his undoing; his system tends inevitably towards some kind a mystic union into which the world, individual men, and the very values from which we started all disappear without trace. But, complains Sorley, 'The one purpose which, so far as I can see, justifies the field of havoc through which the world passes to better things, is the creation of those values which only free minds can realise. And if free minds, when perfected, are to pass away, even for absorption in God, then that value is lost.'[99] On the other hand a mere pluralism of distinct selves will not do either, for contra that scheme, we must recognize something further, not itself a centre of life nor made by any finite mind, namely the order connecting these minds in and through which they all live. This includes not just the system of relations that allows inter-subjective intercourse and knowledge of a shared world, the 'laws of nature', but also the realm of values, valid for personal life but not themselves the product of any finite mind.[100] However, if both metaphysical extremes are equally unacceptable, parity ceases to hold as we advance further. In assessing the case for idealism, Sorley distinguished between two different varieties, the Platonic and the Berkeleyan; the one which looks to interpret reality as an order of objective or absolute thought, and tends to emphasize the unity of reality and lead to monism, and the other which holds the essence of reality to lie in the nature of personality or consciousness and tends to stress plurality.[101] Like Rashdall's, Sorley's idealism falls closer to this later type.

10.1.3 McTaggart

10.1.3.1 Further determination of the Absolute One last figure from the Personal Idealist tradition, meriting rather more extensive consideration than the others, was the Cambridge philosopher McTaggart who, as well as a dedicated scholar of Hegel, was the creator in his own right of an original metaphysical system. His position was unusual, and it might be questioned whether he really deserves classification alongside the other

---

[97] *Moral Values*, 117. [98] *Moral Values*, 436. [99] *Moral Values*, 515.
[100] *Moral Values*, 370. [101] *Moral Values*, 477.

figures considered above, but notwithstanding some very real differences, there are also powerful points of similarity that bind him to the personalist mainstream.

McTaggart arrived early on at his basic metaphysical system to which, despite considerable change in the argument he offered for it, he adhered throughout his life. Initially the position was arrived at through criticism of the final step in Hegel's system employing that system's own methodology. McTaggart agrees with Hegel that the natural progress of thought commits us to the existence of an Absolute which possesses both unity and differentiation in such a way that the whole is in some sense contained within each of its many differentiations, but not with his way of securing this arrangement, viz. through the notion of a single self-positing spirit. He sees two flaws in Hegel's reasoning. It is the fact that the unity is in some way present in each of its parts themselves, branding them uniquely and essentially *its* parts, that distinguishes a whole from a mere aggregate of elements with no essential relation to one another or to the sum they accidentally make up. But if a unity of many different parts collectively, how can a whole at the same time reside in each of its parts severally? This is possible, suggests McTaggart, only through the introduction of a new category, consciousness, which is able to represent to itself the unity to which it belongs. Something may be a unity *in* its parts through being so *for* its parts and, and for this reason Hegel should have concluded that the finite differentiations of his system were all individual spirits, or consciousnesses.[102] But although the unity is for the individuals we are not required to say that the individuals are for the unity—indeed, to do so could only blur the distinction between them—and so his other error was to suppose that the whole to which they belong is itself some kind of super-person.[103] Instead McTaggart argues that we need to think of the Absolute as a community of individual spirits. Their multiplicity accounts for its differentiation, while its unity is explained, not by some overarching individual or experience encompassing them all, but simply by the fact that they form an inter-related community.

10.1.3.2 The argument for idealism McTaggart's magnum opus, *The Nature of Existence*, which sets out his system in detail, did not appear until the end of his life. It had been his original intention to expand greatly on the dialectical approach of his early work, but at some time during the interval he abandoned this line of attack, and the book that he finally published advanced its case via a method which, on the surface at least, would seem to owe more to his younger Cambridge contemporaries Moore and Russell than to Hegel.[104] But the magnitude of this switch should not be exaggerated, for not only is the conclusion towards which he works unaltered, but the concepts, methods, and

---

[102]   *Studies in Hegelian Cosmology*, 13.

[103]   *Studies in Hegelian Cosmology*, 59–60.

[104]   The original drafts bear the title *Dialectic of Existence*, and in 1910 or 1911 he was giving lectures in which he professed to prove dialectically some of the results which subsequently appeared in the *Nature of Existence*, but at some point between then and its publication in 1921 the plan was dropped (Broad, *Examination*, I:13). For his later view of Hegelian dialectic see *Nature of Existence* §§47–51.

arguments employed are all (as we shall see) more Hegelian than they appear on the surface.

At the centre of *The Nature of Existence* lies an argument that McTaggart develops concerning the infinite divisibility of substance which works simultaneously as an attack on the reality of matter and as a defence of idealism. According to this argument there are two general principles concerning substance which everyone must accept. The first, which he terms the Principle of Sufficient Description, holds that there must exist for every object a distinctive and wholly general description of its nature. This follows from the fact that every individual being must have its own unique character in virtue of which it exists as a separate being. The second, the Principle of Infinite Divisibility, holds that every substance is divisible into substances which are themselves further divisible into substances, in a process that may be carried on without end. We cannot, of course, specify in advance in what this division might consist for inevitably it takes us into depths of their nature beyond our current knowledge, but the inherent difficulty of picturing to ourselves a simple substance without partitionable content recommends the principle to us, as a self-evident yet synthetic axiom.

Together these two rules call for an infinite number of sufficient descriptions; one for each of the endless number of distinct substances. But can we be sure that this is really possible? We certainly cannot begin to imagine what all these descriptions might be. In view of this difficulty McTaggart is unwilling to rest content in the mere possibility that the required descriptions might *just happen* to be available, and to be sure that the demand is met, he holds instead that it must be possible somehow to *derive* them one from another. But how might such a derivation work? Perhaps the most obvious way to attempt this would be in an ascending fashion, using sufficient descriptions of parts to construct sufficient descriptions of the wholes to which they belong, but clearly if substance is infinitely divisible this procedure could never even get started. Upwards approaches thus ruled out, the only alternative, suggests McTaggart, would be to try derive the required descriptions in a descending fashion using descriptions of a given whole somehow to construct descriptions of their parts. If substance is to exist at all, he concludes, it must be structured in some way as to permit such downwards derivation of the sufficient descriptions of its infinitely many substance-parts.

But what kind of a structuring might this be? McTaggart presents an abstract schemata, which he calls a Determining Correspondence System, in which parts are so related to wholes as to give to each a sufficient description referring only to the whole from which it came. This he suggests is the only kind of design which could meet the abstract requirements set out.

How might this sketch be filled out? What might a Determining Correspondence System amount to? McTaggart puts forward as a possibility on this scheme a universe in which there exists nothing but atemporal and immaterial selves who do nothing but perceive each other and themselves. If A and B are two such individuals, A will consist of A's perception of B (or, in McTaggart's symbolism, $A!B$) and A's perception of himself (*A!A*). At the next level *A*'s perception of *B* will consist in *A*'s perception of *B*'s perception of *A* (*A!B!A*) and *A*'s perception of *B*'s perception of himself (*A!B!B*), while *A*'s perception of himself will consist of his perception of his perception of *B* (*A! A!B*) and his perception of his perception of himself (*A!A!A*). This system meets McTaggart's requirement since, starting with sufficient description of *A* and *B*, it is possible to derive sufficient descriptions of each of their infinite parts.

Such a universe, urges McTaggart, is at least possible. But, he goes on to claim, it is in fact the *only* possible system, for none other, and especially not one involving the existence of matter or sense data[105] is able to satisfy the demand set out for infinitely divisible yet generally describable reality. At first glance McTaggart's argument looks weak, for using spatial qualities it would seem easy enough to meet the requirement of infinite divisibility—we could identify the parts of a repeatedly bisected line as, say, the longest part, the shortest part of the longest part, the shortest part of the shortest part of the longest part, and so on—but central to McTaggart's contention that neither matter nor sense data can pass the test is his insistence that any attempt to do so must be based solely on the non-spatial qualities of things. He argues in a manner reminiscent of Leibniz that all spatial properties require a non-spatial basis, but once one is restricted to non-spatial qualities, such as colours and smells, it does indeed become hard to see how one could construct a system of endless implication comparable to that which he proposes of mutually perceiving minds. McTaggart concludes that, for all it may appear to be otherwise, ultimate reality consists in nothing but a timeless realm of mutually perceiving immaterial selves. This idealism, understood as the assertion that nothing exists but spirit, is an ontological one akin to that of Berkeley, Leibniz, and (he thinks) Hegel, not an epistemological one like that of Kant or the neo-Hegelians.[106]

10.1.3.3 The unreality of time McTaggart's system is a *timeless* one, like that of the Absolute Idealists, and although that system itself has been wholly forgotten, modern philosophy continues to remember his argument for the unreality of time. The argument begins by noting that the ways in which we speak about time fall into two very different kinds. Because a single set of events may be placed in a given order using either of these ways of speaking, he calls them the *A* and the *B* series respectively. The *A* series picks events out by the characterizations past, present, and future (and their cognates), while the *B* series orders events under the relations before, after, and simultaneous with (and their cognates). The principal difference between the series is that the *A* series statements change their truth-value according to the time at which they are uttered (though it was once false, it is now true, to say that the lives of

---

[105] Sense data was a form of being postulated by many philosophers in the early twentieth century, the immediate object of our sensory experiences, yet reducible neither to mind nor to matter. McTaggart is accommodating himself here to contemporary Cambridge philosophy.

[106] *Nature of Existence*, §52. A characterization most of them would, of course, reject. To the extent that McTaggart's system bears similarities to that of Leibniz it is reasonable to suggest the influence of his Trinity tutor James Ward, whose own system was Leibnizian.

McTaggart and his wife are both past), while the *B* series statements are timelessly true or false (it was, is and always will be true to say that McTaggart died before his wife.)

The proof of the unreality of time is divided into two stages. To begin with McTaggart urges that the reality of the *A* series is crucial to the reality of time, that is to say, that the *B* series alone cannot account for it. The problem he holds is that there could be no change without the *A* series, but that without change there could be no time. The *B* series alone cannot account for change because change is more than just the possession of different properties at different times. Though no doubt essential to it, this alone does not capture the true passage or dynamism of change; for that we need the flow of time expressed by the *A* series.

The second stage of the proof urges that, for all its importance to change and time, the *A* series is in itself thoroughly contradictory and impossible. What prompts McTaggart to say this is that, although past, present, and future are all incompatible characteristics, every event must nonetheless possess them all. The most obvious response to this paradoxical assertion is to attempt to dismiss it by pointing out that no event need ever have more than one of these determinations at any time. No event is past, present, and future at once, rather, for instance, it may be that it was future, is present, and will be past. But that, argues McTaggart, anticipating the objection, is just to say that its futurity is past, its presence present, and its pastness future, creating three new problems where before we had only one. Any attempt to circumvent the paradox by resting within a fixed temporal perspective, McTaggart immediately undoes by insisting on rewriting its claim in perspectiveless mode. Given its contradictory nature, concludes McTaggart, the *A* series must be deemed unreal, but if it is to be dismissed, then so too must time itself be.

10.1.3.4 C series and error If the conclusions which McTaggart reaches are correct, it is clear that the real nature of the universe differs very much from the nature which it appears *prima facie* to possess; for if he is right, though the universe seems to house matter and sense data it in fact contains nothing but spirits, while the only non-reflexive objects of our perception are other selves (and their parts), selves which though they appear to be made up of, not merely perceptions, but also, judgements, assumptions, sensations, volitions, and emotions, are in reality composed of nothing but perceptions. Moreover, although the world seems to be in time in reality it is timeless. There is then a great deal of error in our everyday view of the world, and it is this which McTaggart next sets himself to explain. The theory he develops to do so is complicated, and not easy to summarize, but essential to his final metaphysical conclusions.

He argues that error must be a species of perception, namely misperception—for perception, he has concluded, is all that selves may do. But what kind of a misperception might it be? He suggests that the most pervasive error we make, and one from which all others follow, is to see things as in *time*. We see events as forming a time series when in fact they form no such series at all. How does this come about? McTaggart argues that although time itself is unreal there must nonetheless exist a real series which serves as a basis for our perception of things as temporal; for no more than any other misperception can that be a pure fiction, pulled out of thin air. To misperceive is to take one thing for another, not to invent. This real series, which he supposes we misperceive as a *temporal* series, he calls the *C* series. But where does the *C* series come from? We begin to understand this if we switch our attention from the object of acts of misperception to their subject, the perceiver. Insofar as McTaggart's Determining Correspondence System consists in a community of spirits each made up of perceptions of each other's parts it seems to leave no room for error. However, he argues, once the requirements of Determining Correspondence have been met, there is nothing to preclude the possibility that spirits might also be divided in *other* ways, and there is no reason why the parts formed in these ways need be regarded as accurate perceptions. He therefore suggests that a subject's perceptual errors be thought of as a series of what he calls Fragmentary Parts strung out along a dimension of division other than that of the Determining Correspondence System. With the most illusory at one end and the least illusory at the other these parts can be arranged into what he calls a Misperception Series. In response to the question how a set of erroneous perception can together make up an accurate one, he suggests that the series be thought of as an Inclusion Series. To explain, a ruler may be divided into twelve separate sections each one inch long, but alternatively it may divided into a series of twelve overlapping sections of one inch, two inches, three inches, and so on, from which series any term except the last might be simply removed without losing the whole length. If all members of the Misperception Series form a similarly overlapping sequence the result of taking away a misperception from a correct perception can never be or involve a further mispercep-tion.[107] It is when we consider how such a series would regard *itself* that we reach the heart of McTaggart's theory of error. He argues that, if it is to represent itself at all, an inclusion series must misrepresent its members as exclusive of one another, as appearing to have no content in common, but that since this is just how temporally distinct perceptions manifest themselves to us, to so regard it is to view it as precisely a temporal series.[108] In this way the inclusion series becomes the *C* series for the temporal misperception of ourselves. The heart of error, McTaggart is claiming, is that in self-perception we inevitably misconstrue ourselves as temporal. From this point every-thing else swiftly follows. Once we perceive ourselves as in time, we perceive the world as in time, and once we misperceive the world as in time, he argues, all the other errors follow too.

    McTaggart's account of misperception has a second and very important application. It secures for him a doctrine of immortality and pre-existence. (McTaggart held that no good argument for immortality could fail to bring in pre-existence as well, for as he wryly comments in *Some Dogmas of Religion*, 'If the universe got on without me a

---

[107] *Nature of Existence*, §558–66.   [108] *Nature of Existence*, §§579–80, 588.

hundred years ago, what reason could be given for denying that it might get on without me a hundred years hence.'[109]) It might be objected that McTaggart's view that time is but an appearance of an underlying timeless reality precludes the possibility of genuine immortality, offering only atemporal eternity, which is something very different altogether. McTaggart was sensitive to this criticism and admits that in the strictest sense we are not immortal, but he goes on to argue that nonetheless on his theory it can be shown that we *appear* to be immortal, just as we *appear* to exist in time, and that this fact captures all that we need or desire. He suggests that we correlate the time series and the Misperception Series of his system. Were that the case, as time progressed, we would find ourselves getting ever closer to a final state of wholly adequate perception, in which the illusion of time itself would be overcome and the eternity of the world perceived. Eternity would become a condition that to creatures bounded within the illusion of time itself appeared to be in the future. Yet it would be a future which arrived at, could never go on to appear present or past, since to reach it would be precisely to see through it and transcend the misperception which is time. On this view it would appear to us as though eternity, or timelessness, were the final or culminating moment of time. It would be the end of history, our future, and our destiny. In this way, for McTaggart, the claim that eternity awaits us in the future, though not wholly true, has an important measure of truth in it; 'the whole is, not really future, since nothing is really temporal, but as really future as my breakfast tomorrow is future'.[110]

10.1.3.5 Love Immortality was for McTaggart an immensely important belief, held from an early age and bound up with the very high value he placed on love and friendship. We all feel that our loves are special and mourn their passing, hoping perhaps for a future life in which we shall be reunited. To McTaggart past and future lives meant not only the possibility of re-encountering our friends but the certainty of doing so, for he believed friendships are not accidental but rather structures built into the very fabric of the universe, the substance of Determining Correspondence itself. Advancing what he considered to be the most important of all his doctrines, he argued that the mutual perceptions linking the community of finite spirits that make up ultimate reality are at the same time relationships of *love*, and thus that spirits are eternally bound together in interlocking systems of loving perception which, if enjoyed in the here and now, will only be enjoyed more fully in the timeless hereafter.[111]

McTaggart has a very distinctive understanding of the nature of love not uncon-nected with the metaphysical role he gives it. He makes a sharp distinction between its object and its cause, arguing that love for the individual while it may be caused by certain characteristics is not necessarily held in respect of them—a great passion may be

[109] *Some Dogmas of Religion*, 114.   [110] *Philosophical Studies*, 289.
[111] For further details see Mander, 'On McTaggart on Love'.

inspired by a very minor cause. Indeed he suggests that genuine love for individuals is not held in respect of any characteristics, we may love one person but need not love another identical one, nor are we obliged to cease loving that person even if they change in respect of characteristics we most admire. Love is a direct relationship between individuals involving a realist rather than a representationalist species of perception.

That the relationships at the heart of the universe are ones of love, holding outside the appearances of space, time, and matter, was a doctrine he had put forward at the very start of his career in 'Further Determination of the Absolute', a paper printed in 1893 for private circulation,[112] and it was the doctrine too with which he concluded, capping a system which is as complex as it is idiosyncratic. In his assertion of the fundamental reality of finite selves and their individual relationships, he offers a pluralistic Personal Idealism to outstrip any, similar in some regards to Rashdall's. But notwithstanding this, the unity of his cosmos of interconnected loving spirits should not be underestimated. It would be a little simplistic but not wholly wrong to say that where analytic thinkers see parts as making up wholes, monists think of wholes as prior to parts. But if so, we should observe that Determining Correspondence is McTaggart's version of this latter view, for it is precisely the doctrine that the specific nature or identity of a substance's parts is determined by relationship to the whole to which they belong, not *vice versa*.[113]

10.2 The further development of absolutism

10.2.1 Bernard Bosanquet

While our attention has shifted from the earliest advances of monistic absolutism to the more personalist systems which emerged subsequently in reaction to that, it should not be supposed that absolutism remained in the meanwhile dormant. The further advance of that metaphysic is best illustrated through the work of Bernard Bosanquet who, although an early convert to the cause for whom Bradley's *Appearance and Reality* was 'the gospel',[114] did not publish his own views on metaphysics until relatively late in his career permitting them to take on board the many developments in the subject that had taken place in the meanwhile. His two sets of Gifford Lectures appeared in 1912 and 1913 respectively as *The Principle of Individuality and Value* and *The Value and Destiny of the Individual*. The detailed consideration already undertaken of his other views prepares us well for the main results, since there was no radical departure, although much subtle elaboration.[115]

---

[112]   Lowes Dickinson, *McTaggart*, 36.

[113]   It should be noted however, that it is only with considerable qualification that McTaggart is prepared to accept the notion that the universe is an 'organic unity' (*Nature of Existence*, §§149–54).

[114]   Muirhead, *Bernard Bosanquet and his Friends*, 97.

[115]   See above pp.47, 81, 134–5, Chapters 8.4, 9.2.

Metaphysical results are achieved, for Bosanquet, by the application of a principle to a datum or source material. The basis from which we are thus to work he calls simply 'experience', but this should not mislead us, for though experiential, the programme is not that of classical empiricism. It is a mistake argues Bosanquet to suppose that reality is just 'given' to us in our simplest or most immediate, sensory, experiences; for only by the 'work' of our minds can we ever reach it. The coherence and stability that characterize reality and in which the mind may find rest are to be got hold of not 'by withdrawing from the intercourse and implications of life', but through the 'arduous task' of thinking things through and continually broadening our grasp.[116] Rather than something that comes between us and the experience of reality, our thought is the very path by which we arrive at such experience.

More specifically, the thought principle which we must apply to experience he calls 'individuality'. As we shall see in Chapter 13, individuality is a principle as applicable to value-theory as it is to first philosophy, but even with respect to its metaphysical employment there is more than one way of looking at the notion. In one guise it appears as the principle of the concrete universal, which we have already discussed.[117] It is the urge towards unity-in-diversity that binds concrete reality together as the various different manifestations of an underlying idea. In another slightly different guise, suggests Bosanquet, it is the same as the principle of non-contradiction which acts as a drive to ever-expanding all-inclusiveness.[118] Whatever is finite is, for that very reason self-contradictory. Since contradiction is a mark of incompleteness, it therefore points beyond itself, to its wider context, carrying inside it an impulse to its own transcendence.[119]

The terminal point of this application of the principle of individuality to experience Bosanquet calls the 'Absolute'. A self-determining completeness in which the contradiction of finitude is overcome and thought completed, 'It bears this name because it does not permit of being referred to or put in relation with anything other than itself, that is to say, of being treated as dependent on anything other than itself.'[120] Exactly what sort of a thing this signifies remains vague, but it is clear that for Bosanquet the Absolute is not a mind, and it is not God—although it bears many of the marks of both.

The pressing need to develop experience through the application of the principle of individuality comes not from outside but from the very nature of thought itself. Not something (like the weather) which just happens, thought is purposive—it attempts to express reality. But not something (like a job applicant) whose fate rests in the hands of others, it marks its own efforts—the solution to poor thinking lies in more thought. Specifically, it carries within it its own inner drive (or *nisus*, to use Bosanquet's term)

---

[116] *Principle of Individuality and Value*, 7.
[117] *Principle of Individuality and Value*, ch.II. See above Chapter 8.4.3.
[118] 'Non-contradiction . . . is the principle of individuality' (*Value and Destiny of Individual*, 76).
[119] *Principle of Individuality and Value*, 44.
[120] 'The Part Played By Aesthetic in The Development Of Modern Philosophy', 378.

towards coherence and completeness, or truth. And because there is no final distinction between mind and world this must be understood at the same time as a tendency within reality itself. In this way we find at the heart of Bosanquet's metaphysics a fundamental teleology.[121] Forestalling misunderstanding, however, we should note that this teleology is not *temporal*. The claim is not that perfected being will come into existence at some future date; for that would be to accept the reality of time, and Bosanquet does not regard time as ultimately real.[122] Indeed, rather than think of the Absolute as in time, we do better to think of time as in the Absolute. Not some future 'heaven' that awaits us, the Absolute is something in which we here and now already participate.[123]

Instead of temporally, the teleology of the Absolute manifests itself in a hierarchy of beings and states, a ranked scale of how far various different modes of experience get towards expressing the all-inclusive individuality of the Absolute. We can construct a ladder or scale up from the natural world, through living creatures, to the lower stages of mind, and finally on up to its highest reaches. There is a temptation to identify these uppermost modes of mind with the maximum achievable for any individual conscious-ness, but in fact, as there is 'teleology below [finite] consciousness', there is also teleology above mental life as we know it,[124] and the peaks of being, the '"worlds" of spiritual values through participation in which we realize our true selves, largely transcend what any given unit can fairly be said to be conscious of'.[125] It is in this sense that Bosanquet speaks of the Absolute as the 'high-water mark' of the various fluctua-tions in consciousness across peoples and times.[126]

10.2.2 *Further Absolute Idealists*

If perhaps the most fully articulated, Bosanquet's Absolute Idealist metaphysics was nonetheless typical of a whole set of similar systems put forward in the first quarter of the twentieth century amounting to something like an Absolute Idealist orthodoxy. This sense of 'party line' is perhaps strongest with A.E. Taylor's 1903 book, *The Elements of Metaphysics*, for (like those we have already examined in ethics) this is a *textbook*, rather than an independent account of the author's own viewpoint; not that it leaves its readers in any doubt about that stance. Written in the belief that there obtains sufficient agreement among contemporary philosophers (if not on details then on general principles) to constitute a kind of canon that students ought to know, it outlines a generic monistic idealism. Taylor had been for some years (1891–8) a colleague of Bradley's at Merton, and it is to Bradley that the greatest debt is owed—indeed, at times, with its emphasis on non-conceptual immediate experience

---

[121] *Principle of Individuality and Value*, ch.IV.
[122] 'Time and the Absolute', 119. McTaggart as we saw *does* claim something quite similar to this.
[123] *Value and Destiny of Individual*, 258.
[124] *Principle of Individuality and Value*, 153ff.
[125] Hoernlé, 'On Bosanquet's "Idealism"', 584.
[126] *Principle of Individuality and Value*, 378.

as our sole point of contact with reality, its use of the law of non-contradiction as the supreme metaphysical criterion for reality, its subsequent development of a doctrine of degrees of reality, and its assertion of the inadequacy of relational thought to ever capture ultimate reality,[127] it serves almost as a commentary on *Appearance and Reality*— but liberal use too is made of Royce, Ward, Stout, Bosanquet, and McTaggart.

Generally unsympathetic to Kant,[128] Taylor continues the subordination of epistemology to metaphysics. 'Since the conditions under which truth is obtainable depend, in the last resort, on the character of that reality which knowledge apprehends, it is clear that the problems of the Theory of Knowledge, so far as they do not come under the scope of ordinary logic (the theory of the estimation of evidence), are metaphysical in their nature.'[129] Turning Kant's critique of the ontological argument to another use, he argues for idealism based on the lack of any difference between our thought of a real and of an imaginary object.[130] To say that 'Reality is experience' is to commit one's self to two further points, that it is 'uniquely individual' and 'through and through purposive', for both are inseparable characteristics of experience as first we meet with it.[131] But fully developed to result in the Absolute—that infinite individual whose elements are all lesser individuals, that final end which sums all lesser purposes—the appeal is far from any brute trust in individual or personal consciousness. Self is but a limited appearance, not sharply demarcated from not-self, and inapplicable to the Absolute.[132]

Haldane's, *The Pathway to Reality*, reproducing his 1902–3 Gifford Lectures, was another metaphysical treatise of the same period to disclaim originality; but in this case not because what is offered was a survey of contemporary debates, but rather on the grounds that it saw itself as simply the re-presentation of a single ancient thought, first set out in Aristotle, subsequently re-discovered by the German idealists, and now expressed again in a form fit for modern times.[133] That thought, of course, is the idealist one that reality exists only as an object for some subject,[134] or as Haldane later put it that, 'There is no world apart from knowledge for which it is there.'[135] Though perhaps expounded with more enthusiasm than clarity, the influence of Hegel is strong

---

[127] *Elements*, 54–6; *Elements*, 19–22; *Elements*, 104–20; *Elements*, 140–57.
[128] *Elements*, 39, 69, 134, 242.
[129] *Elements*, 16.
[130] *Elements*, 24.
[131] *Elements*, 58.
[132] *Elements*, 337, 343.
[133] *Pathway*, 1, 14, 18, 169.
[134] *Pathway*, 32.
[135] *Human Experience*, 22. 'behind knowledge we cannot go; there is no standard of truth save in its own process' (Haldane's Preface to *Hegel's Science of Logic*, 14). 'The relation of mind to nature is a foundational one, and it lies in this, that there can be no meaning in any object-world that is not object-world for a knower. If there can be no meaning for the object there can be accordingly no existence for it. For existence involves meaning, and is not a fact unless it is significant' (*Reign of Relativity*, 173); 'experience is ... the ultimate reality behind which you cannot get' (*Pathway*, 88).

throughout.[136] It explains, for instance, the return to Aristotle, whose essential message, that the universal exists in and though the particular, that reality is to be found only in the indissoluble union of the universal of thought and the particular of sense,[137] Haldane (like Green) holds that Hegel first taught the world to read correctly.[138]

The experience we enjoy is, of course, finite, but as we process it in our thinking, we mount through a stairway of categories from lower to higher ranges of understanding—levels of knowledge which are at the same time levels of truth and reality—passing in the end from the finite to the infinite. The finite Haldane understands in Hegelian fashion as that which is limited from outside itself, and in so far as we apprehend the world through the abstract distinctions and contrasts of thought, or conceive of ourselves in distinction from the other selves around us, we remain at this level of the finite. But once we come to see the self as the real source of these categorizations which therefore fall within it, as something higher than these oppositions which go to the make-up of its own finitude, 'reason takes us beyond ourselves' and we mount to a conception of *mind itself* as the ultimately real, with the finite self as just one of the stages through which it comprehends its own content. 'Not a thing to be laid on the dissecting table and taken to pieces',[139] since itself presupposed as the basis of all analysis, this basic experience of union between universal and particular, or between subject and object, Haldane follows Hegel in calling 'Spirit' or 'Geist'.[140] Could we consistently thus see reality, *sub specie aeternitatis* and beyond the limits of our finitude, 'we should have become as God is'. God must be Absolute all-inclusive Mind, since by 'God' we may understand whatever in the end turns out to be most real, and that proves to be Mind Itself.[141]

Mackenzie's *Outlines of Metaphysics*, appeared only two years before Haldane's *Pathway* and offers yet another slightly different perspective on the same basic scheme. He advances a version of Objective Idealism (the view that 'the whole system of reality—and not merely the world as we know it—is constituted by thought-determinations')[142] close to that of his teacher, Edward Caird,[143] which basic stance he then attempts to fill out by charting the development of experience and its ideal construction, from its least to its most developed phase, from the perceptual through the scientific, ethical, and aesthetic to the religious sphere. This short work was intended as a kind of sketch for a more thorough treatment, which, much delayed, finally appeared in 1917, under the title *Elements of Constructive Philosophy*, and constitutes Mackenzie's chief metaphysical effort. He begins by seeking to locate the most basic presupposition of judgement and inference, which he finds in the idea of objective

---

[136] 'All that is in these lectures I have either taken or adapted from Hegel' (*Pathway*, 309); 'I am content to say that I am a Hegelian and wish to be called so' (*Pathway*, 407).
[137] *Pathway*, 52–3, 169–70.
[138] *Pathway*, 169.
[139] *Pathway*, 88.
[140] *Pathway*, 79–80.
[141] *Pathway*, 391–2, 353, 335, 19.
[142] *Outlines*, 34.
[143] *Lectures on Humanism*, 232.

order.[144] It is of the very essence of mind to discover and to create structure or arrangement, and the work of philosophy we may therefore understand as the effort to locate its several different kinds and place them in order themselves, ranking them by their various degrees of comprehensivness and organic unity. He then works through a range of different species of organization, from the numerical and spatio-temporal, through the causal, to that of consciousness and value, leading finally to the conception of the universe as a completely ordered self-explanatory system, or *Cosmos*. Since it is only from the last or highest point of view that the universe can be understood as fully ordered, the actual world that we know must itself be regarded as but a 'partial expression of that eternal process through which the perfect whole unfolds itself', and human life but 'the partial manifestation of the life of an eternal spirit' progressively revealing itself to us.[145] That our universe really amounts to such a cosmos remains, admits Mackenzie, something of an hypothesis or hope, but the degree of order to be found in the world we already know offers some assurance of a more perfect order in the whole of which we know it to be but a fragment. Some of that order, of course, is up to us, and here too there is reason to be optimistic: 'we can gradually increase our knowledge and our insight, and we can gradually make life more sane and beautiful; and there is no real reason for supposing that there is any absolute limit to the progress that may thus be made'.[146]

This general conception of the Absolute was shared by Henry Jones, another of Caird's pupils, and although he wrote no specific treatise on metaphysics, the outlines of his position are clear enough to see in his Gifford lectures, *A Faith that Enquires* (1922). His commitment to monism is secure. To deny the existence of a unity that makes the universe a rational whole, to hand everything over to chaos, he thinks, is to abandon oneself to a hopeless and irrational scepticism. (The intermediate option of *Pluralism*, of a system which makes room for contingency, is dismissed out of hand as 'one of the most inept of all metaphysical theories'.)[147] But like others, Jones is keen to contrast this monism with that to be found in Bradley. In Bradley's Absolute differences are not so much reconciled or surmounted as absorbed and eliminated. Everything disappears into his Absolute, which transmutes them and defeats itself in doing so.[148] The triumph of idealism had been to prove the essential bond of the object world with the subject, but to represent that insight as the thesis that everything resolves into experience is to run the risk of taking half a truth and turning it into a falsehood, and the task now must be demonstrate the co-relative point, to demonstrate that the ideal world leaves full room for objective reality and finite difference.[149]

---

[144]   *Elements of Constructive Philosophy*, 62, 79, 94.
[145]   *Elements of Constructive Philosophy*, 444 and 445.
[146]   *Elements of Constructive Philosophy*, 479.
[147]   *Faith that Enquires*, 81–2.
[148]   'The Working Faith of the Social Reformer', 70–6. For similar comments from Haldane and Mackenzie see *Pathway*, 396; and *Outlines*, 151.
[149]   'The Working Faith of the Social Reformer', 78.

10.3 Life and finite individuality: the Aristotelian Society debate

Although the division between Absolute and Personal Idealism which we have now outlined runs throughout the late nineteenth- and early twentieth-century years, there was only one point at which there occurred a direct head-to-head debate between the two schools, a symposium organized by the Aristotelian Society between Bosanquet and Pringle-Pattison which took place in London in July 1918.[150] It was a clash which had been brewing for thirty-odd years, ever since Seth Pringle-Pattison published his *Hegelianism and Personality* in 1887, and Bosanquet his *Logic* in 1888. However, the immediate cause of the symposium was this. In chapter 14 of his 1917 Gifford Lectures, *The Idea of God*, Pringle-Pattison sharply criticized the account of individuality which had been set out in Bosanquet's own Gifford Lectures of four years earlier, *The Value and Destiny of the Individual*. In particular he objected that Bosanquet's account made the individual merely adjectival of reality as a whole, rather than a substantive in its own right. So a symposium between them was organized.[151] The chief participants to the debate were joined for the occasion by two additional figures, Richard Burdon Haldane and George Frederick Stout.

The debate (which runs to 119 pages in the printed volume) is quite far-reaching and covers several different topics. Indeed, it has something of the quality of a marital dispute where, whatever the initial occasion or starting point, each party brings up *all* the other things they have been secretly harbouring over the years—connected or not. For while it starts with the question of whether selves are best understood adjectivally or substantivally, almost immediately it becomes clear that these terms are just pegs, and really both philosophers are exploring; seeking to develop new concepts and categories to express their meaning which at the same time problematize any simple dichotomies that we might employ.

To begin by looking at what Bosanquet says about the key term here, 'finite individual', it should be noted that he is happy enough to follow Aristotle and the great bulk of philosophical tradition in taking the 'individual'—primary substance—as

---

[150]   Entitled 'Do finite individuals possess a substantive or an adjectival mode of being?' it was published (together with a second symposium) in a volume, *Life and Infinite Individuality*. Citations are taken from this combined volume, which can be found listed in the Bibliography with the works of both B. Bosanquet and A. Seth Pringle-Pattison.

[151]   Bosanquet, *The Value and Destiny of the Individual*, see especially chs.II, IX; Pringle-Pattison, *The Idea of God*, ch.XIV. Pringle-Pattison's question which suggested the title for the symposium can be found at p.272. Despite their differences, their correspondence shows that there was never any professional nor personal animosity between them; indeed Pringle-Pattison was the person who first put Bosanquet forward for the lectureship (*Bernard Bosanquet and his Friends*, 129–30). Pringle-Pattison was by no means the only person at the time to worry about Bosanquet's treatment of the self here. The complaints of Henry Jones will be considered in the next chapter (see pp.428–9) and we should note also Webb's criticisms of Bosanquet's conception of persons as 'adjectival' in his *Divine Personality and Human Life*, ch.IX. Even if all personal characteristics are 'universal', Webb argues, 'the principle of unity according to which they are combined in an individual Personality is in each case unique' (234).

what is most fundamentally real. To be an individual is to be *one*, an indivisible whole. However, the construction '*finite* individual' he takes as pretty much a contradiction in terms.[152] He is driven to do so in view of the Hegelian conception he adopts of the difference between the finite and the infinite, for which he gives credit to Bradley's account in his *Ethical Studies*; a discussion which we have already had occasion to note.[153] According to this way of thinking, the finite is that which is opposed by another; bounded or limited from the outside. In consequence, its opposite, the infinite, is not the endless or *un*limited, for that is either nonsense, or just some covert and disingenuous way of talking about what is really finite. The opposite of the finite, the infinite, is rather that whose unity holds *within* itself. Instead of limitation from without, it holds itself together from within. Instead of forming one among many parts of something wider, it is a totality, an indivisible whole. In short, to be infinite is the same as to be individual or real; while conversely to be finite is to fall short of both individuality and reality. In this sense for Bosanquet to say that the finite individual is adjectival is to say that it is unreal or provisional, an appearance. What reality, nature, and value it has are all to be found only in the wider (and infinite) systematic whole in relation to which it lies and towards which it points.[154] In other words what we have here, what Bosanquet is working towards, is a coming together—a cross-fertilization, one might say—of the relationship between a thing and its *properties* with the relationship between a thing and its *appearances*. In so far as anything is finite, it is merely apparent; what we understand as its *finite* nature should rather be understood as its *appearance*.

We get another angle on Bosanquet's thinking here if we examine the way in which the connection between a thing and its properties is brought together with a *second* relationship, that which we find between a *whole* and its *parts*. Traditional metaphysical thinking allows us to separate properties from one another and from their subjects, but holds these to be distinctions of thought only. In reality they are neither so sharply marked off from one another, nor capable of such separate existence. Now, in Bosanquet's judgement the situation with respect to wholes and parts is scarcely different. We may single out a subject which is less than its whole, but given that reality faces us with a continuous scale of parts within parts and wholes within wholes, our choices signify nothing but conventions—it is, he notes, a seamless passage from the Sahara, down to any region of it, down to any grain of sand in it.[155] Moreover, our conventions must be judged but provisional in the sense that any full understanding of our selection needs must bring in the wider context from which it has been taken. In this way any point or differentiable content within a given whole—be it what we would traditionally regard as a part or as a property—can be taken on its own and made an adjective of the whole; treated as one of the various aspects or regions through which the whole expresses itself. The process of abstraction is in each case the same—

[152] *Life and Infinite Individuality*, 181.   [153] *Ethical Studies*, 74ff. See above p.185.
[154] *Life and Infinite Individuality*, 179.   [155] *Life and Infinite Individuality*, 79.

be it part or property, what is separated off can only be what it is or do what it does on condition of the presence of an entire system of implicit factors, the rest of its context. In this way he argues that although it is somewhat to extend the usage of the term 'adjective', any part may be thought of as an adjective of the whole to which it belongs. 'It is plain,' he suggests, 'that the dog's tail qualifies the dog.'[156] Its tail is not simply *part* of the dog but a *property* of the whole animal—a dog is a be-tailed creature.[157]

The claim about finitude and the claim about parts come together in Bosanquet's general theory of judgement, already discussed,[158] according to which there is only one ultimate subject—Reality—to which all things are referred.[159] In this sense everything, including the finite individual, is a predicate, or part of a predicate, of the one true subject. Instead of 'S is P', we attribute the S–P connection of reality as a whole and say, 'Reality is such that at or in S it is P'. In short, all finite reality is adjectival—by which Bosanquet tells us he means, it is 'something which has its main being and value as a qualification of a whole which includes it'[160]—to the only possible subject of judgement.

Pringle-Pattison rejects wholly Bosanquet's general theory of judgement. He accuses it of abolishing singular statements altogether to replace them with hypothetical or universal ones. It mistakes properties for actual things, abstractions for realities; an error perfectly illustrated by Bosanquet's failure to recognize the difference between parts and properties, the former something concrete the latter something abstract.[161] Pringle-Pattison complains that Bosanquet ignores 'the concrete texture of existence' in favour of 'the abstractions of intellect'[162] and, where Bosanquet shies away from 'numerical identity',[163] his own account positively celebrates it. 'Every existent is a "this," a "one," a being in a strict sense unique,'[164] he tells us; it is 'a "this" as well as a "what," a being possessing qualities and not a mere conflux of universals.'[165]

But immediately there is a surprise. If much of the force in Bosanquet's claim that finite individuals are only provisionally substantival and ultimately adjectival comes from his holism, we might expect in Pringle-Pattison a rejection of that. But far from it. He is as opposed as Bosanquet to what might be described as the 'rationalist' sense of substance; to the notion of an independent and self-subsistent 'metaphysical atom'. Rejecting what he calls 'pluralism', Pringle-Pattison is happy to admit that any individual thing 'qualifies' or 'characterizes' the nature of the whole in which it is to be found.[166] The mere individual as some kind of self-contained unit is a fiction, 'a

---

[156] *Life and Infinite Individuality*, 81.   [157] Cf. Bosanquet, *Logic*, II:257–8.
[158] See above pp.310–12.   [159] *Life and Infinite Individuality*, 80.
[160] *Life and Infinite Individuality*, 85.
[161] Pringle-Pattison takes particular exception to this conflation of parts with properties, noting that 'although there may seem to be only a verbal change in the form of expression, we have passed in reality . . . from the general relation of whole and part to the specific and quite different category of substance and accident, thing and quality' (*Life and Infinite Individuality*, 104–5).
[162] *Life and Infinite Individuality*, 106.   [163] *Life and Infinite Individuality*, 108.
[164] *Life and Infinite Individuality*, 106.   [165] *Life and Infinite Individuality*, 106–7.
[166] *Life and Infinite Individuality*, 104.

piece of covert materialism'.[167] So, whatever contrast he is trying to draw with Bosanquet, he does not think that anything can exist independently of its surroundings. Substance is organic to its wider context. The debate is not between holism and individualism. The question is rather how, recognizing the contextual–holistic nature of the finite individual, we should then characterize it?

What Pringle-Pattison advocates instead is what he describes as the Aristotelian sense of substance; substance understood as a subject of predicates not itself a predicate.[168] Talk of the bearer of properties might suggest some notion of substratum—the sort of things sometimes attributed to Locke—but Pringle-Pattison is clear that that is not his meaning either.[169] Yet beyond these rejections of Bosanquet, rationalism, and Locke it is not entirely clear what positive general conception of substance he *is* advancing.

Although both philosophers are prepared to set their stands on a general ground, it is with respect to the nature of selves that the real differences between them emerge. For Bosanquet the finite self is something incomplete and imperfect, defects which can be corrected only through a process of expansion. He offers a couple of illustrations of this. First there is our belief in our own unity. We all think of ourselves as unified but, while this is something demanded by both thought and action, it is not, he urges, anything we find in our own experience.[170] We encounter there nothing which is not 'frag-mentary and provisional',[171] a point Hume would be ready enough to agree with. Like an incomprehensible detail in a painting that falls into place as we step back and see the whole picture, unity emerges only when we broaden our view to take in more than just our selves as we experience them. Secondly there is our belief in our own freedom. We think ourselves free but, he urges, in almost everything we will we find ourselves frustrated (either by the world or by our own nature.) Only when we raise our sights and join with a more universal and necessary will which includes but goes beyond our own can we find true freedom, that is, willing without obstruction.[172] In these and other ways, Bosanquet concludes, we come to learn that finite selves are not merely *related* to the world around but owe their very nature and reality to that wider context. Correcting the gaps and flaws which are the mark of their finitude would take us into a wider sphere, and ultimately into the widest sphere of all. He offers the example of a philosophical system. Changing a limited and flawed philosophical idea into a full and perfect philosophical system would involve a massive expansion to incorporate the many partial truths that we recognize in other philosophies.[173] It is just the same with the self—'If I possessed myself entirely,' Bosanquet argues, 'I should be the Absolute.'[174]

For Pringle-Pattison the illustration of a philosophical system could scarcely have been worse; confusing 'an impersonal system of thought and the life-course of a moral

---

[167] *Life and Infinite Individuality*, 110.
[168] 'Every real individual must possess a substantive existence in the Aristotelian sense' (*Idea of God*, 282).
[169] *Idea of God*, 383, 385.
[170] *Life and Infinite Individuality*, 92.
[171] *Life and Infinite Individuality*, 93.   [172] *Life and Infinite Individuality*, 95.
[173] *Life and Infinite Individuality*, 99.   [174] *Life and Infinite Individuality*, 88.

personality',[175] it perfectly illustrates his complaint. He objects that Bosanquet, like Spinoza, sees mind simply as a complex of ideas; that he can offer no account of the unity which makes each individual mind a separate centre of thought and action.[176] He offers us nothing but abstract thoughts without a thinker.

For Pringle-Pattison the key needed to understand substance is, as we saw, its particularity. The general category of substance, he finds himself hard-pressed to explain further, but in the more specific case of selves he regards the situation as more promising, for here he links the uniqueness of substance to the notion of lived consciousness or subjectivity, the 'this' of experiential inwardness. A self is a being which exists not just in itself but 'for itself', it views the world 'from its own centre'.[177] 'He seems never to look at them from the inside, if I may so express myself,'[178] laments Pringle-Pattison of Bosanquet's treatment of finite selves. Each self he insists is 'a unique focalisation of the universe'.[179] The concept of the first person point of view, the perspective from within—*what it is like to be something or other*, to use the popular phenomenological jargon—is a familiar one in contemporary debates over materialist or functionalist reductionism in the philosophy of mind. However, observing the same concept at work in this wholly *idealist* context reminds us that the dichotomy between perspectival and perspectiveless accounts is, in fact, quite distinct from any more ontological categories.

Bosanquet does not actually *deny* that there exist selves in Pringle-Pattison's sense, but he does challenge their ultimate reality and value. When we think of such beings, numerically distinct yet existing 'side-by-side' with one another, we forget the abstraction involved in doing so. We focus on the self which feels or acts but, without contents to feel or objects to act on, units of this kind are mere empty forms and to identify our selves with such shadows is to take an abstraction for reality.

We better see the sense in which for Bosanquet we are left focusing on an abstraction, when we come to understand that for him there are more ways of existing that just numerical identity; all of which are ignored by Pringle-Pattison. The lesson to learn is that we exist in more ways—along more dimensions—than simply that which is picked out by numerical identity. 'The reality of the finite individual is not confined to his temporal existence,'[180] Bosanquet tells us. He clearly identifies several of these ways. To start with there is what he calls our *lateral* rather than our *linear* identity—the identity we share *at a time* with others rather than *over* time with ourselves.[181] It is in this context that we need to understand what he says about the communal or group mind. For Bosanquet a first real step on the path to the Absolute is the coming together of minds that we find in a society. As they participate in its moral life and adapt themselves to its common functions, the selves come to comprise something more genuinely

---

[175] *Life and Infinite Individuality*, 110.   [176] *Life and Infinite Individuality*, 105.
[177] *Idea of God*, 285, 288.   [178] *Life and Infinite Individuality*, 113.
[179] *Life and Infinite Individuality*, 109.   [180] *Life and Infinite Individuality*, 100.
[181] *Life and Infinite Individuality*, 94, 96.

individual, such that could line up all their minds 'side-by-side', as it were, they would look, not like the identical units that form an accidental conglomeration, but like the interlocking parts of a machine or the interacting organs in a body.[182] Bosanquet calls this a 'communal mind', but it is not he insists something over and above the members.[183] The point is just that the mental states of different community members may have more in common with and more connections to each other than have the past, present and future mental states of a single member, and, since we are happy to speak of an identity or continuity stretching across the latter kind of states, consistency requires us to admit it stretching between the former kind also.[184]

Besides our lateral identity, there is also what we might call our *causal* identity. Are we not real, suggests Bosanquet, as far as extends the influence of our character, thoughts, and actions?[185] We know a person thought the actions and thought they create or bring about, but if so, why place an arbitrary spatio-temporal limit on the range and type of effects that may be considered? Socrates' friends met him in his discussions with them, but if so, he lives on, for the same ideas have not yet finished speaking to us. Likewise, if the measure of Martin Luther King lies in the goal he strove for, his 'moral life' did not end with his death, for his assassination and legacy were as important in helping to realize that as anything completed within the compass of his thirty-nine years. Again it is undeniable that the plans of kings or rulers continue to shape lives long after their power of direct effect has been brought to a close, but even mundanely each one us who takes on the influence of another person we admire, who 'tries to do what they would have done', continues their life as truly as if they themselves had acted indirectly, perhaps, by letter, advice, or example.

Again, there is what we might call our *typical* identity. In so far as we manage to express the Absolute, we may live on in other similar expressions which come after us; we may live on in others of the same type.[186] Why hold it merely a metaphor when someone says, 'I can see your father in you'? 'Our distinctnesses are indifferent to the real spiritual unities, which transcend us at every point,' Bosanquet insists.[187]

A key to understanding what lies at the heart of the 1918 debate is found when we note the curious fact that Bosanquet and Pringle-Pattison in fact accuse each other of the very same fault. As far as they see it, each takes his stand on *concrete* reality, while his opponent reifies what is only an *abstraction*. It is a fair guess that when we find two

---

[182]   *Life and Infinite Individuality*, 82.
[183]   'The communal mind is not a ghost hovering over a nation; it is the minds of individuals in which the common stuff gives varied expression to the qualities and functions of the whole' (*Life and Infinite Individuality*, 185).
[184]   *Life and Infinite Individuality*, 185.
[185]   *Life and Infinite Individuality*, 100, 193–4.
[186]   *Life and Infinite Individuality*, 102. Without explicitly referring to Bosanquet, Pringle-Pattison who youngest son was killed during the Great War, takes great exception to this last suggestion that we should not grieve at the loss of loved ones because we find the same characteristics elsewhere in other people (*Life and Infinite Individuality*, 124).
[187]   *Value and Destiny of Individual*, 60.

opposing positions each claiming the same terminological high ground, that there is some equivocation going on. And indeed that is just what we find. Each accuses the other of 'abstraction' but they mean really rather different things by that. This becomes quite clear if we revisit the charge-sheet. Abstraction for Pringle-Pattison is a matter of pure generality without instantiation; of redness in itself as opposed to this or that particular red thing, of humanity in itself rather than this or that particular human being. He sees Bosanquet as advancing universality without particularity, 'what' without 'that', content without existence. The concrete is that which is particular. Abstraction for Bosanquet is understood rather differently; it is a matter of ignoring or portioning off aspects or sides of some individual's being to leave only a thin, one-sided, and ghost-like remainder. Suppose I were to ask you to think of my car, but to ignore its make, colour, age, and condition. You might find the task a little hard, the thing you are being asked to imagine too 'abstract'. This is Bosanquet's complaint. For Bosanquet, to be concrete something has to be complete. The difference then would seem to be this, between generality and incompleteness.

Lying behind this difference about abstraction lies a difference in their views about experience. Pringle-Pattison feels that in experience he has a direct and unmediated contact with reality. He says, 'The existence of the self for the self is an experienced certainty; it is, in a sense, the ground on which we stand.'[188] We take our foundation, he urges, in 'living experience'.[189] Such a stance is natural and attractive but it cannot really sustain serious weight, and Bosanquet has no such confidence in immediate experience. He does not *deny* that we have such experience; he is content, for example, to speak of 'the finite self as we experience it',[190] or 'beings such as I experience myself to be'.[191] But such experiences are hardly a touchstone with reality, and focus on identity over time, he complains, can have the effect of 'blinding us' to that which 'lies behind the visible scene'.[192] One problem is that such immediate experience is already highly abstractive, for we see with our minds as much as with our eyes, that is to say, experience comes to us already screened or filtered through our theories and concepts, disregarding a variety of aspects and sides to a thing's being as 'inessential' or 'irrelevant'. Moreover, the experience we appeal to is mute. In this connection it is to be noted that Pringle-Pattison's appeal to the first person perspective furnishes him no real *account* of subjects of predication. He says they are neither substrata, nor 'metaphysical atoms', but what they *are*, he can't say. While Pringle-Pattison holds out here for the inexpressible contact with reality marked by the intuition of 'this-here-now', Bosanquet sides with Hegel in his critique of the barren emptiness of sense-certainty. Useful comparison may also be made here with Bradley's contrast between 'this' and 'thisness',

---

[188] *Life and Infinite Individuality*, 114.
[189] *Life and Finite Individuality*, 115. 'No supposed result of speculative theory can override a certainty based on direct experience' (*Idea of God*, 288).
[190] *Life and Infinite Individuality*, 86.
[191] *Life and Infinite Individuality*, 88.   [192] *Life and Infinite Individuality*, 90.

the former our genuine point of contact with given reality, the later the incoherence into which we fall when we try to express it, forcing us insofar as we wish to *understand* individuality to do so instead in terms of completeness.[193]

One of the several directions in which the debate moves off concerns what gets termed the 'confluence of selves'. Because he sees individual selves as pragmatic units only, provisional divisions within a deeper unity which embraces them all, Bosanquet is able to endorse a degree of fluidity between them; a degree of overlap or combination. Were we able to render fully consistent our view of ourselves, he thinks, it would thereby expand to the Absolute itself, uniting with many other similar selves.[194] Haldane concurs that the higher up we go through the various stages and levels of knowledge 'the less do we encounter that hard and fast distinction of selves'[195] so typical of the lower levels.

Pringle-Pattison, on the other hand, will have none of this. He objects that all talk of 'blending or absorption depends entirely on material analogies which can have no application in the case of selves'.[196] Selves may overlap in content, but not in existence; that is, they may think the same thoughts or feel the same feelings, but for all that qualitative identity they remain numerically distinct individuals. To put the same point another way, any greater self that contained the content of others could do so only by destroying their very self-hood. To offer an analogy, it would be like a growing city that over-runs and swallows up the autonomous villages around it dissolving their identity in its. The ascent to the Absolute, that to Bosanquet seems a path of enrichment, in Pringle-Pattison's eyes looks more like a course of destruction.

But is the kind of arrangement Bosanquet describes really so sharply at odds with the world we know? To change the analogy, we might move from urban planning to the business world. We might think of a parent company—perhaps a multi-national corporation—and its sub-companies, some of which might themselves have sub-companies. Not only can companies fall under other ones, but they may come together or apart (mergers, and divisions) or overlap (perhaps they share a legal department). They may even be divided differently for different purposes (one company for production, say, but two for marketing). However, these further relationships do not necessarily destroy their original identities.[197] So long as we rely on a supposed awareness of ourselves as complete and unified, notions such as those of the union of

---

[193] See above p.290.

[194] 'If we possessed our self we should be the absolute; for certainly we should then include or be blended with innumerable other selves' (*Life and Infinite Individuality*, 96; cf. 99).

[195] *Life and Infinite Individuality*, 177.

[196] *Life and Infinite Individuality*, 121. 'The existence of an individual centre of knowledge and feeling is, in itself, an enrichment of the universe' he says; 'To merge or blend such centres is simply to put out the lights out one by one' (*Life and Infinite Individuality*, 122).

[197] It is natural to turn to metaphors in trying to understand the highly abstract difference between Bosanquet and Pringle-Pattison, but interestingly Haldane even wonders how much their disagreement is one simply of preferred metaphors (*Life and Infinite Individuality*, 151).

minds (or indeed their division) prove impossible to entertain. But once this grip is loosened conceptual space is gained.

In addition to the matter of its reality, another important thread running throughout the debate concerns the *value* of the finite individual. Indeed, both philosophers agree that of all the issues they touch upon this is really the most important—we fight over the reality only of what *matters*. Moreover, it is here on the issue of value that the greatest difference emerges between them. For all that their debate shows them to be in many ways far closer together on questions of metaphysics than their initial statements, or the crude summaries of others, might suggest, when it comes to their different understandings of what gives value to the universe they find themselves very far apart indeed. In both cases their overall objection to the other is more ethical than ontological, the whole debate taking on a moral fervour and weight even through its most abstract and technical sections.

For Pringle-Pattison the locus of value in the universe is finite individuals; spirits are what matter and things only matter because they matter to spirits.[198] The aim of the universe is soul-making, that is, the bringing forth and nurturing of finite beings—not, to be sure, as they are now, but as God knows and intends them to become, yet finite souls nonetheless.[199] To his way of thinking the very concept of value presupposes the reality of finite wills with a genuine choice between good or evil; something which calls for a distinction between them and God, or the universe at large. Neither error nor sin make sense unless we be different enough from the spirit of the whole to make it possible for us to stand in opposition to it. On the Absolute model ethics becomes an illusion, for if we are all somehow parts or components of a divine reality, already perfect, what is there for us either to choose or to overcome? We may understand virtue as surrender on the part of the selfish-will to a higher law, but 'what is the merit or value,' Pringle-Pattison asks, 'in [such] self-surrender if the whole process is a make-believe on the part of the Absolute,'[200] if there is nothing really to be overcome?

Bosanquet, for his part, finds the Personal Idealist conception of value fearfully narrow and limited. Finite individuals cannot be the last word in what matters. As an idealist he holds there is no reality beyond thought, but that does not mean that there cannot be values higher than *our* highest ones. 'I cannot believe that the supreme end of the Absolute is to give rise to beings such as I experience myself to be,'[201] he says; on such a view temporal self-identity becomes a kind of 'fetish'[202]—we might obtain personal survival, but devoid of all that would give it value.[203] We exist in other ways

---

[198] 'There are no values apart from their realization, that is, apart from consciousness. Spirits are the bearers, the home, of values, so far as the finite world is concerned' (*The Idea of Immortality*, 157). Pringle-Pattison's conception of value in relation to finite selves can be usefully compared to that expressed in McTaggart's 'The Individualism of Value'. (see below pp.464–6).

[199] *Life and Infinite Individuality*, 120.   [200] *Life and Infinite Individuality*, 115.

[201] *Life and Infinite Individuality*, 88.   [202] *Life and Infinite Individuality*, 99.

[203] *Life and Infinite Individuality,* 194. Wittgenstein had a similar intuition (*Tractatus Logico-Philosophicus*, § 6.4312).

than simply as entities over time, and these ways may be more valuable, as well as more permanent. If individuals matter they do not do so intrinsically; rather 'the value of the particularity is indirect, and depends on what it helps to realise'.[204] Nor is Bosanquet unaware of the need for opposition in the construction of any viable ethical theory. However, he places it in a different dimension to Pringle-Pattison. Rather than the finite will surrendering itself to others, or to the infinite will of God, the apparent or superficial will must surrender itself to the true or General Will. Pringle-Pattison may object that this is just 'a game which the Absolute plays with itself', but (Bosanquet would reply) unless our duty can be expressed as 'the true good of our true selves' what reason can there ever be for us to pursue it?

10.4 Encounter with the New Realism

10.4.1 The challenge to Idealism

Green's critique of traditional empirical realism left idealism in dominance of the field, but in the new century that supremacy was challenged. Leading the charge was the Cambridge philosopher, G.E. Moore, whose 1903 paper, 'The Refutation of Idealism'[205] marked a crucial juncture in the history of British philosophy. The fact that it addresses itself to Berkelean rather than Kantian or Hegelian idealism, however, demonstrates that it was of significance less as a critique of existing systems than as a manifesto for a positive alternative; and the representative realism which it advocated certainly found much support in Cambridge, from such figures as G.F. Stout, B. Russell, and C.D. Broad.

In Oxford the response to Idealism was slightly different. Rejecting all intermediaries or 'representatives' in perception, Cook Wilson developed a kind of naive realism that harked back to Thomas Reid.[206] Attacking the idealistic account of relations, he urged a theory of knowledge as direct non-inferential 'apprehension' of some object by a distinct subject. This basic position that 'knowing in no way alters or modifies the thing known'[207] (sometimes called 'Oxford Realism')[208] was further developed by H.A. Prichard in a 1906 article, 'Appearances and Reality', and in his 1909 book *Kant's Theory of Knowledge*, which presents a realist critique of Kant's idealism.[209]

This second kind of reaction to idealism, which became known generally as 'the new realism',[210] was most closely associated, however, with Samuel Alexander. In a

---

[204] *Value and Destiny of Individual*, 27.   [205] *Mind*, 1903.

[206] Cook Wilson had been a student of both Green and Lotze. From the 1880s onwards he was very influential in Oxford, but eschewing publication, this was almost entirely through his teaching and students. His lecture notes and letters appeared posthumously in a volume titled *Statement and Inference* (1926).

[207] *Kant's Theory of Knowledge*, 118.

[208] For further details see Marion, 'Oxford Realism'.

[209] Bosanquet criticizes this book in the 2nd edition of his *Logic* (301–22).

[210] Like British Idealism, the view had its trans-Atlantic equivalent. See *The New Realism* (1912) by six American authors Walter Taylor Marvin, Ralph Barton Perry, Edward Gleason Spaulding, W. P. Montague, Edwin Holt, and Walter B. Pitkin.

series of articles from 1908 onwards and given perhaps clearest expression in his 1914 address to the British Academy, he advanced a version of direct realism, holding fast to our pre-reflective experience that 'mind and its object are two separate existences connected together by the relation of togetherness or comprescence',[211] where 'compresence' is understood as an association comparable to that in which two physical things stand alongside one another, any difference in the resulting complex a function of the terms themselves and not their linkage. Indeed, recalling the dependence of mind on its base structure in the brain, he argues that we may even say that the knowledge relation is nothing but the comprescence between one physical object and another, when the first has acquired the additional property of consciousness. Central to Alexander's whole position is a sharp distinction between the mental act of perception and its object.

10.4.2 Idealist responses

Either implicitly or explicitly many historians have taken the emergence of Cambridge representative realism and the new realism to mark the end of British Idealism. But this was not the case at all, and one of the most interesting aspects of its history concerns the nature of the response idealism made in the new century to the fresh challenges which presented themselves; for the reaction was far from one of simple rejection. Mackenzie, for example, in his 1906 paper 'The New Realism and the Old Idealism', finds Moore's rejection of subjective idealism wholly legitimate, and even allows that he is justified, to a degree, in reading British Idealism that way. It *has been* more subjective that it would like to think—he cites T.H. Green[212] and even Bradley. But Mackenzie continues, falling back on his old teacher Caird, in so far as that has been the case it has been no true idealism. Moore wants to separate consciousness and its object. Thought without content is obviously vacuous, Mackenzie replies, but we might well be tempted to follow Moore and suppose that objects can exist without consciousness of them. For surely the world that we know is not something in my mind, but something we all may apprehend? However, this contrast between private or subjective and public or shared is not at all the same as that between ideal and non-ideal, the contrast Bradley indicated between idea as fact and idea as meaning, and to be an idealist with respect to this latter sense of 'idea' is to recognize the presence of meaning not only in our current thinking, but throughout the whole field of our experience; passing beyond the contents of any individual mind. In dismissing subjective idealism, realism does a valuable service; it reminds us that true idealism does not depend even in the slightest degree, upon the principle that '*esse* is *percipi*'.[213]

We must not say, as Berkeley does, that cups and saucers and stars and planets exist in people's mind, or even in some hypothetical divine mind. We must not even say, as Kant does, that time and space are only forms of our consciousness. Personally, I am disposed even to add that we

---

[211] 'Basis of Realism', 283.
[212] This, as we saw above (p.362) was a charge repeated by Pringle-Pattison.
[213] 'The New Realism and the Old Idealism', 314.

must not say, with Mr Bradley, that the objects of our experience have only degrees of reality. Idealism, as I understand it, admits the reality of all the objects of our experience. It leaves us our cups and saucers, our suns and planets, our primroses and skylarks, our time and space, undisturbed. What it denies is that any of these things are to be regarded as distinct and independent realities, separable from one another and from us. It maintains that they can only be interpreted as parts of a whole; that that whole is a living whole; and that its ultimate interpretation can only be found in the development of intelligence within it.[214]

By the time Bosanquet came to write on metaphysics, realism was well established and on the ascendant, and it is at first sight surprising to see how far he seems to have taken it on board; so much so that McTaggart objected that his position was dualist, if not actually materialist.[215] Muirhead too doubted whether 'idealism' was really the right name for it,[216] a point Bosanquet himself was quite happy to concede—coming to prefer the name 'speculative philosophy'.[217] Key texts here are his *The Distinction between Mind and its Objects* (1913)—written in response to Alexander—and *The Meeting of Extremes in Contemporary Philosophy* (1921).

Bosanquet generally opposes any view that sees nature as existing only in or for mind and not in its own right. We must not libel nature by saying that she borrows her content and meaning from us, when in truth it is the other way.[218] For this reason he rejects any theory which would reduce the material world to nothing more than an object for or state of the human—or any other—mind. This takes in the subjective idealism of Berkeley,[219] but leaves him scarcely more supportive of objective versions such as transcendental idealism,[220] or Panpsychism.[221]

In addition to opposing much that we might expect idealists to support, we also find Bosanquet endorsing various realist ideas we might expect any idealist to reject.[222] For example, he is happy to speak of consciousness as a late comer on the cosmic scene, the

[214] 'The New Realism and the Old Idealism', 326–7.

[215] Review of *Principle of Individuality and Value*, 421–2.

[216] 'Bernard Bosanquet', 399.

[217] *Meeting of Extremes*, 2. 'Speculative Philosophy' was, of course, the name Hegel preferred for his own subject (*Phenomenology of Spirit*, §56).

[218] *Principle of Individuality and Value*, 367. 'There is nothing to be afraid of in finding that the operative content, the actual being of the soul, comes from the environment' (*Psychology of the Moral Self*, 10).

[219] See, for example, *Meeting of Extremes*, 2–7. Although he is not always wholly consistent on this, e.g. consider, 'The whole world, for each of us, *is* our course of consciousness in so far as this is regarded as a system of objects which we are obliged to think' (*Essentials of Logic*, 14–5).

[220] Like all the British Idealists, Bosanquet wholly rejected Kant's or any similar system in so far as it was understood as turning the world we experience into some mental representation and leaving ultimate reality as some unknowable *ding-an-sich*. See for example *Meeting of Extremes*, ch.7.

[221] *Principle of Individuality and Value*, 363–6. Not only does Panpsychism fail to do justice to the basic opposition of mind and nature, but the minds which it postulates do no real work. If the role of mind in nature is not so much to do as to appreciate that is something much more effectively achievable by us than it could possibly be by things themselves. 'Suppose a mountain or a lake to have a dim subjectivity of its own, this consciousness can neither guide itself, nor again appreciate itself as the poet and artist can appreciate it' (*Principle of Individuality and Value*, 365).

[222] Although, he makes clear that, if this is his position, it is materialism or externalism 'with a difference'; materialism 'as the fullness and genuine purport of concrete idealism' (*Principle of Individuality and Value*, 319).

function of complex material organization,[223] while Moore's 'Refutation of Idealism' is welcomed for its rejection of the idea that spatial objects in themselves are quite different from how they appear to us, and for its insistence on the reality and objectivity of sensa.[224] And in a similar vein Alexander's realism is approved because, having freed itself from the old materialist prejudice that only spatial properties are real, it can admit the reality of universals.[225] Interestingly, the same conciliatory tone may also be noted in Mackenzie's 1917 *Elements of Constructive Philosophy*. He too finds much to applaud in the new realism, noting that it has done great service in opposing subjectivism and that its view of universals brings it close to the idealism of Plato, even—he dares to suggest—of a correctly interpreted Hegel.[226]

Nonetheless there is plenty of textual evidence to the fact that Bosanquet was and remained an idealist. 'I do not doubt that anything which can ultimately *be*, must be of the nature of mind or experience, and, therefore, that reality must ultimately be conceived after this manner,'[227] he says in his Gifford lectures, while he speaks of the Absolute always as the 'supreme', 'complete', or 'perfect' *experience*.[228] He wholly rejects the dualist model of mind as one thing set opposite or alongside one or more others. Consciousness is more like an 'atmosphere' that 'includes' its objects. As we move from a smaller to a larger room our mind itself seems to expand, not just the range of things which it confronts. Mind is a kind of world or panorama which includes its objects within it. It belongs to the very nature of mind to be a whole, while an object by its very nature is always a fragment.[229] Though prepared to draw some working distinction between mind and object, the reality of universals is sufficient proof that the objects of mind are at bottom continuous in nature with it, universals being precisely the currency of thought.[230] He insists that the fundamental ground for placing mind at the centre of reality is not the subjective idealist's refusal to distinguish between act and object, his prejudice that mind can apprehend only what is part of itself, but rather the insight that a universe severed from the life of mind can never fulfil the conditions of self-existence; mind is a world, its object always something fragmentary.[231]

---

[223] *Principle of Individuality and Value*, 196.   [224] *Meeting*, 4–6.

[225] *Distinction between Mind and its Objects*, 21.

[226] *Elements*, 161–2. However, while recognizing that there is some value in the pluralism that commonly goes with it, he insists that in the end thought cannot rest content with the lack of ultimate order which such pluralism brings with it, and that cosmic unity therefore remains its ideal (*Elements*, 143).

[227] *Principle of Individuality and Value*, 135.

[228] For example, *Principle of Individuality and Value*, 256, 391, 393. Two further pieces of evidence. A remark which Bosanquet made in a letter to C.C. J. Webb in 1923: 'I didn't say anything about Naturalism [in a previous letter]. I don't think it important; the universe is so obviously experience, and it must all be of one tissue' (*Bernard Bosanquet and his Friends*, 24). Elsewhere Bosanquet speaks approvingly of 'the old lesson of Hegel and his sympathisers—that the universe is a single spirit, of whom or of which all appearances are manifestations; that all its manifestations fall within a single experience, compact of experiences; that all of it is life and activity, and that outside this living experience there can be nothing' (Review of five books of Italian idealism, 367).

[229] *Distinction between Mind and its Objects*, 27–8.

[230] *Distinction between Mind and its Objects*, 34–6.

[231] *Distinction between Mind and its Objects*, 38.

With pointers in either direction it is hard to get to the bottom of Bosanquet's view (and one might be tempted here by a comparison with Edward Caird, whose metaphysics shows similar contradictory tendencies). But his position seems to be as follows. The Absolute is the unified totality of all things. It manifests itself in everything, including nature and mind. It is in a sense the deeper principle behind them both. They are not, however, completely separate or independent manifestations. Neither could exist wholly without the other and there occurs much two-way traffic between them, as each influences the other—although it must be admitted too that just where we draw the line between them is grey and fluctuates with context.[232] In particular we must acknowledge that nature, in any interesting sense, is coloured by mind. Mind gives to it secondary and tertiary qualities (e.g. aesthetic ones).[233] Although both are manifestations of the Absolute, it needs to be added that mind is a derivative or indirect manifestation, for Bosanquet sees mind as emerging out of matter. (To offer an analogy, the process is perhaps a bit like creating a garden; something one does by planting seeds which then grow into beautiful colours and shapes). Nature gives to mind both its being and its content; thoroughly presupposing the mechanical nature from which it emerges, it has no special 'filling' of its own, not even a priori principles of knowledge or of morality. At this point, however, it is vital to appreciate that although the Absolute manifests itself in all things, it does not manifest itself *equally* in all things. Crucially (reversing the order preferred by reductionistic or evolutionary thinkers) Bosanquet is convinced that the later, the more complex, the more developed the manifestation, the more revelatory we may take it of the true nature of the Absolute. Hence that mind comes after matter is not only not a problem for, but a proof of, his idealism. Although a late product, mind is not epiphenomenal, rather it is the very key. In a similar fashion he thinks we best understand mind if we focus on the highest levels of its conscious life (e.g. the social, religious, or aesthetic consciousness) rather than the lowest.[234] But this does not mean the Absolute is or is similar to a finite mind, since Bosanquet, like Bradley, regards everyday consciousness as contradictory (set in debilitating opposition to the not-self). As we leave the contradiction of consciousness behind—although not its positive harmonizing aspects[235]—we leave behind the idea of *a mind* as a kind of *thing*, and end up with something more like *mind itself*, the quality or activity.[236]

Idealists, then, responded to the resurgence of realism. Nor should that response be thought an irrelevance, the last cry of a few old idealist dinosaurs. For even if the overall direction of philosophical thought continued ultimately in the direction of realism, the on-going debate did manage to produce a certain amount of vacillation and even

---

[232] There occurs, Bosanquet argues, 'a constant transposition of content between the self and the not-self' (*Psychology of the Moral Self*, 8; cf. Bradley, *Appearance and Reality*, 79).

[233] *Principle of Individuality and Value*, 366.

[234] *Principle of Individuality and Value*, 269–70.

[235] *Principle of Individuality and Value*, ch.VI.

[236] *Principle of Individuality and Value*, ch.X.

'back-sliding' in the realist camp. Prichard certainly became dissatisfied with his early position, his later thoughts unable to settle in any clear-cut positive account of perception.[237] But an even greater apostasy we find in the figure of H.W.B. Joseph. Joseph came up to Oxford in 1886 to New College, where Cook Wilson held sway, and so not unnaturally began his career as a realist. His 1906 work *An Introduction to Logic* is solidly Aristotelian. But from this starting point for which 'to be' is one thing and 'to be perceived' quite another, he became increasingly assailed by doubts, in part about secondary qualities, but especially about space which he found difficult to regard as something independent of all consciousness.[238] These doubts reached their head in his 1929 British Academy address on the idealism of Kant and Berkeley. In this lecture the detailed arguments of each are examined and found wanting but, Joseph admits, that hardly refutes idealism itself. Holding that the discoveries of contemporary physics already leave our common-sense realism 'rudely shaken', he argues that space is something which can make no sense except to perceiving minds, 'for it is infinite and infinitely divisible, and therefore neither a genuine whole nor with genuine unit-part'. How, he asks, can we make sense of 'real' size or solidity except in terms which refer us back to the sensory experience?[239] In consequence, real things, he concludes, though certainly not private like pains or sounds, are perhaps best thought of as similarly 'bound up' with the knowing and perceiving of them.[240] Even if the world we know is *found in* not *fashioned by* our knowing, it may yet be the creation of some greater intelligence in whose nature our minds somehow participate. Though tentative and vague, this was nonetheless a return to idealism; even if in his later years Joseph tended more and more towards a kind of Platonism.[241]

Undoubtedly during the early years of the twentieth century these waters became very muddied indeed. We see an interesting example of this in a 1933 essay by R.G. Collingwood on Bradley's metaphysics. Correctly noting that for Bradley, unimpeded by some mental intermediary standing between us and it, we enjoy direct contact with reality (albeit of a lowly degree and much in need of transformation), he suggests that *Appearance and Reality* 'instead of the last word of a decaying Idealism, is the manifesto of a new Realism'—a realism that went on in different ways to influence Cook Wilson, Prichard, Russell, and Moore.[242] But this judgement is anachronistic. Idealism became increasingly phenomenal, and its dispute with realism when Collingwood came up to Oxford in 1908 had largely become one about whether there could be any immediate awareness of non-mental objects. But idealism in 1893, idealism as

---

[237] Prichard's later thoughts may be found in his posthumous *Knowledge and Perception* (1950).

[238] 'Psychological Explanation of the Development of the Perception of External Objects', 468. Joseph's lectures on 'Things in Space' remain unpublished New College Library.

[239] 'On Occupying Space', 336–9.

[240] 'A Comparison of Kant's idealism with that of Berkeley', 233–4.

[241] Collingwood, *Autobiography*, 21.

[242] 'The Metaphysics of F.H. Bradley', 245–6. Unpublished at the time, this essay was first published in the 2005 edition of Collingwood's *An Essay on Philosophical Method*.

we find it in Green, Caird, or Henry Jones, was a very different affair. The point at issue then was not whether we were in direct contact with reality—that was never in question—but what was the correct account of its nature; whether it was something to be found by the application of thought *to* sense, or something to be found by scrapping away the distortions of thought *from* sense.[243] *Appearance and Reality* did not presage new realism, instead new realism found its way back to the essential insights that had characterized idealism at its beginning—which is why so many of the original idealists were sympathetic to it.

---

[243] Insofar as he leant towards the second of these, when most of the others leant towards the first, there is, of course, a second and rather different sense in which Bradley was a 'realist' to their 'idealism'. But that is not the point Collingwood is trying to make here.

11

Developments in Idealist Philosophy of Religion

It has already been examined how—flowing out of the religious doubts of the late nineteenth century—philosophy of religion was one of the central pillars of the idealistic movement. As that century ended and the new one started religious concerns changed, but the subject continued to be important and to form a key component of idealism. The larger part (although by no means all) of this development was associated with the Personal Idealist branch of the movement whose metaphysical doctrines were discussed in the previous chapter. Alongside their intuitive faith in the moral consciousness, they tended to set a similar trust in religious feeling, and this led to a different emphasis than before. For where the first wave of idealists had been concerned to wrench the *possibility* of faith from out of the hands of a hostile naturalism, the second-wave—born into an idealistic confidence—were more concerned with the religious *adequacy* of what they could find. Questions of worship, prayer, immortality, dogma, and sin began to reassert themselves, as philosophy of religion become more personal, spiritual, and experiential; less historical, social, and moral.

At the root, however, remained metaphysics; and in particular a central knot of puzzles regarding the nature and inter-relations of the triad: universe, God, and self. As shall be seen below, different philosophers took different lines here, allegiances becoming complex and blurred, and to help steer a path through this debate, it is useful to distinguish five different positions. For some (such as Green and Caird) the Absolute was the universe or Reality as a whole, and identified with God. Others (such as Bradley and Bosanquet) took the same view of the Absolute but rejected the identity with God, relegating the divine instead to some sort of appearance of the Absolute. Those unhappy with either of these positions tended to move off in one or other of three directions. Some (such as Rashdall) kept the term 'Absolute' to refer to the whole universe, but loosened its tight bound unity so that it became more like a pluralistic system which could include both finite spirits and God. Others (such as Webb) retained the title 'Absolute' to refer exclusively to God, but loosened its claims to holistic completeness so as to allow finite spirits to sit in some measure of independence alongside, or in relation to, it. And finally some (such as James Seth and W.R. Sorley) pretty much ceased using the term 'Absolute' altogether, as more of a hindrance than a help in thinking through such matters.

11.1 Personalism

11.1.1 James Seth

James Seth's *Ethical Principles*—whose final section treats the metaphysical implications of morality—provides an early example, both typical and influential, of personalist philosophy of religion. We must, he argues there, accept the existence of both an intellectual and a moral order—that there is an objective rational world and an objective moral law—but how do these two systems stand to one another? The former hardly manifests the latter; indeed, if evolutionary theory is correct in its assertion that strength, guile, and luck are what win out in the end, they seem positively opposed. But is this really a view we can accept? Can reality be so divided against itself? It must be wondered whether this oppositional dualism may not be met by reducing both man and nature to some deeper unity, whether both may not be seen as ultimately compatible expressions of some common source—God?

In Kant's hands this line of reasoning takes the form of an argument that God must exist as a distributor of rewards and punishments. More specifically, for Kant, the goal of moral life consists in a perfect happiness that results from perfect virtue, and he insists that whatever ought to be the case must be possible to realize, but clearly within the compass of the world we know there is no guarantee of any coincidence between virtue and happiness. To rectify this situation we are forced to postulate not merely enough time to become righteous (i.e. immortality) but also a deity who will grant us the grace to do so and ensure that our subsequent efforts result in happiness. There is something 'inadequate', 'unworthy', and 'external' about this *deus ex machina* argument, complains Seth. It makes God not much better than 'a chief-of-police of the moral universe'.[1] A more promising line of thought is found if we trace through Greek and Christian thought the idea of providence, of a divinely crafted universe that 'knows no ultimate distinction between the course of the world and the course of the moral life, but sees all things working together for good'.[2] To suppose the universe not foreign or indifferent to our ethical life, but crafted for and conducive to it, is essential if that morality is to have meaning, and therefore a necessary metaphysical presupposition of it. Just as an intellectual being may insist on the rationality of existence—the coincidence of inconceivability and impossibility—so an essentially moral being has a claim on the universe to be a medium, and not an obstacle, to his proper life.[3] This

---

[1] *Ethical Principles*, 410.
[2] *Ethical Principles*, 416.
[3] Bradley considers a similar argument in *Appearance and Reality* (139–40) but was more equivocal. See above Chapter 6.1.7.

'ultimate and inalienable human right' is, Seth quickly points out, no promise of happiness, only of the chance to realize oneself morally. To deny the claim, however, 'is either to naturalise, that is, to de-moralise man, or to convict the universe of failure to perfect its own work, to say that, in the end, the part contradicts the whole.'[4] The ethical life is a sham and a dead end in any universe not specifically designed for morality. To this line of argument Seth adds a further consideration, that were the universe ethical in its most fundamental structure, this fact might be brought in to explain the undeniable objective validity of ethics.[5]

But if there exists a divine principle that brings in line what *is* with what *ought to be*, just what is its nature? What more can we say about the 'God' whose existence we have proved? Seth argues that it must be personal. 'Since the moral ideal is an ideal of personality,' he suggests, 'must not the moral reality, the reality of which that ideal is the after-reflection as well as the prophetic hint, be the perfection of personality, the supreme Person whose image we, as persons, bear and are slowly and with effort inscribing on our natural individuality?'[6] Seth is well aware of the difficulties of such an assertion from the Absolute Idealist perspective. For one thing, personhood, as an essentially finite notion—surely self is always limited by its correlative not-self?—seems inapplicable to the infinite. But following Lotze, Seth replies to this objection, in a move that owes much also to Descartes' celebrated conception of the finite as the negation of the infinite not *vice versa*, that the finite kind of personality which we experience is but an imperfect form of, and hence no guide to, ideal or infinite personality.[7] Another charge might be that to assert the personality of God seems unduly anthropomorphic; a looking out at the universe and seeing ourselves reflected back. But here too Seth is prepared to fight his corner. Absolute Idealism's conception of 'God' he finds completely inadequate; either an empty abstraction or pantheistic whole, it is at bottom self-contradictory. Its Absolute is supposed to be more 'subject' than 'object', but idealism fails properly to carry through that thought; 'if we are to find the key to the interpretation of the Absolute in the subject rather than in the object, with what right do we exclude the ethical and emotional elements of the subject's life, and retain only the intellectual?'[8] Absolute Idealism fails properly to understand the relationship between man and God, which is moral not metaphysical, a communion of wills not an identity of substance; 'the union and communion not only of thought with Thought, but of will with Will'.[9]

Kant appeals to morality to argue for immortality, as well as to secure free will and divinity. 'Ought' implies 'can', and hence an infinite obligation implies an infinite ability to fulfil it, he argues. But an infinite moral ideal cannot be realized in a finite time, and so it follows that man, as the subject of such an ideal, must have available

---

[4] *Ethical Principles*, 418.   [5] *Ethical Principles*, 420.   [6] *Ethical Principles*, 424.
[7] *Ethical Principles*, 443–4; Descartes, *Meditation* III; Lotze, *Microcosmus*, bk.IX/ch.iv/§4 (Volume II 678–88).
[8] *Ethical Principles*, 441.   [9] *Ethical Principles*, 387.

infinite time for the task of its realization.[10] Seth is generally sympathetic with this case, but wishes to broaden it out, insisting that the essence of the argument is independent of any particular view of the ethical life. Indeed, the question of whether we are immortal is really just another aspect of our previous question whether morality finds correlate in the nature of reality.[11] Kant's real deduction of immortality is from the transcendental source and significance of the moral ideal. There is a timeless significance to moral action; 'In every moral act . . . man transcends the limits of the present life, and becomes already a citizen of an eternal world.'[12] Can it be that just as we develop, everything is given up? Is life not a training for something more? Is it all thrown away? The rhetorical questions come thick and fast here and probably replace actual argument.

But even if we grant immortality, need it be personal or individual in type? We might think here of the corporate immortality, the continuance and moral progress of tribe and species, discussed by John Caird. Alongside straightforward factual scepticism that doubts whether we really do see any advance or permanence in history, more theoretically Seth objects that moral gain could never be preserved, since it consists in improvement in character, and character cannot be transferred. The hard-won experience and growth of a lifetime must be started over again by the next generation. The good can be nothing over and above the good of individuals, like myself, but if there is no permanent good for me, neither can there be for them.[13]

11.1.2 J.R. Illingworth

It is no surprise to find that one of the Personal Idealists most strongly concerned with religious questions was the theologian, J.R. Illingworth. Coming up to Corpus Christi College Oxford in 1867, in 1872 Illingworth was appointed a Fellow of Jesus College and simultaneously a tutor at the newly established Keble College, which academic career he continued until 1883, when ill-health obliged him to take up instead the clerical living at Longworth, a small village some ten miles outside Oxford. His philosophical education was in the newly ascendant idealism, but his sympathies were clearly with what (evoking the earlier split within Hegel's followers) he characterized as the Greenites of the right rather than the Greenites of the left.[14] Like Seth, he too defends what he regards as Kant's moral argument for the existence of God, but he takes a slightly different line, holding that the existence of God may be derived from two central and undeniable facts of consciousness: freedom and morality. The experience of freedom is an inalienable component of the experience of personhood. It is in part a matter of self-determination,[15] but it also involves an element of real choice and

---

[10] *Ethical Principles*, 449. see Kant, *Critique of Practical Reason*, pt.I/bk.II/ch.II/§4 (126–8).

[11] *Ethical Principles*, 453.

[12] *Ethical Principles*, 449–50.

[13] *Ethical Principles*, 456–60.

[14] A.L. Illingworth, *Life and Work of John Richardson Illingworth*, 90.

[15] 'I possess this peculiarity—that, whereas all other things in the world are necessarily determined by external agencies or causes, I have the power to make the external influences which affect my conduct my own,

contingency.[16] Although free, however, we cannot simply do as we choose; for to be a person is to feel also a sense of duty, to be conscious of an obligation upon our conduct. Such is the experience of all people, urges Illingworth, at least in every civilized race.[17] The imperative is not a physical necessity, for we can disobey; it does not originate from within, for we cannot simply unmake it;[18] and it cannot be the voice of others, for it goes above and beyond any law that men make. (It speaks to motives, for example and asks for superogatory things no external law would demand). 'The inevitable inference must be that it is the voice of a personal God,' Illingworth concludes.[19]

We have already seen how strongly Illingworth bangs the drum for human personality, and we find him an equally fervent advocate of personality in God. Men drew a conception of God, he suggests, from the most real, most active, and most valuable thing they know; themselves. This might sound like a crude anthropomorphism, but that impression is diminished by the stress he places on the developing nature of our concept of person. Eschewing any simplistic appeal to immediate experience, he admits that the growth in our understanding of this concept has been gradual and, indeed, slow. This gives him, in reviewing that history, an opportunity to stress the great contribution of Christianity—the Incarnation especially, but also the offerings of Augustine, Luther, and Kant[20]—and even more importantly it means that the concepts of human and divine personality have developed in tandem. This has two notable corollaries.

The first consequence is that personhood becomes a degree notion not an absolute one. Although personality is the thing we know best in the world, we are still far from understanding all that it implies, only dimly aware of its depths and undeveloped potential. And evoking such higher levels, we may suppose that in God alone is found perfect personality, of which ours is but an imperfect copy. This is Lotze's argument, already encountered above in Seth.[21] The second consequence is more specific to Illingworth. He argues that the high-water mark of the attempt to understand personhood is the Christian doctrine of the Trinity. Human personality, he suggests, is essentially triune consisting in subject, object, and their relation.[22] Its first manifestation, in the family, is also triune consisting in father, mother, and child.[23] If we are to

---

before allowing them to do so, thereby converting them from alien forces into inner laws; so that when determined by them I am not determined from without but from within' (*Personality Human and Divine*, 104–5).

[16] *Divine Immanence*, 194–5; *Personality Human and Divine*, 104–7.

[17] *Personality Human and Divine*, 108.

[18] If the moral law does not originate from within, it must be internalized if it is to have any value. 'I act, as Kant says, not from the law, but from the consciousness of the law. However strongly, therefore, positive law may urge me to act I must appropriate it and make it *my* law before it can do so' (*Personality Human and Divine*, 107). Thus Illingworth seeks to reconcile a divine account of ethics with a Kantian stress on moral autonomy.

[19] *Personality Human and Divine*, 110–11.

[20] *Personality Human and Divine*, 8–23.

[21] *Personality Human and Divine*, 52–3. See above p.400. For further occurrences of this 'perfect personality' argument see Upton, *Lectures on the Bases of Religious Belief*, 363; and Webb, *God and Personality*, 18–19, 106–7.

[22] *Personality Human and Divine*, 69.

[23] *Personality Human and Divine*, 71.

think of God as personal, it must be as possessing in transcendent perfection the same properties that are imperfectly possessed by us; and as our own personality is triune in nature so must God's be.[24] Notable here is the fact that Illingworth thinks the inference goes from humanity to God; doubtful critics, of course, will see it running in reverse.

We have already seen in the previous chapter how Illingworth regards knowledge holistically, placing great emphasis on intuition and emotion. We find the same in his religious epistemology. In *Divine Immanence* (1898) he argues that we 'feel' that the material world is a revelation of spirit. The underlying feeling itself is hard to describe more precisely, but undeniable and, unless good reason can be given for discrediting it, 'weighty evidence of a spiritual reality behind material things'.[25] This may seem weak, but he readily allows that belief in a personal God is primarily instinctive and only secondarily rational.[26] He allows that Kant demonstrated the inadequacy of the traditional theistic arguments, but has little worry that this might undermine the belief itself. Indeed, rather perversely, its immunity to rational critique becomes an argument in its own right. 'The persistence of a belief, whose negative supports have been removed, is an additional evidence of its inherent strength.'[27] Quite reversing the position of John Caird or T.H. Green, for Illingworth the ethical and religious striving for God take precedence over and determine the intellectual. Reason alone will not secure faith. For instance, he argues that we cannot know God unless we have already a 'moral affinity' with him. If we are to know God as a person, we must begin with a *desire* to know him (his self, as distinct from simply his works or manifestations in nature). This desire must be both intense and sincere. 'Further, moral affinity is an essential of personal intimacy. A man cannot understand a character with which he has no accord. And affinity with a Holy Being implies a progressive and lifelong effort of the will.'[28]

Illingworth is an idealist. Matter and Spirit are known only in combination with each other.[29] Matter 'as we know it, is everywhere and always fused by mind'[30]—the argument here is very Berkleyan—but Spirit too we know only in connection with matter. We cannot untangle their relative contribution to 'experience' and to think of either by themselves is to make an unwarranted abstraction.[31] None the less they represent two 'very distinct phases of our total experience', 'perfectly separable in thought',[32] and far from equal or symmetrical. Illingworth urges that while spirit is of no use to matter, matter is of great use to spirit. Indeed, Matter is only there for spirit. That is its purpose.[33] This apparent dualism that verges on epiphenomenalism shows itself even more strongly in his consideration of the relationship between God and the universe. He argues at great length that God is manifest in all nature, especially in the

[24] *Personality Human and Divine*, 74.   [25] *Divine Immanence*, 50.
[26] *Personality Human and Divine*, 81–2.   [27] *Personality Human and Divine*, 84.
[28] *Personality Human and Divine*, 120–1.   [29] *Divine Immanence*, 2.
[30] *Divine Immanence*, 4.   [31] *Divine Immanence*, 5.   [32] *Divine Immanence*, 6.
[33] *Divine Immanence*, 9.

incarnation, but he is quite emphatic in rejecting any suggestion of pantheism that this might be thought to imply. 'Spirit which is merely immanent in matter, without also transcending it, cannot be spirit at all' he argues; 'it is only another aspect of matter, having neither self-identity nor freedom. Pantheism is thus really indistinguishable from materialism; it is merely materialism grown sentimental, but no more tenable for its change of name.'[34] He suggests instead that we model divine immanence on our immanence in the world. More specifically, just as humans have two degrees of immanence, in our body and in our works, so the best model for God is a Trinitarian one in which he has two degrees of immanence, in his Son (akin to our immanence in our body) and in his creation (akin to our immanence in our works.)[35]

11.1.3 Hastings Rashdall

Further development of the Seth/Illingworth argument for God's existence from the objective validity of ethics may be found a decade or so later in Hastings Rashdall's 1907 *The Theory of Good and Evil*. To take seriously the moral consciousness is to commit us *directly* to a number of presuppositions, Rashdall argues, such as, that selves are real, that they act, and that ethical conviction is not mere subjective feeling, but at a deeper level it makes further *indirect* commitments also. For example, we may say that there is real truth and falsity in ethical judgement, but this rules out any naturalism; for naturalism, whatever account it offers of our ethical convictions, never quite dismisses the scepticism that haunts it. And there are positive implications as well as negative ones. We may say there is absolute value, but where and in what manner does the ethical ideal exist? Problematic here is the fact that each person thinks differently about ethics. Difference of opinion with most questions is of little matter, for in most cases we can believe in a common object over which people disagree. But this is not possible in ethics, for the moral ideal is not a thing or property. 'A moral ideal can exist nowhere and nohow but in a mind,' argues Rashdall. But if the ideal is not to be found, wholly and completely, in any individual human mind, that leaves only God's. 'Our moral ideal can only claim objective validity in so far as it can rationally be regarded as the revelation of a moral ideal eternally existing in the mind of God'.[36] Rashdall's argument here represents an advance on Illingworth's, for he makes clear that his question is not where conscience comes from, or why it has the content it does, but wherefrom it derives its validity or binding force.

This was not Rashdall's only argument for the existence of God. In the 1902 Henry Sturt *Personal Idealism* volume we find him developing a more metaphysical case for the existence of a universal knower.[37] Things only exist as perceived, but what about all the things that no one has ever seen or even thought of?[38] If science is not to be just 'a mass of illusion', we must accept their reality too but, if it is absurd for matter to exist without mind, it certainly cannot be for transient minds such as ours that these parts of

---

[34] *Divine Immanence*, 69.   [35] *Divine Immanence*, 72–3.   [36] *Theory of Good and Evil*, II: 212.
[37] 'Personality: Human and Divine', 376.   [38] *Philosophy and Religion*, 16.

world are or were real, so we must posit another mind, God, to sustain the universe; 'we cannot explain the world without the supposition of one universal Mind in which and for which all so-called material things exist, and always have existed.'[39] The very fact that there are things which I do not know proves the existence of a universal knower. In this argument, with its distinctive echoes of both Berkeley and Green, we see a clear example of the subjective epistemological thinking that some members of the school were to concede had contaminated the older purer idealist stream.[40]

Rashdall strongly opposes the monist view that human selves are parts or aspects of the one divine mind. This fails to distinguish between the being of *things* and the being of *persons*. The essence of a person is whatever he is *for himself*, not whatever he may be *for another*. 'All the fallacies of our anti-individualist thinkers come from talking as though the essence of a person lay in what can be known about him, and not in his own knowledge, his own experience of himself.'[41] However alike experiences may be, they are forever distinct; my toothache is forever my toothache and can never become yours. Were two spirits to undergo exactly the same experience, they would still be two and not one.[42] 'To talk of one self-conscious being including or containing in himself or being identical with other selves is to use language which is (as it appears to me) wholly meaningless and self-contradictory, for the essence of being a self is to distinguish oneself from other selves.'[43] God's knowledge of other selves does not exhaust or constitute their being, as it does for material things. God knows the self as a being that is real in its own right, something more than just his knowledge of it. The same basic conditions which apply regarding selves' relations to each other, thinks Rashdall, hold of God's relation to them.

Of all the Personal Idealists, Rashdall is closest to the extreme pluralism of McTaggart,[44] and a forceful advocate of the 'imperviousness' of all souls, finite and infinite. Insofar as he has a use for the term, the 'Absolute' for Rashdall was the whole system which comprised both God and finite spirits.[45] But to critics, like Webb, to thus treat God as but one element of the universe as a whole, which must therefore limit and condition him, amounts in effect to the admission of a finite God.[46]

11.1.4 W.R. Sorley

Nowhere is the methodological shift that characterizes Personal Idealism more clearly displayed than in the 1914–15 Gifford lectures of Sorley (who in 1900 had succeeded Henry Sidgwick in the Knightbridge Professorship of Moral Philosophy at Cambridge)

---

[39] *Philosophy and Religion*, 19.
[40] Mackenzie, 'The New Realism and the Old Idealism', 312; Pringle-Pattison, *The Idea of God*, 190–9.
[41] 'Personality: Human and Divine', 383.
[42] 'Personality: Human and Divine', 384.
[43] 'Personality: Human and Divine', 388.
[44] The principal difference between these two is that Rashdall thinks God creates souls whereas for McTaggart souls are eternal.
[45] 'Personality: Human and Divine', 392–3.
[46] *God and Personality*, 135.

entitled *Moral Values and the Idea of God* (published 1918). Where Green moves from metaphysics to ethics, he explicitly reverses matters and hopes to move from ethics to metaphysics. In this vein he offers two arguments for the existence of God, neither original.

Sorley explicitly endorses Hasting Rashdall's argument that the moral standard itself constitutes a reason for belief in God, because its objective validity can be explained no other way than by holding it grounded in the mind of God itself; for

the validity of these values or laws, or of this ideal, however, does not depend upon their recognition: it is objective and eternal: and how could this eternal validity stand alone, not embodied in matter and neither seen nor realized by finite minds unless there were an Eternal Mind whose thought and will are therein expressed? God must therefore exist and his nature must be goodness.[47]

Regarding this as a species of cosmological argument, he commends the fact that it holds no hostages to factual reality—we do not have to show that the world is a certain way, since truths about how things ought to be hold regardless of how they are, or of whether such truths are recognized. As with Rashdall, Sorley's 'how-else-but-in-God?' step involves more rhetoric than argument.

If this argument from morality is like the cosmological argument, he endorses too the more familiar Kantian case from morality. According to this line of thinking, God is called in as, we might say, the cosmic guarantee of alignment between the moral and the natural—which Kant regards as two realms, but Sorley prefers to regard as two ways of looking at the same order.[48] But there is further advance beyond Kant, for just what it means for them to be in line, for the world to meet the ethical ideal, is something on which there can be different views. A first thought might be that this must be a world which instantiates those values, a world where everyone is happy or at least where the virtuous are happy. Since the world we experience is obviously not like this, the only way to meet this standard would be to posit a future life where all is well, treating this life as but a temporary local aberration of a wider cosmic harmony. This is Kant's view, but such a drastic discontinuity between reality in general and everything we actually experience is not plausible. Nor is it necessary, thinks Sorley, for deeper reflection on value suggests a different answer. The moral nature of agents is not a fixed quantity but something changing, and the moral ideal something to be realized first and foremost, not by changing *the world*, but transforming *ourselves*. The mere distribution of pleasure and alleviation of pain would not by itself perfect the universe were *we* to remain as we are, indeed the reverse, for paradoxically human growth itself seems to require a degree of opposition or resistance. A perfect world is not one where we get what we want or deserve, but one that allows us to want or deserve better than we currently do. A universe in line with the moral ideal is thus one that provides a medium for moral growth, for the realization of goodness, one that exhibits a teleological

---

[47] *Moral Values and the Idea of God*, 349.   [48] *Moral Values and the Idea of God*, 336.

structure towards that ideal. The progress cannot be lawlike, some unconscious and inevitable development towards the good, for there can be no true goodness that is not *freely* grasped, hence the only possible teleology towards the good must be a system of free agents set within a world that encourages and trains them in that direction, that is, a world of struggle. Such a two-sided scheme of free agents in a challenging environment rules out spiritual pluralism which accepts only the agents, and also monism which cannot countenance the necessary opposition between these two elements, but most significantly this view of the world requires us to regard it as an intelligently designed system, thereby proving the existence of a deity.

That God is infinite or unlimited by outside forces, Sorley admits; although he thinks this not incompatible with his creation of beings who, while owing their existence and power to him, can nonetheless act counter to his purposes. Insofar as he creates them that way and voluntarily withdraws from them, the result would be a kind of *self*-limitation.[49] However, to call such a God the 'Absolute' would be misleading, for that implies having nothing outside oneself with which one is related and, although there is nothing outside of God in the sense of being independent of his nature or his will, his creation gives rise to distinct finite beings who stand in real relations to him. Nor should we really apply the term to the whole of reality, for it implies perfection, and the whole contains many elements which are not yet ideal.[50] It is only working towards perfection.

11.1.5 C.C.J. Webb

Cook-Wilson voices the ordinary religious consciousness when he observes, 'We don't want merely inferred friends. Could we possibly be satisfied with an inferred God?'[51] And this intuition was shared by his more idealist pupil, Webb,[52] whose argument for the existence of God stresses that religious experience (like moral and aesthetic experience) must be taken seriously. He offers an analogy. Had we no appreciation at all of poetry, or no ear whatsoever for music, we could know nothing of Shakespeare as a poet, or Beethoven as a musician. We might know a few facts about them, but we would not know either the poet or the musician.[53] Similarly it is

only in and through a religious experience have we any knowledge of God; what are called 'arguments for the existence of God' will never prove to those who lack such an experience the existence of God, but only at most the need of assuming, in order to account for our experiences other than religious, a designing Mind, or a Necessary Being, or an Absolute Reality.[54]

---

[49] *Moral Values and the Idea of God*, 483–4.   [50] *Moral Values and the Idea of God*, 485–6.

[51] *Statement and Inference*, II:853.

[52] Maintaining an entirely Oxford based career, Webb entered Christ Church in 1884 and was appointed a Fellow of Magdalen College in 1889, where he taught until appointment in 1920 as the first Professor of the Philosophy of the Christian Religion, based at Oriel. Two sets of his Gifford lectures were published as *God and Personality* (1918) and *Divine Personality and Human Life* (1920).

[53] *God and Personality*, 151.

[54] *God and Personality*, 152.

What matters about religion is given in religious experience. He argues for an immediate apprehension of the personality of God, as well as of other selves, as from an idealist point of view he opposes both naturalism and panlogicism, seeking to preserve the person 'from dissolution either into movements of matter or into categories of thought'.[55]

We have seen how the debate over immanence and transcendence dominates religious philosophy during the period. As late as 1924 Webb still confesses himself torn: 'About the problem involved in these questions: Is God the Absolute? Is the Absolute God? My thoughts continually revolve, but I could not honestly say that I am satisfied with any suggestion that I can offer towards its solution.'[56] On the one hand the tendency to immanence, the identification of God and creation, runs headlong up against our actual religious experience, whose characteristic attitude of *worship* is nonsense if God is but some extension of ourselves. But neither can we be content with any God who, being only part of the whole of reality, is finite and, like anything finite, thereby transcended and transmuted in the Absolute. Webb has strong sympathy with the religious urge that would be satisfied with nothing less than the totality, 'no conception of God which takes him for less than the ultimate Reality will satisfy the demands of the religious consciousness...in Religion we seek to place ourselves effectively in touch with what nevertheless must, it would seem, already include us within itself.'[57] Consequently he complains against both Bradley and Bosanquet and against Rashdall who, in their different ways separate God and the Absolute (the former as appearance, the latter as part).

This dispute over the immanence or transcendence of God is, Webb thinks, one with the dispute over his personality.[58] Highlighting the facts that 'person' is a concept only lately to appear in intellectual history, and even later to find application to God, he nevertheless argues strongly for a 'personal God'. This restricts our metaphysics in more than one direction; extreme immanence and extreme transcendence alike he argues would destroy personal relations (such as prayer or worship) between human and divine, because on neither scheme is there scope for reciprocation from God to us.[59] Only theism can really grasp the personality of God. The claim of Christianity to be the most highly developed of the religions lies in the emphasis it gives to the personality of God, which adds to the intelligibility and efficacy of such notions as sin, forgiveness, justice, sacrifice.[60] But we cannot think of God as having personality in the same sense as do the people around us. For if one of the reasons for thinking him personal lies in our relations with him, it can hardly be denied that there is a very great difference between our intercourse with God and with men. However we understand God's transcendence, it must not be so taken as to be inconsistent with his immanence

---

[55] *Divine Personality and Human Life*, 193; see chs. 8 and 9.
[56] 'Outline of a Philosophy of Religion' 349.   [57] *God and Personality*, 137–8.
[58] *God and Personality*, 213.   [59] *God and Personality*, 68–75.
[60] *God and Personality*, ch.X.

in the human soul, so that the relationship between our personality and God's is not exclusive in the way that it is between two human personalities.[61] The key to bringing these two together is an 'instrumental' grasp of personality. The demand is for a 'God with whom we can stand in personal relations' rather than for a 'personal God.' Religion is not concerned with the inner mental life of God. So long as we can stand in personal relations with him, which are neither figurative nor illusory, his thoughts and ways may be quite other than ours.[62] So long as God passes what might be described as a theological version of a Turing Test—we communicate, he responds—we have all we need, and there is no further need to speculate about the precise nature of whatever lies on the other side.

11.1.6 A.S. Pringle-Pattison

Pringle-Pattison, in a sense the 'head' of the Personal Idealist thinkers, had probably the most complex philosophy of religion of them all. Like the others, he takes our intuitions of value as foundational; the lesson to learn from the history of modern philosophy is that the atheism or scepticism to which Hume's philosophy leads us can be met only by a Kantian assertion of the reality of 'moral personality' (and all that implies—God, freedom, and immortality.) In this affirmation we find the heart of all idealism.[63] In its own terms it stands without need of further support as a revelation of or intuition into the true spiritual nature of reality—'Spiritual truth is judged by the spiritual nature of man' insists Pringle-Pattison and 'its authority lies in its own content'[64]—but from outside it looks more like a species of irrationalism. For this reason he insists that it must be accompanied by a refutation of naturalism and shown to be the proper outcome of a rational account of nature in which, as we have seen, he thinks biology comes to the fore.[65]

The precise form which Pringle-Pattison gives to the Personal Idealist moral argument is interesting. For him our metaphysical, and especially our moral, criteria are themselves arguments for the existence of a reality which meets them. Hume famously argues that we may infer no more in any cause than necessary for its effect, from which it follows that were we simply finite we could never reach beyond our own finitude. But, in truth, we are not. Man is not merely finite, but rather 'a finite-infinite being, conscious of finitude only through the presence of an infinite nature within him'.[66] 'The presence of the ideal is the reality of God within us.'[67] We find this suggestion in Descartes' Third Meditation, in certain versions of the cosmological argument from contingency, but more broadly construed it is the argument *a contingentia mundi* which, in Pringle-Pattison's view, Bosanquet rightly describes as present in all idealism.[68]

---

[61] 'Outline', 353–4.   [62] *God and Personality*, 153–4.   [63] *Idea of God*, 46.
[64] Letter to A.J. Balfour, included in G.F. Barbour's Memoir in *The Balfour Lectures on Realism*, 110.
[65] *Idea of God*, 48.   [66] *Idea of God*, 247.   [67] *Idea of God*, 246.
[68] *Idea of God*, 251.

That Pringle-Pattison can endorse the argument he finds in Bosanquet may make us wonder at his conception of God. And it is noteworthy. In many ways it turns out to be much like Bosanquet's, not clearly separate from the world at all. For example, he criticizes the traditional cosmological argument. To think God might be found at the furthest end of a chain of phenomenal causes is to treat him as just one more phenomenal thing, when in truth, 'God is cause only in the sense of ground, that is to say, the Being whose nature is expressed in the system as a whole.'[69] 'As soon as we begin to treat God and man as two independent facts, we lose our hold upon the experienced fact, which is *the existence of the one in the other and through the other*.'[70] We can only create problems for ourselves if we try to think of God 'as a solitary unit apart from the universe in which he expresses himself'.[71] 'God, then, becomes an abstraction if separated from the universe of his manifestation, just as the finite subjects have no independent subsistence outside of the universal Life which mediates itself to them in a world of objects.'[72] Pringle-Pattison was even content to speak in this connection of the Absolute—'As soon as men began to reflect a little on what was meant by the term,' he says, 'it became evident that the ultimate object of philosophy always is, and must be, the Absolute.'[73] For him the term 'Absolute' means, like the term 'God', the universe as a whole.[74]

Not surprisingly such a perspective renders him lukewarm too on the personality of God. The whole is spiritual, and as such better thought of as personal rather than impersonal, but it is not a person as co-ordinate with us.

But by the existence of the personality of God we do not mean the existence of a self-consciousness so conceived. We mean that the universe is to be thought of, in the last resort, as an Experience and not as an abstract content—an experience not limited to the intermittent and fragmentary glimpses of this and the other finite consciousness, but resuming the whole life of the world in a fashion which is-necessarily incomprehensible save by the Absolute itself.[75]

A sense of how far Pringle-Pattison is from more 'orthodox' personalisms can be seen from his criticisms of the American idealist Howison.[76] In Howison's spiritual pluralism God is treated as one further soul in the universe, even if superior to all the others. But Pringle-Pattison objects that we cannot understand the infinite–finite relation in the same way as the finite–finite relation. If we insist on doing so, we reduce God to our level, and so end up with something more like the pluralistic atheism of McTaggart. It is true that self-conscious individuals can not be coerced but only invited into goodness, 'still the relation between the finite spirit and its inspiring source must be, in the end, incapable of statement in terms of the relation of one finite individual to another'.[77] God is not simply one more self among many, not even *primus inter pares*.

---

[69] *Idea of God*, 302.   [70] *Idea of God*, 254.   [71] *Idea of God*, 310.   [72] *Idea of God*, 314.
[73] 'New Theory of the Absolute', 131.   [74] See e.g. *Idea of God*, 259.
[75] *Idea of God*, 390.   [76] *Idea of God*, 319–21.   [77] *Idea of God*, 320.

Reviewing points such as those we have made above, it would be tempting to say that for Pringle-Pattison God just is the system as a whole, and certainly some critics of more orthodox persuasion felt he never really advanced beyond Hegelian pantheism.[78] But there is more to the matter than that, for he clearly and forcefully rejects the thought present in some Absolute Idealisms that the human goal or consummation lies in somehow joining or fusing with the divine whole.

Because I desire to be made more and more in the likeness of God, I do not therefore desire to *be* God. The development of a personality in knowledge and goodness does not take place through confluence with other personalities, nor is its goal and consummation to yield up its proper being and be 'blended with innumerable other selves' in the Absolute. In spite of Professor Bosanquet's fresh attempts at justification, and in spite of the ecstatic utterances of the mystics, I maintain that the idea of blending or absorption depends entirely on material analogies which can have no application in the case of selves.[79]

To meaningfully submit our wills to God's requires there to be two distinct wills,[80] a thought which precludes us from reading in a wholly Bradlean or Bosanquetian manner the claim that, 'we may conceive God as an experience in which the universe is felt and apprehended as an ultimately harmonious whole'.[81]

Like almost everyone who has ever considered the question, Pringle-Pattison argues for a mid-point between immanence and transcendence which, since a mid-point varies vastly according to where one sets the extremes, tells us little. But it is possible to cash out this formula in more detail. He distinguishes his doctrine of the immanence of God from any 'lower pantheism', which he regards as equivalent to atheism and undermining of value.[82] There is more to God than just his manifestations in nature, even in human nature. His transcendence, however, is a matter not of *ontology* but of *value*. We must think of a moral, rather than an ontological, separation of the deity. 'The infinite greatness and richness of the containing life, as compared with anything as yet appropriated by the finite creature.'[83] But even this transcendence is also limited. While the perfection of God outstrips that of his creatures, it is something which also in measure resides immanently in us. It is the same in kind with our value and outstrips only what we have appropriated *as yet*.[84] What is given in one hand is immediately clawed back with the other, and in the end it must be confessed Pringle-Pattison's exact view on God remains hard to pinpoint with precision.

Pringle-Pattison wrote twice on the subject of immortality. In *Life and Finite Individuality* part of his intention in insisting on the substantival nature of the self is to

---

[78] Inge, *Mysticism in Religion*, 155.   [79] *Idea of God*, 429.   [80] *Two Lectures on Theism*, 47.
[81] *Idea of God*, 314.
[82] *Idea of God*, 219, 221–2, 254; 'Immanence and Transcendence', 5. The distinction comes from Tennyson's poem, 'The Higher Pantheism', famously satirised by Swinburne in his poem 'The Higher Pantheism in a Nutshell'.
[83] *Idea of God*, 255.   [84] *Idea of God*, 255.

take a stand on its *reality*,[85] and he admits that such substantiality implies also the possibility of a genuine personal immortality—of the kind Bosanquet rejects. But on a closer look we see that what Pringle-Pattison is after here is really something rather more subtle than might first suggest itself. For, he insists, selves are not necessarily or intrinsically immortal.[86] We can demand and find proof of the permanence of our values in the universe,[87] but the permanence of finite beings cannot be guaranteed. There are two main points he is making here. In the first place, he holds that individuality is a question of *degree*, ranging up from the simplest to the most sophisticated entities.[88] There can be no simple dichotomy between types of entities that do and types of entities that do not survive. In the second place, he argues that individuality is something which each particular organism has to *achieve*. We are given an opportunity, but effort is required to make good of it and 'continuous self-maintenance' to conserve it.[89] Otherwise he warns 'mere sloth and self-indulgence may induce a condition of moral flabbiness in which a man becomes little more than a loosely associated group of appetites and habits.'[90] The genuine individual lives on, but we must fight to become—and remain—such individuals.

In a subsequent set of Gifford lectures, which appeared in 1922 under the title *The Idea of Immortality*, he revisited the subject. Continuing to hold that the truest view of the universe is that given by morality, he argues that God manifests himself in the world generally, but more so in spirits, even more so in value, and most of all in love. But if the locus of love, and more widely of value, is precisely the unique and individual spirit, we may surely conclude that we 'were not made to be broken up and cast aside and to be replaced by relays of others in a continual *succession*.'[91] Although we cannot say that selves are by nature immortal, neither can we rule out the possibility of universal restoration.[92] Pringle-Pattison has difficulties, however, with the temporal aspects of the question. Making a distinction between mere prolongation of existence and 'eternal life', he insists that the former has no value except as a way to lay hold of the later, but he also recognizes that we cannot discard duration altogether, least the 'eternal now' just shrinks to a mathematical point.[93]

11.2 Gifford and the Gifford Lectures

We have now considered the variety of ways in which the Personal Idealists responded to the religious philosophy of the first Absolute Idealists. But naturally there was

---

[85] In *Idea of God* he argues against the notion of selves as mere appearance not least on the simple Cartesian ground that 'There cannot be illusion or mere appearance, unless souls or finite selves really exist as such, to be the seats or victims of this illusion' (*Idea of God*, 277).

[86] 'Do Finite Individuals possess a Substantive or an Adjectival mode of Being?' in *Life and Finite Individuality* (ed. W.H. Wildon Carr), 110. This view he associates with the discredited doctrine of soul as independent substances, whose reintroduction by McTaggart he laments.

[87] *Life and Finite Individuality*, 112.   [88] *Life and Finite Individuality*, 107.

[89] *Life and Finite Individuality*, 111.   [90] *Life and Finite Individuality*, 125.

[91] *Idea of Immortality*, 191.   [92] *Idea of Immortality*, 203.   [93] *Idea of Immortality*, 205.

evolution on this side also, and so we must now turn to consider developments in philosophy of religion from this more orthodox wing. Before we do so, however, a brief interlude is in order. Already it will have been noticed how much of importance in metaphysics and philosophy of religion was first put forward in Gifford lectures, and the story must be told of this lectureship so vital to the flourishing of constructive philosophy in Britain.

A series of lectures on natural theology which, begun in 1888, continue unbroken to this day, the Gifford lectures have had a profound impact on the course of British Philosophy. They were set up in fulfilment of the bequest of a Scottish lawyer, Adam Gifford, who after his death in 1887 left the massive sum of £80,000 to the four Scottish Universities of Edinburgh, Glasgow, St Andrews, and Aberdeen, with the object to found 'a lectureship or popular chair for promoting, advancing, teaching, and diffusing the study of natural theology in the widest sense of that term'. Open to those of any denomination or no denomination at all, he insisted that 'the lectures are to treat their subject as strictly natural science, the greatest of all possible sciences, indeed, in one sense, the only science, that of Infinite Being, without reference to or reliance upon any supposed special or exceptional or so called miraculous revelation'. In their early days the lectures were dominated by the British Idealists, and (encouraging precisely that fusion of metaphysical and religious thought which is their mark) became the place where they had the time and leisure to fully expand their metaphysical and religious systems. A prestigious invitation, many took it as an opportunity to set down their own personal metaphysical systems, and thus the series facilitated what became a great flowering of speculative philosophy in Britain.

Gifford himself was an interesting person. Born in 1820, and educated at Edinburgh University, he was called to the Bar in 1849, rising ultimately to the Court of Session as Lord Gifford. For all his success, his heart was never entirely with his profession, his true interests lying with philosophy, to which as he grew older he devoted more and more of his time. His views were not dissimilar from many who were to take up his lectureships. Influenced by Emerson and Spinoza and arguing that there is more to reality than just matter, he urged that God is the substance of all forces and powers, of all beings, even of our very souls, their thoughts and actions. God is everything and we creatures but parts of the infinite.[94]

11.3 Absolutism

11.3.1 William Wallace and A.C. Bradley

Gifford's own philosophy was without influence, but there were other more noted Absolute Idealists who continued to develop the religious philosophy of the pioneers.

---

[94] For a history of the Gifford lectures see L. Witham, *The Measure of God*. For a full list of Gifford lectures up to 1986, a discussion of their significance, John Gifford's memoir of his brother and a selection from his addresses, see S.L. Jaki, *Lord Gifford and his Lectures*. Well known locally in his day, Gifford's views were given even wider circulation when they were discussed by J.H. Stirling in his own 1889 series of Gifford Lectures, *Philosophy and Theology*.

One was William Wallace. Although he is remembered now only as a Hegel scholar, Wallace was a key figure in the British Idealist movement more generally. This has been obscured because he eschewed publication of his own original philosophical thought, but it was a testament to the high regard in which he was held that he was appointed Gifford Lecturer in the University of Glasgow for 1893 and 1894 lecturing respectively on 'Natural Theology' and 'The Relation of Religion to Morality'. He contemplated publishing these lectures and, it seems, began revising them with that end in mind, but his early death prevented him from completing the work. Edward Caird collected together the available bits and pieces for posthumous publication in 1898, and the resulting material it must be admitted is patchy and unsystematic; but the reason for this lies not solely in its unfinished state, for Wallace's own style is discursive, subtle, and only gently persuasive; he but rarely advances bold positions or direct arguments.

The key features of Wallace's philosophy of religion emerge clearly enough, nonetheless. He rejects the older natural theology of Paley, which focused on specific manifestations of design in nature, in favour of a broader philosophical approach which takes 'the surveillance of the whole over the members, or rather the spirit of the whole, awaking in each of these members, and making them aware of their mutual dependence.'[95] He thus endorses the Kantian idea that God is not really an object of knowledge or science, for neither first cause nor final end may properly be understood as just one further term in a sequence.[96] God is not something behind or beyond other objects. Instead Wallace presses for a strong form of immanence. The lesson of modern philosophy is that 'of the world itself as immanent in God and God immanent in the world.'[97] Any individual thing, it is true, is less than God—only the whole is wholly divine—but all in their various degree express and involve Him.[98] 'If it be true even of the human artist, that into his work he puts something of himself... it is more emphatically true of the Divine Artist or Artifice.... The world is not merely his work: it is, as Plato dared to say long ago in bold metaphor, his own only offspring, his only-begotten, the gradually realizing and realized image of himself.'[99]

For Wallace, the heart and significance of Christianity is that it is illustrative of this immanence—all other elements of the faith recede into the background—and crucial to this message is an appreciation that Christ's nature was not unique or contrary to anything in our own being. What he shows us is 'the bringing into one of God and man: the discovery that the supernatural is in the natural, the spiritual in the physical: the eternal life as the truth and basis of this... the immanence of the divine, not as a new and imported element in human life, a special bit of man peculiarly holy, but as the truth and life in life.'[100]

---

[95] *Lectures and Essays*, 19.   [96] *Lectures and Essays*, 40.   [97] *Lectures and Essays*, 140.
[98] *Lectures and Essays*, 41.   [99] *Lectures and Essays*, 142.
[100] *Lectures and Essays*, 49–50; also *Lectures and Essays*, 91.

God is revealed to reside in man. But lest this be misunderstood, we must remember two things about man. First, we must recall that man is a still-evolving creature, so that any lesson we may wish to draw from his nature can be provisional only. 'We do not know what we are, because we know not yet what we shall be,' warns Wallace.[101] Second, it must not be forgotten that man is an essentially social creature, that he is always more than we find in any one individual. Wallace particularly stresses the social nature of reason, but there is an important point here also for understanding the nature of God. For even if God is in man, not every feature of human life can be applied to God. We must remember that, 'personality can only belong to a member of a world, to one who is not everything, but stands in contact and relation with others outside himself. Such a position cannot belong to the Absolute or Infinite. We cannot indeed say that the absolute is impersonal, but we may at least say he is something more than a person.'[102]

Another figure to develop the religious side of Absolute Idealism was A.C. Bradley, the younger brother of F.H. Bradley. Graduating from Balliol in 1876 he was appointed a Lecturer of the college, first in English, and then in Philosophy. In 1882 he took up the Chair of Literature and History at University College Liverpool, and in 1890 the Chair of English Literature and Language at Glasgow University. In 1900 he retired, but in 1901 he was elected to the Professorship of Poetry at Oxford, a post he held until 1906. He is today best known from his literary work—his *Shakespearean Tragedy* (1904) and his *Oxford Lectures on Poetry* (1909)—but in 1907 and 1908 he delivered two courses of Gifford lectures at Glasgow University. He argued there that the essence of religion lies neither in speculation nor feeling, but in worship. It starts from the subjective or human end, our aspirations and ideals themselves defining its object, the infinite, as the completion of all that we value highest and serve most devotedly. Using this ideal standard he finds defective any positions, such as those of Mill and Seeley,[103] which refuse to recognize the infinite, eternal, and transcendent, directing themselves solely towards nature or humanity. But the ideal has also a positive side, and the position which Bradley himself defends is both idealist and immanentist, one in which man is viewed as 'deity inchoate' striving for 'absolute' community or union with God. The sketch of Absolute Idealist metaphysics offered is too swift and inadequately argued to be anything other than an example of the genre rather than any advance on it, indeed the position claimed differs hardly at all from that of his brother or of Bernard Bosanquet, whose obituary he wrote for the *Proceedings of the British Academy*. He had been in the process of revising and rewriting his Gifford lectures for publication during his final years but ill-health prevented him from ever completing the task. The first set of lectures was published posthumously in 1940 as *Ideals of*

---

[101]   *Lectures and Essays*, 142.
[102]   *Lectures and Essays*, 278.
[103]   Mill, *Three Essays on Religion*; Seeley, *Natural Religion*. John Robert Seeley was an academic and essayist more famous as the author of *Ecce Homo* (1866), a notorious life of Christ that focused only on his humanity.

Religion, but appearing as it did some thirty years after its initial presentation, the work was very much out of its time, and had no influence.

11.3.2 Bernard Bosanquet

Although belonging to the same metaphysical tradition as Wallace and Bradley, compared to theirs, Bernard Bosanquet's philosophy of religion was an altogether more complicated affair.[104] The son of a minister and originally destined for the Church, Bosanquet left behind orthodox Christianity on coming up to Jowett's Balliol but, recalled his wife, he remained 'fundamentally religious by nature as well as by education, and never lost his hold upon the ultimate realities of faith.'[105] This is important, for there is always a suspicion (sometimes justified) that those who would reinterpret religion seek really to downplay or downgrade it. Nothing could be further from the truth in this case. However he may have understood it, the absolute centrality of religious orientation was never in doubt for Bosanquet. 'A man's real religion,' he urged, 'is that set of objects, habits, and convictions, whatever it may prove to be, which he would die for rather than abandon, or at least would feel himself excommunicated from humanity if he did abandon.'[106] Or to put it more concisely, it 'is the only thing that makes life worth living at all'.[107]

11.3.2.1 The religious consciousness Bosanquet seeks to analyse what he calls 'the religious consciousness',[108] a term whose import he never precisely fixed, but which invites comparison both with his notion of 'the aesthetic consciousness' and with Caird's notion of 'moral life'.[109] It is used with something of the same historical descriptive force, but it is also normative, setting out an ideal of what spirituality *ought* to be, but from which actual practice may diverge.

Even if, as we shall see below, they do not differ in *content*,[110] Bosanquet is in no doubt that the philosophical and the religious consciousness are quite different *modes of apprehension*. Unlike reason, 'Faith in the ordinary sense is a kind of feeling,' he says. It is 'immediate'.[111] Another crucial factor about religious faith is that it is *social*. Belief is a communal activity. Ethnographic and historical research confirms the universality of this point,[112] but in the modern Christian consciousness it is indissolubly linked to the

---

[104]   For further discussion see Sweet, 'Bernard Bosanquet and the Nature of Religious Belief'; Sprigge, 'Bosanquet and Religion'.

[105]   Helen Bosanquet, *Bernard Bosanquet, A Short Account of his Life*, 25, cf. 8, 24. (See also *Bernard Bosanquet and his Friends*, 238–9).

[106]   'Philosophy of Religion', 456.

[107]   *What Religion Is*, vii.

[108]   *Value and Destiny of the Individual*, ch.VIII.

[109]   See above Chapters 6.3.1 and 9.2.1.

[110]   'The substantive problem of the philosophy of religion being inseparable from the general theory of reality' ('Philosophy of Religion', 454).

[111]   'Philosophy of Religion', 456.

[112]   'from the beginning religion displays itself as a social phenomenon, depending on a sense of union or communion between a group of human beings and their god' ('Philosophy of Religion', 455).

contribution of St Paul, for whom faith in the risen Christ by which alone we may be saved amounts to the spiritual oneness of all believers in and with Christ, the participation of all Christians in the living body of the Lord, outlined in his first letter to the Corinthians which, Bosanquet reminds us, itself echoes Plato.[113] And how could it be otherwise? There might seem to exist individualistic religions,[114] but they must be pronounced degenerate, for spirits in unity with God must be in unity with one another, hence religion involves the unity of men.[115] Indeed what we are saved from in religion is precisely our own isolation.[116] 'Wherever a man is so carried beyond himself whether for any other being, or for a cause or for a nation, that his personal fate seems to him as nothing in comparison of the happiness or triumph of the other, there you have the universal basis and structure of religion.'[117]

Although natural and universal, the religious consciousness for Bosanquet is not something fixed and timeless, some eternal truth never to be tampered with. It is rather dynamic and constantly changing. In his 1891 essay, 'How to read the New Testament', opposing the orthodox view that Christianity emerged fully fledged out of the mouth of Jesus, he presents it as having had a four-stage evolution.[118] In 1894 Caird extended this thesis to cover all religions, an extension with which Bosanquet agreed, publishing in 1895 what was in effect a paraphrase of that view, including an endorsement of Christianity as the 'Absolute Religion'.[119]

11.3.2.2 Critique of traditional religion All that has been said so far concerns the *form* of the religious consciousness, but what of its *content*? What is it that we do or should believe? Here the normative and revisionary side of Bosanquet's thought comes to a head, as he advocates a thoroughly non-supernatural and immanentist faith. He rejects all of the traditional mythologies and metaphysical pictures of Christianity, replacing them with something more subtle. Religion tells us that there is *more* to life than we in our more naturalistic or egoistic minds might think; its life is fuller, richer, and more significant. But it does not do so by positing some *extra* world; the difference is one of the *same* world transformed. In an important essay, already considered, 'On the True Conception of Another World', he connects this understanding of the *religious* vision with the *philosophical* vision of thinkers like Plato, Kant, and Hegel whose aim was only ever to draw a distinction *within* the world we know, not *between* the world we know and some other world.[120]

---

[113] 'How to read the New Testament', 151–2; I Corinthians 12; Plato, *Republic*, V:462c–e.

[114] One might think here of eastern meditation, or Newman's restricted spirituality of myself and my Creator alone.

[115] *What Religion Is*, 29.

[116] *What Religion Is*, 6.

[117] *What Religion Is*, 5.

[118] 'How to read the New Testament', 141–57.

[119] 'The Evolution of Religion'; see also 'Philosophy of Religion', 457.

[120] 'On the True Conception of Another World', xviii, xxx–xxxiv. See above pp.47, 81.

Religion teaches the union of the finite and infinite.[121] But what is the infinite? To most minds the infinite stands for something unreal, distant, and irrelevant, but Hegel offers us an alternative understanding that would allow us to fix it as what is most real and precious in life.[122] The infinite is that without limit, and with 'common infinity'—Hegel's *false* infinite—this is taken as enumeration without end. His rival idea of the infinite is totally opposed to this. 'Its root-idea is self-completeness or satisfaction. That which is "infinite" is without boundary, because it does not refer beyond itself for justification.'[123] 'The finite is that which presents itself as incomplete; the infinite that which presents itself as complete.' If false infinity is pictured by a line, true infinity is represented by a circle.[124] And crucially this true infinity, far from being remote, is 'present, concrete, and real'.[125]

Metaphysically, Bosanquet's rejection of other-worldly theology amounts to a rejection of any sort of belief in the existence of a personal god dwelling in some separate realm[126] in favour of the conception of an 'immanent divinity'.[127] 'We are spirits, and our life is one with that of the Spirit which is the whole and the good,' he urges.[128] Most believers would find it hard to imagine a more radical change than abandoning belief in an external personal God, but interestingly Bosanquet regards the alteration as little more than verbal.[129] What matters in both beliefs is the same, what differs the dressing only. Similarly, in his discussion of Huxley's agnosticism, he complains that the domain of interest the agnostic picks out is not worth fixing on as a special issue, for even if it is unknown, it is not what matters. And what matters is known.[130]

Such insouciance is only possible, of course, because he treats lightly things others might want to hold essential. For instance, one loss that we might complain of would be prayer; how can we pray if there is no personal God to address ourselves to? Bosanquet replies that prayer consists in openness to the good.[131] Its value, like that of worship (another casualty) is *instrumental* only.[132] Again, one might think of immortality. What prospect can there be for survival beyond the here and now if the here and now are all there is? Bosanquet's vision in this regard is not entirely without hope, but any promise held out is both timeless and impersonal. He holds that were I to realize the Absolute, my nature and being would become so transformed that I would no longer be what I experience as myself, so, although I do truly belong in the timeless Absolute and in that sense have eternal life,[133] this is not as the finite individual I know myself to be. With regard to the kind of life we currently enjoy, no one can

---

[121] *What Religion Is*, 62.   [122] 'On the True Conception of Another World', xxiv.
[123] 'On the True Conception of Another World', xxvi.
[124] 'On the True Conception of Another World', xxvii.
[125] 'On the True Conception of Another World', xxviii.
[126] The Civilization of Christendom', 81.   [127] The Civilization of Christendom', 84.
[128] *What Religion Is*, 25.   [129] 'Old Problems under New Names', 108–15.
[130] 'Are We Agnostics?'.   [131] "Old Problems under New Names', 122–4.
[132] *What Religion Is*, ch.VII.
[133] Bosanquet refers approvingly to 'the eternity of all spirits in God' (102).

conclusively say whether or not there awaits any further consciousness for each of us—we may or we may not get 'another slice of the pie'—but even if our span may be extended, since the eternity of the Absolute must take us beyond our finite conscious selves, we are not in any ultimate or final sense a permanent feature of the universe.[134] Nor argues Bosanquet, in a thought that harks back to Caird's 'corporate immortality', is this the kind of continuance that matters. We seek the preservation and growth of goodness, but 'to identify the conservation of values with the permanence or survival of given personalities,' says Bosanquet, 'is to my mind an extraordinary assumption.'[135]

Traditional religion thinks of God as revealing himself through miracles or through sacred scripture. But Bosanquet rejects miracles and takes a wholly naturalistic herme- neutical approach to the New Testament.[136] This does not mean, however, that he rejects revelation, for the shift from an external to an immanent God calls for a fundamental shift in the idea of revelation too. God reveals himself in the world. More especially, since God is spirit and, as such, exists through the medium of finite minds, revelation consists in the realization of God in man's intelligent nature.[137] Instead of looking for miraculous revelation we should simply look at human devel- opment; *education* is for Bosanquet a greater miracle than the *resurrection*.[138] Such a conception of revelation is especially geared to Christianity with its stress on the immanence of Christ in his Church and in its members.

Bosanquet's immanentist anti-supernaturalism comes out most strongly as we enter the field of religious ethics. He rejects future distributive justice, since that makes us complacent and narrows our sense of duty.[139] In addition future immortality is unlikely, and a Kantian understanding of ethics makes such prudentialism self-defeat- ing.[140] He rejects too Divine Command Theory; God's commands and the Bible reflect rather than create morality.[141] This is not to deny that we must obey the will of God, but simply to point out that the will of God is revealed in our own will.[142] Specifically it is to be found in the will of our higher or social self, he argues, explicitly endorsing the doctrine set out in Bradley's theory of My Station and its Duties;[143] we do the will of God in doing our civic duty. Religion teaches precisely the unity

---

[134] Bosanquet's position is laid out in more detail in Lectures IX and X of his *The Value and Destiny of the Individual*. Although he sometimes speaks as though unification with the Absolute were something towards which we are moving in time, his considered position is that this is how things timelessly are; our ontological rather than our temporal destiny.

[135] *Principle of Individuality and Value*, 21 note.

[136] 'Old Problems under New Names', 116; 'How to read the New Testament'.

[137] The Evolution of Religion', 443; 'On the True Conception of Another World', xxxi, xxxii; 'The Civilization of Christendom', 83.

[138] 'Are We Agnostics?', 143.

[139] 'The Kingdom of God on Earth', 108–9.

[140] 'The Kingdom of God on Earth', 109–11.

[141] 'The Kingdom of God on Earth', 113.

[142] 'The Kingdom of God on Earth', 116.

[143] We find the same faith at the very end of his life. In clear echo of Bradley's *Ethical Studies* (79) he says 'You cannot be a whole unless you join a whole' (*What Religion Is*, 12).

between God and man—try to break it up into its respective parts and you destroy it.[144] 'You will not be helped by trying to divide up the unity and tell how much comes from "you" and how much from "God."'[145] Hence the coming of the kingdom of God consists, not in a future distant heaven, but in moral and civic regeneration here and now. Restored from misinterpretation, the doctrine of Jesus can command our allegiance, but not unquestioningly so. Bosanquet worries about Jesus' warnings against worldliness—we must not neglect this world, he counters.[146]

As we have already seen, Bosanquet was not the only Idealist to reinterpret orthodox belief, but where others did this largely in a spirit of sympathy with traditional religious institutions, more than any of the other Idealists, Bosanquet disapproves strongly of the Church itself which is guardian of all these old 'fairy tales'. Like Bradley,[147] whose father was also a clergyman in the Church of England, he seems to have developed a distaste for the traditional forms. He suggests that Jesus himself saw that a spiritual religion should have no truck with priestly classes or exclusive membership lists,[148] and he rejects special priestly authority about revelation.[149] Where the revelation is in and through humanity at large rather than some private book, no scholarly cabal can claim to be the sole authority. Generally he allows that the church may contribute to the Kingdom of God, but thinks family and state more important.[150] Quite how little importance he attaches to established religion can be seen in, 'The Future of Religious Observance', in which he speculates on the future of organized religious ritual. He values the social function of church membership, and the time set aside for more worthy thoughts, feelings, and pursuits; but such things can be provided in other ways.[151] He wonders if it even means anything in the modern world to call oneself a 'Christian'.[152] He is, to be sure, a great supporter of Christendom, but what he values most in it is its civilization, and that he thinks has ancient (Greek and Roman) origins.[153]

11.3.2.3 The metaphysical grounds of religion In denying that there is another higher world, we may fear that Bosanquet has 'levelled down' rather than 'levelled up'. There are two parts to this concern over his stance: one asking, isn't this just naturalism? the other challenging, isn't this just ethics? To take the first objection, it is certainly the case that Bosanquet's spiritual vision seems more naturalistic than that of the other Idealists. But simply to leave matters there would be misleading. For as we saw in the previous chapter, Bosanquet is an Absolute Idealist, and religious consciousness in its highest levels he regards as having insight into that Absolute which, if thoroughly immanent in

---

[144] *What Religion Is*, 21.   [145] *What Religion Is*, 20.
[146] 'How to read the New Testament', 146.   [147] See above ch.5 note 207.
[148] 'How to read the New Testament', 145.   [149] 'The Kingdom of God on Earth', 114.
[150] 'The Kingdom of God on Earth', 123.   [151] 'The Future of Religious Observance', 3–5.
[152] 'Are We Agnostics?', 127.
[153] See 'Some thoughts on the Transition from Paganism to Christianity'; 'The Civilization of Christendom'.

the natural and human world, is certainly not reducible to it, any more than is an oak to an acorn. As the highest reality we can conceive and the greatest possible source of our satisfaction, Bosanquet's Absolute plays much the same role as God.

To be sure, the Absolute is not the same as God traditionally conceived. 'Father, Son, Holy Spirit, Lord Omnipotent, Creator, Providence—none of these terms can apply to a Universe or an Absolute which has nothing outside it,' Bosanquet admits.[154] Paradoxically, its very perfection disqualifies it, for 'The whole considered as perfection in which the antagonism of good and evil is unnoted, is not what religion means by God.'[155] For Bosanquet, the God of religion is an appearance of reality rather than the whole of reality itself.[156]

In the end for Bosanquet the term 'God' gets divided; in part it refers to the traditional conception which, for all its value, is ultimately dismissed as 'appearance', in part it becomes identified with 'The Good', which is regarded almost in the manner of Plato, and in part it becomes the Absolute, the totality of all things.

11.3.2.4 Morality and the problem of evil To take the second objection, insofar as the Spirit of God is the Spirit of the Good, Bosanquet can appear to be replacing transcendent private spirituality with an imminent social morality. He speaks as though civic morality might take the place of religion. We saw the very same charge raised against Bradley's philosophy of religion in Chapter 5, and Bosanquet's answer to this objection is essentially and consciously the same as that which Bradley gave. Morality *aims* at goodness, he says, religion is committed to its *reality*.[157] It recognizes goodness as the one real thing that there is.[158] In this way ethics is founded on religion, rather than *vice versa*.

The crucial test for such a position lies, of course, in its response to the problem of evil. How can anyone possibly remain committed to the ultimate reality and triumph of Goodness, when there is manifestly so much evil all around? Green, the Cairds and Bradley might all be judged too swift and superficial here, encouraging the Personal Idealists in their alternate response, but the same can hardly be said of Bosanquet, for this is a topic which exercises him greatly.

Much of Bosanquet's second set of Gifford lectures, *The Value and Destiny of the Individual*, is devoted to the problem of evil. Overall he endorses a 'greater good' answer; the pain we endure may well be the occasion of the emergence of some greater good and on the grand scheme of things 'worth it'. He insists that the universe is a 'vale of soul-making'.[159] We must live in the 'world of claims and counterclaims' but out of such conflict, progress is achieved; just as, in the metaphysical sphere, contradiction is the engine of growth towards harmony. Though they must still be fought against, pain

---

[154] *Value and Destiny of the Individual*, 249.   [155] *Value and Destiny of the Individual*, 251.
[156] *Value and Destiny of the Individual*, 255.   [157] 'The Kingdom of God on Earth', 124ff.
[158] 'Are we Agnostics?', 149. See also Chapter 13.1.3 below.
[159] The phrase comes from Keats, in a letter to his brother and sister, 21 April 1819.

and badness are not some sort of mistake in the cosmos—things that ideally would be cut away—but rather necessary preconditions of all that is good.[160]

It is easy to think we have the measure of this answer, but Bosanquet's understanding of it is subtle, and much of what he says is designed to challenge our too easy assumption as to its meaning. One crucial point to stress is that Bosanquet (like Bradley) does not think that time is real; the perfection of the Absolute is therefore not something future. This sharply contrasts his view with that of two other key Absolute theorists, Caird and Green. Another jolt to understanding comes from his resistance to any assumption of 'individual' justice; we should not expect in the overall scheme each to reap our own rewards.[161] Overall, suffering is vindicated, but the vindication need not feed down into individual cases.[162] A further difficulty is this. In supposing that everything in the end is for the best all too often we assume we know here and now which things are good and which bad, which things compensate and which call for compensation, but in an interconnected universe Bosanquet challenges, can we ever really know this? If we try to think through the implications for cosmic value of any element, we soon become unstuck, for each case is individual.[163] Moreover, Bosanquet argues, not only are we unaware of how much or how little each thing or event contributes to the value of reality as a whole, we do not really even know *what the correct scale is*. Part of his point here is to develop Green's ideas about the evolution of values; is it not absurd to use our current values to judge the Absolute? We know what things we desire now, but will such valuations hold good at the end? In particular, Bosanquet objects to reducing the question of the overall 'value' of the universe to a hedonic one about the balance of pleasure over pain. If pain facilitates the emergence of things that rank highly on other values scales (for example, truth, nobility, or beauty) why assume that the 'best' universe will have less pain than pleasure.[164] The 'perfection' of the universe is a standard even above the notions of 'moral good and evil', he suggests.[165]

In the end thinks Bosanquet all is perfect and evil has no ultimate reality. It is commonly objected that no moral conception which denied the reality of evil could ever be accepted, for if it is to be vanquished we must take that which we oppose as something real. But, Bosanquet responds, it is impossible that anything absolutely real

[160] 'The Affinity of Philosophy and Casework', 179–80.

[161] Like 'system', 'organisation', or 'individuality', 'justice' is a term whose proper application is to wholes and not parts. As we shall see, Jones takes exception to this (see below pp.429–30). For Bosanquet's general treatment of justice see below pp.500–1.

[162] In this connection it should be noted that one of the few doctrines in Christianity which meets with Bosanquet's approval is that of vicarious atonement (*Value and Destiny of the Individual*, 147). It may be wondered if this can be squared with his squeamishness elsewhere about punishing someone for a very old offence (*Life and Finite Individuality*, 100) but Bosanquet's point (presumably) is that even if in the last analysis of metaphysics no solid distinction can be drawn between who benefits and who pays, where pragmatic factors force us to adopt a system of justice based on makeshift judgements of personal identity it is simply unfair to admit some partial identities whilst rejecting others no more partial than they.

[163] *What Religion Is*, 60–2.

[164] *Value and Destiny of the Individual*, 182.

[165] *Value and Destiny of the Individual*, 217–18; see also *Principle of Individuality and Value*, 244–6.

could ever be extinguished,[166] and so we must not confuse the undeniable, 'evil is a fact', with the mistaken, 'evil is absolutely real'.[167] The truth of the matter is, 'not that evil *is* good, but that it is made out of the same stuff as good; the stuff of life, its passions and values. It is evil when it is evil, that is, when it is antagonistic to good, and impairs our values or will to them. But the same stuff is not evil in its positive nature.'[168]

But if at the highest level evil is absorbed into perfection, at a lower level it is still to be resisted. Why, we might ask? Why must there be soul-making? Why is the universe not such that everything appears to be as good as it ultimately is? Bosanquet responds that apparent evil is inevitable, an ineliminable consequence of the finite/infinite appearance/reality matrix. Were everything already perfect, this would already be for us the Absolute. There is no chance of a finite, but wholly suffering-free, universe. Indeed, rather than exempt us from it, religion guarantees suffering. Religion is a force for good. But in that case it cannot intrude into our lives in any way that would serve to weaken our moral fibre. It follows that the religious life is essentially one of conflict, struggle, questioning, and doubt—and hence too of suffering—something we must fight for; not some kind of safety net which we may passively receive.[169]

11.3.2.5 The rationality of religious belief Before leaving Bosanquet, note should be taken of the 'rationality' of religious belief. In what sense for him is faith 'reasonable'? His system leaves much room for rationality in religion; specific dogma may be challenged as irrational superstition, while the core commitment is in some sense shared out between social ethics and metaphysics, two assuredly rational pursuits. But notwithstanding these points one of the most interesting features of Bosanquet's view of religion is his lack of interest in rationality. As noted at the outset, we find in his writings a considerable emphasis on accepting religious experience as it stands and not probing it with reason.[170] 'Religion, being a very full experience, is a subject matter highly essential to philosophy, but philosophy, as the theoretical interpretation, is not necessary to religion, nor any component of it. The religious consciousness stands on its own foundation, and needs no support from philosophical theory.'[171] Religion, he urges, offers an *experience* of God, not a *proof* of him.[172] To attempt an analogy: it is as though someone were to say to us, I can see you are crying but how do you know you are sad? Crying is an expression of sadness, an experience of sadness. It is not, to be sure, sadness itself; sadness is more than crying. It is perhaps, in a way, the cause of our crying. But it is simply wrong-headed to try to think of crying as more-or-less-good-evidence for our sadness.

---

[166] *Some Suggestions in Ethics*, 91.   [167] *Some Suggestions in Ethics*, 96.
[168] *Some Suggestions in Ethics*, 113.
[169] *Principle of Individuality and Value*, 277; *What Religion Is*, 53–4.
[170] See *What Religion Is*, 12, 19, 63.   [171] *Value and Destiny of the Individual*, 232.
[172] *Value and Destiny of the Individual*, 256.

Linked with this is an emphasis on deciding for oneself in sincerity and pureness of heart on religious matters.[173] In a manner reminiscent of Kierkergaard's claim that it matters more how we believe than what we believe, Bosanquet suggests, 'What a man's religion brings him, and what he cannot help receiving when he places himself humbly and sincerely in the attitude of religious faith, I should venture to suggest, let him hold to without scruple. It will be the nearest thing to truth that he can make his own.'[174] For Bosanquet, religion just is whatever we most care for, so there can be no consciousness without religion.[175]

11.3.3 Henry Jones

One reason why it is instructive to conclude this account of Absolute Idealist religion with a consideration of Henry Jones, is that he demonstrates a species of motivation unlike any yet considered. Jones' religious philosophy did not emerge as some kind of response to the 'Victorian crisis of faith'. He never had such doubts. Rather the conventional faith of his early years was, without hiatus, transformed into idealist religion. Born in great poverty in a small village in North Wales, in 1852, Jones was brought up in a small two-room cottage adjacent to the Calvinistic Methodist Chapel, of which his family were deeply committed members, and whose life and creed dominated their world. It was an upbringing too of deep biblical knowledge, which Jones in his turn acquired, and can be clearly seen in all his subsequent writing. By supreme personal effort he managed to acquire enough learning to win a scholarship to Bangor teacher training college and became a schoolmaster, but his deeper ambition was always to become a minister in the Church, and it was with this goal that in 1875 he returned to study in order to gain a scholarship to Glasgow University. Once in Glasgow, however, Jones came under a new influence; that of Edward Caird. And the effect was life-changing. Looking back on it, he chose to speak in terms the full significance of which requires us to remember their specific use in communities such as that which he came from, saying, 'I was born in Llangernyw in 1852, and born again in 1876 in Edward Caird's class-room.'[176] In more detail he explained:

Old things passed away, never to return. There was never any direct negative criticism of the traditional beliefs which we had, like others, accepted without examination or criticism. We were led, rather, to assume a new attitude of mind; and articles of our creed simply became obsolete. When I entered the moral philosophy class, the story of Jonah gave me no difficulty: and had Jonah been credited with swallowing the whale, I should have had no difficulty. . . . Before the end of the session, miracles had lost their interest for me, and the legal and vindictive creed in which I had been nurtured had passed away like a cloud. I wanted to shorten the creed

---

[173] *What Religion Is,* 32.   [174] *What Religion Is,* 29–30.
[175] *Value and Destiny of the Individual,* 236.
[176] Hetherington, *The Life and Letters of Sir Henry Jones,* 20n.

so that it should consist of one article only: 'I believe in a God who is omnipotent love, and I dedicate myself to his service.'[177]

The fervour which Jones formerly felt for Calvinism was redirected towards the idealism that had freed him from it, which he proceeded to propound at every opportunity with the same vigour and enthusiasm,[178] the passion now deployed on behalf of a more liberal, social, and rational species of faith. Though never a member of that denomination, he lectured regularly at Oxford's Unitarian Manchester College, and published in its *Hibbert Journal*.[179]

Moving from the biographical to the philosophical, it is most illuminating to view Jones as trying to bring together the two traditions of Absolute and Personal Idealism, as attempting to find a path between those for whom all limited phenomena point beyond themselves to their completion in an all-encompassing ideal whole, and those who take as a non-negotiable axiom the actual experience of the finite self. The way Jones repeatedly presents this division—and, as always with Jones, the brush is a broad one—is as a clash between the two notions of 'divine immanence' and 'divine transcendence'. Rejecting Deism, we must recognize a continuity between the finite and the infinite; we must recognize that, 'All is one scheme, and God is the meaning of it.'[180] But is this to be done by raising up the finite to the level of the infinite, or by bringing down the infinite to the level of the finite? Both are problematic. An excess of divine immanence heads towards a pantheistic equation between God and nature that leaves no room for the exercise of genuine morality but, on the other hand, an excess of divine transcendence, in clearing space for a moral arena external to God, threatens to do away with the very perfection and omnipotence of that God.[181]

Jones' answer is that we need *both* immanence and transcendence—the religious consciousness 'can yield up neither of the two conceptions, except with its own life'[182]—for he insists they are not, as they first seem to be, incompatible with each other; rather each implies and therefore requires the other, as but different phases or aspects of the same truth.[183] Put as baldly as this, such an answer is, of course, too cryptic to make much sense, and one way to put a bit more flesh on the thought is to try to unpack some of his agreements and disagreements with both parties.

11.3.3.1 Rationality and religion We can begin with what he takes to be a common fault. In Jones' eyes reconciliation between Absolute and Personal Idealists may be

---

[177] *Old Memories*, 134.

[178] 'Idealism was for Jones an intensely religious philosophy which he *preached* in university lecture theatres and public halls around the world' (Boucher, 'Practical Hegelianism: Henry Jones' Lecture Tour of Australia', 424).

[179] He was retained as a College lecturer for many years, giving various series including, 'The Philosophy of Martineau in Relation to the Idealism of the Present Day', 1905; 'The Working Faith of the Social Reformer', 1905; 'The Religion of Idealism', 1906; 'Divine Transcendence', 1907. See 'Divine Transcendence' (3–4) for his estimate of the importance of the College.

[180] 'Divine Immanence', 748.   [181] 'Divine Immanence', 750.
[182] 'Divine Immanence', 751.   [183] 'Divine Immanence', 766.

effected by a stricter adherence to rational principles, from which he senses a falling off
in both camps. This alleged failing is most obvious in the case of the Personal Idealists
who combine a distrust of what they see as the extravagant claims of reason with a faith
in the immediate and un-analysable deliverances of experience and feeling, on which
they ground their belief in ethics, freedom, and the self. In their hands, complained
Jones (writing in 1902–3), 'Philosophy, in this country, is no longer an attempt to
interpret the world of reality as an inter-related whole, but an examination of human
knowledge; constructive metaphysics has sunk into Epistemology.'[184] He is here of
course re-visiting his earlier 1893 objection to Pringle-Pattison.[185]

But the fault is not all one-sided and Absolute Idealism too breaks faith with reason,
albeit in a more complicated fashion. At a surface level, both Bradley and Bosanquet
display a willingness to simply detach religious faith from rational enquiry and treat it as
a more or less practical self-supporting attitude. As we have already seen, for Bosanquet
religion offers an experience of God, not a proof of him, while for Bradley faith is an
essentially volitional stance that is able to hold in tension and 'live through' the
contradictions of the religious hypothesis. But Jones takes religion too seriously for
that. Against a similar proposal by Lotze, he complains that in no other department
would we be prepared to sacrifice truth for pragmatic value.[186] Unable perhaps quite to
shake his Calvinistic concern with *belief*, he is disquieted to find his is an age that trusts
to the *practicalities* of faith—something manifested in the social reform taking place all
around—but fights shy of its *theory*; an age of religion but not theology.[187]

Such trust is not the whole story for, of course, at a deeper level, both Bradley and
Bosanquet pursue rational enquiry to its very end, which is the Absolute. But even
here, thinks Jones they have not properly understood its nature. For conceiving it as an
abstract principle of comprehensive unity, both take it in a fashion that is ultimately
self-destructive, albeit in slightly different ways. Bradley, of course, with his notion of
'thought's suicide' believes in a reality beyond thought, something Jones will have no
truck with.[188] And, while Bosanquet would not follow such trans-rationalism, the
process of reason leads him to an abstract washing out of all fine differences (or so Jones
wants to claim) which our own thinking, at least, is powerless to follow.

Against both sets of sceptics—and very much in the spirit of the earliest Idealists—
T.H. Green, John Caird, and his own teacher, Edward Caird—Jones asserts a strong
faith in the power of reason to solve all questions; 'there are no problems which reason
is entitled to ask that do not lie within the power of reason to solve'.[189] And this
emphatically extends to religion: 'I believe with all my heart that religion, yea, the

---

[184] 'The Present Attitude of Reflective Thought towards Religion', 232–3.
[185] See above p.360.
[186] *Faith that Enquires*, 23.
[187] 'The Present Attitude of Reflective Thought Towards Religion', 239.
[188] 'I doubt whether there can be anything unintelligible except that which is irrational, and I doubt if
anything real is irrational except as misunderstood'(*Faith that Enquires*, 5).
[189] 'Are Moral and Religious Beliefs Capable of Proof?', 98.

Christian religion in its essence, is rational through and through.'[190] Indeed, he sums up the central message of his Gifford Lectures, *A Faith that Enquires*, as 'Let man seek God by way of pure reason, and he will find him.'[191]

To speak of 'faith' in the power of reason is perhaps a little misleading for, unlike a brute religious conviction, Jones' confidence in the potential of thinking is itself securely grounded. Reason can deal with any problem, he argues, because there are no problems except where we find at least apparent incompatibility, and there is no incompatibility except where opposites meet within a wider reconciling unity.[192] The debt here to the logic of Caird and Hegel is obvious. Appeal to 'reason' may also be misunderstood unless we grasp that what Jones has in mind at this juncture is not the narrow abstractions of science or syllogism, but the broader process in which the whole self attempts to make sense of our experience as a whole; 'In every case of knowing, *all* the powers of mind are employed,'[193] he insists, and we are taken always beyond what first appears, for 'no *human* mind observes the whole of a fact at any time'.[194] As such, reasoning is something one might find in poetry just as well as in philosophy.[195]

11.3.3.2 Jones and Bosanquet In order to appreciate precisely how Jones thinks that the more strenuous application of reason may help us find a path between Absolutism and Personalism, we can compare his position to those of Bosanquet and Pringle-Pattison. Beginning with Bosanquet, the similarity that strikes with greatest force is that both philosophers have a fundamentally moral and social conception of religion. Religion for Bosanquet is neither an internal affair, nor an other-worldly one; rather it consists in the transformation of this world, specifically in its moral regeneration. And with this Jones agrees; 'morality *is* religion operative,' he says, 'It is divine service.'[196] God is immanent in human nature and so human relationships, from the individual or familial up to the civic and national, are not purely secular but take on a moral and a spiritual worth, as the means by which God reveals himself.[197] 'His 'Kingdom will come', says Jones, 'with the development of the more secular forces on which the well-being of mankind depends.'[198] The equation, naturally, may just as well be read the other way round: 'the religious life is nothing but *the secular life devoted to the Best we know.*'[199]

But Jones does not *simply* follow Bosanquet. Against the charge that he has just *replaced* religion by civic morality, Bosanquet follows Bradley in holding that if for ethics the good is something *to be realized*, for religion it is something, already and in spite of appearance to the contrary, emphatically *actual*. Jones rejects this answer, for to say that only the divine *is* as it *ought* to be, and every moral act of ours merely *aims at* that ideal, is in effect to condemn all our acts as 'failures',[200] to doom us always to try

[190] 'Are Moral and Religious Beliefs Capable of Proof?', 114.   [191] *Faith that Enquires*, vii.
[192] 'Divine Transcendence', 12.   [193] *Faith that Enquires*, 65.   [194] *Faith that Enquires*, 66.
[195] See above pp.352–5.   [196] 'Education of the Citizen', 249.
[197] 'Divine Transcendence', 8.   [198] *Faith that Enquires*, vii.
[199] 'Are Moral and Religious Beliefs Capable of Proof?', 98.   [200] *Faith that Enquires*, 159.

and never to succeed. In opposing Hegel's conception of philosophy as the successor to religion, Bradley rejects any view of faith as 'failed philosophy', but himself making it the successor to morality, he in turn condemns ethics as 'failed religion'. Jones' humanity is too large to allow that and urges compromise. While we know no single fact *absolutely* it by no means follows that we know *nothing* of it, and what holds of cognition, he suggests, holds equally of morality; though we may never *fully* realize the moral ideal that is not to say we do not realize it *at all*.[201] Bradley and Bosanquet here are victim to a deep misconception about the nature of morality. It is not some sort of *precursor* to religion, it is religion itself, in practice. Morality is not, nor does it aim to be, some accomplished achievement or the reaching of some fixed goal, rather it is always and essentially a *process*, whose ongoing operation *is* the moral ideal itself. The mistake of the alternative view Jones regards as the remnant of some unhealthy 'Platonic' reification of ideas which would have us aim at some abstract universal good, when in truth our aim is always and only the good as particularized in this or that duty.[202]

Shifting from ethical to more metaphysical comparisons, another obvious point of similarity is that both Jones and Bosanquet believe in some form in the Absolute; the totality of being conceived as ideal. But from the point of view of religion, this comparison takes us only so far. For Bosanquet, the Absolute is emphatically not God; and of course Bradley concurs. But Jones by contrast insists on identifying God with the Absolute.[203] Even more problematically he insists at the same time on a conception of the divine as personal. As he lay dying Jones said: 'The ultimate meaning of Reality is Love. If that is true, there must be a soul, a personal God, to do the loving. The task of philosophy is to justify that view.'[204] In consequence Jones' Absolute—more like the eternal self-consciousness of Green or Caird than the supra-relational whole of Bradley or the unified totality of Bosanquet—turns out to be a personal form of being. Indeed, he specifically opposes what he describes as Bradley's 'pantheism' on the grounds of its irreconcilability with the idea of a God both personal and individual.[205] That is, he confesses, the matter on which he differs 'most deeply' from Bradley.[206]

For Bradley and Bosanquet the unconditioned nature of the infinite means that it cannot be personal, and for Jones this error is as much one about the nature of personality as it is about the nature of the Absolute. This comes out clearly in his opposition to Bosanquet's treatment of finite individuality.[207] He objects that the

---

[201] *Faith that Enquires*, 160.

[202] *Faith that Enquires*, 161–4. See also 'The Ethical Ideal in Shakespeare', 205.

[203] 'The God of religion is the same as the Absolute of philosophy' (*Faith that Enquires*, 244).

[204] Hetherington, *Life and Letters of Sir Henry Jones*, 154. Belief in the personality of God capable of standing in relation to us he elsewhere describes as 'vital for religion' (*Faith that Enquires*, 320).

[205] *Faith that Enquires*, 320.

[206] *Faith that Enquires*, 315. The half-way assertion that God is super-personal (*Appearance and Reality*, 531) is one to which he can attach no definite meaning at all, Jones complains—and many surely would agree (*Faith that Enquires*, 315).

[207] *Faith that Enquires*, ch.XI; see also Hetherington, *Life and Letters of Henry Jones*, 167–8; Muirhead, *Bosanquet and his Friends*, 233.

doctrine of the infinite-in-finite, in which all things have a *nisus* to their completion in a wider whole, translates for Bosanquet into a process in which finite things transcend themselves, becoming utterly transmuted and lost; their individual reality in effect denied.[208] And he locates the underlying problem in a mistaken assumption on Bosanquet's part that finite and infinite contradict each other.[209] The accusation is made that he thinks of man as nothing more than a 'finite centre' whose identity is lost when we pass outside its boundary into its wider context; when in truth man does not have to go beyond himself at all to find the infinite, for he already is the infinite, in process.[210] Of course, both Bradley and Bosanquet would firmly resist this charge, and in one sense it is monumentally unfair—a quick glance at what they say on the subject of the infinite confirms that neither of them thought this—but in another sense there is some ground to Jones' complaints that they tend to over-emphasize the finitude of actual experience, from which they court a species of transcendence that looks decidedly un-Hegelian.

If the difference between Jones and Bosanquet is still a bit vague, it gains even more focus when we turn to look at the problem of evil. Like Bosanquet's, Jones' Absolutism commits him to a belief in the perfection of the whole, though neither imagine that that absolves them from giving any account of evil. But Jones feels that Bosanquet's own efforts in this direction do not take evil seriously enough.[211] Despite committing to the ultimate goodness (in some sense) of the whole, Bosanquet doubts all 'local valuations'. Can we really judge that specific things and events are good and bad, he worries, or that the values we employ are really those by which the final assessment is made? Jones, by contrast, remains defiantly bound to the finite perspective in addressing this question, and insists that each felt evil must be justified in comprehensible human terms. No doctrine of God which requires us to dismiss as unreal the experienced imperfections and tragedies of human existence can possibly stand as true; it is simply inconsistent with the facts we know, he says; in a somewhat brute appeal to actual experience.[212] As to the justification of evil itself, the answer Jones himself gives is remarkably conventional. The purpose of our lives is to learn goodness,[213] but 'where there is no real evil to resist . . . there cannot be good',[214] a need met by natural evil, which provides an opportunity for growth, and by moral evil, which results from our misuse of the independent free will necessary for moral goodness itself.[215]

Their greatest difference between the two philosophers on the problem of evil concerns what we might call 'cosmic justice'. Bosanquet rejects any call for 'individual' justice; we should not expect the balance in the overall scheme of things to filter down to any correlation between our own virtue or vice and our own happiness or suffering. Jones disagrees: 'justice on the whole and to the whole, which is not justice to any constituent of that whole, seems to me unsatisfactory from every point of view,' he

---

[208] *Faith that Enquires*, 187.   [209] *Faith that Enquires*, 178.   [210] *Faith that Enquires*, 190.
[211] *Faith that Enquires*, 202.   [212] 'Divine Transcendence', 11.   [213] *Faith that Enquires*, 223.
[214] *Principles of Citizenship*, 45.   [215] *Faith that Enquires*, 246.

complains.[216] Pursuit of such justice leads Jones in the end to adopt a theory of personal immortality like that of many of the other Personal Idealists. Immortality he suggests is an implication of our religious nature; it 'extends man's spiritual chances.'[217] For people die in their sins and if death ends everything then their lives can be called nothing but failures, not simply on their part, but also of God's purpose for them. 'It is not possible to maintain the limitless love and power of God if the soul be not immortal,'[218] urges Jones in a universalist hope far distant from the narrow religion of his youth.

11.3.3.3 Jones and Personalism The coincidence of many of Jones' belief with those of the Personal Idealists will no doubt have been registered, but for all his agreements with it,[219] in the end he opposes that position. No suggestion that the individual self is something independently real, an autonomous starting point that exists it its own right, can possibly stand more than initial scrutiny. For the self exists only in so far as it finds itself in a wider context; it draws its content, its whole life, from its surroundings. A person, says Jones, 'is always the centre, the owner, the user of a world; and he is most fully and truly a person whose world is widest and richest'. By contrast, 'He approaches extinction in the degree in which he is shut up within himself.'[220] This was a message he repeated again and again:

Man's soul is mediated by the vast scheme in which he lives. His environment is the treasury from which he draws every item of his knowledge, and his world is the laboratory wherein he achieves his character. Sever him from his world, isolate him, call his self 'impervious,' let the world's waves beat about his soul as around a rock-bound island, and his mind will be dark, his will unformed, and wholly impotent for either good or evil.[221]

What we have above, it will readily be recognized, is simply a more metaphysical and theological application of the 'social conception of the individual' familiar in all British Idealist moral and political philosophy. But in our context the word 'impervious' here is especially significant, a clear reference to Pringle-Pattison who notoriously used the term to characterize the non-overlapping nature of selves. And while it is true that he later distanced himself from such an extreme view, holding not that selves are unrelated, but that each enjoys its own life,[222] even this lesser position Jones would reject. Although valid between finite individuals, between man and God, the familiar opposition between 'mine' and 'yours' does not hold. We cannot say of anything 'If God's then not man's' or 'if man's then not God's', for God is 'the essence of our essence and

---

[216] *Faith that Enquires*, 177.   [217] *Faith that Enquires*, 344.   [218] *Faith that Enquires*, 347.
[219] Particularly striking is the following: 'Persons are the most solitary things in the world, even though they are capable of the deepest communion' ('Nature and Aims of Philosophy', 165).
[220] *Principles of Citizenship*, 61.
[221] 'The Immanence of God and the Individuality of Man', 31.
[222] *Hegelianism and Personality*, 216; *Idea of God*, 389n. Although Pringle-Pattison rejects the term, Rashdall, McTaggart, or Howison would all be happy to retain it.

life of our life'.[223] The spiritual life is one in which a man gives up his whole self before God, in a process which paradoxically turns out to be not death but life, for 'the indwelling of God sustains, enriches, liberates, [and] enlarges the personality of man'.[224]

From another angle, the issue is again that of the relation between morality and religion. At first glance morality and religion seem opposed in the sense that morality implies a certain individualism—we are each responsible for our own acts—while religion seems to break down these barriers—everything is given up before, and handed over to, God.[225] But the opposition is an illusion, the result of thinking in terms of extreme abstractions. To affirm either the unity of the divine and human, or their independence, is destroy religion as a doctrine of the concurrence of finite and infinite will. Echoing Pringle-Pattison, Jones insists that there can be no coming together of wills unless they are first distinct and free, but adds too that unless they come together they cannot even be separate, for neither makes sense on its own.[226] In their mistaken fear that inclusion within the Absolute would overwhelm the self, the Personal Idealists were merely repeating an earlier error on the part of Martineau who had felt that the only way to avoid merging man and God was wholly to sever them; hence his horror of pantheism.[227] But, in truth, only in so far as they are taken together as part of a broader unity is it even possible to pick them out as distinguishable components. Isolated, man is nothing at all, so his continuity with God and nature is not the undoing but the making of him. In God we find our freedom and ourselves.[228]

11.3.3.4 The problem of Jesus Many of these issues come to a head in Jones' discussion of Jesus. Neither Bosanquet nor Pringle-Pattison was especially interested in Jesus.[229] Jones, by contrast, could not be more so—and here again his upbringing is a relevant factor.

His account is notable. In the first place it is wholly anti-supernatural. 'The moment religious faith is made to rest upon the supernatural and the superhuman, the moment that things divine do not express themselves in the ordinary world and in the ordinary life of man,—religion becomes indistinguishable from superstition.'[230] Jesus' impor-

---

[223] 'The Immanence of God and the Individuality of Man', 36. In similar vein Muirhead argues that God is not personal in any sense that excludes other minds (*Social Purpose*, 106).

[224] 'The Immanence of God and the Individuality of Man', 39.

[225] *Faith that Enquires*, 153–4.

[226] *Faith that Enquires*, 317.

[227] 'The Philosophy of Martineau in Relation to the Idealism of the Present Day', 23.

[228] 'The Philosophy of Martineau in Relation to the Idealism of the Present Day', 35.

[229] 'The double nature is a figment of theologians' argues Bosanquet ('The Evolution of Religion', 443) but he never explores the 'speculative import' that he hints might attach to the notion of incarnation in the light of Hegelian immanentism ('On the True Conception of Another World', xxxiv). For Pringle-Pattison, the incarnation, 'Whatever else it may mean, . . . means at least this—that in the conditions of the highest human life we have access, as nowhere else, to the inmost nature of the divine' (*Idea of God*, 157) but while we need to think of God in terms of Christ, we don't have to say Christ is God (*Philosophy of Religion*, 252).

[230] 'Idealism of Jesus', 88.

tance is not as a miracle worker; even the final miracle of his death and resurrection fails to interest much. 'Judicial arrangements' or 'punitive atonement' are 'inadequate' and 'irrelevant' for bringing us to God, argues Jones, and when in 'conversion' we turn to God we create no new relation with him but merely recognize a closeness which existed from the beginning.[231] All that matters is the lesson Christ teaches, partly through his words, but mainly through his very being—in other words, the incarnation—for 'the essential message of Christianity is that a perfect humanity is the most perfect revelation of God; or that the humanity of God and the divinity of man are two aspects of the same truth.'[232] What Jesus has to teach is the idealization of man, the revelation of the intrinsic splendour of his nature as a child of God,[233] Sonship and fathership standing as metaphors for the *unifying* love of God to man and man to God.[234] His message is that of the *unity* of the divine and human nature, in short, idealism.[235] If it seems absurd (and philoso-centric) to suggest that Jesus came to preach idealism, Jones would no doubt reply that the same essential truth manifests itself in different guises in all times and places, so that we could just as easily say that idealism finally arrives at what Christianity was saying all along.

But what of Jesus' own nature? The story is told how on not receiving an expected repeat invitation to preach at a chapel in Anglesey, enquiry was made as to what the difficulty might be. The reply came back that they were reluctant to make a second invitation, rumour having reached them that Jones was a heretic who denied the divinity of Christ. 'I deny the divinity of Christ,' he objected indignantly, 'I do not deny the divinity of any man!'[236] And that of course was the problem. Asked whether Christ were human or divine, Jones would say both. But asked if he was unique in being so, he would say not. To Jones, Christ manifests something in the highest form, true in lesser degree of us all. For were it otherwise, his value to us would be destroyed. If we make Jesus unique the very message of his being—that human nature is ideal, that we are much more than we take ourselves to be—is obscured and contradicted.[237] We find this view of Christ in T.H. Green, John Caird, and Edward Caird, but with reference to the specific issue we have been considering here, the figure of Christ stands forth in denial of the position that, in being taken up in the divine nature, finite human life is destroyed; a position which, in their different ways, both Bosanquet and Pringle-Pattison seem to endorse; Bosanquet concluding that it

---

[231] 'Idealism of Jesus', 92.

[232] 'The Philosophy of Martineau in Relation to the Idealism of the Present Day', 15 n.1. Jesus exemplifies incarnation, but by no means exhausts it, a point with which Bosanquet was in full agreement (*Bernard Bosanquet and his Friends*, 215).

[233] 'Idealism of Jesus', 93.

[234] 'Idealism of Jesus', 95.

[235] 'Idealism of Jesus', 96.

[236] This story is told by Hetherington, *Life and Letters of Henry Jones*, 43.

[237] 'I believe that Jesus was divine. But when it is said that the splendour with which he was clothed, and which was divine, was his *only*, that it made him stand absolutely alone in the world, I must demur' ('Idealism of Jesus', 102).

is destroyed, Pringle-Pattison that it is not taken up. Idealism to Jones rejects any such either/or for a both/and.

At the end of this discussion we are left with something of a paradox. David Stove and others have presented philosophical idealism as a kind of gentle exit for those no longer able to stay but not quite ready to leave the comfort of religion; a weakened substitute of reduced content easier to swallow than the hard edges of traditional belief systems.[238] Whether idealism's demands on belief were really less or easier could be debated at length, but one thing which it is important to recognize is that that was *not how it seemed to the Idealists themselves.* Henry Jones is a case in point. Reflecting on his Calvinistic Methodist upbringing and his later more flexible religious views, it would be tempting to speak of a *falling away* from faith, but that—emphatically—was not his own view: As he put it in his autobiography, 'I think my religious views are less crude now as well as shorter than they were in those days; but the essentials of the faith, the hypothesis in which I would fain say that my life rests, and without which the world would seem to me to be a wild chaos and the life of man a tragic blunder—*that* remains the same.'[239] Rather than a retreat, it was the reverse. By escaping Calvinism to idealism Jones felt he had broken through the outer form of religion to its essence.

11.4 McTaggart's atheism

11.4.1 Methodological points

It would be easy to think that the British neo-Hegelians, be they Personal or Absolute Idealists, all advanced a religious worldview; but this was not quite the case; and no study of idealist philosophy of religion could be complete without a consideration of McTaggart, as vigorous an atheist as they were theists.

As well as on this specific point of doctrine McTaggart's thought also offers a vital corrective in its general approach to philosophy. Too often in studying the figures discussed in this chapter the reader is struck with a discomfiting sense of complacent optimism or rhetorical vagueness, but few have warned so clearly of the dangers of such sloppy metaphysics, or in their own work strived so hard to avoid it, than McTaggart. The issue is partly one of style. In all McTaggart's writing he takes the very greatest care to express himself with maximum clarity and precision. G.E. Moore, that Jeremiah of clarity, attests to this fact,[240] but nothing could be more obvious to the reader himself as he turns from the prose of Bradley, Caird, Jones, or Pringle-Pattison to that of McTaggart; it is like a sharp and very welcome breath of fresh air. But the issue is not solely stylistic. The ethically driven argumentation and rhetorical presentation of much idealist writing plants in many minds a suspicion of wishful thinking. Very aware of this danger, in his 1906 book *Some Dogmas of Religion*, McTaggart offers an extended

---

[238] Stove, 'Idealism: A Victorian Horror-Story', 87–96.   [239] *Old Memories*, 59.
[240] Moore, Obituary Notice: McTaggart, 271.

discussion of what might best be described as the ethics of belief, in which he argues for a ruthlessly objective and value neutral approach that sets him apart from his contemporaries. If asked why I should believe a certain metaphysical dogma, there are a number of equally unacceptable answers, each of which we must resist, he argues. First, some people claim to believe things on the basis of an immediate certainty, without the need of arguments. As far as the person themselves is concerned, this is decisive—if I am thus certain, I have all the justification I can desire—but for others who do not share this insight it is useless, and if I refuse to accept criticism, I forfeit my right to criticize others. McTaggart does not dispute that immediate certainty has a place in philosophy, but its revelations must be universally shared, and most metaphysical and religious dogmas are not. Secondly, it is sometimes urged that we should believe things because most people, or most unsophisticated people, do so. Often, no doubt, the majority are right, and often too sophistication does corrupt thought, but in both of these matters the converse is equally possible, counters McTaggart. In rejecting untutored belief as a court of appeal, McTaggart cuts across both the intuitive consciousness (moral and religious) of the personalists and the common sense of Moore. Thirdly, it is sometimes said that we ought to believe certain things because the consequences of not doing so are just too awful to contemplate. Certain beliefs would make us miserable, or immoral, or would render morality and practical action absurd. Though few would be happy to see it put so brutally this is recognizable as a form of argument we have encountered several times so far in the British Idealist tradition. McTaggart objects that, while much may seem to us unbearable to believe, there is probably no dogma that has not been found acceptable by *some* people. But, more fundamentally, he charges that whether or not we welcome any given belief has nothing to do with its *truth*. Fourthly, it is sometimes suggested that we should believe certain dogmas because of the miraculous warrant associated with them. For instance, many of those who preached the Christian Gospel are said to have had the power to perform miracles, while the Koran is believed to be a miracle itself. McTaggart has little to add beyond endorsement to Hume's famous discussion of this matter, arguing that even if we could be sure that the miracle really did occur, it hardly follows that the associated dogma is true. The problem is that, except in a few cases (for example, the resurrection of Christ and the doctrine of our own resurrection) there is no logical connection between the former and the latter.

11.4.2 The comfort of metaphysics

The strength of McTaggart's warnings against loose metaphysics is perhaps to be explained by his equally strong sense of the temptations to the same. He is typical of the British Idealists in the very great importance he placed on finding an adequate metaphysics, but perhaps more than any of them he understood that the desire to do so is not just intellectual, but *practical and emotional*. McTaggart was an unashamed advocate of the practical significance of metaphysics. He speaks of 'the tremendous effect on our welfare, and the welfare of our fellow beings, of those aspects of reality with which religion and philosophy are concerned.'[241] Dealing with doctrines the difference between the truth and falsity of which is for us the difference between happiness or misery, 'The utility of Metaphysic is to be found,' he claims, 'in the comfort it can give us.'[242] His conviction in the genuine power of philosophy to offer such reassurance and hope led him to republish his doctrine on immortality for the War bereaved, and throughout his Cambridge career to give additional classes on philosophy to non-philosophers.

Such a view of the practical significance of metaphysics would find few supporters today, facing two sorts of objection. First, conceiving of metaphysics as some kind of extension to science, its results might be thought value neutral. The only worth such matters have, it might be said, comes from us, from the attitude we take towards them. McTaggart is not entirely without sympathy to this point. He accepts that things only have value in relation to conscious observers, and he allows that notions such as God and immortality may please some but not others. However, he would not allow that we can adopt any attitude we like to the world. If we embrace and welcome the pain of others, that does not make pain a good thing, it makes us evil. Taking a different line, it might be objected that metaphysics, as a wholly non-empirical subject, by its nature deals with things that lack all experiential import and hence that the results of metaphysics, however much they may satisfy our intellectual curiosity, can have no practical significance. Against this, McTaggart would no doubt have responded, that even if ultimate reality falls outside of our current experience it should not be assumed that that will always be the case, and if the veil of perception may one day be pierced, our beliefs about what lies beyond it become of very direct and immediate consequence to our present happiness.

11.4.3 Atheism

Given the great potential of any answer to reassure or disappoint us, we need to ask if God exists. But before we discuss McTaggart's atheism, it is necessary to consider his overall conception of religion in general and Christianity in particular. He defines religion as an emotion resting on a conviction of a harmony between ourselves and the universe at large,[243] a belief (to put it otherwise) that the universe is on the whole a good place.[244] There is much to be said for this definition. It is wide enough to include most systems we would be inclined to call religions,[245] but at a time when religion and metaphysics were being radically rethought, it is a rather reactionary definition, in that it excludes several more liberal accounts. For instance, it deliberately leaves out accounts of religion in terms of morality or accounts which see religion as a matter of our attitude towards the universe.[246] In its insistence on dogma as an essential

---

[241] *Philosophical Studies*, 37.   [242] *Philosophical Studies*, 184.
[243] *Some Dogmas of Religion*, 3.   [244] *Some Dogmas of Religion*, 11.
[245] It would even include, it should be noted, his own metaphysical worldview. See section 11.4.4 below.
[246] *Some Dogmas of Religion*, 6–11. In making these exclusions McTaggart has in mind Matthew Arnold and Lowes Dickinson respectively, but parallels are easily discernible among his fellow Idealists also.

component McTaggart's might even be thought a somewhat old-fashioned—narrowly cognitive and doctrinal—definition of religion.

He takes a similarly reactionary view of theism, of which Christianity is the only type he considers. God is defined as personal, supreme, and good.[247] He declines to call the Absolute 'God' on a variety of grounds. First, he thinks that it offends against ordinary usage. In this he is no doubt right, but while ordinary usage is important, few people would think that it should always be given the last word in questions of philosophical theology. Second, he objects that this way of speaking renders the question of whether or not God exists a trivial one, equivalent to whether or not the universe exists. Third, he objects that it directly contravenes the facts of our finite personality; the Absolute cannot be a person, since we, as parts of the Absolute are all persons, and no person can include another as one of its parts.[248] Clearly on this last point he stands with Rashdall and Pringle-Pattison.

McTaggart's arguments for atheism may usefully be divided into three distinct classes. First, there are the arguments in his *Studies in Hegelian Cosmology* to the effect that Hegelianism does not lead to Christianity. Already noted in a previous chapter, this difference of opinion with fellow Idealists such as Wallace or Caird, reminds us that there was no monolithic 'British Idealist reading of Hegel'.

Secondly, there are his indirect attacks to the effect that the world is a very different place from that suggested by traditional theology; there is no time, no material world, and no free will. While not direct refutations of theism these results serve to undermine fundamentally the traditional believers' worldview. McTaggart's attacks on material reality and on time have already been considered in the previous chapter, but a word is in order here about his rejection of free will.[249] He argues for a deterministic scheme, together with a Humean understanding of freedom to the effect that we have liberty in so far as we are not constrained. But if not especially original, this discussion of free will should not be passed by without note. Of particular interest here is the fact that he decouples entirely from the question of free will that of physicalism—let no one think he has secured free will simply by denying materialism—joining the rare class of those who are both determinist and idealist; a class that includes Rashdall as well as Leibniz (although the latter would certainly dispute his own claim to admission).

In addition to these two indirect attacks, McTaggart offers a series of direct attacks on the theistic hypothesis. His strategy works by trying to fix an acceptable version of the hypothesis itself. Looking again at the definition of God, personality and goodness are taken to be non-negotiable, but he notes that the property of being supreme is ambiguous. A supreme God may be omnipotent, in which case he must have created the universe, or he may simply be extremely powerful, in which case he may or may not be the creator. This gives McTaggart three possible hypotheses; an omnipotent and

---

[247] *Some Dogmas of Religion*, 186.
[248] *Some Dogmas of Religion*, 187–8; *Studies in Hegelian Cosmology*, 84–5; *Nature of Existence*, §§401–4.
[249] *Some Dogmas of Religion*, ch.V.

creative God, a non-omnipotent and creative God, or a non-omnipotent and non-creative God. He considers each in turn.

According to McTaggart, 'an omnipotent person is one who can do anything'.[250] Not surprisingly he rejects this as nonsense, because such a God would not be bound by the laws of logic, like identity, contradiction, or excluded middle. He therefore concludes that if there is a God, he must be merely very powerful rather than omnipotent. This is a conclusion that has been endorsed, on both logical and biblical grounds, by some recent philosophers of religion; although against it the objection may be made that (with some logical care) we can find a perfectly good sense of omnipotence without embracing the sort of absurdities McTaggart fears. The attempted reply undoubtedly meets with many difficulties which are all familiar and need not be discussed here, but McTaggart himself raises one problem, typical of its day but little considered now, which is worthy of note. He objects that personality and omnipotence are incompatible.[251] The argument is that personhood requires an Other, a not-self, which inevitably must limit it. Lotze's response to this sort of objection, that this condition holds only of finite and not infinite selves, is not taken up.[252]

The possibility of a non-omnipotent and creative God is ruled out by McTaggart because of the existence of evil, which he regards as an insuperable problem not just for an allegedly omnipotent God but even for a non-omnipotent creative God.[253] He argues that since God created the universe, there should be nothing in the universe to act as a barrier to his will. Were there such a barrier, since it too must be something that God willed, we would then have to conclude that he had not in fact willed absolute goodness at all. It is to be noted that one of the most familiar responses to the problem of evil, the free will defence, is not available to McTaggart. In *The Nature of Existence* he offers a further argument against the idea of a creative God. He argues that the universe could not have been made by a God since it is made up of a number of selves which by their very nature are non-created primary parts.[254]

The third and final hypothesis is that of a non-omnipotent and non-creative God. Such a being would be, in effect, nothing more than a very powerful spirit, who controlled but did not create the world in which he found himself.[255] In *The Nature of Existence* McTaggart attacks this hypothesis on the grounds that power or control require the reality of time, which he denies. The weakened suggestion there might exist some spirit which *seemed* to be in charge of the universe, he considers at least possible, although of little religious value.[256] Asking whether it is a possibility in fact realized, he dismisses all of the traditional arguments for the existence of God.[257] This last discussion is standard, and adds nothing new to the debate, but in truth it hardly

[250] *Some Dogmas of Religion*, 202.   [251] *Some Dogmas of Religion*, 202–8.

[252] Lotze, *Microcosmus*, bk.IX/ch.iv/§4 (Volume II, 678–88).

[253] *Some Dogmas of Religion*, 223–34.

[254] *Nature of Existence*, §492.   [255] *Some Dogmas of Religion*, 235.

[256] *Nature of Existence*, §§496–8.   [257] *Some Dogmas of Religion*, 190–202, 238–250.

matters, for given how little he will concede, by this stage the hypothesis has lost most if not all of its interest for us.

11.4.4 Surrogates for religion

To leave matters here, however, would be misleading in so far as it might suggest that for McTaggart the universe is a religiously blank zone, a realm wholly without spiritual significance. But that is very far from being the truth.

If one criterion for taking a religious view of the universe is the admission of mystical experience, then one fact from McTaggart's own life needs to be recorded. For in his youth and periodically he had such an experience, which he referred to as the 'Saul' feeling in reference to the poem by Browning of that name, whose closing section he felt best described the way it took possession of him. Not a mere feeling or thought but capable of bringing about sensory alteration, he seems to have understood it as an intuition that love, the personal love of one soul for another, sums up or is the essence of reality.[258] It was for him a confirmation of the truth of his philosophy and it undoubtedly influenced his thinking; Geach memorably describes him as someone who, having taken a look at the end of the book, worked out backwards his answer from that.[259]

Of course, too great a weight must not be placed on any point of personal biography, but really this youthful vision just serves to illuminate for us a point of crucial importance about McTaggart's metaphysical system more generally which, once realized, cannot but take centre stage; and this is that his universe is in many respects a deeply religious one. And we must recall here his definition of religion as an emotion resting on a conviction of a harmony between ourselves and the universe at large.[260] It is not so, to be sure, in any conventional sense; but his timeless paradise in our future where spirits are joined, and indeed reunited, in love is surely not distant from many Christian visions of heaven. And although with out any 'ruler' his system of loving spirits is not so far from polytheism, or a distribution of deity through a plurality of persons rather than just one. Armour has described it as 'an expanded trinity', which metaphor is perfectly apt, although it would doubtless have embarrassed McTaggart.[261] His embarrassment, however, would be limited, for despite the claims to atheism, he himself would have been happy to allow that a philosophical vision could so capture our hearts and imaginations that it transports us beyond ourselves, for as he says in the concluding lines of *Studies in Hegelian Dialectic*, 'All true philosophy must be mystical, not indeed in its methods, but in its final conclusions'.[262]

---

[258] Lowes Dickinson, *McTaggart*, 46, 92–8. The section McTaggart refers to begins with the lines, 'I know not too well how I found my way home in the night'.

[259] *Truth, Love and Immortality*, 15.

[260] See above p.435.

[261] Mackenzie, *Elements of Constructive Philosophy*, 436. Armour, 'The Idealist Philosophers' God', 447.

[262] *Studies in Hegelian Dialectic*, 255.

12

Developments in Idealist Logic

It has been considered how, expounding and developing the thoughts of Kant and Hegel, the Idealists went on to create a new and complex logic worthy of consideration in its own right; but, as in other fields, idealistic thinking on this front was never static and the process of development continued into the twentieth century. This chapter outlines some of that evolution. In some measure the further advance which took place did so in response to new and rival ideas in logic which were emerging around it—many destined to dominate the discipline during the coming century—but more often this ferment was simply ignored and the development is best understood as an internal one, an inward-looking process by which the stream of idealistic logic increasingly disconnected itself from the main current of contemporary logical thought.

12.1 The coherence theory of truth

For Green, the test of whether a thing is 'real' lies in its ability to fit with the rest of our experience and with the experiences of others. Bradley too used coherence and comprehensiveness as a criterion of adequacy—reality is a unified whole and, therefore, the closer any experience or judgement approximates to this, the truer it must be held. Bosanquet went even further; for him the truth of any judgement consists precisely in its contribution to the systematic coherence of the body of knowledge as a whole. In this way the coherence theory became something like the 'official' theory of truth for monistic idealism; a point which may be illustrated by one further example. Henry Jones, in his lectures 'The Working Faith of the Social Reformer', by way of criticism of the dangers of metaphor, takes issue with the 'foundationalist' model of knowledge. Descartes' project fails, he argues, since there are no underpinning ideas which do not imply others, no thoughts which may make secure claims to either meaning or truth on their own.[1] For this reason knowledge should be regarded less like

---

[1] 'Working Faith of the Social Reformer', 43.

a building and more like a solar system—'an equipoise of elements which sustain one another'—where ideas possess meaning, not in their own right, but only in relation to others. Here we have, urges Jones, 'the most significant of all discoveries of modern Epistemology[2]—that an idea is an idea, and a judgement is true or false, in virtue of their relation to a *system* of ideas or judgements; that their certainty rests not in themselves, but in the system of knowledge of which they are a part; and that their certainty grows as the system of knowledge expands.'[3]

12.1.1 H.H. Joachim

Despite its key role in Absolute Idealist thought, however, the coherence theory of truth remained for a very long time without either explicit recognition or detailed development in its own right. The person to change that was Joachim who in 1906 published *The Nature of Truth*, a work whose significance was precisely to put into systematic form the ideas of coherence which had thus far been merely implicit.

Joachim begins the book by dismissing alternative accounts, starting with the notion of truth as correspondence. The tempting thought that the 'correspondence' of two things is somehow elucidated when understood as a one-to-one relation between their parts, he quashes on the grounds that such sub-correlations inevitably appeal to the function or place of each element in the whole to which it belongs, so that instead of the isomorphism of the individual components accounting for the correspondence between the wholes, any explanation to be had runs the other way round.[4] But spurious claim to illumination aside, what is really wrong with the correspondence theory is that it requires us to hold, not simply that truth involves two corresponding wholes, but that one is in some sense 'mental' or *representing* while the other in some way 'real' or *represented*. Yet such a division is impossible to make, it turns out, for however we look at it, *both* sides of the relation display *both* characteristics.[5] Suppose I make a judgement about the reality I perceive. We might think it easy enough to distinguish here the *corresponding* from the *corresponded to*, but judgement exists more objectively that we first suppose—'The "purely personal" would be strictly incommunicable,' Joachim argues[6]—while perceived reality is always in large part our own contribution. Again, we might take the case of a scientific theory that supposedly 'mirrors' the facts. But what are these 'facts' except a set of judgements, like those of the theory itself, turning truth into a relation between semantic entities, rather than one between semantic entities and natural objects?[7] At the root of these worries lies Joachim's contention that the theory requires, not just that there obtain a correspondence between items, but further that this must be 'for' a mind. 'Truth,' he insists, 'is not truth at all except in so far as it is recognised, i.e. except in so far as it is the living

---

[2] The subject to which, we should remember, he was earlier so opposed! See above p.360.
[3] 'Working Faith of the Social Reformer', 44.
[4] *Nature of Truth*, 9–12.   [5] *Nature of Truth*, 19.
[6] *Nature of Truth*, 24.   [7] *Nature of Truth*, 28.

experience of a mind.'[8] Against the suggestion that thought or judgement might correspond to perception, he offers the further interesting objection that identity of structure is impossible where the relations hold between different materials; between ideas, on the one hand, and perceptions, on the other. The reasoning behind this claim invokes the characteristically idealist thesis that there can be no purely external relations; the doctrine that the nature of any relation depends on precisely what entities it relates makes it impossible ever to have exactly the same relations holding between different sets of things.[9]

By 1906 the assumption that truth must be experienced or judged was becoming increasingly controversial. Joachim thus moves on to consider a view which he finds in recent writings of Russell and Moore[10]—their earliest departures from idealism—according to which truth and falsity, since they seem to hold whether or not we recognize them (the notes of a chord are in harmony whether I hear them or not), are to be taken as immediate characteristics ('flavours') of objective universals; more specifically, of eternal and unchangeable 'propositions'. The difference between them is immediate and intuitively apprehended.[11] While admitting that there is indeed a *sense* in which experiencing makes no difference to the facts (what we intuit is independent of any particular act of intuition, 'here and now')[12] Joachim rejects this new theory on the grounds that it involves a *complete* severance of the experienced from experience. Known reality cannot exist in a purely external relation to the knowing subject, he complains. The natural reply that this is a theory which speaks, not of the *world as known*, but of the *world in itself*, is dismissed with an Hegelian wave of hand—'Truth *in itself*, truth neither known nor recognized, may be anything you please. You can say what you like about it, and it is not worth any one's while to contradict you; for it remains beyond all and any knowledge, and is a mere name for nothing.'[13] Joachim is equally sceptical of the notion of intuition to which this theory appeals. The bare fact that an apprehension is 'immediate' does not, he says, create any presumption in favour of its truth. On the contrary, it rouses suspicion, in so far as 'immediate intuition' is often just the last resort in defence of a conviction which the believer cannot justify nor yet abandon.[14]

From this point Joachim moves on to argue that, in rejecting the two previous theories, we must, in effect, have been employing our own positive understanding of truth. This, he ventures, is the notion of truth as coherence, which holds any thing true

---

[8] *Nature of Truth*, 14.

[9] As an Idealist Joachim formulates this argument as one to rule out any correspondence between thoughts and perceptions, but if sound, it would be equally effective against taking the correspondence relation as one that held between ideal and material reality.

[10] The targets are, for Russell: *A Critical Exposition of the Philosophy of Leibniz*, *The Principles of Mathematics*, 'On Denoting' and for Moore: 'The Nature of Judgement', 'The Refutation of Idealism', *Principia Ethica*.

[11] *Nature of Truth*, 37–8.

[12] *Nature of Truth*, 52.

[13] *Nature of Truth*, 51.

[14] *Nature of Truth*, 55.

in so far as it may be thought-out or conceived, fully, clearly, and logically, which is the same as to say in so far as it may be brought to fit harmoniously within a larger network; 'systematic coherence'. Something is true if it belongs to a 'significant whole', one in which 'all its constituent elements reciprocally involve one another, or reciprocally determine one another's being as contributory features in a single concrete meaning'.[15] Rejecting the distinction between necessary and contingent truth,[16] the coherence he advocates is more than just logical or *formal* 'consistency' or 'validity', for in concrete experience form and matter cannot be intelligibly separated one from another and considered apart.[17] It takes in any kind of relation whereby one judgement calls for or rules out another. This is, moreover, an account of the *nature* of truth, not simply (as for Bradley) of the *criterion* for it.

Without natural boundaries, any frameworks of belief to which we appeal must themselves be thought of as expanding outwards until we reach finally the whole of knowledge; systematic, self-contained, and unique in its all-inclusiveness. 'The truth itself is one, and whole, and complete, and . . . all thinking and all experience moves within its recognition and subject to its manifest authority,'[18] Joachim concludes. Be our focus on judgement or meaning, and be our focus on entailment or presupposition, each truth, in the end, connects to all truth. But since this whole process of contextualization is a matter of more or less, truth also must be a matter of more or less, and so the theory involves also a doctrine of degrees of truth and reality.[19]

Crucial to the coherence theory is the fact that the whole in which judgements find their truth is no mere sum or aggregation of single truths. Such an arrangement, Joachim says, would be 'as if one were to treat the Choral Symphony as a *collection* of beautiful sounds, Othello as an *aggregate* of fine ideas, or a picture by Rembrant as a *sum* of colours and lines'.[20] Instead the relationships between the judgements are internal, each having the nature it does through its relation to the others. In consequence, the holism which we find in truth extends also to meaning, and each individual judgement must be thought of really as an abbreviated, and in that regard, inadequate, statement of a meaning whose sufficient expression would ideally bring in the whole system of knowledge. But if this falsifies all judgement as partial, it must be added, that we are not thereby completely severed from reality; our concepts can to some extent express the whole, for each judgement is 'subject to a complex mass of conditions unexpressed and yet implied,' from which 'inarticulate background' it draws its meaning.[21]

One of the most notable points about *The Nature of Truth* is that, although written by a representative of the idealist school and supportive of the coherence theory, it is frank about (and indeed highly perceptive of) the problems which attend that theory, the last chapter of the book being devoted to its critique. In this respect it stands, comparable with Seth Pringle-Pattison's *Hegelianism and Personality*, as a landmark of internal

---

[15] *Nature of Truth*, 66.   [16] *Nature of Truth*, 67 n1.
[17] *Nature of Truth*, 170, also 76.   [18] *Nature of Truth*, 178.
[19] *Nature of Truth*, 85ff.   [20] *Nature of Truth*, 100.   [21] *Nature of Truth*, 107.

criticism on the part of the idealist movement, eclipsing anything mounted by its opponents from outside.

Joachim finds two main problems with the theory he has outlined. The first concerns error. According to such an holistic theory—and this is what happens with both Bradley and Bosanquet[22]—error is understood as defective truth. 'There are no roads which are such that to take them is *eo ipso* to lose one's way; and there are no judgements so constituted that the person who makes them must be in error.'[23] Error is a matter of taking, as the last word, a fragment out of context which, reconnected, would look very different. It is partial or incomplete knowledge, which takes itself as final truth. Both components of this formulation are necessary, stresses Joachim. A mere part of the truth may be incorporated as a harmless moment within a wider vision. It is precisely our confidence in its adequacy *as it is* which 'constitutes the distinctive character of error'. But therein, he argues, lies 'its power for mischief. [For] this feature is never annulled and never converted into an element of the fuller knowledge'.[24] What we precipitately believed may come to be assimilated into a greater truth, but not our rash and premature belief in it. He illustrates this via the case of Spinoza,[25] who tries to account for error by suggesting that what to God is experienced as a unified true thought, distributed over many minds would to them appear mutilated and false. However, if the unified divine thought constitutes the genuine reality here, then the existence of these many erring minds is, if truth be told, but an illusion, while if their plurality is last word, what mistake do they make in their thinking? Either way, the explanation of error dissolves.

'The erring subject's confident belief in the truth of his knowledge distinctively characterizes error, and converts a partial apprehension of the truth into falsity. It is this feature which refuses to be absorbed in fuller knowledge, and which makes the fact of error a problem for Metaphysics.'[26] It is not enough to say that error consists in partial truth, for properly understood in context, that is, as part of a wider account, a partial truth has nothing to reproach itself for. Taken wrongly, as itself something independent or complete that may stand on its own, it *is* an error, but what can it mean to 'take it wrongly' except that someone holds an erroneous belief about it—a second error called in to explain the first? Regress ensues, as the error itself keeps always one step ahead. The result is failure. If the ultimate coherence of the Absolute includes everything, it must embrace even its partial or lesser forms of experience, its error. It must make clear how they are somehow necessary to and taken up in the self-assertion of the whole. But no metaphysical theory could ever explain this, being itself precisely one of those limited visions and not completed truth.[27]

The second problem Joachim locates is that the coherence theory ends up postulating a kind of truth that human knowledge can never reach; an ideal system too high

[22] Bradley, *Essays on Truth and Reality*, 245–92; Bosanquet, *Logic*, I:383.
[23] *Nature of Truth*, 143.   [24] *Nature of Truth*, 145.   [25] *Nature of Truth*, 157–62.
[26] *Nature of Truth*, 162.   [27] *Nature of Truth*, 171.

above our heads to be of any real use. None of the things we ordinarily 'know' come out as true on this reckoning. Joachim objects to the notion of a wholly mind-independent truth—it would be nothing to us—but recognizes that the coherence theory is in its own way just as fatally divorced from real epistemology. Human knowledge, knowledge as it is for us, is always about an 'other', something independent of the individual knowing subject, to which truth in the end *for us* is always a matter of correspondence.[28] But this lesser truth also stubbornly fails to find any neat incorporation in the whole. If how and why 'this self-diremption of the one significant whole,'[29] this apparent gap between knower and known, opens up in the first place remains mysterious, the further explanation of how it may be overcome is equally beyond us, Joachim admits.

The coherence theory, Joachim concludes, 'may thus be said to suffer shipwreck at the very entrance to the harbour.'[30] But if not wholly true, he continues, this fact in itself, though unsettling, does not prevent it from being truer than rival theories—perhaps as true as any theory can be—nor does it undermine the arguments adduced in its support.

12.1.2 Russell and Moore

Capturing the attention of both critics and supporters of the theory, Joachim's book sparked off, and became the central focus of, considerable debate. Since it put forward detailed criticisms of them, it is not surprising that both Russell and Moore undertook to refute Joachim's account. Russell wrote two reviews, but his fullest response was in an Aristotelian Society paper entitled 'On the Nature of Truth'.[31] Re-iterating his own allegiance to the alternative correspondence theory, he made a number of celebrated objections. To start with, in criticism of the notion that there might exist degrees of truth, he raises a worry, which Joachim himself had raised, that 'if no partial truth is quite true, it cannot be quite true that no partial truth is quite true', for the statement itself claims only to be one small part and not the whole of truth.[32] Russell is suggesting that there is something absurd in this, something self-undermining, but that is not so. An induction from the history of science tell us that our current scientific beliefs will eventually be abandoned for better theories, but there is nothing absurd in believing them until that happens. More specifically, as Bradley had already pointed out in *Appearance and Reality* several years before, it is perfectly rational to believe a half-truth so long as we think it the best we can have; so long as we think it truer than its denial and than any possible rival.[33]

A second, more substantial, complaint Russell raises was that for all we know there might exist more than one maximally coherent system. This has become known as the

---

[28] *Nature of Truth*, 174–5.   [29] *Nature of Truth*, 172.   [30] *Nature of Truth*, 171.
[31] A shortened and rewritten version appeared in his *Philosophical Essays*.
[32] *Philosophical Essays*, 133.
[33] See above Chapter 8.3.11.

'Bishop Stubbs objection'[34] for as Russell puts it, what is there to stop us constructing a whole world of propositions radiating outwards from the false statement that 'Bishop Stubbs was hanged for murder'?[35] There is, he worries, 'no evidence that a system of false propositions might not, as in a good novel, be just as coherent as the system which is the whole truth'.[36] Our intuition tells us that there is one and only one truth, but it seems that there could exist many different coherent systems all contrary to each other.

Joachim would reply, as Russell notes, that we must appeal to *experience*, that we are not creating or choosing systems *in vacuo*, but rather we start from our given experiences which we then try to make as coherent as possible. Broadening out from this point of departure until everything has been incorporated into it, we must end with one completely coherent experience.[37] To this, however, Russell objects that, taking 'experience' in a loose sense, as well as 'true' experiences, we all have many 'false' or 'imaginary' ones, such as the picture of Bishop Stubbs hanged that comes to mind on reading the offending sentence, and by what right may these be excluded from any opening set? To be sure, we give no credence to them, even at the start, but if we are to restrict ourselves to experiences we *believe* as opposed to those we disbelieve, that seems to be appealing to some new further sense of truth.[38] But Russell here is resting on a distinction between experience and belief that the idealists would not admit. There must be some starting point, but since all experience involves judgement, it is absurd to insist that we begin from mere experience unmarked by belief—there is no such state. We start from the world as it seems to us, a world in which Stubbs dying in his bed already fits far more readily than Stubbs dying on the gallows, and from this point it is hardly surprising that as our belief system expands it does so in a net of coherence around the former rather than the latter idea.

In the second part of his essay Russell argues against what he takes to be the fundamental error at the root of the whole theory, the principle he terms *the axiom of internal relations*.[39] He locates it as the source both of the view that the sum of truths is a 'significant whole' and of the position that nothing is quite true except the whole.[40] This axiom Russell then just assimilates to Bradley's general position on relations. We have already considered his objections to that standpoint in Chapter 4, but the point is worth noting here, for Russell's fusing of the theory of truth and the theory of relations, as well as his fusing of Joachim and Bradley, were influential and set opinions on these matters for many years to come.

Moore[41] in his reply focuses on Joachim's criticism of his and Russell's theory of mind-independent propositions, locating three claims on which they differ: first, that there exist truths and facts never experienced, second, that some truths and facts we do

---

[34] Walker, *The Coherence Theory of Truth*, 3–4, 143–4.
[35] William Stubbs (1825–1901) was the eminently respectable and recently deceased Bishop of Oxford.
[36] *Philosophical Essays*, 136.   [37] *Nature of Truth*, 78.
[38] *Philosophical Essays*, 137–8.   [39] *Philosophical Essays*, 139.
[40] *Philosophical Essays*, 140.   [41] 'Mr Joachim's Nature of Truth', 231.

experience exist unexperienced at other times and third, that different people may grasp the same fact. He thinks all three true (although he is prepared to *defend* only the third) and urges that Joachim has done nothing to *refute* any of them, for his 'case' that facts cannot be separated from the experience of them is no more than an application of the thesis that all relations are internal, but this he has simply *asserted*. Nothing has been offered, Moore counters, to refute his and Russell's thesis is that some relations (specifically the knowledge relation) are purely external.[42]

Agreeing that they do indeed differ on these points, in reply, Joachim attempts again to refute the notion of external relations on which his rejection of these positions rests. 'What the theory requires seems to me as contradictory as an "evil virtue" or a "round square"' he says, 'for if the relation really unites . . . the *relata* thus united are *eo ipso* not absolutely independent Simples, but interdependent features of a whole'.[43] In the end, he maintains, 'every difference in the universe is vital to every other and to the unity of the whole'.[44]

12.1.3 Bradley and Bosanquet

Quickly Bradley himself was drawn into this debate. In 1909 he published an article in *Mind*, 'On Truth and Coherence', rebutting recent criticisms of Joachim, like those of Russell's 1906 Aristotelian Society paper discussed above, which had in passing taken sideswipes at him. As early as his *Logic* Bradley had urged that the 'idea of system is the goal of our thoughts',[45] and now (whilst insisting that it is not coherence alone, but coherence and comprehensiveness that do the work)[46] he once again defends the view that, 'Perfect truth . . . must realize the idea of a systematic whole'.[47] Reality is a harmonious system and so the more our thinking exhibits that character the truer it will be; even if, paradoxically, the same fact prevents it from ever becoming completely true, since the abstract nature of thought bars it in the end from entry into that ultimate coherent system which is the Real. So long as it remains thought it must strive to represent the world as coherently as possible, even if the pursuit of coherence—which is but the reverse of the flight from all abstraction—in the end must lead it to renounce representation altogether.

Russell had complained that, linking judgements to other judgements rather than to facts, the coherence theory divorces belief from reality. It can only have astounded Bradley to find himself accused of such an error, for no one could have insisted more strongly that all knowledge is grounded in experience. But this point must be understood correctly, for he also insists at the same time that all experience is subject to interpretation. 'No given fact is sacrosanct,' he argues, 'With every fact of perception or memory a modified interpretation is in principle possible, and no such fact therefore

---

[42] 'Mr Joachim's Nature of Truth', 234.   [43] 'A Reply to Mr Moore', 412.
[44] 'A Reply to Mr Moore', 414.   [45] *Principles of Logic*, 487.
[46] *Essays on Truth and Reality*, 202–3; *Essays on Truth and Reality*, 223.
[47] *Essays on Truth and Reality*, 223; see also *Essays on Truth and Reality*, 202.

is given free from all possibility of error.'[48] He is here repeating an old objection against correspondence, which needs such facts with which to set up its correlations. To be sure, there are truths with which I begin and which I never have to discard, truths without which I would scarcely know how to order my world, but, 'it is quite another thing to maintain that every single one of these judgements is in principle infallible. The absolute indispensable fact is in my view the mere creature of false theory.'[49] As Quine in the twentieth century famously argued, any belief whatsoever may be rejected if one is prepared to make radical enough compensating adjustments to the rest of one's belief-set.

In the same paper Bradley considers also Russell's Bishop Stubbs objection. He responds that the objection fails properly to appreciate the comprehensiveness condition.[50] Side-by-side the actual world and the imaginary Bishop Stubbs world seem a match for each other, but if we are to take a genuinely comprehensive view, we must include all of our manifold imaginations, not just one selected example. That done says Bradley, all the imaginings cancel each other out, but no opposite experience appears to cancel out our actual experience, and for this reason what he calls 'our real world' must win out any day.

Bosanquet also was responding to the general ambient debate, when in 1911 he defended the coherence theory in the second edition of his *Logic*. 'Our doctrine of truth is . . . wholly immanent. There is no external standard,'[51] he argues; meaning that ideas are judged true, not by appeal to something outside them, but by their own interrelations. It is this difference, he urges, that makes the fundamental contrast between coherence and correspondence theories. Put otherwise, the theory holds that truth is individual, that the principle of non-contradiction holds, that the truth is the whole, that coherence is the test of truth and reality, or that truth is its own criterion, suggests Bosanquet, offering these five statements as all saying the same basic thing.[52] The set of equivalences may look doubtful, but takes on a more reasonable aspect as we remember that Bosanquet (like Bradley) understands the prohibition of contradiction as grounded in a positive principle of harmony or individuality, understood as including within it, comprehensiveness;[53] the drive which seeks to connect ideas together and which, since it can stop nowhere short of the whole body of our experience, recognizes no authority outside of itself.

But if judgements are only ever compared against other judgements, what can be left of his earlier claim[54] that judgement refers to a reality beyond the act itself? We can allow that reality is independent of judgement in two senses, Bosanquet replies. First, since reality is not just my reality, the experience with which my judgements are compared is not simply my own. We must hold that there exists an experience which is higher than ours, an ultimate reality, with which my ideas must cohere. But if we allow

---

[48] *Essays on Truth and Reality*, 204.   [49] *Essays on Truth and Reality*, 211.
[50] *Essays on Truth and Reality*, 214.   [51] *Logic*, II:265.
[52] *Logic*, II:266–7.   [53] *Logic*, II:267.   [54] See Chapter 8.3.2.

talk of two elements here, we must remember that they are not independent of each other in the sense of original and copy. Rather, in its own small way, ours contributes to, or is an element in, the other; even if that other stretches vastly beyond anything it incorporates. Our primary point of contact with this wider whole is through immediate experience or feeling, and this gives a second sense in which we may say reality is independent of judgement. For our immediate experience has about it an individuality, a unity of existence and quality, which reflective judgement can never match, however much our intellectual world seeks to reproduce it.[55] (Clearly Bosanquet is much influenced by Bradley here.) Although in a broad sense we never pass outside experience, in a narrower sense abstract cognition aligning itself with more concrete experience feels as though it is facing an element relatively independent of it.

Bosanquet agrees that the root of Russell and Moore's realist substitution of correspondence for coherence lies in their rejection of internal relations, for it is this that allows their propositions to face the facts one by one rather than seek truth as a coherent whole.[56] Since the notion of 'internal' relations suggests some sort of complexity of parts within their terms, Bosanquet prefers the term 'relevant relations', defining them as ones 'which are connected with the properties of their terms, so that any alteration of relations involves an alteration of properties, and vice versa.'[57] This is not, however, the thesis that relations are to be reduced to adjectives or qualities, for they may be as substantive as their own terms.[58] In defence of such relations, Bosanquet argues that connections and associations always hold in a context or framework of some sort; for example distance relations hold only of things in space, while moral relations presuppose some moral community. Terms are not wholly external but share a common property on which their relation depends, the relation expressing their relative positions within such a complex or system. Moreover—and 'this is really the all-important argument,' he says[59]—such positionality itself determines their behaviour and character. If relations made no difference to their terms, that would be to say things behave without reference to the complex in which they belong.

Finally Bosanquet argues that the doctrine of truth as coherence does not fail in quite the way Joachim argues in the second of his two objections.[60] If, as we have allowed, there is a sense in which thought is said to be 'about' some 'other', larger than itself, it must be allowed too that it makes no attempt to capture this greater whole within its own limited resources.[61] It is not a mouse trying to eat an elephant. The 'failure' of coherence theory is not a failure to represent or correspond to some higher reality; it lies simply in the fact that thought or judgement is not reality itself, but just an *appearance* of reality.[62] The ultimate, complete or perfect coherence that Joachim seems to demand is neither intelligible, nor essential to finished truth. 'The perfection of truth is not within its own character, but must lie in a reality different in kind.'[63]

---

[55] *Logic*, II:264–5.   [56] *Logic*, II:277.   [57] *Logic*, II:277.
[58] *Logic*, II:279.   [59] *Logic*, II:278.   [60] See above p.443–4.
[61] *Logic*, II:289.   [62] *Logic*, II:290.   [63] *Logic*, II:290.

Complete coherence is not an intelligible expression. 'Coherence is the substitute, possible only in a system of predicates and relations, for the immediate unity, transcending mediateness, which we are compelled to ascribe to a perfect reality.'[64] Joachim complained that the coherence theory of truth could never, *by its own admission*, rise above correspondence. But Bosanquet responds that there is no return to correspondence here, for once we understand that no experience short of the Absolute is altogether itself, we see and accept that not even the highest truth could be quite true. The fullest completeness of truth lies in 'a more perfect form of experience, which is beyond itself,' and which 'is not truth in the form of truth'.[65] Unusually perhaps for him, the general character of Bosanquet's response here is to appeal to a reality beyond discursive thought, not so far from the doctrine Bradley termed 'thought's suicide'. But as Ralph Walker notes,[66] Joachim rejects this idea, demonstrating to us once again how mistaken Russell was to take him to be speaking for Bradley, or even Bosanquet.

12.2 The debate with pragmatism

In the early years of the twentieth century there arose a new theory of truth, which came to be known as 'pragmatism'. An anti-realist theory which held that truth could be understood only in terms of what it meant for experience or practice, in America this was most closely associated with C.S. Peirce, William James, and John Dewey (although only the latter two were much recognized in Britain), while in Britain the movement found its own exponent in the figure of F.C.S. Schiller. His position, which he referred to at various times as humanism, voluntarism, and personalism, as well as pragmatism, defined itself, almost as much as by its debt to James, in terms of its opposition to Absolute Idealism; Bradley, in particular, standing as the target for many of his numerous articles. Personal Idealism, by contrast, with its distrust of metaphysical abstractions and its emphasis on volition, was regarded as more of an ally. Indeed, Schiller contributed an article to the 1902 Henry Sturt volume, *Personal Idealism*.

A loose doctrine held in different forms by different figures, pragmatism is much harder to capture than its various caricatures (truth is utility, truth is cash-value) imply. It was also only gradually that it made itself felt on the philosophical scene. In 1906 Joachim was still content to ignore the theory—'It is not easy to discern the meaning of its advocates through the noise of their advocacy,' he complained[67]—but increasingly this ceased to be possible.[68] Bradley, in particular, was drawn into the debate. In part this was because there were several respects in which what he had been arguing stood

---

[64] *Logic*, II:290n.   [65] *Logic*, II:291.   [66] Walker, 'Joachim on the Nature of Truth', 185.
[67] *Nature of Truth*, 3.
[68] Key publications here include: Dewey, *Studies in Logical Theory*, 1903; Schiller, *Humanism*, 1903; James, *Pragmatism*, 1907; James, *The Meaning of Truth*, 1909; Dewey, 'Reality and the Criterion for the Truth of Ideas', *Mind*, 16:63, 1907, 317–42; Schiller, *Studies in Humanism*, 1907; Schiller, *Plato or Protagoras?*, 1908.

not so far from the position pragmatists themselves were developing. A fellow critic of correspondence, he was able to agree with their insistence that truth be not separated utterly from our procedures for determining it. 'Truth indeed must not become transcendent,' he admits.[69] Rather, he suggests (echoing Peirce), truth is what satisfies the intellect. In truth, the intellect finds a rest and contentment that is its own proper end or good. That which contradicts either experience or other beliefs, or which falls short in meaning or explanation, on the other hand, produces in the intellect a sense of uneasiness or dissatisfaction, in which state it cannot remain. Such ideas leave us with a 'certain felt need'[70] that must be met, and so we search for a state in which the intellect can rest contented.[71] Full intellectual satisfaction is impossible, as we have seen, and so Bradley admits that in the real world our acceptance criteria are ultimately pragmatic, a matter of saving phenomena or serving our purposes. We have already explored in a previous chapter how this works for science, and in particular for psychology.[72]

In these ways it might be easy to mistake Bradley for a pragmatist. But despite calls from figures such as Schiller and William James to join their camp, he never felt able to call himself a pragmatist. Part of his problem was that of finding a single clear doctrine to sign up to. Their views represent something more like a collection of tendencies, he complains, than a single doctrine.[73] What we must make of the theory depends, of course, on what we understand by the term 'practice'. But this is left hopelessly vague. Understood in some very narrow way by reference to one artificially isolated part of life, our material needs and projects, it seems obviously incorrect; for surely a thing could be useful, but false. Construed more generously, to take in our culture and our general interest in the world around us, it is more plausible, but it ceases to claim anything distinctive. *Of course*, truth is related to life. How could it not be? Thus Bradley worries that in its more personal or individual forms pragmatism will simply give up on objectivity and slide into relativism. There is a world of difference between holding that truth is what works *for me now* and holding that truth is what works *for us all on the whole*. His objection to James at least is reduced in so far as James commits himself to something more like the latter.[74] But satisfaction for us all on the whole includes acceptability to the intellectual side of our nature, reducing the difference between the theory and its more traditional rivals.

For all their criticism of it, Bradley accuses the pragmatists of having made the same mistake the correspondence theorists do. As the realist thinks he has the ability to put his hand on 'perceived reality' and proposes to declare whatever matches it 'true', so the pragmatist claims to know what it would be for some idea to 'work' or 'serve' and offers to call 'true' whatever does so. Although both claim to be defining truth, they understand it as that which subserves something else, the known or working world, something grasped more securely than the ideal realm that gets designated 'true' or

---

[69]   *Essays on Truth and Reality*, 128.   [70]   *Essays on Truth and Reality*, 311.
[71]   *Appearance and Reality*, 509; *Essays on Truth and Reality*, 1, 2, 242.   [72]   See above pp.116–18.
[73]   *Essays on Truth and Reality*, 73.   [74]   *Essays on Truth and Reality*, 71, 129.

'false' in relation to it. A wedge is forced between thought and knowledge, between experience and reality, as truth becomes some kind of extra property which thoughts may or may not have, when in actual fact reality is found within thought itself.[75]

In the end for all his agreement Bradley stands at great remove from pragmatism. True ideas work, he admits. But they are not true because they work; rather they work because they are true.[76] For however unattainable it may be to us, Bradley believes in absolute truth. Even if not one which we can properly enter, there remains a 'supreme court' of metaphysics in which our judgements are assessed for absolute truth, such that however widespread or inevitable it may be, the use of the pragmatic is always a kind of 'second best'. Knowledge aims to reproduce or recreate the way things really are, and practical reasoning for all its inevitability remains something different from inquiry into the state of ultimate reality. Their orientations are quite different. For Bradley first principles or metaphysics is central to everything, but the pragmatists want to dislodge its centrality.[77] The apparent closeness of Bradley and pragmatism is to an extent coincidental—Bradley seems to agree with them that truth satisfies the intellect, but this is down to the fundamental nature of *reality* (of which we are, of course, a continuous part) not the fundamental nature of *truth*; it is a practical criterion of truth not its defining essence.[78]

Bosanquet is similarly two-sided in his attitude towards pragmatism. In a section added to the second edition of his *Logic*, he suggests that 'the treatment of thought as a system...of adaptations evolved in response to the needs of practice, has in principle adopted and popularised the coherence theory of truth'.[79] Opposing any goal which hopes to relate the mental to some non-mental realm, it rightly seeks to bring different elements of experienced life into line with one another. However, by 'restricting the coherence which is to be the standard to the coherence of adaptation with external action', [80] it breaks apart experience and unduly narrows its application, for it is the *whole* of experience we must develop, not just our experience of action. 'Thought is essentially the nisus of experience as a world to completion of its world.'[81] For the pragmatist, our thinking is always born out of a special need or purpose, which creates our problem and sets the standard of its success. Bosanquet does not deny that we all have specific motives, but 'in knowledge the true and widest-reaching motive,' he argues, (following Russell) is 'scientific curiosity. It is the impulse of the mind to know, by which all private motives and unique tensions are superseded.'[82]

---

[75] *Essays on Truth and Reality*, 110–11.
[76] *Essays on Truth and Reality*, 76.
[77] Pragmatism, in James' words, is *'the attitude of looking away from first things, principles, "categories," supposed necessities; and of looking toward last things, fruits, consequences, facts'* (*Pragmatism*, 54–5).
[78] Candlish 'Scepticism, Ideal Experiment, and Priorities', §II.
[79] *Logic*, II:269.
[80] *Logic*, II:269.
[81] *Logic*, II:272.
[82] 'The Relation of Coherence', 267.

Moving forward some years to Mackenzie's 1928 work, *Fundamental Problems of Life*, we find a similar welcome for pragmatism—extended now to correspondence also—as a valuable step on the way towards the coherence theory. Serving practical needs or matching experienced reality are just *parts* of what it is to be true. 'I am disposed to regard all the three leading theories of Truth as having a place in the actual quest for Truth,' he says, 'But the coherence theory is the most comprehensive of the three, and may be said to include the other two.'[83] Once again, former enemies become allies. But if, in the end, as an Absolute Idealist, Mackenzie's preferred theory is coherence, times have changed for he now admits that this theory can be *tested* only by the gradual application other two theories—that is only in so far as ideas are found to work and to correspond.

Bradley, Bosanquet, and Mackenzie all advanced versions of the coherence theory, but not all idealist opponents to pragmatism were of the same stamp. McTaggart, for example, was of the view that truth consists in a relation of correspondence to fact. The only thing that makes it true that 'This table is square' is the fact that it *is* square.[84] Completeness, system, satisfaction, and practical success may all be characteristics of true belief, but they do not make for truth. In his review of James' *Pragmatism,* McTaggart, like Bradley, is worried by the lack of precision,[85] but more substantively he complains that surely not all true beliefs work or bring success (what if the shock of recognizing that it is my friend and not some stranger who is being eaten by a lion causes me to misfire my gun and shoot him rather than the lion?) and that the truth is not always and simply a form of the good, something we *ought* to believe. (We are content to say things like, 'Smith is a fool, but happily his wife thinks him a wise man' or, 'That boy is exceptionally clever, and unfortunately he knows it.')[86] Rejecting the idea of any sort of truth that floats apart from the knowing of it, since all our knowing is in time, James concludes that reality is essentially temporal—still in the making—in contrast to the Absolutist or rationalist view of it as complete and timeless.[87] But McTaggart complains that this to confuse views about truth and views about reality. Allowing that knowledge takes place in time, it is possible (as Moore and Russell do) to embrace timeless truth because one rejects the connection between knowledge and reality; but it is equally possible, suggests McTaggart, to see the timelessness of reality in independent metaphysical terms, and embrace it at the same time as maintaining the essential connection of knowledge and the known.[88]

---

[83] *Fundamental Problems*, 31.

[84] *Nature of Existence*, §§9–10.

[85] McTaggart's review of *Pragmatism*, 105. For instance, does the truth of 'I have a bad headache' lie in the difference it makes to my action, which might perhaps be none, or in the sensations I experience, which is presumably considerable?

[86] McTaggart's review of *Pragmatism*, 107, 108.

[87] *Pragmatism,* 257.

[88] McTaggart's review of *Pragmatism*, 109.

12.3 Bosanquet *Implication and Linear Inference*

The topic of much of his earliest work, although he went on to embrace other concerns, logic was a discipline Bosanquet never really left behind. We have already noted the substantial additions made for the second edition of his *Logic*, which came out in 1911, and some nine years later in *Implication and Linear Inference* he returned to the subject again. While not inaugurating any radical new departures, the book much clarifies his underlying ideas as well as demonstrating the continued life of 'idealist logic'.

Still understanding by 'inference' any operation at all through which knowledge extends itself,[89] he begins by setting out his own preferred understanding of the process, which he terms 'systematic'.[90] Eschewing traditional argument-forms, with this conception the stress is on coherence, as we 'build up' judgements into a 'system' connected seamlessly to the rest of our knowledge and then 'read off' its implications, or to put it slightly differently, as we attempt to transfer to specified particulars the certainty that attaches to the whole, in a sort of 'this or nothing at all' move. Says Bosanquet, 'implication rightly judged is guaranteed by the whole system of reality. If you deny it, you leave nothing standing'.[91] Resistance is possible, up to a point, but while we can just about imagine an entire physical theory coming to shipwreck on a single failed prediction, no implication could ever be so unwelcome as to overturn *everything* we believe about reality.

This understanding he contrasts with what he calls the 'linear' conception of inference to be found in many ordinary textbooks. This fallacious way of regarding matters is typical both of those who advocate models of deduction based on syllogism and of those who advocate models of induction based on simple enumeration. According to this 'bead-theory' of inference,[92] we reason by moving along chains of ideas whose relations to one another remain always formal and external. Its fundamental mistake is to treat terms as mutually independent, unable to modify each other's content or come together in any more systematic whole. That is, it admits the basic facts of conjunction or exclusion of predicates within individual subjects, but without investigation into the explanations or necessary connections behind this. 'In such arguments you get, technically recognised, no bearing of the import of one term upon another at all. They are, so to speak, in capsules, and all you can do with them is to note which lie in the same drawer, and which refuse to do so.'[93] As reagents in chemical synthesis may combine to produce new products, thoughts together create wholes which are more than mere aggregates, but in linear inference different premises—and conclusions too—are all kept separate, unable to modify or shed further light on each other.

---

[89] *Implication*, 2.   [90] *Implication*, 24.   [91] *Implication*, 11.
[92] To use an expression from Costello's review of *Implication*, 403.   [93] *Implication*, 26.

An interesting corollary of Bosanquet's alternative approach is the way in which he deals with necessary or a priori inferences. If all inference proceeds on the same logical basis, namely system, rather than sharply bracketing these off in some distinct 'formal' domain, we must recognize instead that their difference is one of degree only. Propositions or inferences we think of as a priori are merely those in which the extreme simplicity and abstractness of the relations perceived render it particularly easy to 'read off' the results. 'The a priori is merely what comes clear and connected out of the mass of the a posteriori.'[94] Bosanquet criticizes in particular the formality and symbolism of recent logic for the delusive appearance of isolated self-evidence or necessity which it helps to create,[95] but his point is not that necessity should be given up. He wishes only to abolish delusory short-cuts to it, urging instead that, reunited with their content, mere formalities should take up their place alongside the rest of our knowledge. For the task of knowledge remains the task of connecting together each thing known and, following that project through, argues Bosanquet, what to present understanding seems contingent will, in a deepest and widest understanding, be seen in the end as a genuinely essential element in the whole system.

Notable also is Bosanquet's discussion in his penultimate chapter of the relationship between logic and psychology. The extreme psychologism of the classical British empiricists and of such figures as Mill and Spencer has now, he notes, been widely rejected,[96] and he restates the principal objections to it. According to that view the laws of logic are simply psychological phenomena (laws of thought) which must therefore be determined empirically[97] and, worse, there is no guarantee that any such laws of thought conform to the actual laws of reality itself, for this approach would 'cut the connection between the laws of logic and the real world.'[98] But, taken to its extreme, opposition to any psychologism of this type leads us to 'pure logic' which takes as its subject matter meanings only, propositions without any reference at all to psychical life.[99] Neither route attracts; indeed Bosanquet finds a disquieting affinity between an extreme 'logicism' such as this and the extreme 'psychologism' it sets out by rejecting. Both sever the real from the ideal, holding 'that functions of actual thinking are not necessarily to be considered as expressions of the truth of things'.[100] Ideas, psychologism says, may be psychologically necessary without being true of reality. Truth, pure logic says, may be logically necessary, regardless of the habits of human thinking.[101] Bosanquet's alternative suggestion tries to find a middle path. 'Truth' he suggests 'is reality as it makes itself known through particular minds in the form of ideas.'[102] Thought unfolds according to its own proper nature, but the principles at work behind

---

[94] *Implication*, 127.   [95] *Implication*, 159.
[96] *Implication*, 141–2. He cites Husserl's, *Logical Investigations* (see Volume I, chs 3–8) although, noting a similarly anti-psychologistic passage from Bradley, he points out that Husserl's criticisms of British philosophy were written without knowledge of how contemporary British Idealist thinking had already taken issue with the psychologism of such figures as Mill and Spencer.
[97] *Implication*, 143.   [98] *Implication*, 144.   [99] *Implication*, 144.
[100] *Implication*, 147.   [101] *Implication*, 148.   [102] *Implication*, 150.

thought are the same as those at work behind reality itself. Here again we may draw illuminating connection with Bradley. Though striking out against psychologism, in the end, Bradley was not quite so anti-psychologistic as he first seems, and a similar thing must be said of Bosanquet. Logic deals with universals, but a complete logic cannot wholly ignore psychology. 'This is not to base logic upon psychology in the sense of accepting mental facts and habits as the evidence for real laws; it might rather be described as exploring the psychological field in search of the complete and continuous developments in which the thinking function proper reveals its nisus and ideal—the spirit of truth.'[103]

12.4 Bradley's *Logic* revisited

We have already discussed Bradley's *Principles of Logic*[104] which was first published in 1883. However, Bradley's opinions did not remain unchanged, any more than did Bosanquet's, and there occurred many developments which found their way into subsequent books and articles. Of particular significance in this regard was Bernard Bosanquet's book *Knowledge and Reality*, a detailed criticism of the *Principles*, published just two years after its first appearance. In the end, but not until 1922, there appeared a second edition of the *Principles* incorporating Bradley's various changes of mind. This second edition leaves the basic text unchanged, but has a great many footnotes and twelve terminal essays, vastly expanding the whole. Many of the changes are minor, but many are substantial, for by that time, and in no small part as the result of Bosanquet's criticisms,[105] Bradley had come to feel that there were numerous places in the first edition where he had gone badly wrong. Some of the most important of these second edition changes can be noted here.

12.4.1 Floating ideas

No doubt the most significant change concerned 'floating ideas'. To say (as Bradley had in the first edition) that the mind abstracts from what is given it in perception some universal content which it then applies to reality makes it seem as though there were two tasks which we must carry out in order to judge, as though the mind's coming to have ideas and its subsequent use of them were distinct and separable functions. In the first edition of the *Principles* Bradley certainly talked in this way as though one and the same content could be affirmed, hoped, questioned, etc., even that an idea might be 'held before the mind without any judgment'.[106] 'Affirmation, or judgment, consists in saying, This idea is no mere idea, but is a quality of the real,' he said then, 'The act attaches the floating adjective to the nature of the world, and, at the same time, tells me it was there already.'[107] But soon after the book appeared[108] he changed his position

---

[103] *Implication*, 161.   [104] see Chapter 8.3.   [105] *Principles of Logic*, viii.
[106] *Principles of Logic*, 76–7.   [107] *Principles of Logic*, 11.
[108] The change is clear by the time of *Appearance and Reality*, ten years later, but seems to have occurred even earlier.

and argued that abstraction and reference were indistinguishable aspects of a single process, and that nowhere can we find any such 'floating ideas'.

> Now a thought only 'in my head', or a bare idea separated from all relation to the real world, is a false abstraction. For we have seen that to hold a thought is, more or less vaguely, to refer it to Reality. And hence an idea, wholly un-referred, would be a self-contradiction.[109]

> There is no and there can not be any such thing as a *mere* idea, an idea outside any judgment and standing or floating by itself. We have here again not an actual fact but an unreal abstraction. The essence of an idea consists always in the loosening of 'what' from 'that.' But, apart from some transference, some reference elsewhere of the 'what,' no such loosening is possible.[110]

Bradley's retraction here could be viewed as simply his coming to a fuller recognition of his basic thesis that ideas are signs or symbols. For as such it is their essence to refer beyond themselves; assertion is built into them from the start. To put the point in another way, ideas can only be ideas in the context of a judgement, but all judgements in their nature make a claim.

However, there is more to the point that just this. Ideas do not simply *try* to refer, thinks Bradley, they *succeed* in doing so. But an idea can only refer if there is something in the world to which it does refer, and so in a sense it must be conceded that all ideas are true. A comparison is helpful here. Frege, since he holds that a name could have sense but no reference, would allow a singular thought even where there existed no corresponding object. Bradley, in rejecting all such floating ideas, ideas un-referred to any object, holds that singular thought requires the presence of the actual object.[111] *Reality itself* enters into the judgement. The objects of our thinking are not intentional objects, but reality itself.

> A judgment, we assume naturally, says something about some fact or reality. If we asserted or denied about anything else, our judgment would seem to be a frivolous pretence. We must not only say something, but it must also be about something actual that we say it.[112]

But floating ideas were rejected not simply because they ran counter to his theory of reference and judgement. Bradley came to appreciate that, introducing a kind of dualism between pure thought and reality, they were incompatible with the kind of idealism he wished to develop. As Bradley sees it, both thought and its object originate in a single experience and however distinct they may appear to become, there remains a continuity between thought and its perceptual ground or context. Floating ideas were rejected also because they were incompatible with Bradley's coherentism. For if we may start from ideas floating free of any reference to reality, we might construct around them systems as extensive and coherent as those we currently endorse,

---

[109] *Appearance and Reality*, 350.
[110] *Principles of Logic*, 640; cf *Appearance and Reality*, 324; *Essays on Truth and Reality*, 28–64.
[111] As we saw above, for Bradley, though none is wholly so, all thought is in some measure singular or categorical.
[112] *Principles of Logic*, 41.

yet these would not thereby be true.[113] This (as we saw) was Russell's famous Bishop Stubbs objection to the coherence theory of truth. An insistence that all ideas first be anchored in or referred to reality effectively blocks this objection to coherentism.

Of course, the thought that ideas may be simply held before the mind without judging is itself plausible, so if Bradley is to reject it, he will have some explaining to do. In this regard, he adopts a two-fold strategy. In the first place he holds that surface grammar often misleads us as to the true logical form of a judgement. Although the thought must be referred to reality, 'the ideal content may be applied subject to more or less transformation; its struggling and conditional character may escape our notice, or may again be realised with more or less transformation'.[114] Bradley had already allowed that a single word—'Wolf!' 'Fire!' etc.—might really be an implicit judgement;[115] and in a similar way he suggests that, although I might take myself simply to imagine, say, a unicorn or a tree in winter, there will really always be involved some judgement or other, perhaps, that unicorns are white or that trees in winter look sad. Bare entertaining is not possible; thought is always for some purpose, which involves judgement and, with analysis, that may be uncovered.

A central role here is given to the notion of what Bradley calls 'my real world', the universe of things continuous in space with my body, and in time with the states and actions of that body.[116] This notion provides him with a tool whereby many thoughts, which seem at first to float are, on analysis found to refer implicitly to my real world. For example, a question seeks a truth which we take to be already there,[117] while something is called 'imaginary' only by exclusion from this real world.[118]

The second part of the response to the apparent possibility of floating ideas is to expand the realm of possible reference. My real world is not the only one. In addition to this narrow sphere, Bradley says, there are the worlds of duty, of religion, of hope and desire, of dreams, madness, and drunkenness, of politics or commerce, of art and imagination, 'all counting as elements in the total of reality'.[119] Reality is the sum total of all these different realities. Ideas which seem but entertained with respect to the here and now may be true of some other reality; 'Because there are many worlds, the idea which floats suspended above one of them is attached to another.'[120]

---

[113]   Holdcroft, 'Bradley and Floating Ideas', 171ff.

[114]   *Appearance and Reality*, 324.

[115]   They are to be understood as shorthands for such assertions as 'Here is a wolf' or 'There is a fire' (*Principles of Logic*, 56–7).

[116]   *Essays on Truth and Reality*, 460.

[117]   *Essays on Truth and Reality*, 36.

[118]   *Essays on Truth and Reality*, 47.

[119]   *Essays on Truth and Reality*, 31.

[120]   *Essays on Truth and Reality*, 32. Although it comes into its own here as a device to assist in his rejection of floating ideas, this (it should be noted) was not a new idea but something Bradley had already used in the first edition of the *Principles*. For considering there how best to analyse the claim that 'The wrath of the Homeric Gods is fearful' in view of his thesis that judgement must affirm something of some reality, he responds that, 'In Homer it *is* so; and surely a poem, surely any imagination, surely dreams and delusions, and surely much more our words and our names are all of them facts of a certain kind' (*Principles of Logic*, 42).

12.4.2 Restricted subject of judgement

In the early logic all judgement has as its subject reality as a whole. This distinctive position with respect to the subject of judgement was one which Bradley felt called for modification in the second edition of the *Principles*. Without denying that it is reality as a whole that is always the 'ultimate subject' of our judgements, Bradley came to feel that this common referent is not quite the undifferentiated whole it first seems. Rather judgements have also what he variously calls a 'special' or 'limited' or 'selected' subject—the point at which reality as a whole presents itself to us in perception, the point at which we feel ourselves called upon to qualify it as we do.[121]

12.4.3 Negation

Bradley's account of negative judgement was one of the aspects of his logic that came under the most sustained attack by Bernard Bosanquet, in Chapter V of his *Logic and Knowledge*, and later on for the second edition of the *Principles*, Bradley modified his views accepting many of Bosanquet's criticisms.[122]

In general, it can be said that the doctrine of floating ideas was an unfortunate intrusion into the system, whose removal improved consistency. But it did necessitate one or two changes elsewhere in the system, for example, in his view of negation; for in the first edition Bradley describes negation as something 'subjective', in so far as what is rejected is merely a 'suggestion'. He says that 'the process takes place in the unsubstantial region of ideal experiment. And the steps of that experiment are not even asserted to exist in the world outside our heads.'[123] However, if there are no floating ideas, ideas can not be simply 'suggested' or 'entertained', all we can do with them is to affirm them. Negation is, perhaps, more 'reflective', in the sense that we tend to make assertions before we make denials, but such prior awareness is (Bradley acknowledges) irrelevant to the logical point at issue.[124] Instead he seeks to solve the problem by appeal to the distinction which his further reflections on judgement in general had already encouraged him to draw between reality in general and the 'special subject' of a judgement. He suggests that negation does involve a rejection or denial, but 'the content which it denies is never excluded absolutely. Far from falling nowhere, that content qualifies elsewhere the Universe.'[125] What he had earlier called the 'suggested synthesis' does in fact apply to some reality, and hence does not float, but nothing is actually asserted of the special subject.

Another problem with Bradley's first edition account comes out in his treatment of double negation. It is a generally accepted axiom that double negation is equivalent to

---

[121] *Principles of Logic*, 39 n.14, 629, 662. See Sprigge, *James and Bradley*, 301; Ferreira, *Bradley and the Structure of Knowledge*, 26. The change was one of those made in response to Bosanquet's criticisms (see *Knowledge and Reality*, 5ff).

[122] *Principles of Logic*, 125 n.1; Terminal Essay VI.

[123] *Principles of Logic*, 120.

[124] *Principles of Logic*, 665.

[125] *Principles of Logic*, 665.

affirmation, that, not-not-A is equivalent to A. However, it might be objected that Bradley's understanding of negation precludes him from this principle, for the contrary of a contrary need not be the original. (Think of colours: a contrary of red might be green, but a contrary of green might be yellow.)

In the first edition of the *Principles* Bradley attempts to preserve the axiom of double negation by insisting that, although we might use any positive ground, y, to deny that A is b, if we then choose to deny our denial the choice of ground is limited to b itself, since any other ground, z, might be just as exclusive of b as y, leaving us no further on.[126] However, in the second edition he withdraws this solution deferring to Bosanquet's alternative response.[127] He now suggests that introducing a special subject into the judgement in the manner just considered above in effect implies a dichotomy—a 'this' as opposed to a 'that'—and thus he urges, 'disjunction within a whole is the one way in and by which in the end negation becomes intelligible'.[128] The negation is under-laid by an exclusive disjunction (The tree is either x or yellow), such that when we implicitly assert the positive ground (The tree is x) we can then conclude our negative assertion (The tree is not yellow). Viewed in this way negation (like many other forms of judgement) is seen to involve an aspect of inference.

This seems a retraction of his earlier view that negative judgement has a wholly positive basis, for while something that is merely contrary to yellow (green) can be positive, the exclusive disjunction of yellow (not yellow) has a negativity about it. Even if we read it as itself a disjunction of positive options (blue or red or orange, etc.) the further assumption of completeness (not anything else) involves negation. Bradley's own understanding of the situation is more nuanced, however. He suggests that perhaps it is better to say that all judgements are both positive and negative at the same time; that there is no sharp line between positive and negative. 'Negation everywhere has a ground, not on one side merely but on both sides.'[129]

12.4.4 *Collective judgement*

By the time of the second edition, Bradley had become unhappy with his account of collective judgement and withdrew it, deferring again to Bosanquet.[130] The problem he says is 'that all counting presupposes and depends on a qualitative Whole, and that Collective Judgment asserts a generic connection within its group. Hence no mere particulars can be counted.'[131] For example, we never count just people, books, or cars, but rather people *in the boat*, books *in the pile*, or cars *in the queue*, but in doing so we make them all instances of a type or kind. However, since universal judgements also

---

[126] *Principles of Logic*, 159.

[127] *Principles of Logic*, 167 n.25.

[128] *Principles of Logic*, 662 'Negation...implies at its base a disjunction which is real' (*Principles of Logic*, 666).

[129] *Principles of Logic*, 664.

[130] *Principles of Logic*, 110 n.37, 368 n.2 referring to Bosanquet *Knowledge and Reality*, 76ff and *Logic*, I:152ff, 209ff.

[131] *Principles of Logic*, 368 n.2.

pick out members of a type or kind (e.g. all members of the type: animal) this is to remove the difference he earlier insisted on between collective and universal judgement.

12.4.5 Inference

As with the theory of judgement, so it was with inference that there were certain changes of view between the first and the second editions of the *Principles*. As well as the numerous footnote comments, Bradley wrote a complete new essay on inference for the revised edition. Here a new way of describing inference (which had occurred in the first edition[132] but in a more minor role) comes to the fore. 'Every inference,' Bradley says, 'is the ideal self-development of a given object taken as real.'[133] The term 'object' here is used in a very loose sense to cover any set of facts or conditions, expressible as premises, which the mind takes together as one object of thought. This presents itself to us in ideal form—that is to say, it comes before the mind—as something real, as one part of the actual universe. But always reality is more than it seems to be; 'what in any particular case this object is, and how its limits really are defined, cannot be taken as appearing in those forms of language which serve as its expression'.[134] Below its surface it carries with it traces of the wider whole to which it belongs and with which it is continuous. In inference, we penetrate to these deeper levels, or the object reveals its hidden depths to us. (Bradley sees no fundamental difference between these two for, driven by an inner logic which needs must lay bare the structure lying below what is explicitly presented to us, the process is one of 'discovery' rather than 'creation'.) But because the object only is what it is insofar as it is an element in a wider connected whole, in thus revealing itself, it takes us beyond our original and explicit starting point to a new insight which forms the conclusion of our inference; even if, in another sense, all the time, it has done no more than develop itself.

12.5 Joachim *Logical Studies*

Enough has been said to demonstrate that idealist thought on logic carried on long after the emergence of the new 'mathematical logic' at the turn of the century, even if that was a development that rendered it increasingly disconnected from the mainstream. However, it is not always realized for just how long that process continued, and in this connection our story returns to the figure of Joachim, with whom the chapter began. In 1919 Joachim was elected Wykeham Professor of Logic at Oxford, succeeding the realist John Cook Wilson in a reversal of fortune comparable to that ten years earlier in which J.A. Smith succeeded Thomas Case to the Waynflete Chair of metaphysics.[135] Joachim held the post until his retirement in 1935, his lectures from 1927 onwards receiving posthumous publication in 1948 under the title *Logical Studies*.

---

[132] *Principles of Logic*, 487, 489, 493–4.   [133] *Principles of Logic*, 598.
[134] *Principles of Logic*, 598.   [135] See below p.532.

The book opens with an attempt to characterize the discipline of logic itself which makes very clear just how much distance had by this time opened up between idealist and non-idealist conceptions of the subject. In so far as it disregards almost entirely those questions and ideas that were occupying other more analytically minded logicians, the species of inquiry which Joachim champions is, in the words of Stuart Hampshire, a contemporary reviewer of decidedly non-idealist stamp, 'wholly different in method and purpose from anything which either the layman or most philosophers would now call logic'.[136] The subject matter of logic, for Joachim, is 'knowledge-or-truth'.[137] This is something at once wholly concrete, in the sense that it abstracts off neither object nor subject of experience, dealing rather with 'reality-as-known', and at the same time deeply abstract, in the sense that it seeks to uncover, not specifics, but the universal structural principles of intelligibility and intelligence in one.[138] This understanding is to be contrasted with the common conception of logic as a study of the laws or forms of thinking. That errs in two ways; in suggesting that logic deals with thoughts rather than things it renders it subjective, while in suggesting that it is formal, that is, organizing but not supplying material, it separates it fatally from the rest of our cognition, from sense and from feeling.[139] Turning from subject matter to methodology, the proper technique of logic is 'critical-and-reflective analysis',[140] thinks Joachim, but this should not be understood as the decomposition or reduction of some 'complex' into relatively simpler elements, for the clarification or explanation that such a process appears to offer is in fact illusory. The problem is that only by focusing on artificial abstractions—mathematical or geometrical constructions, for example—can such aggregates ever be found, and 'within our experience no one-of-many, or no whole-of-parts, is ever a mere aggregate or sum'.[141] They have parts, to be sure, but viewed out of context these parts take on a quite different character; as surely as the vinegar that brought the meal to life but on its own tastes just sour. If we stick to the genuine wholes we meet with in actual experience, argues Joachim, the only way to explain them is, retaining their unity, to deal with their parts *in situ*, as it were, never losing sight of their position in the structural unity or plan of the whole, their connection with all the other parts. Such an approach Joachim designates as *simultaneously* analytic and synthetic.[142]

What drives the rejected conception of analysis is not simply a belief that elements are unaffected by combination or dissolution, but a belief that elements are clearer, more certain, or more intelligible, than complexes. It is to this belief Joachim turns in the second section of the book as he argues against all theories of knowledge which make a firm distinction between intuitive or immediate cognition and discursive or inferential cognition. There can never be, he insists, anything more than a relative distinction between knowledge that supports and knowledge that is supported by other

---

[136] Hampshire, Review of *Logical Studies*, 168.   [137] *Logical Studies*, 20.
[138] *Logical Studies*, 13–15.   [139] *Logical Studies*, 18.
[140] *Logical Studies*, 27.   [141] *Logical Studies*, 33.   [142] *Logical Studies*, 38.

knowledge. He proceeds by attempting to establish the impossibility of ever finding any *datum* upon which such a distinction might rest. Looking to perception and feeling, the case he outlines is familiar enough, but with respect to supposed a priori truths matters are, of course, harder and he adopts a variety of strategies. Taking a truth like Descartes' *cogito*, for example, he argues that nothing can be pulled out of the Cartesian insight substantive enough to support anything else—I may exist, alright, but *what* exists or for *how long* I have no idea at all.[143] By contrast, geometrical truths, such as 'the angles at the base of an isosceles triangle are equal to each other', have more content, he allows, but he nonetheless urges that their self-evidence depends upon the geometrical system of which they are part, robbing them of their apparent isolation and simplicity.[144] We might dispute that this kind of dependence obtains in *all* cases. Surely, we might object, there hold instances of pure analyticity that stand quite on their own without the support of surrounding beliefs—'the thing that is A and B is A' to take a possible example—but Joachim would deny that such abstract claims are ever made outside logic textbooks. They have no possible application to actual experience, in other words, no place in knowledge.

With the dismissal of any firm datum for knowledge, the book's final section returns to the topic of Joachim's earlier work, the coherence theory of truth. Rejecting both what he calls the subjectivist position, which regards truth as a property of psychological 'ideas' or complexes thereof, and what he terms the objectivist position, which regards it as a property of abstract 'propositions', he asserts the idealist conception of truth as 'a synthesis of fact with idea' or 'the ideal expansion of a fact'.[145] On this mode truth and falsity can figure only in concrete experience or judgement, but this is never the private experience of any one individual. What marks out the idealist conception most clearly from the other two is its rejection of their common assumption that truth and falsity are incompatible predicates. To the Idealist every judgement is both true and false—neither absolutely, but both in some degree or other.[146] A judgement is true because it contributes to a wider infinite whole of knowledge, but as much as it could never be that whole all by itself neither could it ever exist entirely separate from it. A complete falsehood, something that overlapped at no point with knowledge, that drew not in the slightest on anything whatsoever that we think or believe about reality, would not be a judgement at all. Although continuing to hold that the existence of error remains an insoluble puzzle on the idealist scheme, Joachim's attitude softens somewhat in this later work as he suggests the problem may simply be assimilated to the more general mystery of the two-fold nature of truth—eternal yet appearing in time, infinite but finding expression in finite judgement—something that it is coherent to accept, even without being able to offer any further 'how' or 'why'.[147]

---

[143] *Logical Studies*, 138. [144] *Logical Studies*, 166.
[145] *Logical Studies*, 182. The rejection of propositions constitutes one of the very few points in the book where Joachim engages with contemporary non-idealist logic, in the case with Russell.
[146] *Logical Studies*, 263.
[147] *Logical Studies*, 269.

13

Developments in Idealist Ethics

Although not destined to produce any new systems of equivalent stature to those of Green, Bradley, and Caird, no more than was the case with idealist logic, did idealist ethics simply cease at the turn of the century. But here the story to be told is of a rather different character, both internally with respect to the idealist movement considered by itself, and externally with respect to the wider philosophical culture. Bosanquet's, Bradley's, and Joachim's later pronouncements on logic are of interest, but they were essentially refinements or developments. There was no great question or problem or controversy that exercised their attention. By contrast later idealist thinking on ethical matters is marked by a number of fundamental disagreements and divergences, as the apparent consensus of the latter years of the century began to come apart. Moreover, while later logical thought was, as we saw, marked by an increasing distance and isolation from the work that others in the discipline were doing, idealist ethicists were more in tune with what was being written outside their own tradition. To be sure they maintained their allegiance and in consequence their opponents often *thought* them out of touch, but they did engage with the changing landscape of ethical thought around them. Indeed, out of that process, there were even developed new systems of idealist ethics. It is with these changes that the following chapter is concerned.

13.1 Individualist versus holistic ethics

Of the various in-house differences, none were greater than that between the Personal and the Absolute Idealists, whose significance for metaphysics and religion has already been explored, but which extended into ethics as well. That it should have done so is hardly surprising, for one thing the Idealists agreed on was that ethics is grounded in metaphysics. But if so, given the metaphysical distance between these two systems, it was only to be excepted that there should open up a similar ethical gap. There was no direct debate across the divine in this domain, like those Pringle-Pattison entered into with Ritchie and with Bosanquet, but the gap may still be seen very clearly if we consider the contrasting ethical philosophies of McTaggart and Bosanquet.

13.1.1 McTaggart

Personal Idealism was never simply, or even primarily, a metaphysical doctrine. It was at root an ethical protest. In personalist eyes, the territorial claims of the Absolute threatened to lose the discrete value of the individual within that of the whole, to blur even the distinction between good and evil. Ethics, they insisted, requires real individuals with real agency.[1]

This much was common to all Personal Idealists, but in a 1908 paper entitled 'Individualism of Value' McTaggart took the argument even further, urging not simply that persons *have* value but that *all* value is personal; specifically, that nothing is ultimately good or bad except conscious beings and their conscious states.[2] His point is not the *epistemological* one that nothing can have value unless recognized by some individual as having it—the happiness of a kitten or a child may be good without they or anyone else acknowledging that it is[3]—but rather the *personalist* one that the only items in the universe which possess intrinsic value are the conscious states of individuals.

The argument he offers in support of this individualism is essentially an appeal to experience. Whatever disputes there may be about value, the only candidates for intrinsic value that get suggested with any regularity—pleasure, virtue, self-realization, knowledge—are all states of conscious beings. Of course, one might propose other things which are not; and McTaggart explicitly considers G.E. Moore's famous suggestion in *Principia Ethica* that a beautiful world of which no one ever had or will have any experience or awareness would still possess value.[4] Moore's stance has persuaded some. It is but an intuition, however, and McTaggart's confident intuition of the opposite has convinced a great many others; it is hard to see why if there were no conscious beings to enjoy it Moore's unperceived beauty would have any value at all.[5]

The issue to which McTaggart addresses himself, however, is not so much the *truth* of this way of thinking as its *implications*. The key consequence to draw out is that if the only things of value are individual selves, then the only way to estimate the overall worth of anything is simply to *aggregate* the selves it contains. The worth of the universe, for example, is just the sum total of the separate values of the selves which it contains. Collections of valuable items win no further worth; no extra value over and above the total of the values they bring together. There is a strong anti-holism here. The point is not to deny, however, that the collection in question may possess some deeper metaphysical unity—indeed McTaggart in his own way is sympathetic to the

---

[1]   Insofar as they held freedom compatible with determinism, McTaggart and Rashdall might be cited as exceptions to this claim (see above p.472 and p.367), but both would have held firm to the claim that it is we who act and not the Absolute that acts through us.

[2]   'The Individualism of Value', 97.

[3]   'The Individualism of Value', 99.

[4]   *Principia Ethica*, §50.

[5]   'The Individualism of Value', 101.

idea that the universe forms a coherent whole[6]—only to insist that even where various elements of reality are all bound together as one unit, it does not follow that their various values are too.[7] The anti-holism is one of value. The divorce McTaggart introduces here between metaphysics and value is significant, not least as a sign of the times. Where for Absolutist Idealists these spheres must always map onto each other, McTaggart finds value individualistic even where ontology is not; embracing a divorce between fact and value that was typical also of idealism's growing number of critics.

The universe as a whole will have intrinsic value only if it is itself a person or conscious being. And this, McTaggart quite correctly points out, is really a much rarer doctrine than one might think—that which Green and Caird would have been prepared to call 'the eternal consciousness' or 'God' they would have balked at describing as a 'person'. But even if the universe were a person, continues McTaggart in a further twist of the individualist argument, our calculations of its overall value would have to proceed in a very different way from our calculations of its overall content. Its overall ontological content would be a sum of that of its components. But in such a universe I would be part of another person, and whatever greater being I might contribute to, I would remain also a finite consciousness with an existence and value of my own. It must therefore be concluded, urges McTaggart, that 'if within God's consciousness there are x finite consciousnesses, the total number of consciousnesses is neither one nor x. It is one plus x.'[8] Drawing the implication of this point for value, it must further follow that my value is not part of the value of this greater consciousness, for the greater consciousness forms a new self with a new value which must be *added* to all the other values which the universe already contains, if we want to arrive at the sum of all value that obtains. The calculation we make of the total ontological content of the universe and that we make of its total value are quite different in form.

And what holds of the universe holds too of any other aggregate, such as a society. A group of selves collectively can have no more intrinsic value than is found by summing that of each of its members separately.[9] Here too McTaggart thinks Idealists have tended to go wrong, attributing to the whole more value than is found in the parts. Nor is the point merely academic. McTaggart admits that nothing in his own doctrine has implications for the specifics of political or social doctrine, but he suggests that much of the force behind Socialism has lain not in economic or political theory but in the 'foolish exaggeration' of a rhetoric of value that would make the state almost an object of religion. Of this tendency he is utterly condemning.

---

[6] He was not, of course, an absolutist. But his necessitarianism, combined with his determining-correspondence system composed of relations of love are enough to constitute his universe a strong Hegelian unity.

[7] 'The Individualism of Value', 97.

[8] 'The Individualism of Value', 104.

[9] *Nature of Existence*, §§789–90.

if what I have said is true, it will follow that, whatever activity it is desirable for the State to have, it will only be desirable as a means, and that the activity, and the State itself, can have no value but as a means. And a religion which fastens itself on a means has not risen above fetish-worship. Compared with worship of the State, zoolatry is rational and dignified. A bull or a crocodile may not have great intrinsic value, but it has some, for it is a conscious being. The state has none. It would be as reasonable to worship a sewage pipe, which also possesses considerable value as a means.[10]

The mistake of which McTaggart accuses his contemporaries is, he appreciates, widespread and hence some diagnosis is called for. One error which is commonly made, he suggests, is a confusion between this true and plausible thesis of the individu-alism of value and the similar-sounding, but false and implausible, notion that the value of a self is independent of other selves. Idealists have been at the forefront in criticism of this second doctrine, rejecting any suggestion that self-realization could be a solitary project. But there is no need to abandon their entirely valid insights. McTaggart offers a parallel example; though we may speak loosely of the drunkenness of a town, drunkenness can only be the quality of a man, not a town, but for all that, a man's drunkenness may well *depend* on his environment; the example of his family, the pressure of his friends, the low price of alcohol, the high number of pubs, and so on. In the same we way, although we say that all value resides in individuals, we may still hold that it *depends* on their relations to other selves.[11] The origination and manifestation of value involves others, but its proper possessor is the individual himself. From the fact that much, perhaps the greater part, of value comes through relations to others, Idealists have been mislead into thinking that that value resides in the *relations* themselves, or a least in the whole comprising of the relations and the terms; but in truth what actually has value is the state of being one of the terms in such a relation, not the relation itself. Thus, suggests McTaggart, taking another example, if A loves B, although there is only one relation involved, there obtain two goods; the state of A's loving B and the state of B's being loved by A.[12]

These general findings on the nature of value McTaggart went on to apply to his own universe of timeless loving spirits, whose metaphysics has been outlined in previous chapters. He inquires into the value of its final stage (which appears to us as future.) Freed from all error and puzzlement (although not all ignorance) and feeling love for those selves we perceive directly, affection for those selves we perceive indirectly, and reverence for ourselves, all of which are sources of great pleasure, McTaggart concludes that this condition will be an unmixed good of very great order.[13] Because unbounded,[14] he decides that the value of the final stages is infinitely greater than that of the aggregate of values of the pre-final stages.[15]

---

[10] 'The Individualism of Value', 109.

[11] *Nature of Existence*, §791.

[12] 'The Individualism of Value', 107.

[13] *Nature of Existence*, §830, §839, 844.

[14] In this sense we may call it 'infinite' (*Nature of Existence*, §885).

[15] *Nature of Existence*, §892. This allows us to say that the universe *as a whole* is good.

But it is not perfect. This is in part because his summative conception of value does not allow for an upper limit to goodness.[16] There can be no best world. But there is also a second, rather different, reason. It cannot be a state wholly without evil, because of the 'sympathetic pain' which memory must cause us to feel for the suffering undergone in the pre-final stages by those whom we love.[17] We may reach heaven, but we cannot simply forget the tears and struggle it took to get there. McTaggart is developing here worries that had long concerned him. In *Studies in Hegelian Dialectic* he had pointed out that any attempt to save the Hegelian claim that whatever is real is rational from refutation by the incoherence and evil of the world around us through declaring such features mere delusions or appearances, while it might dissolve the initial problem, could only cause it to reappear at a higher level, since a universe marred by such appearances and errors is hardly fully rational.[18] Nor was McTaggart the only person to arrive at this problem. For it will be recognized that the difficulty here has an exact equivalent in Joachim's discussion of error which we have already examined; the content of our false belief may be re-distributed among various other truths, but there still remains the falsehood of our first having taken it to be true.[19] How can we square the perfection of reality with our experience of imperfection? What answer can there be which does not itself taint reality? McTaggart clearly sees that this puzzle is but a secular version of the traditional problem of evil.[20] Unprepared to conjure the reality of evil away, his great intellectual honesty precludes for him any form of perfectionism; Absolute Idealism and theism alike.

13.1.2 Bosanquet

If McTaggart's individualism about value represents one extreme of the spectrum, at the opposite end we find the value philosophy of Bernard Bosanquet. The initial appearance is one of apparent agreement. Green famously declared, 'Our ultimate standard of worth is an ideal of *personal* worth. All other values are relative to values for, of, or in a person.'[21] And Bosanquet is prepared to endorse that claim. However, he insists that we err badly if we take it to mean, as McTaggart does, that 'Nothing has value but the conscious states of conscious beings; and the value of the universe has no unity but that of a sum of these values.'[22] We must understand and accept the caution that there can be no value in anything less than personal consciousness, he grants, but it must be remembered too that a person is something much more than its given self at any moment, and Green's warning by itself does not settle the question of whether

---

[16] *Nature of Existence*, §§814–17, §852, §887.
[17] *Nature of Existence*, §838, §893, §899.
[18] *Studies in Hegelian Dialectic*, §153. See above p.443.
[19] See above p.50.
[20] *Studies in Hegelian Dialectic*, §159.
[21] *Prolegomena*, §184.
[22] *Principle of Individuality and Value*, 302.

consciousness is best valued as given in separate momentary fragments, or as combined together into greater wholes.[23]

In part the disagreement here is metaphysical. Contra McTaggart, Bosanquet holds that we simply cannot find a sense of finite individual robust enough to stand on its own and evaluate,[24] for as we have seen to his mind the finite individual always points beyond itself to the whole. If we reflect upon the full range of threads that bind, really we find no greater unity *within* one self than we do *between* different selves. If a man denies his unity with others, it must be disputed whether he may really lay claim to his own self-unity. But given he does claim this, he may equally be challenged whether he can deny the further stages of individuality continuous with that point. There is no reason for drawing a line around a set of linked terms if they bear as many links of the same kind to the vast sea of terms outside the set.[25]

Without explicitly mentioning Bosanquet, McTaggart considers this last question when he returned to the issue in *The Nature of Existence*. Could not the atomism of value be carried further, he wonders? If societies have no more value than that of the selves they bring together, should selves be thought to have any more value than the individual mental states they collect?[26] Relying on our natural tendency to think of the value of such mental states as qualifying the self that contains them, rather than to any larger unit that contains the self—we praise *McTaggart* for his philosophical ideas not *Cambridge University*—he persists in thinking that selves and not their states are what properly bear value.[27]

But metaphysical issues aside, Bosanquet was unsympathetic to the thought that values ever could be summed in any simple arithmetical way.[28] With a word of direct contradiction to McTaggart, he endorses what he regards as Plato's view of the State in his *Republic*, namely, that the value of a society lies in its happiness as a whole, not in the happiness of the separate individuals that compose it.[29] An aggregate of the latter would simply miss the essential quality of the former, as eating some bread followed by some cheese would miss the essential quality of eating a cheese sandwich. He insists, moreover, that holistic valuation incorporates and thus takes over from the individualistic method, so where we rise to think of the value of the whole we must abandon our old habits of thinking in terms of the value of the parts. In this way and directly contra McTaggart's principle by which the value of any self is determined, he says, 'You cannot add the value which it retains, in spite of its shortcoming, to the value which it has in the complete being which it implies. If a thing, seen as you see it, is worth

---

[23] *Principle of Individuality and Value*, 312.

[24] *Principle of Individuality and Value*, 271.

[25] *Principle of Individuality and Value*, 309. For more on the different sense of identity which Bosanquet believes may be applied to an individual see pp.386–7 above.

[26] *Nature of Existence*, §792ff.

[27] *Nature of Existence*, §§795–8. He acknowledges, however, that this view can be harder to sustain where we think of their states as past or future ones.

[28] Sprigge, *The God of Metaphysics*, 328.

[29] *Principle of Individuality and Value*, 313.

two, but properly seen is worth ten, you cannot add the two to the ten in counting its full value.'[30] In effect, he is objecting, McTaggart is advocating a species of double-counting.

13.1.3 Bosanquet's metaphysics of value

In order properly to understand how Bosanquet comes to advance a position so opposed to McTaggart's we need to look at his underlying grasp of the nature of value, which (in contrast to McTaggart's direct and intuitive approach) is very abstract and metaphysical. In *The Principle of Individuality and Value* Bosanquet makes the case for a single criterion which, in the sense that the more real a thing, the more true and the more valuable, is applicable equally to reality, truth, and value.[31] Nor should this three-way coincidence be thought so odd; for surely truth *is* at least a species of value,[32] and no idealist can hold these two 'ideal' realms in the end finally separate from reality itself. The relevant title chapter—'Individuality as the Logical Criterion of Value'—makes it clear that the criterion or standard Bosanquet champions, that of positive non-contradiction,[33] is the very same principle we have seen at work in his metaphysics.[34] And thus the imperative towards higher value is just one further instance of the 'development of experience', under its own natural *nissus*, towards comprehensive consistency.[35] According to this way of thinking, the good or valuable is that which pleases, but pleasure or satisfaction is a function of the logical stability of the whole desired—that what is more real and at one with itself is also that which gives us a more complete and durable satisfaction[36]—and thus things are said to have 'value' in as far as they possesses a stable structure, in as far as their components 'confirm and sustain one another.'[37] This idea extends to all value, including the aesthetic—where it is, perhaps, easier to appreciate. In 'the valuation of beauty,' suggests Bosanquet, 'we are quiet, sane, and harmonious'.[38] Part of Bosanquet's case here is an appeal to a unified view of human nature which will not admit irreducibly different forms of satisfaction—aesthetic, moral, metaphysical, etc.—but merely a single kind, differently stressed or applied.

---

[30] *Principle of Individuality and Value*, 310.

[31] *Principle of Individuality and Value*, 298.

[32] *Some Suggestions in Ethics*, 61.

[33] Like Bradley, Bosanquet rejects the notion of a bare or merely negative judgement; any significant negation must assert something positive (*Logic*, I:283). In consequence the apparently negative claim that reality does not contradict itself, may equally and more truly be thought of as a positive principle of harmony or individuality (*Principle of Individuality and Value*, 44–52, 267).

[34] Bosanquet should not be thought a lone voice here. Bradley too argues that 'the practical standard seems to be the same as what is used for theory. It is individuality, the harmonious or consistent existence of our contents' (*Appearance and Reality*, 131).

[35] *Principle of Individuality and Value*, 298.

[36] *Principle of Individuality and Value*, 298–9.

[37] *Principle of Individuality and Value*, xxxi.

[38] *Some Suggestions in Ethics*, 61.

It is crucial to establishing this thesis that Bosanquet show questions of value to be as objective and discursive as those of metaphysics. With respect to the first, he argues that the fact that different people all value things differently demonstrates, not that value is subjective as opposed to metaphysical, but rather that finite minds differ in the degree and direction of their development.[39] With respect to the second, against those who think value something simple or basic, he insists that it is as amenable to logical argument as other questions. This comes out especially in his disagreement with G.E. Moore, to be considered below.[40]

The significance of the equation which Bosanquet is attempting to establish should not be downplayed. Where McTaggart feels that wholly different principles may be at work in metaphysics and ontology, and where even Bradley fights to show that our greatest theoretical satisfaction constitutes also our greatest practical satisfaction, Bosanquet strolls easily across the apparent gap, confident that there is no great dividing line between the real and the good, that the marks of genuine being (coherence and comprehensiveness) are equally those of value and thus that whatever is ultimate in logico-metaphysical terms is supreme in evaluative terms also.

Far from a novel creation, Bosanquet's theory of value is one with a long pedigree. The sense in which his absolute is 'perfect' is similar to the metaphysical sense in which Spinoza's universe is 'perfect', but Bosanquet himself prefers a more ancient comparison. It was, he reminds us, Plato's conclusion that 'objects of our likings possess as much of satisfactoriness—which we identify with value—as they possess of reality and trueness'.[41] His form of the Good was not only the supreme object ethically but also metaphysically. However, where Plato's self-predication thesis judges the good itself to be good, Bosanquet is more circumspect. If the universe itself is thought of as some sort of finished mind, then, judged comparatively to the lesser minds it contains, as both embodying and providing their standard, it may be regarded as relatively good. But viewed in itself, though complete or perfect, it is not really good, because it is not on one side of that contrast between what is and what is not as it ought to be; the 'good' as opposed to the 'bad'. Strictly, you do not value the universe itself, rather it is the standard by which you measure other things. The whole is always the unit of value.[42]

13.1.4 Bosanquet's ethics

Translating the abstractions of metaphysical value theory into the concrete specificities of real life, what sort of a moral philosophy did Bosanquet advance? The answer to this question is that in the specifics of ethical life itself he broke little new ground. We have already noted that in the 1890s he specified the content of the will of God, by setting out Bradley's doctrine of My Station and its Duties, and some twenty years later in

---

[39] *Principle of Individuality and Value*, 300.   [40] See below pp.480–1.
[41] *Principle of Individuality and Value*, 317.
[42] *Principle of Individuality and Value*, 310.

Some Suggestions in Ethics (1918) we find him advocating substantially the same position.[43]

There is a distinctive and interesting communal life, which seems rather in fact to absorb individuals and to provide them with purposes and values, than to be itself deducible from an accumulation of private lots, as it were, or claimable portions, of welfare, each lot to each individual. This . . . single social life . . . is hard to represent as merely derivative from the separate claims of individuals to welfare. . . . It has rather the air of something new; of something which comes out of the co-operation of individuals, but reveals a fresh character in them, and exhibits them as something, which, qua mere units set side by side, they would not appear to be.[44]

But it would be wrong to dismiss Bosanquet's ethics as wholly derivative, for the same volume reveals that he had several more unique contributions as well. For example in the essay 'Living for Others' he moves beyond familiar (perhaps by this point, clichéd) idealist notions of sacrifice and dying to live. Whatever we do involves some loss and some gain, he observes, and so 'the law of sacrifice has no special relation to actions in favour of other persons. It refers to something wider and deeper than living for others. The secret is that values are impersonal, and to live for them means self-sacrifice certainly, but primarily for impersonal ends, and only secondarily and incidentally for ends which involve the furtherance of others' existence and happiness.'[45] I must renounce *my* good for *the* good. In saying that values are impersonal, Bosanquet does not mean to deny, of course, that they are revealed in and through people, merely to insist that 'they are imperatives or notes of perfection to which the persons as facts are subordinate'.[46] 'Persons are to love like facts to truth, a medium in which something is revealed greater and deeper than the particulars concerned.'[47]

Two examples may illustrate this attitude further. In 'Unvisited Tombs' Bosanquet reflects on how nearly all mankind rest in forgotten graves and leave behind them common undistinguished work.[48] We are wrong to regret this fact, he argues; devoted to value itself it matters not who enjoys it or who brings it about, and a man should be quite content to have the work of his life carried on by others. We should feel no need for individual survival to continue our efforts, or to complete our projects, only that they should be continued or completed.[49] Bosanquet is here returning to an idea already expressed in his debate with Pringle-Pattison. A further illustration of his impersonal conception of value is to be found in his insistence that worth should not be limited to *homo sapiens*.[50] Traditional religion served us badly when it drew a sharp

---

[43] More explicitly in a 1922 letter to Webb he describes himself as only ever a popularizer of Bradley's ethics (*Bernard Bosanquet and his Friends*, 238).

[44] *Some Suggestions in Ethics*, 35–6.

[45] *Some Suggestions in Ethics*, 7.

[46] *Some Suggestions in Ethics*, 11.

[47] *Some Suggestions in Ethics*, 12.

[48] *Some Suggestions in Ethics*, 87.

[49] *Some Suggestions in Ethics*, 84ff.

[50] *Some Suggestions in Ethics*, 73.

distinction between man and the lower animals, he argues, for 'as between social classes, so in the community of the universe, the higher and the lower both nourish and colour one another, and the total resulting experience is far richer and more solid than it could be if *per impossibile* any part of the whole could be removed'.[51] When our interest is in what they convey, not the vehicles themselves, it is a mistake to get hung up on any one particular type.

13.1.5 McTaggart and Bosanquet on freedom

Before we leave McTaggart and Bosanquet there is one last interesting point of comparison to make between them. This concerns their differing views of freedom. McTaggart's ethics were presented as an example of the Personal Idealist vision, but on the issue of freedom he differed sharply from them. They asserted contingency, even counter-causal autonomy, but in his 1906 *Some Dogmas of Religion* McTaggart argues strongly against Free Will or, as he more precisely puts it, indeterminism; the view that actions are not completely determined by prior motives or volitions.[52] Instead he affirms the universal rule of necessity.[53] Against the charge that this would undermine morality, McTaggart insists it is enough that we have the power to bring about good or evil through the exercise of our will.[54] Against the thought that, since wholly predictable, the result would not really be a *choice*, McTaggart responds that so long as will is genuinely effective of the outcome, predictability is irrelevant—'I can see no absurdity in a choice which is preceded by a perfect knowledge that it would be made.'[55] Presumably, God's choices are like this. Proponents of free will often present moral responsibility and social interaction as things which cannot be explained on the determinist system. McTaggart's scheme is of interest for the way he turns that argument on its head pressing that in so far as these can be explained it is on the determinist system alone. Without determinism there could be no moral responsibility[56]—we could not pass from the value of the action to the value of the agent—and without the ability to predict future action there could be no coherent interaction with other people.[57] We may punish or praise to deter and reform in the way we train a dog or a child; a possibility the indeterminist cannot explain at all.[58]

---

[51] *Some Suggestions in Ethics*, 74.

[52] *Some Dogmas of Religion*, 143.

[53] It might be wondered what sense can be made of determinism given that McTaggart denies the reality of *time*. Of particular significance in this regard is a 1914 paper on 'The Meaning of Causality' in which he argues that causality is nothing more than a relation of determination between existents. It is a relation of reciprocal implication; effect implies cause as much as cause implies effect. It is often held to have a sort of asymmetry, but McTaggart denies that cause determines effect in a way effect never determines cause (the difference more usually coming down to one of description) and it has no essential connection to time or explanation (*Some Dogmas of Religion*, 165).

[54] *Some Dogmas of Religion*, 152.

[55] *Some Dogmas of Religion*, 171.

[56] *Some Dogmas of Religion*, 178.

[57] *Some Dogmas of Religion*, 182ff.

[58] *Some Dogmas of Religion*, 184.

There are interesting comparisons to be made with Bosanquet here because for all the great difference between them on the metaphysics of the universe and the value of persons, they come much closer to one another on the issue of freedom. Indeed, we find something almost like cross-over, as McTaggart takes a position one might expect from an absolutist and Bosanquet makes claims that would not be out of place for a personalist. Unlike McTaggart, Bosanquet is prepared to say that there exists free will.[59] Of course, one must not hang too much on words and no more than McTaggart does Bosanquet believe in indeterminism or mere voluntarism—which is nothing but 'blind impulse'[60]—but neither does he wish to embrace a law-like universe of rigid necessity.

In his metaphysics Bosanquet stresses the continuity of the universe and the uniform applicability of rational law to everything. But does not such a perspective conflict with the element of mind and individuality towards which he regards the universe as moving? Is not individuality at odds with universality? Does not mentality demand a variation which is incompatible with the uniformity of nature? Bosanquet replies that uniformity (properly understood) is no obstacle to individual spontaneity or freedom. Freedom does not have to violate law or impose some sort of distinction between us and nature. Freedom requires variability. But mere '*de facto* variability'[61] is not enough; it has to be of the right sort. Caprice is the very opposite of freedom; what is needed is systematic or law-like variability. Our interest is in 'explicable variation'[62] and this is something which especially characterizes the mental rather than the physical—although there can be no sharp discontinuity here. Our thoughts are ever different, but always explicable. Only the lowest sort of law rules out variability, but such bare uniformity hardly deserves to be called law at all.

The difference between the two philosophers emerges clearly if we consider the question of whether predictability destroys choice. McTaggart, as we saw, finds little to worry about here. Bosanquet is more sceptical. He does not oppose prediction of human action in principle because that would place a discontinuity between us and the natural world and because, to a degree, it is already possible; we often can more or less predict what action will be taken by those whose character we know well. But he stresses that we would need a vast amount of knowledge taking in the entire context; that the kinds of truths we would need to know go beyond the simply natural to the moral, aesthetic, religious, and suchlike; and that in trying to predict action, it needs to be remembered that human reasoning brings with it new processes beyond the simply mechanical or calculating—it is synthetic and manifests a spontaneity akin to that of artistic creativity.[63] Taking over the Hegelian notion of freedom as 'thinking will', as a

---

[59] *Value and Destiny of the Individual*, 9.
[60] *Value and Destiny of the Individual*, 123.
[61] *Principle of Individuality and Value*, 94.
[62] *Principle of Individuality and Value*, 95.
[63] *Principle of Individuality and Value*, 115, 331.

form of rational teleology rather than a species of causation,[64] he argues that the 'secret' of will lies in the fact that 'mind has always more in it than is before it . . . So for every given situation there is a larger and more effective point of view than that given, and because the spirit of the whole . . . is always in the mind, it can always, in principle, find clues to new possibilities in every given situation.'[65] As the *nissus* towards a whole which transcends its present or past states, 'thinking will' resists law without relinquishing explicability. It defeats any simplification that attempts to tie its current state in any law-like way to its actions, because the 'current state' to which we appeal in explanation of those actions can never be wholly set out, but keeps always one step ahead of our analysis. A further attempt to bring out this point may be found in a paper Bosanquet gave on Charity Organisation Society (COS) casework in which he argues that, rather than thinking in terms of typical problems calling for stock remedies, every situation must be looked at individually and a solution found specific to that problem, for each subject and caseworker are unique with 'inexhaustible' depths or potentialities that any simply generic approach must miss. Although Bosanquet is as ready as any idealist to acknowledge their importance in our formation, we are more than just the product of our history and social context, not because we have some core 'soul', but because we point towards a greater Absolute. It is the resultant 'infinity of mind' which grounds the individual freedom that the COS was so keen to preserve.[66]

13.2 Evolution and ethics

The McTaggart–Bosanquet difference of opinion was an issue internal to idealism, but in that respect it was unusual, for after 1900 most of the stimulation to ethical thought came from outside the idealist camp. For example, we already saw how the early Idealists, such as Pringle-Pattison and Ritchie responded to the challenges of evolutionary theory, but evolution continued to be a dominant theme into the twentieth century, and Idealists continued to be called upon for a response.

W.R. Sorley in his short 1904 book, *Recent Tendencies in Ethics*, argues that we must distinguish the *evolution of ethics*, the idea that values have developed over time, from the *ethics of evolution*, the idea that Darwin's evolutionary theory gives us somehow or other a standard or criterion of value.[67] Idealists, he argues, have long since advocated the former, they dispute only the latter—although in this regard he also makes the important observation that there is no single position against which to take a stand here, for not even the evolutionists themselves agree about the ethical significance of the doctrine; Darwin, Spencer, Stephen, Huxley, and Nietzsche all offering very different ethical accounts.[68]

---

[64] Hegel, *Logic*, §53.
[65] *Value and Destiny of the Individual*, xxiv; see also x, 110–27.
[66] 'The Affinity of Philosophy and Casework' esp. 162–72.
[67] *Recent Tendencies*, 36–7.   [68] *Recent Tendencies*, 51.

Considering the ways in which ethicists have sought to extend Darwin's theory, Sorley suggests that we may distinguish between three different kinds of competition. The theory may be taken from the natural world and applied to competition between individual human beings, to competition between human groups, and to competition between ideas (in which class we may also include institutions, customs, and habits.) Starting with the last of these, it must be recognized, objects Sorley, that ideas are deliberately accepted or rejected for mental and conceptual reasons, in full consciousness of the end sought, whereas natural selection is an involuntary, physical, and purposeless process.[69] Moreover, the triumph of ideas is a much more rapid process than natural selection could effect.[70] In conflict between human groups too purposive selection enters in. Societies carefully seek out the modifications that will help them thrive or defeat their neighbours; these are not simply stumbled upon by chance.[71] Conscious competition between individuals also sees more than just natural selection at work, he argues.[72] He concludes that natural selection is only really applicable in the very lowest levels of the world, and that the processes of life itself in its higher ranges pass beyond it into the sphere of conscious purposive selection.[73]

By the end of the first decade of the twentieth century the 'old' evolution had been joined by a 'new' variety, that of Henri Bergson.[74] Embracing the historical facts of change and growth, Bergson objects to Darwin's particular system as overly mechanical. Yet he objects equally to those systems he regards as 'teleological' on the grounds that they too present a fixed and inevitable universe. Instead he proposes his own theory of 'creative evolution', driven by what he terms the *élan vital*. This gives to the universe a forward motion not wholly unlike that of freedom or creativity.

Bergson's developing universe presented something of a conundrum for Idealists. There was much in it for them to approve. His account of conscious life as characterized by non-linear time (*durée réelle*) rather than the spatialized conception we construct for ourselves in thought, was welcomed by Personal Idealists like Pringle-Pattison as wholly accurate to the phenomenology of finite experience.[75] His opposition to mechanism, in holding that the past does not determine the future, was not far either from the Bosanquet's Absolutist thought that everything moves beyond itself.[76] But switching from the individual to the global perspective, matters were rather different. For if he opposed the driven-from-behind aspect of Darwinian evolution, Bergson was

---

[69] *Recent Tendencies*, 60.   [70] *Recent Tendencies*, 63.   [71] *Recent Tendencies*, 64.

[72] *Recent Tendencies*, 65.

[73] *Recent Tendencies*, 67. Indeed, emboldened by these differences, Sorley suggests that even in animal life we can find aspects of behaviour that call for some sort of 'choosing' and that cannot be explained in a wholly natural way, hints that mark the beginnings of the end of the reign of natural selection (*Recent Tendencies*, 66). Similar ideas may be found in Ritchie, although he is more sympathetic to Darwinism, insofar as he tends to read the introduction of conscious purpose as a development rather than a refutation of evolution.

[74] *Creative Evolution* was published in 1907 and translated into English in 1911.

[75] *Idea of God*, 371.

[76] *Idea of God*, 368; *Principle of Individuality and Value*, 355.

not really any more amenable to the drawn-from-the-front teleology of idealistic evolution, and his system seemed to many of them irrational and contingent. What James described as the open or unfinished character of his universe, however much it might seem to hold from within, could not really be true of the whole. The universe itself could not *grow*. Without regarding it as the unfolding of something already achieved, there can be no explanation of development in the universe, and importantly no guarantee that its processes point towards the eventual realization of the highest values. That such is its tendency might seem obvious, wrote Mackenzie in 1924, but even so, 'it is only an idealistic system, such as that of Leibniz or that of Hegel, that seems capable of giving us any sure basis for such a belief'.[77]

Bergson's understanding of this 'creative evolution' was closely linked to his rejection of thought in favour of intuition. In this regard, William James in his 1910 article, 'Bradley or Bergson?' found important similarities, but also a crucial parting of the ways. Both Bradley and Bergson think of reality as a harmonious one-in-many, he notes, first given in feeling or intuition, but then lost in conceptualization or thought. The choice we face is that between giving up on concepts and (with Bergson) returning to a kind of empirical intuition, or sticking with thought until it eventually undoes its own damage and points (as Bradley would have) to a super-relational reality. That, for James, this is a choice between knowing life 'in its thick fullness and activity' or knowing some 'trans-conceptual evaporation like the absolute' leaves no doubt where his sympathies lie;[78] but for other Idealists whether or not to follow Bergson was a more difficult question. His anti-intellectualist advocacy of intuition could not endear him to the more rational parties. His 'attempt to assign a secondary place to knowledge, and to bring back the real to the felt, seems to me to invite the inquirer to travel along a dubious path,' warned Haldane.[79] But on the other hand in so far as he was opposing all analysis—the compartmentalism of cognition—his orientation was not so far from the unified conception the Idealists loosely referred to as 'experience'. This was Pringle-Pattison's point when he wrote to Haldane, of Bergson, that it was 'useless to appeal to intuition *unless one takes intuition as equivalent to the larger reason.*'[80]

13.3 The influence of Nietzsche

As well as the continued discussion of old challenges, the period after 1895 saw the appearance of new themes also. One such introduction was the philosophy of Nietzsche. In a process not wholly dissimilar to that by which Kant and Hegel made their way into native philosophy, the ideas of Nietzsche, while they were all the rage in continental Europe, made only slow inroads into British thought and were largely kept at bay until after the Great War. Receipt of his ideas second-hand either from hysterical

---

[77] *Ultimate Values*, 73.   [78] 'Bradley or Bergson?', 32.
[79] *Universities and National Life*, 115–16.
[80] Barbour's memoir of Pringle-Pattison, 17—my italics; see also Sorley, *Moral Values,* 255–80.

opponents or from controversialist disciples, together with poor quality, badly-chosen, and slow-to-emerge translations no doubt assisted an inward-looking native temperament in this matter.[81] But in this context (in which he was largely neglected by other philosophers), it is interesting to see the work of Idealists in bringing Nietzsche's ideas to greater public knowledge.

William Wallace's idealism did not exclude an interest in other traditions,[82] and in 1896 he reviewed the opening two volumes of the first English translation of *The Works of Nietzsche*. The following year he also reviewed separately the translation of *Thus Spake Zarathustra*. He was intending to write a detailed criticism of Nietzsche but was prevented from doing so by his early death later that same year; all that was completed, the beginning chapter, was included by Caird in his *Lectures and Essays*. 'Report of Nietzsche on this side of the channel has been heard now and again,' wrote Wallace in his 1896 review, 'but of knowledge, as distinct from notoriety, there has been no great amount,'[83] and in consequence, with the aim of making good that gap, his writings are almost entirely expository. But, of course, the very choice of what one takes time to expound in detail is a philosophical one and claiming that, however extravagant his views, 'Nietzsche is always at least honest, pure and thorough', Wallace expresses the hope that his own efforts have been enough perhaps 'to excite a desire to hear more'.[84]

But if Wallace merely heralded, the first serious philosophical engagement came a year later from another Idealist, Pringle-Pattison. In 1897–8 he published a pair of articles on Nietzsche; the first biographical, the second expounding his thought. 'Though Nietzsche's paradoxes and epigrams are hardly likely to take an important or permanent place in the movement of modern thought',[85] nonetheless, he advertised, 'An attempt at greater precision is made in the following pages, in the belief that, however preposterous Nietzsche's theories may be, his conclusions and the steps by which he reached them form an instructive chapter in the history of ideas.'[86]

Pringle-Pattison approves of Nietzsche's attack on pure altruism as self-contradictory. The only possible moral motive is satisfaction or perfection of the self; altruism and self-sacrifice enter in only insofar as the self that we try to realize or perfect is a higher one, one that finds its own satisfaction in the common good.[87] Nietzsche's error is

---

[81] Max Nordau's *Degeneration* (1895) prejudiced many against Nietzsche before he was even read, nor was he much better served by his earliest British disciples, Thomas Common and Alexander Tille. Other early names to note here include John Davidson, Havelock Ellis, G.B. Shaw and W.B. Yeats. For detailed discussion see Thatcher, *Nietzsche in England*. After the war his work was widely taken up although not, for the most part, by professional philosophers.

[82] It is worth noting that Wallace also wrote, in 1890, a life of Schopenhauer,

[83] Review of *The Works of Nietzsche*, 75.

[84] 'Nietzsche's Criticism of Morality', 541.

[85] 'Life and Opinions of Friedrich Nietzsche', 254.

[86] 'Life and Opinions of Friedrich Nietzsche', 255.

[87] 'Life and Opinions of Friedrich Nietzsche', 291–2.

rather his individualism, which he pursues 'to the verge of anarchism'.[88] In utter indifference to the masses, Nietzsche's superman pursues an isolated path leading in the end to self-destruction and madness. The discipline we need is not that of selfishness but that of service, in which we lose our lives to find them. Nietzsche derides such Christianized ethics as the life-denying morality of slaves. But such criticism touches only the Christian ideal in its worst extreme of medieval asceticism, responds Pringle-Pattison, and in its true overall affect on human civilization it has shown itself to be a progressive and life-affirming force.[89]

As much as with Nietzsche's ethical views, Pringle-Pattison takes issue with their metaphysical basis. Nietzsche falls into a naturalism that destroys morality of any kind. He fails to grasp that human life means primarily emancipation from our lower animal being, the control of natural impulse through self-consciousness. 'It is the break with instinct that first renders *human* life possible,' says Pringle-Pattison.[90] The same separation makes also for reason, and thus he complains that Nietzsche's naturalism leads him as well to an absurd denial of the validity of the distinction between truth and falsehood.[91] In the end Nietzsche refutes himself; 'a conclusion which involves the complete disintegration both of morality and of knowledge is, at most, a *reductio ad absurdum* of the premises which lead to it'.[92]

Countering the prevalent hysteria, Pringle-Pattison tries to locate Nietzsche within the philosophical tradition. He is less original than either his supporters or his critics suppose. That happiness not the goal in life is a message that Idealists long ago learned from Carlyle,[93] but Nietzsche's own debts reach back much further. In essence, his ethical theory is that of Callicles in the *Gorgias*, while his subjective theory of knowledge, his substitution of the beneficial for the true, is that of Protagoras in the *Theatetus*.[94] For his refutation we need only re-read our Plato.

Another Idealist to engage with Nietzsche on more than one occasion was J.S. Mackenzie who, while insisting that many of his statements are too exaggerated to take seriously, nonetheless recognized his call to stand 'above morality' as one able to find a sympathetic ear in several quarters, and therefore not to be ignored.[95] He treats him mainly as a foil, an example of extreme individualism and self-centredness, representative of the mistaken view that egoism and altruism are opposed,[96] and (as did Pringle-Pattison) in the end any challenge is met in effect by neutering it. He dismisses Nietzsche's 'transvaluation of all values' project as just another of the recurrent phases of doubt, scepticism and reinvestigation of the foundations of value that have regularly

[88] 'Life and Opinions of Friedrich Nietzsche', 304.
[89] 'Life and Opinions of Friedrich Nietzsche', 292.
[90] 'Life and Opinions of Friedrich Nietzsche', 314.
[91] 'Life and Opinions of Friedrich Nietzsche', 318.
[92] 'Life and Opinions of Friedrich Nietzsche', 319.
[93] 'Life and Opinions of Friedrich Nietzsche', 297. See for example Carlyle, *Past and Present*, bk.3 ch.4.
[94] 'Life and Opinions of Friedrich Nietzsche', 319.
[95] 'Use of Moral Ideas', 11.
[96] 'Idea of Progress', 209–11.

occurred through intellectual history.[97] A further sign of Nietzsche's growing inroads into ethical thought occurs in the brief introduction to his philosophy to be found in Sorley's 1904 *Recent Tendencies in Ethics* which, stressing his debt to evolutionary theory,[98] sees Nietzsche as a wholly biological thinker who takes natural selection as the sole test of ethics.[99] But this growing concern of Idealists with Nietzsche, as well as their diagnosis of his failings, culminates in Muirhead's *German Philosophy and the War*. Published in 1915, this book is best understood in the context of the controversy surrounding idealism and the Great War, however, and will therefore be discussed in the final chapter.

13.4 G.E. Moore

Contemporary analytic philosophy dates the beginning of its own engagement with ethics from the publication of G.E. Moore's *Principia Ethica* in 1903, and undoubtedly this was a landmark book. Even an Idealist like Muirhead acknowledged the great influence that it had had: 'ethical discussion in the later years of the nineteenth century suffered from a certain torpor. The book which more than any other may be said to have the credit of awaking it from its dogmatic slumbers was G.E. Moore's *Principia Ethica*.'[100]

Moore writes in the Preface that the main object of the book might be expressed by modifying one of Kant's famous titles and calling it a 'Prolegomena to any future ethics that can pretend to be a scientific',[101] but the implicit pretension behind such a suggestion that he saw himself also as offering a replacement for *Green*'s great work would certainly not have been be lost on Moore's first readers. And (although that is only one of its targets) it certainly contains much criticism of the idealist school, which was still at that time the dominant mode of ethical thought.

For instance, its main contention was that good is indefinable, a simple notion, like yellow—to be grasped in intuition or not at all.[102] While the Idealists did not think we could offer any neat formula to capture it, they did think that good was a complex notion whose content could be progressively unfolded through the work of reason. Any attempt to define the good, in any way, Moore terms the 'naturalistic fallacy'— and he specifically accuses Green of having committed it in holding that '*the* common characteristic of the good is that it satisfies some desire',[103] (although it seems mischievous to represent this as an attempt at *definition*, certainly in anything like Moore's own

---

[97] 'The Meaning of Good and Evil', 252.

[98] *Recent Tendencies*, 47.

[99] *Recent Tendencies*, 67.

[100] *Rule and End in Morals*, 10.

[101] *Principia Ethica*, ix.

[102] *Principia Ethica*, §6. Not that this claim was original to him; he clearly acknowledges its presence in his teacher Sidgwick (*Principia Ethica*, §14).

[103] *Principia Ethica*, §84. The reference is to *Prolegomena*, §171. Moore adds the italics.

understanding of that term.) Repudiation of the naturalistic fallacy involved for Moore the rejection of all 'metaphysical ethics'. Within this term he includes the Stoics, Spinoza, Kant, but especially those whose views are due to the influence of Hegel, that is the Idealists.[104] Varying his illustration, he attacks also the view of Mackenzie, equally committed to a system in which the ideal is bound up with the real, and whom he further accuses of making the contradictory claim that the 'true self' or 'rational universe', though already *eternally real*, is nonetheless something we must *bring about* for the future.[105] Central to the Christian message (as Bradley noted) this paradox is hardly unique to idealism, and perhaps only McTaggart really faced it. Moore's overall position was consequentialist—not hedonistic, to be sure, but it did assess the consequences of actions. This placed him at even further distance from idealism; for while Green was not wholly unconcerned with consequences, in general the idealist ethic of self-realization was an ethic of *character* rather than of action.

But it is possible to overstress both Moore's differences with idealism and his negative impact upon idealist ethics. On at least one key point he is in line with them.[106] Moore argues that value of a whole is not a sum of the value of its parts, giving the example of beauty.[107] Value is an organic whole. Noting the importance of this idea in idealism, however, Moore seeks to distinguish his own precise conception; rejecting any implication that the individual constituents lack meaning or value apart from the whole.[108]

Turning to the Idealists themselves, Bernard Bosanquet (for one) was unimpressed; indeed the notion of organic wholes was about the only thing he found to approve of in Moore's new system.[109] In a 1904 review, locating the heart of *Principia Ethica* to be the non-definability of good as proved by the naturalistic fallacy, Bosanquet complains that, using a 'manifestly false'[110] theory of definition, based on a doctrine of the non-essentiality of relation, Moore has effectively gagged ethical science.[111] If definition is by analysis only, 'the determination of one aspect by "others," which for an Idealist is the obvious foundation of all science' becomes something utterly extraneous that cannot touch a thing's nature. To refuse on the mere basis of a theory of definitional judgement even to consider the great metaphysical ethics of history 'seems to me', complains Bosanquet, 'an abuse of ingenuity'.[112] Nine years later, in *Value and Destiny of the Individual*, revisiting Moore's claim that good cannot be defined, Bosanquet expands, 'Definable, I should urge, is just what it is; describable, perhaps, is what it is not.' We cannot exhaustively enumerate its components for 'that would be indeed to construct the universe a priori, to deduce the detail of its components from the single

---

[104] *Principia Ethica*, §66.   [105] *Principia Ethica*, §§67, 70.
[106] Although not *all* of them. As we saw above, McTaggart disagreed.
[107] *Principia Ethica*, §18.
[108] *Principia Ethica*, §22.
[109] *Principle of Individuality and Value*, 304.
[110] Review of *Principia Ethica*, 259.
[111] Review of *Principia Ethica*, 260.   [112] Review of *Principia Ethica*, 261.

fundamental character of satisfactoriness'. And so, if definition is taken narrowly to mean analysis of elements then it is indefinable, but if it means 'the exposition of the universal character of any whole' then good is perfectly definable. It is precisely 'the harmony of all being'.[113] A few more years and Bosanquet's opposition hardened even further. To say value is an indefinable quality like yellow 'seems merely to be saying that it is a thing you cannot explain...a mere mark of ignorance'. To be able to recognize it, but not say how 'indicates as a rule a want of attention'.[114] Everything must have a structure and that inevitably links it to the rest of reality; you cannot draw a line around it and say 'here its connection with the rest of reality stops'.[115]

Mackenzie's attitude was similar. For him 'good' is something *thought* not sensed (because necessary) and something *complex* not simple (because it has an opposite).[116] Like Bosanquet, he approves of Moore's organicism,[117] although he would like to see it extended from ethics to metaphysics. But he finds a tension between it and the indefinability claim. Why is the only kind of definition analysis into parts? If there are such things as organic wholes, must there not also be what we might call 'contextual definition'; definition by reference to wider surroundings?[118] He also takes issue with Moore's fundamentally realist conception of value. There is a big difference between perceiving something as yellow and perceiving something as good. In the latter, but not the former, case we may later be persuaded, or persuade ourselves, to see it differently—placing it among that class of objects which depend for their existence upon the way in which they are regarded. This gives us a *prima facie* case against any purely realist interpretation.[119]

But not all the Idealists were hostile. Rashdall agrees with Moore that Good is undefinable,[120] pointing out only that this advances nothing new—the same point may be found in many previous thinkers, he notes, including Cudworth, Plato, and Aristotle.[121] Sorley does not go quite so far as to say with Moore that good is indefinable, but does see it as an irreducible and basic aspect of experience.[122] But the Idealist most strongly influenced by Moore was his Cambridge contemporary, McTaggart. Not everything was approved. He rejects the organicism of value (the most popular aspect of Moore with the others) and he rejects also Moore's unperceived

---

[113] *Value and Destiny of the Individual*, 194.

[114] *Some Suggestions in Ethics*, 47.

[115] *Some Suggestions in Ethics*, 48.

[116] 'The Meaning of Good and Evil', 253–5.

[117] As does W.R. Sorley who cites Moore in support of his own organicism about value, the view that 'we cannot get at the value of the whole simply by adding together the values of its constituent parts' (*Moral Values and Idea of God*, 155n).

[118] Review of *Principia Ethica*, 380.

[119] *Ultimate Values*, 122–3.

[120] *Theory of Good and Evil*, I:135–6 n.

[121] Note the complete contrast here with Bosanquet.

[122] *Moral Values and the Idea of God*, 25.

yet still valuable world,[123] but he follows completely Moore's central claim, that Good and evil are indefinable.[124] We can only appeal to intuition. He gives a list of qualities that possess value (knowledge, virtue, emotions such as love, pleasure, fullness of life, and harmony) not so dissimilar from that which Moore himself proposes.[125]

13.5 Intuitionism

In the early years of the century Oxford produced its own brand of intuitonism. Its founding father was H.A. Prichard whose famous 1912 article 'Does Moral Philosophy rest on a mistake?' argues that the discipline has hitherto consisted 'in an attempt to answer an improper question', viz. *why* a given course of action is obligatory.[126] To show that it would be in our interests or would lead to our happiness, while it may make us *wish* to do it, does nothing to show that we *ought* to do it. And although we may get nearer to an answer by suggesting that it brings about some good (perhaps our own happiness or that of other people) we do so only on the further problematic assumption that we have a duty to bring about that which is good. This he regards as false to our common sense intuitions; we do not think that we ought to pay our debts or to tell the truth because this will originate some further good state of affairs. Indeed, we do not derive our sense of obligation from anything further. Rather we see directly and immediately that certain actions are in and of themselves obligatory or forbidden, right or wrong.

His 1928 Inaugural lecture *Duty and Interest* develops this attack with specific reference to Green. For Green, to think an action our duty is to think it conducive to the good of the society of which we are members and to think of the good of that whole as also our own good. But this, complains Prichard, 'really amounts to resolving the idea of duty into the idea of conduciveness to our advantage, or, in other words, resolving the moral "ought" into the non-moral "ought".'[127] Green tries to deduce the idea that some action is a duty from ideas which do not involve the notion of duty, and all such attempts from their very nature must fail.[128] Something's being to our advantage is wholly irrelevant to the moral issue of whether it is our *duty*. Instead of trying to explain moral convictions as the outcome of some doubtful reasoning process from non-moral starting points, it would be better to account for them by means of

---

[123] 'The Individualism of Value', 100. Here it is instructive to contrast his response to Moore's suggestion; that there is no value here because there is no mind enjoying the beauty, with Mackenzie's more genuinely idealist response; that a thing's beauty depends in part on its being perceived as beautiful. For Mackenzie something has value only because it is experienced as having it, while for McTaggart the presence of value is unaffected by whether it is recognized or not, although all that does have value are mental states themselves.

[124] *Nature of Existence*, §787.

[125] *Nature of Existence*, §§813, 838, 850–1; *Principia Ethica*, §113.

[126] It is ironic that a new line of thought should be initiated by almost exactly repeating the question first asked by Bradley. But that it could be so is itself perhaps illuminating.

[127] 'Duty and Interest', 43.

[128] 'Duty and Interest', 47.

some basic pre-existing capacity for moral knowledge.[129] Prichard also planned to write a book on moral obligation, the uncompleted fragments of which include a critique of Green's *Lectures on Political Obligation*. There the charge is repeated that, paradoxically, as much as Hobbes, Green thinks we always act for our own good (though, admittedly, he has a different conception of what that involves); a view which is not only non-moral, but false.[130] He objects also to Green's dismissal of natural rights and obligations, which he reads as the claim that these cannot exist independent of a government's order, a position he dismisses as 'drastic' and 'totally at variance with our ordinary convictions'.[131]

Prichard's intuitionism was continued by his pupil E.F. Carritt. Taking the existence of duties as self-evident,[132] his 1928 *The Theory of Morals* objects to any teleological theory which attempts to explain rightness in terms of goodness, criticizing along the way many of the key elements of idealist ethics. Against the notion of self-realization he complains that it is not the ideal or universal self that acts for good or ill but the empirical self, and it no more aims at self-realization than pleasure, it just tries to do the right thing—a course of action that may involve *sacrificing* what seems its own self-development.[133] The Common Good is dismissed as both obscure and ambiguous.[134] It represents Green's attempt to avoid the traditional opposition between the 'good' of the agent and the 'good 'of others, but rather than accounting for this, as he should, in terms of the opposition between what is right (duty) and what the agent desires, Green tries to bridge the gap by asserting that what is 'truly good' for one is always 'truly good' for all.[135] Against the idealist theory of rights, like Prichard, Carritt takes issue with the notion that rights require recognition.[136] The Rights recognition thesis also comes under fire from W.D. Ross, whose book, *The Right and the Good*, published two years later, represents the culmination of this Oxford intuitionism. He objects that you can only *recognize* what is already there.[137]

Historically idealism saw itself as something that had arisen in opposition to the intuitionism of the common-sense school (together with its then alternative, utilitarianism), but by the time intuitionism came round again in a new guise most of the original Idealists were dead. However, one figure from the generation of Green remained, J.H. Muirhead, and in his 1932 *Rule and End in Morals* he engaged with the new lines of thought. While the new intuitionists defined themselves in part by their clear rejection of the preceding idealist ethics, it is interesting to see just how sympathetic Muirhead was to them—although we could well complain that his

---

[129] 'Duty and Interest', 48.   [130] 'Green: Political Obligation', 247–8.
[131] 'Green: Political Obligation', 230.
[132] *Theory of Morals*, §28.
[133] *Theory of Morals*, §49.
[134] *Theory of Morals*, §§53–5.
[135] *Theory of Morals*, §56.
[136] *Theory of Morals*, §78.   [137] *The Right and the Good*, 51.

generous idealist spirit encourages perhaps too great a stress on convergence, and too little detail. One may wonder if he is really prepared to disagree with anyone.[138]

We can allow with intuitionism that there is 'self-evidence' and 'immediate apprehension' of obligation,[139] suggests Muirhead, but that is quite compatible with holding that we may appeal to thought to uncover the *ground* of this obligation, not explicitly present to consciousness.[140] He continues to urge that the Good is the most fundamental notion in ethics. 'To attempt,' he writes, 'to cut off one's judgments of the Right and obligatory from their background in the objective Goods or values of human life is as impossible as to cut off our judgments of truth from their background of the objective reality of the world to which they refer.'[141] But in the end Muirhead finds any hard distinction between the two chief moral notions impossible to accept, nor he admits, do we want to make either merely instrumental or reducible to the other. He came to hold that the relationship between the good and the right (between 'rule' and 'end') was a close and organic one.

13.6 Two late flowerings of idealist ethics

13.6.1 H.J. Paton

We have seen how the old Idealists responded to the new currents of thought around them, but what were the prospects in such a critical climate for original idealist work in ethics? We get a good sense of how idealism fared in this regard if we look in a bit more detail at two of its late flowerings: Paton and Joseph. H.J. Paton studied at Glasgow, where (in his own words) 'Sir Henry Jones, who was something of a prophet, contrived to give me the impression that after ages of confusion and error the truth, as expounded by Hegel and clarified by T.H. Green and Edward Caird, had at last been discovered so that little remained to be done in philosophy except to elaborate some further details.'[142] Resolving to add a few of those finishing touches, he took the well-established idealist path to Balliol, where he was taught by J.A. Smith. A job at Queen's College, Oxford was followed in 1925–6 by a research fellowship at the University of California during which he wrote his first work, *The Good Will*.

Published in 1927, this was an independent foray into ethics, distinctly idealist in style, but taking themes further in new directions. He is open about his idealistic

---

[138]   In advance of the emergence of Oxford intuitionism, but heading in a similar direction (though less conciliatory) is Bosanquet. He appreciates that the right is not simply the good—the one cannot be read off from the other—but persists in seeing them as connected; 'The right for me is that form or case of the good which, all things considered, I am able to embody in my scheme of life and my daily conduct' (*Some Suggestions in Ethics*, 152). He sees too a role for immediate apprehension, but insists that 'self-evidence is of one kind only, and depends on the relation of propositions to experience as a whole. There is no special kind of intuition which refers to propositions affecting conduct' (*Some Suggestions in Ethics*, 157).

[139]   *Rule and End in Morals*, 102.
[140]   *Rule and End in Morals*, 103.
[141]   *Rule and End in Morals*, 103.
[142]   *Contemporary British Philosophy: Third Series*, 338–9.

allegiance: 'it will be obvious how much I owe to such writers as Kant and Aristotle, and above all to Plato; and in more recent times to the great tradition, written and unwritten, of English idealism, which has had its centre primarily in the University of Oxford'.[143] To this is supplemented the Italian idealist tradition of Croce and Gentile. Endorsing the idealist stance that reality is experience, able alike to enjoy and to reflect upon itself, he finds the objections of realists like Moore nothing more than 'dogmatic assertion and personal prejudice'.[144]

As truth exists only for a mind which thinks, he argues, so value and goodness exist only for a mind which *wills*; and this, of course, places him in direct opposition to Moore who had argued specifically against theories which locate the good in will-ing,[145] and more generally against *any* attempt to define goodness. Thus Paton attacks Moore's indefinability thesis. He rejects both its metaphysical presupposition—'I do not believe that anything is simple in the sense in which Mr Moore seems to use the word. A thing taken apart from its relations to everything else, and at the same time deprived of all internal differences, is just nothing at all, and the intuition which is alleged to apprehend it is also nothing at all'[146]—and its assumption that all definition proceeds by analysis of a thing into its parts; the true definition of anything always takes us 'beyond it', he counters.[147]

But this is only one half of Paton's case; for the self-same understanding of definition leads him to think, in true idealist fashion, that mind is self-transcendent, something continually straining 'beyond itself'. It is what it is only in relation to a wider whole. This is true not merely of thought, but of wiling, which is a process of self-mediation, self-transcendence, self-realization.[148] In consequence, just as thought seeks out an ever more coherent and comprehensive view of reality, so too from its very nature does the will continually strive to effect the widest possible coherence in action; coherence of project, desire, and effort, not just within a single life, but with the lives of others too. To be good, therefore, is to be not merely an object of will, but the object of a coherent will, the degree of goodness proportionate to the degree of coherence. As Paton puts it, 'goodness belongs to the coherent will' and 'moral goodness in particular belongs to a will which is coherent as a member of an all-inclusive society of coherent wills'.[149] In short, as indicated by the book's sub-title, *A Study in the Coherence Theory of Goodness*, we have from the side of moral philosophy, a parallel working out of the coherence theory of truth so favoured by Idealists. What this amounts to is a new realization of the theory of the common good. 'It is essential to recognise that the goodness of which we speak arises in our relations to others considered not merely as others, but as members of the same society, as cooperating in a common activity and sharing in a common good.'[150] Unsurprisingly the metaphysic with which this is most in harmony (although Paton does not offer to prove it) is an Absolute Idealist one in

---

[143] *The Good Will*, 8. [144] *The Good Will*, 47. [145] *Principia Ethica*, §77 ff.
[146] *The Good Will*, 38. [147] *The Good Will*, 41. [148] *The Good Will*, 108–9.
[149] *The Good Will*, 20. [150] *The Good Will*, 310.

which 'reality is nothing other than spirit itself, which overcomes the abstract antithesis of subject and object'.[151] However, Paton's idealism was (as he later described it) 'a cautious one, not unmixed with some realism in regard to physical objects', finding in its doctrine of the provisional, partial, or incomplete nature of knowledge a *via media* between scepticism and dogmatism.[152]

As the intuitionist, Caritt, pointed out shortly afterwards, Paton's proposal suffers from several of the same defects as the coherence theory of truth itself. Coherence with actual desires and wills can be no guarantee of rightness, when so much of actual moral life is defective, yet if we specify some better set of ideal desires, then all we say is that right actions are those which cohere with other right actions. Nor is it clear that we may isolate a single sense of coherence at work here, especially as we move from the individual to the common domain. In single-minded dedication to his chosen path in life, the actions and desires of a 'good burglar' cohere among themselves, but while those of a 'good man' cohere with the actions and desires of others around him, there is no common species of 'coherence' here.[153]

13.6.2 H.W.B. Joseph

Although he discusses Moore, Paton fails to engage with other recent developments. His concern is with goodness only, and he assumes that right is to be understood in relation to goodness and not *vice versa*. But if this placed him at a distance from contemporary debates, the same can hardly be said, however, of the next idealist to consider, H.W.B. Joseph. We have already seen[154] how, in metaphysics, Joseph returned from the realist camp to the idealist fold. Here we have to observe that this prodigal movement extended to ethical theory also.

Both Cambridge and Oxford intuitionism had sought to free ethics from the shackles of metaphysical speculation, and Joseph begins his reaction with a strongly idealist reassertion of the necessity to ethics of 'a metaphysical foundation'.[155] A wholly scientific or naturalistic view of human nature, such as we find in behaviourism, raises insurmountable problems for ethics; specifically it is inconsistent with freedom of action and the real unity of the acting self.[156] So long as we take the world and all that occurs in it to be as physical science describes it for us, we must simply give up the language of action and of ethics. But since, when fully thought through, this world-view is inconsistent also with the very possibility of thought and knowledge, we may choose ethics over science and 'we are not required to make our ethical theory consistent at all points with the scientific account of the world'.[157] With a view to any positive alternative, he is cautious; 'Of the relation of mind to nature it cannot be said that any wholly satisfying account has been suggested,' he admits.[158] But he is prepared to venture a broadly idealist answer of monistic stamp: 'I do not believe either

---

[151] *The Good Will*, 428.   [152] 'Fifty Years of Philosophy', 347.
[153] *The Theory of Morals*, §58–9.   [154] See above p.396.   [155] *Some Problems*, 15.
[156] *Some Problems*, 1.   [157] *Some Problems*, 15.   [158] *Some Problems*, 40.

that there is a real world independent of mind altogether, or that my mind is independent of that mind of which the world is not independent. The relation of the knowing mind to what it knows is not one of accidental conjunction.'[159]

Though commonly categorized as an adherent,[160] Joseph opposed intuitionism. He finds Prichard's system of irreducible duty, unconnected to any goodness (either of the act itself or produced by it) 'absurd'. To hold duty in this sense basic or ultimate, is to hold it arbitrary and 'irrational'. Duty must have a basis in value.[161] He suggests that the mistaken view stems in part from an ambiguity in the term 'right'. Admittedly, in one sense to say that an action is 'right' is just another way of saying we *ought* to do it, in which case rightness cannot possibly be the *ground* of obligation. But we also use the term to indicate some character of the act, in virtue of which we ought to do it, and in this use it does indicate a species of goodness.[162] Rejected too is the thought that an action could be right or wrong without regard to motive, for it is impossible to identify an action without specifying a motive. Motive is an integral part of action. Returning to an idealist anti-abstractionism, Joseph holds that even if the bodily movement involved might be the same, with a different motive it would be the manifestation of a different act in a moral sense.[163]

But if the heart of ethics lies in goodness, where is that goodness to be located? Joseph is unsympathetic to the consequentialist suggestion that the rightness of actions lies in the goodness of their outcomes.[164] And thus Moore's 'utilitarian' intuitionism is found no more favourable. He takes issue also with Moore's claim of idefinability. Moore has, he suggests, confused simplicity and unity. Whatever is simple cannot be analysed or defined, to be sure, but there occurs unity without simplicity. He suggests, by way of illustration, the health of a body, the perfection of God or the goodness of a poem; their unity does not exclude complexity, and it as wrong to think of these goodnesses, as it is of goodness in general, as a simple quality things either have or lack.[165] Goodness is rather a 'form' or 'character'.[166] Perhaps Moore should have seen this, for it is not far from his doctrine of value as an 'organic whole', in which the value of the whole is not the sum of the values of the parts. But while Joseph applauds Moore's recognition of this fact, he takes issue with the insistence that parts nonetheless have intrinsic value. Rather than some species of magic arithmetic in which the whole comes out greater than the parts, the parts have no value *as mere parts*, only as taken together. Making a vital distinction, he insists, this is not to deny the very plausible notion that wholes get their value from the *natures* of their individual parts, only that that value is itself derived by aggregation of the individual *values* of those parts.[167]

[159] *Some Problems*, 42.
[160] See e.g. Warnock, *Ethics since 1900*, 56; Dancy, 'From Intuitionism to Emotivism', 695.
[161] *Some Problems*, 26.   [162] *Some Problems*, 59.
[163] *Some Problems*, 38.   [164] *Some Problems*, 26.
[165] *Some Problems*, 77–80.   [166] *Some Problems*, 83, 84.   [167] *Some Problems*, 84–5.

From the objective perspective of Moore, the good we must realize is just good, and the notion of 'my good' a meaningless one.[168] Joseph disagrees. If some good is realized in my life it seems quite correct to describe it as 'mine'. Indeed why else would we bring something about unless we thought it our own good?[169] But what then, it may be asked, can we make of the notion of 'duty'—the demand that we do that which, potentially at least, conflicts with what we perceive to be our own good? At this point the full extent of Joseph's return to Idealism becomes manifest, as he appeals to the notion of the common good; a form of being in which 'each man's life would be good not independently of and prior to the rest, but through and as belonging to the realization of their common purpose'.[170] As part of such a system our duties cease to be just an unconnected 'heap',[171] and we find too the explanation we need of obligation in the thought that we may act for a good which, although not in quite the sense that our own personal losses or gains, successes or failures are so, may nonetheless be *our* good.[172] The goodness of right actions lies not in their motives, nor in their consequences, nor brute in themselves, but rather suggests Joseph, in 'the system which the act forms with its context'. In judging a rule of action not just as it is in itself, by its motives, or by its consequences, but with reference to 'the whole form of life in some community, to which all the actions manifesting this rule would belong'— how it would compare to any other—he returns to a holistic notion of the good not inaccurately thought of as a concrete universal. But if in this fashion Idealism is seen to have survived the recent challenge to its hegemony, it emerges rather smaller and more modest; a form of life manifesting such common good is, Joseph admits, perhaps easier to achieve on a humble scale (such as family) than on a grander one (such as a nation or the whole world).[173]

---

[168] *Principia Ethica*, §59. [169] *Some Problems*, 116. [170] *Some Problems*, 119.
[171] *Some Problems*, 107. [172] *Some Problems*, 119. [173] *Some Problems*, 134.

14

Developments in Idealist Political and Social Philosophy

The present chapter examines British Idealist work in political philosophy during the second half of the movement's history. There occurred no sharp break, but rather a gradual shift of emphasis as the initial work of articulating an idealist social philosophy gave way to the twin tasks of exploring in detail its practical implications and defending it against a growing number of critics. The work too became increasingly polemical. Not content simply to theorize about the society in which they found themselves, Idealists took upon themselves the duty to exhort, encourage, or inspire it to realize its greater potential.

14.1 Bernard Bosanquet

14.1.1 Political philosophy

Bosanquet's *Philosophical Theory of the State*, first published in 1899, may be regarded as a kind of watershed in the history of British Idealist thought on political and social matters, insofar as it drew heavily on the previous work of Green and Bradley and, achieving an almost iconic status, went on to influence thinking on these questions for years afterwards.[1] In many ways it represents the highpoint of British Idealist political philosophy; more detailed and systematic than anything else before or after it.

Bosanquet himself describes his book as one of 'social philosophy',[2] but this term calls for further consideration since, during the period under discussion, we find extreme fluidity in the terms 'political philosophy', 'political science', 'sociology', 'social theory', 'science of society', 'social ethics', and the like. We have already seen how Mackenzie urged the development of a discipline called 'social philosophy'— distinct from yet closely connected to ethics and encompassing economics, politics, and education—which would investigate the fundamental nature and aims of society.

---

[1] It should be noted that the canonical idealist texts in political and ethical philosophy exercised a much longer-lasting influence—extending well into the 1930s and even the 1940s—than did those in logic or metaphysics.

[2] *Philosophical Theory of the State*, Preface vii.

Bosanquet supported this ambition—he lectured first for the London Ethical Society and then for the more academic but short-lived London School of Ethics and Social Philosophy spear-headed by Muirhead[3]—and his *Philosophical Theory of the State* falls within Mackenzie's general scheme; although its focus is principally on political rather than more broadly based social questions.

But the philosophical was not the only method in vogue at the time for investigating social questions, and note must be taken of another line of tradition, most commonly called 'sociology', which runs from Comte (who coined the term) through Spencer to Hobhouse (who was made Britain's first professor in the subject in 1907). In his second chapter, Bosanquet seeks to bring out the limitations of, as well as to distinguish his own work from, this more empirical tradition. This he does by investigating some of the analogies its thinkers have employed. It has often been hoped that social science might provide explanatory completeness and predictive power analogous to that of astronomy or mathematical physics. The subject has even been called 'social physics'. But, challenges Bosanquet, is all science quantitative natural science?[4] Another very important analogy has been that of biology, most notably in the work of Spencer. Extending the evolutionary approach of modern biology to the social sphere has, Bosanquet admits, been very fruitful, especially its emphasis on the continuity of nature and the role of competition, but, he complains, it has also promoted an unfortunate pattern of explaining the higher in terms of the lower; a habit encouraged by our unfortunate natural tendency to take as more 'real' whatever comes first or is designated a 'cause'.[5] A third discipline to have offered itself as a model is that of economics, as for example in Marx's materialist view of history and society; but economic life is only one part of human life and the contrast between material facts and ideas can have no ultimate standing.[6] Despite Comte's desire to banish it, psychology has figured strongly in modern French sociology, and certainly when dealing with social 'facts', you cannot avoid bringing in mind.[7] But social philosophy cannot reduce itself to psychology either, for like biology it explains the higher by the lower, whereas philosophy works from the other end.[8]

Bosanquet's comparisons should not be taken too negatively here. He is not opposed to strictly empirical sociology. He wants simply to point out its inability to address those questions he wishes to tackle, questions better suited to a more philosophical method. Philosophy takes a broader and larger vision. It 'is critical throughout; it desires to establish degrees of value, degrees of reality, degrees of completeness and coherence'. And its purpose is 'ethical'—although that term should

---

[3] Muirhead, *Bernard Bosanquet and his Friends*, 92–3. The London School of Ethics and Social Philosophy functioned from 1897 to 1900. See Mackillop, 'The London School of Ethics and Social Philosophy'.

[4] *Philosophical Theory of the State*, 19.

[5] *Philosophical Theory of the State*, 20.

[6] *Philosophical Theory of the State*, 28.

[7] *Philosophical Theory of the State*, 39–40.

[8] *Philosophical Theory of the State*, 46–7.

not be taken too narrowly.[9] It is enough to see that the disciplines are different; although 'different' here does not mean isolated and separate, for certainly philosophy and sociology supplement each other. 'Philosophy gives a significance to sociology; sociology vitalises philosophy.'[10]

14.1.2 Ancient Greece and the nature of society

While in some form there is 'state' wherever there are people, there are two historical manifestations of statehood—with two associated philosophies—in which Bosanquet takes an especial interest. The modern nation-state and its chief theorist Rousseau we shall look at in a moment, but first we need to think about the Greek city state as described by Plato and Aristotle. For they were the first to capture the fundamental nature of society, thinks Bosanquet, continuing and expanding on the central impor-tance already accorded to classical political philosophy by idealist historians such as Nettleship, Caird, and A.C. Bradley.[11]

Bosanquet insists that 'there is no sound political philosophy which is not an embodiment of Plato's conception'.[12] For Plato there is an exact parallel between the structure and unity of a human being and the structure and unity of society, both perfect harmonizations of different functions.[13] Each class of people possesses a distinc-tive type of character and all must be coherently adjusted together into an organic whole, whose proper model is either mind—'the outward organisation of society is really as it were a body which at every point and in every movement expresses the characteristics of a mind'[14]—or, less abstractly, the human individual as a whole; 'This great comparison of the relation between human beings in society to that between the parts of a living body was introduced into moral thought by Plato, and has been, perhaps, the most fruitful of all moral ideas.'[15] Aristotle too (fearing that Plato's abolition of the family produces too much homogeneity) insists that society is a union of different functions.[16] Aristotle's state is an organic unity prior to the individ-ual, such that man makes no sense apart from it; which is why Aristotle describes him as by nature a political animal.[17] Bosanquet sees the ideas of Hegel, Green, and Bradley as repeating these old truths; Aristotle's concept of *ergon* (function) becomes Bradley's 'My Station and its Duties' such that, 'man really does not exist as man without *some*

---

[9] *Philosophical Theory of the State*, 47.

[10] *Philosophical Theory of the State*, 48. For further discussion of this topic see Collini, 'Sociology and Idealism' and Boucher and Vincent, *British Idealism and Political Theory*, ch. 3.

[11] See above sections 3.5.3 and 3.5.6.

[12] *Philosophical Theory of the State*, 6.

[13] *Republic*, V:462.

[14] *Philosophical Theory of the State*, 6–7.

[15] 'How to Read the New Testament', 151.

[16] *Politics*, 1261a25. It will be remembered that A.C. Bradley also notes this point ('Aristotle's Conception of the State', 205).

[17] *Politics*, 1253a5.

station and duties'.[18] For Bosanquet, the Greeks showed that the individual cannot be regarded as an atom, but attains genuine individuality only as something organic to the communal whole. Society is a system of minds not just of things,[19] but a system of minds, taken seriously, requires a system of ideas, some dominant some subordinate, making its unity much like that of an individual mind.[20]

Along with this theory of society and its relation to individuals Bosanquet finds in ancient Greek thinking a theory of the good life. The precise form of that life is set by the nature of the human mind as rational. Humans are driven by intolerance of contradiction, in practical as well as theoretical affairs, and this striving for harmony fuels a growth or advance in character, according to which the 'good' is a matter of the complete realization of the individual soul, 'the perfection of human personality'.[21] But if it is to succeed, this process of development cannot occur in *isolation*; 'The fundamental idea of Greek political philosophy, as we find it in Plato and Aristotle, is that the human mind can only attain its full and proper life in a community of minds.'[22] Only playing our part in a social whole that fulfils others too, may we find our own fulfilment. This, of course, is the notion Green re-discovers in his theory of the common good. It is important that the thoroughly *moral* nature of this ideal not be lost sight of. Advancement in our material well-being, although it may help us on the way, is not an intrinsic part of the good life; Bosanquet is quite explicit, for example, that in itself moving people from poor to better housing, unless it also facilitates an improved form of life or character, brings them no nearer to a better life.[23]

14.1.3 The General Will

The political ideas of the ancient world passed away, but coincident with the emergence of the contemporary nation-state was a rebirth of modern political philosophy, whose decisive figure is Rousseau. Bosanquet arrives at Rousseau's great contribution through criticism of a class he calls 'prima facie theories' or 'theories of the first look'.[24] We can trace back such views at least to Hobbes and Locke, but in more recent times they are associated with Bentham, Spencer, and J.S. Mill. Their distinguishing character is to take individual human beings as distinct units, and try to build from there. But in this, thinks Bosanquet, they face an impossible task. None of these theories are able adequately to explain political obligation. If I do not wish to comply, what authority over me have others—even a majority—besides that of force or coercion? But surely my

---

[18] 'Kingdom of God on Earth', 116.

[19] Sweet, *Idealism and Rights*, 159–60.

[20] *Philosophical Theory of the State*, 158.

[21] *Philosophical Theory of the State*, 189. Bosanquet is here quoting Green from his *Lectures on the Principles of Political Obligation* (§11 note), himself quoting Henrici, although the notion of 'human perfection' appears often enough in Green's own *Prolegomena* (see above Chapter 6 note 74).

[22] *Philosophical Theory of the State*, 6.

[23] *Philosophical Theory of the State*, 185.

[24] *Philosophical Theory of the State*, 75. Contemporary thought would most naturally call these 'individualist' but, as we have seen, that term for Bosanquet has quite other meanings.

political obedience to the legitimate rule of others should be construed as a matter of moral rather than prudential submission? The lesson to be learned, argues Bosanquet, is that we need to dismantle the whole distinction between self and others inherent in the atomistic individualism of 'first look' theories.

He suggests as a more promising approach, that of Rousseau, which for all its inconsistency, '[breaks] through to the root of the whole matter'.[25] His high opinion of Rousseau compares with Green's, but contrasts with Caird's rather lower estimate. However, what he has in mind here is not the theory of social contract, but the theory of General Will. The way in which Bosanquet employs Rousseau's ideas may be set out as follows.

Adopting his notion of the *volonté générale*, as distinct from the *volonté de tous*, Bosanquet claims Rousseau showed that will not force is the basis of the state—his words here echoing Green's.[26] The state expresses the General Will and commands, therefore, the obedience of all. The General Will 'by definition aims at the public welfare',[27] Bosanquet argues; it is 'in the last resort, the ineradicable impulse of an intelligent being to a good extending beyond itself... a common good'[28] or 'common interest'.[29]

At the same time Bosanquet distinguishes between an individual's Actual Will and their Real Will. What we consciously desire from moment to moment constantly changes, and can never amount to 'a full statement of what we want'.[30] Our will as we apply it 'in the trivial routine of daily life' 'implies or suggests'[31] more than itself. To get that something further we must bring in all the other things we want, and then mutually harmonize and adjust them. We then need to bring in what other people want, and again, mutually harmonize and adjust. In this fashion we arrive at the Real Will. The process is in large part one of rationalization, and as well as the 'true' or 'real' will, Bosanquet speaks of it as the 'rational' will.[32] In some respects it is the difference between what we want *at any time* and what we want *sub specie aeternitas*, inviting comparison with Bradley's critical contrast between utilitarian or momentary satisfaction and the satisfaction of one's life as a whole. The two wills are almost exact opposites: our Actual Will is narrow, arbitrary, self-contradictory, aimed at apparent interests and wants, particular, private and casual, while our Real Will is complete, rational, true, aimed at real interests and permanent wants, universal, shared, and purposive.[33]

---

[25] *Philosophical Theory of the State*, 79.
[26] 'Les Idées Politiques de Rousseau', 323, 329. The Section G heading to Green's *Lectures on the Principles of Political Obligation*, 'Will, Not Force, is the Basis of the State', was in fact chosen by Nettleship, but it reflects perfectly Green's meaning. See, for example, §136.
[27] *Philosophical Theory of the State*, 101 n2.
[28] *Philosophical Theory of the State*, 102.
[29] *Philosophical Theory of the State*, 104.
[30] *Philosophical Theory of the State*, 111.
[31] *Philosophical Theory of the State*, 100.
[32] *Philosophical Theory of the State*, 100.
[33] Nicholson, *Political Philosophy of the British Idealists*, 204.

Bosanquet then connects these two distinctions, paralleling (or perhaps even identifying) the Real Will and the General Will. As in the individual the Real Will goes beyond, yet essentially manifests itself through, the Actual Will, so in society the General Will goes beyond, yet essentially manifests itself through, the Will of All; the General Will is, we might say, the Real Will of society. Commentators have glossed this step of the argument differently. Sweet[34] argues that my private will, fully rational and informed, would take in the wills of others and thus be the General Will. Nicholson argues that because we are social beings, we recognize the General Will as our true will.[35] Tyler envisions two transitions taking place, from my actual to my real will and then from my real will to the General Will.[36] But if the precise details may be debated, the general import is perfectly clear. The individual's Real Will is identified with the General Will of society; our individual good is found (as Green would put it) in the common good, or (in Bradley's words) in my station and its duties. And the chief payout for political philosophy from such an identification is that it allows us to make sense of political obligation. Theories of the first look became unstuck with the paradox of what could ever justify one person or group's coercion of another. However, on Bosanquet's model, we can make sense of this; the exercise of government is really one aspect of ourselves (the better/higher) coercing the other (the worse/lower), a matter of 'making ourselves' do something 'for our own good'. An illustration may help. Under the influence of a strong desire we may be sorely tempted to lie or steal or cheat, but (let us suppose) good moral habits win out and we simply can't bring ourselves to do so. Looking back, we see a narrow escape, and are glad that our better self took over the reins. In the same way a state which compels those of its members who do not explicitly agree with it, may still claim to be acting in their name, if it genuinely represents their real will, what they would want if they rationally thought things through.

14.1.4 The state

If there exists a General Will that can justify the coercive structures of society it becomes, of course, a matter of supreme importance to determine its content. But can the General Will be known? And if so, how? Rousseau insisted that it can only be ascertained by the direct votes of everyone[37] (he rejects both the idea of representation and the idea that any one group might be awarded control) but Bosanquet, for all his support of the basic idea, objects that this method simply delivers the Will of All (which is merely a sum of individual interests) and not the General Will (which aims at a common shared interest). For this reason he prefers Hegel's alternative solution that the

---

[34] Sweet, *Idealism and Rights*, 131.
[35] Nicholson, *Political Philosophy of the British Idealists*, 208; Sweet, *Idealism and Rights*, 132 n.90.
[36] Tyler, *Idealist Political Philosophy*, 142–3.
[37] *The Social Contract*, bk IV ch.II.

General Will is not expressed *immediately* but *mediately* in 'sittlichkeit',[38] a term which he uses to indicate the expression of a society's values and beliefs through the whole range of its institutions and practices from political, to legal, to economic, to social. Bosanquet broadly agrees.[39]

From identifying the Real Will with social sittlichkeit, Bosanquet makes the short further step of identifying it with the state.[40] This equation has resulted in much debate, and so it must be looked at very carefully. But to start we should just note his definition of 'state', which is very wide. Far from the narrow organs of political power, he gives to the term a reference even broader than he does to the term 'society'.

I use the term 'State' in the full sense of what it means as a living whole, not the mere legal and political fabric, but the complex of lives and activities, considered as the body of which that is the framework. 'Society' I take to mean the same body as the State, but *minus* the attribute of exercising what is in the last resort absolute physical compulsion.[41]

In criticism Hobhouse complains that Bosanquet confuses state and society.[42] And although the term 'confusion' seems inappropriate here—for Bosanquet is quite deliberately and consciously adopting this wide sense—we may well wonder with Hobhouse whether it is helpful to abandon the more common and narrower sense? What lies behind Hobhouse's complaint is fear. For the state is a coercive force, and in identifying it with something larger than individuals, government or even civil society, we seem to be creating an abstract monster with a life of its own to pursue without regard to, and even at the expense of, our individual selves. Hobhouse sees it as an alien will that can overwhelm our own. That there is something amiss with this reading here is suggested by the fact that on points of specific policy it is almost always Hobhouse who urges greater state intervention and Bosanquet who, in the name of individual autonomy and self-reliance, opposes it.[43] And indeed in unpacking Hobhouse's reading of Bosanquet's sense of the state, there is no small irony. For he has arrived at something which is almost the exact reverse of Bosanquet's meaning. Rather than an abstract obstacle threatening and at odds with individual liberty, Bosanquet's state is a concrete vehicle for personal self-realization, the very path to free individual fulfilment. It is not an end in itself. It is not the Absolute.[44] The state is the servant of society, not *vice versa*, for there is more to life than life-in-the-state.[45] (Comparison with Bradley's 'Ideal Morality' is instructive here.) To be sure, in as much as it is an individual, the state has an ethical goal which it must pursue, and in that sense it is a moral agent, like those

---

[38] *The Philosophy of Right*, Part II (esp §258); see also Taylor, *Hegel*, 372–88. The term is commonly rendered as 'ethical life'.

[39] *Philosophical Theory of the State*, 246.

[40] *Philosophical Theory of the State*, 144.

[41] *Principle of Individuality and Value*, 311, n.1.

[42] *Metaphysical Theory of the State*, 75–6.

[43] Collini, 'Hobhouse, Bosanquet and the State', 87.

[44] Tyler, *Idealist Political Philosophy*, 153.

[45] Panagokou, 'Defending Bosanquet's Philosophical Theory of the State', 36.

who live in it. But it must be remembered that there is a fundamental difference between the morality of the individual and that of the state. The one 'works out the detail of his duty on the basis of recognized rights within a previously ordered and organized society'; the duty of the other is precisely 'to provide and sustain, at all hazards, the organized society within which the individual is to live'.[46] Although he does not believe that the General Will can be ascertained by voting, Bosanquet does believe in democracy.[47] The General Will evolves primarily through changes in *people*, not through changes in laws or governments—the latter transitions are more likely to *reflect* adjustments that have *already* taken place in society.

14.1.5 State authority, freedom, and rights

How on this model are we to conceive the complex knot of relations between state and individual? For Bosanquet, the state has absolute authority over the individual. Its end is a moral one; to bring about the common good. And since we, because of our 'animal limitations',[48] will not do this alone, it is justified in exerting force over us. There is no limit in principle to its jurisdiction.

But all of this is only one half of the story. For the state is made up of individuals and, from their point of view, the only possible goal is freedom. The consciousness that distinguishes us from other creatures is bound up with our will, such that it may fairly be said that freedom 'is the true nature of mind',[49] and for Bosanquet, 'the whole political philosophy of Kant, Hegel, and Fichte is founded on the idea of freedom as the essence of man, first announced . . . by Rousseau'.[50] But we must distinguish here between simple or negative 'juristic liberty' and positive 'political liberty',[51] understood in the sense of self-determination. There is, Bosanquet admits, a degree of metaphorical extension in calling the latter 'freedom'—by it we are delivered not from *others* but from an inhibiting part of *ourselves*—but even if restrictions are called for to put us in a position to realize, not merely our day-to-day will, but our real will, it is nonetheless true that 'the 'higher' liberty is also in fact the 'larger' liberty, presenting the greater area to activity and the more extensive choice to self-determination'.[52]

Against the absolute authority of the state is set the absolute demand for freedom. In any 'theory of the first look' this would be a plain contradiction, but on Bosanquet's system that is no longer the case. The precise way in which they are fitted together forms the subject of Bosanquet's theory of rights. Rights are not freedoms *from the state* for those whose natural condition is liberty, but rather freedoms found *in the state* by those who would otherwise have none. Bosanquet adopts a 'teleological', or moral,

---

[46] 'Patriotism in the Perfect State', 137.
[47] Nicholson, *Political Philosophy of the British Idealists*, 214.
[48] *Philosophical Theory of the State*, 171.
[49] *Philosophical Theory of the State*, 133.
[50] *Philosophical Theory of the State*, 221.
[51] *Philosophical Theory of the State*, 125–8.
[52] *Philosophical Theory of the State*, 128.

conception of rights; they exist in virtue of an 'end'. We have rights to those things necessary for the realization of the common good at which each individual aims. They are 'powers instrumental to making the best of human capacities'.[53] In consequence of the socially situated nature of such human fulfilment, he provides an account of rights that is based on identifying one's 'station' or function in society and the duties that follow from it. One acquires rights to such powers as are needed to fulfil the positions one has within the social order, and they attach to the role not the individual per se.[54] For how could anyone settle what rights people have as mere biological creatures without taking into account their social character and situation, its functions and needs? Like Green, Bosanquet further argues that there exist no rights prior to or independent of the state; rights require recognition by the state.[55] But rights are not a merely social or legal creation, whatever arbitrary rule a society might settle on, for they are essentially moral in aim designed to bring about 'the perfection of human personality'.[56]

It might be asked whether we have the right to defy or resist the state? Bosanquet replies that any set of institutions that embodies the conditions necessary for obtaining the good life has an absolute claim on our obedience—we have no right to act immorally, nor to rebel against that system whose function is precisely the 'mainte-nance' (i.e. the creation and preservation) of our rights[57]—but where that claim to represent us is fraudulent, where those who would have us obey them do not speak for the Real Will or promote the common good, matters are altered.[58] Resistance may be justified. We have no standing right to disobey or rebel against the state, however, and any resistance we contemplate must be weighed up against the value of preserving social order. In consequence, Bosanquet doubts whether political disobedience is ever justified so long as there exists the democratic alternative of constitutional change.[59]

14.1.6 Applications of Bosanquet's political theory

The state is a moral agent. It aims to promote morality; it commands absolute authority; and there is, further, no limit to its sphere of influence. With such guiding principles the question of state interference ought to be easy, but in fact it becomes very complex, for Bosanquet argues (as did Green) that the state cannot directly promote morality. It cannot determine the free will of individuals; their motives, which alone give true value to action, falling outside the scope of its direct control.[60] All it can do is to try to bring about the conditions most likely to promote goodness. Where circum-stances make the best life difficult or impossible, it must try to remove those obstacles

---

[53] *Philosophical Theory of the State*, 195.
[54] Sweet, *Idealism and Rights*, 65. A right is 'a power secured in order to fill a position' (*Philosophical Theory of the State*, 196).
[55] *Philosophical Theory of the State*, 188.
[56] *Philosophical Theory of the State*, 189. See above note 21.
[57] *Philosophical Theory of the State*, ch.VIII §6.
[58] *Philosophical Theory of the State*, 139.
[59] *Philosophical Theory of the State*, 199.
[60] *Philosophical Theory of the State*, 175–6.

and smooth the passage. This Bosanquet describes as the 'principle of the hindrance of hindrances'.[61] In this way state action can create opportunities, and he held that there should be no a priori limitation on the ways in which it might be employed to promote social well-being—allowing it to act both positively and negatively to remove barriers to the best common life. But Bosanquet is very aware of its power to destabilize and demoralize human character. Indeed, of all the Idealists, he is perhaps the most circumspect and fearful of state intervention.[62] The state has a right to force its way into private life, and may achieve much of value by doing so, but extreme care must be taken in administering this 'dangerous drug' of violence,[63] lest it undermine its own efforts. Indiscriminate aid is capable of doing 'very serious mischief'.[64]

Since this balance is one that must be settled on a case by case basis rather than by simple appeal to some blanket general principle,[65] we get a better handle on this so-far very abstract consideration, if we turn to look at some practical applications; beginning with private property. For the basic justification of exclusive ownership, he follows Green. In order to express our will we need to have 'a power of moulding the material world in the service of ideas',[66] which power translates as property. A being wholly without property has no effective will. Moreover, private property encourages responsibility.[67]

But the universal need for property does not extend either to its unlimited acquisition, or to its equal distribution regardless of character, capacity or need.[68] Although he does not advocate complete *laissez faire* and welcomes schemes of worker ownership, Bosanquet had no ambitions towards socialist redistribution. Part of the argument for this comes from his Platonic ideas of differential social function; we all have different roles to play in our community with different property requirements. 'It is plain that there cannot be all-round identity of function, at any rate in a civilised society; and, therefore, the apparatus possessed by individuals for their functions, what we call property, must be different.'[69] But even more importantly, Bosanquet thinks that any attempt simply to grant welfare to all would work to undermine any imperative to self-improvement, which would be disastrous for human character. He allows both charity and state aid, but insists that it must never be such as to act as a disincentive to self-sufficiency. This was precisely what the COS was set up to ensure, for what the effects of any charitable action might be cannot be stated generally, but only ascertained

---

[61] *Philosophical Theory of the State*, 177–87.

[62] Bosanquet himself worries that Green is too tentative about such interference (*Philosophical Theory of the State*, ix, 267–70).

[63] *Philosophical Theory of the State*, 171.

[64] 'The Affinity of Philosophy and Casework', 170.

[65] *Philosophical Theory of the State*, 179.

[66] *Philosophical Theory of the State*, 281.

[67] *Aspects of the Social Problem*, 311, 312.

[68] 'The Principle of Private Property', 311.

[69] 'Three Lectures on Social Ideals', 200.

on a case by case basis.[70] That aid might do more harm than good was a very serious danger in his eyes:

I believe in the reality of the general will, and in the consequent right and duty of civilised society to exercise initiative through the State with a view to the fullest development of the life of its members. But I am also absolutely convinced that the application of this initiative to guarantee without protest the existence of all individuals brought into being, instead of leaving the responsibility to the uttermost possible extent on the parents and the individuals themselves, is an abuse fatal to character and ultimately destructive of social life. The abolition of the struggle for existence, in the sense in which alone that term applies to human societies, means, so far as I can see, the divorce of existence from human qualities; and to favour the existence of human beings without human qualities is the ultimate inferno to which any society can descend.[71]

Turning from property to the question of punishment,[72] which Bosanquet characterizes as a societal 'shudder of repudiation',[73] a communal condemnation or annulment of wrongdoing, we find that he is basically a retributivist. 'Punishment is the "negation" of a bad will by the reaction of the social will for good,' he says. 'This is its nature and character, and this sums up its value.'[74] The fundamental truth 'that wrong demands negation' is most clearly demonstrated in Kant's famous thought-experiment highlighting our obligation to execute the last criminals.[75] We are liable for punishment only where we are a member of a society and rebel against its rules, which is to rebel against ourselves, making it in a sense our own will returning back on ourselves. As when we stumble and hurt our foot we may look up and see we are off the path, punishment 'brings us to our senses'—it is, we might think, a warning signal we leave for ourselves in case we ever need it one day. It needs to be distinguished from private vengeance, and is not more clearly understood by being traced back to its historical origins.

Reform and deterrence are 'expansions [or] outgrowths of its central character,' suggests Bosanquet. He has no wish to deny their function, but insists they must not be allowed to become ends in their own right.[76] Thus, it is certainly to be hoped that punishment will educate (though it has limited power to do so—it cannot, for example, make people moral) but taken alone as a justification of punishment, it must be objected that the reform theory does not respect individuals as agents or ends in themselves. It rather treats them as patients, their crimes merely natural evils, like a disease, to be cured.[77] What might be a kindness to creatures incapable of having rights, applied to responsible human beings is an 'insult'. 'It leads to the notion that the

---

[70] Thomas, 'Philosophy and Ideology in Bernard Bosanquet's Political Philosophy', 115.

[71] *Aspects of the Social Problem*, 290–1.

[72] For further discussion of Bosanquet's theory of punishment see Tyler, 'This Dangerous Drug of Violence'.

[73] *Some Suggestions in Ethics*, 193.

[74] *Some Suggestions in Ethics*, 195.

[75] *Some Suggestions in Ethics*, 197; *Philosophical Theory of the State*, 211.

[76] *Some Suggestions in Ethics*, 195.

[77] *Philosophical Theory of the State*, 206.

State may take hold of any man, whose life or ideas are thought capable of improvement, and set to work to ameliorate them by forcible treatment.'[78] By contrast retributive theory takes seriously the notion of an offender.[79] A criminal who sets himself against the system of rights which he shares with others (and thus against himself) is entitled to 'recognition of his hostile will'.[80] His punishment is a right of which he should not be defrauded by being turned from an offender into a patient.[81] The value of deterrence should not be denied either, thinks Bosanquet. Indeed, he admits that is the main source of the *scales* of punishment; for although retribution calls for some sort of parity, the state cannot estimate levels of either pain or guilt,[82] while there is much data about what levels of deterrence are effective. But deterrence cannot constitute the justification of punishment itself, for let loose from our retributivist sense of justice or desert, its logic would take us straight back to 'the savage cruelties of obsolete penal codes' which were based purely on fear.[83]

The issue of justice itself, which this last point raises and which is a central topic in contemporary theory of politics, received little specific attention from idealist philosophers. Bosanquet was an exception, although the dismissive attitude he adopts is typical enough and his account serves well to explain their broader lack of interest. For Bosanquet justice is a comparative notion; it is the demand that people be treated equally according to a common rule. Injustice is a matter of not keeping to the rule, or making arbitrary exceptions. Its defects are two. First, it is individualistic in so far as it works from a direct surface comparison of individuals. But there are deeper (if less immediately apparent) standards, like patriotism or the common good, that call on us to give all we can and not to compare our advantages or burdens with those of others.[84] Second, even where we meet the primary demands of justice by keeping to a rule, the rule itself can bring in its own injustice, for simplistic exception-less principles inevitably break down, demanding equal treatment in what are really unequal cases.[85]

'Justice is certainly not the highest point of view,' concludes Bosanquet; but if we do consider it among the lower of social values we should remember too that its claims are only 'transformed' by higher ones, not 'cancelled' by them.[86] For instance, with regard to self-sacrifice, we should remember 'that in order to sacrifice himself a man must first have possessed himself. . . . A man can only surrender what is recognised as his.'[87] The state must genuinely grant to all, those goods it calls its citizens to stand up or to die for.

---

[78] *Philosophical Theory of the State*, 207.
[79] *Philosophical Theory of the State*, 208.
[80] *Philosophical Theory of the State*, 207.
[81] *Philosophical Theory of the State*, 211.
[82] *Philosophical Theory of the State*, 212.
[83] *Some Suggestions in Ethics*, 202.
[84] 'Three Lectures on Social Ideals', 198.
[85] 'Three Lectures on Social Ideals', 197, 210. For example, levying the same tax on those who can afford to pay and on those who can't.
[86] 'Three Lectures on Social Ideals', 198.
[87] 'Three Lectures on Social Ideals', 211.

Bosanquet draws a distinction between the 'rough Justice of the social necessity' and 'ideal Justice'. Though they may be the best we can manage, the crude rules of justice we come up with inevitably suffer limitations, but this suggests (even if it is for us something practically unachievable) the notion of a perfect justice, one that involves 'a comparative weighing of the difficulties of every individual case'. For example, instead of a blanket obligation on everyone, the call to serve would be precisely adjusted 'to every inequality of situation and of mental and bodily fitness'.[88] It is possible to regard the whole social system as an attempt to do just this, in which case, 'ideal Justice would practically coincide with a perfect social system'.[89] Modifying each rule for every difference would result in a massively complex system, from which the character of general rule would have vanished altogether.[90] Thus we see that the greatest thinkers on justice in the end move away from any simple rules by which to compare individuals; in the end 'it is the whole system that dictates his functions to every individual; and the law of Justice is that he should be what his special duty demands, however hard or humble may be the place so assigned'.[91]

14.1.7 Objections to Bosanquet's political theory

Such high abstractions set many alarm bells ringing. Some critics were themselves Idealists. For example one hostile voice was the Personal Idealist, Hastings Rashdall, who in his 1899 review, complained that in overlaying the theories of Plato and Aristotle with the ideas of Hegelianism, Bosanquet had mixed up insights 'common to all modern politics' with a host of further points ranging from the questionable, through the absurd, the vague and the nebulous, to the unhelpful. For example, if augmenting Rousseau's notion that it is our duty to obey the wish dominant in our society, Bosanquet wishes to add the proviso, only insofar as it really does tend to the general good, would it not be simpler to say just that, rather than attempt to show that that somehow is what actually is willed? It may be true that, in a sense, in the ideal state, the individual only ever obeys himself, but surely 'there are simpler and less misleading ways of expressing that truth,' opposes Rashdall.[92]

Other critics came from wholly outside the idealist camp. Most prominent among these was L.T. Hobhouse, whose *The Metaphysical Theory of the State: A Criticism* (1918) was directed explicitly at Bosanquet, whom he accuses of the worst of Hegelian Statism.[93] His criticisms were not especially good—Bosananquet was much caricatured and misinterpreted—but they were influential. The mud that was first thrown tended

---

[88] 'Three Lectures on Social Ideals', 206.
[89] 'Three Lectures on Social Ideals', 206.
[90] 'Three Lectures on Social Ideals', 207.
[91] 'Three Lectures on Social Ideals', 209.
[92] Rashdall, Review of *Philosophical Theory of the State*, 544–5.
[93] One of the interesting features of this book is how at the same time as trying to assimilate Bosanquet to Hegel, he seeks to distance him from Bradley or Green, who he sees as immune from most of the criticisms (*Metaphysical Theory of the State*, 24, 83, 99, 118–25).

to stick, the criticisms repeated years later,[94] and Bosanquet's reputation still bears the mark. It is therefore worth our while to consider the details of Hobhouse's critique.

We come quickly to the heart of the matter if we take up Bosanquet's two key terms, the Real Will and the General Will. In what sense (if any) do these exist? Hobhouse rejects the very idea of a *real* as opposed to an *apparent* will. A person's will is what it is, and that's all. We can allow that there are certain things, not currently willed, but which we *would* or *might* will were we more rational, but to allow that these have anything more than an ideal or hypothetical mode of being is to take an essentially unreal abstraction for something real. He objects that Bosanquet (and Hegel behind him) have failed to distinguish the ideal and the actual.[95]

In part Bosanquet would respond to such concerns by assimilating the case to other known and comparable experiences. It is, he suggests, similar to the way in which there can be distance between what we say and what we really mean, or between what we demand and what we really want. When such distance occurs something really is meant and something really is wanted.[96] But at a deeper level Bosanquet would simply reject Hobhouse's implicit equation between being ideal and being unreal. The point is not simply that for Idealists ideas are real, but more specifically that this objection forgets that to Bosanquet the individual itself is an essentially ideal or hypothetical being; its essence is to go beyond itself, it *is* what it is *becoming*.[97] Hobhouse and Bosanquet employ quite opposite senses of 'real'. Far from regarding it, as Hobhouse does, the *equivalent* of 'actual', for Bosanquet, 'real' is a term that *contrasts* with 'actual'. 'Real' for Bosanquet is a *teleological* notion; we really are, not what we actually happen to be, but what we might or will become; our essence is given in our end or goal.

Turning to the General Will, Bosanquet admits that there is quite some difficulty in seeing how this can be something real.[98] How can society have a 'will' when it is not a mind? Surely the only wills are those of the individuals in the society? Bosanquet's reply to this is that in a very real sense society *is* a mind. The point (as we have already seen) was one he got from Plato,[99] who would organize the state precisely as he thinks mind is organized, and in chapter seven of the *Philosophical Theory of the State* Bosanquet attempts to explain. He draws a distinction between mere association (where things simply find themselves together) and organization (where things are shaped by the very principle of unity that binds them as one),[100] and urging that both mind and society are organizations, he suggests that society has the same type of unity as a mind, that of an interconnected structure of ideas. He gives the example of a school, whose reality lies

---

[94] See for example Joad, *Liberty Today*, 182 and Popper, *The Open Society and its Enemies*, ch.12.

[95] *Metaphysical Theory of the State*, 17, 45.

[96] *Philosophical Theory of the State*, 110.

[97] Sweet, *Idealism and Rights*, 131.

[98] *Philosophical Theory of the State*, 110.

[99] As Bosanquet sees it, for Plato 'the social life and experience is that of one mind in a number of bodies, whose consciousnesses, formally separate, are materially identical in very different degrees' (*Principle of Individuality and Value*, 314).

[100] *Philosophical Theory of the State*, 146ff.

not in its buildings, but 'in the fact that certain living minds are connected in a certain way'.[101] Insofar as they share interconnected goals and ideas, minds can overlap (in the same way sets with shared membership overlap) and in this sense constitute a further mind.

We should not get carried away, however. Bosanquet is quite clear that there is no 'social brain' apart from the brains of individuals,[102] and he never attributes *personality* to the state.[103] How then does the union work? In 'Reality of the General Will' he explains. A mind is not just an unconnected set of ideas, but an *organized* set, that is, it manifests certain dominant ideas. Similarly a society is more than just an unconnected set of sets of ideas, for a measure of common beliefs, values, and goals among its members is necessary for the stable unity of any society. Insofar as we share a common life we share, not just ideas, but patterns of dominance among them. Or rather we should say harmoniously combined sets and patterns. For like the various parts of a machine, our differing ideas and patterns of dominance all fit together. Just as an individual's leading ideas are *their* will, so the shared leading ideas in society are *its* General Will. Rather than the reification of some monstrous *abstraction*, the General Will is a thoroughly *concrete* universal, despite the fact that it is not willed in its entirety by any individual. Indeed, no individual knows it in full,[104] for it is only gradually emerging from unconsciousness into reflective consciousness.[105]

14.2 Henry Jones

14.2.1 *The study of society*

We looked already at one of Henry Jones' early papers, 'The Social Organism', which he contributed to the *Essays in Philosophical Criticism* volume, but social and political issues remained at the centre of his work, and so we have now to consider some of his subsequent writings on these topics. Repeating the earlier calls of both Mackenzie and Bosanquet, in a series of Dunkin Lectures given first at Manchester College Oxford in 1904 under the title 'The Working Faith of the Social Reformer', Jones made a further appeal for the systematic study of social questions. At this present time, he complained, the study of society 'is less in evidence in our universities than the study of algae or protozoa'.[106] History, economics, ethics (though all useful) are none quite what is needed to help the social reformer, however; rather what is called for is 'a philosophy of political or social life'.[107]

[101] *Philosophical Theory of the State*, 159.
[102] 'Reality of the General Will', 321.
[103] Thomas 'Philosophy and Ideology in Bernard Bosanquet's Political Philosophy', 110.
[104] 'Reality of the General Will', 328.
[105] 'Reality of the General Will', 331.
[106] 'Working Faith of the Social Reformer', 20.
[107] 'Working Faith of the Social Reformer', 21.

One of the greatest obstacles to the creation of such a science, he suggests, has been the role of 'metaphorical hypotheses' which lead to the distortion of fact and the generation of endless controversy and confusion. He gives, as an example, the issue of how much of society's ills depend on, or (more positively) how much improvement could be achieved by focusing on, 'character' and how much on 'environment'?[108] The debate gets polarized between two extreme views: according to one, we need but change the external conditions and change of heart will follow, while according to the other all this alteration would be irrelevant and make no difference to people because change must come from within, so we must first teach people industry, thrift, sobriety, and such like.[109] The mistake, suggests Jones, is to think of 'character' and 'environment' as though they were two physical things, separate and able to compete, cooperate, or undermine each other, for in truth, 'What we call character from one point of view, we call environment from another. Character and environment are not even separate elements, far less are they independent, isolated, externally interacting objects.'[110] There is no robust distinction to make between character and environment, and so the question of priority really is impossible to frame. We need to get away from the use of *exclusive* categories.[111] Modern psychology is clear in telling us that we find nothing in our individual personality not answering to the environment in which we grow up; it is our social context that gives us the character we have.[112] Take away from the 'individual' all he has borrowed from 'the world' and he could think no specific thought, form no purposes, seek no good, speak no language. But the same is true if you take away from the 'world' all that the 'individual' contributes to it; nothing is left beyond a brute 'something' devoid of either meaning or order.[113]

It is important to appreciate that this two-way relation is a *dynamic* one, 'a process by which the outer world is formed anew within the individual's mind and will, or by which the individual forms himself through taking the world into himself as his own content'.[114] At the beginning individual and world are more or less external to each other, and only potentially a unity. Gradually, however, character develops and takes into itself the nature of its environment. This is of great significance to the social reformer, for character, although plastic at first, once fixed, becomes very hard to change. Thus schemes of reform to the already depraved or corrupted have little effect, or even make things worse.[115] The converse side of the story is that the power of society over unformed childhood is very great indeed,[116] making the quality of the

---

[108] 'Working Faith of the Social Reformer', 46.
[109] 'Working Faith of the Social Reformer', 47.
[110] 'Working Faith of the Social Reformer', 48.
[111] 'Working Faith of the Social Reformer', 49.
[112] 'Working Faith of the Social Reformer', 49–51.
[113] 'Working Faith of the Social Reformer', 51.
[114] 'Working Faith of the Social Reformer', 52.
[115] 'Working Faith of the Social Reformer', 54–5. Jones does not, of course, think it *impossible* to change such people, or that we should do nothing for them.
[116] 'Working Faith of the Social Reformer', 56.

surrounding educative influence that any community imparts a matter of overwhelming importance. People have been blinded to this last point by another metaphor, this time the biological idea of heredity—the belief that acquired characteristics can be inherited, and thus that the children of dissolute parents have themselves a inborn tendency to vice.[117] Reviewing the evidence Jones comes out firmly against this notion. 'The conclusion to which we are thus led, by our consideration of heredity in its relation to the child, is that *character* cannot be transmitted. . . . Each child is a new beginning; and the way to virtue, so far as internal conditions are concerned, is as open to the child of the wicked as it is to the child of the virtuous.'[118]

14.2.2 The evolution of spirit

In 1908 Jones gave a lecture tour of Australia,[119] the substance of which he subsequently published under the title *Idealism as a Practical Creed*. He here sets out a view of history as the development of the spirit of freedom; a conception (as we have already noted) to be found in both Bosanquet and Caird, and in Hegel before them.[120] 'Civilization is nothing but the process of revealing and realizing the Nature of Man,' argues Jones, 'and the revelation is still going on.'[121]

This history, he suggests, has three stages which he designates with a biblical reference, first the blade, then the ear, after that the full corn.[122] At the earliest period in the life of a man or society there seems hardly to be any freedom at all; everything about life is determined for us by social tradition. The first fruits of spiritual growth beyond this state challenge the authority of the social world, as rejecting or turning away from it, freedom is construed negatively in terms of *independence from* society.[123] From Socrates to the French Revolution freedom is conceived in this way. But freedom which is merely freedom *from* the world is only a preliminary stage on the way to true freedom.[124] The next stage has its prophets, the 'poet-philosophers' Hegel, Goethe, Carlyle, and Wordsworth—idealists who see that Spirit is not opposed to the world but rather its very life-blood, that 'the natural world is itself the symbol or phenomenal manifestation of Spirit'.[125] But if spirit is manifest in unthinking nature it is even more so in humanity, and it is here that we must look for its fullest and most developed incarnation. Man must be realized not apart from society, but precisely *through* it. Recognition of this truth, which Jones believed the philosophers of his own age to have reached, constitutes the culminating stage of freedom.

---

[117] 'Working Faith of the Social Reformer', 56. For further discussion see Boucher, 'Henry Jones: Idealism as a Practical Creed', 144–9.

[118] 'The Child and Heredity', 176.

[119] For detailed discussion see Boucher, 'Practical Hegelianism'.

[120] See sections 6.3.2 and 14.1.5 above.

[121] *Idealism as a Practical Creed*, 34.

[122] Mark 4:28.

[123] *Idealism as a Practical Creed*, 59.

[124] *Idealism as a Practical Creed*, 8.

[125] *Idealism as a Practical Creed*, 106.

In other words, Jones, like the other Idealists we have already examined, is offering a social account of the individual and his fulfilment. Metaphysically, he opposes the atomistic conception of self, holding that individuals together form an organic unity. 'The mutual implication of State and citizen has the unity and intensity of a single life.'[126] But if 'the substance of [man's] soul is social',[127] the significance of this answer stretches beyond metaphysics to ethics, and it is in similarly holistic fashion that the individual finds his true end in the state. 'The law within and the law without may coincide. Man may be obedient and yet free, and the more obedient because he is free.'[128] With another deliberate religious echo, he suggests that perfect freedom is service.[129] In a social context man finds himself in his 'station and its duties'.[130] Moreover, in setting out this historical framework, Jones reminds us that the human society in question is trans-historical. Heirs to the achievements of the past and the organs of far-reaching future purposes, we are bound up not simply with our con-temporaries, but are 'member[s] of a moral partnership which contains the living and the dead'—the community of humanity itself.[131]

14.2.3 The idealist conception

This story presupposes a number of core idealist conceptions worth bringing out more explicitly. In the first place, of course, it takes a *teleological* understanding of the historical evolution of society and morals. Historical sequence remains unintelligible if we look only backwards for its causal origins. Instead we need to see where it is heading. 'The ideal—not the "average"—is the true type. It is only when we "know what we shall be," which is not as yet, that we shall know what we are.'[132] But such a change in perspective leads to a switch in the kinds of cause to which we attribute social growth. We must look not to events but to ideas, for 'ideals are the forces of the moral world and the master-powers in the world we see.'[133] Jones is particularly impressed by the way in which the accumulated experience and ideas of the past are carried forward to create and enrich those of the present. A key element in this process is literature, although equally important are institutions, which are thoroughly shaped by their past and 'which are really nothing but embodied ideas'.[134]

From the story he tells Jones draws important practical lessons. Society is not stuck in a rut, nor is it blindly lurching forward. Rather it is progressing under its own inherent

---

[126]   *The Principles of Citizenship*, 90.

[127]   *Idealism as a Practical Creed*, 55.

[128]   *Idealism as a Practical Creed*, 108.

[129]   *Idealism as a Practical Creed*, 87. 'O God . . . whose service is perfect freedom' reads the Collect for Peace in the Book of Common Prayer.

[130]   *Idealism as a Practical Creed*, 117.

[131]   'Is the Order of Nature Opposed to the Moral Life?', 10.

[132]   *The Principles of Citizenship*, 86; also 114.

[133]   *The Principles of Citizenship*, 14.

[134]   'The Library as a Maker of Character', 222. Cf. D.G. Ritchie, 'Ideas can only be productive in full benefit, if they are fixed in institutions' (*Darwinism and Politics*, 38).

steam. And only with great care should we interfere. He is therefore opposed to revolutionary change. Progress, including individual moral progress, must always be steady; there can be no jumps or sudden changes. Jones is no mere conservative, but he does think the reformer must find the way things are 'tending'[135] and work with it not against it. In this manner the practical and the speculative are allies and 'a philosopher's thinking will lose neither range nor force from having a practical purpose to serve— provided always that the purpose be broad enough and he makes the universe an accomplice in his plot'.[136]

A third point to note is that the history of the world can only be thought of as the history of freedom on a peculiar (idealist) conception of freedom, that is, as self-legislation.[137] Jones argues that we should not ask wholly abstract or static questions like, 'Does man have free will or not?' Such questions distort the facts and can only ever be answered, 'Both Yes and No'. Freedom, it must be recognized, is a matter of degree and also a process; man 'is not bond or free, rational or irrational; but he is moving from promise to fulfilment. . . . He is *becoming* free, and *acquiring* reason; and it is only because he can *become*, that we can call him either free or rational.'[138]

There is no hope that we will arrive at the right conception of freedom, unless we have (fourthly) the correct idealist conception of personality. As we have already shown both with regards to the character–environment debate and earlier with regards to his philosophy of religion, for Jones, our person-hood needs to be understood as comprehensive not isolated. The more we are distinguished from others, the less we are in ourselves.[139]

14.2.4 State and individual

Jones' general conception of the relations between state and individual, and of the nature and scope of intervention and rights, follow broadly familiar lines. To begin with we should note that the state is not just the government, but includes such social structures as, for example, the world of business. In his 1905 lectures, *Social Responsibilities*, delivered to businessmen in Glasgow, he insisted that much depends on them. They have a duty, he tells them, to bring about conditions of labour that '*make* men and not destroy them'.[140] For Jones the state is a moral agent;[141] it aims to make us moral;[142] and 'It is only on moral grounds that we can determine the nature and limits

---

[135] 'Working Faith of the Social Reformer', 26–33.
[136] Henry Jones, 'Francis Hutcheson', 20. Cf Edward Caird above p.209.
[137] *The Principles of Citizenship*, 56. On the true sense of freedom see esp. *Idealism as a Practical Creed*, Chs.III–VI.
[138] *Idealism as a Practical Creed*, 38–9; also 'Working Faith of the Social Reformer', 45–6; *Principles of Citizenship*, 83.
[139] See above section 11.3.3.3. *The Principles of Citizenship*, 57–61.
[140] 'Social Responsibilities', 305.
[141] *The Principles of Citizenship*, 46.
[142] 'Moral Aspect of the Fiscal Question', 122–3.

of its functions.'[143] The test of a successful society is not material prosperity, but moral growth. Such a notion conjures fears of an unfortunate citizenry spied upon by some moral police or forced to sit some intrusive moral exam, but in fact the test Jones has in mind is more benign. The criterion of the successful action of the state is the effective freedom of its citizens.[144]

Jones wants to give great power to the state. He argues that no limits on what it may do can be fixed beforehand. 'I am not able to see that there is anything which the State may not do, or any department of man's life, however private, into which its entrance would be an invasion and interference,'[145] he allows. Such power, of course, must be wisely used, but the only relevant test for this is whether it in fact succeeds in bringing about moral transformation. Critics worried about excessive state interference in private lives often fail to realize that the state already limits us in countless way, notes Jones, but on the whole it limits only our ability to do what is wrong or stupid;[146] and this is no violation of rights, 'for the liberty to do wrong is not a right, but the perversion of a right and its negation'.[147]

Turning to the question of rights, for Jones, these are not natural or fixed, but socially determined. Moreover rights imply duties. The two are co-relative, the same thing looked at from different points of view.[148] For all that, Jones takes individual rights seriously.

There remains in the moral life of the citizens an intensely individual element which the State must never over-ride.... But, on the other hand, the sovereignty of the individual's will and all its sacredness come from its identification with a wider will. His rights are rooted in the rights of others.... Hence, the individual can resist the will of the community or the extension of the functions of his city or State only when he has identified his own will with a will that is more universal, more concrete, and the source of higher imperatives than either. And this means that he can resist the State only for the good of the State, and never *merely* for his own profit.[149]

Jones sees real limits to state interference, but these limits are only those imposed by its own end or supreme purpose.[150] The aim is to *moralize social relations as they stand*.[151] But the State cannot enforce or manipulate morality. There can be no coercion to be moral. Compulsion and freedom are incompatible, and any intervention which

---

[143] 'Working Faith of the Social Reformer', 114. 'It is a wrong to the State to regard it as a mere organ of secular force, and its policy as having no ethical character. It never is a mere secular force, and its might, in reference to its own citizens, is always measured by its moral right; for it itself is nothing else than the embodied conscience of the people' ('Moral Aspect of the Fiscal Question', 123).

[144] 'Working Faith of the Social Reformer', 113.

[145] *The Principles of Citizenship*, 136–7. 'So far as I can see, a good and wise State cannot have too much liberty or power or sovereignty, nor an evil and foolish one too little' (*The Principles of Citizenship*, 63).

[146] 'Working Faith of the Social Reformer', 107.

[147] 'Working Faith of the Social Reformer', 108.

[148] *The Principles of Citizenship*, 109.

[149] 'Working Faith of the Social Reformer', 113–14.

[150] *The Principles of Citizenship*, 132.

[151] 'Working Faith of the Social Reformer', 114.

undermines our character is self-defeating. The state cannot make us righteous, any more than can a father make his children good,[152] but it can create circumstances favourable to a good life. In this way,

The good State is like a good gardener, who secures for his plants the best soil and the best exposure for sunshine, air, and rain, and who then waits—not fashioning nor forming flower or fruit, but eliciting the activities of the life which bursts into them. His aim limits his meddling.[153]

Somewhat at a distance from Green and Bosanquet, Jones argues that state interference or provision of goods does not always tend to undermine or nullify individual moral effort in the same direction; legislation need not always impede spontaneity.[154] 'The action of the State cannot be merely negative, and cannot be confined to the external conditions of its citizens' lives, but must enter within,' he argues, 'it does not stop at the outward act and the mere intention but affects the motive and penetrates the self and becomes a living part of its structure.'[155] He suggests that the positive function of the state is becoming more and more prominent as civilization grows, and the range of its exercise extending.[156] Such intrusion is inevitable. The state cannot altogether avoid educating its people, and it is not possible simply to affect outer action without influencing inner motives. The only question is whether it does so well or ill.[157] Besides, Jones argues, the whole distinction between outer action and inner motive is not ultimate.[158]

Given Jones' holism and his support for state intervention, one might fear that in his political philosophy the individual just serves the state. But one of the most distinctive aspects of his system is the thorough *reciprocity* he finds between individual and state. Giving full reign to his literary fondness for a strong turn of phrase, Jones delights in arguing that everything goes both ways.

If the nature of the individual is essentially social, *the nature of society is essentially individual.*[159]

The State *is* the citizen 'writ large,' and the citizen *is* the State writ small. There is, in the final resort, no good State except where there are good citizens, nor good citizens except in a good State. Every citizen is responsible for his State; and the State is responsible for every one of its citizens.[160]

The power of the good State empowers the citizen, and the power of the good citizen empowers the State.[161]

The significance of this reciprocity is that it provides a sense in which the state *can be assessed*. Citizens must serve the state, and are judged by how well they do so, but he

---

[152] 'Moral Aspect of the Fiscal Question', 122.
[153] *The Principles of Citizenship*, 137.
[154] *The Principles of Citizenship*, 128.
[155] *The Principles of Citizenship*, 131–2.
[156] *The Principles of Citizenship*, 152.
[157] *The Principles of Citizenship*, 123, 126.
[158] *The Principles of Citizenship*, 127.
[159] 'Social and Individual Evolution', 233–4.
[160] *The Principles of Citizenship*, 109.
[161] *The Principles of Citizenship*, 89.

wholly rejects the charge that we are just means to its end, for a state that fails to serve it citizens is equally a failing one, for that is how *it* is judged; 'a State [is] a good State, and a citizen a good citizen precisely in the degree to which they are for one and another *both* means and ends.'[162] In view of the common charge that the idealist state is held to no account, this reciprocal principle of measurement is important to note.

14.2.5 *Socialism and individualism*

Like most of the other Idealists Jones was forced to address the pressing debate of the age, the quarrel between individualism and socialism. As did his teacher, Caird, he tries to dissolve the clash. In *Social Responsibilities*, his lectures to businessmen, he argues that as opposites or extremes both positions are mistaken; the former in wishing individuals to be free as far as possible from the interference of society, the latter in wishing to replace as far as possible private with municipal or state action. Their common error is a failure to see that the individual and the state share one life, such that each in repressing its opposite is really destroying itself. Whether he recognizes it or not the individual depends vitally on society, but society can only act through its own strong and healthy individuals.[163] In philosophical terms he argues that the dichotomy between individualism and socialism is a spurious one; 'the distinction of private from public good is, in the moral sphere, entirely false'.[164]

Not only have the terms of the debate been misunderstood, but also the underlying principles at issue. 'This social problem is material or economical only on the surface,' he argues, 'In its deeper bearings it is ethical.'[165] At one level idealism seems unwilling to advocate *any* specific social change, but at a more fundamental level *all* must be changed. Thus idealism does not align itself to the simplistic party politician. It would conserve most of our current social institutions, like property and the family,[166] but all would be moralized and reformed.[167] Progress comes not from destroying social relations but from transforming them ethically.[168]

Jones was in fact unhappy about the Labour Party insofar as it appealed to class interest rather than the common good. Through class interest, he thought, people 'become unconscious enemies of the common weal', 'they strike at the heart of the common good',[169] and simply repeat, this time in reverse, the past errors of the privileged.[170] And any socialism which called for widespread nationalization or the abolition of property was equally to be rejected. The appropriation of the means of

---

[162] *The Principles of Citizenship*, 53.
[163] 'Social Responsibilities', 270–2.
[164] 'Social and Individual Evolution', 237.
[165] 'Working Faith of the Social Reformer', 93.
[166] 'Idealism and Politics', 215.
[167] 'Idealism and Politics', 216.
[168] 'Social Responsibilities', 286.
[169] 'Moral Aspect of the Fiscal Question', 134.
[170] 'Social Responsibilities', 298; See also 'The Corruption of the Citizenship of the Working Man', esp.175–7; also Hetherington, *The Life and Letters of Sir Henry Jones*, 92.

industry by the state would reduce the individual to an unhealthy *dependence* upon it,[171] while private property is necessary for moral self-realization.[172] 'Let the individual own nothing but himself and he will not have a self to own.'[173] Property is in this sense an institution of the state, something the state ought to protect him in claiming.[174] 'Private property . . . is an institution wherein the individual finds a rule of action in society and society a rule of action in the individual.'[175] So even 'private property' is an example of the concurrent growth of both the subjective and the objective aspects of spirit.[176]

14.3 J.H. Muirhead

Muirhead studied under T.H. Green at Balliol and his social philosophy faithfully follows his teacher. Indeed, one of his first works, *Service of the State* (1908), is precisely an exposition of Green's political thought;[177] but even his own contribution to the field, *Social Purpose*, which he co-authored in 1918 with one of Henry Jones' pupils, H.J.W. Hetherington, is thoroughly orthodox, with all of the key idealist elements in place. Muirhead wrote chapters I–V, VII, and XIII, from which all the quotations below are drawn.

As might be expected Muirhead repudiates any individualist conception of society justified by the notion of a social contract; for that is to think of the civic order 'as in its essence a compromise' between the freedom and independence which is ours by natural right and the threats to them which result from communal life, as something 'in spite of which rather than that by means of which individuality is to be realized.'[178] Instead we must understand ourselves as essentially social: 'To deny one's citizenship is to deny one's humanity.'[179] What makes something an individual is not its singular or separable nature but the fact that it 'focuses' reality at a particular point, responding to the environmental forces around it in such a way that, 'at the same time it maintains its own nature, and is an essential part of the whole' within which those forces act.[180] To be noted is the way in which Muirhead makes use of the concrete universal in defence of this conception. Were socialization mere imitation of those around us, there would be no whole at all, merely an aggregate of identical individuals; but a more genuine universality is gained through the way in which we all in fact adapt differently to our

---

[171] 'Social Responsibilities', 285.
[172] 'Working Faith of the Social Reformer', 96–100. He is here basically following Green.
[173] 'Working Faith of the Social Reformer', 94.
[174] 'Working Faith of the Social Reformer', 98.
[175] 'Working Faith of the Social Reformer', 99.
[176] 'Working Faith of the Social Reformer', 100.
[177] Muirhead's estimate of Green is comparable to and near contemporaneous with that of John MacCunn, in his *Six Radical Thinkers*.
[178] *Social Purpose*, 37.
[179] *Social Purpose*, 97.
[180] *Social Purpose*, 102.

different situations; 'all real society is co-operation, the embodiment of an idea or universal in a particular form determined by one's place in a whole. Where co-operation ceases and mere imitation begins, there is an end to sociality.'[181] Nonetheless in his insistence to deny any 'original spark', Muirhead at times makes us seem little else but a conduit for higher things. 'Personality is merely the point where the vitality of which society is the great repository condenses and manifests itself in triumphant form, and it would be strange indeed if the strength of societies and that of the personalities which is fed from it were in inverse proportion to each other.'[182]

As each individual is bound to society, society itself is conceived as an organic individual. He admits that 'institutions are not men', but insists that 'On the other hand living institutions . . . represent the past efforts and the present co-operation of many individuals directed to a single and continuous purpose, and on this account may claim an individuality of their own of even a higher kind than of any single person.'[183] Developing Bosanquet's Platonic comparison between the state and the human body, he suggests that, 'As living organisms develop a central nervous system to co-ordinate the parts and assign them their places, so human life has evolved the State to secure individuals their functions and their corresponding rights.'[184]

Given that individuals are social so is their fulfilment. As 'there is more in the mind than is before the mind' so 'behind the will to the particular good there is the consciousness (or if it be preferred, the subconsciousness) of its relation to a whole of good of which it is only the partial realization'.[185] Whether or not we know it, we will the greater social or common good; although we could equally say that it wills us. There is no need to assume some further will over and above the wills of those that make up any society, simply that their willing is something more complex than we might first suppose, specifically that 'underlying the ends which the individual sets before himself in a social world, there is a reference to a wider end than they commonly represent, and that this is none other than the maintenance of the social structure itself'.[186]

Arousing suspicions of statism, Muirhead has a very high opinion of the state; it is 'the chief secular instrument and the highest as yet developed organ of the spirit'. But the state is not to be deified, it is not, as Hobbes taught, a God upon earth,[187] and its greatness is merely our own; it can be great only by our being so.[188] Indeed rather than working as one unit to bring specific things about, the best it can do is to work to set us free individually each to do the best we can. Idealism's great insight was that, 'The

---

[181]   *Social Purpose*, 99–100.
[182]   *Social Purpose*, 109.
[183]   Editor's Preface to *Birmingham Institutions*, vii.
[184]   'Philosophy and Social Reform', 10.
[185]   *Social Purpose*, 65.
[186]   *Social Purpose*, 87.
[187]   'Philosophy and Social Reform', 10.
[188]   'Philosophy and Social Reform', 22.

ultimate source of social betterment lay in the individual's power of responding to improved external conditions by utilizing them for self-improvement as a member of a civilized society and as himself a contributor to its further civilization. What the State could do was to remove hindrances to the free action of what for lack of a better name moralists call "conscience"—a faculty that might be deadened rather than quickened by hasty ill-considered collectivism.'[189]

One central theme of *Social Purpose*, the reality of the General Will, is something Muirhead finds empirically confirmed by the contemporaneous international catastrophe; 'individuals and nations who threw themselves into the great war at the beginning did so from various motives, to find later that they had been caught up into a larger purpose than they were aware of, pointing to issues unconnected and even inconsistent with their original aims'.[190] That there should be a common will among many individual wills is, of course, puzzling. Where Bosanquet looks to psychology and the presence of common dominating ideas, Muirhead stresses in particular the role of unifying social customs and habits.[191]

Hobhouse's critique of the General Will had considerable influence, and as late as 1924 Muirhead felt it worth returning to the issue and defending the General Will against Hobhouse's attack. Where Hobhouse directed his fire upon Bosanquet alone, Muirhead stresses (quite correctly) the continuity of Bosanquet's view with that of Bradley and Green,[192] while to the charge that this is an unduly 'metaphysical' theory, Muirhead makes the reply—a point which Bradley himself made in *Appearance and Reality*—that *all* such accounts are metaphysical. It is disingenuous of critics to suggest that theirs are not; they simply have a *different* metaphysics.[193] Perhaps most interesting of all is Muirhead's linkage of the General Will with the Concrete Universal.[194] There is no need for us to deny the metaphysical distinctness of persons, for the unity of purpose that makes for the General Will is qualitative not numerical, but it is not a single property the same in all instances, like the common greenness of leaves, but rather a single idea or function variously manifested in its many different appearances;[195] somewhat as throughout a variety of different tasks we may at each point describe what someone is doing as 'making supper'. One advance Muirhead makes beyond Green is to champion the cause of *democracy*. Idealism is faith in the progress of spirit, and nowhere may we see such providence more at work than behind the rise of democracy.[196] An instance of 'the extension of the domain of will and intelligence over that of instinct and custom,'[197] in its growth 'a candle has been lighted that can

[189] *Reflections by a Journeyman*, 160–1.
[190] *Social Purpose*, 83.
[191] *Social Purpose*, 84.
[192] 'Recent Criticism of the Idealist theory of the General Will', 171–2.
[193] 'Recent Criticism of the Idealist theory of the General Will', 174.
[194] 'Recent Criticism of the Idealist theory of the General Will', 24.
[195] 'Recent Criticism of the Idealist theory of the General Will', 238.
[196] 'Philosophy and Social Reform', 13.
[197] *Social Purpose*, 108.

never be put out.'[198] But, warns Muirhead, 'Before democracy can succeed as a form of government it must succeed as a form of life.'[199] So long as social life is conceived as a rivalry among individuals for goods, political democracy in any real sense will be impossible; we need to cultivate a sense of the common good, the virtues of self-sacrifice, patience and charity, to educate people in citizenship. Indeed more generally at the root of most current social problems lies the fact that there has occurred material growth without a corresponding spiritual growth; 'the body has gone ahead of the spirit'.[200]

One of the principal virtues of democracy is its basis in equality—although Muir-head is quick to qualify this; it champions equality, 'not in the sense of any qualitative or quantitative identity of actual goods, but in the sense of the equal right of all to the development of such capacity for good as nature has endowed them with.'[201] What is needed is an equalization of opportunity 'whose formula is not 'I am as good as you are' nor even 'You are as good as I' but rather 'Neither of us is as good as we ought to be and as we shall be when by one another's aid we shall come to our rights'.'[202] In a similar vein Muirhead opposes the suggestion that we abolish all class distinctions, objecting we must not confuse social inequality with the division of industrial labour. Differentiation and specialization are essential to society,[203] he argues, linking the point again to that of concrete universality; greater unity is achieved not by making everyone the same, but by making them more and more different yet connected.[204]

14.4 R.B. Haldane

No one illustrates better than R.B. Haldane the Idealist combination of theory and praxis. He studied in Edinburgh and Germany, and was an early convert to the idealist doctrine, but instead of academia he went into affairs. He began to study law and, after his father's death in 1877, went to live in London. He was called to the English Bar in 1879, establishing a successful practice, and being appointed Queen's Counsel in 1890. In 1885 he was elected to parliament, as a liberal for East Lothian, and thus began a parallel political career. In 1905 he became minister for the War Office, in 1911 he was elevated to the peerage, and in 1912 he was made Lord Chancellor. This post he held until 1915 when, attacked as too 'pro-Germany', he was forced to resign.[205] Through-out his busy political career, however, he continued with his philosophy; his efforts acknowledged by others in the field as worthy of the fullest attention, and not simply

---

[198] 'Spirit of Democracy', 429.
[199] 'Spirit of Democracy', 429.
[200] 'Philosophy and Social Reform', 15.
[201] 'Spirit of Democracy', 428–9.
[202] 'Spirit of Democracy', 431.
[203] 'Philosophy and Social Reform', 19.
[204] 'Philosophy and Social Reform', 20.
[205] See below p.552.

those of an amateur (as was rather the case with A.J. Balfour, Britain's other notable philosopher-politician.) Nor were these two strands of his life set simply side-by-side in parallel, rather each informed the other.

Haldane was involved in the emergence of what became known as 'new liberalism', a broad political movement which sought to augment classical liberal thinking with a greater positive role for the state whilst at the same time avoiding the extremes of socialism. If he went further than Green in his advocacy of state intervention, the goal remained thoroughly Greenian in conception—the 'fight for emancipation from conditions which deny fair play to the collective energy for the good of society as a whole.'[206] The traditional liberal aim of freedom for the individual from interference largely achieved, he argued, politics 'has now to win for him the conditions of freedom in a more subtle and far-reaching sense, of the freedom from that ignorance and unnatural lowness of moral and social ideal which are promoted by bad surroundings amid which too many of our fellow-countrymen are born and grow up'.[207] Such thoughts caused Haldane from 1920 onwards to move increasingly towards the Labour party, and he was briefly Lord Chancellor again in Ramsay MacDonald's 1924 government.

The state should be engaged on a two-fold task, Haldane believed, to build-up and nurture every citizen and at the same time restrain all those who would exploit or drag him down;[208] although it should be added that duties go both ways, and only through our reciprocal contribution to society do we earn the right to such concern from it.[209] In concrete terms what such a view meant was that all should be allowed a living wage, a decent home, and an adequate education,[210] but implicit too was a striving towards equality. The state, Haldane argued, must be furnished 'with the means of in some measure modifying the advantages which one man has over another, and the inequalities which must always arise from diversity of natural capacity'.[211] This was radical, but there were limits to the redistribution Haldane envisioned. Indeed, toning down his earlier position, by the time of the Great War we find him arguing that, although Christianity brought in the idea of the equal (infinite) value of each human being, by nature people are born with unequal advantages (talent, beauty, brains, health, etc.) which can never be done away with. Thus he opposes Bolshevism. People can, however, be given equality of opportunity of developing what is in them[212]— especially children (hence the importance of education) and women (he was closely

[206] 'The New Liberalism', 141–1. It is to the words of Green's 'Liberal Legislation' address that Haldane turns in attempting further to explicate this notion (ibid. 135–7).

[207] 'Liberal Party and its Prospects', 155.

[208] 'Future of Democracy', 9.

[209] 'Every man and woman is, after all, a citizen in a State. Therefore let us see to it that there is not lacking that interest in the larger life of the social whole which is the justification of a real title to have a voice and a vote' ('Conduct of Life', 22).

[210] 'Future of Democracy', 9–10. See below pp.517–21 for more on education.

[211] 'The Liberal Creed', 467.

[212] 'Future of Democracy', 8–9.

involved in promoting female suffrage.) For all his support of Green, on one key point—temperance—Haldane was at odds with him. He felt it addressed only the symptoms not the source of the disease. 'The cause of drunkenness, and half-a-dozen social evils, is ignorance, bad housing, and poverty,'[213] he argued; solve these problems and temperance will follow.

Lying behind this interventionist programme for social progress is a particular idealist model of society, by now familiar, as something both unified and spiritual. Rather than an aggregate of mutually exclusive human particles standing in external relations, people form a community in the sense that each man belongs to an ethical and political environment with which he is continuous and on which he depends for his nature and existence. The whole is not an entity *apart from* its members, it simply consists in the members each with their various stations and duties, but it is a genuine whole because it is only as members of such a unit that the individuals exist with the nature they do, each 'pulse-beats of the whole system'.[214] 'Individual they are, but completely real, even as individual, only in their relation to organic and social wholes in which they are members, such as the family, the city, the state.'[215]

In attempting to explain this, Haldane helps himself to the familiar metaphor of biological organism. Living beings, he argues, display 'this remarkable feature, that the life of the whole is present in each of the parts'. A body, for example, is made of countless cells, 'but these cells act together in maintaining the common life of the organism'.[216] The same he thinks holds of a society. But metaphors only take us part of the way, and he insists that social wholes cannot be completely captured in biological language *alone*, for biology 'does not take account of conscious purpose and of the intelligence and volition which are characteristic of persons as distinguished from organisms'.[217] Just as 'the living organism is more and other than a mechanism', so 'the intelligent and moral human being is more and other than a merely living organism'.[218] We share the holism of *biology*, but we have the added feature of *purpose* or *intent*; and what binds people together more than anything 'is a certain sameness in general purpose'.[219]

In a 1913 address, 'Higher Nationality', Haldane approaches this notion of unity from another angle. 'The law forms only a small part of the system of rules by which the conduct of the citizens of a state is regulated,'[220] he argues, 'if its full significance is to be appreciated, larger conceptions than those of the mere lawyer are essential.'[221] There is *conscience*, but that is private.[222] However, besides these two, 'There is a more

---

[213] 'Future of Democracy', 11.
[214] 'Higher Nationality', 122.
[215] 'Higher Nationality', 121.
[216] *Pathway*, 42.
[217] 'The Meaning of Truth in History', 47.
[218] 'Nature of the State,' 766.
[219] 'Nature of the State', 766–7.
[220] 'Higher Nationality', 112.
[221] 'Higher Nationality', 113.
[222] 'Higher Nationality', 113.

extensive system of guidance which regulates conduct and which differs from both in its character and sanction. It applies, like law, to all the members of a society alike, without distinction of persons. It resembles the morality of conscience in that it is enforced by no legal compulsion.'[223] In English there is no name for it, continues Haldane, but the Germans call it 'Sittlichkeit' and it covers 'the system of habitual or customary conduct, ethical rather than legal, which embraces all those obligations of the citizen which it is "bad form" or "not the thing" to disregard.'[224] It includes all the social institutions in and by which the individual life is influenced such as are the family, the school, the church, the legislature, and the executive.[225] It is this unthinking or automatic sense of obligation that is 'the chief foundation of society,' urges Haldane.[226] It is sometimes thought that (as opposed to the individual will that constantly changes) the communal will is static. But this is a mistake.[227] Public opinion is never static, but constantly changes and develops.[228] It can manifest in different ways, varying in form and strength, but in its highest form it is something 'affording the most real freedom of thought and action for those who in daily life habitually act in harmony with the General Will'.[229]

The last sentence here reminds us that Haldane's Sittlichkeit is, of course, a relative of Rousseau's doctrine of the General Will. And like Rousseau, Haldane thinks that the general opinion must prevail. But the general opinion is not just the numerical or mechanical outcome of a set of ballot boxes on a particular day. We have to look below the surface of the moment. It is not revealed in any single institution, practice, standard, tradition, or culture—but in all of these together and more; in the common spirit they express. While there can be no other standard than that of democracy, like lawyers—and Haldane is here drawing on his other career—the statesmen in charge of a nation 'must do their best to advise and guide their clients, and they must judge whether these clients have, in the utterances of fevered moments, really expressed themselves'.[230] A distinction, for instance, must be drawn between a true General Will and a momentary or mob will.[231]

14.5 Idealism and education

We have already seen how strongly the Idealists focused on education, and this focus continued into the later period. Two general features stand out. The first is their view of the content of education. Given the idealist emphasis on service to society, it might

---

[223] 'Higher Nationality', 114.
[224] 'Higher Nationality', 115.
[225] 'Higher Nationality', 116.
[226] 'Higher Nationality', 116.
[227] 'Nature of the State', 768.
[228] 'Nature of the State', 769.
[229] 'Higher Nationality', 118.
[230] 'Nature of the State', 772.
[231] 'Nature of the State', 773.

perhaps be expected that they would advocate vocational or professional education, such as would allow citizens to take up more effectively their station in society. But that was very far from their view. In an 1897 address to the students at Glasgow entitled, 'General and Professional Education', John Caird argued for the value of higher education of a broad and cultural type rather than one more narrowly focused towards future employment, on the threefold grounds that this is necessary for us to first find our professional vocation, that it works against the subsequent narrowing of the mind that a career tends to bring and that it better fits us for social duties outside our workplace. For these reasons he suggested young people 'should be made to breathe for a term of years an intellectual atmosphere other and purer than that which but too often pervades the world on which they are about to enter'.[232] This potential for a community to be educated through the elevated spirit which pervades it was expressed too by his brother Edward in one of his Lay Sermons to the students of Balliol. Our greatest educator is the moral tone of the community in which we find ourselves, he argued, and, 'A man who has once lived in a society where the moral and intellectual tone was high, has by that very fact had his courage raised to attempt things of which he otherwise would never have dreamed.'[233]

The second general feature to note is the Idealists had a conception of education as *teaching*, not just *learning*. For illustration of this we may look again to John Caird, this time to an 1894 address, 'The Personal Element in Teaching', in which he says that the inspired lecture is to mere book learning 'as the living spirit to the dead letter'.[234] The point is important not least because what the Idealists themselves believed on this score they practised also. Although they were writers, it is crucial to remember that all[235] of the British Idealists were also *teachers*; and in case of figures like Nettleship, Green, and the Cairds, primarily so. Their own educational efforts themselves manifested the ideas they attempted to spread with such zeal, and their influence was very largely through their pupils, rather than their readers.

A key figure to focus on in this regard is Henry Jones. Himself the beneficiary of precisely the kind of educational opportunities for the poor which he later worked so hard to extend, and also someone who had trained as a teacher before serving briefly as the master of an Elementary School, Henry Jones did much to lobby for education, especially in his native Wales. He supported compulsory state education, education for women, and adult education. He was a key player in the movement which resulted in the Welsh Intermediate Education Act (1889), and he served on both the 1916–17 Royal Commission on University Education in Wales—which was chaired by Haldane—and on the 1918 departmental committee on adult education, in which year he also visited the United States as a member of the British University Investigative Committee.

---

[232] *University Addresses*, 381–2.
[233] *Lay Sermons*, 19.
[234] *University Addresses,* 367. Cf. Jones, 'The Library as a Maker of Character', 219.
[235] With the exception of Bradley.

The philosophy which lay behind this involvement was that moral education was a right, and consequently that the state had a duty to educate people; but that such education should allow citizens to develop and set free their latent capacities, rather than regiment or subdue them. They should not be educated for the sake of the state (as he felt was the case in Germany) nor for industrialization (as he felt was too often the case in Britain), rather 'the true education of the citizen, the education which is the best for him and also for the state, is that which educates him *for his own sake*; and not for any ulterior purpose. It must terminate in him.'[236]

Like Jones, throughout his career Haldane was involved in education. Some of his earliest political efforts were with the Universities in Scotland Bill (1889) and with the University of London Bill (1897), while later he was closely involved in the granting of university status to several of the provincial colleges: Birmingham (1900), Liverpool (1903), Manchester (1903), Leeds (1904), Sheffield (1905), and Bristol (1909). (He became the second chancellor of Bristol University from 1912 until his death.) He chaired both the Royal Commission on London University (1909–13)[237] and the Royal Commission into University Education in Wales (1916–17), the latter on which Henry Jones also served. He was involved in the setting up of the London School of Economics (LSE) (1895), the Workers' Educational Association (WEA) (1903), and Imperial College (1907). He also helped to establish The British Institute of Adult Education (which came into being in 1921 at his home at Queen Anne's Gate, London).[238]

The credo behind Haldane's educational work was a belief that 'to all men and women the State should give the right to get such instruction as would free them from the depressing effects of circumstances for which they were not responsible, and which were preventing them from individually having a real chance in life'.[239] Echoing Green's suggestion that being uneducated is akin to being crippled, he argued, 'knowledge is power more really to-day than ever before.... You are hopelessly handicapped in the race of life unless you have knowledge, and it must be the concern of the State, in driving after the ideal of equality, to secure that every man and woman has a chance of knowing.'[240] But the freedom education brings is, of course, an idealist freedom; that is, a freedom to serve, and for this reason people need not just abstract knowledge, but a moral education which tells them 'that their own lives are a trust to be carried out for the benefit of those around them as well as for themselves'.[241]

---

[236] *The Principles of Citizenship*, 133. 'To employ education for the formation of the soul for any purpose other than its own direct good is to pervert the uses of education. Its value and end is to emancipate, not to enslave. Education is the condition of freedom, as freedom is the condition of all the virtues' ('Education of the Citizen', 239).

[237] One of whose recommendations was that Birkbeck College be admitted into the University of London for part-time and evening students. In 1919 he became President of the College, working for this aim, which was achieved in 1920. He remained its President until his death in 1928.

[238] For further details on all these see Lockwood, 'Haldane and Education'.

[239] *Autobiography*, 301.

[240] 'Future of Democracy', 10. cf. Green, 'Liberal Legislation and Freedom of Contract', 374–5.

[241] 'Future of Democracy', 21.

Haldane spoke of the 'double function of our educational institutions, the imparting of culture for culture's sake on the one hand, and the application of science to the training of our captains of industry on the other',[242] but how to achieve this was a matter on which his ideas changed. In early writings he suggests that the German system had succeeded far better than the British in meeting this two-fold aim with its separation of technical and classical education,[243] and he was especially keen to introduce into Britain the German *Technische Hochschule* model;[244] something which he finally did with the creation of Imperial College. However, by his 1912 Bristol University address, he was more amenable to the thought that a single institution could unify both elements,[245] and even later, we find him complaining of the division between humanities and the sciences, claiming that too early a separation (at secondary school level) has served Germany badly.[246] In a near contemporaneous address, Muirhead, on the eve of the transition of Mason's College (where he was Professor of Philosophy) into Birmingham University, reflecting on 'the function which a University performs in opening the minds of the men and women who come within its influence to new ideals as to the meaning of life, and in enabling them to understand and enjoy the best things which it has to offer',[247] urged a similarly liberal education that combines science with art and literature, knowledge with feeling, yoked together by philosophy in the practical moral service of humanity.

A great many of the Idealists were concerned to promote education for women. Together with Henry Nettleship, R.L. Nettleship's brother, Green set up the Association for the Higher Education of Women in Oxford. An early success was the establishment in 1876 of a university college in Bristol (which later became Bristol University), open to both men and women. Green was a member of its council.[248] Caird too was a tireless campaigner for women's education. From 1868 he offered short courses of lectures to women, in 1877 these being done more systematically under the Glasgow Association for the Higher Education of Women (chaired by his brother, John). In 1883 the Association developed into Queen Margaret College, for which Caird continued to lecture and on whose Governing Board he served. Only in 1892 were women finally admitted into the University, into which the College was then incorporated.[249] After coming to Balliol he joined the Oxford Association for the Higher Education of Women and was its President for the last ten years of his life. He was Chair of the Oxford Home Students committee—which looked after the other women students in Oxford, and served as vice-president of the Council of Somerville

---

[242] *Education and Empire*, x.

[243] *Education and Empire*, 27.

[244] *Education and Empire*, 24ff.

[245] 'The Civic University', 89–90.

[246] *Education After the War*, 3, 22. Jones too was ambivalent about German education, clear about the advance it had given them, but lamenting its lack of moral basis ('The Education of the Citizen', 229–41).

[247] 'Liberal Education', 139.

[248] Gordon and White, *Philosophers as Educational Reformers*, 84.

[249] Jones and Muirhead, *Life and Philosophy of Edward Caird*, 96–101.

College. He was one of the hundred and forty MA's who in 1895 presented a proposal to Hebdomadal Council to admit women to degrees.[250] The proposal was rejected, and in the end Oxford did not allow women to attain degrees until 1922.

Women were not only recipients of education, but (outside the universities) in large part its providers. These women teachers needed training, and in this connection mention should be made of Millicent Mackenzie.[251] In 1892 University College Cardiff established a department for the training of women as secondary school teachers and she was appointed as its first Head; elevated in 1904 to Associate Professor of Education and in 1910 to full Professor (thereby making her the first woman professor in Britain[252]), which position she held until her retirement in 1915. In 1898 she married the philosopher J.S. Mackenzie, whose idealist views she shared. Her most important book, *Hegel's Educational Theory and Practice*, which was published in 1909, is a notable early foray into a still neglected area. Admitting that Hegel wrote no specific treatise on education, she nevertheless argues that it is possible to piece together his philosophy of education drawing on his general philosophical writings, his letters, and the addresses which he delivered as Rector of the Nürnberg Gymnasium. She argues that for Hegel education was essential in the evolutionary process whereby we come to a self-conscious realization of our relation to the universe at large; a breaking away of self-estrangement from our purely natural life to a higher spiritual life; a losing one's life in order to find it. The emphasis is on the training of intellect and moral character rather than the senses or the imagination, and for this purpose, in the matter of curriculum, Hegel argued for the pre-eminent place of classics. Mackenzie's book is basically exposition but, although supportive, it is not without an awareness of the difficulties of Hegel's position, such as his disparaging view of women's education (women, he claims, can be trained only in 'picture thinking' unlike men who can be trained in 'thought') and his overemphasis on the intellectual side of mind at the expense of feeling.

14.6 Idealism and international relations

The political philosophy of the Idealists revolved around the state. But what connection has this with the nation-state of actual political life? And what bearing has it on issues of nationalism or internationalism? From the beginning, and increasingly so, these questions pressed themselves; fed also by contemporary events, for this was the period of the expansion of empires, the first and second Boer Wars, and the Great War.[253]

---

[250] Jones and Muirhead, *Life and Philosophy of Edward Caird*, 150–2.

[251] For more details see *John Stuart Mackenzie*, ch.IX.

[252] An achievement sometimes mistakenly attributed to Caroline Spurgeon (1869–1942) who appointed Professor of English Literature at London University in 1913.

[253] The last of these will be discussed in more detail in the next chapter.

Some of Muirhead's earliest writings were on the topic of imperialism. To begin with, he insists, we must separate all historical questions of how or by what right the empire was won, from questions concerning the responsibilities it now entails.[254] We have a duty of care and nurture, part of our 'obligation to the wider whole of Humanity'.[255] This duty is to develop (not 'reconstruct') the moral, industrial, and spiritual ideas of some four or five hundred million people, in best accord with their own races;[256] not to destroy their own forms of the General Will, but foster what is best in them.[257] Our mission must be to teach European ideas of truth, justice, and science, for 'Justice is justice, and science is science, all the world over'.[258] But to go beyond this and make Europe the model in all things is to go too far. More often than not, we have not done enough to understand the people we are trying to educate.[259] We need to encourage in them a sense of loyalty to us and of dependence on the institutions of government we have brought them, for security, prosperity, and freedom,[260] but once the people *know* what good governance is, matters may be trusted to them.[261] He reminds readers that Green was clear that people need to be not just passive recipients of protection, but active participants in self-government, if the state is to earn their loyalty.[262] For the British empire this is still theory, an aspiration, but however distant a goal, it is an ideal that must never be lost sight of.[263]

Henry Jones also endorsed a species of self-critical and benevolent imperialism. He was as ready as Muirhead to admit historical wrongs. After the 1899–1902 Boer War, for example, he allowed that Britain's 'blatant imperialism and reckless greed' had 'left a stain upon the national honour'.[264] And during the Great War he conceded that it was not 'to convert the heathen' or 'to spread civilisation' that we took our empire but rather 'in the way of business', and in that cause, 'We have been as ruthless, and we have been as ready to plead "the rights of the higher civilisation over the lower," as the German people are to day.'[265]

But notwithstanding these admissions, Jones thought empire a high calling. He praises journalists who have helped create 'the throb of the larger Citizenship'. 'It is

---

[254] *The Service of State*, 106.

[255] *Social Purpose*, 265.

[256] *The Service of State*, 106.

[257] *The Service of State*, 107.

[258] 'What Imperialism Means', 249.

[259] 'What Imperialism Means', 250.

[260] *The Service of State*, 109.

[261] *The Service of State*, 110.

[262] *The Service of State*, 11. *Lectures on Principles of Political Obligation*, §122. In consequence Green approves of the way in which the British in India have left native traditions largely to function in their own way encouraging natural indigenous development (§90).

[263] *The Service of State*, 112.

[264] 'Idealism and Politics', 184.

[265] 'Why we are fighting', 56. The War evoked a similar admission by A.C. Bradley: 'In our Empire-making we did things we cannot justify, and the Empire made becomes an object of envy and a cause of war' ('International Morality: The United States Of Europe', 59).

owing to you, in great part,' he says 'that our people is one people and our Empire one Empire. Nay, you bind nation to nation, and involve the fate of one in the fate of all the others.'[266] The ultimate justification or not of empire lies in the way in which it discharges the great responsibility it has to raise up its subject peoples. For Jones the true individual—the individual for whose sake the state exists—is not what each of us is, but what he has it in him to become. But the nurturing duties of states towards their citizens hold equally of empires towards their contained nations which, he thinks, is something we cannot keep too constantly in view in dealing with India or other underdeveloped nations.[267] Our sole imperial duty is to help the nations we govern to become all that they have in them to become. Not only are the interests of the empire one with those of its subject nations, they are equally harmonious with those of other non-subject nations. 'The British Empire, by its political and social progress, by its science and inventions and industrial enterprise, has benefited every country with which it has held intercourse. And other nations have done the same to us. Their good is ours, and ours theirs.'[268] Gradually co-operation in common ends and mutual service come to replace rivalry and antagonism, and if a measure of egoism must remain (for a nation cannot without contradiction sacrifice itself) it becomes an 'enlightened egoism', 'which recognises that the good which is exclusive is a false good'.[269] Jones therefore opposes protectionism.

A similarly high-minded imperialism is advocated by Mackenzie. Writing in 1900, it seemed to him that almost overnight people had woken up to find themselves members, not simply of a country but of an empire.[270] If just as a generation ago the moral consciousness of society had largely shifted from an individualistic to a social perspective,[271] it was time again for a further 'expansion of interest'. The need was to wake up to the fact that 'we have relations and obligations all over the surface of the earth', and thus that we must treat our empire not just as a commercial asset or national adornment but embrace instead a 'true imperialism' which involves 'the recognition that we have our part to play with others in the great task of advancing humanity, that we have to join heartily with others in the promotion of peace, liberty, justice, and enlightenment, to which we hope all nations will be more and more devoted'.[272]

For Edward Caird, the ethical growth that takes us from family, to community to nation cannot stop there but must end in the cause of humanity as a whole, not 'as a mere aggregate of individuals, but rather as a growing social unity, a family of nations which, in spite of their differences and oppositions, are very gradually, but still certainly, being drawn together, and made into the members of one organism, a

[266] 'Journalism and Citizenship', 65.
[267] *Principles of Citizenship*, 145.
[268] 'Moral Aspects of the Fiscal Question', 146.
[269] 'Moral Aspects of the Fiscal Question', 147.
[270] 'The Source of Moral Obligation', 469.
[271] 'The Source of Moral Obligation', 468.
[272] 'The Source of Moral Obligation', 477–8.

world community, in which each has a special function to discharge'.[273] Admitting that at present 'this still remains in great part an idea'[274] and that, 'The world as a whole does not at present look much like such a society',[275] he nonetheless saw in the political developments of his day encouraging signs of movement in that direction.[276]

Specifically Caird saw a large role for the British empire in that globalizing mission. 'We have become the great colonising nation, and the nation that has shown the greatest power of gaining the mastery over uncivilised races' with whom we have made an effort 'such as perhaps hardly any other nation has made, to make our government tend to the good of the governed'.[277] And he told his students, 'There is no harm, rather there is the greatest good, in our being full of zeal for the imperial glory of England, if and so far as that glory is the glory of greater service, the glory of raising barbarous races to civilization and Christianity, the glory of extending the empire of peace and justice among men.'[278] Well he might say so, for the Balliol of his mastership had done much to fuel its expansion—in one address (c.1899) Caird reflected upon the enormous contribution that Balliol men had made to society and to the empire, far outstripping any other educational institution.[279]

But if the Master of Balliol is confident, he is not complacent. Nor does he think that imperialism may be given *carte blanche*. Patriotism can never be a matter of 'my country right or wrong', for we are not simply servants, but members, of our state, each with a degree of responsibility for the direction in which the whole is going.[280] We must hold our nation to account. Moreover, when we do so, by no means does everything look well. Our overseas activities have suffered from an unfortunate 'mingling of higher and lower motives, of gain and gospel, which have often caused us to be accused of hypocrisy by other nations'.[281] For imperialism pursued with thoughts 'of selfish triumph, of commercial success and material aggrandisement and military glory'[282] is to be abhorred. Such reservations make it clear that Caird was no die-hard imperialist (in the Kipling mould) and they are what lay behind his opposition to British action in the Boer War and his protest against the award of an honorary doctorate to Cecil Rhodes.[283]

---

[273] *Lay Sermons*, 61.

[274] *Lay Sermons*, 61.

[275] *Lay Sermons*, 42.

[276] *Lay Sermons*, 62. Ritchie too approves the existence of a few great 'empires' as a possible staging post towards a future 'world-federation' ('War and Peace', 151).

[277] *Lay Sermons*, 113–14.

[278] *Lay Sermons*, 254.

[279] *Life and Philosophy of Edward Caird*, 375–6.

[280] *Lay Sermons*, 117.

[281] *Lay Sermons*, 115.

[282] *Lay Sermons*, 254.

[283] In a letter preserved in the Bodleian Library which the Vice-Chancellor refused to publish in the *Oxford Gazette*, but which subsequently appeared in *The Times* for 20 June 1899, eighty-eight members of Congregation (the body of Oxford academics) including Edward Caird, E. Abott, J.A. Smith, F.C.S. Schiller, C.C.J. Webb, H.H. Joachim, J. Burnet, Hastings Rashdall, H.W.B. Joseph, and James Drummond expressed their regret at his receiving a degree. It was rumoured that the Proctors, both liberals, would protest during the ceremony. But Lord Kitchener stepped in threatening not to take *his* degree if Rhodes was prevented

Like Green, Bosanquet was sceptical about a universal brotherhood of men. Though to be admitted as an ethical ideal,[284] the notion of all mankind as a single community is far from fact. There is no political unity larger than the state. Nothing in Bosanquet's writing rules out a world-state *in principle*, he merely thought that the limits of shared common life were *de facto* fixed by the nation-state.[285] In fact he gave cautious welcome to the League of Nations.[286] But given that there is no 'world community' it is a mistake to regard the morality of states as functioning like that of the individuals within them. He would not deny that states have moral duties to each other, or that their normal relations are ones of co-operation rather than competition,[287] but the situation is more than just a 'scaling up' of the ordinary case. For example, existing solely for the sake of its citizens, the state has an absolute duty to protect itself and its resources from external aggression, in a way no individual could claim an absolute right to self-defence or private property.

In his article on 'Higher Nationality', an address delivered before the American bar association at Montreal, Haldane too considered the prospects for a world-state, asking whether the binding force—the shared social life—that holds *within* nations might not hold also *between* nations?[288] 'There is, I think, nothing in the real nature of nationality that precludes such a possibility,'[289] he says, but there is a very long road to travel before we can get there.[290] A world union, an international sittlichkeit, would be the ideal, but this is most likely to come about first by smaller unions of countries, and in this connection he suggests that 'Canada and Great Britain on the one hand and the United States on the other, with their common language, their common interests, and their common ends, form something resembling a single society'.[291] This is also the context for his endorsement of the suggestion of an Imperial University, a sort of 'post-graduate research college, where students from every part of the empire could come to carry their scientific training further than is possible in the less specialised colonial and other Universities'.[292] He suggests the newly constituted University of London might play that role.

---

from taking his. Jones and Muirhead, *Life and Philosophy of Edward Caird*, 153–4; Symonds, *Oxford and Empire*, 163. In September 1899, Caird wrote again to *The Times* on the subject of the war. It is worth noting that not all Idealists took this line—Haldane was a strong supporter of the Boer War (*Autobiography*, 135–9).

[284] *Philosophical Theory of the State*, 305.

[285] 'The Function of the State in Promoting the Unity of Mankind', 294. Although the belief that man will inevitably advance to a single political body he regards as a 'naive form of optimism' akin to that which looks forward to the removal of all evil (ibid. 299).

[286] *Philosophical Theory of the State*, lix–lxi.

[287] 'The Function of the State in Promoting the Unity of Mankind', 277.

[288] 'Higher Nationality', 126.

[289] 'Higher Nationality', 127.

[290] 'Higher Nationality', 128.

[291] 'Higher Nationality', 129, 101. Haldane's account of this trans-Atlantic proposal is worth comparing with A.C. Bradley's consideration of Kant's suggestion of a united states of Europe ('International Morality: The United States of Europe', 67ff). Bosanquet thinks such unions lack the necessary spirit of community to ever succeed ('Patriotism in the Perfect State', 136–7).

[292] *Education and Empire*, 36.

15

The After-Life of Idealism

Much time is spent tracing the origins of intellectual movements, rather less time examining their endings; but since ideas decline as much as they rise there is value to be had from investigating the latter process also. The final chapter of this study undertakes that task with respect to the British Idealist movement, casting a spotlight on areas that have received scarcely any scholarly attention up to now. Looking at a range of texts and figures it will be demonstrated that idealism, or idealistically influenced thinking, continued far into the twentieth century—long after new schools of thought might be considered to have 'replaced' it. It became fragmented, cautious and diluted with other lines of thinking, but it continued to exist as a kind of 'counter-current' to the language- and logic-based style of philosophy that came forward to take centre stage. That it suffered a massive decline in popularity cannot be denied, however, and the second half of this chapter turns to consider some of the factors behind that reversal of fortune. This it will be argued was in great part the result of external rather than internal factors, of changing intellectual fashions rather than philosophical arguments mounted against it.

15.1 The long decline of British Idealism

Puzzles arise from the moment we attempt to date the demise of British Idealism. We fixed with some degree of satisfaction when it began, and arguably the turn of the century marks its high point, but when did it *end*?

A variety of dates might be proposed. We might suggest 1903, the year which saw the appearance of Russell's *Principles of Mathematics*, as well as Moore's *Principia Ethica* and 'The Refutation of Idealism', works which simultaneously attacked idealism and inaugurated the new 'analytic' philosophy commonly regarded as characterizing the twentieth century. Certainly this was regarded as a new and exciting departure,[1]

---

[1] For C.D. Broad's sense of the mood at the time see his 'Autobiography' (49–50). For a retrospective assessment of the new philosophical uprising see A.J. Ayer, *The Revolution in Philosophy*.

certainly idealism was felt by some to be in decline as early as 1906,[2] and certainly conventional histories, where they mention idealism at all, tend to leave off their accounts at this point, switching attention to the new players on the field; but unlike, for example, the reign of a monarch, the beginning of a new research programme in philosophy is not at all the same thing as the end of its predecessor and, as we have already seen in the second half of this book, much interesting idealist work was done after 1903.[3] On this point histories of philosophy may fairly be charged with misleading by omission.

Some later dates might be considered. Perhaps the Great War of 1914–18, whose carnage so scarred the European consciousness and which for many left fatally under-mined any grand optimism about states, civilization, and the universe, of the kind that so characterized idealism? Again one might suggest the years 1923–5 which, with the deaths of Jones, Bosanquet, Bradley, James Seth, and McTaggart, seemed like some-thing of the passing of an age? Or one might suggest the thirties during which the Logical Positivists thundered out their message that metaphysics, the very heart of idealism, was meaningless? There is plausibility in all three suggestions; but it is possible also to find significant idealist work done after each of these dates.

In truth the later years offer us a complex and contradictory picture. On the one hand it is undeniable that the movement's strong popular support was followed by an equally robust rejection. Many new philosophers cast off completely the idealism of their teachers, which had come to seem complacent or irrelevant, and the school withered; first argued against, then ridiculed, and finally just ignored.[4] As philosophy moved on, the twentieth century was marked for the large part by a lack of interest in those questions of metaphysics, history of philosophy and political philosophy so vitally important to the Idealists. Antipathy to the immediate past gave way to dismissal, as a version of the history of British Philosophy began to be taught that jumped straight from Mill to Russell.[5] This had the result that even today most philosophers know nothing of British Idealism; it comes to them as a genuine surprise to learn of this 'idealist aberration' in the great British empirical tradition.

The problem with this received narrative is that it tells only one half of the true story. The history of idealist philosophy after its heyday has remained largely unknown, and closer investigation reveals something unexpected. The prevailing attitude is that the school died out and ceased to matter. But neither of these things are true. Idealism

---

[2] G.B. Foster review of *Evolution of Theology in the Greek Philosophers*, 762.

[3] Paton, for example, testifies that up until the war idealism was still felt generally to be in the ascendant—'to say that it was already on the wane would be, I think, to judge by hindsight rather than to express the feeling of the time'—and that 'For philosophers generally, at least outside Cambridge, Bradley and, in a lesser degree, Bosanquet were the dominant figures even to those who opposed them' ('Fifty Years of British Philosophy', 341–3).

[4] By 1930 C.D. Broad felt able to dismiss Green in a sentence as 'a thoroughly second-rate thinker' (*Five Types of Ethical Theory*, 144).

[5] E.g. J. Lewis, *History of Philosophy*; W. Matson, *A History of Philosophy*; A. Kenny, *A Brief History of Western Philosophy*.

continued to live on long after its 'refutation'. Works continued to be produced, ideas to be developed, and disputes engaged in. Its decline was a very long drawn-out affair. This continuance of Idealism is crucial, not least because it formed the context in which students were still taught and against which many of them developed their own views. This period is also worth exploring, insofar as it is perhaps typical of intellectual movements more generally; once assimilated, ideas live on in intellectual culture for far longer than is commonly appreciated.

15.1.1 The longevity of idealist literature

There are a number of different ways in which we may bring out this 'after-life' of Idealism. One is by examination of the literature, by looking at the philosophical discussions that were actually taking place during these years. To be sure, new topics began to fill up the pages of the philosophical journals. But even if they no longer dominated, it is still possible to find articles on and discussions of such topics as idealism and realism, idealism and pragmatism, the Absolute, the General Will, the concrete universal, the reality of time, Bradley, and Bosanquet well into the 1920s, even the 1930s. To take but one group of writings; who, we must ask, were the British Logical Positivists objecting to in the 1930s if not the last few remaining idealists? In his 1936 *Language, Truth and Logic* Ayer memorably lays into Bradley whose *Appearance and Reality* was published in 1893, some forty-three years earlier—such an attack could have had no relevance for Ayer's readers unless they felt that there were still at work around them modern representatives of the same errors.

Another factor which belies the supposed disappearance of interest is the persistent republication into the 1920s, 1930s, and even 1940s of many classic and key idealist texts, such as Green's *Prolegomena* and *Lectures on Political Obligation*, or Bradley's *Ethical Studies* and *Appearance and Reality*.[6] These books continued to be read and taught, even if to an increasing unsympathetic audience.

The lasting presence of idealism—at least in a teaching context—is further reflected in the history of textbooks dealing with it. The ethical textbooks of Muirhead, Mackenzie, and James Seth continued to enjoy success well into the twentieth century. Another long-running book was A.E. Taylor's *Elements of Metaphysics*, also used for a many years as a textbook.[7]

---

[6] *Prolegomena to Ethics*—1883, 1884, 1891,1899, 1907 (5th edn), 1911, 1919, 1925, 1929, 1931, 1949, 2003 (ed. D. Brink); *Lectures on the Principles of Political Obligation*—1885–8, 1895, 1901, 1907, 1913, 1917, 1921, 1924, 1927, 1931, 1941, 1948, 1950, 1986 (ed. P. Harris and J. Morrow), 2002; *Ethical Studies*—1876, 1927 (2nd edn), 1935, 1951, 1952, 1959, 1962, 1988 (ed. R. Wollheim), 1990; *Appearance and Reality*—1893, 1897 (2nd edn), 1899, 1902, 1908, 1916, 1920, 1925, 1930 (9th impression, corrected), 1946, 1955, 1959, 1963, 1969 (ed. R. Wollheim), 2002.

[7] Muirhead's *Elements* 1892, 1894, 1910, 1932 (4th edn); MacKenzie's *Manual* 1893, 1894, 1897, 1900, 1915, 1929 (6th edn); Seth's *Study* 1894, 1895, 1898, 1899, 1900, 1902, 1904, 1905, 1907, 1908, 1909, 1911, 1914, 1918, 1921, 1924, 1926, 1928 (18th edn). Taylor's *Elements* 1903, 1909, 1912, 1915, 1920, 1921, 1924, 1927, 1930, 1936, 1940, 1946, 1952 (13th edn) 1962. As Taylor's career developed he gradually left behind his early Bradleyan views, arriving eventually at a position of ethical theism. The change was largely

There was even a demand for new textbooks exclusively devoted to the topic. We might consider, for example, C.R. Morris' *Idealistic Logic*, described on its publication in 1933 as a 'useful and timely book' by the decidedly non-idealist Susan Stebbing.[8] Nor was Morris himself a committed idealist,[9] having studied under Prichard at Trinity, but the book grew out of lectures given whilst a Fellow and tutor at Balliol (during A.D. Lindsay's mastership) and presented idealism in detail as a serious, and still 'live', option. Taking a broad understanding of the subject, and holding that it is best understood by 'reflecting on the debt which any Idealistic Logic must owe to Kant',[10] the book begins with a detailed historical discussion of the way in which traditional Aristotelian logic gave way to Kant's rival account of the forms which determine experience and judgement. Most recognizably indebted to Bradley and to Joachim, the 'idealistic logic' which Morris presents as having developed from this break emphasizes the notion that no judgement is wholly a priori or wholly a posteriori, and the consequent principle that validity in inference cannot be set out beforehand but determined only through the examination of instances of actual reasoning. Its conception of thought as 'system-producing' leads it inevitably to a coherence theory of truth, but Morris questions the easy appeal to comprehensiveness as a test to settle between rival coherent theories, on the grounds that a thorough commitment to 'system' precludes belief in any bank of 'brute facts' available to be more or less comprehended by rival theories as some sort of deciding 'test'.[11] It is noteworthy that the 'objections' to idealist logic that Morris considers in the second half of the book derive from the reactionary realism of Cook Wilson, not the emerging mathematical or symbolic logic. It is noteworthy too that Morris' own final conclusions are sceptical; its doctrine of the corrigibility of all judgement leaves idealist logic unable to deal adequately with mathematical reasoning while its coherence theory leaves it unable to allow for the role in knowledge of direct apprehension (such as perception or other non-sensuous intuition).[12]

In a similar vein, note may be taken of the Cambridge philosopher A.C. Ewing's 1934 book, *Idealism; a Critical Survey*. Written in an era and place which had become decidedly unsympathetic to idealism, while the book has perhaps the sense of assessing and summing up something that has come to its end, its topic is certainly not presented as mere ancient history. Rather, it offers a careful and thorough survey of the subject, with textually grounded examinations of epistemological idealism, Kantian idealism,

---

complete by the time he returned from Canada to Britain in 1908 taking up the Chair at St Andrews vacated by Bernard Bosanquet. His new position was most fully expressed in his Gifford lectures, *The Faith of A Moralist*.

[8] Review of *Idealistic Logic*, 368.

[9] It is notable, however, that in his later career he continued the idealist tradition of service to education serving as Vice-Chancellor of Leeds University.

[10] *Idealist Logic*, v.

[11] *Idealist Logic*, 185.

[12] *Idealist Logic*, 292–302, 302–15.

the internality of relations, the coherence theory of truth and the idealist theory of perception. The standpoint is realist, rejecting the traditional arguments for the mind-dependent nature of reality, but it is a standpoint at the same time 'in deep sympathy' with its subject, believing that the realists, in wholly rejecting idealism, had 'gone too far.' For, as Ewing says, 'it is most unlikely that the school which dominated thought in this country for so long and still numbers so many adherents has nothing to give that its opponents have overlooked'.[13] For example, strongly rejecting the contemporary dismissal of metaphysics, he argues that, although knowing is more like discovering than making, the constructive activity of mind cannot simply be ignored and a kind of 'methodological idealism' in which we grasp only how things are to a knowing mind retains its force. Again, after a careful analysis of various different senses in which it has been put forward, he rejects the internality of relations, but he nonetheless argues for a view of causality as logical entailment and for the dependence of an object's qualitative character on its relations, positions which together entail a view of the world as something like an intelligible system. For this reason he urges that coherence, while it can not constitute the nature of truth, may still function as an important criterion for it.[14]

15.1.2 Twentieth-century idealist philosophers

Turning from works to people, another simple point which helps us to appreciate the persistence of idealism is to note just how far into the twentieth century stretched the lives of many of those we have discussed in this book. Consider the following list of death dates: Haldane 1928, MacCunn 1929, Pringle-Pattison 1931, Sorley, Mackenzie, A.C. Bradley, Boyce Gibson, 1935, Joachim 1938, J.A. Smith 1939, J.H. Muirhead 1940, H.W.B. Joseph 1943, A.E. Taylor 1945. In most of these cases the publication of new material continued right up to their deaths (and indeed beyond!) as can be seen from the following list of late works: Mackenzie's *Cosmic Problems* (1931), Muirhead's *The Platonic Tradition* (1931), Pringle-Pattison's *The Balfour Lectures* (1933), McTaggart's *Philosophical Studies* (1934), Bradley's *Collected Essays* (1935), Muirhead's *Rule and End in Morals* (1939), Joachim's *Logical Studies* (1948).

More importantly, however, it needs to be seen that the idealist story does not end with these people, for if we look at their pupils, or those otherwise influenced by them, we see its influence continuing for many years afterwards. Although something of a catalogue of names and far from a full analysis of their respective contributions, the following paragraphs attempt to give a sense of just how far into the twentieth century idealist philosophy stretched.[15] One thing to note in this register is that as idealism

---

[13]   *Idealism*, 1.
[14]   Ewing's sympathy with the idealistic worldview continued throughout his life. He went on to write two useful and well-respected commentaries on Kant and edited a reader on the subject of idealism in 1957. Also worth consulting are his articles 'The Necessity of Metaphysics' and 'The Significance of Idealism for the Present Day'.
[15]   This list is not complete. A fuller picture might add literary figures such as T.S. Eliot, who studied for a while at Merton; those who took their influence abroad such as Brand Blanshard, who studied under Joseph

collapsed there was a tendency for people to carve off aspects from it, that is, to give up on the central idealist notion of the thoroughgoing unity of knowledge and hold instead that the doctrine was useful in just this or that specific area, such as the philosophy of history, the philosophy of religion, or the vindication of objective value.[16]

An interesting figure with whom to begin, May Sinclair (1863–1946), is testament to the penetration of idealism beyond merely professional circles.[17] She was educated mostly at home, but in 1881 sent for a year to Cheltenham Ladies College, where, as one of the older pupils, the headmistress, Dorothea Beale, encouraged her in the reading of philosophy, and especially the idealism of Plato, Kant, Fichte, Green, and Caird, in which she found a position to satisfy her philosophical and religious questions. She is today best remembered for her fiction[18] and her efforts on behalf of women's suffrage,[19] but her early interest in philosophy continued throughout her life. The 1890s saw an article in support of Green's metaphysics and ethics and a lengthy philosophical poem defending the claims of idealism against its rivals.[20] But it was not until the new century that she really took up arms in vindication of idealism, writing two substantial books to that end. Certainly, by this point, apology was what was needed, for as she noted in her Preface to the first, *Defence of Idealism* (1917), 'There is a certain embarrassment in coming forward with an Apology for Idealistic Monism at the present moment. You can not be sure whether you are putting in an appearance too late or much too early.'[21] The book (which she later described as a 'light-hearted essay' but is nonetheless carefully argued) is an attempt on behalf of idealism to deal with the contemporary challenges of vitalism and pragmatism, and marked throughout by a strong interest in psychoanalysis (very much the fashion of the age). The book was well received, and Sinclair afterwards became a member of the Aristotelian Society and was even invited by Muirhead to contribute to his *Contemporary British Philosophy* volume.[22] Her second book, *The New Idealism*, which appeared five years later in 1922, attempts to formulate an idealism that could withstand the 'new realism' of Russell, Whitehead, and Alexander, a position for which she had great respect and which had, she thought, successfully brought out many weaknesses of the older idealism. In particular it had taught the need to take space and time seriously and not to dismiss them as mere antinomies. Central to her reconstructive effort is a distinction she draws

---

and Joachim and who met Bradley (see his 'Bradley; Some Memories and Impressions'); those such as Alexander and Whitehead who went on to develop idealisms of a very different stamp; or those simply out of sympathy with modern philosophy, such as Ruth Saw or C.E.M. Joad, who kept interest in idealism alive.

[16] I owe this observation to Leslie Armour.

[17] For biographical details see Suzanne Raitt, *May Sinclair; A Modern Victorian*.

[18] Of philosophical note is the short-story 'The Finding of the Absolute' in her collection *Uncanny Stories*.

[19] That the pro-suffrage, May Sinclair, and the anti-suffrage, Mrs Humphry Ward, could both with rights claim the mantle of idealism demonstrates that its political legacy was a complex one.

[20] 'The Ethical and Religious Import of Idealism', 'Guyon; A Philosophical Dialogue'.

[21] *Defence of Idealism*, vii.

[22] Raitt, *May Sinclair*, 42n. She declined the invitation.

between primary and secondary consciousness; between on the one hand, the objects, events, relations, and conditions which are immediately present to mind, and on the other, such further observation, reflection, judgement, inference, and belief as mind exercises upon them. The realist is right, she argues, to attempt to draw a line between knower and known; this must fall not between consciousness and its objects, however, but rather within consciousness itself, between its primary and secondary forms.

John Alexander Smith (1863–1939), who was educated at Edinburgh and Balliol, where he was for a long time a tutor before he became Waynflete Professor in 1910, is an interesting figure because he was no idealist from the start. He had for a time defended realism, but by his own admission, even at his election he lacked a philosophy of his own.[23] After his appointment but before taking up the post, however, he fell under the influence of the Italian Hegelian idealists, Croce and Gentile, and began both to introduce their ideas into Britain and to defend a similar position himself.[24] Many at Oxford were unhappy. In the first decade of the new century, with Cook Wilson and Thomas Case in the Wykeham and Waynflete chairs respectively, Oxford Realism seemed to be winning the day. And in the polarized atmosphere of the time, Smith's conversion was regarded as a setback. It seemed as though the broad-based modern thinker that many had thought they were to get in this figurehead post had just slipped back into the clutches of the old idealism.[25] But really there was not much truth in this. For what Smith brought was mainly new, not a continuation of the old, which by his own admission, he knew little about. Though Balliol educated, his allegiance to Nettleship and Caird was more personal than philosophical and, preferring classical philosophy, he had only 'dipped into' Hegel, while Green and Bradley had 'passed over [his] head'.[26] Smith's two courses of Gifford Lectures (1929–30 and 1931) on 'The Heritage of Idealism' were never published, but a sense of his position may be gained from his contribution to the second series of Muirhead's *Contemporary British Philosophy*, where he characterizes his idealism in three theses; that reality is something essentially in process or historical (unlike the stationary or immobile Absolute of Bradley and Bosanquet), that history is something essentially spiritual, and that spirit is something which most freely and fully manifests itself in self-consciousness.[27] Occupying the Waynflete chair for twenty-five years his influence was considerable, both on colleagues (such as Collingwood) and on pupils (such as H.J. Paton and E.E. Harris.)[28]

---

[23] 'Philosophy as the Development of the Notion and Reality of Self-Consciousness', 228–9.

[24] As well as in metaphysics and the philosophy of history, Smith followed the Italians in their interest in art. The bulk of his aesthetic output, however, remained unpublished.

[25] This feeling of regression was only compounded when nine years later Joachim was awarded the Wykeham Professorship.

[26] 'Philosophy as the Development of the Notion and Reality of Self-Consciousness', 230.

[27] 'Philosophy as the Development of the Notion and Reality of Self-Consciousness', 234–44.

[28] First taught by the South African idealist A.R. Lord, and then in 1931 proceeding to Oxford where he studied under H.H. Joachim, as well as Smith, Errol Harris continued to speak out for idealism from a variety of South African and American university positions until his death in 2009.

May Sinclair's female voice in the cause of idealism was unusual, but it was not unique, for the movement's support of women's education won it a second champion, in the figure of Hilda Oakeley (1867–1950).[29] Oakeley was educated at home in Northumberland, after which she moved to London where she attended Bernard Bosanquet's university extension lectures, earning a prize for her essay on Aristotle. With his support, from there she went on, in 1894, at the comparatively late age of twenty-seven, to Somerville College; where, in her last two years, she took essays to Caird, and heard lectures by Cook Wilson, Wallace, and Bosanquet.[30] Becoming an Oxford Idealist, she was inspired to a career in education; involved first in adult education in London, before taking up a post in 1899 as head of the newly founded Royal Victoria College at McGill, Canada's first residential college for women. At McGill she also lectured in philosophy. Returning to Britain in 1905, she took posts teaching philosophy at Manchester University and then as Warden at King's College for Women in Kensington, moving to the Strand when it was amalgamated with King's College in 1914. From 1915 to 1921 she was resident warden of the Passmore Edwards (later Mary Ward) Settlement; after which period she returned to lecturing in Philosophy at Kings, until her retirement in 1931. Throughout her busy career she continued to write, remaining within the idealist fold. Highlighting the notions of personality and of history, her developments of the idealistic tradition were perhaps typical of her times. But if she came to doubt that the nation itself should be regarded as any sort of inevitably progressive unity, her underlying commitment to idealism itself remained in the form of a belief in the *possibility* of such endless progress. Where a realist conception of history as rooted in and therefore bounded by the natural order must regard it as inevitably repetitive, to the idealist for whom history itself can never be separated from the work of productive intelligence there always exist new possibilities, just as there do for creative thinking.[31]

Norman Kemp Smith (1872–1958) graduated from St Andrews in 1893 where he was taught by John Burnet, A.S. Pringle-Pattison, and Henry Jones.[32] After a year in Jena and periods spent as assistant in Glasgow to both Henry Jones and Robert Adamson, he worked from 1906 to 1916 at Princeton, before finishing his career in the Chair at Edinburgh, where he succeeded his old teacher Pringle-Pattison. Much of his effort went into the history of philosophy, and it is for his scholarly efforts on Kant, Hume, and Descartes that he is best known today. But he was also an independent thinker. His *Prolegomena to an Idealist Theory of Knowledge* (1924) presents what he calls 'an idealist theory of knowledge on realist lines',[33] but the great bulk of the book is taken up with the latter element, as he develops a theory of perception much

[29] For biographical details see Oakeley, *My Adventures in Education*.
[30] A course of lectures on 'The Theory of the State' given at Manchester College Oxford.
[31] Oakeley, *Should Nations Survive?*, 103–6.
[32] Pringle-Pattison was there from 1887 to 1891, before taking up the chair at Edinburgh. He was replaced by Henry Jones who was there from 1891 to 1894 before taking up the chair at Glasgow.
[33] *Prolegomena to an Idealist Theory of Knowledge*, ix.

influenced by Samuel Alexander and G.F. Stout which strongly asserts the independent reality of space and time. Idealism *is* advanced, but only in the final chapter of the book, and in a much chastened and modest form; for previous idealisms he thinks, 'have been apt to overreach themselves', saying with Berkeley that material reality is mind-dependent, or with Bradley and Bosanquet that everything is experience, when all the facts warrant us to assert is that Mind and Nature stand in relations of mutual implication. Kemp Smith suggests that nature's bringing forth of creatures appreciative of truth, beauty, and goodness is best understood, not as some sort of accident, but purposively, as an act of self-revelation of nature's part.[34] Knowledge is possible, mind is able progressively to penetrate to the real, because it is not finally independent of it but integrally bound up with it, ministered to and upheld by it.[35] Thus idealism enters as a high-level metaphysical thesis suggesting that spiritual values have a determining role at the cosmic or universal scale, and set against naturalism only as a religious opposes a secular worldview and not as an anti-realist opposes a realist worldview.[36]

Another late idealist was J.E. Turner (1875–1947). Obtaining his BA and MA from Liverpool where John MacCunn held the chair, he went on to teach there until his retirement in 1941.[37] His doctoral thesis, published in 1925 under the title, *A Theory of Direct Realism and the Relation of Realism to Idealism*, shows perfectly the coming together of these two streams of thought. The bulk of the book is taken up with a strong defence of naive realism in perception. Indeed he opines that the 'marked tendency towards Realism which is so characteristic of twentieth-century speculation has not yet, in my opinion, gone far enough',[38] complaining that recent systems (including, for example, Kemp Smith's) have conceded more than is necessary to subjectivism and phenomenalism. But, urging that the material universe is only part of reality and the theory of perception only part of philosophy, this account he then seeks to embed within a wider Hegelian idealist conception of the universe. Resistance to such a proposal stems, he argues, from a mistaken understanding of idealism as a doctrine, principally in the theory of knowledge, which declares the world to be both mental and subjective; an understanding which, however common it may have become, was very far from that of Hegel and the early British Idealists. Finite experience, argues Turner, is always self-transcendent, continually expanding itself in every direction to overcome its temporary limitations, a process which (Hegel teaches us) must culminate in the end with the 'Absolute Idea'—objective, universal, systematic, and complete.[39] What this comes to is the universality or immanence of reason, the equation of rationality and actuality, and in this way we arrive at the notion of a universe 'which is certainly directly present

---

[34] *Prolegomena to an Idealist Theory of Knowledge*, 230–3.

[35] *Prolegomena to an Idealist Theory of Knowledge*, 237.

[36] *Prolegomena to an Idealist Theory of Knowledge*, 4.

[37] Before joining the Department Turner taught for the University's Extension Board. He was made a Reader in 1926.

[38] *A Theory of Direct Realism*, 7.

[39] *A Theory of Direct Realism*, 273, 278.

to perception, but which can be truly apprehended only by thought', as 'realism expands into a more profound idealism'.[40] Turner's idealist sympathies are further displayed in his attachment to constructive philosophy of religion where, in his 1926 *Personality and Reality*, he puts forward an argument for the existence of what he terms a 'supreme self'. Fusing cosmological and teleological lines of thought, he urges that the material world, being purely mechanical, could not have evolved of its own accord. That it has nonetheless advanced in a direction of ever-increasing rationality and perfection, 'implies the real existence of a mind which so dominates the whole realm of matter as progressively to embody therein, by means of perfectly definite, unalterable, and indestructible mechanisms, its own constructive—if not indeed creative— ideas'.[41] He contrasts his view with both the spiritual pluralism of McTaggart and the super-personal Absolute of Bosanquet. The Supreme Self (or God) must be *distinguished* from the whole of reality (or Absolute) although this is not to say they are *separate*, since the former is essentially something which expresses itself through the life of the latter.

A.D. Lindsay (1879–1952) studied at Glasgow and then University College Oxford. After a Clark Fellowship at Glasgow (1902), a Shaw Fellowship in Edinburgh (1903), and a post as assistant lecturer in philosophy (alongside Samuel Alexander) at Manchester (1904–6), he came finally to Balliol where he taught philosophy until 1922 and, was among other things, involved in setting up the degree of PPE.[42] From there he relocated to Glasgow University, taking the chair made vacant by Henry Jones' death, before returning to Balliol in 1924 as Master, which post he held until 1949. He was briefly Oxford's Vice-Chancellor from 1935 to 1938. Elevated to the peerage in 1945, in 1949 Baron Lindsay of Birker became the first Principal of the University College of North Staffordshire, which later became Keele University.

In his time first student of and then junior colleague to both Henry Jones and Edward Caird,[43] Lindsay's debt to their blend of idealism can be seen in his 1922 Glasgow inaugural lecture 'Idealism'.[44] Locating the two main objections to idealism of recent years as those directed against the unity of all things and the dependence of the known on its knowing, he argues that neither of these positions belong to the true spirit of idealism, which is something to found in the common ground between its four great influences—Plato, Spinoza, Kant, and Hegel—namely, a 'combination of the critical spirit of scientific inquiry with an unhesitating belief in the reality of moral experience'.[45] Any philosophy which stands by the value and importance of ideals must commit also to those differences and distinctions upon which they depend;

---

[40] *A Theory of Direct Realism*, 320.

[41] *Personality and Reality*, 158.

[42] The Oxford PPE degree (commonly called 'Modern Greats' in its early years) started in 1920.

[43] Although a student at University College, he had been sent to Caird at Balliol for philosophy tutorials.

[44] With a revised set of opening remarks, this was reprinted in *Journal of Philosophical Studies* in 1926 under the title 'The Idealism of Caird and Jones'.

[45] 'The Idealism of Caird and Jones', 178.

distinctions between knowledge and opinion, good and evil, the actual and the ideal, and so forth. But turning its face from the 'patient examination and testing of the significance of moral values' subjective idealism runs after an impossible magic short-cut to the truth.[46]

R.F. Alfred Hoernlé (1880–1943) was a student at Balliol from 1899 to 1903 where he came under the influence of Edward Caird and J.A. Smith.[47] Following his first position as an assistant to Bosanquet at St Andrews, his career included posts at Cape Town, Newcastle-upon-Tyne, Harvard, Newcastle again and finally Wittwaterstrand. Never a dogmatist, his was a synoptic conception of philosophy resting on 'the assumption that truth has many sides, and that to the whole truth on any subject every point of view has some contribution to make',[48] but the general drift of his thinking was idealist in direction; although like his early mentor, Bosanquet, he came himself to prefer the term 'speculative philosophy'.[49] His 1924 book, *Idealism as a Philosophical Doctrine* (expanded in 1927 under the title, *Idealism as a Philosophy*) is of interest and value for its recognition of the breadth that the term 'idealism' had come to take in by this stage. After an historical introduction outlining the development of the concept 'idea' from its Platonic origins, through its neo-Platonic/Augustinian phase, to the modern Lockean 'way of ideas', he examines modern idealism in both its spiritual pluralism (Berkeley, Ward, McTaggart) and its absolute (Kant, Hegel, Bradley) forms. To thus divide matters might make it seem as through the cardinal issue were numerical (the many *versus* the one) but in the end Hoernlé adopts a Bosanquetian idealism which seeks only to do justice to the whole of experience, allowing for its connectedness but recognizing too its diversity, for example, allowing that we experience a world of material things very different from our ideas or feelings, but allowing too that our experience includes the worlds of art, morality, and religion which cannot properly be understood or appreciated except in terms of the ideas that make them what they are.[50]

Note has already been taken of H.J. Paton's (1887–1969) work of idealist ethics, *The Good Will*, but his is a name worth mentioning again in this context, since he continued to be a source of idealist influence long afterwards. In 1927 he was appointed to the chair of logic and rhetoric at Glasgow, and in 1937 to the White's Chair of Moral Philosophy at Oxford (which he held until 1952). Becoming convinced that there was 'some flaw in the idealist doctrines, which could be corrected only by going back to the fountain-head',[51] he devoted himself to Kant, for which scholarly work he became best known. But he remained out of sympathy with modern philosophical develop-

[46] 'The Idealism of Caird and Jones', 180.
[47] For further discussion of Hoernlé's ethics see W. Sweet, 'British Idealism and Ethical Thought in South Africa and India', 294–303.
[48] 'On the way to a synoptic philosophy', 138.
[49] 'On the way to a synoptic philosophy', 155; *Idealism*, 18.
[50] *Idealism*,147–8, 174–81.
[51] 'Fifty Years of Philosophy', 348.

ments, and even into the 1950s continued to strike an idealist note defending, for example, the by-then unpopular conception of metaphysics as concerned with the Whole—holding out even on behalf of those much-derided initial capital letters.[52] But the idealism he came to in the end was more Platonic than Hegelian; an idealism in which, rising from the sensible to the intellectual, the Forms of things are alone what is truly intelligible and the source of all intelligibility in everything else.[53]

H.J.W. Hetherington (1888–1965) was one of Henry Jones' Glasgow pupils (1905–1910) then his assistant (1910–1914, apart from a short time in 1912 when he was at Merton College studying with H.H. Joachim) and an idealist very much in the mould of his teacher. He held positions at Sheffield, Cardiff, and Exeter, before succeeding A.D. Lindsay as Professor of Moral Philosophy at Glasgow. The Idealist dynasty of that distinguished chair, which had been occupied by both Jones and Caird before Lindsay, he continued from 1924 to 1927, but after that he moved into university management becoming Vice-Chancellor at Liverpool (1927–36) and then Principal at Glasgow (1936–61)—a position once held by the idealist John Caird. In recognition of his services to education, which included support for adult education, he was knighted in 1936.[54] The increasingly administrative nature of his career meant that, after *Social Purpose* (which he published in 1918 with J.H. Muirhead) and Jones' *Life and letters* (which he published in 1924) he spent less and less time on academic philosophy. It is no doubt figures such as Hetherington, Baillie, and Lindsay that Quinton has in mind when he quips that a remarkable number of Idealists overcame the spectre of unemployment that loomed from its waning popularity by being vice-chancellors.[55] But it must be remembered that for them this was not an alternative to their philosophy, but a practical continuation of it, a further putting into practice of Idealism's commitment to bring about social progress through education.

One important point to note, the further away we move from its origins in Green, Bradley, and Caird, is just how wide the notion of 'idealism' becomes. This is well illustrated by the figure of Sir Sarvepalli Radhakrishnan (1888–1975).[56] Invited by J.H. Muirhead to write a book on Indian philosophy for the Library of Philosophy series, the success of the work led to an invitation in 1926 to Manchester College Oxford to give the Upton Lectures (subsequently published as *The Hindu View of Life*) and in 1929 to Manchester and London to give the Hibbert Lectures (subsequently published as *An Idealist View of Life*). Idealism in Radhakrishnan's hands becomes very broad indeed, a wide river underlying all the greatest philosophical and religious ideas in both Eastern and Western thought, of which Hegelian idealism is seen

[52] *The Modern Predicament*, 65–6.
[53] *The Modern Predicament*, 246–50.
[54] For further detail on Hetherington see C. Illingworth, *University Statesman: Sir Hector Hetherington*.
[55] 'Absolute Idealism', 125–6.
[56] Elected as the second President of India (1962–67) Radhakrishnan also illustrates the connection between idealism and statesmanship that we saw in R.B. Haldane. For further discussion of Radhakrishnan's ethics see W. Sweet, 'British Idealism and Ethical Thought in South Africa and India', 310–20.

as but one current.[57] Thinking back to a figure like Caird, it might be said that idealism preached such inclusiveness from the start, but it is nonetheless true that increasingly the family began to be seen as including members the early idealists would not have recognized.[58] Dividing idealism into three broad types: subjective, objective (either Personal or Absolute in form), and axiological, Radhakrishnan's own form of the doctrine was of the third type and stressed both the reality of value and the teleological nature of reality.

The breadth of twentieth-century idealism is further illustrated by another high profile figure to carry it forward, R.G. Collingwood (1889–1943). Collingwood owed much to his father who, as a student of Bosanquet in the 1890s had been influenced on leaving Oxford to take up social work, and he was himself an Oxford product. But Collingwod's philosophy is better understood as a reaction to his youthful realism, under the influence of Italian idealism, than any conscious continuity with the earlier British Idealist tradition. Coming up to University College in 1908 (where he was tutored by E.F. Carritt and influenced also by Cook Wilson), and taking up a fellowship at Pembroke in 1912, he was first a realist.[59] This realism was subsequently rejected, Collingwood himself tells us, in part on traditional idealist grounds, that to say knowledge makes no difference implies a grasp of things in themselves,[60] and in part because of its failure to appreciate history.[61] In place of the old 'logic of propositions' he proposed his own 'logic of questions and answers' in which every statement must be regarded as the 'answer' to some specific historically determined 'question',[62] which historical contexuality must be thought of as shaping its meaning, truth, and consistency with other statements.[63] Collingwood's focus on understanding things historically links him to the British Idealist tradition, but at that time anyone who rejected realism was labelled an 'idealist', and Collingwood felt himself to have arrived at a position quite unlike anything in the school of Green.[64] He certainly disavowed the term 'idealist'.[65] And in truth his historicism owed more to his study of Vico, Croce, Gentile, and de Ruggiero; a discovery made at about the same time as J.A. Smith's

---

[57] *Idealist View of Life*, 16.

[58] For example, the more realist Alexander earns a place within the fold for his emergent teleology (*Idealist View of Life*, 321ff).

[59] *Autobiography*, 22.

[60] *Autobiography*, 44.

[61] *Autobiography*, 22, 28.

[62] A position which Stein Helgeby observes (*Action as History*, 79 n) was interestingly anticipated by C.R. Morris, *Idealistic Logic*, 117, 157.

[63] *Autobiography*, 37–9.

[64] *Autobiography*, 56. Matters are complicated by the fact that, after his rejection of realism, Collingwood's own position did not remain constant. Some (but not all) commentators have suggested that between his 1933 *An Essay on Philosophical Method* and his 1940 *An Essay on Metaphysics*, he moved from a position not so very different to that of mainstream British Idealism towards the kind of view described here. The *Autobiography* itself, it should be noted, dates from 1939. For opposing views on this point contrast Donagan, *Later Philosophy of R.G. Collingwood* (chs.1, 10) and Connelly, *Method, Metaphysics and Politics* (ch.1).

[65] See his correspondence with Gilbert Ryle, in *Essay on Philosophical Method*, 256.

and no doubt encouraged by it.[66] As with Smith there are points of connection with traditional British Idealism, but overall Collingwood's position was very different. That it was no part of his system to exclude non-mental reality distanced him from some, but not all, of the British Idealists—figures such as Caird, Jones, and Bosanquet had been equally keen to hold onto '*bona fide* nature'.[67] But more distancing was his rejection of the overarching intellectualism and rationalism so characteristic of all that school; for based on a conceptual relativism that rejected any God's eye perspective and bound all thought to its historical context of production, his own anti-realism was not an ontological thesis but a fundamentally epistemological one; the position that there is no presuppositionless knowledge.[68]

A figure more clearly connected to the classical tradition of British Idealism was G.R.G. Mure (1893–1979). His education was at Merton and when, in 1919 his former tutor H.H. Joachim was appointed Wykeham Professor of Logic, he recommended Mure to succeed him as the College Philosophy Tutor. Bradley, of course, was a colleague also; although by now an old man, Mure knew him only slightly. After the Second World War in 1947 he became warden of the College. A wholehearted supporter of a view which by that time was rapidly losing favour in the philosophical world, he became a kind of lone voice for an Oxford that had passed, dismissed by most of his Oxford colleagues as a mere reactionary; the last of the Oxford Hegelians. Continuing to teach through the study of standard texts, contemporary philosophy was either ignored or dismissed. Indeed his teaching was so out of touch that it was rumoured in the 1930s that the examiners put in special questions 'for Merton men'.[69] It was principally as a scholar of Hegel that he made his name—writing three books and many articles on the philosopher. But Mure was not only a champion of Hegelian idealism, he was also a critic of modern philosophy. In 1958 he published *Retreat from Truth*, a wide ranging and passionate attack on contemporary British Philosophy, in which he saw a deeply regrettable regression and turning away from the speculative thought of the earlier Absolute Idealists; a falling away he attempted in the book to trace to the overly practical preoccupation of the British and the general poverty of modern cultural life. For Mure, the philosopher was one engaged in the construction of systems which dealt with serious questions of ultimate reality, not a piecemeal conceptual under-labourer for science, and certainly no mere mouthpiece of common sense or dissolver of linguistic puzzles. The book had its supporters, but it is intemperately passionate in tone—modern philosophy is derided as 'naive', 'absurd', and a

[66] In 1936 Collingwood followed Smith as Waynflete Professor of Metaphysics until his retirement in 1941; giving Italian idealism a voice in Oxford for over thirty years.

[67] The phrase is Bosanquet's (*Principle of Individuality and Value*, 135) repeated in Collingwood's unpublished 1935 essay 'Realism and Idealism'.

[68] Collingwood would never have accepted Jones' dismissal of epistemology. The notion that metaphysics concerns the fundamental presuppositions of the scientific thinking of an age, combined with the fact that scientific thinking is never finished, led Brian Carr to describe Collingwood's position as 'metaphysical relativism' (*Metaphysics, An Introduction*, 7).

[69] Walsh, 'Geoffrey Reginald Gilchrist Mure', 8.

'product of spiritual sterility'[70] and he ends by saying that if he now had an intelligent son coming up to Oxford he would not be sorry if he chose not to study philosophy there[71]—and crude in the characterization of its targets—the analytic style of Russell, the ordinary language philosophy of Ryle, and Wittgenstein's philosophy, are all lumped together as merely deficient variants of the British empirical tradition of Locke and Hume—and these two facts together ensured that among those to whom it was addressed it met with little attention, and less approval. Mure's own positive philosophical position, which he termed 'objective idealism', was set out in his last book, *Idealist Epilogue*, published in 1978 a few months before his death.

C.A. Campbell (1897–1974) was a student at both Glasgow where Jones was professor, and Balliol where A.D. Lindsay was tutor, before taking posts at Glasgow, Bangor, then Glasgow again, where in 1938 he took the Chair of Logic and Rhetoric which he occupied until 1961. Following his tutors his was a reactionary stance. 'The reaction in contemporary thought against idealism seems to me to have passed beyond all reasonable bounds,'[72] he complained. But he was not content simply to set out old truths. Much influenced by Bradley, he attempted in his *Scepticism and Construction* (1931) to move beyond that position, extending Bradlean scepticism to make reality almost wholly beyond knowledge. Rejecting the rational Absolute of more orthodox idealists, in a sort of return to Kant, ultimate reality is judged supra-rational, supra-relational, and unknowable by the intellect. As itself the ground of being, he allows that that 'the Absolute of Bradley may well be regarded as the philosophical counterpart of the God of Religion'.[73] But alongside scepticism there is construction. At the same time he urges that we can reach thoughts which, if not ultimately true, may become as true as anything can be; final phenomenal truths, or intellectually incorrigible principles (to use terms found in Bradley).[74] One such truth concerns freedom, where we find Campbell moving in a direction quite other than that of Bradley and the other idealists (although not without precedent in Personal Idealism.) Without denying that the idealists' sense of positive freedom, the removal of obstacles to self-development, represents a genuine and important *kind* of freedom, he nonetheless separates himself from them in holding that *real* freedom, the sort required for moral responsibilities, requires 'open possibilities'.[75] Rejecting Green's solution to the problem (that heredity and environment have no power to undermine freedom, since only factors consciously taken up as motives can determine actions) he opts for an introspectively derived libertarianism in which the individual self has absolute freedom (even from its own character) to choose from among alternate possibilities. For this reason he rejects the arguments of those such as

---

[70] *Retreat from Truth*, vii, viii.
[71] *Retreat from Truth*, 250.
[72] *Scepticism and Construction*, ix.
[73] *Scepticism and Construction*, 311.
[74] *Scepticism and Construction*, 112.
[75] *Scepticism and Construction*, 127n. See also 'In Defence of Free Will' and 'Self-Activity and its Modes'.

Bradley who would deny the genuine individuality or real self-subsistence of finite individuals.[76] Never quite able to fully subscribe to a doctrine of Absolute mind or spirit, he nonetheless remained deeply influenced by and sympathetic to it, and in this way—though swimming against the tide—he continued as an important conduit of idealist influence; even into the 1960s, it being the case that, 'A major part of the honours programme in philosophy at Glasgow University during his tenure involved the logic and metaphysics of Bradley.'[77]

A further (albeit somewhat diluted) continuation of the idealist tradition may be observed in the early work of Michael Oakeshott (1901–90), whose 1933 *Experience and its Modes*, self-confessed in its debt to Hegel and Bradley, works from within a thoroughly idealist understanding of experience. 'Experience,' he begins, in thoroughly idealist fashion, 'stands for the concrete whole which analysis divides into "experiencing" and "what is experienced". Experiencing and what is experienced are, taken separately, meaningless abstractions; they cannot, in fact, be separated.'[78] Nor, to press the anti-abstractionism further, may we locate any realm of mere sensation or perception unmediated by thought or judgement. The book sets out a scheme according to which, absolutely coherent reality or experience as a whole can be grasped only through limited moments or 'modes'. Though there are in principle infinitely many, we know chiefly three; the historical, the scientific, and the practical, each self-contained and 'self-developing' according to its own logic, but because abstractions, none able to bring us to a full or lasting satisfaction. But unlike most other Idealists Oakeshott makes no attempts to rank these limited modes of appearance. Although Collingwood, Joachim, and Sorley all thought highly of it, and although Oakeshott himself went on to exert greater influence as a political philosopher, *Experience and its Modes* was a work out of its time and made little impact.

A last figure to mention is W.H. Walsh (1913–86) who was educated at Merton, where he was influenced into idealist ways of thought by his tutor G.R.G. Mure. After a short spell at Dundee, on Mure's elevation to Warden, he then taught at Merton until 1960, when he became Professor of Logic and Metaphysics at Edinburgh (which post he held until 1979). By this point the idealist tradition was highly diluted—indeed Walsh was never really an idealist himself, but his case is interesting as an example of how far ideas can carry, for encouraged by his training, he championed and explored various idealist themes—unpopular elsewhere—such as metaphysics and history of philosophy, including the study of Bradley, Kant, and Hegel.

15.2 Idealist histories of philosophy

As idealism grew to be an established feature in the philosophical landscape, it became too a suitable topic for inclusion in histories and surveys of the discipline. The earliest of

---

[76] *Scepticism and Construction*, 178–9. See also 'In Defence of Free Will' and 'Self-Activity and its Modes'.
[77] Maclachlan, 'Campbell', 146.
[78] *Experience and its Modes*, 9.

these mentions are brief and of no great moment,[79] but in the course of time they came to be written by idealists themselves, taking on the form of institutional autobiography, which gives them extra significance. These historians were, of course, partisan, but that hardly diminishes their interest to us now.

James Seth's, *English Philosophers and Schools of Philosophy* (1912)[80] finds the antecedents of the movement in the mid-nineteenth century spiritual awakening of Coleridge, Newman, Ferrier, and Grote, and characterizes the movement itself by short summaries of Stirling, Caird, Green, and Bradley. With considerable use of quotation he stresses particularly the independence of the last three from Hegel. W.R. Sorley's *A History of English Philosophy* (1920)[81] offers a similar role call of idealists—Ferrier, Stirling, Green, Wallace, Caird, Bradley, and Bosanquet. Today, nearly a century later, the only one of these names known to those not specific students of the period is Bradley's, rendering him the *de facto* representative of idealism in modern eyes, however, Sorley stresses the controversial nature at the time of Bradley's contribution; to some his work was the 'finest exposition' of idealism, but to many others what he had proposed was 'its dissolution'. Sorely emphasizes how fundamentally at odds Bradley is to Caird and Green; if his argument about relations is sound, it is the undoing of their positions.[82] Of the importance of Bradley's work, however, there can be no doubt. *Appearance and Reality*, Sorley says, 'has probably exerted more influence upon metaphysical thinking in English-speaking countries than any other treatise of the last thirty years'.[83] In both Seth and Sorley, Personal Idealism receives the most cursory of mentions, which is interesting given their own affiliations, but this is a gap made up for by Webb. His 1915 *History of Philosophy* gives equal, if brief, weight to both Green's Absolute Idealism and the Personalist reaction against it, and this even-handed treatment is continued in his 1933, *A Study of Religious Thought in England from 1850*, which as well as a chapter on Absolute Idealism also contains one on Personal Idealism.

---

[79] One of the earliest was Belfort Bax whose 1886 *History of Philosophy* was perhaps the first to mention the idealists. Although both an idealist and a socialist, Belfort Bax never really belonged to the British Idealist tradition as such. Educated in Germany under Edward Von Hartman, his idealism is an anti-intellectualism from Schopenhauer, while his socialism is broadly Marxist. To the final chapter of his history detailing 'Recent and Current philosophy'—which covers Hartmann, Lotze, Dühring, Lange, Comte, Mill, Lewes, and Spencer—are added four pages on the new 'Neo-Hegelian School' which has 'rudely shaken of late' the orthodoxy of British Empiricism (ibid. 390). Correctly locating their lineage in Plato, Aristotle, Kant. and Hegel, Bax dissents from their position on account of his disagreement with the last of these—he is unable to accept that consciousness can overcome *all* distinctions—but he allows that they are 'by far the most important school existing at present' (ibid. 393). Another early, but equally brief entry on the new School may be found in Archibald Alexander's *A Short History of Philosophy* (1907), to whom they stand as worthy demonstrators of continued interest in speculative enquiry (ibid. 581).

[80] 'English' here refers to English language, not nationality, the book appearing as part of a series on English Literature.

[81] As with Seth's book the restriction here is to language not nationality, and for a similar reason—the book grew out of a series of chapters contributed to the *Cambridge History of English Literature*.

[82] *History of English Philosophy*, 292.

[83] *History of English Philosophy*, 291.

Muirhead's *The Platonic Tradition in Anglo-Saxon Philosophy*, which appeared in 1931 and was the first dedicated chronicle of the British Idealism movement, is perhaps the most interesting of all the histories for, no mere compendium of past names and doctrines, this work has a very definite thesis to advance. Specifically it argues that the school of Green, far from simply a recent alien interloper displacing native empiricism, was in fact the continuation of a long idealist tradition which goes back to the Cambridge Platonists.[84] And as well as more recent thinkers, the book contains ground-breaking discussions of Cudworth, Norris, Collier, and Carlyle. The omission of Coleridge is merely apparent, for Muirhead in researching his book, came to see Coleridge as so important and found so much new material on him, that in the end he became the dedicated subject of a separate book, *Coleridge as Philosopher*, which appeared the year before. This book should be considered as part of the larger project of *The Platonic Tradition*. A second important element in Muirhead's account sets out the history of how Hegel came to England. This might seem to cut against his main thesis, but Muirhead has no wish to *deny* the influence of Hegel, only to point out that it was planted in (unconsciously) receptive soil, that it called back the surface streams already flowing underground. He also points out that the idealist movement was stimulated at least as much by the Jowett-inspired Plato revival, as by German thought. In discussing idealism itself, rather than write again on Green and Caird,[85] Muirhead discusses the Pringle-Pattison and Haldane volume, *Essays in Philosophical Criticism*, rightly showing its importance and typicality. He also looks at Pringle-Pattison's *Hegelianism and Personality* as the chief internal critique of idealism. But his main discussion concentrates on Bradley, exploring the evolution over time of his philosophical views. This is a thorough and weighty engagement of eighty-five pages, with serious criticisms and, set alongside Cambell's *Scepticism and Construction* of the same year, reminds us that forty years after it was published, *Appearance and Reality* was still exerting considerable influence. Muirhead's history is also valuable for its discussion of the parallel American idealist movement.[86] Also notable is the concluding chapter, 'What is Dead and What is Alive in Idealism', with its clear sense that history has now moved on and its five point summary of what Muirhead thinks will last from the 'Platonic tradition'.[87] Generally, no doubt, Muirhead very much overstates his case

---

[84] Essentially the same point had been made earlier by Sorley (*History of English Philosophy,* 300) who urged, not only the fact that there is a long idealist tradition in Herbert of Cherbury, More, Cudworth, Norris, Shaftesbury, and Reid, but also that there is more subtlety and variety in the philosophies of Hobbes, Locke, Hume, Mill, and Spencer than the simple label 'empiricism' might convey.

[85] Which he had already done in *The Service of the State* (1908) and in *The Life and Philosophy of Edward Caird* (1921).

[86] As noted in the Preface space prevents us from discussing this movement. But in this specific context, mention might be made of two further American histories, A.K. Rogers' *English and American Philosophy since 1800* (1922) and Watts Cunningham's more specific *The Idealistic Argument in Recent British and American Philosophy* (1933).

[87] The chapter title is in echo of Croce's 1907 book *What is Living and What is Dead in the Philosophy of Hegel.*

(and his story is only the more implausible for his insistence on excluding Britain's most famous idealist—Berkeley!) but he has an important point to make. The reaction against idealism was strong, and many in the early twentieth century were keen to dismiss what they had usurped as an embarrassing, foreign, and short-lived aberration, best forgotten now the country had returned to its usual empiricism and common sense. But Muirhead is right that the history of British philosophy is far more complex and multi-faceted than the simple canon of Bacon, Locke, Berkeley, Hume, Mill, and Russell still served up to this day to the majority of undergraduates.

15.3 Reasons for the eclipse of idealism

The material covered in the previous two sections should be taken only as corrective to the extreme view that idealism disappeared without trace in the twentieth century, not as a rejection of the claim that it suffered massive reversal of fortune; for, however drawn-out its after-life, it cannot be denied that in the main idealism failed to hold its ground. Idealists today are rare, Absolute Idealists even rarer, and it is worth considering some of the various factors that brought about this decline in population.

15.3.1 Analytic philosophy

Histories of philosophy tend to present each new school of philosophy as arising by refutation of its predecessor, and in this way it is easy to think that idealism was disproved by what we now call linguistic or analytic philosophy. This is certainly the popular understanding of what happened. There is much one could doubt about this story, such as the thought of a single 'analytic school' (the Platonic Russell, the scientisticly-minded Positivists, and the school of ordinary language were all very different) the suggestion that the new thinking was in any sense a return to native habits of thought (indebted as it was to such figures as Peano, Frege, Cantor, Poincaré, the Vienna Circle, and Wittgenstein, this is a most implausible claim) or the idea that idealism just died (as we have seen, it certainly did not), but we may question too the very idea that analytic philosophy 'refuted' idealism. Recent historical scholarship has done much to discredit this simple triumphalist story.[88]

Russell and Moore produced some celebrated arguments against idealism. And there can be no doubting their vigour. But it must also be appreciated that, as the opening salvos of a war they went on to win, these attacks have been remembered as more powerful and decisive then they really were, either historically or philosophically. They were the announcement of a new and, to many, a more exiting way of doing philosophy, and at the end of the day they carried people with them. But that is not the same as refutation. Russell certainly didn't 'win' his debate with Bradley. Indeed, at the last he was reduced to mere assertion; radically different in kind from terms it is

---

[88] See, e.g., P. Hylton, *Russell, Idealism and the Emergence of Analytic Philosophy*, N.Griffin, *Russell's Idealist Apprenticeship*, S.Candlish, *The Russell/Bradley Dispute*.

simply the business of relations to relate, was his bottom line.[89] Likewise, Moore's celebrated attack on Bradley's theory of thinking, his 1899 paper 'The Nature of Judgement', for all its importance as the vehicle by means of which Moore first articulated his theory of propositions and concepts, is hopelessly misdirected as an critique of Bradley. The extreme psychologistic reading it takes of the doctrine that judgement consists in some part of an idea's content considered apart from its existence and referred to the reality as a whole, whereby what we do is regarded as an act of abstraction which itself presupposes a prior judgement setting in train an infinite regress, quite mangles Bradley's meaning; as he himself pointed out in a subsequent letter to Moore. Without ruling out that there *could* occur a prior judgement he denied that there *need* do so, for typically the reference of a content away to reality and its separation from the original presentation in which it occurs are not two separate events.[90] Nor was Moore's famous 'Refutation of Idealism' paper any better targeted, for it was addressed to subjective and not objective idealism, we should remember.

The new analytic philosophers thought all idealists hopelessly out of touch, complaining that they did not really understand the new philosophy. But in many respects this accusation would be better reversed. As we have seen, figures like Bosanquet, Mackenzie, and Muirhead very much had their fingers on the pulse of contemporary philosophy, while the charge is more likely to stick that the young analytic philosophers had not really understood the idealism they attacked. Nor perhaps, it must be allowed, were they very bothered to, for there were other reasons that took them away from idealism.

15.3.2 *The decline of religion*

History suggests that a sense of purpose is the lifeblood of philosophy, the best work that which cuts new ground, but it is equally true that perpetual revolution is impossible, and this can only mean that the thinkers who come after intellectual revolutionaries are at a disadvantage. Even so partisan an advocate of the new philosophy as Warnock saw this correctly, discerning that *ennui* rather than frontal attack played the greater role in idealism's decline.[91]

---

[89] For Russell relational terms simply denote universals, a *sui generis* form of being, whose mode of operation we can never understand. Relations are distinct from and every bit as real as their terms, but as soon as we stop to look at them in isolation they cease to function, forcing us to make an unhappy distinction between the relation actually relating (as when, for example, it is used in some proposition) and the relation in itself. 'A loves B' expresses a relation but 'A, loves, B' is just a list of three terms. 'A proposition . . . is essentially a unity,' he notes, but 'when analysis has destroyed the unity, no enumeration of constituents will restore the proposition.' As to the precise nature of what it is that the analysis has undone he confesses himself able to offer 'no clear account' (*Principles of Mathematics*, §54).

[90] 'The Nature of Judgement' 177–9; For Bradley's letter to Moore see his *Collected Works* 4: 176–7. Bradley's rejection of 'floating ideas' (see above pp.455–7) makes the point quite obvious, although how sensitive Moore was to the progressive refinements in Bradley's position is unclear.

[91] Warnock, *English Philosophy since 1900*, 11.

A good example of this concerns religion. We have seen that one of the great engines behind the growth of idealism was religion. In an age of increasing scientific and historical knowledge, many people found traditional religion untenable. The more rational religion of idealism came to their aid. But as threats grown familiar become less threatening, secularism was more and more embraced, and David Stove has argued that by 1940 the supply had simply dried up of people feeling any need for the sort of spiritual balm that idealism offered.[92] Indeed, writing even earlier in 1913 Haldane testifies to this change. 'In my time we were troubled about our orthodoxy more, I think, than you are to-day,' he told his audience, 'It was in the Victorian period, a period in which we seemed to be bidden to choose between the scientific view of life and the religious view.'[93] A choice that to previous generations was unbearable, increasingly came to be made.

Certainly Stove is correct that a wholly scientific conception of the universe, once almost completely intolerable, became more and more to be accepted. But it would be wrong to take that as the complete story. If, for many, the conflict between the modern and the religious worldviews was solved by rejecting faith, religious belief certainly did not disappear, and one reason for that is that many others met the puzzle by dissolving the threat itself, by finding a way to combine both; a development in which idealism itself played a large contributory part. Nowhere is this better illustrated than by the case of Darwin's theory of evolution. The initial shock to religion from the appearance of this new viewpoint should not be denied, but what is all too often forgotten is how quickly the religious outlook settled down to accommodate Darwin's theory as compatible with its most central beliefs. Idealist philosophy of religion was at the forefront of this process, in its demonstration of how an evolving universe might yet be compatible with a deeper spiritual teleology. Generally idealism played a vital role in showing religious belief how to both loosen and broaden its tenets in such a way as to avoid head-on collision with a scientific view of reality; for as we have seen throughout this study, if in one sense idealism rejects material reality it must immediately be added that in another it wholeheartedly embraces it. It is certainly not in the business of substituting ghosts for material objects.

Stove regards this supply and demand episode from history as a demonstration of how idealism became irrelevant to the modern world, but were his thesis correct we would expect to see in later manifestations of the school a declining interest in its spiritual applications, and in fact we see no such thing. While faith in the idealistic view of such matters as perception, truth, universals, or relations began to fall away, its promise of a universe in which value, order, and purpose 'count in the universe as they count for us'[94] continued to find supporters. Idealism was not a way to bow out from religion by steps with one's dignity intact but rather the path from an orthodox to a

---

[92] Stove, 'Idealism: A Victorian Horror-Story', 96.
[93] 'Conduct of life', 13.
[94] *Appearance and Reality*, 488.

more liberal creed and to suppose the need for a non-supernatural religion localized to the late nineteenth century is to confuse a striking local example with the more general truth it instances. The hiatus to Christian faith brought about by late nineteenth-century scientific and scholarly advances was a local event, but the attempt to find a worldview that can accommodate rationality or science without losing the moral or spiritual is perennial.

15.3.3 The growth of science

Idealism became less appealing; but where loyalties are changed, decline in attractive-ness is only ever half the story. It was Imre Lakatos who, in his philosophy of science, pointed out that a research programme is never given up but where it is felt that there exists a more promising rival. And that was certainly the case with idealism. Rival philosophies appeared, against which idealism was or appeared relatively disadvantaged (and certainly here we must distinguish between perceived defects and actual defects) and thus idealism did not simply suffer from internal shortcomings it also in a sense lost out to competition.

  In considering this process we can best start with science. Realist and pragmatist philosophy not only modelled itself on science, but engaged with it at all levels, develop-ing a worldview that could sit happily with its latest results. The Idealists, by contrast, and quite unlike the Kantian and Hegelian sources from which they drew their inspiration, had little interest in science.[95] Moreover, on the few occasions they did cast their eyes in that direction the materialistic mechanistic beast against which they railed bore little relation to actual contemporary findings. In a new century where scientific knowledge was forging ahead, this lack of interest was a large part of their undoing. Philosophers interested in contemporary science—Henry Sturt and Abraham Wolf, for example—expressed concern, and even figures sympathetic to idealism such as J.A. Stewart were able to appreciate the problem; Speculative idealism looked simply out of touch.[96]

---

[95] In this matter, as Paton notes, there were geographical differences too. Unlike their colleagues at Cambridge, Oxford realist philosophers of the early twentieth century were largely content to continue in the scientific ignorance of their idealist forbears ('Fifty Years of Philosophy', 345).

[96] 'Those who began philosophy in the eighties will remember how, in passing from, say, the *Data of Ethics* to the *Prolegomena to Ethics*, they seemed to pass into another world, and how impossible it was to bring into one focus treatises which professed to deal with the same material. The idealists had no knowledge of or sympathy with science; and the scientific men had no philosophical training. And years had to elapse before the deficiencies on both sides could be made good. Probably this would have been effected much earlier but for the rising influence of Hegelianism, which for a time carried men's minds off in quite another direction' (Sturt, 'The Line of Advance in Philosophy', 36–7). 'One result of Kant's Idealism and Comte's Positivism has been an increasing distrust in human knowledge, a growing suspicion of the foundations of science. In a sense, this was the very opposite of what these philosophers really intended. But then results sometimes have this disagreeable way of showing no respect even for the best intentions' (Wolf 'Natural Realism and Present Tendencies in Philosophy', 141). See also Stewart, 'The Attitude of Speculative Idealism to Natural Science'. Principally a classical scholar, Stewart, whose first class in *literae Humaniores* was awarded in the same year (1870) as Bosanquet's and who followed William Wallace in Oxford's White's Chair of Moral Philosophy (1897–1923), was never a fully fledged member of the idealist school although his Platonism and love of poetry placed him in a certain affinity with it.

Truth in history is always complex and, without retracting them, the statements of the previous paragraph require qualification; for to the general idealist distain for science there were exceptions. And it is important that we look at these for they show that, whatever might have been true in practice, idealism was not *in principle* opposed to science. We may begin with geometry, one of the foundational tools of science, in which idealism's champion was a surprising figure—Bertrand Russell. The fact that shortly afterwards in a sort of reverse Damascus road transition he was to become one of the school's sharpest critics does not alter the fact that his first philosophical book, *An Essay on the Foundations of Geometry* (1897), was written in defence of Hegelian idealism.[97] To those who kept abreast of such things the nineteenth-century development of non-Euclidean geometries was a threat to idealism, for Kant had claimed that space, which we experience as Euclidean, was a necessary a priori imposition on our part. But the appearance of coherent alternatives seemed to suggest that the actual geometry of space itself is a contingent and empirical matter. In defence of idealism, Russell argued that even if Kant had gone too far and that the question of whether space was Euclidean, Lobatchevskyan, Riemannian, or Kleinian could only be settled empirically, a priori necessity might still be maintained for the lesser claim that the possibility of experience required some form of externality of constant curvature (i.e. some variety of homogeneous space.) Thus far, Kant, but the position Russell goes on to develop owes more to Hegel. He holds that geometry, the study of relative, infinitely divisible and unbounded space, because it deals with what is but an abstraction from experience, is inevitably subject to contradictions, contradictions which can be overcome only by an increasingly concrete view of things, as the addition of matter takes us into kinematics, dynamics, and then full mechanics.[98]

Even more radical than the new schemes of geometry were Einstein's Special (1905) and General (1916) Theories of Relativity which attracted much attention in the early years of the twentieth century, as they entered into scientific and general culture. There were many popular publications contributing to that process, including the English translation of Einstein's own *Relativity* (1920) and Bertrand Russell's *ABC of Relativity* (1925), but another very important text was produced by the idealist, R.B. Haldane. The relativity of being to knowledge had long been a theme of Haldane's thought and, seeing in Einstein's theory a confirmation of this, in 1921 he published *The Reign of Relativity* which elaborated the idea and looked in more detail at the philosophical consequences of Einstein's position. He took pains to learn the science in question, even discussing the theory with Einstein himself[99] and, given the contemporary interest in the subject, the book was immediately and immensely successful.

[97] For more discussion see Hylton, *Russell, Idealism and the Emergence of Analytic Philosophy*, 72–101; Griffin, *Russell's Idealist Apprenticeship*, ch.4.

[98] *Foundations of Geometry*, 188–201. For further details of this envisioned transition from geometry to physics see the material from Russell's notebooks reproduced in *Russell on Metaphysics* (ed. Stephen Mumford), 37–51.

[99] On Haldane's support for Einstein see Philipp Frank, *Einstein; his Life and Times*, 187–90.

(A third edition was called for within the space of a year.) Einstein's thesis that our physical measurements depend upon our frame of reference, illustrates for Haldane, in the case of physics, a truth which he thinks holds of knowledge more generally, that what is known depends always upon the knower.[100] The book thus carries over Haldane's earlier idealist stance, that reality is a unified whole whose being is to be known, but goes on to urge that it may be known to finite minds only from various limited points of view, such as those of the physicist, mathematician, or biologist. These different points of view are distinct and irreducible (morality can no more be resolved into mathematics than life into mechanism) and each but partial glimpses of the whole, not to be treated as either final or complete. While he gives a clear and detailed account of Relativity Theory itself, Haldane does tend to read a great deal into it; modern scholarship by contrast has much reduced the *philosophical* import of Einstein's work.

Another area of science that attracted idealists was biology, many of them being drawn to its ideas of evolution and organicism. For no one was this more so than John Scott Haldane, younger brother of R.B. Haldane, and elder brother of the philosophical writer Elizabeth Sanderson Haldane. Educated at the University of Edinburgh, from which he graduated in medicine in 1884, his career was as a working physiologist—his particular specialism was respiration—however, throughout his life he was also deeply interested in philosophy, on which he wrote several important works. Nor were these twin paths unconnected; his philosophy both guided and was inspired by his science, as he attempted to clarify the philosophical basis of biology. His first philosophical work was a contribution, 'The Relation of Philosophy to Science', co-written with his brother, to the seminal volume *Essays in Philosophical Criticism* (1883). Accepting Kant's thesis that it is our categories which structure experience, they argued that those of physics were not in every case prior, and that in particular biology could not be understood in terms of the physical and chemical sciences alone. John Scott Haldane went on to defend and augment this general position in a series of works, culminating in his 1927–8 Gifford lectures, published in 1929 as *The Sciences and Philosophy*. He argues there that there exists a hierarchy of non-reducible sciences differentiated by the degree to which they abstract from concrete experience. Biology is higher than physical science, because with organic life a new factor comes into being. This is not a matter of some additional 'vital force', but of the fact that biology studies living organisms as wholes which cannot be analysed just into the sum of their separate components, of the fact that what makes anything the organism it is is a matter not just of its parts and their inter-relations but of the relations between it and its surrounding environment, and of the fact that biological behaviour is ineliminably purposive. But as biology stands above physical science so, he holds, does psychology stand above biology. The unity of experience characteristic of conscious life can no more be explained in biological terms, than mechanistically or by the postulation of a 'soul'.

---

[100] *Reign of Relativity*, 34, 125.

Here Haldane argues that personality is the key concept which, like life, he understands not as self-contained and complete but rather as something extending over its environment. Our context makes us who we are. At the highest, least abstracted level, we arrive at an all-inclusive personality, which is both the only true reality and the realization of our highest values. This we may call 'God'. Though he admits his deep debt to post-Kantianism, opposes materialism, and asserts the reality of value, Haldane rejects the notion that we can construct the world out of mere ideas, which for him are just further abstractions from concrete experience, and thus he prefers in the end to describe his position as realistic rather than idealistic. His ultimate allegiance, however, is in no doubt, as he himself summarized: 'The conclusion forced upon me in the course of a life devoted to natural science is that the universe as it is assumed to be in physical science is only an idealized world, while the real universe is the spiritual universe, in which spiritual values count for everything.'[101]

Two last figures to add to this story, respected scientists who subsequently made successful moves into the popular presentation of contemporary physics, are Arthur Eddington and James Jeans. Both were keen to explore the middle ground between science and philosophy where they felt modern advances had strengthened rather than weakened the case for religion, a confidence in each case grounded in a kind of idealism. However, with neither thinker was this clearly of Kantian-Hegelian lineage. Eddington's *The Nature of the Physical World* (his 1926–7 Gifford Lectures), chiefly remembered today for its memorable introductory contrast between the two tables of common sense and of modern science,[102] played a crucial role in introducing to a wider audience not just relativity but quantum theory. For all its instrumental advance, the metaphysical import of this last in particular was, for Eddington, sceptical; and he contrasts 'the cycle of physics, where we run round and round like a kitten chasing its tail and never reach the world-stuff at all',[103] with our own power of introspection, which yields direct and indubitable knowledge of our own minds.[104] Beyond consciousness we find we must postulate sub-consciousness, and further beyond that 'something indefinite but yet continuous with our mental nature'.[105] In concluding that ultimate reality is made of such basic 'mind-stuff',[106]—only here and there (in minds like ours) to be thought of as raising islands of consciousness—Eddington reasons in part from exclusion. 'We liken it to our conscious feelings because, now that we are convinced of the formal and symbolic character of the entities of physics, there is nothing else to liken it to.'[107] The thought that the world we experience is but a symbol of some 'more behind' relates this idealism back to that of Carlyle, but its

[101] J.S. Haldane, *The Sciences and Philosophy*, 273.
[102] *Nature of the Physical World*, xi–xiii.
[103] *Nature of the Physical World*, 280.
[104] *Nature of the Physical World*, 281.
[105] *Nature of the Physical World*, 280.
[106] *Nature of the Physical World*, 276.
[107] *Nature of the Physical World*, 280.

subjective scepticism owes more to Berkeley than either Kant or Hegel. Jeans too felt that quantum theory had brought us to a world 'very different from the full-blooded matter and the forbidding materialism of the Victorian scientist'.[108] But in so far as he regarded the new reality revealed as mathematical—'The Great Architect of the Universe now begins to appear as a pure mathematician' his creation 'more like a great thought than like a great machine'[109]—his was a more purely Platonic idealism.

The work of Jeans, Eddington, the Haldane brothers, as well as the early efforts of Bertrand Russell, are important to note insofar as they prove that idealism was not *in principle* opposed to modern science, but it remained the case that the bulk of idealist work ignored science and that was a large part in its undoing.

15.3.4 *New departures in logic*

It was not only with scientific progress that idealism seemed out of touch; there were advances too within the philosophical sphere that appeared to bypass it. In no area was this more true than logic. The new century saw the development of innovative modes of logical thinking; the mathematical techniques of Frege, Whitehead, and Russell, which developed into the symbolic logic familiar to all contemporary philosophers. The Idealists failed almost entirely to engage with this process, and as a result they were hopelessly left behind, their own logic-work looking more and more irrelevant.[110] In this way one of the changes that really 'did for' idealism was *the new logic*.

Given that idealism was (as we have seen) surprisingly well able to deal with *other* advances in philosophy—in, say, metaphysics (the new realism) or ethics (G.E. Moore and intuitionism)—partly by agreeing, partly by disagreeing, but always remaining in dialogue with the new ideas, it is worth asking why it was unable to do the same here. The answer is relatively straightforward. All the great advances of the new logic were *formal*, but the idealists set their face from the start against any formal logic. Nor was this some arbitrary or traditionalist prejudice, for as we saw, the very idea of such a logic— precisely delineated definitions, the mere relations of disembodied concepts only—was opposed to everything they believed in. The continuity they saw between form and matter was not distinct from that to which they were committed between thought and reality. In other domains there was perhaps room for debate, but here there was no middle ground between death or conversion.[111]

---

[108] 'The New World-Picture of Modern Physics', 15.

[109] *Mysterious Universe*, 122, 137.

[110] The only exception to this neglect was the American idealist, Josiah Royce.

[111] To be fair, it should be noted that in Oxford at least, resistance to mathematical logic sprang as much from commitment to Aristotelianism, as from idealism—the study of Aristotle was enshrined in the Greats syllabus, which at this point nearly all students took, and was for most of them their only exposure to formal logic. The realist Cook Wilson too was an opponent and (in the words of A.J. Ayer) 'sat like Canute rebuking the advancing tide of mathematical logic,' while Joseph's *An Introduction to Logic* (written in 1906 when he was still a realist) is similarly Aristotelian in its resistance to formal innovations (Ayer, *Part of My Life*, 77). For further details see M. Marion 'Oxford Realism: Knowledge and Perception'.

15.3.5 Politics and the war

As has been documented in numerous fields, the Great War precipitated many far-reaching changes in the European consciousness. Among these and calling for our attention here was the effect of the war on British Idealist philosophy, for the movement's decline in popularity was in no small part accelerated by that catastrophe. There were perhaps two aspects to this story. We will consider the counter-reaction it produced against philosophy of a generally idealist character further below, but we may begin with the more localized counter-reaction that sprung up in Britain against specifically *German* philosophy.[112]

The anti-German feeling unleashed by the war—a reaction typified in Haldane's fall from political grace—led to a backlash against everything German. Unfortunately for it, British Idealist philosophy was less able to hide its German ancestry than the British Monarchy, and so it too found itself under a cloud of xenophobic suspicion. Specifically its political philosophy came under attack, for it was seen to follow Hegel, and Hegel (the accusation went) was the chief inspiration behind Germany's recent militaristic and nationalistic stance, on which all blame for the war fell. Crucial in this connection was a book we have already considered, Hobhouse's *The Metaphysical Theory of the State* (1918). In the Dedication he describes how in the summer of 1917, sitting in his garden in Highgate reading Hegel's political philosophy, he was disturbed by an air raid. Returning to his work he thought that, 'In the bombing of London I had just witnessed the visible and tangible outcome of a false and wicked doctrine, the foundations of which lay, as I believe, in the book before me.'[113] For, he argued, Hegel and his disciples (Bosanquet in England, no less than Treitschke in Germany) set up the state as a higher end than the individual, 'Yet when the state is set up an entity superior and indifferent to component individuals it becomes a false god, and its worship the abomination of desolation, as seen at Ypres or on the Somme.'[114] In the fevered atmosphere of war, however, it was not simply the opponents of idealism who spoke thus. Sorley has no qualms about tracing such an extreme collectivist view of the state back to Hegel and Fiche[115] for whom 'war and preparation for war are the continual and necessary business of a State.'[116] Similarly, while doubting that Prussian militarism was due, in any great extent, to philosophical theory,[117] Mackenzie also acknowledged the contributory roles that Fichte and Hegel had played in the recent elevation of the

---

[112] For further details see John Morrow, 'British Idealism, 'German Philosophy' and the First World War'. Although it is beyond the scope of this book to consider them, it should be noted that these debates were echoed in North America. John Dewey (who up until 1901 had himself been an idealist) spoke for the prosecution in his *German Philosophy and Politics* (1915), while John Watson spoke for the defence in his 'German Philosophy and Politics' and 'German Philosophy and the War'. Watson's further reflections on political philosophy may be found in *The State in Peace and War* (1919).

[113] *Metaphysical Theory of the State*, 6.
[114] *Metaphysical Theory of the State*, 136.
[115] 'The State and Morality', 39–45.
[116] 'The State and Morality', 55.
[117] 'Might and Right', 58.

idea of the nation-state. 'The doctrine that [Hegel] . . . whispered prepared the way for that which Treitschke proclaimed from the housetop,'[118] he argues; although least anyone feel too complacent, he points out the echoes of such views to be found Britain's own Carlyle—another source of inspiration for idealism.[119] In these and other widely repeated accusations idealism was judged guilty, at least by association, if not directly, of aggressive nationalism and war-mongering.

A small number spoke out against this widespread reaction, however. They included some Idealists, like J.H. Muirhead, who gave a series of lectures in his own University of Birmingham, subsequently published as *German Philosophy in Relation to the War* (1915).[120] Seeking to avert the 'danger of doing a grave injustice to what was in essence a great constructive effort of thought by associating it with the present orgy of violence and ruthless destruction', Muirhead tried to argue that while the current struggle was indeed a war of ideals, 'these things have come upon us, not because German thought has been faithful to its great philosophical tradition, but because it has broken away from its spirit and falsified its results. It is a story, not of a continuous development, but of a reaction—a great rebellion and apostasy'.[121] Indeed ironically, while throughout the nineteenth century Germany has been moving away from its early idealism, noted Muirhead, British thought has moved in the opposite direction. He acknowledged that Kant, Fichte, and Hegel had indeed been influential on the *early* Prussian State, but maintained that this had been beneficial. However, since then there had been a violent reaction against idealism; the pessimism of Schopenhauer, the materialism of Feuerbach, the Darwinism of Haeckel, the egoism of Stirner, all culminating in the irrationalism of Nietzsche. Nietzsche is called to account most severely for his naturalism. His substitution for conscious reflection on experience of unconscious instinct results in an self-centred blindness that seeks only power. In his thought, because it protects the weak from the strong, the general populace from the true individual, conventional social morality is derided in favour of the doctrine of the superman, and war is upheld as a purifier and refresher of states. Muirhead admits, to be fair, that there is a kind of nobility in what is being proclaimed,[122] however, he thinks it all but drowned under Nietzsche's exaggerated presentation and, moreover, open to serious abuse—for the greatest sin of all he finds in contemporary writers such as Treitschke and von Bernhardi who have extended these ideas in even more destructive directions.[123]

---

[118] 'Might and Right', 60.

[119] 'Might and Right', 68ff.

[120] He also gave a single lecture outlining in shorter form the same case under the title *German Philosophy and the War*.

[121] *German Philosophy in Relation to the War*, 2–3.

[122] *German Philosophy in Relation to the War*, 78.

[123] Heinrich von Treitschke (1834–1896) was a nationalist German historian and political writer.

In a paper published in the *Hibbert Journal*, entitled 'Why We Are Fighting', Henry Jones too acquits Hegel and the idealist tradition of any guilt. It is true that Hegel greatly magnified the importance of the nation-state, but this is not in itself an error. The mistake comes in forgetting that precisely because it is so important, we must respect the rights of *all* states, even small ones,[124] for Hegel never had one state only before his mind. 'He knew that in the end all the independent and sovereign States must stand at the bar of World-Spirit.'[125] The root of the present trouble is indeed to be found in ideas but, for Jones, Germany's undoing has been, not idealism, but rather the 'starving spiritual diet of physical science and mechanical invention' that has come to replace it,[126] and in so far as this has affected the whole country and not just its leaders or philosophers he ventures that 'The Germans have deserved their Emperor and their Nietzsche.'[127] But his view is not wholly one-sided, for he adds that if we British fight out of noble duty, it should not be forgotten that our moral authority on this point stems from the uncomfortable fact that aggrandizing and exploitative imperialism is something which we ourselves are only just beginning to put behind us. Only lately have we begun to respect the rights of small nations and the liberties of those we govern.[128]

A.C. Bradley stresses that Kant, Hegel, and Lotze did not rest state authority in force, finding that idea only in Nietzsche, and blaming industrialization and militarization rather than philosophy for the current German state of mind.[129] Bosanquet too thinks that from its erstwhile heights German intellectual culture has 'degenerated' into a creed of violence and self-interest.[130] But in neither of these last two, it should be noted, is the disapproval of militarism unqualified. Bosanquet insists that where there is no higher community, war is the only and proper arbiter, and that 'for war, as for all other evils and accidents, there is a good deal to be said'.[131] And, though admitting that war, like tragedy, is certainly an evil, A.C. Bradley does not regard it as unmitigatedly so; arguing that 'if the disappearance of either meant the disappearance, or even a lowering, of those noble and glorious energies of the soul which appear in both and are in part the cause of both, the life of perpetual peace would be a poor thing, superficially less terrible perhaps than the present life, but much less great and good'.[132]

Given its disunified response and the climate of the times, both political and philosophical, in the end perhaps it is unsurprising that idealism was not very successful in defeating the charge against it, that as a philosophy it was dangerously associated with

---

[124] 'Why We Are fighting', 64.
[125] 'Why We Are fighting', 63.
[126] 'Why We Are fighting', 65.
[127] 'Why We Are fighting', 60.
[128] 'Why We Are fighting', 57.
[129] 'International Morality: The United States Of Europe', 74–7.
[130] 'Patriotism in the Perfect State,' 140.
[131] 'Patriotism in the Perfect State', 143.
[132] 'International Morality: The United States Of Europe', 64–5.

statism and militarism. And so this remained an important reason for the decline in idealism's fortunes, not least because charges once made tend to stick. In this connection it is interesting to see Muirhead, in his Herbert Spencer Lecture *The Man Versus the State*, delivered in Oxford in March 1939, on the eve of the *Second* World War, repeating much the same case as he made in 1915.[133] The problem behind the current situation, he argues, is not that Hitler's Germany has absorbed too much Hegel, but that it has turned its back on him.

Undoubtedly the accusation that it was somehow German or statist did much to undermine idealism at the time of the Great War, but of far greater damage to its cause was the more general change in consciousness which resulted from that immense catastrophe. The moral philosophy of idealism was a religious one of *service and sacrifice*, their politics one of *nation*, both set within a narrative of constant historical progress. But nationalism of any kind seemed implicated in the disaster which had just taken place, as the country fell under a new mood far removed from that of idealism. For idealism had a distinctive tone, which if its supporters called optimistic, its critics were more likely to decry as complacent. This tone grew as the movement itself developed, a fact that can be seen in the increasing use of the moral argument for the existence of God. If Green and Caird use metaphysics to ground their moral optimism, the later Idealists (like Sorley) use their moral certainty to ground their metaphysical theories. As reason presupposes the rationality of things, so our faith in morality assures us that the universe must be a harmonious place. Valid or not, this became a hard argument to press after a war whose equal extremes of pointlessness and destruction seemed to proclaim the very opposite, and to suggest to many the thought that value itself might be a sham. As one commentator has put it, 'The war produced a general loss of faith; in God, in church, in state, in civilisation itself'.[134] Also, we might add, in the power of philosophy. Ethical scepticism and nihilism, so alien in the nineteenth century, so common in the twentieth, began to raise their heads. Of course, the war itself did not create these feelings and doubts—already the Edwardians were throwing off what they regarded as the moralistic complacency of their Victorian predecessors—but it did give a very powerful boost to them.

In its First World War context the 1916 expulsion of the pacifist Bertrand Russell from his Trinity College lectureship, in which McTaggart took a leading part, has been seen almost as a representation of the clash between the new and the old in philosophy; idealism's last attempt to push away the realism fated to replace it.[135] But at the end of this long study, the appropriateness of that simplistic picture is quite exploded. Vague stories may still circulate about a foreign monster called 'idealism' which invaded Britain and was slain by Russell, Moore, and the other brave pioneers of analysis. Yet one of things which becomes clear from studying the facts is that

---

[133] It is notable that Dewey's *German Philosophy and Politics* was also republished 1942.
[134] Robbins, *The British Hegelians*, 106.
[135] For a full account of this episode see Hardy, *Bertrand Russell and Trinity*.

no such creature ever existed, nor was it ever 'slain'. Idealism was never some kind of homogeneous doctrine and the effect of realizing this is to blunt many of the classic attacks. Their target—idealism—instead of a monolithic bloc becomes better understood as a many-headed hydra as likely, with one of its voices, to agree with any challenge as, with another, to resist it. At the same time many of the criticisms of idealism put forward by its opponents are seen to be mirrored in debates which were *already* occurring (often with greater sophistication) *within* idealism itself.

Chronology

1855	T.H. Green enters Balliol W.R. Sorley born J.H. Muirhead born		
1856	R.B. Haldane born A.Seth Pringle-Pattison born		Crimean War ends
1857	Edward Caird returns to Glasgow University		Indian Mutiny
1858	Hastings Rashdall born		Brunel's 'Great Eastern'
1859		Charles Darwin, *Origin of Species*	Italian Unification
1860	James Seth born J.S. Mackenzie born Edward Caird enters Balliol T.H. Green Fellow at Balliol		
1861		J.S. Mill, *Utilitarianism*	American Civil War starts Death of Prince Albert
1862	John Caird Professor at Glasgow University	H. Spencer, *First Principles*	
1863	J.A. Smith born May Sinclair born		
1864	Edward Caird Fellow at Merton R.L. Nettleship enters Balliol		
1865	C.C.J. Webb born W. Wallace enters Balliol F.H. Bradley enters University College	J. Hutchison Stirling, *The Secret of Hegel* Edward Caird, 'Plato and the Other Companions of Socrates'	American Civil War ends Death of Abraham Lincoln
1866	J.M.E. McTaggart born Edward Caird Professor at Glasgow University John Watson enters Glasgow University	Edward Caird, *Ethical Philosophy* T.H. Green, 'The Philosophy of Aristotle'	
1867	Bernard Bosanquet enters Balliol W. Wallace Fellow at Merton Hilda Oakeley born	Karl Marx, *Das Capital*	The Second Reform Bill

1868	H.H. Joachim born	T.H. Green, 'Popular Philosophy in its Relation to Life'	
1869	A.E. Taylor born A.C. Bradley enters Balliol R.L. Nettleship Fellow at Balliol D.G. Ritchie enters Edinburgh University		The Suez Canal opened
1870	Bosanquet Fellow at University College Bradley Fellow at Merton		Death of Charles Dickens First Education Act (establishment of elementary schools nationwide) Married Women's Property Act
1871		Charles Darwin, *The Descent of Man* Benjamin Jowett, *Dialogues of Plato*	The Universities Test Act
1872	James Black Baillie born Bertrand Russell born J. MacCunn enters Balliol R.B. Haldane enters Edinburgh University John Watson Professor Queen's University		
1873	John Caird Principal Glasgow University Death of J.S. Mill G.E. Moore born A.S. Pringle-Pattison enters Edinburgh University		Death of David Livingstone
1874	A.C. Bradley Fellow at Balliol D.G. Ritchie enters Balliol	H. Sidgwick, *Methods of Ethics* T.H. Green, *Introduction to Hume's Treatise of Human Nature* W. Wallace, *The Logic of Hegel* F.H. Bradley, *The Presuppositions of Critical History*	Factory Act
1875	Henry Jones enters Glasgow University		Mason's College Birmingham founded

1876	Green elected to Oxford Town Council James Seth enters Edinburgh University	F.H. Bradley, *Ethical Studies* H. Spencer, *Principles of Sociology*	Death of Harriet Martineau University College Bristol founded
1877	J.S. MacKenzie enters Glasgow University T.H. Green White's Professor of Moral Philosophy at Oxford	F.H. Bradley, *Mr Sidgwick's Hedonism* Edward Caird, *A Critical Account of the Philosophy of Kant*	
1878	D.G. Ritchie Fellow at Jesus		Salvation Army founded Factory Act
1879	R.B. Haldane called to the Bar A.D. Lindsay born	R. Adamson, *On the Philosophy of Kant*	
1880		A.C. Bradley, 'Aristotle's Conception of the State' R.L. Nettleship, 'The Theory of Education in the *Republic* of Plato' John Caird, *An Introduction to the Philosophy of Religion*	Death of George Eliot First Boer War starts
1881	Bernard Bosanquet resigns Fellowship John MacCunn Professor at Liverpool	T.H. Green, 'Liberal Legislation and Freedom of Contract' John Watson, *Kant and his English Critics*	Death of Thomas Carlyle Death of Benjamin Disraeli First Boer War ends University College Liverpool founded
1882	Death of T.H. Green W. Wallace White's Professor of Moral Philosophy Oxford (vice Green) A.C. Bradley Professor at Liverpool	A.S. Pringle-Pattison, *The Development from Kant to Hegel* W. Wallace, *Kant*	Married Women's Property Act
1883	Pringle-Pattison Professor at Cardiff W.R. Sorley Fellow Trinity College Cambridge	F.H. Bradley, *The Principles of Logic* T.H. Green, *Prolegomena to Ethics* Edward Caird, *Hegel* A.S. Pringle-Pattison and R.B. Haldane, *Essays in Philosophical Criticism*	Death of Karl Marx Eruption of Krakatoa University College Cardiff founded

1884	Henry Jones Professor University College of North Wales		Third Reform Act Gordon killed at Khartoum
1885	R.B. Haldane elected to Parliament J.H. Muirhead enters Manchester New College, London J.M.E. McTaggart enters Trinity College Cambridge C.C.J. Webb enters Christ Church Bernard Bosanquet, *Knowledge and Reality*	W.R. Sorley, *The Ethics of Naturalism* A.S. Pringle-Pattison, *Scottish Philosophy* T.H. Green, *The Works of Thomas Hill Green* Edward Caird, *The Social Philosophy of Comte*	
1886	J.S. Mackenzie enters Trinity College Cambridge James Seth Professor at Dalhousie, NS		
1887	A.S. Pringle-Pattison Professor at St Andrews	A.S. Pringle-Pattison, *Hegelianism and Personality*	Queen Victoria's Golden Jubilee
1888	W.R. Sorley Professor at Cardiff (vice Pringle-Pattison)	Bernard Bosanquet, *Logic, or the Morphology of Knowledge* John Caird, *Spinoza*	Death of Matthew Arnold
1889	R.G. Collingwood born C.C.J. Webb Fellow Magdalen College	Edward Caird, *The Critical Philosophy of Immanuel Kant* Bernard Bosanquet, Essays and Addresses D.G. Ritchie, *Darwinism and Politics*	Death of Robert Browning
1890	H.H. Joachim Fellow at Merton J.S. Mackenzie Fellow Trinity College Cambridge A.C. Bradley Professor at Glasgow University	J.S. Mackenzie, *An Introduction to Social Philosophy* W. Wallace, *Schopenhauer*	Death of J.H. Newman
1891	A.S. Pringle-Pattison Professor at Edinburgh Henry Jones Professor St Andrews (vice Pringle-Pattison) J.M.E. McTaggart Fellow Trinity College Cambridge A.E. Taylor Fellow Merton College	James Seth, *Freedom as Ethical Postulate* Henry Jones, *Browning as a Philosophical and Religious Teacher* D.G. Ritchie, *Principles of State Interference*	Factory Act

1892	Death of R.L. Nettleship	J.H. Muirhead, *The Elements of Ethics*
	James Seth Professor at Brown	Bernard Bosanquet, *History of Aesthetic*
	H.H. Joachim lecturer at St Andrews	Edward Caird, *Essays on Literature and Philosophy*
1893	Edward Caird Master of Balliol (vice Jowett)	Bernard Bosanquet, *The Civilization of Christendom*
	G.R.G. Mure born	Edward Caird, *The Evolution of Religion*
		F.H. Bradley, *Appearance and Reality*
		D.G. Ritchie, *Darwin and Hegel*
		J.S. Mackenzie, *Manual of Ethics*
		J.M.E. McTaggart, 'Further Determination of the Absolute'
1894	Henry Jones Professor at Glasgow University (vice Caird)	James Seth, *A Study of Ethical Principles*
	W.R. Sorley Professor at Aberdeen	D.G. Ritchie, *Natural Rights*
	D.G. Ritchie Professor at St Andrews (vice Jones)	R.J. Illingworth, *Personality Human and Divine*
	Joachim lecturer at Balliol	J. MacCunn, *Ethics of Citizenship*
1895	J.S. Mackenzie Professor at Cardiff (Vice Sorley)	T.H. Green, *Principles of Political Obligation*
		Bernard Bosanquet (ed.), *Aspects of the Social Problem*
		Bernard Bosanquet, *The Essentials of Logic*
		Bernard Bosanquet, *A Companion to Plato's Republic*
		Henry Jones, *The Philosophy of Lotze*
1896	James Seth Professor at Cornell	J.M.E. McTaggart, *Studies in the Hegelian Dialectic*
	J.H. Muirhead Professor at Mason College (later Birmingham University)	
1897	Death of W. Wallace	R.L. Nettleship, *Philosophical Lectures and Remains*	Queen Victoria's Diamond Jubilee
	H.H. Joachim Fellow at Merton (vice Wallace)		

		Bernard Bosanquet, *Psychology of the Moral Self* Bertrand Russell, *An Essay on the Foundations of Geometry* A.S. Pringle-Pattison, *Man's Place in the Cosmos*	
1898	James Seth Professor at Edinburgh Death of John Caird	W. Wallace, *Lecture and Essays on Natural Theology and Ethics* John Caird, *University Addresses* John Caird, *University Sermons* R.J. Illingworth, *Divine Immanence* R.L. Nettleship, *Philosophical Lectures and Remains*	Death of Gladstone
1899	Edward Caird opposes honorary degree for Cecil Rhodes	Josiah Royce, *The World and the Individual* John Caird, *The Fundamental Ideas of Christianity* James Ward, *Naturalism and Agnosticism* Bernard Bosanquet, *The Philosophical Theory of the State*	Second Boer War starts
1900	W.R. Sorley Knightbridge Professor of Philosophy at Cambridge (vice Sidgwick)	J.H. Muirhead, *Chapters from Aristotle's Ethics* J. MacCunn, *Making of Character*	Death of John Ruskin Boxer rebellion Labour Party founded
1901	A.C. Bradley Professor of Poetry at Oxford	H.H. Joachim, *A Study of the Ethics of Spinoza* A.E. Taylor, *The Problem of Conduct* James Black Baillie, *The Origin and Significance of Hegel's Logic* J.M.E. McTaggart, *Studies in Hegelian Cosmology*	Death of Queen Victoria Factory Act
1902	Death of Robert Adamson	D.G. Ritchie, *Studies in Political and Social Ethics* J.H. Muirhead, *Philosophy and Life, and Other Essays* H. Sturt (ed), *Personal Idealism* J.S. Mackenzie, *Outlines of Metaphysics*	Second Boer War ends

1903	Death of D.G. Ritchie	A.E. Taylor, *Elements of Metaphysics*	
	Bernard Bosanquet Professor at St Andrews	R.B. Haldane, *The Pathway to Reality*	
		Bertrand Russell, *Principles of Mathematics*	
		G.E. Moore, *Principia Ethica*	
1904		W.R. Sorley, *Recent Tendencies in Ethics*	
		Edward Caird, *The Evolution of Theology in the Greek Philosophers*	
1905		D.G. Ritchie, *Philosophical Studies*	Einstein's theory of Special Relativity
		Bertrand Russell, 'On Denoting'	
1906	A.C. Bradley retires	H.H. Joachim, *The Nature of Truth*	
	A.D. Lindsay lecturer at Balliol	James Black Baillie, *Outline of the Idealistic Construction of Experience*	
		J.M.E. McTaggart, *Some Dogmas of Religion*	
1907		J.S. Mackenzie, *Lectures on Humanism*	
		Hastings Rashdall, *The Theory of Good and Evil*	
		Edward Caird, *Lay Sermons and Addresses*	
		A.S. Pringle-Pattison, *The Philosophical Radicals*	
1908	Death of Edward Caird	J.H. Muirhead, *The Service of the State*	
	Bernard Bosanquet retires		
	A.E. Taylor Professor St Andrews (vice Bosanquet)		
1909	Death of James Hutchinson Stirling	Henry Jones, *Idealism as a Practical Creed*	Bleriot flies the Channel
		Hastings Rashdall, *Philosophy and Religion*	
1910	J.A. Smith Waynflete Professor of Metaphysics at Oxford	J.M.E. McTaggart, *A Commentary on Hegel's Logic*	Death of Leo Tolstoy
		Henry Jones, *Working Faith of a Social Reformer*	Death of Edward VII
1911	J. MacCunn retires	James Ward, *The Realm of Ends or Pluralism and Theism*	
		R.J. Illingworth, *Divine Transcendence*	
		W.R. Sorley, *The Moral Life and Moral Worth*	

1912	R.B. Haldane Lord Chancellor	Bernard Bosanquet, *The Principle of Individuality and Value* Hastings Rashdall, *The Problem of Evil* James Seth, *English Philosophers and Schools of Philosophy*	
1913		Bernard Bosanquet, *The Value and Destiny of the Individual* Bernard Bosanquet, *The Distinction between Mind and its Objects* Hastings Rashdall, *Ethics*	
1914		Hastings Rashdall, *Is Conscience an Emotion?* F.H. Bradley, *Essays on Truth and Reality*	The Great War starts Panama Canal opens
1915	R.B. Haldane resigns Lord Chancellorship J.S. Mackenzie retires	J.H. Muirhead, *German Philosophy in relation to the War* Bernard Bosanquet, *Three Lectures on Aesthetic* C.C.J. Webb, *History of Philosophy*	
1916		R.G. Collingwood, *Religion and Philosophy* A.S. Pringle-Pattison, *The Idea of God*	
1917		J.S. Mackenzie, *Elements of Constructive Philosophy* Bernard Bosanquet, *Social and International Ideals* May Sinclair, *Defence of Idealism*	
1918		J.H. Muirhead and H.J.W. Hetherington, *Social Purpose* W.R. Sorley, *Moral Values and the Idea of God* Bernard Bosanquet, *Some Suggestions in Ethics* J.S. Mackenzie, *Outlines of Social Philosophy* C.C.J. Webb, *God and Personality* W.H. Wildon Carr (ed.), *Life and Finite Individuality*	Fourth Reform Act (female suffrage)
1919	H.H. Joachim Wykeham Chair of Logic at Oxford (vice Cook Wilson) A.S. Pringle-Pattison retires	Henry Jones, *The Principles of Citizenship*	End of the Great War

1920		Bernard Bosanquet, *Implication and Linear Inference* Bernard Bosanquet, *What Religion Is* W.R. Sorley, *A History of English Philosophy* C.C.J. Webb, *Divine Personality and Human Life* Hastings Rashdall, *The Moral Argument for Personal Immortality*	
1921		James Black Baillie, *Studies in Human Nature* J.M.E. McTaggart, *The Nature of Existence (I)* R.B. Haldane, *The Reign of Relativity* Bernard Bosanquet, *Meeting of Extremes in Contemporary Philosophy*	
1922	Death of Henry Jones J.H. Muirhead retires A.D. Lindsay Professor at Glasgow University (vice Jones)	Henry Jones, *A Faith that Enquires* R.B. Haldane, *The Philosophy of Humanism* A.S. Pringle-Pattison, *The Idea of Immortality*	The Irish Free State established The BBC founded
1923	Death of Bernard Bosanquet		
1924	R.B. Haldane Lord Chancellor Death of F.H. Bradley Death of Hastings Rashdall Death of James Seth John Watson retires H.J.W. Hetherington Professor at Glasgow University (vice Lindsay) A.D. Lindsay Master of Balliol	J.S. Mackenzie, *Ultimate Values* R.F.A. Hoernlé, *Idealism as a Philosophical Doctrine* R.G. Collingwood, *Speculum Mentis* N. Kemp Smith, *Prolegomena to an Idealist Theory of Knowledge*	
1925	Death of J.M.E. McTaggart Death of James Ward	R.G. Collingwood, *Outlines of a Philosophy of Art*	
1926		R.B. Haldane, *Human Experience* A.E. Taylor, *Plato, the Man and his Work* James Seth, *Essays in Ethics and Religion*	
1927		J.M.E. McTaggart, *The Nature of Existence (II)*	

		Bernard Bosanquet, *Science and Philosophy and Other Essays* H.J. Paton, *The Good Will* James Ward, *Essays in Philosophy*	
1928	Death of R.B. Haldane Death of J. MacCunn	J.H. Muirhead, *The Use of Philosophy* Hastings Rashdall, *Ideas and Ideals* J.S. Mackenzie, *Fundamental Problems of Life*	
1929		J.S. Haldane, *The Sciences and Philosophy*	Wall Street Crash
1930		F.H. Bradley, *Aphorisms* J.H. Muirhead, *Coleridge as Philosopher* A.S. Pringle-Pattison, *Studies in The Philosophy of Religion* Hastings Rashdall, *God and Man* A.E. Taylor, *The Faith of a Moralist*	
1931	Death of A.S. Pringle-Pattison	J.H. Muirhead, *The Platonic Tradition in Anglo-Saxon Philosophy* J.S. Mackenzie, *Cosmic Problems* C.A. Campbell, *Scepticism and Construction* H.W.B. Joseph, *Some Problems in Ethics*	
1932		J.H. Muirhead, *Rule and End in Morals*	
1933	W.R. Sorley retires	A.S. Pringle-Pattison, *The Balfour Lectures on Realism* C.C.J. Webb, *A Study of Religious Thought in England from 1850* C.R. Morris, *Idealist Logic* R.G. Collingwood, *An Essay on Philosophical Method*	
1934	Death of John Watson	C.C.J. Webb, *Religion and Theism* J.M.E. McTaggart, *Philosophical Studies* A.E. Taylor, *Philosophical Studies* A.C. Bradley, *Oxford Lectures on Poetry* A.C. Ewing, *Idealism, a Critical Survey*	

1935	R.G. Collingwood Waynflete Professor of Metaphysics at Oxford (vice J.A. Smith) Death of W.R. Sorley Death of J.S. Mackenzie Death of A.C. Bradley H.H. Joachim retires	F.H. Bradley, *Collected Essays*	
1936			Death of George V Abdication of Edward VIII
1937			Factory Act
1938	Death of H.H. Joachim C.A. Campbell Professor at Glasgow University		
1939	Death of J.A. Smith Death of John Watson		Start of Second World War
1940	Death of J.H. Muirhead Death of James Black Baillie	A.C. Bradley, *Ideals of Religion*	
1941	A.E. Taylor retires		
1942		J.H. Muirhead, *Reflections of a Journeyman in Philosophy*	
1943	Death of R.G. Collingwood Death of H.W.B. Joseph		
1944			
1945	Death of A.E. Taylor		End of Second World War
1946	Death of May Sinclair		
1947			
1948		H.H. Joachim, *Logical Studies*	

Bibliography

Dates in square brackets denote dates of original publication or original composition.

1. Writings of the British Idealists

Bernard Bosanquet (1848–1923)

——. (1883) 'Logic as the Science of Knowledge' in A. Seth and R.B. Haldane (eds) *Essays in Philosophical Criticism*, pp.67–101.

——. (1885) *Knowledge and Reality*, London: Kegan Paul, Trench and Trubner.

——. [1886] 'On the True Conception of Another World' in B.Bosanquet (ed.) *Introduction to Hegel's Aesthetik or Philosophy of Fine Art*, 2nd edn 1905, pp.xv–xxxv.

——. (1888) 'The Home Arts and Industries Association: Aims and Objects' *Charity Organization Review*, 4, pp.135–7.

——. (1888) 'The Philosophical Importance of a True Theory of Identity' *Mind*, 13, pp.356–69.

——. [1888] *Logic, or the Morphology of Knowledge*, Oxford: Clarendon Press, 2nd edn 1911.

——. (1889) 'Individual and Social Reform' in *Essays and Addresses*, London: Swann Sonnenschein, pp.24–47.

——. (1889) 'Artistic Handwork in Education' in *Essays and Addresses*, pp.71–91.

——. (1889) 'The Kingdom of God on Earth' in *Essays and Addresses*, pp.108–30.

——. (1889) 'How to Read the New Testament' in *Essays and Addresses*, pp.131–61.

——. [1889] 'The Part Played by Aesthetic in the Development of Modern Philosophy' *Proceedings of the Aristotelian Society*, 1. Reprinted in his *Science and Philosophy*, pp.367–91.

——. [1892] *A History of Aesthetic*, London: George Allen and Unwin, 2nd edn 1904, 1949 impression.

——. (1893) 'The Future of Religious Observance' in *The Civilisation of Christendom*, London: Swann Sonnenschein, pp.1–26.

——. (1893) 'Some thoughts on the Transition from Paganism to Christianity' in *The Civilisation of Christendom*, pp.27–62.

——. (1893) 'The Civilization of Christendom' in *The Civilisation of Christendom*, pp.63–99.

——. (1893) 'Old Problems under New Names' in *The Civilisation of Christendom*, pp.100–26.

——. (1893) 'Are We Agnostics?' in *The Civilisation of Christendom*, pp.127–59.

——. [1894] 'On the Nature of Aesthetic Emotion' *Mind*, 3. Reprinted in his *Science and Philosophy*, pp.392–406.

——. (1895) 'The Duties of Citizenship' in B. Bosanquet (ed.) *Aspects of The Social Problem*, London: Macmillan, pp.1–27.

——. (1895) 'The Principle of Private Property' in B. Bosanquet (ed.) *Aspects of The Social Problem*, pp.308–18.

——. (1895) 'The Reality of the General Will' in B. Bosanquet (ed.) *Aspects of the Social Problem*, pp.319–32.

——. (1895) 'Socialism and Natural Selection' in B. Bosanquet (ed.) *Aspects of The Social Problem* pp.289–307.

——. [1895] *The Essentials of Logic*, London: Macmillan, 1928 impression.

——. (1895) 'The Evolution of Religion' *International Journal of Ethics*, 5, pp.432–44.

——. (1895) A *Companion to Plato's Republic*, London: Rivington Percival.

——. [1896] 'Time and the Absolute' *Proceedings of the Aristotelian Society*, 3. Reprinted in his *Science and Philosophy*, pp.113–22.

——. (1897) *The Psychology of the Moral Self*, London: Macmillan.

——. [1899] *The Philosophical Theory of the State*, London: Macmillan, 4th edn, 1923.

——. (1900) *The Education of the Young in Republic of Plato*, Cambridge: Cambridge University Press.

——. (1902) 'Philosophy of Religion' in J.M. Baldwin (ed), *Dictionary of Philosophy and Psychology*, London: Macmillan, Volume Two, pp.454–8.

——. (1903) 'Plato's Conception of Death' *Hibbert Journal*, 2, pp.98–109.

——. [1903] 'The Practical Value of Moral Philosophy' St Andrews inaugural address. Reprinted in his *Science and Philosophy*, pp.135–49.

——. (1904) 'Review of Moore's' *Principia Ethica' Mind*, 13, pp. 254–61.

——. (1912) 'Les Idées Politiques de Rousseau' *Revue de Métaphysique et de Morale*, 20, pp.321–40.

——. (1912) *The Principle of Individuality and Value*, London: Macmillan.

——. (1913) *The Value and Destiny of the Individual*, London: Macmillan.

——. (1913) *The Distinction between Mind and its Objects*, Manchester: Sherratt and Hughes.

——. (1914) 'The Philosophy of Eucken' *Quarterly Review*, No.439, pp.365–79.

——. [1914–5] 'Science and Philosophy' *Proceedings of the Aristotelian Society*, 15. Reprinted in his *Science and Philosophy*, pp.15–33.

——. (1915) *Three Lectures on Aesthetic*, London: Macmillan.

——. (1915) 'Patriotism in the Perfect State' in *The International Crisis in its Ethical and Psychological Aspects*, Oxford: Humphrey Milford, pp.132–54.

——. [1917–18] 'Do Finite Individuals possess a Substantive or an Adjectival mode of Being?' *Proceedings of the Aristotelian Society*, 18. Reprinted in W.H Wildon Carr (ed.) *Life and Finite Individuality, Proceedings of the Aristotelian Society Supplementary volume 1*, 1918, pp.75–194.

——. (1917) 'The Relation of Coherence to Immediacy and Specific Purpose' *The Philosophical Review*, 26, pp. 259–73.

——. (1917) 'The Affinity of Philosophy and Casework' in *Social and International Ideals, Being Studies in Patriotism*, London: Macmillan, pp.161–82.

——. (1917) 'Three Lectures on Social Ideals' in *Social and International Ideals, Being Studies in Patriotism*, pp.189–249.

——. (1917) 'The Function of the State in Promoting the Unity of Mankind' in *Social and International Ideals, Being Studies in Patriotism*, pp.270–301.

——. (1918) *Some Suggestions in Ethics*, London: Macmillan.

——. (1919) 'Croce's Aesthetic' *Proceedings of the British Academy*, 9. Reprinted in his *Science and Philosophy*, pp.407–37.

——. (1920) 'Review of five books of Italian idealism' *Mind*, 24, pp.367–70.

——. (1920) *Implication and Linear Inference*, London: Macmillan.

——. (1920) *What Religion is*, London: Macmillan.

——. (1921) *The Meeting of Extremes in Contemporary Philosophy*, London: Macmillan.

——. (1924) 'Life and Philosophy' in J.H Muirhead (ed.) *Contemporary British Philosophy: First Series*, pp.51–74.

——. (1927) *Science and Philosophy and other essays*, London: George Allen and Unwin.

——. (1935) *Bernard Bosanquet and his friends, Letters illustrating the Sources and the Development of his Philosophical Opinions*, J.H. Muirhead (ed.), London: George Allen and Unwin.

A.C. Bradley (1851–1935)

——. (1880) 'Aristotle's Conception of the State' in A.E. Abbott (ed.), *Hellenica; Essays on Greek Poetry, Philosophy, History and Religion*, London: Rivingtons, pp.181–243.

——. [1909] *Oxford Lectures on Poetry*, London: Macmillan, 1934.

——. (1915) 'International Morality: The United States of Europe' in *The International Crisis in its Ethical and Psychological Aspects*, Oxford: Humphrey Milford, pp.46–77.

——. (1921–3) 'Bernard Bosanquet' *Proceedings of the British Academy*, 10, pp.563–72.

——. (1940) *Ideals of Religion*, London: Macmillan.

F.H. Bradley (1846–1924)

——. [1874] *The Presuppositions of Critical History*, Oxford: James Parker. Reprinted in his *Collected Essays*, pp.1–70.

——. [1876] *Ethical Studies*, Oxford: Clarendon Press. 2nd edn, 1927.

——. [1877] *Mr Sidgwick's Hedonism*, London: King and Co. Reprinted in his *Collected Essays*, pp.71–128.

——. [1883] *The Principles of Logic*, Oxford: Clarendon Press. 2nd edn 1922.

——. [1893] *Appearance and Reality*, Oxford: Clarendon Press. 2nd edn 1897.

——. [1900] 'A Defence of Phenomenalism in Psychology' *Mind*, 9. Reprinted in his *Collected Essays*, pp. 364–86.

——. (1914) *Essays on Truth and Reality*, Oxford: Clarendon Press.

——. [1930] *Aphorisms*, Oxford: The Clarendon Press. Reprinted in G. Stock (ed.) *The Presuppositions of Critical History and Aphorisms*, Bristol: Thoemmes Press, 1993.

——. (1935) *Collected Essays*, Oxford: Clarendon Press.

——. (1983) 'F.H.Bradley: An Unpublished Note on Christian Morality' *Religious Studies*, 19, pp.175–83.

——. (1999) *Collected Work of F.H.Bradley*, edited by C.A. Keene (volumes 1–5) and W.J. Mander (volumes 6–12), Bristol: Thoemmes Press.

Edward Caird (1835–1908)

——. (1865) 'Plato and the Other Companions of Socrates' *The North British Review*, 43, pp.351–84.

——. (1866) *Ethical Philosophy*, Glasgow: James Maclehose.

——. [*c*.1866] 'Reform and the Reformation' in C. Tyler (ed.) *Unpublished Manuscripts in British Idealism*, Exeter: Imprint Academic 2008, vol. 2, pp.1–39.

——. (1875) 'Review of Sidgwick's *The Methods of Ethics*' *Academy*, 7, pp.611–14.

——. [1876] 'Cartesianism' in *Encyclopaedia Britannica*, 9th edn. Reprinted in his *Essays on Literature and Philosophy*, vol. 2, pp. 267–383.

——. [1877] 'Rousseau' *Contemporary Review*, 30. Reprinted in his *Essays on Literature and Philosophy*, vol. 1, pp. 105–46.

——. (1877) *A Critical Account of the Philosophy of Kant*, Glasgow: James Maclehose.

——. [c.1877–93], *Lectures on Moral Philosophy* in C. Tyler (ed.) *Unpublished Manuscripts in British Idealism*, Exeter: Imprint Academic 2008, vol. 2, pp.40–152.

——. (1879) 'Mr. Balfour on Transcendentalism' *Mind*, 4, pp. 111–15.

——. [1879] 'The Social Philosophy and Religion of Comte' *Contemporary Review*, vols 35–6 (four parts). Reprinted in 1885 as *The Social Philosophy of Comte*, Glasgow: James Maclehose, 2nd edn 1893.

——. [1880] 'Wordsworth' *Fraser's Magazine*, 21. Reprinted in his *Essays on Literature and Philosophy*, vol. 1, pp. 147–89.

——. [1881] 'The Problem of Philosophy at the Present Time' Glasgow: James Maclehose. Reprinted in his *Essays on Literature and Philosophy*, vol. 1, pp. 190–229.

——. [1883] 'Metaphysic' in *Encyclopaedia Britannica*, 9th edn. Reprinted in his *Essays on Literature and Philosophy*, vol. 2, pp. 384–539.

——. (1883) 'Professor Green's Last Work' *Mind*, 8, pp. 544–61.

——. (1883) *Hegel*, Edinburgh: William Blackwood.

——. [1886] 'Goethe and Philosophy' *Contemporary Review*, 50. Reprinted in his *Essays on Literature and Philosophy*, vol. 1, pp.54–104.

——. [c.1887–8] 'Lecture on Political Economy' in C. Tyler (ed.) *Unpublished Manuscripts in British Idealism*, Exeter: Imprint Academic 2008, vol. 2, pp.153–63.

——. (1888) *The Moral Aspect of the Economical Problem*, London: Swan Sonnenschein, Lowrey.

——. (1889) *The Critical Philosophy of Immanuel Kant*, Glasgow: James Maclehose.

——. (1892) 'The Genius of Carlyle' in his *Essays on Literature and Philosophy*, vol. 1, pp.230–67.

——. (1892) *Essays on Literature and Philosophy*, Glasgow: James Maclehose.

——. (1893) *The Evolution of Religion*, Glasgow: James Maclehose.

——. (1894) 'Plato's Republic as the Earliest Educational Treatise' Bangor: Jarvis and Foster.

——. [1897] 'The Present State of the Controversy between Individualism and Socialism' Glasgow: James Maclehose. Reprinted in D. Boucher (ed.) *The British Idealists*, Cambridge: Cambridge University Press, 1997, pp.173–94.

——. (1903–4) 'Idealism and the Theory of Knowledge' *Proceedings of the British Academy*, 2, pp.95–108.

——. (1904) *The Evolution of Theology in the Greek Philosophers*, Glasgow: James Maclehose.

——. (1907) *Lay Sermons and Addresses*, Glasgow: James Maclehose.

John Caird (1820–1898)

——. [1880] 'Corporate Immortality' in *Scotch Sermons*, London: Macmillan. Reprinted in his *University Sermons*, pp.176–95.

——. (1880) 'Union with God' in *Scotch Sermons*, pp.18–35.

——. [1880] *An Introduction to Philosophy of Religion*, Glasgow: James Maclehose, 1891.

——. (1888) *Spinoza*, Edinburgh: William Blackwood.

——. (1898) *University Addresses*, Glasgow: James Maclehose.

——. (1898) *University Sermons*, Glasgow: James Maclehose.

——. [1899] *The Fundamental Ideas of Christianity*, Glasgow: James Maclehose, 1915.

——. (1906) *Essays for Sunday Reading*, London: Pitman and Sons.

T.H. Green (1836–1882)

——. [*c*.1858] 'Essay on Christian Dogma' in *Works* III, pp.161–85.

——. [1858] 'The Force of Circumstances' in *Works* III, pp.3–10.

——. [1862] 'An Estimate of the Value and Influence of Works of Fiction in Modern Times' in *Works* III, pp.20–45.

——. [1866] 'The Philosophy of Aristotle' *North British Review*, 45. Reprinted in his *Works* III, pp.46–91.

——. [1867] 'Four Lectures on the English Revolution' in *Works* III, pp.277–364.

——. [1868] 'Popular Philosophy in its Relation to Life' *North British Review*, 48. Reprinted in his *Works* III, pp.92–125.

——. [1870] 'The Witness of God' in *Works* III, pp.230–52.

——. [1874] *Introduction to Hume's Treatise of Human Nature* (two parts). Reprinted in his *Works* I, pp.1–371.

——. [*c*.1874–6] 'Lectures on Kant' in *Works* II, pp.1–155.

——. [*c*.1874–5] 'Lectures on Logic' in *Works* II, pp.157–306.

——. [1877] 'Faith' in *Works* III, pp.253–76.

——. [1877] 'Review of Edward Caird's *The Philosophy of Kant*' *Academy*, 12. Reprinted in his *Works* III, pp.126–37.

——. [1877–9] 'Mr Herbert Spencer and Mr G.H. Lewes' *Contemporary Review*, 31–2. Reprinted in his *Works* I, pp.373–520.

——. [1879] 'On the Different Senses of "Freedom" as Applied to Will and to the Moral Progress of Man' in *Works* II, pp.307–33.

——. [1879–80] 'Lectures on the Principles of Political Obligation' in *Works* II, pp.335–553. Subsequently published as a separate volume.

——. [1880] 'Review of John Caird's *Introduction to the Philosophy of Religion*' *Academy*, 18. Reprinted in his *Works* III, pp.138–46.

——. [1881] 'Liberal Legislation and Freedom of Contract' in Works III, pp.365–86.

——. [1881] 'Review of J. Watson's *Kant and his English Critics*' *Academy*, 10. Reprinted in his *Works* III, pp.147–58.

——. (1882) 'Can there be a Natural Science of Man?' *Mind*, 7, pp. 1–29, 161–85, 321–48. Reprinted in his *Prolegomena to Ethics*.

——. [1883] *Prolegomena to Ethics*, Oxford: Clarendon Press, 5th edn 1907.

——. [1883] *The Witness of God and Faith: two lay sermons*, edited with an introductory notice by Arnold Toynbee, London: Longmans Green. Both sermons reprinted in his *Works* III, pp.230–52 and 253–76.

——. (1885) 'The Incarnation' in *Works* III, pp.207–20.

——. (1885) 'The World is Nigh Thee' in *Works* III, pp.221–9.

——. (1885–8) *Works of T. H. Green*, edited together with a Memoir by R.L. Nettleship, 3 vols, London: Longmans Green.

——. (1997) *Collected Works of T. H. Green*, edited by R.L. Nettleship and P.P. Nicholson, 5 vols, Bristol: Thoemmes Press.

R.B. Haldane (1856–1928)

——. (1883) 'The Relation of Philosophy to Science' (with J.S. Hadane) in *Essays in Philosophical Criticism* (edited with A. Seth) London: Longmans Green, pp.41–66.

——. (1888) 'Hegel and his Recent Critics' *Mind*, 13, pp. 585–89.

——. (1888) 'The Liberal Party and its Prospects' *The Contemporary Review*, 53, pp.145–60.

——. (1888) 'The Liberal Creed' *The Contemporary Review*, 54, pp.461–74.

——. (1896) 'The New Liberalism' *The Progressive Review*, 1, pp.132–43.

——. (1902) *Education and Empire*, London: John Murray.

——. (1903–4) *The Pathway to Reality*, London: John Murray.

——. (1910) *Universities and National Life*, London: John Murray.

——. [1912] 'The Civic University' in *The Conduct of Life*, London: John Murray, 1914, pp.63–95.

——. [1913] 'Higher Nationality' in *The Conduct of Life*, pp.99–136.

——. [1913] 'The Conduct of Life' in *The Conduct of Life*, pp.1–27.

——. [1914] 'The Meaning of Truth in History' in *The Conduct of Life*, pp.29–61.

——. (1916) 'Education After the War, with special reference to technical instruction' London: Imperial College.

——. (1918) 'The Future of Democracy; an Address' London: Headly Bros.

——. (1920) 'The Nature of the State' *Contemporary Review*, 117, pp.761–73.

——. [1921] *The Reign of Relativity*, London: John Murray, 3rd edn 1921.

——. (1922) *The Philosophy of Humanism*, London: John Murray.

——. (1926) *Human Experience*, London: John Murray.

——. (1929) *An Autobiography*, London: Hodder and Stoughton.

——. (1929) Preface to *Hegel's Science of Logic*, W.H. Johnson and L.G. Struthers (eds).

H.H. Joachim (1868–1938)

——. (1901) *A Study of the Ethics of Spinoza*, Oxford: Clarendon Press.

——. (1906) *The Nature of Truth*, Oxford: Clarendon Press.

——. (1907) 'A Reply to Mr Moore' *Mind*, 16, pp. 410–15.

——. (1948) *Logical Studies*, Oxford: Clarendon Press.

Henry Jones (1852–1922)

——. (1883) 'The Social Organism' in A. Seth and R.B. Haldane (eds) *Essays in Philosophical Criticism*, pp.187–213.

——. [1891] *Browning as a Philosophical and Religious Teacher*, Glasgow: James Maclehose. 2nd edn 1892.

——. (1891–2) 'Is the Distinction between "is" and "ought" Ultimate and Irreducible?' *Proceedings of the Aristotelian Society*, 2, pp.92–6.

——. (1893) 'The Nature and Aims of Philosophy' *Mind*, 2, pp. 160–73.

——. (1893) 'Idealism and Epistemology' *Mind*, 2, pp. 289–306, 457–72.

——. (1893) 'Is the Order of Nature Opposed to the Moral Life?' (Glasgow inaugural address) Glasgow: James Maclehose.

——. (1895) *The Philosophy of Lotze*, Glasgow: James Maclehose.

——. (1898) 'Social and Individual Evolution' *The New World*, 7. Reprinted in his *Working Faith of the Social Reformer*, pp.227–55.

——. (1902) Introduction to P. Janet and G. Seailles, *A History of the Problems of Philosophy*, London: Macmillan, vol. I, pp.vii–xvi.

——. (1902–4) 'The Present Attitude of Reflective Thought towards Religion' *Hibbert Journal*, 1, pp.228–52; 2, pp.20–43.

——. [1903–4] 'The Moral Aspect of the Fiscal Question' *Hibbert Journal*, 2. Reprinted in his *Working Faith of the Social Reformer*, 1910, pp.115–50.

——. [1905–6] 'The Working Faith of the Social Reformer' *Hibbert Journal*, 4. Reprinted in his *Working Faith of the Social Reformer*, pp.1–114.

——. [1905] 'Social Responsibilities; Lectures to Business Men' Glasgow: James Maclehose. Reprinted in his *Working Faith of the Social Reformer*, pp.257–305.

——. [1905] 'The Child and Heredity' in T. Stephens (ed.) *The Child and Religion* London: Williams and Northgate. Reprinted in his *Working Faith of the Social Reformer*, pp.151–78.

——. (1905) 'The Immortality of the Soul in the Poems of Tennyson and Browning' London: Philip Green.

——. (1905) 'The Philosophy of Martineau in Relation to the Idealism of the Present Day' London: Macmillan.

——. [1905] 'The Library as a Maker of Character' in his *Essays on Literature and Education*, pp.212–24.

——. (1906) 'Francis Hutcheson, a Discourse' Glasgow: James Maclehose.

——. (1906–7) 'Divine Immanence' *Hibbert Journal*, 5, pp.745–67.

——. (1907) 'Idealism and Politics' in *The Contemporary Review*, 42. Reprinted in his *Working Faith of the Social Reformer*, pp.179–225.

——. (1907) 'Divine Transcendence' Manchester: H.Rawson.

——. (1909) *Idealism as a Practical Creed*, Glasgow: James Maclehose.

——. (1909) 'The Idealism of Jesus' *Hibbert Journal*, supplementary volume (*Jesus of Christ?*) pp.81–106.

——. (1910) *Working Faith of the Social Reformer*, London, Macmillan.

——. (1911–2) 'The Corruption of the Citizenship of the Working Man' *Hibbert Journal*, 10, pp.154–78.

——. (1912) 'The Immanence of God and the Individuality of Man' Manchester: H.Rawson.

——. (1913) 'Journalism and Citizenship' in his *Social Powers*, Glasgow: James Maclehose, pp.47–76.

——. (1913) 'Are Moral and Religious Beliefs Capable of Proof?' in his *Social Powers*, pp.77–114.

——. (1914–15) 'Why We Are Fighting' *Hibbert Journal*, 13, pp.50–67.

——. [1917] 'The Education of the Citizen' *Round Table*, June 1917. Reprinted in his *Essays on Literature and Education*, pp.225–81.

——. [1918] 'The Ethical Ideal in Shakespeare' in his *Essays on Literature and Education*, pp.167–211.

——. (1919) *The Principles of Citizenship*, London: Macmillan.

——. (1921) *The Life and Philosophy of Edward Caird* (with J.H. Muirhead) Glasgow: Maclehose, Jackson and Co.

——. (1922) *A Faith that Enquires*, London: Macmillan.

——. (1923) *Old Memories; Autobiography of Sir Henry Jones*, London: Hodder and Stoughton.

——. (1924) H.J.W. Hetherington (ed.) *The Life and Letters of Sir Henry Jones*, London: Hodder and Stoughton.

——. (1924) H.J.W. Hetherington (ed.) *Essays on Literature and Education*, London: Hodder and Stoughton.

John MacCunn (1846–1929)

——. (1894) *Ethics of Citizenship*, Glasgow: James Maclehose.

——. [1900] *Making of Character*, Cambridge: Cambridge University Press, 6th edn 1921.

——. [1907] *Six Radical Thinkers*, London: E.Arnold, 1964.

J.S. Mackenzie (1860–1935)

——. (1890) *An Introduction to Social Philosophy*, Glasgow: James Maclehose.

——. (1893) *Manual of Ethics*, London: W.B.Clive.

——. (1899) 'The Idea of Progress' *International Journal of Ethics*, 9, pp. 195–213.

——. (1900) 'The Source of Moral Obligation' *International Journal of Ethics*, 10, pp.464–78.

——. (1901) 'Use of Moral Ideas in Politics' *International Journal of Ethics*, 12, pp.1–23.

——. (1902) *Outlines of Metaphysics*, London: Macmillan, 2nd edn 1906, 1922 impression.

——. (1904) 'The Infinite and the Perfect' *Mind*, 13, pp.355–78.

——. (1904) 'Review of G.E. Moore's *Principia Ethica*' *International Journal of Ethics*, 14, pp.377–82.

——. [1906] 'The Dangers of Democracy' *International Journal of Ethics*, 16. Reprinted in D. Boucher (ed.) *The British Idealists*, Cambridge: Cambridge University Press, 1997, pp.156–72.

——. (1906) 'The New Realism and the Old Idealism' *Mind*, 15, pp. 308–28.

——. (1907) *Lectures on Humanism*, London: Swan Sonnenschein.

——. (1909) 'Edward Caird as a Philosophical Teacher' *Mind*, 18, pp. 509–37.

——. (1911) 'The Meaning of Good and Evil' *International Journal of Ethics*, 21, pp. 251–68.

——. (1916) 'Might and Right' in *The International Crisis: The Theory of the State*, Oxford: Humphrey Milford, pp.56–91.

——. (1917) *Elements of Constructive Philosophy*, London: George Allen and Unwin.

——. (1918) *Outlines of Social Philosophy*, London: George Allen and Unwin.

——. (1924) *Ultimate Value in the Light of Contemporary Thought*, London: Hodder and Stoughton.

——. (1928) 'Review of F.H. Bradley's *Ethical Studies*' *Mind*, 37, pp.235–6.

——. (1928) *Fundamental Problems of Life*, London: George Allen and Unwin.

——. (1931) *Cosmic Problems, An Essay on Speculative Philosophy*, London: Macmillan.

——. (1936) *John Stuart Mackenzie*, H.M. Mackenzie (ed.), London: Williams and Norgate.

J.M.E. McTaggart (1866–1925)

——. [1893] 'Further Determination of the Absolute' privately printed. Reprinted in his *Studies in Hegelian Cosmology*, ch.IX.

——. (1896) *Studies in the Hegelian Dialectic*, Cambridge: Cambridge University Press.

——. [1897] 'The Conception of Society as an Organism' *International Journal of Ethics*, 7. Reprinted in his *Studies in Hegelian Cosmology*, ch.VII.

——. (1901) *Studies in Hegelian Cosmology*, Cambridge: Cambridge University Press.

——. (1906) *Some Dogmas of Religion*, London: E.Arnold.

——. [1908] 'The Individualism of Value' *International Journal of Ethics*, 18. Reprinted in his *Philosophical Studies*, pp.97–109.

——. (1908) 'Review of W. James' *Pragmatism*' *Mind*, 17, pp. 104–9.

——. (1910) *A Commentary on Hegel's Logic*, Cambridge: Cambridge University Press.

——. (1912) 'Review of B. Bosanquet's *Principle of Individuality and Value*' *Mind*, 21, pp.16–27.

——. (1921–7) *The Nature of Existence*, Cambridge: Cambridge University Press.

——. (1934) *Philosophical Studies*, S.V. Keeling (ed.), London: E.Arnold.

J.H. Muirhead (1855–1940)

——. (1892) *The Elements of Ethics*, London: John Murray.

——. [1899] 'A Liberal Education' in his *Philosophy and Life and Other Essays*, London: Swann Sonnenschein, 1902, pp.137–55.

——. (1900) 'The Family, ' in S. Coit (ed.) *Ethical Democracy: Essays In Social Dynamics*, London: Swan Sonnesnschein, pp.108–27.

——. (1900) *Chapters from Aristotle's Ethics*, London: John Murray.

——. [1900] 'What Imperialism Means' *The Fortnightly Review*. Reprinted in D. Boucher (ed.) *The British Idealists*, Cambridge: Cambridge University Press, 1997, pp.237–52.

——. (1908) *The Service of the State: Four Lectures on the Political Teaching of T.H. Green*, London: John Murray.

——. (1911) Editor's Preface to *Birmingham Institutions; Lectures given at the University*, Birmingham: Cornish Brothers.

——. (1911–12) 'The Corruption of the Citizenship of the Working Man' *Hibbert Journal*, 10, pp.154–78.

——. (1913) 'Philosophy and Social Reform' in *Converging Views of Social Reform*, London: The Collegium, pp.9–22.

——. (1915) *German Philosophy and the War*, Oxford Pamphelets.

——. (1915) *German Philosophy in Relation to the War*, London: John Murray.

——. (1918) *Social Purpose* (with H.J.W. Hetherington), London: Allen and Unwin.

——. (1921) *The Life and Philosophy of Edward Caird* (with H. Jones), Glasgow: Maclehose, Jackson and Co.

——. (1923) 'Bernard Bosanquet' *Mind*, 32, pp. 393–407.

——. (1923–4) 'The Spirit of Democracy' *Hibbert Journal*, 22, 427–35.

——. (1924) 'Recent Criticism of the Idealist theory of the General Will' *Mind*, 33, pp. 166–175, 233–241, 361–368.

——. (1928) *The Use of Philosophy, Californian Addresses*, London: George Allen and Urwin.

——. (1930) *Coleridge as Philosopher*, London: George Allen and Unwin.

——. (1931) *The Platonic Tradition in Anglo-Saxon Philosophy*, London: George Allen and Unwin.

——. (1932) *Rule and End in Morals*, London: Oxford University Press.

——. (1935) *Bernard Bosanquet and his Friends*, London: George Allen and Unwin.

——. (1942) *Reflections by a Journeyman in Philosophy*, London: George Allen and Unwin.

R.L. Nettleship (1846–1892)

——. (1880) 'The Theory of Education in the *Republic* of Plato' in A.E. Abbott (ed.), *Hellenica; Essays on Greek Poetry, Philosophy, History and Religion*, London: Rivingtons, pp.67–180.

——. (1888) Memoir of T.H. Green, in *Works of T. H. Green*, III, pp.xi–clxi.

——. (1897) 'Individuality' in *Philosophical Lectures and Remains*, London: Macmillan, vol. I, pp.33–8.

——. (1897) 'Lectures on Logic' in *Philosophical Lectures and Remains*, vol. I, pp.109–234.

——. (1897) 'Lectures on the "Republic" of Plato' in *Philosophical Lectures and Remains*, vol. II, pp.3–364.

Andrew Seth Pringle-Pattison (1856–1931)

NOTE: He was born Andrew Seth and published under that name until, in 1898, as a condition of accepting a bequest, he added to his own name that of Pringle-Pattison.

——. (1881) 'Hegel: an exposition and criticism' *Mind*, 6, pp 513–30.

——. (1882) *The Development from Kant to Hegel*, London: Williams and Norgate.

——. (1883) 'Philosophy as Criticism of Categories' in *Essays in Philosophical Criticism* (edited with R.B. Haldane) London: Longmans Green, pp.8–40.

——. [1885] *Scottish Philosophy*, Edinburgh: William Blackwood, 3rd edn 1899.

——. [1887] *Hegelianism and Personality*, Edinburgh: William Blackwood. Reprinted New York: Lenox Hill, 1971.

——. [1891] *Balfour Lectures on Realism*, Edinburgh: Blackwood, first published 1933.

——. (1892) 'The Problem of Epistemology' *The Philosophical Review*, 1, pp.504–17.

——. [1893] 'Man's Place in the Cosmos' *Blackwood's Magazine*, 154. Reprinted in *Man's Place in the Cosmos*, pp.1–33.

——. [1894] 'A New Theory of the Absolute' *The Contemporary Review*, 69. Reprinted in *Man's Place in the Cosmos*, pp.129–225.

——. (1894) 'Epistemology and Ontology' *Mind*, 3, pp.568–82.

——. (1895) 'Review of H. Jones' *Critical Account of the Philosophy of Lotze*' *Mind*, 4, pp.515–33.

——. (1897) *Two Lectures on Theism*, Edinburgh: William Blackwood.

——. (1897) *Man's Place in the Cosmos*, Edinburgh: William Blackwood.

——. [1897/8] 'The Life and Opinions of Friedrich Nietzsche' Two articles in *Blackwood's Magazine*, 162 and *The Contemporary Review*, 73 reprinted as one article in the second edition (1902) of his *Man's Place in the Cosmos*, pp.254–319.

——. [1902–3] 'Martineau's Philosophy' *Hibbert Journal*, 1. Reprinted in *The Philosophical Radicals*, Edinburgh: William Blackwood, 1907, pp.78–107.

——. (1909) Preface to *Selected Essays of Thomas Carlyle*, London: Andrew Melrose.

——. (1916) *The Idea of God*, Oxford: Clarendon Press.

——. [1917–18] 'Do Finite Individuals Possess a Substantive or an Adjectival Mode of Being?' *Proceedings of the Aristotelian Society*, 18. Reprinted in W.H. Wildon Carr (ed.), *Life and Finite Individuality*, *Proceedings of the Aristotelian Society Supplementary volume 1*, 1918, pp.75–194.

——. (1919) 'Immanence and Transcendence' in B. H. Streeter (ed.) *The Spirit*, London: Macmillan, pp.1–22.

——. (1922) *The Idea of Immortality*, Oxford: Clarendon Press.

——. (1930) *Studies in the Philosophy of Religion*, Oxford: Clarendon Press.

D.G. Ritchie (1853–1903)

——. (1883) 'Rationality of History' in A.Seth and R.B. Haldane (eds) *Essays in Philosophical Criticism*, pp.126–58.

——. [1886] 'On Plato's *Phaedo*' *Mind*, 11. Reprinted in *Darwin and Hegel*, pp. 109–50.

——. (1887) 'The Moral Function of the State: a paper' London: Women's Printing Society.

——. (1888) 'Review of A. Seth Pringle-Pattison's *Hegelianism and Personality*' *Mind*, 13, pp.256–63.

——. (1888) 'Origin and Validity' *Mind*, 13. Reprinted in *Darwin and Hegel*, pp.1–31.

——. [1889] *Darwinism and Politics*, London: Swann Sonnenschein, 2nd edn 1891.

——. (1890) 'Natural Selection and the Spiritual World' *Westminster Review*, 135. Reprinted in second edition of *Darwinism and Politics*, pp.87–115.

——. [1890–1] 'Darwin and Hegel' *Aristotelian Society*, 1. Reprinted in *Darwin and Hegel*, pp.38–76.

——. [1891] 'Contributions to the History of the Social Contract Theory' *Political Science Quarterly*, 6. Reprinted in *Darwin and Hegel*, pp.196–226.

——. [1891] 'The Rights of Minorities' *International Journal of Ethics*, 1. Reprinted in *Darwin and Hegel*, pp.265–85.

——. (1891) *The Principles of State Interference*, London: Swann Sonnenschein.

——. (1891) 'Locke's Theory of Property' *Economic Review*, 1. Reprinted in *Darwin and Hegel*, pp.178–95.

——. [1892] 'What is Reality?' *Philosophical Review*, 1. Reprinted in *Darwin and Hegel*, pp.77–108.

——. [1892] 'What are Economic Laws?' *Economic Review*, 2. Reprinted in *Darwin and Hegel*, pp.151–77.

——. (1893) 'Note on Heredity as a Factor in Knowledge' in *Darwin and Hegel*, pp.32–37.

——. (1893) *Darwin and Hegel*, London: Swann Sonnenschein.

——. (1894) *Natural Rights*, London: Allen and Unwin.

——. [1896] 'Social Evolution' *International Journal of Ethics*, 6. Reprinted in his *Studies in Political and Social Ethics*, London: Swan Sonnenschein, 1902, pp.1–29.

——. [1900] 'Ethical Democracy: Evolution and Democracy' in S. Coit (ed.) *Ethical Democracy: Essays in Social Dynamics*, London: Swan Sonnesnschein. Reprinted in D. Boucher (ed.) *The British Idealists*, Cambridge: Cambridge University Press, 1997, pp.68–93.

——. (1901) 'War and Peace' *International Journal of Ethics*, 11, pp.137–58.

——. [1902] '*Cogitatio Metaphysica*' in *Philosophical Studies* (edited with a memoir by Robert Latta) London: Macmillan, 1905, pp.66–133.

James Seth (1860–1924)

——. (1891) *Freedom as Ethical Postulate*, Edinburgh: William Blackwood.

——. (1894) *Study of Ethical Principles*, Edinburgh: William Blackwood.

——. (1904–5) 'The Relation of the Ethical to the Aesthetic Element in Literature' *International Journal of Ethics*, 15, pp.162–72.

——. (1912) *English Philosophers and Schools of Philosophy*, London: Dent.

W.R. Sorley (1855–1935)

——. (1885) *On the Ethics of Naturalism*, Edinburgh: William Blackwood. 2nd rev edn, 1904.

——. (1904) *Recent Tendencies in Ethics*, Edinburgh: William Blackwood.

——. (1911) *The Moral Life and Moral Worth*, Cambridge: Cambridge University Press.

——. (1916) 'The State and Morality' in *The International Crisis: The Theory of the State*, Oxford: Humphrey Milford, pp.25–55.

——. [1918] *Moral Values and the Idea of God*, Cambridge: Cambridge University Press. 1924 edn, 1930 reprint.

——. (1920) *A History of English Philosophy*, Cambridge: Cambridge University Press.

A.E. Taylor (1869–1945)

——. (1901) *The Problem of Conduct; A Study in the Phenomenology of Ethics*, London: Macmillan.

——. (1903) *The Elements of Metaphysics*, London: Methuen.

——. [1908] *Plato*, London: Constable, 1911.

——. (1925) 'F.H. Bradley' *Mind*, 34.

——. (1926) *Plato: the Man and his Work*, London: Methuen.

——. (1930) *The Faith of a Moralist*, London: Macmillan.

William Wallace (1843–1897)

——. [1874] *Prolegomena to the Study of Hegel's Philosophy and especially of his Logic*, Oxford: Clarendon Press. 2nd edn, 1931 impression, new pagination.

——. (1880) 'Hegel' in *Enclyopedia Britannica*, 9th edn, pp.616–21.

——. (1880) *Epicureanism*, London: SPCK.

——. (1882) 'Ethics and Sociology' *Mind*, 8, pp.222–50.

——. (1882) *Kant*, Edinburgh: William Blackwood.

——. [1885] 'Lotze' in *Lectures and Essays,* pp.481–510.

——. (1890) *Schopenhauer*, London: Walter Scott.

——. (1895) 'Review of A.J. Balfour's *Foundations of Belief*' *Fortnightly Review*, 63, pp.540–50.

——. (1896) 'Review of *The Works of Nietzsche* volumes VIII and XI' *Academy*, 50, pp.75–7.

——. [1897] 'Review of Nietzsche *Thus Spake Zarathustra*' *International Journal of Ethics*, 7. Reprinted in *Lectures and Essays*, pp.530–41.

——. (1898) 'Nietzsche's Criticism of Morality' in *Lectures and Essays*, pp.511–29.

——. (1898) *Lectures and Essays on Natural Theology*, Oxford: Clarendon Press.

John Watson (1847–1939)

——. (1881) *Kant and his English Critics*, Glasgow:James MacLehose.

——. (1888) *The Philosophy of Kant: as Contained in Extracts from his own Writings*, Glasgow: James Maclehose.

——. (1897) *Christianity and Idealism,* Glasgow: James Maclehose.

——. (1898) *An Outline of Philosophy*, Glasgow: James Maclehose.

——. (1908) *The Philosophy of Kant Explained*, Glasgow: James Maclehose.

——. (1909) 'The Idealism of Edward Caird' *The Philosophical Review*, 18, pp. 147–63, 259–80.

——. (1912) *The Interpretation of Religious Experience*, Glasgow: James Maclehose.

——. (1915) 'German Philosophy and Politics' *Queen's Quarterly*, 22, pp.329–44.

——. (1916) 'German Philosophy and the War' *Queen's Quarterly*, 23, pp.365–79.

——. (1919) *The State in Peace and War*, Glasgow: James Maclehose.

C.C.J. Webb (1865–1954)

——. (1915) *A History of Philosophy*, London: Williams and Norgate.

——. (1918) *God and Personality*, London: Allen and Unwin.

——. (1920) *Divine Personality and Human Life*, London: Allen and Unwin.

——. (1925) 'Outline of a Philosophy of Religion' in J.H. Muirhead (ed.) *Contemporary British Philosophy: second series*, pp.336–59.

——. (1933) *A study of Religious Thought in England from 1850*, Oxford: Clarendon Press.

2. Other Sources Before 1935

Adamson, Robert (1879) *On the Philosophy of Kant*, David Douglas.

——. (1881) 'Kant' *Encyclopedia Britannica*, 9th edn, pp.844–54.

——. (1903) *Development of Modern Philosophy*, William Blackwood.

Alexander, Archibald (1907) *A Short History of Philosophy*, James Maclehose.

Alexander, Samuel (1889) *Moral Order and Progress*, Trübner.

——. (1914) 'The Basis of Realism' *Proceedings of the British Academy*, 6, pp.279–314.

——. (1925) *Art and the Material*, Manchester University Press.

Arnold, Matthew (1873) *Literature and Dogma*, T.Nelson.

Balfour, A.J. (1878) 'Transcendentalism' *Mind*, 3, no.12, pp.480–505. Reproduced as ch.VI of his *A Defence of Philosophic Doubt*, Macmillan, 1879.

Barbour, G.F. (1933) 'Memoir of Andrew Seth Pringle-Patton' in A.S. Pringle-Pattison, *Balfour Lectures on Realism*, pp.3–159.

Belfort Bax, Ernest (1886) *History of Philosophy*, George Bell.

——. (1920) *The Real, the Rational and the Alogical*, Grant Richards.

Bentham, Jeremy (1843) 'Anarchical Fallacies; being an examination of the declaration of rights issued during the French revolution' in *The Works of Jeremy Bentham*, J. Bowring (ed.) William Tait, vol. II.

Bergson, Henri [1907] *Creative Evolution*, Macmillan, 1911.

Bosanquet, Helen (1924) *Bernard Bosanquet, A Short Account of his Life*, Macmillan.

Boyce Gibson, R. (1902) 'The Problem of Freedom in its Relation to Psychology' in Henry Sturt (ed.), *Personal Idealism*, pp.134–92.

——. (1906–7) 'A Peace Policy for the Idealists' *Hibbert Journal*, 5, pp.407–24.

Broad, C.D. (1924) 'Critical and Speculative Philosophy' in J. H. Muirhead (ed.), *Contemporary British Philosophy: Personal Statements: First Series*, pp.77–100.

——. [1927] 'John Mctaggart Ellis McTaggart, 1866–1925' *Proceedings of the British Academy*, 13. Reprinted as an Introduction to second edition of *Some Dogmas of Religion*, 1930, pp.xxv–lii.

——. (1930) *Five Types of Ethical Theory*, Routledge and Kegan Paul.

——. (1933) *An Examination of McTaggart's Philosophy*, Cambridge University Press.

Campbell, C.A. (1931) *Scepticism and Construction*, Macmillan.

Carlyle, Thomas [1827] 'State of German Literature' in *Critical and Miscellaneous Essays*, Chapman and Hall, 1893, eight volumes in four, vol. I.

——. [1832] *Sartor Resartus*, George Bell, 1900.

——. [1837] *The French Revolution*, Chapman and Hall, 1915.

——. [1841] *On Heroes, Hero-Worship and the Heroic in History*, Chapman and Hall, 1893.

——. [1843] *Past and Present*, Chapman and Hall, 1893.

——. [1850] *Latter-Day Pamphlets*, Chapman and Hall, 1870.

Carnap, Rudolf [1931] 'The Elimination of Metaphysics through the Logical Analysis of Language' in A. J. Ayer (ed.), *Logical Positivism*, The Free Press, 1959, pp. 60–81.

Carpenter, J. Estlin (1905) *James Martineau; Theologian and Teacher*, Philip Green.

Carr, Herbert Wildon (1922) *A Theory of Monads*, Macmillan.

Carritt, E.F. (1928) *The Theory of Morals*, Oxford University Press.

Carroll, Lewis (1895) 'What the Tortoise said to Achilles' *Mind*, 4, pp.278–80.

Coleridge, S.T. [1817] *Biographia Literaria*, J.M. Dent 1906.

——. [1830] *On the Constitution of the Church and State*, in *The Complete Works of Samuel Taylor Coleridge* vol. VI, Harper and Brothers, 1854.

Collingwood, R.G. (1925) *Outlines of a Philosophy of Art*, Oxford University Press.

——. [1933] *An Essay on Philosophical Method*, Clarendon Press, rev edn, 2005.

——. [1933] 'The Metaphysics of F.H. Bradley' reprinted in rev edn of his *An Essay on Philosophical Method*, pp.227–52.

Cook Wilson, J. (1926) *Statement and Inference*, Clarendon Press.

Costello H.T. (1921) 'Review of Bosanquet's *Implication and Linear Inference*' *The Journal of Philosophy*, 18, pp.403–17.

Craufurd, Alexander H. (1903) *Recollections of James Martineau*, Simpkin Marshall.

Croce, B. [1907] *What is Living and what is Dead in the Philosophy of Hegel*, Macmillan 1915.

D'Arcy, C.F. (1899) *Idealism and Theology: A Study of Presuppositions*, Hodder and Stoughton.

Darwin, Charles [1859] *The Origin of Species*, J.W Burrow (ed.) Penguin 1968.

——. [1871] *The Descent of Man*, J. Moore and A. Desmond (eds) Penguin 2004.

Descartes, René [1641] *Mediations on First Philosophy*, J. Cottingham (ed.) Cambridge University Press, 1984.

Devaux, Philipe (1932) *Lotze et son Influence sur la Philosophie Anglosaxonne*, M.Lamertin.

Dewey, John (1890) 'On Some Current Conceptions of the Term "self"' *Mind*, 15, pp.58–74.

——. (1891) *Outlines of a Critical Theory of Ethics*, Ann Arbour.

——. (1915) *German Philosophy and Politics*, rev edn, Putnam, 1942.

Drummond, J. and Upton, C.B. (1902) *The Life and Letters of James Martineau*, J. Nisbet.

Eddington, A.S. (1928) *The Nature of the Physical World*, Cambridge University Press.

Eliot, T.S. [1916] *Knowledge and Experience in the Philosophy of F.H.Bradley*. Eliot's doctoral thesis. Faber and Faber, 1964.

——. [1927] 'Francis Herbert Bradley' *Times Literary Supplement*, no.1352, 29 December. Reprinted in his *Selected Prose*, F. Kermode (ed.), Faber and Faber, 1975, pp.196–204.

Ewing, A.C. (1934) *Idealism; a Critical Survey*, Methuen.

Fairbrother, W.H. [1896] *The Philosophy of Thomas Hill Green*, Methuen, 2nd edn 1900.

Ferrier, J.F. (1840) 'The Plagiarisms of S. T. Coleridge' *Blackwood's Magazine*, 4, pp.287–99.

——. (1854) *Institutes of Metaphysics*, W.Blackwood.

——. (1866) *Lectures on Greek Philosophy and other Philosophical Remains*, W.Blackwood.

Foster, G.B. (1906), 'Review of Caird's *Evolution of Theology in the Greek Philosophers*' *The American Journal of Theology*, 10, pp.762–64.

Foster, M.B. (1931) 'The Concrete Universal: Cook Wilson and Bosanquet' *Mind*, 40, pp.1–22.

Frege, Gottlob [1884] *The Foundations of Arithmetic*, trans. J.L. Austin Basil Blackwell, 1974.

Grote, John (1865–1900) *Exploratio Philosophica*, Cambridge University Press.

Grote, John (1870) *An Examination of the Utilitarian Philosophy*, Deighton Bell.

Haldane, Elizabeth Sanderson (1899) *James Frederick Ferrier*, Oliphant Anderson and Ferrier.

Haldane, John Scott (1883) 'The Relation of Philosophy to Science' (with R.B. Hadane) in R.B. Haldane and A.Seth (eds) *Essays in Philosophical Criticism*, Longmans Green, pp.41–66.

——. (1929) *The Sciences and Philosophy*, Hodder and Stoughton.

Hegel, G.W. [1807] *Hegel's Phenomenology of Spirit*, trans. A.V Miller, Oxford University Press, 1977.

——. [1812–16] *The Science of Logic*, trans. W.H Johnson and L.G Struthers, George Allen and Unwin, 1929.

——. [1817] *Hegel's Logic*, trans. William Wallace, Clarendon Press, 1975. (Previously entitled *The Logic of Hegel*).

——. [1817] *Hegel's Philosophy of Mind*, trans. William Wallace with five introductory essays, Clarendon Press, 1894.

——. [1821] *Hegel's Philosophy of Right*, trans. S.W. Dyde, George Bell, 1896.

——. [1832] *Lectures on the Philosophy of Religion, Together With Lectures On The Proofs Of The Existence Of God*, trans. E.B. Speirs, and J. Burdon Sanderson, Kegan Paul, Trench, Trubner, 1895.

——. [1835] *Hegel's Aesthetics, Lectures on Fine Art*, trans. T.M. Knox, Clarendon Press, 1975.

——. [1835] *The Introduction to Hegel's Philosophy of Fine Art*, trans. Bernard Bosanquet, Kegan Paul, Trench and Trubner, 2nd edn 1905.

——. [1837] *Lectures on the Philosophy of History*, trans. J. Sibree, George Bell, 1884.

——. [1840] *Lectures on the History of Philosophy*, trans. E.S. Haldane and F.H. Simson, University of Nebraska Press, 1995 (three volumes).

Herbart, Johann Friedrich (1850) *Lehrbuch zur Einleitung in die Philosophie*, in his *Sammtliche Werke*, vol. I, Leipzig.

Hetherington, H.J.W. (1918) *Social Purpose* (with J.H. Muirhead) George Allen and Unwin.

Hobhouse, L.T. (1918) *The Metaphysical Theory of the State*, George Allen and Unwin.

Hoernlé, R.F.A. (1923) 'On Bosanquet's "Idealism"' *The Philosophical Review*, 32, pp. 567–88.

——. [1924] *Idealism as a Philosophical Doctrine*, Hodder and Stoughton. Expanded under the title, *Idealism as a Philosophy*, 1927.

——. (1925) 'On the Way to a Synoptic Philosophy' in J.H. Muirhead (ed.) *Contemporary British Philosophy: Second series*, George Allen and Unwin, pp.129–56.

Holland, Henry Scott (1921) *Henry Scott Holland: Memoir and Letters*, John Murray.

Husserl, E. [1900–1] *Logical Investigations* (trans. J.N. Findlay, ed. Dermot Moran) Routledge 2001.

Huxley T.H. [1893] 'Evolution and Ethics' *Collected Essays*, vol. IX, Macmillan, 1894, pp.46–116.

Illingworth, A.L. (1917) *Life and Work of John Richardson Illingworth*, John Murray.

Illingworth, R.J. (1894) *Personality Human and Divine*, Macmillan.

——. (1898) *Divine Immanence*, Macmillan.

——. (1911) *Divine Transcendence*, Macmillan.

James, William (1890) *The Principles of Psychology*, Henry Holt.

——. [1907] *Pragmatism; A New Name for Some Old Ways of Thinking*, Longmans Green 1919.

——. (1909) *A Pluralistic Universe*, Longmans Green.

——. (1910) 'Bradley or Bergson?' *Journal of Philosophy*, 7, pp.29–33.

Jamieson, G (1895) *The Great Problem of Substance and its Attributes*, Kegan Paul.

Jeans, J. (1930) *Mysterious Universe*, Cambridge University Press, 2nd edn 1931.

——. (1934) 'The New World-Picture of Modern Physics' Presidential Address, *Report of the 1934 Annual Meeting of the British Association for the Advancement of Science*, pp.1–18.

Jevons, W.S. (1874) *The Principles of Science*, Macmillan.

Joseph, H.W.B. [1906] *An Introduction to Logic*, Clarendon Press, 2nd edn 1916.

——. (1910–1) 'The Psychological Explanation of the Development of the Perception of External Objects' *Mind*, 19–20, pp.305–21, 457–69, 161–80.

——. (1919) 'On Occupying Space' *Mind*, 28, pp.336–9.

——. (1929) 'A comparison of Kant's Idealism with that of Berkeley' *Proceedings of the British Academy*, XV, pp.213–34.

——. (1931) *Some Problems in Ethics*, Oxford University Press.

Jowett, Benjamin [1871] *Dialogues of Plato translated into English with Analyses and Introductions*, Clarendon Press, 3rd edn 1892.

——. [1885] *The Politics of Aristotle*, Clarendon Press.

Kant, Immanuel [1781/7] *Critique of Pure Reason*, P. Guyer and A.W. Wood (eds) Cambridge University Press, 1997.

——. [1783] *Prolegomena to Any Future Metaphysics*, Gary Hatfield (ed.) Cambridge University Press, 1997.

——. [1788] *The Critique of Practical Reason*, trans. Lewis White Beck, Collier Macmillan, 1956.

Kemp Smith, Norman (1924) *Prolegomena to an Idealist Theory of Knowledge*, Macmillan.

——. (1927) 'The nature of universals' *Mind*, 36, pp.137–57, 265–80, 393–422.

Knox, H.V. (1914) 'Has Green answered Locke?' *Mind*, 23, pp.335–48.

Lindsay, A.D. (1922) 'Idealism' Inaugural Lecture (Lindsay papers L127), University of Keele: Special Collections and Archives. (In all but its first page this item was reproduced in that below.)

——. (1926) 'The Idealism of Caird and Jones' *Journal of Philosophical Studies*, 1, pp.171–82.

Lindsay, T.M. (1877) 'Recent Hegelian Contributions to English Philosophy' *Mind*, 2, pp.476–93.

Locke, John [1690] *An Essay Concerning Human Understanding*, P.H. Nidditch (ed.) Clarendon Press, 1975.

Lotze, Hermann [1856–64] *Microcosmus*, trans. E. Hamilton and E.E. Constance Jones, Clark 1885.

——. [1874–9] *System of Philosophy, I: Logic, II: Metaphysic*, trans. R.L. Nettleship, F.H. Peters, F.C. Conybeare, B. Bosanquet T.H. Green, C.A. Whittuck, and A.C. Bradley, Clarendon Press 1884.

——. (1884) *Outlines of Metaphysic*, trans. G.T. Ladd, Ginn Heath.

Lowes Dickinson, G. (1931) *J.M.E. McTaggart*, Cambridge University Press.

Mace, C.A. (1934) 'Representation and Expression' *Analysis*, 1, pp.33–8.

McGilvarey, E.B. (1901) 'The Eternal Consciousness' *Mind*, 10, pp. 489–92.

Mackenzie, Millicent (1909), *Hegel's Educational Thought and Practice*, Swan Sonnenschein.

Martineau, James (1843) 'The Spirit of Life in Jesus Christ' in *Endeavours after the Christian Life* (first series) pp.1–17.

——. (1847) 'Lo! God is here' in *Endeavours after the Christian Life* (second series) pp.69–84.

——. (1885) *Types of Ethical Theory*, Clarendon Press.

——. [1888] *Study of Religion*, Clarendon Press, 2nd edn, 1900.

Mill, John Stuart [1843] *A System of Logic*, Longman's 1884.

——. [1863] *Utilitarianism*, J.M Dent 1910.

——. [1865] *Examination of Sir William Hamilton's Philosophy*, Longmans, Green, Reader and Dyer, 5th edn 1878.

——. [1874] *Three Essays on Religion*, Prometheus Books 1998.

Moore, G.E. (1899) 'The Nature of Judgement' *Mind*, 8, pp.176–93.

——. (1903) 'The Refutation of Idealism' *Mind*, 12, pp.433–53.

——. (1903) *Principia Ethica*, Cambridge University Press.

——. (1907) 'Mr. Joachim's Nature of Truth' *Mind*, 16, pp. 229–35.

——. (1917–8) 'The Conception of Reality' *Proceedings of the Aristotelian Society*, 18, pp.101–20.

——. (1919–20) 'External and Internal Relations' *Proceedings of the Aristotelian Society*, 20, pp.40–62.

——. (1922) *Philosophical Studies*, Kegan Paul, Trench, Trubner.

——. (1925) 'Obituary Notice: McTaggart' *Mind*, 34, pp.269–71.

Morris, C.R. (1933) *Idealistic Logic*, Macmillan.

Oakeley, Hilda [1911] 'Poetry and Freedom' *Church Quarterly Review*, 72. Reprinted in her *History and Progress*, George Allen and Unwin, 1923, pp.91–107.

Oakeshott, M. (1933) *Experience and its Modes*, Cambridge University Press.

Paton, H.J. (1927) *The Good Will,* George Allen and Unwin.

Pattison, Mark (1876) 'Philosophy at Oxford' *Mind*, old series 1, pp.82–97.

Plato, *The Republic.*

Prichard, H.A. (1906) 'Appearances and Reality' *Mind*, 15, pp.223–9.

——. (1909) *Kant's Theory of Knowledge*, Clarendon Press.

——. (1912) 'Does Moral Philosophy Rest on a Mistake?' *Mind*, 21, pp.21–37.

——. [1928] 'Duty and Interest' in his *Moral Writings*, Jim MacAdam (ed.) Oxford University Press, 2002, pp.21–49.

Radhakrishnan, Sarvepalli [1932] *The Idealist View of Life*, George Allen and Unwin, 2nd edn 1937.

Rashdall, Hastings (1899) 'Review of Bosanquet's *Philosophical Theory of the State*' *The Economic Review*, 9, pp.543–46.

——. (1902) 'Personality: Human and Divine' in H. Sturt (ed.) *Personal Idealism*, Macmillan pp.369–93.

——. (1907) *The Theory of Good and Evil*, Clarendon Press.

——. (1909) *Philosophy and Religion*, Duckworth.

——. (1909) 'Professor Watson on Personal Idealism: A Reply' *Mind*, 18, pp.105–17.

Rogers, A.K. (1922) *English and American Philosophy since 1800*, Macmillan.

Ross, W.D. [1930] *The Right and the Good*, P. Stratton-Lake (ed.) Oxford University Press, 2002.

Rousseau, J.J. [1762] *The Social Contract.*

Royce, Josiah (1899–1901) *The World and the Individual*, Macmillan.

Russell, Bertrand [1897] *An Essay on the Foundations of Geometry*, J. Slater (ed.) Routledge 1996.

——. [1900] *A Critical Exposition of the Philosophy of Leibniz*, J. Slater (ed.) Routledge 1992.

——. [1903] *The Principles of Mathematics*, London: George Allen and Unwin, 2nd edn, 1937.

——. (1905) 'On Denoting' *Mind*, 14, pp.479–93.

——. (1906) 'Review of Joachim *The Nature of Truth*' *Mind*, 15, pp.528–33.

——. (1906) 'Review of Joachim *The Nature of Truth*' *Independent Review*, 9, pp.349–53.

——. (1906–7) 'On the Nature of Truth' *Proceedings of the Aristotelian Society*, 7, pp.28–49. The first two parts reprinted as 'The Monistic Theory if Truth' in his *Philosophical Essays*.

——. (1910) 'Some Explanations in Reply to Mr. Bradley' *Mind*, 19, pp.373–8.

——. [1910] *Philosophical Essays*, rev edn George Allen and Unwin 1966.

——. [1914] *Our Knowledge of the External World*, J. Slater (ed.) Routledge 1993.

——. (1925) *ABC of Relativity*, George Allen and Unwin.

Schopenhauer, A. [1851] 'A few words on Pantheism' in *Parerga and Paralipomena*, Oxford University Press, 2000, vol. 2, pp.99–102.

Schwegler [1848] *Handbook of the History of Philosophy*, trans. J.H. Stirling, Edinburgh: Oliver and Boyd, 9th edn, 1884.

Seeley, J.R. (1882) *Natural Religion*, Macmillan.

Sidgwick, A.S. and Sidgwick, E.M. (1906) *Henry Sidgwick: A Memoir*, Macmillan.

Sidgwick, Henry [1874] *Methods of Ethics*, Hackett Publishing 1981.

——. (1901) 'The Philosophy of T.H.Green' *Mind*, 10, pp.18–29.

——. (1905) *Lectures on the Philosophy of Kant, and other Philosophical Lectures and Essays*, Macmillan.

Sigwart, C. [1873] *Logic*, translated by H. Dendy, Swan Sonnenschein, 1895.

Sinclair, M. (1891) 'Guyon: a Philosophical Dialogue' in her *Essays in Verse*, Kegan Paul, Trench and Trübner.

——. (1893) 'The Ethical and Religious Import of Idealism' *The New World*, 2, pp.694–708.

——. (1917) *A Defence of Idealism*, Macmillan.

——. (1922) *The new Idealism*, Macmillan.

——. [1923] *Uncanny Stories*, Wordsworth 2006.

Smith, J.A. (1925) 'Philosophy as the Development of the Notion and Reality of Self-Consciousness' in J.H. Muirhead (ed.) *Contemporary British Philosophy: Second series*, George Allen and Unwin, pp.227–44.

Spencer, Herbert [1860] 'The Social Organism' *The Westminster Review*, 73. Reprinted in his *Essays: Scientific, Political and Speculative*, Williams and Norgate, 1891, Vol. I, pp.265–307.

——. [1862] *First Principles,* Williams and Norgate, 1911.

——. [1876] *Principles of Sociology*, Williams and Norgate, Vol. I. 2nd enlarged edn 1877.

Spinoza, Baruch [1661–76] *The Correspondence of Spinoza*, Abraham Wolf (ed.) Frank Cass, 1966.

Stebbing, S. (1934) 'Review of Morris' *Idealistic Logic*' *Philosophy*, 9, pp.368–70.

Stephen, Leslie (1879) 'Wordsworth's Ethics' *Hours in the Garden: Third Series*, Smith Elder.

——. (1882) *The Science of Ethics*, Smith Elder.

Stewart, J.A. (1902) 'The Attitude of Speculative Idealism to Natural Science' *Mind*, 11, pp.369–76.

Stirling, Amelia Huchison (1912) *James Hutchison Stirling, His Life And Work*, T.Fischer Unwin.

Stirling, James Hutchison [1865] *The Secret of Hegel*, Oliver and Boyd. Rev edn 1898.

——. (1880) 'Criticism of Kant's Main Principles' *Journal of Speculative Philosophy*, 14, pp.257–85, pp.353–76.

——. (1890) *Philosophy and Theology*, T. and T. Clark.

——. (1903) *The Categories*, Oliver and Boyd.

Sturt, Henry (ed.) (1902) *Personal Idealism*, Macmillan.

Sturt, Henry (1904–5) 'The Line of Advance in Philosophy' *Proceedings of the Aristotelian Society*, 5, pp.29–37.

——. (1906) *Idola Theatri: A Criticism of Oxford Thought and Thinkers from the Standpoint of Personal Idealism*, Macmillan.

Symonds, J.A. [1889–1893] *The Memoirs of John Addington Symonds*, Phyllis Grosskurth (ed.) Hutchinson 1984.

——. (1923) *Letters and Papers of John Addington Symonds*, H.F. Brown (ed.) John Murray.

Temple, William (1934) *Nature, Man and God*, Macmillan.

Tolstoy, L. [1896] *What is Art?* trans. A Maude, Walter Scott Publishing Company, 1898.

Toynbee, A. [1879] 'The Ideal Relation of Church and State' in *Lectures on the Industrial Revolution in England, Popular Addresses, Notes and Other Fragments*, pp.231–9.

——. [1882] 'Are Radicals Socialists?' in *Lectures on the Industrial Revolution in England, Popular Addresses, Notes and Other Fragments*, pp. 203–21.

——. (1883) *Progress and Poverty, A Criticism of Mr. Henry George*, Kegan Paul, Trench.

——. (1884) 'The Church and the People' in *Lectures on the Industrial Revolution in England, Popular Addresses, Notes and Other Fragments*, Rivingtons, pp.xxvi–xxvii.

G.H Turnbull, (1926) *The Educational Theory of J.G. Fichte*, Hodder and Stoughton.

Turner, J.E. (1925) *A Theory of Direct Realism*, Macmillan.

——. (1926) *Personality and Reality*, George Allen and Unwin.

Upton, C.B. (1883) 'Review of Green's *Prolegomena to Ethics*' *Modern Review*, 4, p.831.

——. [1894] *Lectures on the Bases of Religious Belief*, Williams and Norgate 1909.

——. (1905) *Dr Martineau's Philosophy; A Survey*, James Nisbet.

Wallace, Alfred Russel (1870) 'The Limits of Natural Selection as Applied to Man' in his *Contributions to the Theory of Natural Selection*, Macmillan, pp.332–71.

Ward, James (1886) 'Psychology' in *Encyclopaedia Britannica*, 9th edn, pp.37–85.

——. (1899) *Naturalism and Agnosticism*, Adam and Charles Black.

——. (1911) *The Realm of Ends or Pluralism and Theism*, Cambridge University Press.

Ward, Mrs Humphry (1890) *Robert Elsmere*, Smith Elder.

——. (1894) *Marcella*, Smith Elder.

Warr, C.L. (1926) *Principal Caird*, T. and T. Clark.

Watts Cunningham, J. (1933) *The Idealistic Argument in Recent British and American Philosophy*, Century.

Wellek, René (1931) *Immanuel Kant in England 1793–1838*, Princeton University Press.

White, William Hale [1881] *The Autobiography of Mark Rutherford*, Oxford World's Classics, 1990.

Wittgenstein, Ludwig (1922) *Tractatus Logico-Philosophicus*, Routledge.

Wolf, Abraham (1908–9) 'Natural Realism and Present Tendencies in Philosophy' *Proceedings of the Aristotelian Society*, 9, pp.141–82.

3. Other Sources After 1935

Acton, H.B. (1936–7) 'The Theory of Concrete Universals' *Mind*, 45, pp.417–31; 46, pp.1–13.

Allard, James W. (1996) 'Degrees of Truth in F.H. Bradley' in W.J. Mander (ed.) *Perspectives on the Logic and Metaphysics of F.H. Bradley*, Thoemmes Press, pp.137–58.

——. (2003) 'Logic as Metaphysics' *Bradley Studies*, 9, pp.26–39.

——. (2005) *The Logical Foundations of Bradley's Metaphysics: Judgment, Inference and Truth*, Cambridge University Press.

——. (2006) 'Bosanquet and the Problem of Inference' in W. Sweet (ed.) *Bernard Bosanquet and the Legacy of Idealism*, University of Toronto Press, pp.73–89.

Anderson, O. (1991) 'The Feminism of T.H. Green' *History of Political Thought*, 12, pp.671–93.

Apata, Gabriel (2001) 'Feeling and Emotion in Bosanquet's Aesthetics' *Bradley Studies*, 7, pp.177–96.

Armour, Leslie (2002) 'The Idealist Philosophers' God' *Laval Théologique et Philosophique*, 58, pp.443–55.

Ayer, A.J. [1936] *Language, Truth and Logic*, Penguin, 1971.

——. (1952) 'Negation' *Journal of Philosophy*, 49, pp.797–815.

—— et al. (1956) *The Revolution in Philosophy*, Macmillan.

——. (1977) *Part of my Life*, Oxford University Press.

Baldwin, T. (1991) 'The Identity Theory of Truth' *Mind*, 100, pp.35–52.

Basile, P (1999) *Experience and Relations; an Examination of F.H. Bradley's Conception of Reality*, Verlag Paul Haupt.

Bengtsson, Jan Olof (2006) *The Worldview of Personalism; Origins and Early Development*, Oxford University Press.

Berlin, I. [1958] 'Two Concepts of Liberty' Inaugural Lecture Oxford University. Reprinted in his *Liberty*, Henry Hardy (ed.) Oxford University Press, 2002, pp.166–217.

Blanshard, B. (1939) *The Nature of Thought*, Allen and Unwin.

——. (1991) 'Bradley; Some Memories and Impressions' in R Ingardia, *Bradley. A Research Bibliography*, Philosophy Documentation Centre, pp.7–16.

Boucher, D. (1989) *The Social and Political Thought of R.G. Collingwood*, Cambridge University Press.

——. (1990) 'Practical Hegelianism: Henry Jones' Lecture Tour of Australia' *Journal of the History of Ideas*, 51, pp. 423–52.

——. (1992) 'Evolution and Politics; The Naturalistic, Ethical and Spiritual Bases of Evolutionary Arguments' *Australian Journal of Philosophy*, 27, pp.87–103.

——. (1995) 'British Idealism and International Theory' *Bulletin of the Hegel Society of Great Britain*, 31, pp.73–89.

——. (ed.) (1997) *The British Idealists*, Cambridge University Press.

——. (2009) 'Henry Jones: Idealism as a Practical Creed' in *The Moral, Social, and Political Philosophy of the British Idealists*, W. Sweet (ed.), Imprint Academic, pp.137–51.

Boucher, D. and Vincent, A. (1993) *A Radical Hegelian*, University of Wales Press.

—— and ——. (2000), *British Idealism and Political Theory*, Edinburgh University Press.

Bradley, James (1979) 'Hegel in Britain, *The Heythrop Journal*, 20, pp.1–24, 163–82.

Broad, C.D. (1959) 'Autobiography' in P.A. Schilpp (ed.) *The Philosophy of C.D. Broad*, Tudor, pp.3–68.

Brock, M.G. and Curthoys, M.C. (eds) (2000) *History of the University of Oxford*, vol. VII, Part 2, Oxford University Press.

Brooks, T. (2003) 'T.H. Green's Theory of Punishment' *History of Political Thought*, 24, pp. 685–701.

Broomfield, Louise (1997) 'Getting Real: In Praise of Bradley's Aphorisms' *Bradley Studies*, 3, pp.47–72.

Campbell, C.A. [1938] 'In Defence of Free Will' Glasgow Inaugural Lecture. Reprinted in *In Defence of Free Will*, George Allen and Unwin, 1967, pp.35–55.

——. [1956] 'Self-Activity and its Modes' in *Contemporary British Philosophy: Personal Statements: Third Series*, H.D. Lewis (ed.) pp. 85–115.

Candlish, Stewart (1984) 'Scepticism, Ideal Experiment, and Priorities' in A. Manser and G. Stock (eds) *The Philosophy of F.H. Bradley*, Oxford University Press, pp.243–67.

——. (1989) 'The Truth about F.H. Bradley' *Mind*, 98, pp.331–48.

——. (2006) *The Russell/Bradley Dispute and its Significance for Twentieth Century Philosophy*, Palgrave Macmillan.

Carr, Brian (1987) *Metaphysics, An Introduction*, Macmillan.

Carter, M. (2003) *T.H. Green and the Development of Ethical Socialism*, Imprint Academic.

Collingwood, R.G. (1938) *The Principles of Art*, Clarendon Press.

——. [1939] *An Autobiography*, Clarendon Paperbacks 2002.

Collini, S. (1976) 'Hobhouse, Bosanquet and the State: Philosophical Idealism and Political Argument in England 1880–1918' *Past and Present*, 72, pp.86–111.

——. (1978) 'Sociology and Idealism in Britain 1880–1920' *Archives Européennes de Sociologie*, 19, pp.3–50.

——. (1979) *Liberalism and sociology: L. T. Hobhouse and political argument in England, 1880–1914*, Cambridge University Press.

Connelly, James (2003) *Method, Metaphysics and Politics. The Political Philosophy of R.G. Collingwood*, Imprint Academic.

Crossley, D.J. (1978) 'The British Idealists on Disjunction' *Idealistic Studies*, 8, pp.115–23.

——. (2004) 'The Unified Theory of Punishment of Green and Bosanquet' *Bradley Studies*, 10, pp.1–14.

Crowell, N. B. (1963) *The Tripple Soul: Browning's Theory of Knowledge*, University of Mexico Press.

——. (1968) *The Convex Glass: The Mind of Robert Browning*, University of Mexico Press.

Dancy, J. (2003) 'From Intuitionism to Emotivism' in Thomas Baldwin (ed.) *The Cambridge History of Philosophy, 1870–1945*, Cambridge University Press, pp.695–705.

den Otter, S. (1996) *British Idealism and Social Explanation*, Clarendon Press.

——. (2006) 'The Restoration of a Citizen Mind: British Idealism, Poor Relief and Charity Organisation Society' in W. Sweet (ed.) *Bernard Bosanquet and the Legacy of Idealism*, University of Toronto Press, pp.33–49.

Desmond, W. (1986) *Art and the Absolute: A Study of Hegel's Aesthetics*, Oxford University Press.

Dimova-Cookson, M. (2001) *T.H. Green's Moral and Political Philosophy, a Phenomenological Perspective*, Palgrave.

Donagan, A. (1962) *The Later Philosophy of R.G. Collingwood*, Clarendon Press.

Dworkin, R. [1991] 'Liberal Community' in his *Sovereign Virtue, the Theory and Practice of Equality*, Harvard University Press, 2000.

Eagleton, T. (2007) *The Meaning of Life*, Oxford University Press.

Ewing, A.C. (1956) 'The Necessity of Metaphysics' in H.D. Lewis (ed.) *Contemporary British Philosophy: Personal Statements, Third Series*, pp.143–64.

——. (1971) 'The Significance of Idealism for the Present Day' *Idealistic Studies*, 1, pp.1–12.

Ferreira, Phillip (1996) 'Bradley's Attack on Associationism' in James Bradley (ed.) *Philosophy After F.H. Bradley*, Thoemmes Press, pp.283–306.

——. (1999) *Bradley and the Structure of Knowledge*, SUNY Press.

——. (2003) 'Green's attack on Formal Logic' *Bradley Studies*, 9, pp.40–51.

——. (2006) 'Bosanquet, Idealism and the Justification of Induction' in W. Sweet (ed.) *Bernard Bosanquet and the Legacy of Idealism*, University of Toronto Press, pp.90–109.

Findlay, J.N. (1958) *Hegel, a re-examination*, George Allen and Unwin.

Frank, Philipp (1947) *Einstein: his Life and Times*, A.A. Knopf.

Freeden, M. (1978) *The New Liberalism*, Clarendon Press, 1978.

Gabbay, D.M. and Woods, J. (2008) *Handbook of the History of Logic, volume IV: British Logic in the Nineteenth Century*, Elsevier.

Gaus, G. (2006) 'The Rights Recognition Thesis: Defending and Extending Green' in M. Dimova Cookson and W.J. Mander (eds) *T.H. Green: Ethics, Metaphysics and Political Philosophy*, Oxford University Press, pp.209–35.

Geach, P.T. (1979) *Truth, Love and Immortality, an introduction to McTaggart's Philosophy*, Hutchinson.

Gibbins, John R. (2007) *John Grote, Cambridge University and the Development of Victorian Thought*, Imprint Academic.

Gordon, P. and White, J. (1979) *Philosophers as Educational Reformers*, Routledge and Kegan Paul.

Greengarten, I.M. (1981) *Thomas Hill Green and the Development of Liberal-Democratic Thought*, University of Toronto Press.

Griffin, N. (1991) *Russell's Idealist Apprenticeship*, Oxford University Press.

——. (1996) 'F.H. Bradley's Contribution to the Development of Logic' in James Bradley (ed.) *Philosophy After F.H. Bradley*, Thoemmes Press, pp.195–230.

Hampshire, Stuart (1949) 'Review of H.H. Joachim's *Logical Studies*' *Philosophy*, 24, pp.167–9.

Hardy, G.H. (1970) *Bertrand Russell and Trinity*, Cambridge University Press.

Harris, Paul (1986) 'Green's Theory of Political Obligation and Disobedience' in A. Vincent (ed.) *The Philosophy of T.H. Green*, Gower Publishing, pp.127–42.

Harrow, J. (2001) 'The English University Settlements 1884–1939: A social movement becalmed?' *Voluntary Action History Society, Seminar Papers Series*.

Helgeby, Stein (2004) *Action as History, the Historical Thought of R.G. Collingwood*, Imprint Academic.

Holdcroft, D. (1997) 'Bradley Collingwood and *The Presuppositions of Critical History*' *Bradley Studies*, 3, pp.5–24.

——. (1998) 'Bradley and Floating Ideas' in G. Stock (ed.) *Appearance versus Reality: New Essays on the Philosophy of F.H. Bradley*, Oxford University Press, pp.163–79.

Hylton, P. (1990) *Russell, Idealism and the Emergence of Analytic Philosophy*, Oxford University Press.

Iiritano, Massimo (2001) 'Death or Dissolution? Croce and Bosanquet on the *Auflösung der Kunst*' *Bradley Studies*, 7, pp.197–213.

Illingworth, C. (1971), *University Statesman: Sir Hector Hetherington*, George Outram.

Inge, W.R. (1947) *Mysticism in Religion*, Hutchinson's University Library.

Irwin, T. (1984) 'Morality and Personality: Kant and Green' in Allen W. Wood (ed.) *Self and Nature in Kant's Philosophy*, Cornell University Press, pp.31–56.

——. (2009) *The Development of Ethics: Volume III*, Oxford University Press.

Jacquette, Dale (1984) 'Bosanquet's Concept of Difficult Beauty' *Journal of Aesthetics and Art Criticism*, 43, pp.79–88.

Jaki, S.L. (1986) *Lord Gifford and his Lectures, A Centenary Retrospect*, Scottish Academic Press.

Joad, C.E.M. (1934) *Liberty Today*, Watts and Co.

Keefe, J. (2007) 'James Ferrier and the Theory of Ignorance' *The Monist*, 90, pp. 297–309.

——. (2007) 'The Return to Berkeley' *British Journal for the History of Philosophy*, 15, pp.101–13.

Keene, C.A. (2009) 'The Interplay of Bradley's Social and Moral Philosophy' in W. Sweet (ed.) *The Moral, Social, and Political Philosophy of the British Idealists*, Imprint Academic, pp.87–110.

Kenny, A. (1998) *A Brief History of Western Philosophy*, Blackwell.

Kuntz, P.K. (1971) Introduction to George Santayana's *Lotze's System of Philosophy*, Indiana University Press, pp.3–94.

Lang, B. (1968) 'Bosanquet's Aesthetic: A History and Philosophy of the Symbol' *Journal of Aesthetics and Art Criticism*, 26, pp.377–87.

Lakatos, I. (1978) *The Methodology of Scientific Research Programmes*, Cambridge University Press.

——. (1978) 'Falsification and the Methodology of Scientific Research Programmes' in his *The Methodology of Scientific Research Programmes, Philosophical Papers Volume I*, J. Worrall and G. Currie (eds), Cambridge University Press.

Leighton, D. (2004) *The Greenian Moment*, Imprint Academic.

Lewis, C.S. [1959] 'Fern Seeds and Elephants' in *C.S. Lewis Essay Collection: Faith, Christianity and the Church*, Harper Collins, 2002, pp.242–54.

Lewis, John (1962) *History of Philosophy*, English Universities Press.

Litzinger, B. (1964) *Times's Revenges: Browning's Reputation as a Thinker*, University of Tennessee Press.

Lockwood, J.F. (1957) 'Haldane and Education' *Public Administration*, 35, pp. 232–44.

MacEwen, Philip (2006) 'Bosanquet, Santayana, and Aesthetics' in W. Sweet (ed.) *Bernard Bosanquet and the Legacy of Idealism*, University of Toronto Press, pp.127–44.

MacKillop, I.D. (1978) 'The London School of Ethics and Social Philosophy: an adult education movement of the 1890s' *History of Education*, 7, pp.119–27.

——. (1986) *The British Ethical Societies*, Cambridge University Press.

Maclachlan, D.L.C. (2005) 'C.A.Campbell' *Thoemmes Enclopedia of Twentieth Century British Philosophers*, vol. I, pp.145–8.

MacNiven, D. (1987) *Bradley's Moral Psychology* Edwin Mellen Press.

Mallinson, J. (2002) *T.S. Eliot's Interpretation of F.H. Bradley*, Kluwer.

Mander, W.J. (1994) *An Introduction to Bradley's Metaphysics*, Clarendon Press.

——. (1996) 'On McTaggart on Love' *History of Philosophy Quarterly*, 13, pp.133–47.

Manser, A. (1983) *Bradley's Logic*, Blackwell.

Marion, M. (2000) 'Oxford Realism: Knowledge and Perception' *British Journal for the History of Philosophy*, 8, p. 299–338, 485–519.

Matson, W. (1968) *A History of Philosophy*, Van Nostrand.

Metz, R. (1938) *A Hundred Years of British Philosophy*, George Allen and Unwin.

Milne, A.J.M. (1962) *The Social Philosophy of English Idealism*, George Allen and Unwin.

Moore, G.E. (1942) 'An Autobiography' in P.A. Schillp (ed.) *The Philosophy of G.E. Moore*, Northwestern University Press.

Morrow, John (1984), 'Liberalism and British Idealist Political Philosophy: A Reassessment' *History of Political Thought*, 5, pp.91–108.

Mure, G.R.G. (1937) 'Oxford and Philosophy', *Philosophy*, 12, pp.291–301.

——. (1958) *Retreat from Truth*, Basil Blackwell.

——. (1961) 'F.H. Bradley: Towards a Portrait' *Encounter*, 16, pp.28–35.

Nash, A.S. (1943) *The University and the Modern World*, Macmillan.

Nicholson, P.P. (1985) 'T.H. Green and State Action: Liquor Legislation' *History of Political Thought*, 6, pp.517–50.

——. (1990) *The Political Philosophy of the British Idealists*, Cambridge University Press.

——. (1995) 'T.H. Green's Doubts about Hegel's Political Philosophy' *Bulletin of the Hegel Society of Great Britain*, 31, pp.61–72.

——. (1998) 'Introduction' *Collected Works of D.G. Ritchie*, vol. I, pp.vii–xlvi.

Oakeley, Hilda (1939) *My Adventures in Education*, Williams and Norgate.

——. (1942) *Should Nations Survive?* George Allen and Unwin.

Panagokou, S. (1999) 'Religious Consciousness and the Realisation of the True Self: Bernard Bosanquet's views on religion in *What Religion Is*' *Bradley Studies*, 5, 139–61.

——. (2005) 'Defending Bosanquet's Philosophical Theory of the State: A Reassessment of the "Bosanquet–Hobhouse Controversy"' *British Journal of Politics and International Relations*, 7, 29–47.

Passmore, J. [1957] *One Hundred Years of Philosophy*, Penguin 1968.

Paton, H.J. (1955) *The Modern Predicament*, George Allen and Unwin.

——. (1956) 'Fifty Years of Philosophy' in H.D. Lewis (ed.) *Contemporary British Philosophy: Personal Statements, Third Series*, pp. 335–54.

Popper, K. (1945) *The Open Society and its Enemies*, Routledge and Kegan Paul.

Prichard, H.A. [1935–7] 'Green: Political Obligation' in his *Moral Writings* Jim MacAdam (ed.) Oxford University Press, 2002, pp.226–52.

——. (1950) *Knowledge and Perception*, Clarendon Press.

Quinton, A. [1971–2] 'Absolute Idealism' *Proceedings of the British Academy*, 57. Reprinted in A. Kenny (ed.) *Rationalism, Empiricism, Idealism*, Oxford University Press, 1986, pp.124–50.

——. (2000) 'T.H. Green's "Metaphysics of Knowledge"' in W.J. Mander (ed.) *Anglo-American Idealism 1865–1927*, Greenwood Press, pp.21–31.

Raitt, Suzanne (2000) *May Sinclair; A Modern Victorian*, Clarendon Press.

Raters, Marie-Louise (2001) 'Unbeautiful Beauty in Hegel and Bosanquet' *Bradley Studies*, 7, pp.162–76.

Reardon, B.M.G. (2004) 'Henry Longueville Mansel' *Oxford Dictionary of National Biography*, Oxford University Press.

Richter, M. [1964] *The Politics of Conscience: T. H. Green and His Age*, Weidenfeld and Nicholson. Reprinted Thoemes Press, 1996.

Robbins, P. (1982) *The British Hegelians 1875–1925*, Garland.

Russell, Bertrand [1946] *History of Western Philosophy*, George Allen and Unwin, 2nd edn 1966.

——. (1956) *Logic and Knowledge*, George Allen and Unwin.

——. [1959] *My Philosophical Development*, Routledge 1985.

——. (2003) *Russell on Metaphysics*, Stephen Mumford (ed.) Routledge.

Saxena, S.K. (1967) *Studies in the Metaphysics of F.H.Bradley*, George Allen and Unwin.

Schneewind, J.B. (1977) *Sidgwick's Ethics and Victorian Moral Philosophy*, Clarendon Press.

Scott, J.W. (2004) 'Mackenzie, John Stuart (1860–1935)' revised Mark J. Schofield, *Oxford Dictionary of National Biography*, Oxford University Press.

Scruton, R. (1981) *A Short History of Modern Philosophy*, Routledge.

Sell, A.P.F. (1995) *Philosophical Idealism and Christian Belief*, University of Wales Press.

Sellars, W. [1956] 'Empiricism and the Philosophy of Mind' *Minnesota Studies in the Philosophy of Science*, 1. Reprinted in his *Science, Perception and Reality*, Routledge and Kegan Paul, 1963, pp.127–96.

Sievers, K. (1996) 'Inference and the Criterion of System' in W.J. Mander (ed.) *Perspectives on the Logic and Metaphysics of F.H. Bradley*, Thoemmes Press, pp.243–67.

Simhony, A. (1990) 'T.H. Green's Theory of Positive Freedom' *Political Studies*, 39:2, pp.303–20.

——. (2006) 'Rights that Bind: T.H. Green on Rights and Community' in M. Dimova Cookson and W.J. Mander (eds) *T.H. Green: Ethics, Metaphysics and Political Philosophy*, Oxford University Press, pp.236–61.

——. (2010) 'T.H. Green was no consequentialist of any kind' *Collingwood Studies*, 15, pp.7–27.

Sprigge, T.L.S. (1993) *James and Bradley; American Truth and British Reality*, Open Court.

——. (2006) 'Bosanquet and Religion' in W. Sweet (ed.) *Bernard Bosanquet and the Legacy of British Idealism*, University of Toronto Press, pp.178–205.

——. (2006) *The God of Metaphysics*, Oxford University Press.

Stern, Robert (2007) 'Hegel, British Idealism and the Curious Case of the Concrete Universal' *British Journal for the History of Philosophy*, 15, pp.115–53.

Stock, G. (1984) 'Bradley's Theory of Judgment' in A. Manser and G. Stock (eds) *The Philosophy of F.H. Bradley*, Clarendon Press, pp.131–54.

——. (1985) 'Negation: Bradley and Wittgenstein' *Philosophy*, 60, pp.465–76.

Stormer, G.D. (1979) 'Hegel and the Secret of James Hutchison Stirling' *Idealistic Studies*, 9, pp.33–54.

Stove, David (1991) 'Idealism: A Victorian Horror-Story' in his *The Plato Cult*, Blackwell, pp.83–177.

Sweet, W. (1997) *Idealism and Rights: The Social Ontology of Human Rights in the Political Thought of Bernard Bosanquet*, University Press of America.

——. (2000) 'Bernard Bosanquet and the Nature of Religious Belief' in W.J. Mander (ed.) *Anglo-American Idealism*, Greenwood Press, pp.123–39.

——. (2009) 'British Idealism and Ethical Thought in South Africa and India' in W. Sweet (ed.) *The Moral, Social and Political Philosophy of the British Idealists*, Imprint Academic, pp.289–331.

Symonds, R. (1986) *Oxford and Empire*, Macmillan.

Tacelli, R. (1991) 'Cook Wilson as Critic of Bradley' *History of Philosophy Quarterly*, 8, pp.199–205.

Taylor, C. (1975) *Hegel*, Cambridge University Press.

Thatcher, D.S. (1972) *Nietzsche in England: 1890–1914*, University of Toronto Press.

Thomas, G. (1987) *The Moral Philosophy of T.H. Green*, Clarendon Press.

——. (2000) 'Philosophy and Ideology in Bernard Bosanquet's Political Philosophy' in W.J. Mander (ed.) *Anglo-American Idealism*, Greenwood Press, pp.105–22.

Tillich, P. [1952] *The Courage to Be*, Yale University Press, 2000.

Trott, Elizabeth (2006) 'Bosanquet, Aesthetics, and Education: Warding off Stupidity with Art' in W. Sweet (ed.) *Bernard Bosanquet and the Legacy of British Idealism*, University of Toronto Press, pp.113–26.

Tyler, Colin (1997) *Thomas Hill Green and the Philosophical Foundations of Politics*, Edwin Mellen Press. New expanded edition titled *The Liberal Socialism of Thomas Hill Green. Part I: The Metaphysics of self-relisation and freedom*, Imprint Academic, 2010.

——. (2000) 'This Dangerous Drug of Violence: Making Sense of Bernard Bosanquet's Theory of Punishment' *Collingwood and British Idealism Studies*, 7, pp.114–38.

——. (2005) *Unpublished Manuscripts in British Idealism*, Thoemmes Press.

——. (2006) *Idealist Political Philosophy*, Continuum.

——. (2010) 'Vindicating British Idealism: D.G. Ritchie contra David Weinstein' *Collingwood Studies*, 15, pp.54–75.

Van Fraassen, B. (1980) *The Scientific Image*, Clarendon Press.

Vincent, A. (2006) 'Bosanquet and Social Aesthetics' *Collingwood and British Idealism Studies*, 12, pp. 39–65.

——. (2006) 'Ethics and Metaphysics in the Philosophy of T.H. Green' in M. Dimova Cookson and W.J. Mander (eds) *T.H. Green: Ethics, Metaphysics and Political Philosophy*, Oxford University Press, pp.76–105.

——. (2007) 'German Philosophy and British Public Policy: Richard Burdon Haldane in Theory and Practice' *Journal of the History of Ideas*, 68, pp.157–79.

——. and Plant, R. (1984) *Philosophy, Politics and Citizenship: the life and thought of the British Idealists*, Basil Blackwell.

Walker, R.C.S. (1989) *The Coherence Theory of Truth*, Routledge.

——. (1998) 'Bradley's Theory of Truth' in G. Stock (ed.) *Appearance versus Reality: New Essays on the Philosophy of F.H. Bradley*, Clarendon Press, pp.93–109.

——. (2000) 'Joachim on the Nature of Truth' in W.J. Mander (ed.) *Anglo-American Idealism, 1865–1927*, Greenwood Press, pp.183–97.

Walsh, W.H (1980) 'Geoffrey Reginald Gilchrist Mure' *Postmaster* (Merton College annual magazine) 6, pp.5–11.

——. (2000) 'The Zenith of Greats' in *History of the University of Oxford*, Clarendon Press, Volume VII, Part 2, pp.311–26.

Warnock, G.J. (1958) *English Philosophy since 1900*, Oxford University Press.

——. (1988) 'A Sage for a Time' (review of G. Thomas' *The Moral Philosophy of T.H. Green*) *Times Literary Supplement*, 3 June, p.606.

Warnock, M. (1960) *Ethics Since 1900*, Oxford University Press.

Welchman, J. (1995) *Dewey's Ethical Thought*, Cornell University Press.

Weinstein, D. (2007) *Utilitarianism and the New Liberalism*, Cambridge University Press.

Wempe, B. (1986) *Beyond Equality: A Study of TH Green's Theory of Positive Freedom*, Eburon. New expanded edition titled *T.H. Green's Theory of Positive Freedom*, Imprint Academic, 2004.

Willis, Kirk (1988) 'The introduction and Critical Reception of Hegelian Thought in Britain 1830–1900' *Victorian Studies*, 32, pp.85–111.

Wilson, F. (1998) 'Bradley's Critique of Associationism' *Bradley Studies*, 4, pp.5–59.

Witham, L. (2006) *The Measure of God*, Harper Collins.

Wollheim, R. [1959] *F.H.Bradley*, Penguin Books, 1969.

Index

Page numbers in **bold** denote photographs